Thinking Through The Test

A Study Guide for
The Florida College Basic Skills Exit Tests

Reading and Writing

with Answer Key

Fourth Edition

Elizabeth Schmid Bellas and Peri Poland
Pasco-Hernando Community College

Longman

Boston   Columbus   Indianapolis   New York   San Francisco   Upper Saddle River
Amsterdam   Cape Town   Dubai   London   Madrid   Milan   Munich   Paris   Montreal   Toronto
Delhi   Mexico City   Sao Paulo   Sydney   Hong Kong   Seoul   Singapore   Taipei   Tokyo

Acquisitions Editor: Kate Edwards
Senior Supplements Editor: Donna Campion
Electronic Page Makeup: Grapevine Publishing Services, Inc.

Thinking Through the Test: A Study Guide for The Florida College Basic Skills Exit Tests: Reading and Writing, with Answer Key, Fourth Edition

7 8 9 10–V0CR–16 15 14

Longman
is an imprint of

www.pearsonhighered.com

ISBN 13: 978-0-205-77110-3
ISBN 10:   0-205-77110-6

Contents

PART FOUR: TEST-TAKING STRATEGIES

PART FIVE: EXIT EXAMS

PART SIX: CORRESPONDENCE CHARTS FOR TEST QUESTIONS AND TRACKING SHEETS

PART SEVEN: ANSWER KEYS FOR READING

PART EIGHT: ANSWER KEYS FOR WRITING

PART NINE: APPENDIX

Introduction

"Chance favors the prepared mind."
—Louis Pasteur

For many of you, test taking is a most stressful and fearful task. Weeks and months of hard work and significant learning can seem to fly away in a single test session. You've been polishing your reading and writing skills, and you feel ready to enroll in college-level English classes, but now you have one more challenge ahead of you: to pass the Florida College Basic Skills Test in English. *Thinking Through the Test* will help you get ready.

At this moment, even the mere thought of having to pass a test as important as this one has probably raised your anxiety level! But don't worry: you're not alone. Many students have felt like you have about this test, and still thousands of students successfully pass it every year—you can too! The purpose of *Thinking Through the Test* is to help you prepare for the Florida College Basic Skills Exit Exam by lessening your anxiety and by strengthening your reading and writing skills.

First of all, you should take comfort in the fact that those who write the state exit exam are community college teachers who are actively teaching reading and writing in classrooms throughout the state; therefore, the skills addressed on the exit exam and in this book are the same skills that you are already studying in your classrooms, textbooks, and learning centers. As a consequence, *Thinking Through the Test* not only helps you prepare for the exit exam, but it also helps you become a better reader and writer overall by supporting the instruction and learning that you need to be a more successful college student.

In order to support your classroom instruction and prepare you for the college classroom, passages for the items in this book have been taken from textbooks currently used in freshman college classes. These passages represent a variety of content courses such as biological sciences, social sciences, history, government, and education. Because these passages are taken from college-level textbooks that you could be reading in the near future, they may contain unfamiliar concepts and words and therefore may be more difficult than the passages on the actual state tests, so be sure to use the workbook as an opportunity to apply the new skills you are acquiring from your reading and writing classes.

You'll find *Thinking Through the Test* divided into nine parts:

Part One	Pretests
Part Two	Reading Workbook
Part Three	Writing Workbook
Part Four	Test-Taking Strategies
Part Five	Exit Exams
Part Six	Correspondence Charts for Test Questions and Tracking Sheets

One of the benefits of this book is that all of the practice tests and exercises are very similar to the items you will face on the state tests. Therefore, some of the same passages appear in several different chapters because the state exam also uses a single passage to ask several types of questions. For example, there are ten passages in Chapter One of the Reading Workbook on main ideas; those same passages or portions of them are also in other chapters: the same passage, different questions. This repetition should help you see the connections between skills and questions as well as the benefit of re-reading for better understanding.

Remember to make connections whenever possible; for example, questions about the main idea and the author's purpose often have similar answers. Read the section "Test-Taking Strategies" for more helpful information.

New to the Fourth Edition

For the fourth edition of *Thinking Through the Test*, we have added several new features and enhanced the instructional content.

- Revised Reading and Writing Pretests and 4 Brand-New Exit Exams so you can test and re-test all the reading and writing skills you will need to be successful
- More instruction, examples, and explanations to illustrate each reading and writing skill presented in the various chapters
- A completely revised Inferences Section to distinguish between supporting details and true inferences and conclusions
- New organization of the Language, Sentence, and Grammar Skills sections to help students focus on the most important skills areas, tips for quick success, and questions that most benefit from study
- A brand new Parts of Speech Review Appendix to help students become familiar with the most important grammar concepts before tackling the practice questions
- A fully revised chapter on Part 1 of the Writing Test (~Questions 1–10), focusing on more intensive instruction on Main Ideas and tips for answering the other questions in this section
- A revised Test-Taking Strategies Section located before the practice Exit Exams to provide helpful tips on what to study before the test, how to approach the test, and how to handle test anxiety
- Tracking Sheets for the Practice Exit Exams to help you track your progress and see your strengths and weaknesses

While these features are designed to help you make the most of your learning experience, remember: The more practice you have in *thinking through* your choices, the more likely you are to be successful on the state test and in future college courses.

In the meantime, as you study and practice for the test ahead, remember what baseball legend Ted Williams said: "Just keep going. Everybody gets better if they keep at it."

 # Part One: Pretest—Reading

Instructions: This Pretest has 36 questions. Read each passage below and answer the questions that follow.

Carnivorous plants trap their prey, which may vary from single-celled organisms, small crustaceans, mosquito larvae, and tiny water insects to small tadpoles, large insects, and small amphibians. Carnivorous plants fall into two groups: active and passive trappers.

Active trappers use rapid plant movements to open trap doors or to close traps. Two examples of active trappers are the Venus flytrap and the aquatic and semi-aquatic blad- 5 derworts. The Venus flytrap uses clam-shaped, hinged leaves. Around their unattached edges are many guard hairs and very small nectar glands that attract insects. On the surface of each half are three small trigger hairs and a covering of small digestive glands. An insect attracted to the brightly colored leaf touches the trigger hairs, causing the trap to close quickly. The bladderwort, as its name suggests, has small, elastic, flattened blad- 10 ders with the entrance sealed by a flap of cells. When prey touch the tactile cells on the flap, the trap door opens. The bladder walls spring apart, causing a sucking motion that sweeps a current of water into the bladder. Then the door closes, trapping the prey.

Passive trappers use pitfalls or sticky adhesive traps. Pitcher plants and sundews are ex- amples of passive trappers. Pitcher plants use pitfalls. The leaves are shaped into pitcher- 15 like or funnel-like traps that grow from underground stems. Bright coloration and secretions of nectar attract the insects. When they land and move down the leaf, the insects are unable to back up against the stiff, downward-directed hairs. They fall into watery fluid containing digestive enzymes produced by the leaf. The sundews attract insects to sticky leaves by color, scent, and glistening droplets of adhesive. Sundews have two types 20 of glands on the leaf surface that produce adhesive droplets. Long stalks on the edge of the leaf trap the insect. Shorter stalks slowly bend into the center of the leaf, holding the prey in the digestive area of the leaf. (Adapted from Robert Leo Smith and Thomas M. Smith, *Elements of Ecology*, 5th ed., San Francisco: Benjamin Cummings, 2003.)

1. Which sentence best states the main idea of the passage?
   A. Two examples of active trappers are the Venus flytrap and the aquatic and semi-aquatic bladderworts.
   B. Pitcher plants and sundews are examples of passive trappers.

C. Carnivorous plants fall into two groups: active and passive trappers.
D. Carnivorous plants trap their prey, which may vary from single-celled organisms, small crustaceans, mosquito larvae, and tiny water insects to small tadpoles, large insects, and small amphibians.

2. The overall pattern of organization for this passage is
    A. listing.
    B. classification.
    C. cause and effect.
    D. statement and clarification.

3. The authors' purpose is to
    A. describe Venus flytraps and Pitcher plants.
    B. define active trappers and give examples of each.
    C. explain how different types of carnivorous plants catch their prey.
    D. show the effects of prey landing upon carnivorous plants.

4. What is the relationship between the following sentences? "When prey touch the tactile cells on the flap, the trap door opens. The bladder walls spring apart, causing a sucking motion that sweeps a current of water into the bladder"?
    A. Compare and contrast
    B. Spatial order
    C. Statement and clarification
    D. Process

5. The authors' claim that "Carnivorous plants fall into two groups" is
    A. inadequately supported because it lacks evidence.
    B. adequately supported with relevant details.

6. What is the relationship within the sentence, "When prey touch the tactile cells on the flap, the trap door opens"?
    A. Example
    B. Listing
    C. Cause and effect
    D. Summary

7. The overall tone of the passage is
    A. objective.
    B. admiring.
    C. nostalgic.
    D. reverent.

8. The main idea of paragraph 2 is that
    A. carnivorous plants trap their prey in a complicated process.
    B. active trappers use rapid plant movements to open trap doors or to close traps.
    C. Venus flytraps use an active trapping process to catch their prey.
    D. all active trappers have nectar glands.

9. A conclusion that can be drawn from the passage is that
   A. Pitcher plants have a slower process for capturing their prey than bladderworts.
   B. Venus flytraps are not as common as bladderworts.
   C. bladderworts also use a sticky adhesive to trap their prey.
   D. all passive trappers have small trigger hairs to trap their prey.

Read the passage below and answer the questions that follow.

Karen Silkwood grew up in an unassuming middle-class family in Nederland, Texas, near the Gulf Coast. She baby-sat at her church nursery, earned straight A's through high school, and went to Lamar College on a full scholarship to study medical technology. Marriage, three children, and a divorce intervened, and in 1972 she began working as a laboratory analyst at Kerr-McGee's plutonium processing plant in Crescent, Oklahoma. There the highly poisonous radioactive material was made into fuel rods for nuclear power plants.   5

In the summer of 1974, at age 28, Silkwood was elected a local official of the union that represented many Kerr-McGee workers and began organizing for greater worker safety. She learned of numerous incidents of radioactive contamination at the plant. She also uncovered evidence of significant quantities of missing plutonium. On November 13, Silkwood set out for Oklahoma City to meet a national representative of her union and a *New York Times* reporter, intending to give them documents proving that Kerr-McGee was knowingly manufacturing defective nuclear products. She never made it. Her car was forced off the road, and she died instantly when it crashed into a concrete culvert.   10

    15

Karen Silkwood challenged the power of one of the nation's largest energy corporations. Her brief career as a whistleblower brought together major issues of the 1970s: labor organizing, environmental damage, the safety record of nuclear energy, and the power of corporations over individual citizens. Her **dismissive** treatment by some fellow workers, her employers, and the media also suggested the lack of respect that women had long endured, especially when they moved out of the role of the traditional homemaker. (Jacqueline Jones et al., *Created Equal*, New York: Longman, 2003.)   20

10. Which statement best states the implied main idea of the passage?
    A. Karen Silkwood grew up in an unassuming middle-class family in Nederland, Texas, near the Gulf Coast.
    B. Karen Silkwood was murdered for trying to bring the energy company that she worked for to justice.
    C. Karen Silkwood was a union official and whistleblower who brought attention to many major issues of the 1970s.
    D. Karen Silkwood challenged the power of one of the nation's largest energy corporations.

11. A conclusion that can be drawn from the passage is that
    A. Karen Silkwood was unaware of the effects that radioactive material can have on humans.
    B. Karen Silkwood cared deeply about workers' rights.

    C. most women in the 1970s were not traditional homemakers.
    D. Kerr-McGee was sued for producing defective nuclear products.

12. According to the passage
    A. Karen Silkwood died on November 13, 1974.
    B. Kerr-McGee processed plutonium for nuclear weapons.
    C. Kerr-McGee was unaware that its nuclear products were defective.
    D. Karen Silkwood had a paying job working as a whistleblower.

13. The word **dismissive** in paragraph 3 means
    A. reverent.
    B. careless.
    C. disrespectful.
    D. supportive.

14. The following statement, "Her dismissive treatment by some fellow workers, her employers, and the media also suggested the lack of respect that women had long endured, especially when they moved out of the role of the traditional homemaker," is
    A. a fact.
    B. an opinion.

15. The author's claim that "Karen Silkwood challenged the power of one of the nation's largest energy corporations," is
    A. adequately supported by facts.
    B. inadequately supported by opinions or irrelevant facts.

16. The overall pattern of organization for the entire passage is
    A. compare and contrast.
    B. listing.
    C. spatial order.
    D. time order.

17. The relationship within the sentence, "Her car was forced off the road, and she died instantly when it crashed into a concrete culvert" is one of
    A. statement and clarification.
    B. spatial order.
    C. cause and effect.
    D. example.

18. The authors' purpose in writing the passage was
    A. to show how Karen Silkwood challenged one of the largest energy corporations.
    B. to illustrate how women who worked in careers were not respected in the 1970s.
    C. to warn readers of what could happen when someone challenges a powerful corporation.
    D. to caution readers about the harmful effects of radioactive material.

Read the passage below and answer the questions that follow.

Research in Japan on the personality of the "salarymen" males employed in the fast-paced corporate world, links male personality with the demands of the business world. Salarymen work long hours for the company. They leave home early in the morning and return late at night and thus are nicknamed "7–11 men."

Many Tokyo salarymen eat dinner with their family only a few times a year. After work, 5 they typically spend many hours with fellow workers at expensive nightclubs. Groups of about five to ten men go out together after work. A few drinks and light snacks can result in a tab in the hundreds of dollars for one hour. The corporation picks up the bill. At the club, men relax and have fun after a long day of work. This is ensured by having a trained hostess sit at the table, keeping the conversation moving along in a lightly 10 playful tone. Her job is to flatter and flirt with the men and to make them feel good.

While working as a hostess, one woman found that conversations are full of teasing and banter, with much of it directed at the hostess. This may be viewed as a reaction to their upbringing, with its total control by the mother. Club culture puts the man in control. The hostess can flirt with him but she will never control him. 15

Salarymen's nightclub behavior appears to be linked with their upbringing. Given the near total absence of the father from the home scene, children are raised mainly by the mother. The concentration of maternal attention is especially strong toward sons and their school achievements. The goal is that the boy will do well in school, get into a top university, and then gain employment with a large corporation. These corporations pay well, guarantee 20 lifelong employment, and provide substantial benefits after retirement. Loyalty is required, work hours are long, and the pressure to perform is high. (Adapted from Barbara D. Miller, *Cultural Anthropology*, 2nd ed., Boston: Allyn and Bacon, 2002.)

19. What is the implied main idea of this passage?
    A. Salarymen's behavior is linked to their culture and the demands of their jobs.
    B. Club culture in Japan puts salarymen in control of any situation.
    C. In Japanese corporations, loyalty is required, work hours are long, and the pressure to perform is high.
    D. Salarymen's nightclub behavior appears to be linked with their upbringing.

20. Is the following statement one of fact or opinion? "This may be viewed as a reaction to their upbringing, with its total control by the mother."
    A. Fact
    B. Opinion

21. What is the relationship within the sentence, "Given the near total absence of the father from the home scene, children are raised mainly by the mother"?
    A. Compare and contrast
    B. Time order
    C. Example
    D. Cause and effect

22. The overall pattern of organization for this passage is
    A. listing.
    B. process.
    C. cause and effect.
    D. addition.

23. In this passage, the author is
    A. biased in favor of salarymen.
    B. biased in favor of Japanese mothers.
    C. biased against salarymen.
    D. unbiased.

24. The author's tone in this passage is
    A. critical.
    B. impassioned.
    C. humorous.
    D. straightforward.

25. Which of the following statements provides the best support for the author's claim, "Loyalty is required, work hours are long, and the pressure to perform is high"?
    A. The goal is that the boy will do well in school, get into a top university, and then gain employment with a large corporation.
    B. They leave home early in the morning and return late at night and thus are nicknamed "7–11 men."
    C. Groups of about five to ten men go out together after work.
    D. Given the near total absence of the father from the home scene, children are raised mainly by the mother.

26. What is the relationship between the following sentences? "Many Tokyo salarymen eat dinner with their family only a few times a year. After work, they typically spend many hours with fellow workers at expensive nightclubs."
    A. Addition
    B. Contrast
    C. Cause and effect
    D. Listing

27. Which of the following conclusions cannot be drawn from the passage?
    A. Japanese parents expect their sons to do well in school.
    B. A hostess at a nightclub often endures teasing from salarymen.
    C. Mothers in Japan do not work outside of the home.
    D. Japanese corporations have high expectations for their salarymen.

Read the passage below and answer the questions that follow.

Everywhere it occurred, industrialization drove society from an agricultural to an urban way of life. The old system, in which peasant families worked the fields during the summer and did their cottage industry work in the winter to their own standards and at their own pace, slowly disappeared. In its place came urban life tied to the factory system. The factory was a place where for long hours people did repetitive tasks using machines to process large amounts of raw materials. This was an efficient way to make a lot of high-quality goods cheaply. But the factories were often dangerous places, and the lifestyle connected to them had a terrible effect on the human condition.

In the factory system, the workers worked, and the owners made profits. The owners wanted to make the most they could from their investment and to get the most work they could from their employees. The workers, in turn, felt that they deserved more of the profits because their labor made production possible. This was a situation guaranteed to produce conflict, especially given the wretched conditions the workers faced in the first stages of industrialization.

The early factories were miserable places, featuring bad lighting, lack of ventilation, dangerous machines, and frequent breakdowns. Safety standards were practically nonexistent, and workers in various industries could expect to contract serious diseases; for example, laborers working with lead paint developed lung problems, pewter workers fell ill to palsy, miners suffered black lung disease, and operators of primitive machines lost fingers, hands, and even lives. Not until late in the nineteenth century did health and disability insurance come into effect. In some factories workers who suffered accidents were **deemed** to be at fault; and since there was little job security, a worker could be fired for almost any reason.

The demand for plentiful and cheap labor led to the widespread employment of women and children who worked long hours. Girls as young as 6 years old were used to haul carts of coal in Lancashire mines, and boys and girls of 5 years of age worked in textile mills, where their nimble little fingers could easily untangle jams in the machines. When they were not laboring, the working families lived in horrid conditions in Manchester, England. There were no sanitary, water, or medical services for the workers, and working families were crammed 12 and 15 individuals to a room in damp, dark cellars. Bad diet, alcoholism, cholera, and typhus reduced lifespans in the industrial cities. (Brummet, Palmira, et al., *Civilization: Past and Present*, New York: Longman, 2000.)

28. Which sentence best states the implied main idea of the passage?
    A. Industrialization changed society from an agricultural way of life to an urban life plagued by many problems.
    B. Early factories were miserable places that had numerous problems.
    C. Industrialization was an efficient way to make a lot of high-quality goods cheaply.
    D. Industrialization gave people the opportunity to work at jobs in factories.

29. What is the relationship within the sentence, "In the factory system, the workers worked, and the owners made profits"?
    A. Time order
    B. Addition
    C. Process
    D. Clarification

30. What is the overall pattern of organization?
    A. Listing
    B. Compare and contrast
    C. Example
    D. Cause and effect

31. In this passage, the authors
    A. are biased against the early factory system.
    B. are biased in favor of industrialization.
    C. are biased against agricultural societies.
    D. are unbiased.

32. As used in this sentence from paragraph three, "In some factories workers who suffered accidents were **deemed** to be at fault; and since there was little job security, a worker could be fired for almost any reason," the word **deemed** most nearly means
    A. used.
    B. injured.
    C. believed.
    D. controlled.

33. Which of the following conclusions cannot be drawn from the passage?
    A. Owners of factories exploited their workers.
    B. Industrialization had negative effects upon society.
    C. Industrialization caused a decrease in agriculture.
    D. There were no child labor laws during the beginning of industrialization.

34. What is the authors' tone in this passage?
    A. Optimistic
    B. Critical
    C. Nostalgic
    D. Ironic

35. Which of the following statements is an opinion?
    A. This was a situation guaranteed to produce conflict, especially given the wretched conditions the workers faced in the first stages of industrialization.
    B. The demand for plentiful and cheap labor led to the widespread employment of women and children who worked long hours.
    C. The factory was a place where for long hours people did repetitive tasks using machines to process large amounts of raw materials.
    D. In some factories workers who suffered accidents were deemed to be at fault; and since there was little job security, a worker could be fired for almost any reason.

36. What is the authors' purpose in this passage?
    A. To explain how industrialization replaced agriculture as the main source of employment in the early nineteenth century
    B. To compare industrialized society to agricultural society
    C. To show the early effects of industrialization on society
    D. To describe conditions in early factories

# Part One: Pretest—Writing

Read the entire passage carefully, then answer the questions. (Note: Intentional errors may have been included in the passage.)

(1) _____.

(2) In early autumn of 1991, two hikers working their way along the edge of a melting glacier in the high Alps of northern Italy found what seemed to be the weathered remains of an unlucky mountain climber. (3) Next to him were a bow and several arrows, a wooden backpack, and a metal ax. (4) It was a man clothed in hand-sewn leather, frozen in glacial ice. (5) A closer look turned up a leather pouch and other tools. (6) The "Ice Man" turned out to be a leftover from the Stone Age, a young hunter who may have died from exhaustion and exposure some 5,000 years ago. (7) Although scientists knew that the Ice Man was ancient, they did not know where he was from. (8) In 1994, researchers reported that mitochondrial DNA from the Ice Man closely matched that of central and northern Europeans, not Native Americans. (9) DNA is unlikely to remain intact if it is not carefully preserved. (10) _____ the Ice Man remains frozen in the anatomy department of the University of Innsbruck. (11) Continuing analysis of DNA may provide more clues about his place in human evolution. (12) Scientists have reported DNA from a 65-million-year old dinosaur fossil. (Adapted from Neil A. Campbell, Lawrence G. Mitchell, and Jane B. Reece, *Biology*, 3rd ed., San Francisco: Benjamin Cummings, 2000.)

1. Which of the following sentences, if inserted into the blank labeled number 1, would provide the best thesis statement for the entire passage?
   A. Because it is difficult to obtain uncontaminated samples from fossils, DNA is very challenging.
   B. Science advances by the ebb and flow of ideas.
   C. The analysis of DNA from fossils provides important information about ancient life forms.
   D. The discovery of the "Ice Man" was highly publicized.

2. Which of the numbered sentences is NOT supported by sufficient details?
   A. 9
   B. 2
   C. 7
   D. 3

3. Select the order of sentences 3, 4, and 5 that presents the details in the most logical sequence of ideas. If no change is necessary, select option A.
   A. Next to him were a bow and several arrows, a wooden backpack, and a metal ax. It was a man clothed in hand-sewn leather, frozen in glacial ice. A closer look turned up a leather pouch and other tools.
   B. It was a man clothed in hand-sewn leather, frozen in glacial ice. Next to him were a bow and several arrows, a wooden backpack, and a metal ax. A closer look turned up a leather pouch and other tools.
   C. Next to him were a bow and several arrows, a wooden backpack, and a metal ax. A closer look turned up a leather pouch and other tools. It was a man clothed in hand-sewn leather, frozen in glacial ice.
   D. A closer look turned up a leather pouch and other tools. It was a man clothed in hand-sewn leather, frozen in glacial ice. Next to him were a bow and several arrows, a wooden backpack, and a metal ax.

4. Which numbered sentence is the LEAST relevant to the passage?
   A. 12
   B. 2
   C. 6
   D. 8

5. Which word or phrase, if inserted into the blank in the sentence labeled number 10, would make the relationship between sentences 8, 9, and 11 clear?
   A. In contrast,
   B. However,
   C. Furthermore,
   D. Therefore,

Read the entire passage carefully, then answer the questions. (Note: Intentional errors may have been included in the passage.)

(1) _____ .

(2) Even when your use of a source may be perfectly legal, you may still be violating ethical standards if you do not give credit to the information source. (3) _____ assume that you are writing a research report on genetically modified foods. (4) In your research, you discover a very good paper on the Web. (5) Under copyright and fair use guidelines, you can reproduce portions of this paper without permission. (6) However, does this legal standard mean that you can use someone else's material freely, without giving that person credit? (7) Even though it might be legal under fair use guidelines to reprint the material without notifying the copyright holder, using someone else's material or ideas without giving them credit is plagiarism. (8) There are several systems for citing others' ideas. (9) Plagiarism is serious because it violates several of the reasonable criteria for ethical decision making. (10) It also violates your obligation to society to produce fair and accurate information. (11) Plagiarism violates your obligation to yourself to be truthful. (12) Finally, it violates your obligation to other students and researchers. (13) Students can be expelled from school. (Adapted from Laura J. Gurak, and John M. Lannon, *A Concise Guide to Technical Communication*, New York: Longman, 2001.)

6. Which of the following sentences, if inserted into the blank labeled number 1, would provide the best thesis statement for the entire passage?
   A. Plagiarism is using someone else's words and ideas without giving that person proper credit.
   B. People can lose their jobs if they plagiarize.
   C. Plagiarism violates ethical standards.
   D. Plagiarism is rampant in colleges and universities.

7. Which of the numbered sentences is NOT supported by sufficient details?
   A. 2
   B. 4
   C. 8
   D. 9

8. Select the order of sentences 10, 11, and 12 that presents the details in the most logical sequence of ideas. If no change is necessary, select option A.
   A. It also violates your obligation to society to produce fair and accurate information. Plagiarism violates your obligation to yourself to be truthful. Finally, it violates your obligation to other students and researchers.
   B. It also violates your obligation to society to produce fair and accurate information. Finally, it violates your obligation to other students and researchers. Plagiarism violates your obligation to yourself to be truthful.

    C. Plagiarism violates your obligation to yourself to be truthful. Finally, it violates your obligation to other students and researchers. It also violates your obligation to society to produce fair and accurate information.

    D. Plagiarism violates your obligation to yourself to be truthful. It also violates your obligation to society to produce fair and accurate information. Finally, it violates your obligation to other students and researchers.

9. Which numbered sentence is the LEAST relevant to the passage?
    A. 5
    B. 7
    C. 9
    D. 13

10. Which word or phrase, if inserted into the blank in the sentence labeled number 3, would make the relationship between sentences 2 and 4 clear?
    A. For example,
    B. Therefore,
    C. In addition,
    D. Being that,

11. DIRECTIONS: Choose the most effective word or phrase within the context suggested by the sentence.

Martin's English skills are strong, but his math skills are _____, for he hasn't passed more than one math exam this semester.

    A. impaired
    B. deficient
    C. sufficient
    D. excessive

12. DIRECTIONS: Choose the most effective word or phrase within the context suggested by the sentence.

We have lived near the airport for so long that we are _____ to the noise of planes flying over our house, yet it annoys anyone who visits us.

    A. oblivious
    B. conscious
    C. negligent
    D. realistic

13. DIRECTIONS: Choose the option that corrects an error in the underlined portion(s). If no error exists, choose "No change is necessary."

Diana sat <u>beside</u> a person on the bus <u>who's</u> <u>clothes</u> were soaked with perspiration.
              A   B   C

    A. besides
    B. whose
    C. cloths
    D. No change is necessary.

14. DIRECTIONS: Choose the option that corrects an error in the underlined portion(s). If no error exists, choose "No change is necessary."

Now that Steven is working on improving his health, he is drinking <u>fewer</u> cups of coffee,
$\qquad\qquad\qquad\qquad\qquad\qquad\qquad\qquad\qquad\qquad$ A

cutting down on the <u>amount</u> of calories, and <u>losing</u> weight as a result.
$\qquad\qquad\qquad\quad$ B $\qquad\qquad\qquad\qquad\quad$ C

A. less
B. number
C. loosing
D. No change is necessary.

15. DIRECTIONS: Choose the sentence in which the modifiers are correctly placed.
A. They had a perfect view of the fireworks display sitting on the beach.
B. Sitting on the beach was a perfect view of the fireworks display.
C. Sitting on the beach, they had a perfect view of the fireworks display.

16. DIRECTIONS: Choose the sentence in which the modifiers are correctly placed.
A. Natalie returned the garlic and herb cheese spread to the supermarket that was moldy.
B. Natalie returned the garlic and herb cheese spread that was moldy to the supermarket.
C. The garlic and cheese spread was returned by Natalie that was moldy to the supermarket.

17. DIRECTIONS: Choose the sentence that expresses the thought most clearly and effectively and has no error in structure.
A. Because I have a job now, I can start saving money for a car.
B. Although I have a job now, I can start saving money for a car.
C. Unless I have a job now, I can start saving money for a car.

18. DIRECTIONS: Choose the most effective word or phrase within the context suggested by the sentence.

Jeff's dog is very aggressive; _____, he has to keep Killer in his cage when Jeff has visitors.

A. however
B. otherwise
C. finally
D. therefore

19. DIRECTIONS: Choose the most effective word or phrase within the context suggested by the sentence.

Drinking and driving a car can have several risks, such as harming innocent people, getting arrested, and _____.

A. it can interfere with brain functions.
B. interferes with brain functions.
C. interfering with brain functions.
D. interference with brain functions.

20. DIRECTONS: Choose the sentence that has no errors in structure.
    A. Since my car broke down, I have to figure out how to get to school every day; my choices are to ride the bus, taking a cab, or borrow my aunt's car.
    B. Since my car broke down, I have to figure out how to get to school every day; my choices are riding the bus, taking a cab, or borrow my aunt's car.
    C. Since my car broke down, I have to figure out how to get to school every day; my choices are to ride the bus, take a cab, or borrow my aunt's car.

21. DIRECTIONS: Choose the option that corrects an error in the underlined portion(s). If no error exists, choose "No change is necessary."

    Even though I am not a high school cheerleader anymore, I still help out at my old <u>school sometimes</u> I even cheer along with the cheerleaders just for fun.

    A. school. Sometimes
    B. school, sometimes
    C. school, sometimes,
    D. No change is necessary.

22. DIRECTIONS: Choose the option that corrects an error in the underlined portion(s). If no error exists, choose "No change is necessary."

    In order to retrieve our anchor, I had to perform a perfect <u>dive. If</u> I dove too <u>fast, my</u> body
    A$$B

    would not be able to adjust to the quick increase in <u>pressure, if</u> I drove too slowly, I would
    C

    run out of oxygen.

    A. dive, if
    B. fast. My
    C. pressure; if
    D. No change is necessary.

23. DIRECTIONS: Choose the option that corrects an error in the underlined portion(s). If no error exists, choose "No change is necessary."

    In my house, there is always a task to be <u>accomplished. Such as</u> walking the dog, mowing the lawn, or planning a fishing trip.

    A. accomplished; such as,
    B. accomplished, such as
    C. accomplished such as;
    D. No change is necessary.

24. DIRECTIONS: Choose the option that corrects an error in the underlined portion(s). If no error exists, choose "No change is necessary."

    When my mother first came to the United <u>States. She</u> could not speak a word of
    A

    <u>English; she</u> struggled with the language for a long <u>time, but</u> today she communicates
    B$$C

    in English very well.

A. States, she
B. English, she
C. time but,
D. No change is necessary.

25. DIRECTIONS: Choose the option that corrects an error in the underlined portion(s). If no error exists, choose "No change is necessary."

Jarred had spoke with his parents about going away to school, but they wanted him to go to the local community college.

A. had spoken
B. has spoke
C. speaking
D. No change is necessary.

26. DIRECTIONS: Choose the option that corrects an error in the underlined portion(s). If no error exists, choose "No change is necessary."

Bonnie worked on hiring the caterer and the photographer, and Jennifer is looking for a
        A   B
wedding dress while Dad worried about paying for everything.
                                  C

A. works
B. looked
C. worrying
D. No change is necessary.

27. DIRECTIONS: Choose the option that corrects an error in the underlined portion(s). If no error exists, choose "No change is necessary."

I used every last bit of energy I had to catch up with the ball; then, I dive in the air to make the catch in the end zone.

A. am diving
B. dove
C. had dove
D. No change is necessary.

28. DIRECTIONS: Choose the option that corrects an error in the underlined portion(s). If no error exists, choose "No change is necessary."

Some high schools install video cameras in the halls to see if there are any fights or if there
                             A   B
is any drug sales.
C

A. installs
B. is
C. are
D. No change is necessary.

29. DIRECTIONS: Choose the option that corrects an error in the underlined portion(s). If no error exists, choose "No change is necessary."

Because of the heavy rains from the tropical storm that <u>is</u> moving through the area, neither
                                        A

the grass nor the flowers <u>needs</u> any more water, but the weather service <u>predicts</u> five more
                     B   C

inches of rain within the next three hours.

    A. are
    B. need
    C. predict
    D. No change is necessary.

30. DIRECTIONS: Choose the option that corrects an error in the underlined portion(s). If no error exists, choose "No change is necessary."

Even though each of the children forgot a few of <u>their</u> lines, the audience clapped <u>its</u> hands
                                                 A   B

eagerly to show <u>its</u> appreciation for the performance.
                  C

    A. his or her
    B. their
    C. their
    D. No change is necessary.

31. DIRECTIONS: Choose the option that corrects an error in the underlined portion(s). If no error exists, choose "No change is necessary."

One reason <u>we</u> like living in Florida is that <u>we</u> can play sports outdoors all year round,
               A   B

and <u>you</u> don't have to wear heavy coats.
      C

    A. you
    B. you
    C. we
    D. No change is necessary.

32. DIRECTIONS: Choose the option that corrects an error in the underlined portion(s). If no error exists, choose "No change is necessary."

<u>They</u> are always looking for good places to surf, but to find the most challenging waves,
  A

<u>we</u> have to travel to the northern coast, or <u>they</u> can wait for a big storm and surf at the
 B   C

local beach.

A. We
B. they
C. we
D. No change is necessary.

33. DIRECTIONS: Choose the option that corrects an error in the underlined portion(s). If no error exists, choose "No change is necessary."

At the Dade City car show, <u>they</u> always have such interesting old cars on exhibit.

A. them
B. an antique car exhibit
C. the exhibitors
D. No change is necessary.

34. DIRECTIONS: Choose the option that corrects an error in the underlined portion(s). If no error exists, choose "No change is necessary."

<u>She</u> and <u>I</u> had an argument, so our friends have to relay messages between her and <u>I</u>.
 A   B   C

A. Her
B. me
C. me
D. No change is necessary.

35. DIRECTIONS: Choose the option that corrects an error in the underlined portion(s). If no error exists, choose "No change is necessary."

Flea cocoons can live <u>safe</u> in your home for over a year without eating, surviving <u>easily</u>
                           A   B
most pesticides as they hibernate in their <u>secure</u> shell.
                                                    C

A. safely
B. easy
C. securely
D. No change is necessary.

36. DIRECTIONS: Choose the word or phrase that best completes the sentence.

The weather is getting _____, so we had better go inside.

A. worst
B. worse
C. the worst
D. worser

37. DIRECTIONS: Choose the option that corrects an error in the underlined portion(s). If no error exists, choose "No change is necessary."

    <u>Broccoli</u> contains many cancer-fighting properties including fiber, beta-carotene, and vitamin C.

    A. Brocoli
    B. Brocolli
    C. Broccolli
    D. No change is necessary.

38. DIRECTIONS: Choose the option that corrects an error in the underlined portion(s). If no error exists, choose "No change is necessary."

    As part of my <u>job as</u> an after-school care <u>worker, I</u> am responsible for organizing the
                    A   B
    children's arts and crafts <u>activities, and</u> helping them with their homework.
                          C

    A. job, as
    B. worker I
    C. activities and
    D. No change is necessary.

39. DIRECTIONS: Choose the sentence that is correctly punctuated.
    A. Eric wanted to know where were the team members jerseys.
    B. Eric wanted to know where the team members' jerseys were.
    C. Eric wanted to know where were the team members' jerseys?

40. DIRECTIONS: Choose the option that corrects an error in the underlined portion(s). If no error exists, choose "No change is necessary."

    Many people do not think that the <u>Southern</u> part of Florida represents the <u>south</u> in terms
                                    A   B
    of <u>culture</u> because most of the people living there come from other states or countries.
          C

    A. southern
    B. South
    C. Culture
    D. No change is necessary.

# Part Two:
Reading Workbook

Chapter 1: Concept Skills

SECTION 1 ◆ THE MAIN IDEA

Understanding the author's main point is the most important key to reading comprehension. To help you understand main ideas, you must understand the difference between a main idea, a thesis, and a topic sentence.

Main Idea: The author's most important point in a passage. There are three ways in which main ideas present themselves:

1. **Topic Sentence:** The main idea of a <u>paragraph</u>. Topic sentences are *generally* located at the beginning of a paragraph (first or second sentence).

2. **Thesis or Thesis Statement:** The main idea in a <u>multi-paragraph</u> passage. Thesis statements are generally located in one of four spots:

   • The last sentence of the first paragraph (most common)
   • The first sentence of the first paragraph (2nd most common)
   • The first sentence of the second paragraph (3rd most common)
   • The conclusion (most often seen in narratives, or passages that tell a story)

3. **Implied Main Idea:** If there is no one sentence in the passage that captures the author's main point, then the main idea is implied. Implied main ideas are the hardest to determine because they require the most thinking.

We can visualize main ideas and where they are located as follows:

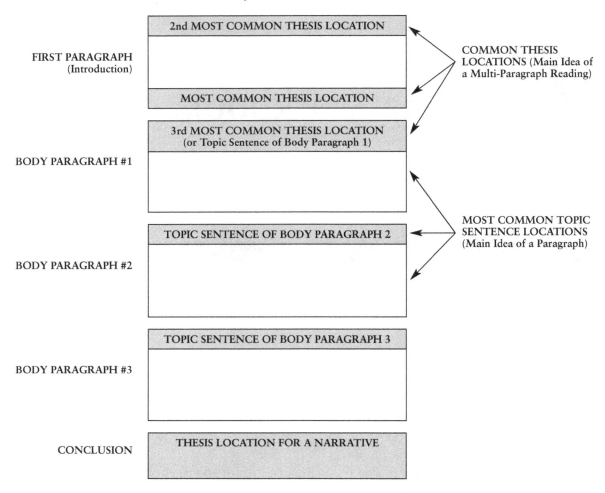

As you can see, each paragraph has a main idea (topic sentence). There is also a main idea for the whole reading selection (thesis statement). If you are unable to find a sentence that expresses a main idea, then the main idea is *implied* and you have to figure it out from the supporting details.

Keep in mind these two questions when looking for the main idea:

1. What is the topic (subject) of the passage?
2. What is the author's most important point about that topic, or what is he/she trying to say about the topic?

A good strategy is to begin reading every passage with these two questions in mind, and then to summarize the author's thesis or main idea in your own words before looking at the answer choices.

Read the following paragraph to find the answers to:

1. What is the topic (subject) of the passage?
2. What is the author's most important point about that topic?

Example #1
One of the most devastating problems facing children today can be found in every segment of society, among the rich or poor, the educated, or illiterate. The effects of child abuse are widespread and often irreversible, and can cause severe physical and psychological effects in children. Infants can suffer permanent brain damage when shaken violently. Abused children often suffer from emotional problems, such as schizophrenia or multiple personality disorders. They tend to become more withdrawn or more aggressive than children who are not abused. They also have a tendency for weaker social skills, as they withdraw from others and become more isolated than their non-abused peers. Such children may grow to be overly timid or to act out their anger and frustration with negative behaviors.

When seeking the topic, look for a key word which is most often repeated in the passage. In this case, "abused children" and "child abuse" appear frequently. But both are very general terms, and could include numerous subtopics such as the causes of child abuse, the solutions for child abuse, etc. On what subtopic of child abuse does this passage focus?

In this passage, there are several examples listed of the effects of child abuse. Therefore, the **topic** of this passage is *The effects of child abuse.*

When looking for a topic, be sure to select a topic that is not too broad and could include a wider scope of ideas than what is discussed in the passage, nor one that is too narrow and excludes information that *is* in the passage.

To find the main idea (or topic sentence, since this is a paragraph), ask yourself, "What is the author's point about the effects of child abuse?"

Look for the answer to the question stated in a general, broad statement that makes a strong point or summarizes the supporting details. In this passage, the broadest statement that summarizes the effects of child abuse is found in the second sentence, "The effects of child abuse are widespread and often irreversible, and can cause severe physical and psychological effects in children."

Remember, **the main idea is a broad and general statement**, and it is *not* a restatement of specific major details.

Check Your Work
When you think you have found the correct main idea, go back and look through the passage. Ask yourself: Do all of the other sentences tell more about this sentence? If they do, then your answer is correct.

Implied Main Ideas
Sometimes an author does not state the main idea in a topic sentence or a thesis statement. In these cases, the reader must infer the main idea by drawing a conclusion.

Think like a detective by looking for clues. Start by answering the two questions:

1. What is the topic? (Who or what is this about?)
2. What is the author's main point about the topic?

Pay close attention to the sentences that support the main idea, called **supporting details**.

The supporting details in the passage on the previous page are:

1. (Abused) infants can suffer permanent brain damage.
2. Abused children often suffer from emotional problems.
3. (Abused children) tend to become more withdrawn or more aggressive.
4. They also have a tendency for weaker social skills.

All of these sentences point out the effects of child abuse. If you had to write your own implied main idea of this passage, it may be something like:

Children who are abused may suffer many permanent and harmful effects.

This sentence would be broad enough to include all of the supporting details listed above.

> **Example #2**
> Although urban poverty is probably more familiar to most people, about one-fifth of poor people live in rural areas and another third in suburban areas. Rural poverty is not as visible as urban poverty. Separated from the mainstream of urban life, the rural poor are largely hidden on farms, on Indian reservations, in open country, and in small towns and villages. Unemployment rates in rural areas are far above the national average. Largely because of the technological revolution in agriculture and other occupations, poorly educated, unskilled rural workers have been left with no means of support. (Adapted from William Kornblum and Joseph Julian, *Social Problems*, 13th ed., Upper Saddle River, NJ: Pearson Prentice Hall, 2009.)
> **Topic:** Rural poverty

There is no topic sentence that expresses the main idea. The entire paragraph is composed of <u>supporting details</u> about rural poverty:

1. . . . about one-fifth of poor people live in rural areas and another third in suburban areas
2. . . . largely hidden on farms, on Indian reservations, in open country, and in small towns and villages.
3. Unemployment rates in rural areas are far above the national average.
4. Largely because of the technological revolution in agriculture and other occupations, poorly educated, unskilled rural workers have been left with no means of support.

All of the supporting details are giving features of rural poverty. A possible implied main idea that includes all of the ideas expressed in the supporting details might be:

Although it is less visible than urban poverty, rural poverty is common and has its own features and causes.

▶▶▌ *Secrets to Success*

- *When looking for the main idea, ask: What is the topic (subject) of the passage?*
- *What is the author's most important point about that topic?*
- *Most often, main ideas of multi-paragraph reading selections (thesis statements) are found in the first paragraph (last sentence or first sentence) or in the first sentence of the second paragraph.*

- *Look for a broad statement that sounds like an important point the author is making.*
- *Ask yourself: Do all of the other sentences tell more about this sentence?*
- *Sometimes an author does not state the main idea in a topic sentence or a thesis statement. In these cases, the reader must infer the main idea by drawing a conclusion.*

SECTION 1 ◆ DIAGNOSTIC: THE MAIN IDEA

Read the passages and apply the strategies described above for finding the main idea. When you are done, check your work with the answers immediately following the diagnostic. Even if you get a perfect score here, go ahead and complete the exercises in this section; they are designed to help build confidence and to give you practice for future test success.

Read the passage below and answer the questions that follow.

Evaluation research on drug education prevention programs done over the last thirty years indicates that these programs have not been effective. In fact, the findings state that these programs essentially had no effect on the drug problem. Although studies of the more recently developed programs are more optimistic, the findings still do not provide strong evidence of highly effective programs.   5

The goals of these programs have been to affect three basic areas: knowledge, attitudes, and behavior. The programs have had some success in increasing knowledge and, to a lesser extent, attitudes towards drugs; however, increases in knowledge and changed attitudes do not mean much if the actual drug behavior is not affected. In fact, those programs that only increase knowledge tend to reduce anxiety and fear of drugs and   10
may actually increase the likelihood of drug use. For example, one approach in the past was to provide students with complete information about all the possibilities of drug abuse, from the names of every street drug, to how the drugs are usually ingested, to detailed descriptions of possible effects of drugs and possible consequences of an overdose. Given the inquiring nature of children, such an approach could well amount   15
to a primer on how to take drugs, not how to avoid them.

The only effective approach to drug education is one in which children come to see that drug abuse constitutes unnecessary and self-abusive consequences. Too often, the real appeal of such drugs as marijuana or alcohol is dismissed by asking children to take up a sport or go bike riding or learn to play a musical instrument. Such suggestions   20
are fine as far as they go, but they often fail to take into account the personal problems that may tempt children into drug abuse.

Education programs that address social influence show the most promise in reducing or delaying onset of drug use. Psychological approaches in which social influences and skills are stressed are more effective than other approaches. The most effective pro-   25
grams in influencing both attitudes and behavior are peer programs that include either refusal skills—with more direct emphasis on behavior—or social and life skills, or both.

The use of scare tactics in any health education program, including drug abuse education programs, is counterproductive. Children soon learn to recognize the difference

between fact and possible fiction. Attempts to equate the dangers of marijuana with   30
those of heroin, suggestions that any drug can kill or permanently impair an individual,
and other dire warnings, no matter how true, are often disregarded as propaganda.
(David J. Anspaugh and Gene Ezell, *Teaching Today's Health*, 7th ed., San Francisco:
Benjamin Cummings, 2004.)

1. What is the topic of the passage?
   A. Drug abuse
   B. Drug education prevention programs
   C. Drug abusers
   D. The effects of drugs on children

2. Which sentence best states the main idea of the entire passage?
   A. The goals of these programs have been to affect three basic areas: knowledge, attitudes, and behavior.
   B. Although studies of the more recently developed programs are more optimistic, the findings still do not provide strong evidence of highly effective programs.
   C. Evaluation research on drug education programs done over the last thirty years indicates that these programs have not been effective.
   D. Education programs that address social influence show the most promise in reducing or delaying onset of drug abuse.

3. Which sentence best states the main idea of the second paragraph?
   A. The goals of these programs have been to affect three basic areas: knowledge, attitudes, and behavior.
   B. Programs that only increase knowledge tend to reduce anxiety and fear of drugs and may actually increase the likelihood of drug use.
   C. The programs have had some success in increasing knowledge and, to a lesser extent, attitudes toward drugs; however, increases in knowledge and changed attitudes do not mean much if the actual drug behavior is not affected.
   D. Given the inquiring nature of children, such an approach could well amount to a primer on how to take drugs, not how to avoid them.

4. Which sentence best states the main idea of the third paragraph?
   A. Children who take up sports or learn a musical instrument will not abuse drugs.
   B. The most effective way to prevent drug abuse is to address personal problems that may tempt children into using drugs.
   C. The most effective approach to drug abuse prevention is successfully convincing children that drug use is unnecessary and harmful.
   D. The consequences of drug abuse are unnecessary and self-abusive.

5. Which sentence best states the main idea of the fourth paragraph?
   A. Psychological approaches in which social influences and skills are stressed are more effective than other approaches.
   B. The most effective programs in influencing both attitudes and behavior are peer programs.
   C. Education programs that influence attitudes towards drugs are most effective.
   D. Education programs that address social influence show the most promise in reducing or delaying onset of drug use.

6. What is the topic of the fifth paragraph?
   A. Health education programs
   B. Scare tactics in drug prevention programs
   C. Propaganda
   D. The dangers of marijuana and heroin

7. Which sentence best states the main idea of the fifth paragraph?
   A. Using scare tactics in drug education programs is not effective.
   B. Children are not affected by drug education.
   C. The warnings about marijuana and heroin are not true.
   D. Drug abuse prevention programs use a lot of propaganda.

Answers to Diagnostic
   1. B   2. C   3. B   4. C   5. D   6. B   7. A

SECTION 1 ◆ EXERCISES: THE MAIN IDEA

Use the following exercises to practice reading for the main idea.

PASSAGE #1

Read the passage and answer the questions that follow.

"Street gangs" are a more formal variety of youth gang. They generally have leaders and a hierarchy of membership roles and responsibilities. They are named, and their members mark their identity with tattoos or "colors." While many street gangs are involved in violence, not all are. An anthropologist who did research among nearly forty street gangs in New York, Los Angeles, and Boston learned much about why individuals join gangs, providing insights that contradict popular thinking on this subject.   5

One common stereotype is that young boys join gangs because they are from homes with no male authority figure with whom they could identify. This study showed that equal numbers of gang members were from intact nuclear households as from those with an absent father. Another common perception is that the gang replaces a missing   10
feeling of family as a motive. This study, again, showed that the same number of gang members reported having close family ties as those who did not.

Those who were gang members shared a personality type called a "defiant individualist." This type has five traits: intense competitiveness, mistrust or wariness, self-reliance, social isolation, and a strong survival instinct. Poverty, especially urban poverty, leads   15
to the development of this type of personality. Many of these youths want to be economically successful, but social conditions channel their interests and skills into illegal pursuits rather than into legal pathways of achievement. (Adapted from Barbara D. Miller, *Cultural Anthropology*, 2nd ed., Boston: Allyn and Bacon, 2002.)

1. Which of the following sentences is the best statement of the main idea in the entire passage?
   A. The reasons individuals join street gangs are not those commonly held.
   B. An anthropologist studied street gangs in New York, Los Angeles, and Boston.

C. Not all street gangs are involved in violence.

D. Street gangs are a type of youth gang that is organized and identifies itself with "colors."

2. The implied main idea of paragraph 3 is that
   A. street gang members are victims of society.
   B. street gang members would be successful if they weren't poor.
   C. street gang members are not competitive.
   D. individuals develop a "defiant individualist" personality type due to urban poverty.

3. The implied meaning of paragraph 2 is that
   A. many gang members have close family ties.
   B. most gang members have no male authority figures in the household.
   C. individuals do not join gangs for the reasons most people think.
   D. people think that the gang is a substitute for a missing family, but this is not true.

PASSAGE #2

Read the passage and answer the questions that follow.

Although many people think of First Ladies as well-dressed homemakers presiding over White House dinners, there is much more to the job. The First Lady has no official government position. Yet she is often at the center of national attention. The media chronicles every word she speaks and every hairstyle she adopts.

Abigail Adams (an early feminist) and Dolly Madison counseled and lobbied their husbands. Edith Galt Wilson was the most powerful First Lady, virtually running the government when her husband, Woodrow, suffered a paralyzing stroke in 1919. Eleanor Roosevelt wrote a nationally syndicated newspaper column and tirelessly traveled and advocated New Deal policies. She became her crippled husband's eyes and ears around the country and urged him to adopt liberal social welfare policies. Lady Bird Johnson chose to focus on one issue, beautification, and most of her successors followed this pattern. Rosalyn Carter chose mental health, Nancy Reagan selected drugs, and Barbara Bush picked literacy.   5

                                                                                    10

In what was perhaps a natural evolution in a society where women have moved into positions formerly held only by males, Hillary Rodham Clinton attained the most responsible and visible leadership position ever held by a First Lady. She had been an influential advisor to the President, playing an active role in the selection of nominees for cabinet and judicial posts, for example. Most publicly, she headed the planning for the President's massive health care reform plan in 1993 and became, along with her husband, its primary advocate. (Adapted from George C. Edwards, Martin P. Wattenberg, and Robert L. Lineberry, *Government in America*, 9th ed., New York: Longman, 2000.)   15

                                                                                    20

4. The implied idea of the entire passage is that
   A. the job of First Lady reflects the role of women in society at the time.
   B. the role of First Lady has become more important in the past 50 years.

    C. First Ladies have taken active roles during their husbands' presidencies.

    D. the media reports all of the First Lady's activities.

5. Which of the following sentences best states the main idea of paragraph 2?

    A. Some First Ladies focused on one issue while others were more involved in helping the President run the government.

    B. Edith Galt Wilson was the most powerful First Lady.

    C. Eleanor Roosevelt helped her husband run the government because he was disabled.

    D. First Ladies are champions of causes.

6. The implied idea of paragraph 3 is that

    A. Hillary Rodham Clinton was a model First Lady.

    B. Hillary Rodham Clinton planned the health care reform plan in 1993.

    C. Hillary Rodham Clinton was well educated.

    D. Hillary Rodham Clinton held the most responsible leadership position of all First Ladies.

PASSAGE #3

Read the passage and answer the questions that follow.

In the 1980s, a long-running TV public service advertisement showed a father confronting his son with what is obviously the boy's drug paraphernalia. The father asks his son incredulously, "Where did you learn to do this?" The son, half in tears, replies, "From you, okay? I learned it from watching you!" Observational learning, which results simply from watching others, clearly appears to be a factor in an adolescent's willingness to experiment with drugs and alcohol.   5

Andrews and her colleagues found that adolescents' relationships with their parents influence whether they will model the substance use patterns of the parents. Specifically, they found that adolescents who had a positive relationship with their mothers modeled her use (or nonuse) of cigarettes, and those who had a close relationship with their fathers modeled the father's marijuana use (or nonuse). Similarly, those who had a negative relationship with their parents were less likely to model their parents' use of drugs or alcohol. Although some of the more complex results of this study depended on the age and sex of the adolescent, the general findings can be understood by thinking about them from the three levels of analysis and their interactions.   10 ... 15

At the level of the brain, observing someone engage in a behavior causes you to store new memories, which involves the hippocampus and related brain systems. These memories later can guide behavior, as they do in all types of imitation. At the level of the person, if you are motivated to observe someone, you are likely to be paying more attention to him or her and, therefore, increasing the likelihood of your learning from them and remembering what you learn. At the level of the group, you are more likely to be captivated by models who have certain attractive characteristics.   20

In this case, adolescents who had a positive relationship with their parents were more likely to do what their parents did; if their parents didn't smoke, the adolescents were less likely to do so. The events at these levels interact. Children who enjoy a positive   25 relationship with their parents may agree with their parents' higher status than do children who have a negative relationship with their parents. Thus, the former group of children probably increases the amount of attention they give to their parents' behavior. (Adapted from Stephen M. Kosslyn and Robin S. Rosenberg, *Psychology*, 2nd ed., Boston: Allyn and Bacon, 2004.)

7. Which of the following sentences is the best statement of the main idea of the entire passage?
   A. Your brain stores memories of observing someone's behavior.
   B. Children who have a positive relationship with their parents pay more attention to the way their parents act.
   C. A parent's use of drugs or alcohol will cause the child to use these substances.
   D. Watching people behaving a certain way on television becomes stored in your memory.

8. The implied main idea of paragraph 4 is that
   A. if a parent smokes, the adolescent will smoke.
   B. the parent-child relationship affects the child's behavior.
   C. children who have a negative relationship with their parents are likely to copy their parents' behavior.
   D. adolescents with positive relationships with their parents almost certainly pay closer attention to the way their parents act.

9. The implied main idea of paragraph 2 is that
   A. substance use or nonuse is dependent on an adolescent's relationship with his or her parents.
   B. adolescents who had negative relationships with their parents did not model the parents' use of alcohol or drugs.
   C. adolescents whose parents use drugs or alcohol may or may not copy their parents.
   D. adolescents who had negative relationships with parents who used drugs or alcohol are better off.

10. The implied main idea of paragraph 3 is that
    A. people are influenced by those who are attractive.
    B. behaviors you have observed become memories that will later influence your behavior.
    C. observational learning affects an individual on three levels.
    D. you will learn from someone you want to pay attention to.

SECTION 2 ◆ SUPPORTING DETAILS

Supporting details are sentences which give more specific information about the main idea. Quite often, main idea questions will include 2 or 3 supporting details as answer choices. Knowing the difference between main ideas and supporting details will help us answer the main idea questions correctly.

Long passages contain one main idea and may have one or several major supporting details. The number of major and minor details varies with each passage. Not every major detail has a minor detail to support it, while some major details may have several minor supporting details.

Major and Minor Details

Major details tell us more information about the main idea.
Minor details tell us more about the major details.

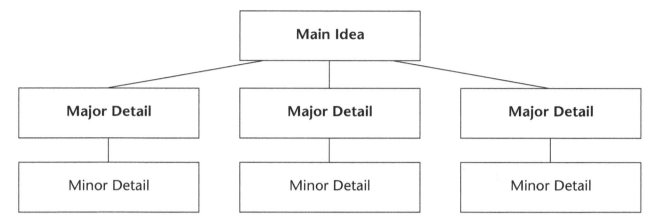

Read the following passage, and ask:
- What is the topic (subject) of the passage?
- What is the author's most important point about that topic?
- Which details support the main idea?

As portions of federal governmental debt become due, the government refinances the debt by selling new bonds. It uses the income from the sale of the new bonds to pay off the current debt, and the new bonds have a later maturity date, which allows them more time to pay off debt. Also, the federal government has the authority to raise taxes to generate funds to pay off its debt when necessary, something that private corporations and banks cannot do to avoid bankruptcy. Another way that the government can deal with its debt is by printing new money. Although printing new dollars may cause inflation, the government can use new dollars to pay off debt or to make interest payments.

Here is a concept map of the passage:

Topic: Governmental Debt

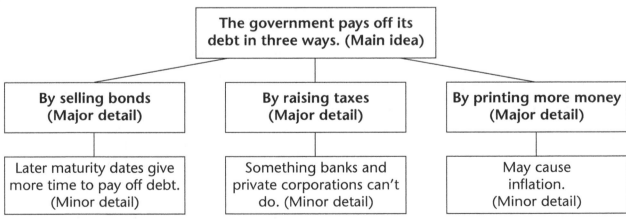

Notice that the three major details explain how (the three ways) the government pays off debt. The other (minor) details explain more about each of the three ways.

Identifying Supporting Details

To find supporting details, pay close attention to the <u>first sentence of each paragraph</u>. They often contain major details that support the main idea. They are also usually topic sentences that tell you what kind of information to expect in the paragraph. Supporting details answer questions such as, *who, what, when, where, why,* and *how*. To find supporting details, look for:

> Reasons
> Examples
> Characteristics
> Analysis and explanations
> People and places
> Senses

▶▶▎ *Secrets to Success*

- *Some answer choices distort the information to give you an answer which sounds right, but is, in fact, inaccurate.*
- *ALWAYS go back and reread the passage to check the facts; do not rely on your memory.*
- *Nearly all supporting detail questions ask about specific facts, and can be answered by finding the information as it is stated in the passage, not inferred or implied.*
- *Supporting detail questions often start out, "According to the passage . . ."*
- *Beware of answer choices that use words like "always," "never," "all," or "none." Unless it is directly stated in the passage, do not assume that these terms apply.*
- *Read questions carefully, looking for words like "except" and "not." Sometimes you are asked to look for the one answer that is not correct.*

SECTION 2 ◆ DIAGNOSTIC: SUPPORTING DETAILS

Read the passages and apply the strategies described above for finding supporting details. When you are done, check your work with the answers immediately following the diagnostic. Even if you get a perfect score here, go ahead and complete the exercises in this section; they are designed to help build confidence and to give you practice for future test success.

Read the passage below and answer the questions that follow.

A single parent may experience a variety of problems. First of all, it may be difficult to meet the emotional needs of the child. There are a variety of ways to express love for a child. Telling a child he or she is loved and demonstrating that love with quality time serve to express love; however, the demands of working and maintaining a home may be so overwhelming that a child's emotional needs may not be met adequately. It also may   5
be hard for the single parent to provide proper supervision for the child. Making arrangements for the child's care and supervision is difficult and costly and may take a large share of the budget. In addition, because women tend to make less money than men, households headed by women can experience financial difficulties. Finally, the single parent may experience unfulfilled emotional and sexual needs. Unmet emotional needs can   10
develop because of the lack of time to seek a relationship. Because most single parents wish to hide their sexual involvement from their child, finding a time and place can present problems. Nevertheless, being a single parent does not have to be a disaster. It is im-

portant that single parents have sufficient financial, material, and emotional support to meet their own and their child's demands. (Adapted from David J. Anspaugh and Gene Ezell, *Teaching Today's Health*, 7th ed., San Francisco: Benjamin Cummings, 2004.)   15

1. Which sentence best states the main idea of the passage? *(This question will also help you to determine the supporting details.)*
   A. Parents must have financial, material, and emotional support to meet their child's demands.
   B. Being a single parent does not have to be a disaster.
   C. A single parent may experience a variety of problems.
   D. Many children of single parents may have needs that are not being met.

2. The first major detail which the authors discuss is
   A. It may be hard for the single parent to provide proper supervision for the child.
   B. Women tend to make less money than men, and households headed by women can experience financial difficulties.
   C. There are a variety of ways to express love for a child.
   D. It may be difficult for single parents to meet the emotional needs of the child.

3. According to the passage, which of the following statements is true?
   A. All single parents experience unfulfilled emotional and sexual needs.
   B. Women tend to make more money than men.
   C. Child care can be difficult and costly.
   D. Households headed by women always experience financial difficulties.

4. According to the passage, single parents
   A. may experience anger or frustration at having their own needs go unmet.
   B. can show their love for the child by telling a child he or she is loved.
   C. cannot maintain a home and a job, and still meet the child's emotional needs.
   D. find that the demands of working and maintaining a home are overwhelming.

5. In the passage, the authors
   A. give reasons why being a single parent is difficult.
   B. explain why single parents have more problems than two-parent families.
   C. tell the effects of single-parent families on children.
   D. tell single parents how to avoid common problems in raising children.

6. Which of the following is *not* one of the problems discussed in the passage?
   A. Children from single-parent families are often left unsupervised.
   B. It may be hard for the single parent to provide proper supervision for the child.
   C. Women tend to make less money than men, and households headed by women can experience financial difficulties.
   D. Single parents may experience unfulfilled emotional and sexual needs.

7. The sentence, "Unmet emotional needs can develop because of lack of time to seek a relationship" (lines 10–11) is a
   A. topic.
   B. topic sentence.
   C. major detail.
   D. minor detail.

Answers to Diagnostic
1. C (The variety of problems described are the major supporting details.)
2. D   3. C   4. B   5. A   6. A   7. D

SECTION 2 ◆ EXERCISES: SUPPORTING DETAILS

Use the following exercises to practice reading for supporting details.

PASSAGE #1

Read the passage and answer the questions that follow.

Do you believe that your Zodiac sign matters? So many people apparently do that the home page for the *Yahoo!* site on the World Wide Web will automatically provide your daily horoscope. But astrology—along with palm reading and tea-leaf reading, and all their relatives—is not a branch of psychology; it is pseudopsychology. Pseudopsychology is superstition or unsupported opinion pretending to be science. Pseudopsychology is not just "bad psychology," which rests on poorly documented observations or badly designed studies and, therefore, has questionable foundations. Pseudopsychology is not psychology at all. It may look and sound like psychology, but it is not science.

Appearances can be misleading. Consider extrasensory perception (ESP). Is this pseudopsychology? ESP refers to a collection of mental abilities that do not rely on the ordinary senses or abilities. Telepathy, for instance, is the ability to read minds. This sounds not only wonderful but magical. No wonder people are fascinated by the possibility that they, too, may have latent, untapped, extraordinary abilities. The evidence that such abilities really exist is shaky. But the mere fact that many experiments on ESP have come up empty does not mean that the experiments themselves are bad or "unscientific." One can conduct a perfectly good experiment, guarding against bias and expectancy of effects, even on ESP. Such research is not necessarily pseudopsychology.

Let's say you wanted to study telepathy. You might arrange to test pairs of participants, with one member of each pair acting as "sender" and the other as "receiver." Both the sender and receiver would look at hands of playing cards that contained the same four cards. The sender would focus on one card (say, an ace), and would "send" the receiver a mental image of the chosen card. The receiver's job would be to guess which card the sender is seeing. By chance alone, with only four cards to choose from, the receiver would guess right about 25% of the time. So the question is, can the receiver do better than mere guesswork? In this study, you would measure the percentage of times the receiver picks the right card, and compare this to what you would expect from guessing alone.

However, what if the sender provided visible clues (accidentally or on purpose) that have nothing to do with ESP, perhaps smiling when "sending" an ace, grimacing when "sending" a two. A better experiment would have sender and receiver in different rooms, thus controlling for such possible problems. Furthermore, what if people have an unconscious bias to prefer red over black cards, which leads both sender and receiver to select them more often than would be dictated by chance? This difficulty can be countered by including a control condition, in which a receiver guesses cards when the

sender is not actually sending. Whether ESP can be considered a valid, reliable phe- 35
nomenon will depend on the results of such studies. If they conclusively show that there
is nothing to it, then people who claim to have ESP or to understand it will be trying
to sell a bill of goods—and will be engaging in pseudopsychology. But as long as proper
studies are under way, we cannot dismiss them as pseudopsychology. (Stephen M. Kosslyn and Robin S. Rosenberg, *Psychology*, 2nd ed., Boston: Allyn and Bacon, 2004.)   40

1. According to the passage, ESP
   A. is a pseudopsychology.
   B. has not as yet been proved or disproved.
   C. is related to astrology and palm reading.
   D. is an ability that everyone can learn to draw on.

2. According to paragraph 1, pseudopsychology is
   A. a branch of psychology.
   B. a science.
   C. a badly designed study.
   D. a superstition.

3. Research experiments on telepathy
   A. must guard against bias.
   B. are difficult to set up.
   C. have shown that telepathy is largely guesswork.
   D. are a waste of time.

4. According to paragraph 4, a better experiment would
   A. eliminate guesswork.
   B. eliminate problems of visible clues and unconscious bias.
   C. use playing cards.
   D. measure the percentage of times the receiver picks the right card.

PASSAGE # 2

Read the passage and answer the questions that follow.

North America has ten species of skunks. The one most people have seen—or at least
smelled—is the abundant and widespread striped skunk. Another species is the spotted
skunk, rarely seen but especially interesting because it illustrates some important concepts about biological species. This particular skunk belongs to a species called the western spotted skunk. The adult is only about the size of a house cat, but it has a potent   5
chemical arsenal that makes up for its small size. Before spraying her potent musk, a female guarding her young usually warns an intruder by raising her tail, stamping her
forefeet, raking the ground with her claws, or even doing a handstand. When all else
fails, she can spray her penetrating odor for three meters with considerable accuracy.

The western spotted skunk inhabits a variety of environments in the United States,   10
from the Pacific coast to the western Great Plains. It is closely related to the eastern
spotted skunk, which occurs throughout the southeastern and midwestern United
States. The ranges of these two species overlap, and the two species look so much alike

that even experts can have a difficult time telling them apart. Both are black with broken white stripes and spots. Individuals of the western species are, on average, slightly smaller, and some have a white tip on the tail, but these and other minor differences in body form are not always present.   15

For many years, biologists debated whether all spotted skunks belong to one species. But in the 1960s, studies of sexual reproduction in these animals showed that they are indeed two species. Reproduction in the eastern spotted skunk is a straightforward affair. Mating occurs in late winter, and young are born between April and July. In marked contrast, the western spotted skunk includes what is called delayed development in its reproductive cycle. Mating takes place in the later summer and early fall, and zygotes begin to develop in the uterus of the female. Further development, however, is temporarily stopped at an early point called the blastocyst stage. Blastocysts remain dormant in the female's uterus throughout the winter months and resume growth in the spring, with the young (usually 5–7) being born in May or June. Because mating occurs at different times of the year for the two species, there is no opportunity for gene flow between populations of eastern and western spotted skunks. Thus, they are separate species, despite the pronounced similarities in their body form and coloration.   30

Spotted skunks show us that looks can be deceiving. Without knowledge of the mating cycles, we could interpret the minor differences between the two species as insignificant and conclude that there is only one species of spotted skunk in North America. (Adapted from Neil A. Campbell, Lawrence G. Mitchell, and Jane B. Reece, *Biology*, 3rd ed., San Francisco: Benjamin Cummings, 2000.)

5. The western spotted skunk and the eastern spotted skunk
   A. are about the size of a house cat.
   B. are not difficult to tell apart.
   C. live in completely different parts of the United States.
   D. belong to the same species.

6. The female western spotted skunk guarding her young warns an intruder by
   A. hissing.
   B. running in circles.
   C. stamping her forefeet.
   D. swishing her tail.

7. Biologists discovered that the two skunks were different species by studying their
   A. migration patterns.
   B. range overlap.
   C. chemical composition of their potent musk sprays.
   D. mating habits.

8. The western spotted skunk's reproductive cycle
   A. occurs in late winter.
   B. occurs at the same time as the eastern spotted skunk.
   C. includes delayed development.
   D. takes longer than the eastern spotted skunk.

9. The eastern and western spotted skunks are interesting because
   A. they live in a variety of environments across the U.S.
   B. they illustrate some important concepts about biological species.
   C. they could become extinct.
   D. they have similar markings.

10. The most important discovery about the North American eastern and western spotted skunks is that
    A. their habitats overlap.
    B. there is more than one species of spotted skunk.
    C. they are difficult to tell apart.
    D. they defend their young similarly.

SECTION 3 ◆ AUTHOR'S PURPOSE

Now that you understand how to find the main idea and supporting details, you can use this knowledge to more easily find the author's purpose. This is because the author's purpose is VERY closely related to the main idea.

Every author has a purpose for writing and a main point that he or she is making about the topic. The three most common reasons for writing are:

- **To entertain** (examples: short stories, novels, poems, jokes, anecdotes)

- **To inform** (examples: newspaper articles, textbooks, reference materials, instruction manuals, legal documents)

- **To persuade** (examples: campaign speeches, advertising, music/art/literary criticism, sales pitches)

More specific purposes may include:

- To state a problem, then offer a solution
- To analyze or discuss an idea
- To explain something
- To criticize or praise something or someone
- To describe something in detail
- To illustrate something
- To define something

Sometimes an author may have more than one purpose when writing. For example, an author may combine a purpose to criticize with a purpose to persuade when trying to convince readers that a change needs to be made in the national health care system.

To find the author's purpose, ask: <u>Why did the author write this?</u> What was he or she trying to accomplish?

Look for Clues

Take a close look at the <u>main idea</u>. It often indicates the author's purpose.

Consider the <u>author's tone</u>. Is the author's "voice" serious or lighthearted? Does the author use emotional language with positive or negative connotations? Certain tones are related to specific purposes. For example, if the author is informing or instructing, the tone will usually be objective, straightforward, matter-of-fact, formal, or neutral. To entertain, authors often use tones that are lighthearted, humorous, amusing, or dramatic. Authors with persuasion in mind may use a tone that is critical, indignant, angry, impassioned, or insistent.

Does the author present mostly <u>facts or opinions</u>? Factual passages tend to be objective and informative, while passages with many opinions tend to be persuasive and biased.

Look for phrases that indicate the <u>author's intent</u>, such as "The goal of this essay . . ." or "It is my intent to show . . ."

Pay attention to the overall <u>pattern of organization</u> the author uses. For example, an author's purpose may be to compare two or more things, or to contrast them. Another may be to define or explain a term, or give the causes or effects of something.

What is the author's primary purpose in the following passages?

> **Example #1**
> Although physics and chemistry are considered separate fields of study, they have much in common. First, both are physical sciences and are concerned with studying and explaining physical occurrences. Second, to study and record these occurrences, each field has developed a precise set of signs and symbols. These might be considered a specialized language. Finally, both fields are closely tied to the field of mathematics and use mathematics in predicting and explaining physical occurrences. (Hewitt, *Conceptual Physics*, 8th ed.)

The primary purpose in the passage above is
   A. to explain the fields of chemistry and physics.
   B. to persuade the reader that physics and chemistry are closely tied to mathematics.
   C. to compare the similarities between chemistry and physics.
   D. to give the reasons why mathematics is related to chemistry and physics.

How to Find the Author's Purpose
First, determine the topic and main idea:

Topic: Physics and Chemistry

Main Idea: Although physics and chemistry are considered separate fields of study, they have much in common.

Then look for the author's **pattern of organization:** The author is comparing the similarities between physics and chemistry.

Consider the **author's tone:** Serious and objective, containing mostly facts.

The correct answer is C, which restates the main idea and the overall pattern of organization.

Example #2

Hate sites began on the Internet in the mid-1990s, and their number expanded rapidly. Now hate groups in general across the nation are on the rise because of the Internet. Hate sites advocate violence toward immigrants, Jews, Arabs, gays, abortion providers, and others. Through the Internet, disturbed minds effectively fuel hatred, violence, sexism, racism, and terrorism. Never before has there been such an intensive way for depraved people to gather to reinforce their prejudices and hatred. (Adapted from Shedletsky and Aitknen, *Human Communication on the Internet*, Boston: Allyn and Bacon, 2004.)

The primary purpose in the passage above is
   A. to show how the number of hate sites on the Internet has increased rapidly.
   B. to show how the Internet has caused the increase of hate groups in general.
   C. to criticize hate groups.
   D. to persuade the reader to not visit hate sites on the Internet.

Topic: Hate sites on the Internet

Main Idea: Hate groups in general across the nation are on the rise because of the Internet.

Pattern of Organization: (Cause and effect) The Internet is the cause of the (effect) increase in the number of hate groups.

The correct answer is B, *To show how the Internet has caused the increase of hate groups in general.*

▶▶▌ *Secrets to Success*

   • *Begin by stating the topic and main idea in your own words, and try to find a topic sentence in the passage.*
   • *Ask: Why did the author write this?*
   • *Look at the overall pattern of organization.*
   • *Pay close attention to the author's tone.*
   • *Look at the language used: is it biased?*
   • *Look for facts and opinions.*

SECTION 3 ◆ DIAGNOSTIC: AUTHOR'S PURPOSE

Read the passages and apply the strategies described above for finding the author's purpose. When you are done, check your work with the answers immediately following the diagnostic. Even if you get a perfect score here, go ahead and complete the exercises in this section; they are designed to help build confidence and to give you practice for future test success.

Read the passages below and answer the questions that follow.

PASSAGE #1

Inside those (television) networks, a growing number of people with Ph.D.'s are injecting the latest in child development theory into new programs. That's the good news.

The bad news is that working these shows into kids' lives in a healthy way remains a challenge. Much of what kids watch remains banal or harmful. Many kids watch too much. There are also troubling socioeconomic factors at work. In lower income homes, for instance, kids watch more and are more likely to have TV in their bedrooms, a practice pediatricians discourage. (Daniel McGinn, *Newsweek*, November 11, 2002.)   5

1. The primary purpose of this passage is to
   A. list the reasons why television is harmful to children.
   B. explain why children in lower income homes watch more television than children in higher income homes.
   C. persuade the reader that making television healthy for children is still a challenge.
   D. inform the reader that child development theory in television is harmful.

PASSAGE #2

Think of your speech as beginning as soon as the audience focuses on you. Similarly, think of it ending not after you have spoken the last sentences, but only after the audience directs its focus away from you. Here are a few suggestions for before and after you give your speech. (DeVito, *Essentials of Human Communication*, 3rd ed., Boston: Allyn and Bacon, 1999.)

2. The author's purpose will probably be to
   A. convince the reader that a speech lasts longer than the spoken part.
   B. instruct the reader on what to do before and after a speech.
   C. explain when a speech really begins.
   D. compare what happens before a speech to what happens afterward.

PASSAGE #3

Public opinion polling sounds scientific with its talk of random samples and sampling error; it is easy to take results for solid fact. But being an informed consumer of polls requires more than just a nuts and bolts knowledge of how they are conducted; you should think about whether the questions are fair and unbiased before making too much of the results. The good—or the harm—that polls do depends on how well the data are collected and how thoughtfully the data are interpreted. (Edwards, Wattenberg, and Lineberry, *Government in America*, 9th ed., New York: Longman, 2000.)   5

3. The main purpose of the passage above is to
   A. narrate a story about public opinion polling.
   B. criticize the use of public opinion polls.
   C. inform the reader about how public opinion polls are conducted.
   D. convince the reader to be an informed consumer of public opinion polls.

PASSAGE #4

During the 1950s, the Cleavers on the television show "Leave It to Beaver" epitomized the American family. In 1960, over 70% of all American households were like the

Cleavers: made up of a breadwinner father, a homemaker mother, and their kids. Today, "traditional" families with a working husband, an unemployed wife, and one or more children make up less than 15% of the nation's households. (Alexander, Lombardi, et al., *Joining a Community of Readers*, New York: Longman, 1998.)   5

4. The authors' primary purpose is
   A. to persuade the reader that American families are not as stable as they used to be.
   B. to contrast the differences between American families of the 1950s and families of today.
   C. to contrast the differences between television show families and real American families.
   D. to inform the readers about the television show families of the 1950s.

PASSAGE #5

Articulation refers to movements of the speech organs as they modify and interrupt the air stream being sent from the lungs. Different movements of the tongue, lips, teeth, palate, or vocal cords produce different sounds. Pronunciation refers to the production of the syllables or words according to some accepted standard, such as the dictionary. (DeVito, *Essentials of Human Communication,* 3rd ed., Boston: Allyn and Bacon, 1999.)

5. The author's primary purpose is
   A. to define the terms *articulation* and *pronunciation.*
   B. to compare the differences between articulation and pronunciation.
   C. to inform the reader about how articulation occurs.
   D. to give examples of articulation.

Answers to Diagnostic
   1. C   2. B   3. D   4. B   5. A

SECTION 3 ◆ EXERCISES: AUTHOR'S PURPOSE

Use the following exercises to practice reading for the author's purpose.

PASSAGE #1
Read the passage and answer the question that follows.

Fungi have a number of practical uses for humans. Most of us have eaten mushrooms although we may not have realized that we were ingesting the fruiting bodies of subterranean fungi. In addition, mushrooms are not the only fungi we eat. The distinctive flavors of certain kinds of cheeses, including Roquefort and blue cheese, come from the fungi used to ripen them. Highly prized by gourmets are truffles, the fruiting bodies of certain mycorrhizal fungi associated with tree roots. The unicellular fungi, the yeasts, are important in food production. Yeasts are used in baking, brewing, and winemaking. Fungi are medically valuable as well. Some fungi produce antibiotics that are used to treat bacterial diseases. In fact, the first antibiotic discovered was penicillin, which is made by the common mold called *Penicillium*. (Adapted from Neil A. Campbell, Lawrence G. Mitchell, and Jane B. Reece, *Biology*, 3rd ed., San Francisco: Benjamin Cummings, 2000.)   5   10

1. The primary purpose of the above passage is to
   A. describe foods that are fungi.
   B. explain how fungi are used to ripen cheeses.
   C. give examples of the uses of fungi.
   D. analyze the medical and nutritional benefits of fungi.

PASSAGE #2

Read the passage and answer the question that follows.

John Castle's lifestyle gives us a glimpse into how the super-rich live. After earning a degree in physics at MIT and an MBA at Harvard, John went into banking and securities, where he made more than $100 million. Wanting to be close to someone famous, John bought President John F. Kennedy's "Winter White House," an oceanfront estate in Palm Beach, Florida. John spent $11 million to remodel the 13,000-square-foot house so it would be more to his liking. Among those changes: adding bathrooms numbers 14 and 15. He likes to show off John F. Kennedy's bed and also the dresser that has the drawer labeled "black underwear," carefully hand-lettered by Rose Kennedy.

If John gets bored at his beachfront estate—or tired of swimming in the Olympic-size pool where JFK swam the weekend before his assassination—he entertains himself by riding one of his thoroughbred horses at his nearby 10-acre ranch. If this fails to ease his boredom, he can relax aboard his custom-built, 45-foot Hinckley yacht. The yacht is a real source of diversion. He once boarded it for an around-the-world trip.

He didn't stay on board, though—just joined the cruise from time to time. A captain and crew kept the vessel sailing in the right direction, and whenever John felt like it, he would fly in and stay a few days. Then he would fly back to the States to direct his business. He did this about a dozen times, flying perhaps 150,000 miles, an interesting way to get around the world.

How much does a custom-built Hinckley yacht cost? John can't tell you. As he says, "I don't want to know what anything costs. When you've got enough money, price doesn't make a difference. That's part of the freedom of being rich." (Adapted from James M. Henslin, *Sociology*, 6th ed., Boston: Allyn and Bacon, 2003.)

2. The primary purpose of the above passage is to
   A. persuade the reader that John Castle's lifestyle should be envied.
   B. describe John Castle's lifestyle as an example of how the super-rich live.
   C. criticize John Castle's squandering his money.
   D. inspire the reader to become wealthy.

PASSAGE #3

Read the passage and answer the question that follows.

The National Child Abuse Prevention and Treatment Act of 1974 defines child abuse and neglect as "physical or mental injury, sexual abuse or exploitation, negligent treatment, or maltreatment of a child under the age of eighteen or the age specified under the child protection law of the state in question, by a person who is responsible for the

child's welfare, under circumstances which indicate that the child's health or welfare 5
is harmed or threatened thereby."

The laws of every state require teachers to report suspected cases of child abuse and
neglect. Every state grants teachers who make such reports immunity from civil and
criminal suits. State laws vary in their requirements, and teachers should become familiar with the laws where they teach. Most states require an oral report to an admin- 10
istrator followed by a written statement. The law will protect teachers who act in good
faith. Teachers should not hesitate to file a report if they believe a student is a victim
of abuse or neglect. In most states teachers can be fined or imprisoned if they do *not*
make the report, and in some states they can be sued for neglect.

A teacher who sees a student exhibit indicators of child abuse and neglect over a period 15
of time should think seriously about why the indicators are present. As in other areas
of the law, the *reasonable person* standard applies: Under similar circumstances, would
a reasonable person suspect abuse or neglect? If your answer is yes, you should make
a report. Remember, the law will protect you if you act in good faith. Do not be blind
to the problem. (Adapted from Joseph W. Newman, *America's Teachers*, 4th ed., 20
Boston: Allyn and Bacon, 2002.)

3. The author's primary purpose in the above passage is to
   A. define child abuse to teachers.
   B. explain state laws regarding child abuse to teachers.
   C. inform teachers about child abuse indicators.
   D. convince teachers that it is their duty to report child abuse.

PASSAGE #4

Read the passage and answer the question that follows.

There are vast cultural differences in what is considered proper when it comes to criticism. In some cultures, being kind to the person is more important than telling the ab-
solute truth, and so members may say things that are complimentary, but untrue, in a
logical sense. Those who come from cultures that are highly individual and competitive,
such as the United States, Germany, and Sweden, may find public criticism a normal 5
part of the learning process. Those who come from cultures that are more collectivist
and that emphasize the group rather than the individual, such as Japan, Mexico, and
Korea, are likely to find giving and receiving public criticism uncomfortable. Thus,
people from individual cultures may readily criticize others and are likely to expect the
same "courtesy" from other listeners. After all, this person might reason, "If I'm going 10
to criticize your skills to help you improve, I expect you to help me in the same way."
Persons from collectivist cultures, on the other hand, may feel that it's more important
to be polite and courteous than to help someone learn a skill. Cultural rules to maintain
peaceful relations among the Japanese and politeness among many Asian cultures may
conflict with the Western classroom cultural norm to voice criticism. 15

The difficulties are compounded when you interpret unexpected behavior through your
own cultural filters. For example, if a speaker who expects comments and criticism
gets none, he or she may interpret the silence to mean that the audience didn't care or

wasn't listening. But they may have been listening very intently. They may simply be operating with a different cultural rule—a rule that says it's impolite to criticize or evaluate another person's work, especially in public. (Adapted from Joseph A. DeVito, *Essentials of Human Communication*, 3rd ed., New York: Longman, 1999.)   20

4. The main purpose of the above passage is to
    A. contrast cultural differences in public criticism.
    B. explain how to criticize effectively.
    C. persuade the reader to respect cultural differences.
    D. describe the effects of cultural miscommunications.

PASSAGE #5

Read the passage and answer the question that follows.

Although many people think of First Ladies as well-dressed homemakers presiding over White House dinners, there is much more to the job. The First Lady has no official government position. Yet she is often at the center of national attention. The media chronicles every word she speaks and every hairstyle she adopts.

Abigail Adams (an early feminist) and Dolly Madison counseled and lobbied their husbands. Edith Galt Wilson was the most powerful First Lady, virtually running the government when her husband, Woodrow, suffered a paralyzing stroke in 1919. Eleanor Roosevelt wrote a nationally syndicated newspaper column and tirelessly traveled and advocated New Deal policies. She became her crippled husband's eyes and ears around the country and urged him to adopt liberal social welfare policies. Lady Bird Johnson chose to focus on one issue, beautification, and most of her successors followed this pattern. Rosalyn Carter chose mental health, Nancy Reagan selected drugs, and Barbara Bush picked literacy.   5   10

In what was perhaps a natural evolution in a society where women have moved into positions formerly held only by males, Hillary Rodham Clinton attained the most responsible and visible leadership position ever held by a First Lady. She had been an influential advisor to the President, playing an active role in the selection of nominees for cabinet and judicial posts, for example. Most publicly, she headed the planning for the President's massive health care reform plan in 1993 and became, along with her husband, its primary advocate. (Adapted from George C. Edwards, Martin P. Wattenberg, and Robert L. Lineberry, *Government in America*, 9th ed., New York: Longman, 2000.)   15   20

5. The main purpose of the above passage is to
    A. contrast the activities of the First Ladies.
    B. explain the way the First Lady does her job.
    C. convince the reader that First Ladies are feminists.
    D. illustrate the public roles of the First Ladies.

PASSAGE #6

Read the passage and answer the question that follows.

President Truman's decision to order the atomic bombings on the Japanese cities of Hiroshima and Nagasaki has been the subject of intense historical debate. Truman's defenders argue that the bombs ended the war quickly, avoiding the necessity of a costly invasion and the probable loss of tens of thousands of Americans' lives and hundreds of Japanese lives. According to some intelligence estimates, an invasion might have cost 268,000 American casualties, with Japanese costs several times that figure.   5

Truman's defenders also argue that Hiroshima and Nagasaki were legitimate targets with both military bases and war industry, and their civilian populations had been showered with leaflets warning them to evacuate. Finally, they argue that two bombs were ultimately necessary to end the war. They note that even after the atomic bomb   10 had fallen on Hiroshima, the Japanese war minister implored the nation's Supreme Council "for one last great battle on Japanese soil—as demanded by the national honor. . . . Would it not be wondrous for this whole nation to be destroyed like a beautiful flower."

Truman's critics argue that the war might have ended even without the atomic   15 bombings. They maintain that the Japanese economy would have been strangled by a continued naval blockade and forced to surrender by conventional firebombing. The revisionists also contend that the President had options apart from using the bombs. They believe that it might have been possible to induce a Japanese surrender by a demonstration of the atomic bomb's power or by providing a more specific   20 warning of the damage it could produce or by guaranteeing the emperor's position in postwar Japan.

The revisionists also believe that estimates of potential American casualties were grossly inflated after the war to justify the bombing. Finally, they argue that the bomb might have been dropped mainly to justify its cost or to scare the Soviet Union. The Soviet   25 Union entered the Japanese war August 8, and some revisionists charge that the bombings were designed to end the war before the Red army could occupy northern China. (Adapted from James Kirby Martin et al., *America and Its Peoples*, 5th ed., New York: Longman, 2004.)

6. The authors' purpose in the above passage is to
   A. describe the effects of the U.S. dropping the atomic bombs on the Japanese.
   B. inform the reader of the reasons for dropping the atomic bombs on Hiroshima and Nagasaki.
   C. persuade the reader that the dropping of atomic bombs on Hiroshima and Nagasaki was wrong.
   D. present the two sides of the debate over the dropping of the atomic bombs on Hiroshima and Nagasaki.

5

PASSAGE #7

Read the passage and answer the question that follows.

A single parent may experience a variety of problems. First of all, it may be difficult to meet the emotional needs of the child. There are a variety of ways to express love for a child. Telling a child he or she is loved and demonstrating that love with quality time serve to express love; however, the demands of working and maintaining a home may be so overwhelming that a child's emotional needs may not be met adequately. It also may be hard for the single parent to provide proper supervision for the child. Making arrangements for the child's care and supervision is difficult and costly and may take a large share of the budget. In addition, because women tend to make less money than men, households headed by women can experience financial difficulties. Finally, the single parent may experience unfulfilled emotional and sexual needs. Unmet emotional needs can develop because of the lack of time to seek a relationship. Because most single parents wish to hide their sexual involvement from their child, finding a time and place can present problems. Nevertheless, being a single parent does not have to be a disaster. It is important that single parents have sufficient financial, material, and emotional support to meet their own and their child's demands. (Adapted from David J. Anspaugh and Gene Ezell, *Teaching Today's Health*, 7th ed., San Francisco: Benjamin Cummings, 2004.)

10
15
20

7. The authors' purpose in the above passage is to
   A. argue the disadvantages of single parenthood.
   B. explain the types of problems single parents have.
   C. convince the reader that children in single parent homes suffer.
   D. give the effects of divorce on children.

PASSAGE #8

Read the passage and answer the question that follows.

Many overweight and obese individuals are trying to lose weight. Although it took several months and years to put on the extra weight, many of them are looking for a quick way to lose that weight. This attitude results in choosing quick-weight-loss diets that are not effective and may be harmful.

Some choose metabolic products, such as herbs or caffeine, to lose weight. Herbs have not been shown to speed the loss of fat, and caffeine shows little promise as a weight-loss aid.

Others go on very-low-calorie diets, which severely restrict nutrients and can result in serious metabolic imbalances. Weight can be lost on this type of diet; much of the weight lost will be lean protein tissue and/or water, not fat. This results in harm to the muscles (including the heart), loss of essential vitamins and minerals through the water loss, and dizziness and fatigue. Further, if one cuts calories, this slows the metabolism; once this person goes off the diet, the metabolism remains slow and the body continues to use few calories—and the pounds come back.

Liquid protein diets operate on the theory that insulin is controlled and therefore more fat is burned. With this type of diet, ketosis will result. Ketosis will increase blood levels of uric acid, a risk factor for gout and kidney stones. There is new research evidence that carbohydrates lead to fat storage and weight; further, the excessive protein in this diet can damage the kidneys and cause osteoporosis.

Prescription drugs, such as Redux and Pondimin (fen-phen), curb hunger by increasing the level of serotonin in the brain. These were intended for the obese, but they were banned in 1997 after the FDA found strong evidence that they could seriously damage the heart.

Some people try crash diets to lose a moderate amount of weight in a very short period. These types of diets can damage several body systems and have been proven not to work because most of these individuals regain their weight. This yo-yo dieting causes many health problems and shortens lifespan. The best way to lose weight is to lose weight slowly (no more than one-half to one pound a week), eat properly and in moderation, and exercise. (Adapted from David J. Anspaugh and Gene Ezell, *Teaching Today's Health*, 7th ed., San Francisco: Benjamin Cummings, 2004.)

8. The main purpose of the above passage is to
   A. describe the various types of quick diets that are ineffective and harmful.
   B. persuade the reader that crash diets are harmful.
   C. describe fad diets.
   D. explain the best way to lose weight.

PASSAGE #9

Read the passage and answer the question that follows.

The dramatic difference between the social status of the Egyptian nobility and that of the common people is reflected in their respective burial rites. The keen Egyptian interest in the afterlife, combined with strikingly materialistic criteria for happiness, made lavish tombs for the pharaohs (Egyptian rulers) seem particularly important. Elaborate goods were buried with the pharaoh to assure him a gracious existence in the world beyond, and a processional causeway linked each pyramid to a temple constructed for the worship of the pharaoh; adjacent to the pyramid was a building to house the special cedar boat that would carry him on his voyage to the land of the dead. The pyramid served as the core of an entire necropolis, or city of the dead, which included small pyramids for the wives and daughters of the pharaoh and mastabas for the nobility. Even a minor royal official spent a considerable portion of his time preparing an elaborate tomb for his afterlife, and he would want his corpse to be mummified because of the Egyptian belief that the *ka*, the spirit of life in each person, periodically returned to the body. The corpse of an average farmer, however, was typically wrapped in a piece of linen and deposited in a cave or pit with only a staff and a pair of sandals to facilitate the journey to the next world; some bodies were even left in the open sand of the desert. (Adapted from Richard L. Greaves, Robert Zaller, and Jennifer Tolbert Roberts, *Civilizations of the West*, 2nd ed., New York: Longman, 1997.)

9. The authors' main purpose in the above passage is to
   A. explain the Egyptian belief in the afterlife.
   B. give reasons for building pyramids for the pharaohs.
   C. show the difference in burial rites according to social status.
   D. describe the lavish tombs of the pharaohs.

PASSAGE #10

Read the passage and answer the question that follows.

"Street gangs" are a more formal variety of youth gang. They generally have leaders and a hierarchy of membership roles and responsibilities. They are named, and their members mark their identity with tattoos or "colors." While many street gangs are involved in violence, not all are. An anthropologist who did research among nearly forty street gangs in New York, Los Angeles, and Boston learned much about why individuals join gangs, providing insights that contradict popular thinking on this subject.

One common stereotype is that young boys join gangs because they are from homes with no male authority figure with whom they could identify. This study showed that equal numbers of gang members were from intact nuclear households as from those with an absent father. Another common perception is that the gang replaces a missing feeling of family as a motive. This study, again, showed that the same number of gang members reported having close family ties as those who did not.

Those who were gang members shared a personality type called a "defiant individualist." This type has five traits: intense competitiveness, mistrust or wariness, self-reliance, social isolation, and a strong survival instinct. Poverty, especially urban poverty, leads to the development of this type of personality. Many of these youths want to be economically successful, but social conditions channel their interests and skills into illegal pursuits rather than into legal pathways of achievement. (Adapted from Barbara D. Miller, *Cultural Anthropology*, 2nd ed., Boston: Allyn and Bacon, 2002.)

10. The main purpose of the above passage is to
    A. discourage youths from joining a gang.
    B. argue that street gang members come from homes with no authority figure.
    C. give reasons why youths join street gangs.
    D. define the typical gang personality type.

KEEP IN MIND ◆ SUMMARY OF CHAPTER 1

Understanding the author's main point is the most important key to comprehension. Keep in mind these two questions when looking for the main idea:

1. What is the topic (subject) of the passage?
2. What is the author's most important point about that topic?

- Most often, main ideas are found in the first paragraph. A second place to look is in the last paragraph. Then check the sentences in the middle.
- Look for a broad statement that sounds like an important point the author is making.
- When you think you have found the correct main idea, go back and look through the passage. Ask yourself: Do all of the other sentences tell more about this sentence? If they do, then your answer is correct.

Sometimes an author does not state the main idea in a topic sentence or a thesis statement. In these cases, the reader must infer the main idea by drawing a conclusion.

Supporting Details

Supporting details are sentences which give more specific information about the main idea. Long passages contain one main idea and may have one or several major supporting details. The number of major and minor details varies with each passage. Not every major detail has a minor detail to support it, while some major details may have several minor supporting details.

Major details tell us more information about the main idea.

Minor details tell us more about the major details.

To find supporting details,

- pay close attention to the <u>first sentence of each paragraph</u>. They often contain major details that support the main idea. They are also usually topic sentences that tell you what kind of information to expect in the paragraph.
- Supporting details answer questions such as *who, what, when, where, why*, and *how*. To find supporting details, look for:

> Reasons
> Examples
> Characteristics
> Analysis and explanations
> People and places
> Senses

Author's Purpose

Every author has a purpose for writing, and a main point that he or she is making about the topic.

- Begin by stating the topic and main idea in your own words, and try to find a topic sentence in the passage.
- Ask: Why did the author write this? Look at the overall pattern of organization.
- Pay close attention to the author's tone.
- Look at the language used: is it biased?
- Look for facts and opinions which may reveal the author's purpose.

All three components—the main idea, supporting details, and author's purpose—work together to convey the author's intended meaning. Knowing these skills will help readers to understand the structural skills covered in the next section.

Chapter 2: Structural Skills

There are more questions concerning organizational patterns than any other skill on the Exit Exam, so understanding this concept is absolutely vital to success on the test. There are actually three different questions on the Exit Exam that concern patterns of organization: overall pattern of organization, relationship between two sentences, and relationship within a sentence. This first section concerns the overall pattern of organization, which is the arrangement of the details in a reading into a clear structure.

The other two Exit Exam questions that concern patterns of organization are covered in the next two sections, but the three question types are closely related. Each pattern of organization has a set of "clue words" or *transitional words* related to its meaning. These transitional words found in and between sentences convey the organizational pattern.

Some Common Patterns of Organization

Chronological Order (Time Order): Arranges information in the order in which the events occurred. (Example: A story about what happened on the day that John F. Kennedy was assassinated.)

Steps In a Process: Arranges information in the order in which the steps occur in a process, much the same as chronological order. The only difference is that instead of discussing events that occurred over a period of time, the author is explaining a process that takes place in a certain order. (Example: The directions for installing computer software.)

Cause and Effect: Shows how one or more events caused another (or several others). (Example: A textbook section on the causes of World War II and its effects on the economy of Europe.)

Compare and Contrast: Shows the way(s) that two or more things are alike (compare) or different (contrast). (Example: A biology report comparing and contrasting how plants and animals convert food to energy.)

Simple Listing (also known as Listing or Addition): Arranges information in a list in no particular order. The key words for this pattern are very similar to those for Time Order and Process. However, the big difference is that with Time Order and Process, you cannot mix up the items or steps. With Simple Listing, you can. (Example: An article showing the various ways that computers are used in engineering and manufacturing is LISTING. An article showing how to install a software patch for your computer is PROCESS.)

Generalization and Example: States a main idea and then gives one or more examples to explain it. (Example: "Plagiarism is a serious infraction in most settings. For instance, students can be suspended or expelled from school.")

Definition and Example: The author uses a term and then explains it with an example. (Example: A term that is defined in a biology textbook: "An **organ** consists of several tissues adapted to perform specific functions as a group. The heart, for example, while mostly muscle, also has epithelial, connective, and nervous tissue." —Campbell et al., *Biology: Concepts & Connections*, 3rd ed., 2000.)

Statement and Clarification: States a broad, general idea and then explains in further detail, without using a specific example. (Example: An ecology text that states a point and follows it with more information: "Forest decline is not a new phenomenon. During the past two centuries, our forests have experienced several declines, with different species affected." —Smith and Smith, *Elements of Ecology*, 5th ed., 2003.)

Spatial Order: Arranges details according to their location in space. (Example: A travel brochure which describes the geography of an island according to location, beginning in the north and ending in the south.)

Classification: Sorts ideas into categories according to similar characteristics. (Example: A health textbook chapter describing the different types of drugs by their function and effects.)

Transitional Words (Key Words)—knowing these makes it much easier to identify the pattern of organization.
- **Chronological Order (Time Order) and Steps in a Process:** first, second, third, etc., finally, and, also, next, then, meanwhile, during, afterward, another. Dates are also clue words for time order.
- **Cause and Effect:** result, effect, cause, consequently, thus, then, if, since, because, therefore, accordingly, results in, leads to, so.
- **Compare and Contrast:** different, whereas, while, although, even though, despite, despite the fact that, opposite, in spite of, but, contrast, instead of, however, nevertheless, yet, unlike, like, alike, similar, both, compare, also.
- **Simple Listing (also known as Listing or Addition):** and, first, second, third, etc., finally, also, next, then, another, moreover, furthermore, in addition.
- **Generalization and Example:** for example, to illustrate, to show, in general, for instance, such as, generally.
- **Statement and Clarification:** to clarify, to explain, to understand, namely, specifically, thus.
- **Spatial Order:** next to, beside, under, over, around, between, outside of, inside of, within, front, side, back, interior, exterior, north, south, east, west.
- **Classification:** types, classifies, classifications, groups, categories, styles.

How to Determine the Overall Pattern of Organization

To determine the correct overall pattern of organization, you must:

- Identify the topic and main idea, and note any transitional words
- For multi-paragraph readings, compare the thesis statement (main idea of the whole reading) to the topic sentences (main idea of each paragraph). See how these main ideas relate, and note any transitional expressions that are common to all of them.
- Think about the author's purpose
- Look for relationships between ideas
- **Learn the transitional phrases associated with each pattern**

> **Example #1**
> While mainland Europe suffered through the Thirty Years' War, England faced serious domestic stress under the first two Stuart kings. Conflict between the first, James I, and his English subjects began immediately after he came to the throne in 1603, but the wily monarch avoided any real constitutional crisis. This fate fell to his son, Charles I, who succeeded his father in 1635. During the next 15 years, misguided royal policies produced steadily mounting opposition, until the country stood at the brink of war. (Brummett et al., *Civilizations Past and Present*, 9th ed., 2000.)

Topic: England's first two Stuart kings

Main Idea: While mainland Europe suffered through the Thirty Years' War, England faced serious domestic stress under the first two Stuart kings.

How are the supporting details arranged?
    A. Listing
    B. Chronological order
    C. Cause and effect
    D. Compare and contrast

Look for transitional phrases to help you decide. (Another clue in this passage is the use of dates in chronological order.)

The correct answer is B. Chronological order.

> **Example #2**
> The heavily populated coastline in the south is the center for business and manufacturing. In the central region, the land grows into rolling hills and pastures for dairy farming and sheep herding. The northern part of the state boasts of its majestic snow-covered mountains and dramatic waterfalls from granite precipices. To the west are the broad plains and rich farmland that are the heart and soul of its people.

Topic: A state's geography

Main Idea (implied): The state has a variety of geographical regions.

What is the overall pattern of organization?
    A. Classification
    B. Cause and effect
    C. Generalization and example
    D. Spatial order

Look at the transitional phrases the author uses (south, central, northern, west).

The correct answer is D. Spatial order.

▶▶| **Secrets to Success**

- *Learn the transitional phrases associated with each pattern.*
- *Identify the topic and main idea.*
- *Focus on the supporting details.*
- *Think about the author's purpose.*
- *Be aware that authors may combine two or more patterns.*
- *When looking for an overall pattern, think about the author's main idea and purpose.*

SECTION 1 ◆ DIAGNOSTIC: PATTERNS OF ORGANIZATION

Read the passages and apply the strategies described above for finding the patterns of organization. When you are done, check your work with the answers immediately following the diagnostic. Even if you get a perfect score here, go ahead and complete the exercises in this section; they are designed to help build confidence and to give you practice for future test success.

Read the following passages to determine the author's overall pattern of organization.

PASSAGE #1

One of the most important results of the Civil War was the freedom gained by southern slaves. In the decade following the defeat of the Confederacy, hundreds of thousands of men and women migrated throughout the South, searching for land, work, and relatives lost through prewar sale. Some former slaves, however, took an even bolder step, leaving the South altogether and traveling west in search of cheap farmland or north seeking industrial employment. While most faced difficult years adjusting to the world of free labor and white prejudice, none would have exchanged their life of freedom for the days of bondage. (Nash and Schultz, *Retracing the Past: Readings in the History of the American People*, 4th ed., New York: Longman, 2000.)   5

1. The author's overall pattern of organization
   A. contrasts the differences between the southern slaves.
   B. lists the changes in the South after the Civil War.
   C. summarizes the changes in slavery.
   D. shows the effects of Civil War upon southern slaves.

PASSAGE #2

Walt Whitman, whose *Leaves of Grass* (1855) was the last of the great literary works of his brief outpouring of genius, was the most romantic and by far the most distinctly American writer of his age. He was born on Long Island, outside of New York City, in 1819. At 13, he left school and became a printer's devil; thereafter he held a succession of newspaper jobs in the metropolitan area. He was an ardent Jacksonian and later a   5

Free Soiler, which got him into hot water with a number of the publishers for whom he worked. (Garraty and Carnes, *The American Nation: A History of the United States,* 10th ed., New York: Longman, 2000.)

2. The author's overall pattern of organization
   A. is a presentation of Walt Whitman's life in chronological order.
   B. explains the reasons why Walt Whitman was not published much.
   C. shows the effects of Whitman's political views.
   D. shows the cause of Whitman's creative genius.

PASSAGE #3

Active listening serves several important functions. First, it helps you, as a listener, check your understanding of what the speaker said and, more important, what he or she meant. Reflecting back on your understanding of what you think the speaker means gives the speaker an opportunity to offer clarification. In this way, future messages will have a better chance of being relevant. Second, through active listening, you let the speaker know that you acknowledge and accept his or her feelings. (Rigolosi and Campion, eds., *The Longman Electronic Test Bank for Developmental Reading,* 2001.)   5

3. The passage is organized by
   A. clarifying an explanation of active listening.
   B. listing the important functions of active listening.
   C. classifying the different functions of active listening.
   D. showing the effects of active listening.

PASSAGE #4

Self-disclosure is a type of communication in which you reveal information about yourself, in which you move information from the hidden self into the open self. Overt statements about the self as well as slips of the tongue, unconscious nonverbal movements, and public confessions would all be considered forms of self-disclosure.

Self-disclosure is information previously unknown by the receiver. This may vary from the relatively commonplace ("I'm really afraid of that French exam") to the extremely significant (I'm so depressed, I feel like committing suicide"). (DeVito, *Essentials of Human Communication,* 3rd ed., Boston: Allyn and Bacon, 1999.)   5

4. The author's overall pattern of organization
   A. lists the types of self-disclosure.
   B. contrasts self-disclosure with other forms of communication.
   C. discusses the importance of self-disclosure in communication.
   D. defines self-disclosure and provides examples.

PASSAGE #5

Presidents and prime ministers govern quite differently. Prime ministers never face divided government, for example. Since they represent the majority party or coalition, they can almost always depend on winning on votes. In addition, party discipline is better in parliamentary systems than in the United States. Prime ministers generally differ from presidents in background as well. They must be party leaders, as we have seen, and they are usually very effective communicators, their skills honed in the rough and tumble of parliamentary debate. In addition, they have had substantial experience dealing with national issues, unlike American governors who may move directly into presidency. Cabinet members, who are usually senior members of parliament, have similar advantages. (Edwards, Wattenberg, and Lineberry, *Government in America*, 9th ed., New York: Longman, 2000.)

5. The author's overall pattern of organization
    A. contrasts the roles of the president and the prime minister.
    B. compares the roles of the president and the prime minister.
    C. lists additional information about the roles of the president and the prime minister.
    D. analyzes which form of government has the most advantages.

PASSAGE #6

Deprived of access to Middle Eastern oil, the American economy sputtered. The price of oil rose to $12 a barrel, up from $3. This sent prices soaring for nearly everything else. Homes were heated with oil, factories were powered with it and utility plants used it to generate electricity. Nylon and other synthetic fibers as well as paints, insecticides, fertilizers, and many plastic products were based on petrochemicals. Above all else, oil was refined into gasoline. By the time of the Yom Kippur War, American car owners were driving more than a trillion miles a year, the major reason why the United States, formerly a major oil exporter, imported one third of its oil. The Arab oil embargo pushed up gas prices; service stations intermittently ran out of gasoline and long lines formed at those that remained open. (Garraty and Carnes, *The American Nation: A History of the United States*, 10th ed., New York: Longman, 2000.)

6. The author's overall pattern of organization
    A. lists examples of products and services dependent upon oil.
    B. shows the effects of the oil embargo on the American economy.
    C. explains why Americans use so much oil.
    D. illustrates ways that oil is used in the United States.

PASSAGE #7

Communicate your information with varying levels of abstraction. For example, in talking about the freedom of the press, you can talk in high-level abstractions about the importance of getting information to the public, by referring to the Bill of Rights, and by relating a free press to the preservation of democracy. You can also talk in low-level abstractions, for example, by citing how a local newspaper was prevented from running a story critical of the town council or about how Lucy Rinaldo was fired from the *Accord Sentinel* after she wrote a story critical of the Mayor. Combining high and low abstractions seems to work best. (DeVito, *Essentials of Human Communication*, 3rd ed., 1999.)

7. The author's overall pattern of organization
   A. shows the effects of high and low level abstractions.
   B. makes a general statement and follows it with specific examples.
   C. compares high level and low level abstractions.
   D. gives a definition of high level and low level abstractions.

Answers to Diagnostic
   1. D   2. A   3. B   4. D   5. A   6. B   7. B

SECTION 1 ◆ EXERCISES: PATTERNS OF ORGANIZATION

Use the following exercises to practice reading for patterns of organization.

PASSAGE #1

Read the passage and answer the question that follows.

Regardless of the type of job you have, you have to divide your time between work
and school. The following suggestions will help you balance these two segments of
your life. First of all, make sure that your supervisor knows you are attending college
and that your job helps pay for it. He or she may be more understanding and helpful
if he or she knows you are a serious student. In addition, try to find a coworker who   5
may be willing to switch work hours or take your hours if you need extra time to study.
Next, if possible, try to build a work schedule around your class schedule. For example,
if you have an eight o'clock class on Tuesday mornings, try not to work until midnight
on Monday night. Finally, allow study time for each class. Make sure you have time
between class sessions to do homework and complete assigned readings. For example,   10
if you have a Tuesday/Thursday class, make sure you have some study time between
the two sessions. (Adapted from Kathleen T. McWhorter, *Study and Critical Thinking
Skills in College*, 5th ed., New York: Longman, 2003.)

1. For this passage, the author uses an organizational pattern that
   A. summarizes the problems of a working student.
   B. gives reasons for attending school full-time instead of working and studying at the same
      time.
   C. discusses how to get along with your supervisor and coworkers.
   D. gives instructions on how to balance work and school time.

PASSAGE #2

Read the passage and answer the question that follows.

Contrary to popular assumption, slavery was not usually based on racism, but on one
of three other factors. The first was debt. In some cultures, an individual who could
not pay a debt could be enslaved by the creditor. The second was crime. Instead of
being killed, a murderer or thief might be enslaved by the family of the victim as compensation for their loss. The third was war and conquest. When one group of people   5

conquered another, they often enslaved some of the vanquished. Historian Gerda Lerner notes that the first people enslaved through warfare were women. When premodern men raided a village or camp, they killed the men, raped the women, and then brought the women back as slaves. The women were valued for sexual purposes, for reproduction, and for their labor. (James M. Henslin, *Sociology*, 6th ed., Boston: Allyn and Bacon, 2003.)   10

2. For this passage, the author uses an organizational pattern that
   A. describes what happened to women after warfare in premodern times.
   B. explains the reasons for slavery.
   C. contrasts premodern and modern forms of slavery.
   D. defines slavery.

PASSAGE #3

Read the passage and answer the question that follows.

Cyberliteracy is not purely a print literacy, nor is Internet literacy purely an oral literacy. Cyberliteracy is an electronic literacy—newly emerging in a new medium—that combines features of both print and the spoken word, and the medium does so in ways that change how we read, speak, think, and interact with others. Once we see that online texts are not exactly written or spoken, we begin to understand that cyberliteracy   5
requires a special form of critical thinking. Communication in the online world is not quite like anything else. Written messages, such as letters (even when written on a computer), are usually created slowly and with reflection, allowing the writer to think and revise even as the document is chugging away at the printer. But electronic *discourse*— talking, conversing, interacting—encourages us to reply quickly, often in a more oral   10
style. In discourse, we blur the normally accepted distinctions, such as writing versus speaking, and conventions, such as punctuation and spelling. Normal rules about writing, editing, and revising a document do not make much sense in this environment. (Adapted from Leonard J. Shedletsky and Joan E. Aitken, *Human Communication on the Internet*, Boston: Allyn and Bacon, 2004.)

3. For this passage, the authors use an organizational pattern that
   A. defines cyberliteracy.
   B. shows similarities between online and written communication.
   C. describes critical thinking.
   D. explains how to become cyberliterate.

PASSAGE #4

Read the passage and answer the questions that follow.

The most boisterous forms of entertainment in the Roman Empire involved the excitement of a roaring crowd. The huge seating capacity of the Circus Maximus, which could probably accommodate a quarter of a million spectators, made chariot races an extremely popular diversion in the city of Rome. Bets were placed both on and off the track, and the seating regulations of the Colosseum, which separated the sexes, did not   5 operate in the Circus, where men and women sat together, heightening the tension and festivity of the atmosphere. An element of danger also contributed to the air of excitement, as ancient chariot races afforded the same kinds of entertaining and often fatal crashes that are common to automobile competitions today. But the tumult of the races was tame in comparison to the spectacles offered in the amphitheaters of the empire, where emperors, local officials, and public-minded citizens vied with one another to give the most memorable shows.   10

Sadism and voyeurism were key elements in Roman entertainment. Savage gladiatorial combats to the death and the feeding of humans to wild beasts are not inventions of Hollywood; they were a staple of Roman entertainment. Most residents of the empire who lived anywhere near a city saw a number of people killed in the arena over their lifetimes. Nearly all would have been mystified by the anxieties people feel today about the make-believe violence in the movies and on television, and the ghoulish curiosity about witnessing bloody deaths that people try to suppress and deny in our own society seems to have caused the Romans no embarrassment. Uninhibitedly, they flocked in great numbers to the arenas of doom. (Adapted from Richard L. Greaves, Robert Zaller, and Jennifer Tolbert Roberts, *Civilizations of the West*, New York: Longman, 1997.)   15   20

4. For this passage, the authors use an overall organizational pattern that
    A. gives the effects of violent entertainment on the Roman people.
    B. explains how gladiators fought in the arena.
    C. gives examples of the forms of entertainment that excited the Romans.
    D. analyzes the reasons Romans enjoyed sadism and voyeurism.

5. The second paragraph is organized by
    A. contrasting the Romans' acceptance of violence to our anxiety about seeing violence in movies and television.
    B. defining sadism.
    C. explaining the key elements of Roman entertainment: sadism and voyeurism.
    D. describing Hollywood gladiator movies.

PASSAGE #5

Read the passage and answer the question that follows.

Nonflowing bodies of water such as lakes become contaminated in stages. First, pollutants such as animal fertilizer, detergents, industrial waste, and sewage are dumped into the water supply. As a result, an accelerated growth of algae occurs. As algae growth skyrockets on a diet of inorganic pollutants, especially nitrogen and phosphorus, a blanket of slime covers the water. Eventual death of the algae results in bacterial decomposition that consumes the oxygen present. This oxygen deficit kills fish and other lake inhabitants, many of which are valuable as food resources, and as recently suggested, disrupts freshwater animals' endocrine systems. Eventually, the body of water becomes contaminated beyond use. (Adapted from David J. Anspaugh and Gene Ezell, *Teaching Today's Health*, 7th ed., San Francisco: Benjamin Cummings, 2004.)   5

6. This paragraph is organized by
   A. listing the types of chemicals that pollute our water.
   B. describing the growth of algae.
   C. defining water pollution.
   D. explaining the process of water contamination.

PASSAGE #6

Read the passage and answer the questions that follow.

One type of anxiety disorder is the panic disorder. The hallmark of panic disorder is the experience of panic attacks, episodes of intense fear or discomfort accompanied by symptoms such as palpitations, breathing difficulties, chest pain, nausea, sweating, dizziness, fear of going crazy or doing something uncontrollable, fear of impending doom, and a sense of unreality. Symptoms reach their peak within a few minutes of the beginning of an attack, which can last from minutes to hours. Often these attacks are not associated with a specific situation or object and may even seem to occur randomly. One study of college students found that 12% of the participants experienced spontaneous panic attacks during their lifetimes. Some people may have episodes of panic attacks, with years of remission; others may have more persistent symptoms. 5 10

People with panic disorder worry constantly about having more attacks, and in their attempts to avoid or minimize panic attacks, they may change their behavior. People may go to great lengths to try to avoid panic attacks, quitting their jobs, avoiding places (such as hot, crowded rooms or events) or activities that increase their heart rate (such as exercise or watching suspenseful movies or sporting events). Some people fear or avoid places that might be difficult to leave should a panic attack occur, for example, a plane or car. They may avoid leaving home or do so only with a close friend or relative. Such fear and avoidance can lead to agoraphobia, a condition in which the avoidance of places or activities restricts daily life. In some cases, people have agoraphobia without panic attacks, avoiding many places because either they fear losing control of themselves in some way (such as losing bladder control) or they fear the occurrence of less severe but still distressing panic symptoms. (Stephen M. Kosslyn and Robin S. Rosenberg, *Psychology*, 2nd ed., Boston: Allyn and Bacon, 2004.) 15 20

7. For this passage, the authors use the overall organizational pattern that
   A. contrasts panic attacks with agoraphobia.
   B. explains one type of disorder, panic disorder.
   C. explains recommended strategies for dealing with panic attacks.
   D. classifies the causes of panic attacks.

8. The second paragraph is organized by
   A. giving examples of things people do to avoid or minimize panic attacks.
   B. defining panic disorder.
   C. giving the steps for treatment.
   D. comparing types of panic avoidance behavior.

PASSAGE #7

Read the passage and answer the questions that follow.

Plagiarism is using someone else's words and ideas without giving that person proper credit. Even when your use of information may be perfectly legal, you may still be violating ethical standards if you do not give credit to the information source.

Assume, for example, that you are writing a class report on genetically modified foods. In your research, you discover a very good paper on the Web. You decide that parts of this paper would complement your report quite nicely. Under copyright and fair use guidelines, you can reproduce portions of this paper without permission. But does this legal standard mean that you can use someone else's material freely, without giving that person credit? Even though it might be legal under fair use guidelines to reprint the material without notifying the copyright holder, using someone else's material or ideas without giving them credit is plagiarism.

Plagiarism is a serious infraction in most settings. Students can be suspended or expelled from school. Researchers can lose their jobs and their standing in the academic community. Most importantly, plagiarism is serious because it violates several of the reasonable criteria for ethical decision making. Plagiarism violates your obligation to yourself to be truthful, and it violates your obligation to society to produce fair and accurate information. It also violates your obligation to other students and researchers. (Adapted from Laura J. Gurak and John M. Lannon, *A Concise Guide to Technical Communication*, New York: Longman, 2001.)

9. For this passage, the authors use the overall organizational pattern that
   A. analyzes a situation in which plagiarism occurs.
   B. lists types of plagiarism.
   C. defines plagiarism.
   D. tells how to use information from the Web.

10. The third paragraph is organized by
   A. describing the effects of plagiarism on students.
   B. defining ethical decision making.
   C. contrasting plagiarism at college and at work.
   D. giving reasons why plagiarism is a serious infraction.

PASSAGE #8

Read the passage and answer the questions that follow.

During the seventeenth and eighteenth centuries, the process of childbirth in colonial America was conducted by women. The typical woman gave birth to her children at home, while female relatives and neighbors clustered at her bedside to offer support and encouragement.

Most women were assisted in childbirth not by a doctor but by a midwife. Most midwives were older women who relied on practical experience in delivering children. One midwife, Martha Ballard, who practiced in Augusta, Maine, delivered 996 babies with only 4 recorded fatalities. Skilled midwives were highly valued. Communities tried to attract experienced midwives by offering a salary or a rent-free house. In addition to assisting in childbirth, midwives helped deliver the offspring of animals, attended the baptisms and burials of infants, and testified in court cases of illegitimate babies.

10

During labor, midwives administered no painkillers, except for alcohol. Pain in childbirth was considered God's punishment for Eve's sin of eating the forbidden fruit in the Garden of Eden. Women were merely advised to have patience, to pray, and during labor, to restrain their groans and cries which upset the people near them.

15

After delivery, new mothers were often treated to a banquet. At one such event, visitors feasted on boiled pork, beef, poultry, roast beef, turkey pie, and tarts. Women from well-to-do families were then expected to spend three to four weeks in bed convalescing. Their attendants kept the fireplace burning and wrapped them in a heavy blanket in order to help them sweat out "poisons." Women from poorer families were generally back at work in one or two days. (Adapted from James Kirby Martin et al., *America and Its Peoples*, New York: Longman, 2004.)

20

11. For this passage, the authors use the overall organizational pattern that
    A. gives religious reasons for pain in childbirth.
    B. illustrates the ways in which women assisted childbirth.
    C. explains the differences between childbirth for rich and poor women.
    D. describes the dangers of childbirth.

12. The second paragraph is organized by
    A. describing midwives.
    B. arguing the advantages of midwives over doctors.
    C. listing the achievements of Martha Ballard.
    D. explaining how the midwife assists in childbirth.

PASSAGE #9

Read the passage and answer the questions that follow.

Deborah Tannen, sociologist and author, explains the differences in the listening behavior of men and women. Women seek to build rapport and establish a closer relationship and so they use listening to achieve these ends. For example, women use more listening cues that let the other person know they are paying attention and are interested. On the other hand, men not only use fewer listening cues but interrupt more and will often change the topic to one they know more about or one that is less relational or people-oriented to one that is more factual, for example, sports, statistics, economic developments, or political problems. Men, research shows, play up their expertise, emphasize it, and use it to dominate the conversation. Women play down their expertise.

5

10

Research shows that men communicate with women in the same way they do with other men. Men are not showing disrespect for their female conversational partners, but are simply communicating as they normally do. Women, too, communicate as they do not only with men but also with other women.

Tannen argues that the goal of a man in conversation is to be accorded respect, and so he seeks to display his knowledge and expertise even if he has to change the topic from one he knows little about to one he knows a great deal about. A woman, on the other hand, seeks to be liked, and so she expresses agreement and less frequently interrupts to take her turn as speaker.   15

Men and women also show that they are listening in different ways. A woman is more apt to give lots of listening cues, such as interjecting "yeah, uh-uh," nodding in agreement, and smiling. A man is more likely to listen quietly, without giving lots of listening cues as feedback. Tannen also argues, however, that men do listen less to women than women listen to men. The reason is that listening places the person in an inferior position whereas speaking places the person in a superior position.   20   25

There is no evidence to show that these differences represent any negative motives on the part of men to prove themselves superior or of women to ingratiate themselves. Rather, these differences in listening are largely the result of the way in which men and women have been socialized. (Adapted from Joseph A. DeVito, *Essentials of Human Communication*, 3rd ed., New York: Longman, 1999.)

13. For this passage, the author uses the overall organizational pattern that
    A. illustrates conversational behaviors of men and women.
    B. argues that men need to prove themselves superior when in conversation.
    C. contrasts the listening behaviors of men and women.
    D. discusses the negative effects of male listening behavior on women.

14. The first paragraph is organized by
    A. offering examples of how men do not listen to women.
    B. contrasting the listening cues used by men and women.
    C. explaining how women use listening to get close to a person.
    D. developing the theory that men do not disrespect female conversational patterns.

📚 Study Hint

The following section of exercises includes some passages that you have already seen in one or more of the previous sections. The purpose of presenting you with the same passages in different sections is two-fold. First, the repetition imitates the state exit exam, which presents you with a passage and then asks you several different types of questions based on that one passage. These sets of questions address different skills. For example, one passage may have the questions about the following skills: main idea, relevance of supporting details, author's purpose, types of organization, word meaning in context.

The state exit test's use of one passage for several questions is the second reason for working with the same passages throughout the workbook. Many of these skills are connected to each other. For example, the author's purpose is closely connected to the pattern of organization and reinforced by tone. So it is important for you to see how one passage uses each of these skills for an overall effect. Study smart; compare these questions to the other sections where the passages also appear, and think about the relationship between the skills.

PASSAGE #10

Read the passage and answer the question that follows.

On April 20, 1999, a school shooting of such immense proportions occurred which radically, if not permanently, altered public thinking and debate about student safety and security. After months of planning and preparation, 18-year-old Eric Harris and 17-year-old Dylan Klebold armed themselves with guns and explosives and headed off to Columbine High School in Littleton, Colorado, to celebrate Adolph Hitler's birthday in a manner fitting their hero. By the time the assault ended with self-inflicted fatal gunshots, a dozen students and one teacher lay dead.

In understanding the horrific actions of schoolyard snipers, it is as important to examine friendships as it is to delve into family background. At Columbine, Harris and Klebold were generally seen as geeks or nerds, from the point of view of any of the large student cliques—the jocks, the punks, etc. Though excluded from mainstream student culture, they banded together and bonded together with several of their fellow outcasts in what they came to call the "Trench Coat Mafia." The image they attempted to create was clearly one of power and dominance—the barbaric incivility, the forces of darkness, the preoccupation with Hitler, the celebration of evil and villainy. Harris and Klebold desperately wanted to feel important; and in the preparations they made to murder their classmates, the two shooters got their wish. For more than a year, they plotted and planned, colluded and conspired to put one over on their schoolmates, teachers, and parents. They amassed an arsenal of weapons, strategized about logistics, and made final preparations—yet, until it was too late, not a single adult got wind of what Harris and Klebold intended to do.

Birds of a feather may kill together. Harris, the leader, would likely have enjoyed the respect and admiration from Klebold, who in turn would have felt uplifted by the praise he received from his revered buddy. In their relationship, the two boys got from one another what was otherwise missing from their lives—they felt special, they gained a sense of belonging, they were united against the world. As Harris remarked, as he and his friend made last-minute preparations to commit mass murder: "This is just a two-man war against everything else." (Adapted from James Alan Fox and Jack Levin, *The Will to Kill*, Boston: Allyn and Bacon, 2001.)

15. For this passage, the authors use the overall organizational pattern that
    A. describes the Columbine High School massacre.
    B. lists the effects of the Columbine High School massacre.
    C. tells the process Harris and Klebold used to prepare for the shootings.
    D. analyzes Harris and Klebold's friendship to understand their crime.

PASSAGE #11

Read the passage and answer the question that follows.

Each of the 2000 or so species of firefly has its own way to signal a mate. When a female sees flashes of light from a male of her species, she reacts with flashes of her own. If the male sees her flashes, he automatically gives another display and flies in the female's direction. Members of both sexes are responding to particular patterns of light flashes characteristic of their species. Some flash more often than others or during different hours, while other species give fewer but longer flashes. Many species produce light of a characteristic color: yellow, bluish-green, or reddish. Mating occurs when the female's display leads a male to her, and most females stop flashing after they mate. But in a few species, a mated female will continue to flash, using a pattern that attracts males of other firefly species. A veritable *femme fatale*, she waits until an alien male gets close, then grabs and eats him. (Adapted from Neil A. Campbell, Lawrence G. Mitchell, and Jane B. Reece, *Biology*, 3rd ed., San Francisco: Benjamin Cummings, 2000.)

16. This paragraph is organized by
    A. explaining the flashing patterns of fireflies.
    B. illustrating the cannablistic female firefly behavior.
    C. describing the process fireflies use to signal mates.
    D. giving examples of the length and color of fireflies' flashes.

PASSAGE #12

Read the passage and answer the questions that follow.

Many overweight and obese individuals are trying to lose weight. Although it took several months and years to put on the extra weight, many of them are looking for a quick way to lose that weight. This attitude results in choosing quick-weight-loss diets that are not effective and may be harmful.

Some choose metabolic products, such as herbs or caffeine, to lose weight. Herbs have not been shown to speed the loss of fat, and caffeine shows little promise as a weight-loss aid.

Others go on very-low-calorie diets, which severely restrict nutrients and can result in serious metabolic imbalances. Weight can be lost on this type of diet; much of the weight lost will be lean protein tissue and/or water, not fat. This results in harm to the muscles (including the heart), loss of essential vitamins and minerals through the water loss, and dizziness and fatigue. Further, if one cuts calories, the metabolism slows; once this person goes off the diet, the metabolism remains slow and the body continues to use few calories—and the pounds come back.

Liquid protein diets operate on the theory that insulin is controlled and therefore more fat is burned. With this type of diet, ketosis will result. Ketosis will increase blood levels of uric acid, a risk factor for gout and kidney stones. There is new research evidence that carbohydrates lead to fat storage and weight; further, the excessive protein in this diet can damage the kidneys and cause osteoporosis. Prescription drugs, such as Redux and Pondimin (fen-phen), curb hunger by increasing the level of serotonin in the brain. These were intended for the obese, but they were banned in 1997 after the FDA found strong evidence that they could seriously damage the heart.

Some people try crash diets to lose a moderate amount of weight in a very short period. These types of diets can damage several body systems and have been proven not to work because most of these individuals regain their weight. This yo-yo dieting causes many health problems and shortens lifespan. The best way to lose weight is to lose weight slowly (no more than one-half to one pound a week), eat properly and in moderation, and exercise. (Adapted from David J. Anspaugh and Gene Ezell, *Teaching Today's Health*, 7th ed., San Francisco: Benjamin Cummings, 2004.)

17. For this passage, the authors use the overall organizational pattern that
    A. explains the effects of many quick-weight-loss diets.
    B. describes the types of quick-weight-loss-diets.
    C. gives the effects of the prescription drugs Redux and Pondimin (fen-phen).
    D. contrasts liquid protein diets with very-low-calorie diets.

18. The third paragraph is organized by
    A. explaining how weight is lost on very-low-calorie diets.
    B. describing the effects of very-low-calorie diets.
    C. defining very-low-calorie diets.
    D. arguing against using a very-low-calorie diet for weight loss.

PASSAGE #13

Read the passage and answer the question that follows.

President Truman's decision to order the atomic bombings on the Japanese cities of Hiroshima and Nagasaki has been the subject of intense historical debate. Truman's defenders argue that the bombs ended the war quickly, avoiding the necessity of a costly invasion and the probable loss of tens of thousands of Americans' lives and hundreds of Japanese lives. According to some intelligence estimates, an invasion might have cost 268,000 American casualties, with Japanese costs several times that figure.   5

Truman's defenders also argue that Hiroshima and Nagasaki were legitimate targets with both military bases and war industry, and their civilian populations had been showered with leaflets warning them to evacuate. Finally, they argue that two bombs were ultimately necessary to end the war. They note that even after the atomic bomb   10 had fallen on Hiroshima, the Japanese war minister implored the nation's Supreme Council "for one last great battle on Japanese soil—as demanded by the national honor. . . . Would it not be wondrous for this whole nation to be destroyed like a beautiful flower."

Truman's critics argue that the war might have ended even without the atomic bomb-   15 ings. They maintain that the Japanese economy would have been strangled by a continued naval blockade and forced to surrender by conventional firebombing. The revisionists also contend that the President had options apart from using the bombs. They believe that it might have been possible to induce a Japanese surrender by a demonstration of the atomic bomb's power or by providing a more specific warning of the   20 damage it could produce or by guaranteeing the emperor's position in postwar Japan.

The revisionists also believe that estimates of potential American casualties were grossly inflated after the war to justify the bombing. Finally, they argue that the bomb might have been dropped mainly to justify its cost or to scare the Soviet Union. The Soviet Union entered the Japanese war August 8, and some revisionists charge that the bomb-   25 ings were designed to end the war before the Red army could occupy northern China. (Adapted from James Kirby Martin et al., *America and Its Peoples*, 5th ed., New York: Longman, 2004.)

19. For this passage, the authors use the overall organizational pattern that
    A. gives reasons that the bombing of Hiroshima and Nagasaki ended the war.
    B. presents the arguments for and against Truman's decision to bomb Hiroshima and Nagasaki.
    C. gives the sequence of events that led to the dropping of the bombs.
    D. explains causes for dropping atomic bombs on Hiroshima and Nagasaki.

PASSAGE #14

Read the passage and answer the question that follows.

Fungi have a number of practical uses for humans. Most of us have eaten mushrooms although we may not have realized that we were ingesting the fruiting bodies of subterranean fungi. In addition, mushrooms are not the only fungi we eat. The distinctive flavors of certain kinds of cheeses, including Roquefort and blue cheese, come from the fungi used to ripen them. Highly prized by gourmets are truffles, the fruiting bodies of certain mycorrhizal fungi associated with tree roots. The unicellular fungi, the yeasts, are important in food production. Yeasts are used in baking, brewing, and winemaking. Fungi are medically valuable as well. Some fungi produce antibiotics that are used to treat bacterial diseases. In fact, the first antibiotic discovered was penicillin, which is made by the common mold called *Penicillium*. (Adapted from Neil A. Campbell, Lawrence G. Mitchell, and Jane B. Reece, *Biology*, 3rd ed., San Francisco: Benjamin Cummings, 2000.)

20. This paragraph is organized by
    A. describing how fungi ripens cheeses.
    B. defining fungi.
    C. classifying the types of fungi.
    D. giving examples of how people use fungi.

SECTION 2 ◆ RELATIONSHIPS *WITHIN* A SENTENCE

This is the second type of question that concerns patterns of organization. With this question, you are expected to understand *how the parts of a sentence relate to one another*. Once again, knowing the transitional words (key words) that go with each pattern is vital for understanding how the parts of a sentence relate so that you can answer these questions correctly. (See the section in this book on Patterns of Organization for a list of patterns and common transitions.)

When you are asked to find the relationship within a sentence, use the following process:

1. **Identify the <u>parts</u> of the sentence, or where the sentence breaks.**
   Many times, although not always, the parts of the sentence are joined by a piece of punctuation: a comma, a colon, dashes, a semicolon, etc.

2. **Look for transitional words (key words) at the beginning of one of the parts.**
   The transitional word will often clarify the relationship between the parts of the sentence.

3. **If there are no key words, try to analyze how the two parts relate.**
   Is one part an example of the other? Does one part contrast with the other? Does one part cause another?

> **Example #1**
> While mainland Europe suffered through the Thirty Years' War, England faced serious domestic stress under the first two Stuart kings.

Using the process outlined above, you can find the parts of the sentence by noting that there is a comma that separates the sentence into two parts: "While mainland Europe suffered through the Thirty Years' War" and "England faced serious domestic stress under the first two Stuart Kings." Next, if you look for transitional words at the beginning of one of the parts, you'll notice the word "while" at the beginning of the first part. That word is a transitional word for the "compare and contrast" pattern. Therefore, the relationship within the sentence is one of contrast, or compare and contrast. The author is showing how the situation of mainland Europe was different from that of the country of England.

Important: The relationship within a sentence has nothing to do with the overall pattern of organization.

> **Example #2 – What is the relationship within the LAST sentence of this paragraph?**
> All college students experience stress, which is *caused* by many factors. For example, a new student who is unfamiliar with the campus may become stressful just trying to find his or her way around on campus to arrive at class on time. *Another* cause of stress in university students is being away from family and friends, an important emotional support system. *Although* both male and female students feel stress, female students are *more likely to* display their feelings *than* male students.

The overall pattern of organization is <u>cause and effect</u> because the passage points out the causes and effects of stress experienced by college students. However, in the last sentence, there is a relationship of compare and contrast <u>within</u> the sentence. The sentence breaks into two parts at the comma, and the word "although" appears at the beginning of the first part. "Although" is a transitional word for compare and contrast. Thus, the author is contrasting the differences between male and female students:

> *Although* both male and female students feel stress, female students are *more likely to* display their feelings *than* male students.

> **Example #3**
> Plagiarism violates your obligation to yourself to be truthful, and it violates your obligation to society to produce fair and accurate information. (Gurak and Lannon, *A Concise Guide to Technical Communication,* New York: Longman, 2001.)

The sentence breaks into two parts at the comma, and the transitional word "and" appears at the beginning of the second part. "And" is a clue word for the addition pattern. Therefore, the relationship within this sentence is one of addition because the author is adding one more detail about the subject.

> **Example #4**
> Children who enjoy a positive relationship with their parents may agree more with their parents' higher status than do children who have a negative relationship with their parents. (Adapted from Stephen M. Kosslyn and Robin S. Rosenberg, *Psychology*, 2nd ed., Boston: Allyn and Bacon, 2004.)

In this sentence, there is no punctuation to indicate where the sentence breaks into parts. Therefore, you must find the parts without that aid. Logically, you'll notice "Children who enjoy a positive relationship with their parents" and "children who have a negative relationship with their parents." Even though there is no transitional word to indicate the relationship within the sentence, logic shows that it is one of compare and contrast because the author is comparing children who have a positive relationship with their parents to children who have a negative relationship.

> **Example #5**
> Although the rainforest is lush, its soils are poor because torrential rains cause soil erosion and intense heat leaches the soil of nutrients and burns off humus or organic matter that is essential for soil fertility. (Brummet, Palmira, et al., *Civilization,* 9th ed., New York: Longman, 2000.)

This final example illustrates another difficulty with identifying relationships within a sentence: sometimes, more than one pattern can be seen because the sentence breaks into more than two parts. When that happens, you must identify the two MAIN parts of the sentence and select the pattern that corresponds to that relationship.

In this sentence, there is a break after the comma, and there is the transitional word "although" at the beginning of the first part. Therefore, you might conclude that the sentence is contrasting the lushness of the rainforest with the poorness of its soils. However, that is not the real point of the sentence. Instead, most of the sentence shows WHY the soil is so poor. Therefore, the MAIN relationship within the sentence is one of cause and effect. The transitional word "because" helps clarify this relationship. When you have to decide upon two patterns, consider the author's purpose: why did he or she write the sentence? Here, the author's purpose is to show what causes the rainforest soil to be poor even though the vegetation (implied) is lush.

▶▶▮ *Secrets to Success*

- *Find where the sentence breaks into parts (usually at a piece of punctuation).*
- *Look for transitional words (clue words for the pattern) at the beginning of one of the parts.*
- *Ask yourself, What is the relationship between the ideas? Are they showing an example of something? Making a comparison? Showing an effect or cause of something? Or perhaps using some other type of relationship?*
- *Be aware that not all sentences have transitional phrases, and some phrases used may not match the relationship that is being shown. For this reason, always ask, What is the relationship between the ideas?*
- *When it looks like there are two patterns within a sentence, try to identify the MAIN relationship by asking yourself why the author wrote the sentence. What is he or she trying to tell you?*

SECTION 2 ◆ DIAGNOSTIC: RELATIONSHIPS *WITHIN* A SENTENCE

Read the passages and apply the strategies described above for finding relationships within sentences. When you are done, check your work with the answers immediately following the diagnostic. Even if you get a perfect score here, go ahead and complete the exercises in this section; they are designed to help build confidence and to give you practice for future test success.

Read the passages below and answer the questions that follow.

PASSAGE #1

One of the most important results of the Civil War was the freedom gained by southern slaves. In the decade following the defeat of the Confederacy, hundreds of thousands of men and women migrated throughout the South searching for land, work, and relatives lost through prewar sale. Some former slaves, however, took an even bolder step, leaving the South altogether and traveling west in search of cheap farmland or north   5
seeking industrial employment. While most faced difficult years adjusting to the world of free labor and white prejudice, none would have exchanged their life of freedom for the days of bondage. (Nash and Schultz, *Retracing the Past: Readings in the History of the American People*, 4th ed., New York: Longman, 2000.)

1. What is the relationship within the sentence, "While most faced difficult years adjusting to the world of free labor and white prejudice, none would have exchanged their life of freedom for the days of bondage"?
   A. Cause and effect
   B. Summary
   C. Contrast
   D. Comparison

2. What is the relationship within the sentence, "In the decade following the defeat of the Confederacy, hundreds of thousands of men and women migrated throughout the South searching for land, work, and relatives lost through prewar sale"?
   A. Cause and effect
   B. Time order
   C. Example
   D. Contrast

PASSAGE #2

Walt Whitman, whose *Leaves of Grass* (1855) was the last of the great literary works of his brief outpouring of genius, was the most romantic and by far the most distinctly American writer of his age. He was born on Long Island, outside of New York City, in 1819. At 13, he left school and became a printer's devil; thereafter he held a succession of newspaper jobs in the metropolitan area. He was an ardent Jacksonian and later a   5
Free Soiler, which got him into hot water with a number of the publishers for whom he worked. (Garraty and Carnes, *The American Nation: A History of the United States*, 10th ed., New York: Longman, 2000.)

3. What is the relationship within the sentence, "He was an ardent Jacksonian and later a Free Soiler, which got him into hot water with a number of the publishers for whom he worked"?
   A. Cause and effect
   B. Addition
   C. Process
   D. Comparison

PASSAGE #3

Self-disclosure is a type of communication in which you reveal information about yourself, in which you move information from the hidden self into the open self. Overt statements about the self as well as slips of the tongue, unconscious nonverbal movements, and public confessions would all be considered forms of self-disclosure.

Self-disclosure is information previously unknown by the receiver. This may vary from   5
the relatively commonplace ("I'm really afraid of that French exam") to the extremely significant ("I'm so depressed, I feel like committing suicide"). (DeVito, *Essentials of Human Communication,* 3rd ed., Boston: Allyn and Bacon, 1999.)

4. What is the relationship within the sentence, "Overt statements about the self as well as slips of the tongue, unconscious nonverbal movements, and public confessions would all be considered forms of self-disclosure"?
   A. Addition
   B. Summary
   C. Example
   D. Definition

5. What is the relationship within the sentence, "This may vary from the relatively commonplace ('I'm really afraid of that French exam') to the extremely significant ('I'm so depressed, I feel like committing suicide')"?
   A. Contrast
   B. Comparison
   C. Example
   D. Definition

PASSAGE #4

Presidents and prime ministers govern quite differently. Prime ministers never face divided government, for example. Since they represent the majority party or coalition, they can almost always depend on winning on votes. In addition, party discipline is better in parliamentary systems than in the United States. Prime ministers generally differ from presidents in background as well. They must be party leaders, as we have seen,   5
and they are usually very effective communicators, their skills honed in the rough and tumble of parliamentary debate. In addition, they have had substantial experience dealing with national issues, unlike American governors who may move directly into presidency. Cabinet members, who are usually senior members of parliament, have similar

advantages. (Edwards, Wattenberg, and Lineberry, *Government in America*, 9th ed.,   10
New York: Longman, 2000.)

6. What is the relationship within the sentence, "Since they represent the majority party or coalition, they can almost always depend on winning on votes"?
   A. Statement and clarification
   B. Addition
   C. Compare and contrast
   D. Cause and effect

7. What is the relationship within the sentence, "In addition, they have had substantial experience dealing with national issues, unlike American governors who may move directly into presidency"?
   A. Addition
   B. Comparison
   C. Contrast
   D. Definition

Answers to Diagnostic

1. C
2. A (This sentence shows time order at the beginning, but the MAIN point of the sentence is to show WHY they were migrating, which is cause and effect.)
3. A
4. C
5. A (This sentence shows examples in the parentheses, but the MAIN point of the sentence is to contrast the two extremes of "commonplace" and "significant.")
6. D
7. C (This sentence shows addition at the beginning, but the MAIN point of the sentence is to contrast prime ministers and presidents.)

📚 *Study Hint*

Just as before, the following section of exercises pulls passages that you have already seen in one or more of the previous sections. Remember, the purpose of presenting you with the same passages in different sections is to imitate the state exit exam, which presents you with a passage and then asks you several different types of questions based on that one passage. Also, many of these skills are connected to each other.

For example, the author's purpose is closely connected to the pattern of organization and reinforced by tone, so it is important for you to see how one passage uses each of these skills for an overall effect. For example, the preceding section, Patterns of Organization, and this section, Relationships Within a Sentence, and the next section, Relationships Between Sentences, are all so closely related that you will benefit from seeing how they tie into each other.

So, study smart. Compare these questions to each of the sections where the passages also appear, and think about the relationships between the skills.

SECTION 2 ◆ EXERCISES: RELATIONSHIPS *WITHIN* A SENTENCE

Use the following exercises to practice reading for relationships within a sentence.

PASSAGE #1

Read the passage and answer the questions that follow.

Contrary to popular assumption, slavery was not usually based on racism, but on one of three other factors. The first was debt. In some cultures, an individual who could not pay a debt could be enslaved by the creditor. The second was crime. Instead of being killed, a murderer or thief might be enslaved by the family of the victim as compensation for their loss. The third was war and conquest. When one group of people 5
conquered another, they often enslaved some of the vanquished. Historian Gerda Lerner notes that the first people enslaved through warfare were women. When premodern men raided a village or camp, they killed the men, raped the women, and then brought the women back as slaves. The women were valued for sexual purposes, for reproduction, and for their labor. (James M. Henslin, *Sociology*, 6th ed., Boston: Allyn and 10
Bacon, 2003.)

1. "When one group of people conquered another, they often enslaved some of the vanquished."
    (lines 5–6)

    The relationship of parts within the sentence above is

    A. contrast.
    B. cause and effect.
    C. process.
    D. summary.

2. "The women were valued for sexual purposes, for reproduction, and for their labor." (lines 9–10)

    The relationship of parts within the sentence above is

    A. summary.
    B. example.
    C. clarification.
    D. listing.

PASSAGE #2

Read the passage and answer the question that follows.

Nonflowing bodies of water such as lakes become contaminated in stages. First, pollutants such as animal fertilizer, detergents, industrial waste, and sewage are dumped into the water supply. As a result, an accelerated growth of algae occurs. As algae growth skyrockets on a diet of inorganic pollutants, especially nitrogen and phosphorus, a blanket of slime covers the water. Eventual death of the algae results in bacterial 5
decomposition that consumes the oxygen present. This oxygen deficit kills fish and other lake inhabitants, many of which are valuable as food resources, and, as recently suggested, disrupts freshwater animals' endocrine systems. Eventually, the body of

water becomes contaminated beyond use. (Adapted from David J. Anspaugh and Gene Ezell, *Teaching Today's Health*, 7th ed., San Francisco: Benjamin Cummings, 2004.)

3. "As algae growth skyrockets on a diet of inorganic pollutants, especially nitrogen and phosphorus, a blanket of slime covers the water." (lines 3–5)

   The relationship of parts within the sentence above is

   A. spatial order.
   B. example.
   C. addition.
   D. cause and effect.

PASSAGE #3

Read the passage and answer the question that follows.

Cyberliteracy is not purely a print literacy, nor is Internet literacy purely an oral literacy. Cyberliteracy is an electronic literacy—newly emerging in a new medium—that combines features of both print and the spoken word, and the medium does so in ways that change how we read, speak, think, and interact with others. Once we see that online texts are not exactly written or spoken, we begin to understand that cyberliteracy requires a special form   5 of critical thinking. Communication in the online world is not quite like anything else. Written messages, such as letters (even when written on a computer), are usually created slowly and with reflection, allowing the writer to think and revise even as the document is chugging away at the printer. But electronic *discourse*—talking, conversing, interacting—encourages us to reply quickly, often in a more oral style. In discourse, we blur the   10 normally accepted distinctions, such as writing versus speaking, and conventions, such as punctuation and spelling. Normal rules about writing, editing, and revising a document do not make much sense in this environment. (Adapted from Leonard J. Shedletsky and Joan E. Aitken, *Human Communication on the Internet*, Boston: Allyn and Bacon, 2004.)

4. "Cyberliteracy is an electronic literacy—newly emerging in a new medium—that combines features of both print and the spoken word, and the medium does so in ways that change how we read, speak, think, and interact with others." (lines 2–4)

   The relationship of parts within the sentence above is

   A. definition.
   B. addition.
   C. cause and effect.
   D. summary.

PASSAGE #4

Read the passage and answer the question that follows.

Research shows that men communicate with women in the same way they do with other men. Men are not showing disrespect for their female conversational partners, but are simply communicating as they normally do. Women, too, communicate as they do not only with men but also with other women. (Adapted from Joseph A. DeVito, *Essentials of Human Communication*, 3rd ed., New York: Longman, 1999.)

5. "Research shows that men communicate with women in the same way they do with other men." (lines 1–2)

    The relationship of parts within the sentence above is

    A. example.
    B. cause and effect.
    C. comparison.
    D. clarification.

PASSAGE #5

Read the passage and answer the questions that follow.

Most women were assisted in childbirth not by a doctor but by a midwife. Most midwives were older women who relied on practical experience in delivering children. One midwife, Martha Ballard, who practiced in Augusta, Maine, delivered 996 babies with only 4 recorded fatalities. Skilled midwives were highly valued. Communities tried to attract experienced midwives by offering a salary or a rent-free house. In addition to   5
assisting in childbirth, midwives helped deliver the offspring of animals, attended the baptisms and burials of infants, and testified in court cases of illegitimate babies.

During labor, midwives administered no painkillers, except for alcohol. Pain in childbirth was considered God's punishment for Eve's sin of eating the forbidden fruit in the Garden of Eden. Women were merely advised to have patience, to pray, and during   10
labor, to restrain their groans and cries, which upset the people near them.

After delivery, new mothers were often treated to a banquet. At one such event, visitors feasted on boiled pork, beef, poultry, roast beef, turkey pie, and tarts. Women from well-to-do families were then expected to spend three to four weeks in bed convalescing. Their attendants kept the fireplace burning and wrapped them in a heavy blanket in   15
order to help them sweat out "poisons." Women from poorer families were generally back at work in one or two days. (Adapted from James Kirby Martin et al., *America and Its Peoples*, New York: Longman, 2004.)

6. What is the relationship between parts of the following sentence?

    "In addition to assisting in childbirth, midwives helped deliver the offspring of animals, attended the baptisms and burials of infants, and testified in court cases of illegitimate babies." (lines 6–8)

    A. Addition
    B. Time
    C. Process
    D. Summary

7. What is the relationship between parts of the following sentence?

    "After delivery, new mothers were often treated to a banquet." (line 13)

    A. Cause and effect
    B. Summary
    C. Addition
    D. Time

PASSAGE #6

Read the passage and answer the question that follows.

Birds of a feather may kill together. Harris, the leader, would likely have enjoyed the respect and admiration from Klebold, who in turn would have felt uplifted by the praise he received from his revered buddy. In their relationship, the two boys got from one another what was otherwise missing from their lives—they felt special, they gained a sense of belonging, they were united against the world. As Harris remarked, as he and his friend made last-minute preparations to commit mass murder: "This is just a two-man war against everything else." (Adapted from James Alan Fox and Jack Levin, *The Will to Kill*, Boston: Allyn and Bacon, 2001.)

    5

8. What is the relationship between parts of the following sentence?

"In their relationship, the two boys got from one another what was otherwise missing from their lives—they felt special, they gained a sense of belonging, they were united against the world." (lines 3–5)

A. Comparison
B. Statement and clarification
C. Contrast
D. Time

PASSAGE #7

Read the passage and answer the question that follows.

Each of the 2000 or so species of firefly has its own way to signal a mate. When a female sees flashes of light from a male of her species, she reacts with flashes of her own. If the male sees her flashes, he automatically gives another display and flies in the female's direction. Members of both sexes are responding to particular patterns of light flashes characteristic of their species. Some flash more often than others or during different hours, while other species give fewer but longer flashes. Many species produce light of a characteristic color: yellow, bluish-green, or reddish. Mating occurs when the female's display leads a male to her, and most females stop flashing after they mate. But in a few species, a mated female will continue to flash, using a pattern that attracts males of other firefly species. A veritable *femme fatale*, she waits until an alien male gets close, then grabs and eats him. (Adapted from Neil A. Campbell, Lawrence G. Mitchell, and Jane B. Reece, *Biology*, 3rd ed., San Francisco: Benjamin Cummings, 2000.)

    5

    10

9. What is the relationship between parts of the following sentence?

"Some flash more often than others or during different hours, while other species give fewer but longer flashes." (lines 5–6)

A. Comparison
B. Addition
C. Contrast
D. Process

PASSAGE #8

Read the passage and answer the question that follows.

The dramatic difference between the social status of the Egyptian nobility and that of the common people is reflected in their respective burial rites. The keen Egyptian interest in the afterlife, combined with strikingly materialistic criteria for happiness, made lavish tombs for the pharaohs (Egyptian rulers) seem particularly important. Elaborate goods were buried with the pharaoh to assure him a gracious existence in the world beyond, and a   5
processional causeway linked each pyramid to a temple constructed for the worship of the pharaoh; adjacent to the pyramid was a building to house the special cedar boat that would carry him on his voyage to the land of the dead. The pyramid served as the core of an entire necropolis, or city of the dead, which included small pyramids for the wives and daughters of the pharaoh and mastabas for the nobility. Even a minor royal official spent a consider-   10
able portion of his time preparing an elaborate tomb for his afterlife, and he would want his corpse to be mummified because of the Egyptian belief that the *ka*, the spirit of life in each person, periodically returned to the body. The corpse of an average farmer, however, was typically wrapped in a piece of linen and deposited in a cave or pit with only a staff and a pair of sandals to facilitate the journey to the next world; some bodies were even left   15
in the open sand of the desert. (Adapted from Richard L. Greaves, Robert Zaller, and Jennifer Tolbert Roberts, *Civilizations of the West*, 2nd ed., New York: Longman, 1997.)

10. What is the relationship between parts of the following sentence?

"Elaborate goods were buried with the pharaoh to assure him a gracious existence in the world beyond, and a processional causeway linked each pyramid to a temple constructed for the worship of the pharaoh; adjacent to the pyramid was a building to house the special cedar boat that would carry him on his voyage to the land of the dead." (lines 4–8)

A. Listing
B. Time
C. Spatial order
D. Addition

SECTION 3 ◆ RELATIONSHIPS *BETWEEN* SENTENCES

As described above in the section *Relationships Within a Sentence*, the same patterns of organization and transitional phrases are used to show the relationship between ideas in two different sentences.

How to Find the Relationship Between Sentences
- Ask: What is the author trying to tell me about the relationship between these two ideas?
- Look at the beginning of the second sentence. Are there any transitional phrases?
- **Be very careful NOT be distracted by the overall pattern or by the pattern *within* one (or both) of the sentences.** The relationship between the two sentences has nothing to do with those.

> **Example #1**
> In the paragraph below, the overall pattern is cause and effect, but the relationship between the first and second sentences is the pattern of generalization and example. The author begins with a broad, general statement (the main idea) and follows it with a specific example:

<u>All college students experience stress, which is *caused* by many factors. For example, a new student who is unfamiliar with the campus may become stressful just trying to find his or her way around on campus to arrive at class on time.</u> *Another* cause of stress in university students is being away from family and friends, an important emotional support system. *Although* both male and female students feel stress, female students are *more likely to* display their feelings *than* male students.

Example #2

What is the relationship between these two sentences?

"For example, a new student who is unfamiliar with the campus may become stressful just trying to find his or her way around on campus to arrive at class on time. *Another* cause of stress in university students is being away from family and friends, an important emotional support system."

The relationship is addition (or simple listing) because the second sentence adds more information to the sentences before it.

Example #3

Tannen argues that the goal of a man in conversation is to be accorded respect, and so he seeks to display his knowledge and expertise even if he has to change the topic from one he knows little about to one he knows a great deal about. A woman, on the other hand, seeks to be liked, so she expresses agreement and less frequently interrupts to take her turn as a speaker. (DeVito, *Essentials of Human Communication,* 3rd ed., Boston: Allyn and Bacon, 1999.)

The second sentence shows a contrasting idea from the first one. Note the transitional phrase, *on the other hand.*

Example #4

Most of us have eaten mushrooms, although we may not have realized that we are ingesting the fruiting bodies of subterranean fungi. In addition, mushrooms are not the only fungi we eat. (Campbell, Mitchell, and Reece, *Biology,* 3rd ed., 2000.)

Here, in the second sentence, the author is adding more details about the subject of the first sentence, so the pattern between the sentences is one of addition.

Example #5

Federal courts ordered registration (for the draft) suspended while several young men filed suit. These men argued that the registration requirement was a gender-based discrimination that violated the due process clause of the Fifth Amendment. (Edwards, Wattenberg, and Lineberry, *Government in America,* 9th ed., New York: Longman, 2000.)

In the absence of any helpful transitions, the reader must try to determine <u>why</u> the author wrote the second sentence. Is it to explain the first one? To add more detailed information to the first one? To show a contrast or similarity to the ideas in the first one?

The author states that the registration for the draft was suspended. In the second sentence, the author tells why registration was suspended. The relationship between these two sentences is one of cause and effect.

▶▶ **Secrets to Success**

- *Learn the common patterns of organization and their transitions (refer to the first section of this chapter).*
- *Read both sentences carefully and paraphrase the ideas in each one.*
- *Look for a relationship that matches one of the common patterns.*
- *Look closely at the beginning of the second sentence for transitional phrases.*
- *Ask: Why did the author write the second sentence? (To add more details? To show an effect or cause? To compare or contrast with something in the first sentence?)*

Study Hint

If the relevant transition word is implied, not provided by being explicitly stated, then insert between the given sentences the word(s) for the choices of relationships listed in the questions option. For example, if option A gives "Cause and effect" as a possible answer, then insert a cause and effect word like "therefore," and then reread the two sentences to see if the word makes sense. If not, go to the next option and insert a word related to its pattern of organization.

Just remember to try a variety of words from any one pattern, for each word expresses a definite relationship.

SECTION 3 ◆ DIAGNOSTIC: RELATIONSHIPS *BETWEEN* SENTENCES

Read the passages and apply the strategies described above for distinguishing relationships between sentences. When you are done, check your work with the answers immediately following the diagnostic. Even if you get a perfect score here, go ahead and complete the exercises in this section; they are designed to help build confidence and to give you practice for future test success.

Read the passages below and answer the questions that follow.

PASSAGE #1

One of the most important results of the Civil War was the freedom gained by southern slaves. In the decade following the defeat of the Confederacy, hundreds of thousands of men and women migrated throughout the South, searching for land, work, and relatives lost through prewar sale. Some former slaves, however, took an even bolder step, leaving the South altogether and traveling west in search of cheap farmland or north 5
seeking industrial employment. While most faced difficult years adjusting to the world of free labor and white prejudice, none would have exchanged their life of freedom for the days of bondage. (Nash and Schultz, *Retracing the Past: Readings in the History of the American People*, 4th ed., New York: Longman, 2000.)

1. What is the relationship between the sentences, "In the decade following the defeat of the Confederacy, hundreds of thousands of men and women migrated throughout the South, searching for land, work, and relatives lost through prewar sale. Some former slaves, however, took an

even bolder step, leaving the South altogether and traveling west in search of cheap farmland or north seeking industrial employment"?

A. Comparison
B. Example
C. Definition
D. Contrast

PASSAGE #2

Walt Whitman, whose *Leaves of Grass* (1855) was the last of the great literary works of his brief outpouring of genius, was the most romantic and by far the most distinctly American writer of his age. He was born on Long Island, outside of New York City, in 1819. At 13, he left school and became a printer's devil; thereafter he held a succession of newspaper jobs in the metropolitan area. He was an ardent Jacksonian and later a   5
Free Soiler, which got him into hot water with a number of the publishers for whom he worked. (Garraty and Carnes, *The American Nation: A History of the United States*, 10th ed., New York: Longman, 2000.)

2. What is the relationship between the sentences, "He was born on Long Island, outside of New York City, in 1819. At 13, he left school and became a printer's devil; thereafter he held a succession of newspaper jobs in the metropolitan area"?

A. Addition
B. Spatial order
C. Time order
D. Statement and clarification

PASSAGE #3

Active listening serves several important functions. First, it helps you, as a listener, check your understanding of what the speaker said and, more important, what he or she meant. Reflecting back on your understanding of what you think the speaker means gives the speaker an opportunity to offer clarification. In this way, future messages will have a better chance of being relevant. Second, through active listening, you let the   5
speaker know that you acknowledge and accept his or her feelings. (Rigolosi and Campion, eds., *The Longman Electronic Test Bank for Developmental Reading*, 2001.)

3. What is the relationship between the sentences, "In this way, future messages will have a better chance of being relevant. Second, through active listening, you let the speaker know that you acknowledge and accept his or her feelings"?

A. Listing
B. Chronological order
C. Process
D. Example

PASSAGE #4

Self-disclosure is a type of communication in which you reveal information about yourself, in which you move information from the hidden self into the open self. Overt

statements about the self as well as slips of the tongue, unconscious nonverbal movements, and public confessions would all be considered forms of self-disclosure.

Self-disclosure is information previously unknown by the receiver. This may vary from   5
the relatively commonplace ("I'm really afraid of that French exam") to the extremely
significant ("I'm so depressed, I feel like committing suicide"). (DeVito, *Essentials of
Human Communication*, 3rd ed., Boston: Allyn and Bacon, 1999.)

4. What is the relationship between the sentences, "Self-disclosure is information previously unknown by the receiver. This may vary from the relatively commonplace ('I'm really afraid of
that French exam') to the extremely significant ('I'm so depressed, I feel like committing suicide')"?
    A. Compare and contrast
    B. Definition and example
    C. Spatial order
    D. Process

5. What is the relationship between the sentences, "Self-disclosure is a type of communication in
which you reveal information about yourself, in which you move information from the hidden
self into the open self. Overt statements about the self as well as slips of the tongue, unconscious nonverbal movements, and public confessions would all be considered forms of self-
disclosure"?
    A. Example
    B. Statement and clarification
    C. Spatial order
    D. Process

PASSAGE #5

Presidents and prime ministers govern quite differently. Prime ministers never face divided
government, for example. Since they represent the majority party or coalition, they can
almost always depend on winning on votes. In addition, party discipline is better in parliamentary systems than in the United States. Prime ministers generally differ from presidents in background as well. They must be party leaders, as we have seen, and they are   5
usually very effective communicators, their skills honed in the rough and tumble of parliamentary debate. In addition, they have had substantial experience dealing with national
issues, unlike American governors who may move directly into presidency. Cabinet members, who are usually senior members of parliament, have similar advantages. (Edwards,
Wattenberg, and Lineberry, *Government in America*, 9th ed., New York: Longman, 2000.)

6. What is the relationship between the sentences, "In addition, they have had substantial experience dealing with national issues, unlike American governors who may move directly into
presidency. Cabinet members, who are usually senior members of parliament, have similar advantages"?
    A. Summary
    B. Generalization and example
    C. Comparison
    D. Contrast

7. What is the relationship between the sentences, "Presidents and prime ministers govern quite differently. Prime ministers never face divided government, for example"?
    A. Summary
    B. Generalization and example
    C. Comparison
    D. Contrast

Answers to Diagnostic
    1. D   2. C   3. A   4. B   5. A   6. C   7. B

SECTION 3 ◆ EXERCISES: RELATIONSHIPS *BETWEEN* SENTENCES

Use the following exercises to practice reading for the relationships between sentences.

PASSAGE #1

Read the passage and answer the questions that follow.

One factor that affects the formation of friendship in prisons is the duration of the sentence. Three stages of short-term (one or two years) inmate adaptation are typical. First, inmates experience uncertainty and fear, based on their images of what life is like in prison. Therefore, they avoid contact with other prisoners and guards as much as possible. The next stage involves the creation of a survival niche. The prisoner has 5 selective interactions with other inmates and may develop a "partnership" with another inmate. Partners hang around together and watch out for each other. Maintaining a close tie with another inmate is difficult. In the third phase, the prisoner anticipates his eventual release, transfers to a minimum security area, increases contact with outside visitors, and begins the transition to the outside. In this stage, partners 10 begin to detach from each other as one of the pair moves toward the outside world. (Adapted from Barbara D. Miller, *Cultural Anthropology*, 2nd ed., Boston: Allyn and Bacon, 2002.)

1. What is the relationship between the sentences, "First, inmates experience uncertainty and fear, based on their images of what life is like in prison. Therefore, they avoid contact with other prisoners and guards as much as possible"? (lines 3–5)
    A. Summary
    B. Comparison
    C. Process
    D. Cause and effect

2. What is the implied relationship between the sentences, "The prisoner has selective interactions with other inmates and may develop a 'partnership' with another inmate. Partners hang around together and watch out for each other"? (lines 5–7)
    A. Comparison
    B. Cause and effect
    C. Statement and clarification
    D. Restatement

PASSAGE #2

Read the passage and answer the question that follows.

As a result of Robert Fulton's construction of the North River Steamboat in 1907, the day of the steamboat had dawned. In the 1820s its major effects were clear. The great Mississippi Valley, in the full tide of its development, was immensely enriched. Produce poured down to New Orleans, which soon ranked with New York and Liverpool among the world's great ports. Only 80,000 tons of freight reached New Orleans from the interior in 1816 and 1817. Later, in 1840 and 1841, more than 542,000 tons of freight were transported. Upriver traffic was affected even more spectacularly. Freight charges plummeted, in some cases to a tenth of what they had been after the War of 1812. Around 1818, coffee cost 16 cents a pound more in Cincinnati than in New Orleans, a decade later less than 3 cents more. The Northwest emerged from self-sufficiency with a rush and became part of the national market. (Adapted from John A. Garraty and Mark C. Carnes, *The American Nation*, 10th ed., New York: Longman, 2000.)   5   10

3. What is the implied relationship between the sentences, "Only 80,000 tons of freight reached New Orleans from the interior in 1816 and 1817. Later, in 1840 and 1841, more than 542,000 tons of freight were transported"? (lines 5–7)
    A. Contrast
    B. Example
    C. Time order
    D. Addition

PASSAGE #3

Read the passage and answer the questions that follow.

Different things motivate different people: A monk is not motivated to make money; an entrepreneur is not motivated to give away all earthly possessions and seek enlightenment on a mountaintop. Moreover, you are not motivated by the same forces day in and day out; rather, motivation comes to the fore when you have a *need* or a *want*. A **need** is a condition that arises from the lack of a requirement. Needs give rise to drives, which push you to reach a particular goal that will reduce the need. For example, lacking nutrients creates a need; hunger is a drive that will lead you to fill that need. In contrast, a **want** is a condition that arises when you have an unmet goal that will not fill a requirement. A want causes the goal to act as an incentive. You might *need* to eat, but you don't *need* a fancier car, although you might desperately *want* one—and the promise of a new car for working hard over the summer would be an incentive for you to put in long hours on the job. You are not necessarily aware of your needs or wants; **implicit motives** are needs and wants that direct your behavior unconsciously. (Adapted from Stephen M. Kosslyn and Robin S. Rosenberg, *Psychology*, 2nd ed., Boston: Allyn and Bacon, 2004.)   5   10

4. Identify the relationship between these two sentences from the above paragraph.

    "Different things motivate different people: A monk is not motivated to make money: an entrepreneur is not motivated to give away all earthly possessions and seek enlightenment on a mountaintop. Moreover, you are not motivated by the same forces day in and day out; rather, motivation comes to the fore when you have a *need* or a *want*." (lines 1–4)

The second sentence

A. exemplifies (is an example of) the first.
B. adds to the first.
C. shows the effect of the first.
D. contrasts with the first.

5. Identify the relationship between these two sentences from the above paragraph.

"Needs give rise to drives, which push you to reach a particular goal that will reduce the need. Lacking nutrients creates a need; hunger is a drive that will lead you to fill that need." (lines 5–7)

The second sentence

A. exemplifies (is an example of) the first.
B. summarizes the first.
C. defines the first.
D. compares with the first.

PASSAGE #4

Read the passage and answer the questions that follow.

North America has ten species of skunks. The one most people have seen—or at least smelled—is the abundant and widespread striped skunk. Another species is the spotted skunk, rarely seen but especially interesting because it illustrates some important concepts about biological species. This particular skunk belongs to a species called the western spotted skunk. The adult is only about the size of a house cat, but it has a potent   5
chemical arsenal that makes up for its small size. Before spraying her potent musk, a female guarding her young usually warns an intruder by raising her tail, stamping her forefeet, raking the ground with her claws, or even doing a handstand. When all else fails, she can spray her penetrating odor for three meters with considerable accuracy.

The western spotted skunk inhabits a variety of environments in the United States,   10
from the Pacific coast to the western Great Plains. It is closely related to the eastern spotted skunk, which occurs throughout the southeastern and midwestern United States. The ranges of these two species overlap, and the two species look so much alike that even experts can have a difficult time telling them apart. Both are black with broken white stripes and spots. Individuals of the western species are, on average, slightly   15
smaller, and some have a white tip on the tail, but these and other minor differences in body form are not always present.

For many years, biologists debated whether all spotted skunks belong to one species. But in the 1960s, studies of sexual reproduction in these animals showed that they are indeed two species. Reproduction in the eastern spotted skunk is a straightforward af-   20
fair. Mating occurs in late winter, and young are born between April and July. In marked contrast, the western spotted skunk includes what is called delayed development in its reproductive cycle. Mating takes place in the later summer and early fall, and zygotes begin to develop in the uterus of the female. Further development, however, is temporarily stopped at an early point called the blastocyst stage. Blastocysts remain   25
dormant in the female's uterus throughout the winter months and resume growth in

the spring, with the young (usually 5–7) being born in May or June. Because mating occurs at different times of the year for the two species, there is no opportunity for gene flow between populations of eastern and western spotted skunks. Thus, they are separate species, despite the pronounced similarities in their body form and coloration.   30

Spotted skunks show us that looks can be deceiving. Without knowledge of the mating cycles, we could interpret the minor differences between the two species as insignificant and conclude that there is only one species of spotted skunk in North America. (Adapted from Neil A. Campbell, Lawrence G. Mitchell, and Jane B. Reece, *Biology*, 3rd ed., San Francisco: Benjamin Cummings, 2000.)

6. Identify the relationship between these two sentences from the first paragraph.

    "Before spraying her potent musk, a female guarding her young usually warns an intruder by raising her tail, stamping her forefeet, raking the ground with her claws, or even doing a handstand. When all else fails, she can spray her penetrating odor for three meters with considerable accuracy." (lines 6–9)

    A. Contrast
    B. Cause and effect
    C. Example
    D. Addition

7. Identify the relationship between these two sentences from the second paragraph.

    "The ranges of these two species overlap, and the two species look so much alike that even experts can have a difficult time telling them apart. Both are black with broken white stripes and spots." (lines 14–16)

    A. Addition
    B. Example
    C. Summary
    D. Comparison

8. Identify the relationship between these two sentences from the third paragraph.

    "Further development, however, is temporarily stopped at an early point called the blastocyst stage. Blastocysts remain dormant in the female's uterus throughout the winter months and resume growth in the spring, with the young (usually 5–7) being born in May or June." (lines 25–28)

    A. Addition
    B. Restatement
    C. Cause and effect
    D. Time order

PASSAGE #5

Read the passage and answer the questions that follow.

In the 1980s, a long-running TV public service advertisement showed a father confronting his son with what is obviously the boy's drug paraphernalia. The father asks his son incredulously, "Where did you learn to do this?" The son, half in tears, replies, "From you, okay? I learned it from watching you!" Observational learning, which results simply from watching others, clearly appears to be a factor in an adolescent's willingness to experiment with drugs and alcohol.

Andrews and her colleagues found that adolescents' relationships with their parents influence whether they will model the substance use patterns of the parents. Specifically, they found that adolescents who had a positive relationship with their mothers modeled her use (or nonuse) of cigarettes, and those who had a close relationship with their fathers modeled the father's marijuana use (or nonuse). Similarly, those who had a negative relationship with their parents were less likely to model their parents' use of drugs or alcohol. Although some of the more complex results of this study depended on the age and sex of the adolescent, the general findings can be understood by thinking about them from the three levels of analysis and their interactions.

At the level of the brain, observing someone engage in a behavior causes you to store new memories, which involves the hippocampus and related brain systems. These memories later can guide behavior, as they do in all types of imitation. At the level of the person, if you are motivated to observe someone, you are likely to be paying more attention to him or her and, therefore, increasing the likelihood of your learning from them and remembering what you learn. At the level of the group, you are more likely to be captivated by models who have certain attractive characteristics.

In this case, adolescents who had a positive relationship with their parents were more likely to do what their parents did; if their parents didn't smoke, the adolescents were less likely to do so. The events at these levels interact. Children who enjoy a positive relationship with their parents may agree with their parents' higher status than do children who have a negative relationship with their parents. Thus, the former group of children probably increases the amount of attention they give to their parents' behavior. (Adapted from Stephen M. Kosslyn and Robin S. Rosenberg, *Psychology,* 2nd ed., Boston: Allyn and Bacon, 2004.)

9. Identify the relationship between these two sentences from the second paragraph.

"Andrews and her colleagues found that adolescents' relationships with their parents influence whether they will model the substance use patterns of the parents. Specifically, they found that adolescents who had a positive relationship with their mothers modeled her use (or nonuse) of cigarettes, and those who had a close relationship with their fathers modeled the father's marijuana use (or nonuse)." (lines 7–11)

A. Addition
B. Cause and effect
C. Generalization and example
D. Statement and clarification

10. Identify the relationship between these two sentences from the third paragraph.

"The events at these levels interact. Children who enjoy a positive relationship with their parents may agree with their parents' higher status than do children who have a negative relationship with their parents." (lines 26–28)

A. Clarification
B. Contrast
C. Cause and effect
D. Summary

KEEP IN MIND ◆ SUMMARY OF CHAPTER 2

The Overall Pattern of Organization

The organizational pattern is the arrangement of the details into a clear structure. You must be able to recognize organizational patterns to understand the author's main point and how the details are related to one another. Knowing the main idea and the author's purpose can help you to identify the overall organizational pattern. To find the overall pattern of organization:

- First identify the topic and main idea, focusing on the supporting details.
- Think about the author's purpose, asking why did the author write this? Learn the transitional phrases associated with each pattern. Be aware that authors may combine two or more patterns.

Relationships Within a Sentence

It is important to identify the MAIN parts of the sentence in order to see how they relate. The possible relationships within a sentence are the same as those for overall pattern of organization. (See the section on Patterns of Organization for a list of patterns and common transitions.)

The relationship within a sentence may not be the same as the overall pattern of organization. To find the relationship within a sentence,

- Find where the sentence breaks into parts (usually at a piece of punctuation).
- Look for transitional words (clue words for the pattern) at the beginning of one of the parts.
- Ask yourself, "What is the relationship between the ideas? Are they showing an example of something? Making a comparison? Showing an effect or cause of something? Or perhaps using some other type of relationship?"
- Be aware that not all sentences have transitional phrases, and some phrases used may not match the relationship that is being shown. For this reason, always ask, "What is the relationship between the ideas?"
- When it looks like there are two patterns within a sentence, try to identify the MAIN relationship by asking yourself why the author wrote the sentence. What is he or she trying to tell you?

Relationships Between Sentences

The same patterns of organization and transitional phrases are used to show the relationship between ideas in two different sentences.

- Learn the common patterns of organization and their transitions.
- Read both sentences carefully and paraphrase the ideas in each one.
- Look for a relationship that matches one of the common patterns.
- Look closely at the beginning of the second sentence for transitional phrases.
- Ask: Why did the author write the second sentence? (To add more details? To show an effect or cause? To compare or contrast with something in the first sentence?)

Chapter 3: Language Skills

SECTION 1 ◆ WORD CHOICE: CONTEXT CLUES

Using context clues correctly can help you to determine the meaning of an unfamiliar word. Context is the language that surrounds a word that helps to determine its meaning. Thus, many vocabulary in context questions may offer more than one correct definition of the word in the answer choices. However, the question is really asking you for <u>the meaning of the word as it is used in the context of the reading passage</u>.

In these types of questions, a good strategy is to read the question first, then go back and reread the sentence that contains the word. If necessary, read the sentences before and after, and even the entire paragraph to help determine the answer which is the closest in meaning to the word.

Example
What is the meaning of the underlined word?

A common <u>lament</u> of many instructors is that students do not spend enough time studying or doing assignments.

lament means:

    a. to grieve
    b. to mourn
    c. complaint
    d. compliment

To answer this question, we should consider several factors:

First of all, dictionary definitions for *lament* include both choices *a* and *b*. So simply knowing a word's meaning may not be able to help you, especially when that word can be used in several different senses. **Always** go back to the sentence to determine which sense is the closest for the context of that sentence. The answer may not be a perfect definition of the word, but one that is the *closest* in meaning.

Also, consider what part of speech *lament* is. Is it a noun? A verb? An adjective? Knowing the part of speech will help you determine the correct meaning.

Lament is used as a noun (a thing) in the sentence above. That eliminates choices *a* and *b*, which begin with "to," indicating an action (a verb).

Substitute a blank in place of the word *lament* and ask which answer choice seems to make most sense.

A common _____ of many instructors is that students do not spend enough time studying or doing assignments.

Which would instructors be most likely to do: complain about students not spending enough time studying or doing assignments, or compliment them? Obviously, instructors are more likely to complain about students not spending enough time on studying or doing assignments.

Another technique is to use other information in the sentence as clues to what the word means. Look for:

1. **Definition:** Often authors will give a definition of the word and set it off using commas, dashes, or parentheses:

Example: The definition of *cosmos* follows in parentheses:

The scientific revolution had reordered Western people's views of the **cosmos** (the universe, which is considered in harmony and well-ordered) and themselves.

Example: The definition of *nobility* follows, set off by dashes:

The **nobility**—kings and their courts—was still predominant.

Example: The definition of *milled* is set off by commas:

The crowd **milled**, moving confused and aimlessly, in the streets.

2. **Synonyms:** Often an author provides another word of similar meaning. Synonyms use the same kinds of punctuation and clue words as definitions. Also look for transitions that indicate the author is comparing two things (see Patterns of Organization for a list of transitions).

Example: A substantial British tax was **levied** (charged) on tea as well as the three-penny Townsend Duty tax. (**Levied** means *charged*.)

Example: Crowds milled in the streets, **harangued**—scolded and criticized—by Adams and his friends. (**Harangued** means *scolded and criticized*.)

Example: For a generation, all of Europe was caught up in the **convulsive**—shuddering—changes. (**Convulsive** means something similar to *shuddering*.)

3. **Antonyms** (words that mean the opposite): Sometimes an author will provide another word of opposite meaning to help you understand the full meaning through contrast. Look for transitions that indicate a contrast (see Patterns of Organization for a list of transitions).

Example: Your essays reveal a good deal about your level of mastery of the course content as well as your ability to organize and **synthesize**; instead of *isolating* skills, you apply them. (The word **synthesize** means the opposite of *isolating*. Notice the transition *instead of*.)

4. **Examples** of the unfamiliar word: Authors often include examples or illustrations of the word to help you understand its meaning. Look for transitions that indicate examples (see Patterns of Organization for a list of transitions).

Example: America could hardly hold a national **referendum**, such as *a direct public vote*, on every policy issue on the government agenda. (A direct public vote is one example of a referendum.)

5. **General sense of the passage:** Many times you must rely on your ability to use the details of the entire passage to reason out the logical meaning of an unknown word.

Example: If Parliament could grant the East India Company a monopoly of the tea trade, it could **parcel** out all or any part of American commerce to whomever it pleased. More important, the act appeared utterly **diabolical** and **dastardly**.

> **parcel** means to distribute
> **diabolical** means evil
> **dastardly** means mean and cowardly

The general sense of the passage tells you that Parliament's act was something negative.

Use Word Structure

Knowing the meanings of prefixes, roots, and suffixes can help determine the meaning of an unknown word. Look for smaller words within bigger words. For example:

> **inaccessible** = in (not) + access (root word) + ible (able to)
> Means: not able to have access to, as in "the building was **inaccessible** to anyone in a wheel-chair."

> **intertropical** = inter (between) + tropic (root word) + al (referring to)
> Means: referring to an area between the tropics, as in "Many of the **intertropical** islands suffered extreme damage from the hurricane."

Most good readers use a combination of <u>all</u> of the strategies listed above to determine the meaning of unfamiliar words.

More Examples

1. Although her house was somewhat orderly, it was far from <u>impeccable</u>. In fact, there was often dirt on the floors and in the sinks.

Note the transitional word "Although" at the beginning of the sentence. It leads you to expect a contrast.

Also, try to substitute your choice in the sentence to see if it makes sense:

> **impeccable** means:
> a. messy
> b. to clean
> c. spotless
> d. sanitation

2. Orlando was a city that had an abundance of theme parks but a <u>dearth</u> of good restaurants.

> **dearth** means:
> a. great amount
> b. shortage
> c. to consider
> d. inspection

This sentence makes a comparison between the number of theme parks and the number of good restaurants. Notice the word "but," which indicates an opposite (an antonym).

An <u>abundance</u> of theme parks means a great many. What is the antonym of abundance?

See if your choice makes sense in the sentence:

> Orlando was a city that had an abundance of theme parks but a _____ of good restaurants.

3. Members of Congress may spend so much of their time servicing their <u>constituencies</u> such as the tobacco industry that they have little time to be involved in the policy making process.

Note the example given, *such as the tobacco industry*, and try to think of a meaning that would match this example.

> **constituencies** means:
> a. offices
> b. contracts
> c. groups of supporters
> d. consultants

Answers to Examples
> 1. C   2. B   3. C

▶▶▎ *Secrets to Success*

- *The answer choices sometimes include more than one correct definition of the word. <u>ALWAYS</u> go back and reread the sentence containing the word in the question to determine which meaning is the closest for the context of that sentence. If necessary, reread the entire paragraph.*
- *Knowing the part of speech will help determine the correct meaning.*
- *Substitute a blank in place of the word, and ask which answer choice seems to make most sense when put into the blank.*
- *Use other information in the sentence as clues to what the word means. Look for synonyms, antonyms, examples, and definitions, and consider the general sense of the passage.*
- *Look for smaller words within bigger words. Use word structure (prefixes, roots, and suffixes) to determine the meaning of a word.*
- *Remember that the correct answer may not be the word's exact meaning, but is the <u>closest</u> of the four choices offered.*
- *Use a combination of <u>all</u> of the strategies listed above to determine the meaning of unfamiliar words.*

SECTION 1 ◆ DIAGNOSTIC: VOCABULARY IN CONTEXT

Read the passages and apply the strategies described above for finding the vocabulary in context. When you are done, check your work with the answers immediately following the diagnostic. Even if you get a perfect score here, go ahead and complete the exercises in this section; they are designed to help build confidence and to give you practice for future test success.

Read the passages and answer the questions that follow.

PASSAGE #1

Prime ministers generally differ from presidents in background as well. They must be party leaders, as we have seen, and they are usually very effective communicators, their skills **honed** in the rough and tumble of parliamentary debate. In addition, they have had substantial experience dealing with national issues, unlike American governors who may move directly into presidency. Cabinet members, who are usually senior members of parliament, have similar advantages. (Edwards, Wattenberg, and Lineberry, *Government in America*, 9th ed., New York: Longman, 2000.)

5

1. As used in the sentence, "They must be party leaders, as we have seen, and they are usually very effective communicators, their skills **honed** in the rough and tumble of parliamentary debate," the word *honed* means
    A. a grindstone.
    B. sharpened.
    C. excited.
    D. argument.

PASSAGE #2

Inside those (television) networks, a growing number of people with Ph.D.'s are injecting the latest in child development theory into new programs. That's the good news. The bad news is that working these shows into kids' lives in a healthy way remains a challenge. Much of what kids watch remains **banal** or harmful. (Daniel McGinn, *Newsweek*, November 11, 2002.)

2. As used in the sentence, "Much of what kids watch remains **banal** or harmful," the word *banal* means
    A. commonplace.
    B. hurtful.
    C. beneficial.
    D. irrelevant.

PASSAGE #3

Emigration to the New World in the seventeenth century was an **arduous** undertaking. The journey required two to six months at sea, with passengers huddled in cramped quarters with little provision for privacy. During the long voyage one could expect minimal—and at times rotten—**provisions**. (Nash and Schultz, *Retracing the Past: Readings in the History of the American People*, 4th ed., New York: Longman, 2000.)

3. As used in the sentence, "Emigration to the New World in the seventeenth century was an **arduous** undertaking," the word *arduous* means
    A. brief.
    B. businesslike.
    C. profitable.
    D. difficult.

4. As used in the sentence, "During the long voyage one could expect minimal—and at times rotten—**provisions**," the word *provisions* means
    A. beds.
    B. money.
    C. food.
    D. social life.

PASSAGE #4

There were two black regiments in the regular army and a number of black national guard units when the war began, and once these outfits were brought up to combat strength, more volunteers were accepted. Indeed, at first, no blacks were **conscripted**; Southerners in particular found the thought of giving large numbers of guns to blacks and teaching them how to use them most disturbing. However, blacks were soon drafted, and once they were, a larger proportion of them than whites were taken. (Garraty and Carnes, *The American Nation: A History of the United States*, 10th ed., New York: Longman, 2000.)   5

5. In the sentence, "Indeed, at first, no blacks were **conscripted**," the word *conscripted* means
    A. successful.
    B. drafted.
    C. freed.
    D. excused.

PASSAGE #5

The last decade of the nineteenth century was a time of upheaval in a century marked by **unprecedented** change. In the Northeast, mammoth factories and the immigrants who labored in them dominated the cities of America's industrial heartland. Throughout the country, an ever-growing network of railroads connected even outlying regions to the **burgeoning** metropolises of the nation. And in these metropolises, financial and industrial cartels, monopolies, and holding companies exercised an economic and political influence unparalleled in American life. (Nash and Schultz, *Retracing the Past: Readings in the History of the American People*, 4th ed., New York: Longman, 2000.)   5

6. In the sentence, "The last decade of the nineteenth century was a time of upheaval in a century marked by **unprecedented** change," the word *unprecedented* means
    A. predictable.
    B. not beneficial.
    C. inside of.
    D. never before matched.

7. In the sentence, "Throughout the country, an ever-growing network of railroads connected even outlying regions to the **burgeoning** metropolises of the nation," the word *burgeoning* means
    A. ordinary.
    B. rich.
    C. growing.
    D. connecting.

Answers to Diagnostic
1. B   2. A   3. D   4. C   5. B   6. D   7. C

📚 *Study Hint*

Have you noticed how difficult many of the passages in this workbook are? That is because these passages have been taken from the very textbooks you may use in your college classrooms, and the language is advanced. This is a very important skill for you to master.

As you read these passages, take the time to work with the words you don't know. Imitate the examples above and make up context clue cards for the words that get in the way of your understanding. Use your dictionary and thesaurus and write out definitions, synonyms, examples, antonyms. Or reword the sentences around the unfamiliar word using your own words to see if you can guess the meaning of the word that you don't know.

The key to understanding begins with words—one word at a time. Invest the time in your own success and develop a strong vocabulary!

SECTION 1 ◆ EXERCISES: CONTEXT CLUES

Use the following exercises to practice reading for vocabulary with context clues.

PASSAGE #1

Read the passage and answer the questions that follow.

Future teachers not only need to consider the kinds of students they will be working with; they also need to think seriously about the kind of work they will be doing. Some prospective teachers, not particularly fond of any academic subject, may <u>gravitate</u> toward elementary, early childhood, or special education, where they believe the emphasis will be on "getting along with the kids." They think much of the school day will be   5
filled with games and activities. The human side of teaching will be fun and rewarding. As for the academic side, surely they will know more than their students. Besides, a number of people—including some teachers and administrators—have told them you don't have to be very smart to be a teacher. They may even have heard that being too bright can hurt.   10

Let me <u>dispel</u> several myths about teaching. In spite of all the publicity about teacher burnout, some people cling to the belief that teaching is a fun job. It is not. Getting through to students can certainly be rewarding, but reaching them takes hour after hour of effort. Fun is not the right word. Listen to the counsel of a Florida teacher: "Teaching is work. It is the hardest job there is. Learning is work. We try to make it   15
enjoyable, interesting, exciting, motivating, relevant, palatable, etc. But any way you slice it, it's work."

Notwithstanding the public outcry over academically <u>incompetent</u> teachers, some people believe another myth. Rudimentary literacy is the only academic qualification teachers of the youngest or least able students must have. It is not. This myth, another   20
holdover from the past, finds no support in the research on teacher effectiveness.

(Joseph W. Newman, *America's Teachers: An Introduction to Education*, 4th ed., Boston: Allyn and Bacon, 2002.)

1. As used in line 3, the word <u>gravitate</u> means
   A. be sympathetic.
   B. be attracted.
   C. be agreeable.
   D. be prejudiced.

2. The word <u>dispel</u> (line 11) means
   A. describe.
   B. explain.
   C. remove.
   D. expose.

3. As used in line 17, <u>incompetent</u> most nearly means
   A. weak.
   B. irresponsible.
   C. unproductive.
   D. inadequate.

PASSAGE #2

Read the passage and answer the questions that follow.

Today television is the most <u>prevalent</u> means used by candidates to reach voters. Thomas Patterson stresses that "today's presidential campaign is essentially a mass media campaign. . . . It is not exaggeration to say that, for the majority of voters, the campaign has little reality apart from its media version."

The most important goal of any media campaign is simply to get attention. Media coverage is determined by two factors: (1) how candidates use their advertising budget, and (2) the "free" attention they get as newsmakers. The first, obviously, is relatively easy to control; the second is more difficult but not impossible. Almost every logistical decision in a campaign—where to eat breakfast, whom to include on the rostrum, when to announce a major policy proposal—is calculated according to its intended media impact. About half the total budget for a presidential or senatorial campaign will be used for television advertising.

Candidates attempt to <u>manipulate</u> their images through advertising and image building, but they have less control over the other aspect of the media news coverage. To be sure, most campaigns have press aides who feed "canned" news releases to reporters. Still, the media largely determine for themselves what is happening in a campaign. Campaign coverage seems to be a constant <u>interplay</u> between hard news about what candidates say and do and the human interest angle, which most journalists think sells newspapers or interests television viewers. (Adapted from George C. Edwards, Martin P. Wattenberg, and Robert L. Lineberry, *Government in America*, 9th ed., New York: Longman, 2000.)

4. As used in line 1, <u>prevalent</u> most nearly means
   A. modern.
   B. common.
   C. ordinary.
   D. powerful.

5. The word <u>manipulate</u> (line 13) most nearly means
   A. control.
   B. use.
   C. apply.
   D. plan.

6. As used in line 17, <u>interplay</u> means
   A. competition.
   B. relationship.
   C. link.
   D. interaction.

PASSAGE #3

Read the passage and answer the questions that follow.

Ignorance of African geography and environment has contributed greatly to the prevailing misconceptions about African culture and history. Many Americans, for instance, have thought of the continent as an immense "jungle." In reality, more than half of the area south of the Sahara consists of grassy plains known as *savanna*, whereas "jungle" or tropical rain forest takes up just seven percent of the land surface.   5

The most <u>habitable</u> areas have been the savannas, their grasslands and trees favoring both human settlement and long-distance trade and agriculture. The northern savanna stretches across the continent just south of the central desert, the Sahara. Other patches of savanna are <u>interspersed</u> among the mountains and lakes of East Africa and another belt of grassland that runs east and west across southern Africa, north and east of the   10
Kalahari Desert.

Between the northern and southern savannas, in the region of the equator, is dense rain forest. Although the rain forest is lush, its soils are poor because torrential rains cause soil <u>erosion</u> and intense heat leaches the soil of nutrients and burns off <u>humus</u> (organic matter) that is essential for soil fertility. The rain forests also harbor insects that carry   15
deadly diseases. Mosquitoes transmit malaria and yellow fever, and the tsetse fly is a carrier of sleeping sickness to which both humans and animals, such as horses and cattle, are susceptible. (Brummet, Palmira, et al., *Civilization*, 9th ed., New York: Longman, 2000.)

7. As used in line 6, <u>habitable</u> most nearly means
   A. livable.
   B. convenient.
   C. spacious.
   D. fertile.

8. The word <u>interspersed</u> in line 9 most nearly means
    A. located.
    B. planted.
    C. scattered.
    D. hidden.

9. As used in line 14, <u>humus</u> means
    A. sewage.
    B. organic matter.
    C. nutrients.
    D. chemicals.

10. The word <u>erosion</u> (line 14) most nearly means
    A. destruction.
    B. pollution.
    C. washing away.
    D. contamination.

SECTION 2 ◆ BIASED LANGUAGE

Authors often choose words that reveal their attitudes toward their subjects. A bias is an attitude that is for or against the subject, and sometimes this bias toward or against something can be very subtle. Being able to recognize the author's use of positive or negative language will help you to determine the author's bias for or against the topic.

When an author uses more opinion than fact or a great deal of positive or negative language to present his or her argument, it is easy to spot bias. However, sometimes bias is not so obvious. One way to recognize subtle bias is to ask yourself if the author considers anything in the text to be <u>in-herently</u> good or bad. In other words, is there anything that the author considers to be *positive* or *negative by its very nature*? For example, an author who writes about how wonderfully adapted cockroaches are to a multitude of environments may be showing bias in favor of creatures that are able to adapt to many environments. That characteristic may seem like an obviously positive feature, but in fact, it is only positive if the author sees it that way. Others may be horrified at the thought that one particular creature could take over after a nuclear disaster. They might consider that feature to be disastrous. Thus, subtle bias can be hard to spot, especially if the bias is one that you share with the author.

If the author does not seem to have either a positive or a negative attitude, then the writing is considered unbiased or neutral. In unbiased writing, the author attempts to balance opposing views without appearing to be for or against the topic.

Bias is very closely related to *tone*. If an author seems to present only the facts with very little opinion or judgment, then the tone is neutral, objective, straightforward, or matter-of-fact. If an author is extremely biased in favor or against something, then the tone will also be extremely positive or negative.

Consider the following when determining the author's bias:

- Is the author's language mostly positive toward the subject?
- Is the author's language mostly negative toward the subject?
- Does the author balance both negative and positive aspects of the topic?
- Does the author present mostly facts or opinions?
- Does the author consider anything in the text to be inherently good or bad?

> **Example #1**
> Hate sites began on the Internet in the mid-1990s, and their number expanded rapidly. Now hate groups in general across the nation are on the rise because of the Internet. Hate sites advocate violence toward immigrants, Jews, Arabs, gays, abortion providers, and others. Through the Internet, disturbed minds effectively fuel hatred, violence, sexism, racism, and terrorism. Never before has there been such an intensive way for depraved people to gather to reinforce their prejudices and hatred. (Adapted from Shedletsky and Aitknen, *Human Communication on the Internet*, Boston: Allyn and Bacon, 2004.)

Begin with stating the topic and main idea:

Topic: Hate sites on the Internet

Main Idea: Increases in hate sites on the Internet have enabled depraved people to express their hatred and prejudice.

Notice the adjectives the author has chosen: *disturbed* minds, *fuel* hatred, *depraved* people.

Ask: Is the author sounding positive or negative toward the subject?

This author clearly shows a negative attitude, or bias, against Internet hate sites.

> **Example #2**
> Efficiency brings dependability. You can expect your burger and fries to taste the same whether you buy them in Los Angles or Beijing. Efficiency also lowers prices. But efficiency does come at a cost. Predictability washes away spontaneity, changing the quality of our lives. It produces a sameness, a bland version of what used to be unique experiences. For good or bad, our lives are being McDonaldized, and the predictability of packaged settings seems to be our social destiny. (Henslin, *Sociology*, 6th ed., Boston: Allyn and Bacon, 2003.)

Topic: Efficiency

Main Idea: Efficiency is changing the quality of our lives to a bland version of what used to be unique experiences.

Ask: Is the author more positive about efficiency or more negative about it? Look at the sentence, "It produces a sameness, a *bland* version of what used to be unique experiences."

This author is biased against efficiency because it produces a "*bland* version of what used to be unique experiences."

Example #3
Harriet Tubman was born a slave in Maryland in 1820 and escaped to Philadelphia in 1849. Her own escape presumably required tremendous courage, but that was just the beginning. Through her work on the Underground Railroad, Harriet Tubman led more than 300 slaves to freedom. During the Civil War, Tubman continued her efforts toward the abolition of slavery by working as a nurse and a spy for the Union forces. Today, Americans of all races consider Harriet Tubman one of the most heroic figures in our country's history. (From K. McWhorter, *Reading Across the Disciplines*, New York: Longman, 2005.)

Topic: Harriet Tubman

Main Idea: Harriet Tubman is considered a heroic figure because of her efforts to abolish slavery.

Does the author use positive or negative language? Notice the phrases: "Her own escape presumably required *tremendous courage*" and "one of the most *heroic* figures . . ."

The author is biased in favor of Harriet Tubman.

▶▶▌ *Secrets to Success*

- *Begin by stating the author's topic and main idea. They may give you a clue to the author's bias.*
- *Look for biased language with positive or negative connotations.*
- *Ask: Is the author sounding positive or negative toward the subject?*
- *Look for a subjective, one-sided viewpoint.*
- *Look for opinions, often present in biased writing.*
- *If the author does not appear to have either a positive or a negative attitude toward the subject, the writing is objective, or unbiased.*

SECTION 2 ◆ DIAGNOSTIC: BIASED LANGUAGE

Read the passages and apply the strategies described above for finding biased language. When you are done, check your work with the answers immediately following the diagnostic. Even if you get a perfect score here, go ahead and complete the exercises in this section; they are designed to help build confidence and to give you practice for future test success.

Read the passages and answer the questions that follow.

PASSAGE #1

Managed care plans have agreements with certain physicians, hospitals, and health care providers to give a range of services to plan members at a reduced cost. There are three basic types of managed care plans: health maintenance organizations (HMOs), point-of-service plans (POSs), and preferred provider organizations (PPOs). The PPO, in my opinion, is the best type of managed care plan because it merges the best features of traditional health insurance and HMOs. As in traditional plans, participants in a PPO may pay premiums, deductibles, and co-payments, but the co-pay under a PPO is

5

lower. The best part of a PPO, though, is its flexibility: participants may choose their physicians and services from a list of preferred providers, or they may go outside the plan for care if they wish. (Adaped from Pruitt and Stein, *Healthstyles*, Boston: Allyn and Bacon, 2001.)   10

1. In the passage above, the author
   A. is biased against managed care plans.
   B. is biased in favor of HMO and POS plans.
   C. is unbiased.
   D. is biased in favor of PPOs.

PASSAGE #2

Plagiarism is a serious infraction in most settings. Students can be suspended or expelled from school. Researchers can lose their jobs and their standing in the academic community. More importantly, plagiarism is serious because it violates several of the reasonable criteria for ethical decision making. Plagiarism violates your obligation to yourself to be truthful, and it violates your obligation to other students and researchers.   5
(Adapted from Gurak and Lannon, *A Concise Guide to Technical Communication*, New York: Longman, 2001.)

2. In the passage above, the author
   A. is unbiased.
   B. is biased against plagiarism.
   C. is biased in favor of plagiarism.
   D. is biased against students and researchers.

PASSAGE #3

Tannen argues that the goal of a man in conversation is to be accorded respect, and so he seeks to display his knowledge and expertise even if he has to change the topic from one he knows little about to one he knows a great deal about. A woman, on the other hand, seeks to be liked, and so she expresses agreement and less frequently interrupts to take her turn as a speaker. (J. DeVito, *Essentials of Human Communication*, 3rd ed., New York: Longman, 1999.)   5

3. In the passage above, the author
   A. is unbiased.
   B. is biased against men's style of conversation.
   C. is biased for women's style of conversation.
   D. is biased against women's style of conversation.

PASSAGE #4

Bush infuriated environmentalists, who had been pleased with Clinton's efforts to protect America's national heritage. And, catering to the interests of oil companies, he fought to promote drilling in the protected Arctic National Wildlife Refuge, even in the face of estimates that there was very little oil there to be found. When his own Environmental Protection Agency (EPA) issued a report in mid-2002 linking the use of fossil fuel to global warming, Bush dismissed the study by declaring that he had the "report put out by the bureaucracy," making it clear that he had no confidence in the judgments of the scientists working for the EPA. (G. Nash et al., *The American People: Creating a Nation and a Society*, 6th ed., New York: Longman, 2004.)

5

4. In this passage, the authors
   A. are unbiased.
   B. are biased in favor of the EPA.
   C. are biased against the actions of President George W. Bush.
   D. are biased against oil drilling.

PASSAGE #5

Clinton was an enormously successful politician. Not only had he escaped conviction in the highly visible—and embarrassing—impeachment case, but he also managed to co-opt Republican issues and seize the political center. When he moved to reconfigure the national welfare system, to limit the number of years a person could receive benefits and to pare down the number of people on welfare rolls, the conservatives were pleased while the liberals were furious. Yet in other ways, he quietly advanced liberal goals, with incremental appropriations, even when he was unable to push major programs, such as his medical insurance scheme, through Congress. (G. Nash et al., *The American People: Creating a Nation and a Society*, 6th ed., New York: Longman, 2004.)

5

5. In this passage, the authors
   A. are biased against welfare reform.
   B. are biased in favor of President Bill Clinton.
   C. are biased against Republicans.
   D. are unbiased.

PASSAGE #6

A report in 2000 observed that many Americans still saw Asian Americans as secretive and inscrutable. That kind of reaction was frustrating. "Too many people in this country continue to see us in simple stereotypes," complained Paul M. Ong, a social policy professor at the University of California at Los Angeles. (G. Nash et al., *The American People: Creating a Nation and a Society*, 6th ed., New York: Longman, 2004.)

6. In this passage, the authors
   A. are unbiased.
   B. are biased in favor of Asian Americans.
   C. are biased against stereotypes.
   D. are biased against Asian Americans.

PASSAGE #7

Along with self-education, employers could help by both providing the facts about sleep to employees and stressing how important an adequate amount of sleep is to everyday performance. Don't equate sleep with laziness; they're two totally different issues. Sleepy workers are more likely to cause accidents, make mistakes, and are more susceptible to heart attacks. Lazy workers, for whatever reason, just don't do their jobs. (Dorrit Walsh, "The Sandman is Dead—Long Live the Sleep-Deprived Walking Zombie," from K. McWhorter, *Reading Across the Disciplines*, New York: Longman, 2005.)

     5

7. In the passage above, the author
    A. is biased against laziness.
    B. is unbiased.
    C. is biased against employers.
    D. is biased in favor of getting an adequate amount of sleep.

Answers to Diagnostic
1. D   2. B   3. A   4. C   5. B   6. C   7. D

SECTION 2 ◆ EXERCISES: BIASED LANGUAGE

Use the following exercises to practice reading for biased language.

PASSAGE #1

Read the passage and answer the questions that follow.

Many overweight and obese individuals are trying to lose weight. Although it took several months and years to put on the extra weight, many of them are looking for a quick way to lose that weight. This attitude results in choosing quick-weight-loss diets that are not effective and may be harmful. Some choose metabolic products, such as herbs or caffeine, to lose weight. Herbs have not been shown to speed the loss of fat, and caffeine shows little promise as a weight-loss aid.

     5

Others go on very-low-calorie diets, which severely restrict nutrients and can result in serious metabolic imbalances. Weight can be lost on this type of diet; much of the weight lost will be lean protein tissue and/or water, not fat. This results in harm to the muscles (including the heart), loss of essential vitamins and minerals through the water loss, and dizziness and fatigue. Further, if one cuts calories, the metabolism slows; once this person goes off the diet, the metabolism remains slow and the body continues to use few calories—and the pounds come back.

     10

Liquid-protein diets operate on the theory that insulin is controlled and therefore more fat is burned. With this type of diet, ketosis will result. Ketosis will increase blood levels of uric acid, a risk factor for gout and kidney stones. There is new research evidence that carbohydrates lead to fat storage and weight; further, the excessive protein in this diet can damage the kidneys and cause osteoporosis.

     15

Prescription drugs, such as Redux and Pondimin (fen-phen), curb hunger by increasing the level of serotonin in the brain. These were intended for the obese, but they were banned in 1997 after the FDA found strong evidence that they could seriously damage the heart. `20`

Some people try crash diets to lose a moderate amount of weight in a very short period. These types of diets can damage several body systems and have been proved not to work because most of these individuals regain their weight. This yo-yo dieting causes many health problems and shortens lifespan. The best way to lose weight is to lose weight slowly (no more than one-half to one pound a week), eat properly and in moderation, and exercise. (Adapted from David J. Anspaugh and Gene Ezell, *Teaching Today's Health*, 7th ed., San Francisco: Benjamin Cummings, 2004.) `25`

1. In this passage, the author expresses a bias in favor of
   A. taking prescription drugs to lose weight.
   B. controlling insulin levels to burn fat.
   C. restricting calories.
   D. losing weight slowly.

2. In this passage, the author is biased against
   A. harmful quick-weight-loss diets.
   B. moderating food choices.
   C. obesity.
   D. research evidence on quick weight-loss diets.

PASSAGE #2

Read the passage and answer the questions that follow.

Television's portrayal of courts and trials is almost as dramatic as its portrayal of detectives and police officers—both often vary from reality. Highly publicized trials are dramatic but rare. The murder trial of O. J. Simpson made headlines for months. Cable News Network even carried much of the pretrial and trial live. But in reality, most cases, even ones in which the evidence is solid, do not go to trial. `5`

If you visit a typical American criminal courtroom, you will rarely see a trial complete with judge and jury. In American courts, 90 percent of all cases begin and end with a guilty plea. Most cases are settled through a process called **plea bargaining**. A plea bargain results from an actual bargain struck between a defendant's lawyer and a prosecutor to the effect that a defendant will plead guilty to a lesser crime (or fewer crimes) in exchange for the state's not prosecuting that defendant for a more serious (or additional) crime. `10`

Critics of the plea-bargaining system believe that it permits many criminals to avoid the full punishment they deserve. The process, however, works to the advantage of both sides; it saves the state the time and money that would otherwise be spent on a trial, and it permits defendants who think they might be convicted of a serious charge to plead guilty to a lesser one. (George C. Edwards, Martin P. Wattenberg, and Robert L. Lineberry, *Government in America*, 9th ed., New York: Longman, 2000.) `15`

3. In this passage, the authors are biased against
   A. live television trial coverage.
   B. the guilty plea.
   C. O. J. Simpson's verdict.
   D. spending money on trials.

4. In this passage, the authors express a bias in favor of
   A. television's portrayal of courts and trials.
   B. detective and police shows on television.
   C. plea bargaining.
   D. trial by jury for every criminal case.

PASSAGE #3

Read the passage and answer the question that follows.

The most common stimulant is caffeine, which is contained in coffee, tea, cola drinks, and even chocolate. Caffeine is a mild stimulant that is often abused. Nonetheless, it is a drug and should be recognized as one that can lead to health problems.

Caffeine is absorbed rather quickly into the bloodstream and reaches a peak blood level in about thirty to sixty minutes. It increases mental alertness and provides a feeling of energy. However, high doses of caffeine can overstimulate and cause nervousness and increased heart rate. Caffeine can also cause sleeplessness, excitement, and irritability. In some cases, high doses of caffeine can induce convulsions.

Coffee or cola drinking, let alone chocolate eating, cannot be considered drug abuse by most commonly accepted standards. But some individuals seek out caffeine for its own sake in over-the-counter products and in illegal substances to produce a caffeine "high." Because it is not considered a dangerous drug, the opportunities for caffeine abuse are often overlooked. (David J. Anspaugh and Gene Ezell, *Teaching Today's Health*, 7th ed., San Francisco: Benjamin Cummings, 2004.)

5. In this passage, the authors have a bias in favor of
   A. eating chocolate and drinking coffee and cola.
   B. considering caffeine a drug.
   C. using caffeine to produce a "high."
   D. using caffeine to increase mental alertness.

PASSAGE #4

Read the passage and answer the questions that follow.

Through the Equal Employment Opportunity Commission, the federal government has classified some interview questions as unlawful. Some of the more important areas about which unlawful questions are frequently asked concern age, marital status, race, religion, nationality, physical condition, and arrest and criminal records. For example, it's legal to ask applicants whether they meet the legal age requirements for the job and could provide proof of that, but it's unlawful to ask their exact age, even in indirect ways.

One strategy to deal with unlawful questions is to answer the part you do not object to and to omit any information you do not want to give. For example, if you're asked the unlawful question concerning what language is spoken at home, you may respond with a statement such as "I have language facility in German and Italian" without specifying a direct answer to the question. Generally, this type of response is preferable to the one that immediately tells the interviewer he or she is asking an unlawful question. In many cases, the interviewer may not even be aware of the legality of various questions and may have no intention of trying to get at information you're not obliged to give.

On the other hand, recognize that in many employment interviews, the unwritten intention is to keep certain people out, whether it's people who are older or those of a particular nationality, religion, and so on. If you're confronted by questions that are unlawful and that you do not want to answer, and if the gentle method described above does not work and your interviewer persists, you might counter by saying that such information is irrelevant to the interview and to the position you're seeking. Be courteous but firm. If the interviewer still persists, though it is doubtful that many would after these direct responses, you might note that these questions are unlawful and that you're not going to answer them. (Adapted from Joseph A. DeVito, *Essentials of Human Communication*, 3rd ed., New York: Longman, 1999.)

6. In this passage, the author is biased against
   A. answering unlawful questions.
   B. answering direct questions.
   C. answering closed questions.
   D. answering for proof of age.

7. In this passage, the author has a bias in favor of
   A. immediately telling the interviewer that he or she is asking an unlawful question.
   B. answering an unlawful question.
   C. developing strategies to deal with unlawful questions.
   D. turning in the employer for asking unlawful questions.

PASSAGE #5

Read the passage and answer the question that follows.

Hate sites began on the Internet in the mid-1990s, and their numbers expanded rapidly. Now hate groups in general across the nation are on the rise because of the Internet. Hate sites advocate violence toward immigrants, Jews, Arabs, gays, abortion providers, and others. Through the Internet, disturbed minds effectively fuel hatred, violence, sexism, racism, and terrorism. Never before has there been such an intensive way for depraved people to gather to reinforce their prejudices and hatred. In one analysis of hate speech sites, the researchers found sophisticated use of persuasive strategies. The hate sites generally started with an objective approach that was straightforward and neutral, in which they reinforced and strengthened the hate ideas that people already have. The Internet provides a forum for people with prejudicial attitudes to speak out and act out. Hatemongers can create an online world where they reign supreme, a world of similar minds, where they can gather with others to feel that their way is right and where they can design severe disruption for the on-ground world. (Adapted from Leonard J. Shedletsky and Joan E. Aitken, *Human Communication on the Internet*, Boston: Allyn and Bacon, 2004.)

8. In this passage, the author is biased against
    A. online commentaries.
    B. online messages among terrorists.
    C. immigrants.
    D. hate sites.

PASSAGE #6

Read the passage and answer the questions that follow.

The thousands of McDonald's restaurants that dot the U.S. landscape—and increasingly the world—have a significance that goes far beyond the convenience of ready-made hamburgers and milk shakes. As sociologist George Ritzer says, our everyday lives are being "McDonaldized."

The McDonaldization of society, the standardization of everyday life, does not refer   5
just to the robotlike assembly of food. Shopping malls offer one-stop shopping in controlled environments. Travel agencies offer "package" tours. They will transport middle-class Americans to ten European capitals in fourteen days. All visitors experience the same hotels, restaurants, and other scheduled sites, and no one need fear meeting a "real" native. *USA Today* spews out McNews—short, bland, unanalytic pieces that   10
can be digested between gulps of the McShake or the McBurger.

Efficiency brings dependability. You can expect your burger and fries to taste the same whether you buy them in Los Angeles or Beijing. Efficiency also lowers prices. But efficiency does come at a cost. Predictability washes away spontaneity, changing the quality of our lives. It produces a sameness, a bland version of what used to be unique   15
experiences. For good or bad, our lives are being McDonaldized, and the predictability of packaged settings seems to be our social destiny. (Adapted from James M. Henslin, *Sociology*, 6th ed., Boston: Allyn and Bacon, 2003.)

9. In this passage, the author has a bias in favor of
    A. package travel tours.
    B. unique experiences.
    C. *USA Today* news reporting.
    D. consistency in food at McDonald's across the world.

10. In this passage, the author is biased against
    A. shopping at a mall.
    B. standardization of everyday life.
    C. McDonald's burgers.
    D. efficiency.

SECTION 3 ◆ AUTHOR'S TONE

An author's choice of words conveys his or her attitude toward the subject. Understanding the author's tone will help you comprehend the author's ideas and feelings toward the topic. To determine the tone, you must pay close attention to the language of the passage. Look for adjectives that describe nouns. Think about the connotation, the emotional tone of the words. Look for opinions and bias. Also think about the main idea and author's purpose. Knowing the author's main point and the purpose for writing can help identify the tone of the passage.

For the Exit Exam, questions about the author's tone can cause problems – not because it is difficult to determine an author's tone, but because the <u>vocabulary words</u> that the Exit Exam uses to describe tone are sometimes difficult. There is nothing worse than understanding clearly what an author's tone is only to get the question wrong because you don't understand the answer choices. Therefore, learning the meanings to as many tone words as you can is vital. Knowing what the tone words mean will help you to choose the correct tone.

Sometimes, students who lack confidence will select an answer to a tone question when they do not know what that tone word means. This happens simply because such students believe the test is harder than it really is, that the test writers are trying to trick them, or that they should choose the most difficult answer. <u>Do not make this mistake!!</u> If you do not know what some tone word means, do NOT select it as the answer unless you are 100% sure that the other answer choices are wrong. Most of the time, you will see an answer choice that matches fairly closely your own estimation of the author's tone.

*<u>NOTE</u>: The word "objective" has nothing to do with a goal or with making an argument against something. Objective means neutral, unbiased, or straightforward. Many academic texts are written in an objective tone because they are fact-based. Make sure that you know this tone word definition in particular because it shows up frequently on the Exit Exam.

COMMON TONE WORDS TO LEARN

Ambivalent	Docile	Ironic	Reverent
Apathetic	Earnest	Irreverent	Righteous
Awestruck	Eloquent	Malicious	Satiric
Callous	Enigmatic	Melancholic	Scornful
Caustic	Erudite	Melodramatic	Smug
Condescending	Farcical	Morose	Solemn
Contemplative	Flippant	Nostalgic	Somber
Contemptuous	Frenzied	Objective	Vindictive
Cynical	Frivolous	Obsequious	

Example:
Efficiency brings dependability. You can expect your burger and fries to taste the same whether you buy them in Los Angeles or Beijing. Efficiency also lowers prices. But efficiency does come at a cost. Predictability washes away spontaneity, changing the quality of our lives. It produces a sameness, a bland version of what used to be unique experiences. For good or bad, our lives are being McDonaldized, and the predictability of packaged settings seems to be our social destiny. (Henslin, *Sociology*, 6th ed., Boston: Allyn and Bacon, 2003.)

Topic: Efficiency

Main Idea: Efficiency is changing the quality of our lives to a bland version of what used to be unique experiences.

Author's Purpose: To criticize how efficiency has negatively changed the quality of our lives.

Author's Language: Notice the choice of words used to describe efficiency: "a *sameness*, a *bland* version."

1. What is the overall tone of this passage?
   A. Humorous
   B. Nostalgic
   C. Sarcastic
   D. Pessimistic

The author's feeling is more pessimistic than any of the other choices, so the correct answer is D. However, if you do not know what pessimistic means, you may have problems with this question. Based on the author's use of language, you may feel that the tone is negative or critical. However, those choices do not appear. You can see how important it is to learn the vocabulary words typically used to describe an author's tone.

> **Example #2**
> Plagiarism is a serious infraction in most settings. Students can be suspended or expelled from school. Researchers can lose their jobs and their standing in the academic community. More importantly, plagiarism is serious because it violates several of the reasonable criteria for ethical decision making. Plagiarism violates your obligation to yourself to be truthful, and it violates your obligation to other students and researchers. (Adapted from Gurak and Lannon, *A Concise Guide to Technical Communication*, New York: Longman, 2001.)

2. What is the overall tone of this passage?
   A. Detached
   B. Objective
   C. Concerned
   D. Reverent

Topic: Plagiarism

Main Idea: Plagiarism is a serious infraction in most settings for many reasons.

Author's Purpose: To show why plagiarism is a serious offense.

Author's Language: Note the language the author uses: "a *serious* infraction" and "*violates* your obligation."

The correct answer is choice C, concerned. Reverent means deeply respectful or worshipful. If you selected that answer because you did not know the meaning, please do not do that on the real Exit Exam! Study the tone words and do not select an answer unless you know what it means.

Example #3

Overt statements about the self as well as slips of the tongue, unconscious nonverbal movements, and public confessions would all be considered forms of self-disclosure. Self-disclosure is information previously unknown by the receiver. This may vary from the relatively commonplace ("I'm really afraid of that French exam") to the extremely significant ("I'm so depressed, I feel like committing suicide"). (DeVito, *Essentials of Human Communication,* 3rd ed., Boston: Allyn and Bacon, 1999.)

3. What is the overall tone of this passage?
   A. Objective
   B. Bitter
   C. Lighthearted
   D. Nostalgic

Topic: Self-disclosure

Main Idea: Self-disclosure is a type of communication in which you reveal information about yourself, in which you move information from the hidden self into the open self.

Author's Purpose: To define and explain self-disclosure and provide examples.

Author's Language: The author uses facts and very few adjectives with a positive or negative connotation. Do not consider quotes in examples as representing the author's feeling; the author is simply repeating what someone else has said. Focus on the author's own words.

The correct answer choice is A, objective. The tone is very factual and straightforward, and does not attempt to sway the reader's attitude about the topic. Again, objective is a very common tone word that has nothing to do with argument or a goal. Make sure you know what this tone word means.

▶▶◀ *Secrets to Success*

- *Learn the meanings to as many tone words as you can.*
- *Pay close attention to the language of the passage.*
- *Look for adjectives that describe nouns.*
- *Think about the connotation, the emotional tone of the words.*
- *Look for opinions.*
- *Think about the main idea and author's purpose.*

SECTION 3 ◆ DIAGNOSTIC: AUTHOR'S TONE

Read the passages and apply the strategies described above for determining the author's tone. When you are done, check your work with the answers immediately following the diagnostic. Even if you get a perfect score here, go ahead and complete the exercises in this section; they are designed to help build confidence and to give you practice for future test success.

Read the passages and choose the word that best describes the author's tone.

PASSAGE #1

The baby died last winter. It was pretty terrible. Little Charlotte (not her real name) lay on a high white bed, surrounded by nurses and doctors pushing drugs into her veins, tubes into her trachea and needles into her heart, trying as hard as they could to take over for her failing body and brain. She was being coded, as they say in ICU. It had happened several times before, but this time it would fail. Her parents, who were working, weren't there. (C. Mitchell, "When Living Is a Fate Worse Than Death," *Newsweek*, 2000, from *Reading Across the Disciplines*, New York: Longman, 2005.)

5

1. The overall tone of this passage is
   A. sorrowful.
   B. ambivalent.
   C. caustic.
   D. malicious.

PASSAGE #2

Nobody is arguing that the huge and growing global environmental and social crisis is entirely the fault of one high-profile burger chain, or even just the whole food industry. McDonald's is, of course, simply a particularly arrogant, shiny and self-important example of a system that values profits at the expense of anything else. Even if McDonald's were to close down tomorrow, someone else would simply slip straight into its position. There is a much more fundamental problem than Big Macs and French fries: capitalism. (Anonymous, "McDonald's Makes a Lot of People Angry for a Lot of Different Reasons," from *Reading Across the Disciplines*, New York: Longman, 2005.)

5

2. The overall tone of this passage is
   A. ironic.
   B. reverent.
   C. critical.
   D. objective.

PASSAGE #3

Harriet Tubman was born a slave in Maryland in 1820 and escaped to Philadelphia in 1849. Her own escape presumably required tremendous courage, but that was just the beginning. Through her work on the Underground Railroad, Harriet Tubman led more than 300 slaves to freedom. During the Civil War, Tubman continued her efforts toward the abolition of slavery by working as a nurse and a spy for the Union forces. Today, Americans of all races consider Harriet Tubman one of the most heroic figures in our country's history. (K. McWhorter, *Reading Across the Disciplines*, New York: Longman, 2005.)

5

3. The overall tone of this passage is
   A. optimistic.
   B. admiring.
   C. pessimistic.
   D. solemn.

PASSAGE #4

In Japan, married women are often supposed to stay at home and clean the house and raise the children. In fact, the Japanese word for wife means "Mrs. In-the-Back-of-the-House." There are even legal incentives to encourage married women to quit full-time jobs, and a married couple is legally required to use the same last name—almost always the husband's. Such an environment presents immense obstacles for women to overcome   5 in order to transform themselves into a meaningful force in Japanese politics. Women find it difficult to be taken seriously by voters, facing prejudice such as that reflected in one male candidate's taunt, "Women can't do anything. They should just shut up." (Edwards, Wattenberg, and Lineberry, *Government in America*, 9th ed., New York: Longman, 2000.)

4. The overall tone of this passage is
    A. serious.
    B. ironic.
    C. objective.
    D. critical.

PASSAGE #5

Inside those (television) networks, a growing number of people with Ph.D.'s are injecting the latest in child development theory into new programs. That's the good news. The bad news is that working these shows into kids' lives in a healthy way remains a challenge. Much of what kids watch remains banal or harmful. Many kids watch too much. There are also troubling socioeconomic factors at work. In lower income homes,   5 for instance, kids watch more and are more likely to have TV in their bedrooms, a practice pediatricians discourage. (Daniel McGinn, *Newsweek*, November 11, 2002.)

5. The overall tone of this passage is
    A. lighthearted.
    B. amused.
    C. angry.
    D. concerned.

Answers to Diagnostic
    1. A   2. C   3. B   4. D   5. D

SECTION 3 ◆ EXERCISES: AUTHOR'S TONE

Use the following exercises to practice reading for author's tone.

PASSAGE #1

Read the passage and answer the question that follows.

Efficiency brings dependability. You can expect your burger and fries to taste the same whether you buy them in Los Angeles or Beijing. Efficiency also lowers prices. But efficiency does come at a cost. Predictability washes away spontaneity, changing the quality of our lives. It produces a sameness, a bland version of what used to be unique experiences. For good or bad, our lives are being McDonaldized, and the predictability of packaged settings seems to be our social destiny. (Adapted from James M. Henslin, *Sociology*, 6th ed., Boston: Allyn and Bacon, 2003.)

5

1. What is the overall tone of this passage?
   A. Humorous
   B. Pessimistic
   C. Critical
   D. Nostalgic

PASSAGE #2

Read the passage and answer the question that follows.

Regardless of the type of job you have, you have to divide your time between work and school. The following suggestions will help you balance these two segments of your life. First of all, make sure that your supervisor knows you are attending college and that your job helps pay for it. He or she may be more understanding and helpful if he or she knows you are a serious student. In addition, try to find a coworker who may be willing to switch work hours or take your hours if you need extra time to study. Next, if possible, try to build a work schedule around your class schedule. For example, if you have an eight-o'clock class on Tuesday mornings, try not to work until midnight on Monday night. Finally, allow study time for each class. Make sure you have time between class sessions to do homework and complete assigned readings. For example, if you have a Tuesday/Thursday class, make sure you have some study time between the two sessions. (Adapted from Kathleen T. McWhorter, *Study and Critical Thinking Skills in College*, 5th ed., New York: Longman, 2003.)

5

10

2. The tone of this passage can best be described as
   A. instructive.
   B. authoritative.
   C. cautionary.
   D. sarcastic.

PASSAGE #3

Read the passage and answer the question that follows.

Each of the 2000 or so species of firefly has its own way to signal a mate. When a female sees flashes of light from a male of her species, she reacts with flashes of her own. If the male sees her flashes, he automatically gives another display and flies in the female's direction. Members of both sexes are responding to particular patterns of light flashes characteristic of their species. Some flash more often than others or during different hours, while other species give fewer but longer flashes. Many species produce light of a characteristic color: yellow, bluish-green, or reddish. Mating occurs when the female's display leads a male to her, and most females stop flashing after they mate. But in a few species, a mated female will continue to flash, using a pattern that attracts males of other

5

firefly species. A veritable *femme fatale*, she waits until an alien male gets close, then grabs and eats him. (Adapted from Neil A. Campbell, Lawrence G. Mitchell, and Jane B. Reece, *Biology*, 3rd ed., San Francisco: Benjamin Cummings, 2000.)   5

3. What is the overall tone of this passage?
   A. Humorous
   B. Objective
   C. Critical
   D. Argumentative

PASSAGE #4

Read the passage and answer the question that follows.

Fungi have a number of practical uses for humans. Most of us have eaten mushrooms although we may not have realized that we were ingesting the fruiting bodies of subterranean fungi. In addition, mushrooms are not the only fungi we eat. The distinctive flavors of certain kinds of cheeses, including Roquefort and blue cheese, come from the fungi used to ripen them. Highly prized by gourmets are truffles, the fruiting bodies of certain myc-   5
orrhizal fungi associated with tree roots. The unicellular fungi, the yeasts, are important in food production. Yeasts are used in baking, brewing, and winemaking. Fungi are medically valuable as well. Some fungi produce antibiotics that are used to treat bacterial diseases. In fact, the first antibiotic discovered was penicillin, which is made by the common mold called *Penicillium*. (Adapted from Neil A. Campbell, Lawrence G. Mitchell, and   10
Jane B. Reece, *Biology*, 3rd ed., San Francisco: Benjamin Cummings, 2000.)

4. The tone of this passage can best be described as
   A. neutral.
   B. respectful.
   C. excited.
   D. boring.

PASSAGE #5

Read the passage and answer the question that follows.

Plagiarism is a serious infraction in most settings. Students can be suspended or expelled from school. Researchers can lose their jobs and their standing in the academic community. Most importantly, plagiarism is serious because it violates several of the reasonable criteria for ethical decision making. Plagiarism violates your obligation to yourself to be truthful, and it violates your obligation to society to produce fair and   5
accurate information. It also violates your obligation to other students and researchers. (Adapted from Laura J. Gurak and John M. Lannon, *A Concise Guide to Technical Communication*, New York: Longman, 2001.)

5. What is the overall tone of this passage?
   A. Cautionary
   B. Defiant
   C. Annoyed
   D. Sad

PASSAGE #6

Read the passage and answer the question that follows.

Truman's critics argue that the war might have ended even without the atomic bombings. They maintain that the Japanese economy would have been strangled by a continued naval blockade and forced to surrender by conventional firebombing. The revisionists also contend that the President had options apart from using the bombs. They believe that it might have been possible to induce a Japanese surrender by a demonstration of the atomic bomb's power or by providing a more specific warning of the damage it could produce or by guaranteeing the emperor's position in postwar Japan. (Adapted from James Kirby Martin et al., *America and Its Peoples*, 5th ed., New York: Longman, 2004.)

5

6. The tone of this passage can best be described as
   A. complaining.
   B. passionate.
   C. neutral.
   D. humorous.

PASSAGE #7

Read the passage and answer the question that follows.

On April 20, 1999, a school shooting of such immense proportions occurred which radically, if not permanently, altered public thinking and debate about student safety and security. After months of planning and preparation, 18-year-old Eric Harris and 17-year-old Dylan Klebold armed themselves with guns and explosives and headed off to Columbine High School in Littleton, Colorado, to celebrate Adolph Hitler's birthday in a manner fitting their hero. By the time the assault ended with self-inflicted fatal gunshots, a dozen students and one teacher lay dead. (Adapted from Neil A. Campbell, Lawrence G. Mitchell, and Jane B. Reece, *Biology*, 3rd ed., San Francisco: Benjamin Cummings, 2000.)

5

7. What is the overall tone of this passage?
   A. Objective
   B. Tragic
   C. Excited
   D. Flattering

PASSAGE #8

Read the passage and answer the question that follows.

We, therefore, the Representatives of the United States of America, in General Congress, Assembled, appealing to the Supreme Judge of the world for the rectitude of our intentions, do, in the Name, and by the Authority of the good People of these Colonies, solemnly publish and declare, That these United Colonies are, and of Right ought to be Free and Independent States; that they are Absolved from all Allegiance to the British Crown, and that all political connection between them and the State of Great Britain, is and ought to be totally dissolved; and that as Free and Independent States, they have full Power to levy War, conclude Peace, contract Alliances, establish Commerce, and

5

to do all other Acts and Things which Independent States may of right do. And for the
support of this Declaration, with a firm reliance on the protection of divine Providence,   5
we mutually pledge to each other our Lives, our Fortunes and our sacred Honor. (From
The Declaration of Independence, in George C. Edwards, Martin P. Wattenberg, and
Robert L. Lineberry, *Government in America*, 9th ed., New York: Longman, 2000.)

8. The tone of this passage can best be described as
    A. reverent.
    B. nostalgic.
    C. objective.
    D. formal.

PASSAGE #9

Read the passage and answer the question that follows.

September 11, 2001

Today, our fellow citizens, our way of life, our very freedom came under attack in a series
of deliberate and deadly terrorist acts. The victims were in airplanes or in their offices: secretaries, business men and women, military and federal workers, moms and dads, friends
and neighbors. Thousands of lives were suddenly ended by evil, despicable acts of terror.   5

The pictures of airplanes flying into buildings, fires burning, huge structures collapsing have
filled us with disbelief, terrible sadness and a quiet, unyielding anger. These acts of mass
murder were intended to frighten our nation into chaos and retreat. But they have failed.

Terrorist attacks can shake the foundations of our biggest buildings, but they cannot
touch the foundation of America. These acts shatter steel but they cannot dent the steel   10
of American resolve.

Today, our nation saw evil, the very worst of human nature, and we responded with
the best of America, with the daring of our rescue workers, with the caring for strangers
and neighbors who came to give blood and helped in any way they could. (From President George W. Bush's speech on September 11, 2001, in James Kirby Martin et al.,
America and Its Peoples, 5th ed., New York: Longman, 2004.)

9. What is the overall tone of this passage?
    A. Impartial
    B. Sympathetic
    C. Inspirational
    D. Graphic

PASSAGE #10

Read the passage and answer the question that follows.

It was a Tiwi custom when an old woman became too feeble to look after herself to
"cover her up." This could only be done by her sons and brothers, and all of them had
to agree beforehand so there would be no feud afterwards. My "mother" was now

completely blind, she was constantly falling over logs or into fires, and they, her senior
clansmen, were in agreement that she would be better out of the way. The method was   5
to dig a hole in the ground in some lonely place, put the old woman in the hole and fill
it in with earth until only her head was showing. Everybody went away for a day or
two and then went back to the hole to discover to their surprise that the old woman
was dead, having been too feeble to raise her arms from the earth. Nobody had "killed"
her; her death in Tiwi eyes was a natural one. She had been alive when her relatives   10
last saw her. I had never seen it done, though I knew it was the custom, so I asked my
brothers if it was necessary for me to attend the "covering up." They said no and that
they would do it, but only after they had my agreement. Of course I agreed, and a week
or two later we heard in our camp that my "mother" was dead, and we walked and
put on the trimmings of mourning. (Adapted from James M. Henslin, *Sociology*, 6th   15
ed., Boston: Allyn and Bacon, 2003.)

10. The tone of this passage can best be described as
    A. graphic.
    B. annoyed.
    C. argumentative.
    D. excited.

KEEP IN MIND ◆ SUMMARY OF CHAPTER 3

Using context clues correctly can help you to determine the meaning of an unfamiliar word. Context
is the language that surrounds a word that helps to determine its meaning. To choose the correct
meaning of the word in the question,

- Always go back and reread the sentence containing the word in the question to determine which
  meaning is the closest for the context of *that sentence*. If necessary, reread the entire paragraph.
- Knowing the part of speech (noun, verb, adjective, etc.) will help determine the correct meaning.
- Substitute a blank in place of the word, and ask which answer choice seems to make most sense
  when put into the blank.
- Use other information in the sentence as clues to what the word means. Look for synonyms,
  antonyms, examples, and definitions, and consider the general sense of the passage.
- Look for smaller words within bigger words. Use word structure (prefixes, roots, and suffixes) to
  determine the meaning of a word.
- Remember that the correct answer may not be the word's exact meaning, but is the **closest** of the
  four choices offered.
- Use a combination of **all** of the strategies listed above to determine the meaning of unfamiliar words.

Biased Language

Authors often choose words that reveal their attitudes toward their subjects. A bias is an attitude that
is for or against the subject. This subjective point of view may have a negative attitude or a positive
one. Being able to recognize the author's use of positive or negative language will help you to determine the author's bias for or against the topic.

If the author does not seem to have either a positive or a negative attitude, then the writing is considered unbiased. In unbiased writing, the author attempts to balance opposing views, without appearing to be for or against the topic. The tone is therefore neutral, objective, straightforward, or matter-of-fact. Consider the following when determining the author's bias:

- Look for biased language with positive or negative connotations.
- Is the author's language mostly positive toward the subject?
- Is the author's language mostly negative toward the subject?
- Does the author balance both the negative and the positive aspects of the topic? Or is the information presented about the topic decidedly one-sided?
- Does the author present mostly facts or opinions?
- Begin by stating the author's topic and main idea. They may give you a clue to the author's bias.
- If the author does not appear to have either a positive or a negative bias toward the subject, the writing is objective, or unbiased.

Author's Tone

Authors choose words to create a tone or feeling. Understanding the author's tone will help you to comprehend the author's ideas and attitude toward the topic.

- Learn the meanings of as many tone words as you can.
- Pay close attention to the language of the passage.
- Look for adjectives that describe nouns.
- Think about the connotation, the emotional tone of the words.
- Look for opinions.
- Think about the main idea and author's purpose.

Chapter 4: Reasoning Skills

SECTION 1 ◆ FACT AND OPINION

In Reading texts and on tests of Reading Comprehension, there are several rules to keep in mind when determining whether a statement is a fact or an opinion. Learning the rules can help you choose the correct answer.

A *fact* is any statement that is verifiable, or provable. It does not necessarily have to be a true statement, but it must be provable by some means.

An *opinion* is not provable. It is a personal belief, a judgment, or an attitude.

All future events are considered opinions because, since they have not yet happened, they are not provable, even when they seem certain to happen.

> **Examples**
> Columbus died in 1506. (A provable fact.)
> He discovered America in 1493. (An incorrect but provable fact.)
> Columbus was a brave and heroic man. (A judgment and an opinion.)
> The discovery of the New World will be remembered throughout history. (Future event, an opinion.)

Beware of opinions in quotes:

"This is the most exciting book you can read," our instructor said.

Even though the statement contains an opinion, the sentence is provable by verifying that the instructor said it. Therefore, it's a fact.

Important: If a statement appears to be half fact and half opinion, and the choices available are only fact and opinion, then choose opinion. If a third option, "fact and opinion" is offered, then choose that one.

▶▶❘ *Secrets to Success*

- *Look for adjectives that describe people, places, things, or events.*
- *Ask: Is this provable?*
- *Don't confuse opinions in quotes with the fact that someone said it.*
- *If a sentence is both fact and opinion, consider it opinion unless you have an option to choose "fact and opinion."*

SECTION 1 ◆ DIAGNOSTIC: FACT AND OPINION

Read the passages and apply the strategies described above for fact and opinion. When you are done, check your work with the answers immediately following the diagnostic. Even if you get a perfect score here, go ahead and complete the exercises in this section; they are designed to help build confidence and to give you practice for future test success.

Read each sentence and choose A for "Fact" or B for "Opinion."

1. The meeting is scheduled for 9:00 a.m. on Wednesday morning.
   A. Fact
   B. Opinion

2. There will be several items on the agenda which we must discuss at the meeting.
   A. Fact
   B. Opinion

3. We have been unable to determine whether or not our e-mails have been received.
   A. Fact
   B. Opinion

4. Sending an e-mail to notify everyone on the committee is the most efficient way to communicate the information about the meeting.
   A. Fact
   B. Opinion

5. Several members of the committee will not be able to attend because of another sales meeting they must attend in Tokyo.
   A. Fact
   B. Opinion

6. The committee meets once a month to discuss important issues and resolve complicated business problems.
   A. Fact
   B. Opinion

7. When the Japanese attend our business meetings, they prefer to begin by socializing and getting to know the members of our committee.
   A. Fact
   B. Opinion

8. After September 11, 2001, many businesses faced extreme hardship and bankruptcy.
   A. Fact
   B. Opinion

9. The U.S. economy suffered one of the worst recessions in its economic history after 9/11.
   A. Fact
   B. Opinion

10. Despite the setbacks, both the stock market and real estate markets have rebounded to become effective investments.
    A. Fact
    B. Opinion

Answers to Diagnostic
1. A   2. B (future event)   3. A   4. B
5. A   6. B   7. A   8. B   9. A   10. A

SECTION 1 ◆ EXERCISES: FACT AND OPINION

Use the following exercises to practice reading for fact and opinion.

PASSAGE #1

Read the passage and answer the question that follows.

As a result of Robert Fulton's construction of the North River Steamboat in 1907, the day of the steamboat had dawned. In the 1820s its major effects were clear. The great Mississippi Valley, in the full tide of its development, was immensely enriched. Produce poured down to New Orleans, which soon ranked with New York and Liverpool among the world's great ports. Only 80,000 tons of freight reached New Orleans from the interior in 1816 and 1817. Later, in 1840 and 1841, more than 542,000 tons of freight were transported. Upriver traffic was affected even more spectacularly. Freight charges plummeted, in some cases to a tenth of what they had been after the War of 1812. Around 1818, coffee cost 16 cents a pound more in Cincinnati than in New Orleans, a decade later less than 3 cents more. The Northwest emerged from self-sufficiency with a rush and became part of the national market. (Adapted from John A. Garraty and Mark C. Carnes, *The American Nation*, 10th ed., New York: Longman, 2000.)

1. Which sentence is a statement of opinion?
   A. Only 80,000 tons of freight reached New Orleans from the interior in 1816 and 1817.
   B. Later, in 1840 and 1841, more than 542,000 tons of freight were transported.
   C. Upriver traffic was affected even more spectacularly.
   D. Around 1818, coffee cost 16 cents a pound more in Cincinnati than in New Orleans, a decade later less than 3 cents more.

PASSAGE #2

Read the passage and answer the question that follows.

The modern science of genetics began in the 1860s when an Augustinian monk named Gregor Mendel discovered the fundamental principles of genetics by breeding garden peas. Mendel lived and worked in an abbey in Brunn, Austria. In a paper published in 1866, Mendel correctly argued that parents pass on to their offspring discrete heritable factors. He stressed that the heritable factors (today called genes) retain their individuality generation after generation. Mendel probably chose to study garden peas because they were easy to grow and available in many readily distinguishable varieties. Also, with pea plants, Mendel was able to exercise strict control over plant matings. As a result, he was always sure of the parentage of new plants. (Adapted from Neil A. Campbell, Lawrence G. Mitchell, and Jane B. Reece, *Biology*, 3rd ed., San Francisco: Benjamin Cummings, 2000.)

2. Which sentence is a statement of opinion?
   A. The modern science of genetics began in the 1860s when an Augustinian monk named Gregor Mendel discovered the fundamental principles of genetics by breeding garden peas.
   B. Mendel lived and worked in an abbey in Brunn, Austria.
   C. Mendel probably chose to study garden peas because they were easy to grow and available in many readily distinguishable varieties.
   D. In a paper published in 1866, Mendel correctly argued that parents pass on to their offspring discrete heritable factors.

PASSAGE #3

Read the passage and answer the questions that follow.

Ignorance of African geography and environment has contributed greatly to the prevailing misconceptions about African culture and history. Many Americans, for instance, have thought of the continent as an immense "jungle." In reality, more than half of the area south of the Sahara consists of grassy plains known as *savanna*, whereas "jungle" or tropical rain forests take up just seven percent of the land surface.   5

The most habitable areas have been the savannas, their grasslands and trees favoring both human settlement and long-distance trade and agriculture. The northern savanna stretches across the continent just south of the central desert, the Sahara. Other patches of savanna are interspersed among the mountains and lakes of East Africa and another belt of grassland that runs east and west across southern Africa, north and east of the   10
Kalahari Desert.

Between the northern and southern savannas, in the region of the equator, is dense rain forest. Although the rain forest is lush, its soils are poor because torrential rains cause soil erosion and intense heat leaches the soil of nutrients and burns off humus or organic matter that is essential for soil fertility. The rain forests also harbor insects that   15
carry deadly diseases. Mosquitoes transmit malaria and yellow fever, and the tsetse fly is a carrier of sleeping sickness to which both humans and animals such as horses and cattle are susceptible. (Brummet, Palmira, et al., *Civilization*, 9th ed., New York: Longman, 2000.)

3. "Ignorance of African geography and environment has contributed greatly to the prevailing misconceptions about African culture and history." (lines 1–2)

The above sentence is a statement of

A. fact.
B. opinion.

4. "Mosquitoes transmit malaria and yellow fever, and the tsetse fly is a carrier of sleeping sickness to which both humans and animals such as horses and cattle are susceptible." (lines 17–19)

   The above sentence is a statement of

   A. fact.
   B. opinion.

5. "Many Americans, for instance, have thought of the continent as an immense 'jungle.'" (lines 2–3)

   The above sentence is a statement of

   A. fact.
   B. opinion.

PASSAGE #4

Read the passage and answer the questions that follow.

Though most precincts now use computer punch cards to record votes, the high-tech age has not yet made much impact on the voting process. There is good reason to expect that this will change in the twenty-first century.

The National Mail Voter Registration Form is available to download on the Federal Election Commission website. Twenty-two states currently accept copies of this application printed from the computer image, signed by the applicant, and mailed in the old-fashioned way. As e-mail becomes ever more popular and "snail mail" fades into a method reserved for packages, the entire voter registration process may someday be conducted mostly through electronic means. In an age where personal computers in the home will be as common as television sets are today, this technology would clearly make registering to vote more user-friendly.

If people can register by computer, the next step is naturally voting by e-mail. A growing trend in the Pacific Coast states has been voting by mail. In 1998, Oregon voters approved a referendum to eliminate traditional polling places and conduct all future elections by mail. In California, 25 percent of the votes cast currently come in via the post office. Again, as e-mail takes the place of regular mail, why not have people cast their votes via cyberspace? It would be less costly for the state, as well as easier for the average citizen—assuming that computer literacy reaches near-universal proportions sometime in the future. The major concerns, of course, are currently being addressed by some of the world's top computer programmers, as commercial enterprises look toward using the Internet to conduct business.

Making voting more user-friendly should encourage turnout, but people will still have to be interested enough in the elections of the future to send in their e-mail ballots. If everyone votes electronically in the convenience of his or her home, the sense of community on election day may be lost, which could lead to lower turnout. (Adapted from George C. Edwards, Martin P. Wattenberg, and Robert L. Lineberry, *Government in America*, 9th ed., New York: Longman, 2000.)

6. "In California, 25 percent of the votes cast currently come in via the post office." (lines 15–16)

   The above sentence is a statement of

   A. fact.
   B. opinion.

7. "If everyone votes electronically in the convenience of his or her home, the sense of community on election day may be lost, which could lead to lower turnout." (lines 23–25)

   The above sentence is a statement of

   A. fact.
   B. opinion.

8. "If people can register by computer, the next step is naturally voting by e-mail." (line 12)

   The above sentence is a statement of

   A. fact.
   B. opinion.

9. The National Mail Voter Registration Form is available to download on the Federal Election Commission website. (lines 4–5)

   The above sentence is a statement of

   A. fact.
   B. opinion.

PASSAGE #5

Read the passage and answer the question that follows.

There is no military conscription at present. The United States has had a volunteer force since 1973. However, President Jimmy Carter asked Congress to require both men and women to register for the draft after the Soviet Union invaded Afghanistan in 1979. Registration was designed to facilitate any eventual conscription. In 1980, Congress reinstated registration for men only, a policy that was not universally popular. 5
Federal courts ordered registration suspended while several young men filed suit. These men argued that the registration requirement was gender-based discrimination that violated the due process clause of the Fifth Amendment.

The Supreme Court ruled in 1981 in *Rostker v. Goldberg* that male-only registration did not violate the Fifth Amendment. The Court found that male-only registration bore 10
a substantial relationship to Congress's goal of ensuring combat readiness and that Congress acted well within its constitutional authority to raise and regulate armies and navies when it authorized the registration of men and not women. Congress, the Court said, was allowed to focus on the question of military need, rather than "equity."
(Adapted from George C. Edwards, Martin P. Wattenberg, and Robert L. Lineberry, *Government in America*, 9th ed., New York: Longman, 2000.)

10. Which sentence is a statement of opinion?
    A. The United States has had a volunteer force since 1973.
    B. In 1980, Congress reinstated registration for men only, a policy that was not universally popular.

C. These men argued that the registration requirement was gender-based discrimination that violated the due process clause of the Fifth Amendment.

D. The Supreme Court ruled in 1981 in *Rostker v. Goldberg* that male-only registration did not violate the Fifth Amendment.

SECTION 2 ◆ INFERENCES AND CONCLUSIONS

Inference and conclusion questions are among the most difficult to answer correctly. This is because they generally require a full reading of the text with complete comprehension, and because they require the reader to "read between the lines" in a logical way to locate the correct answer. To make an **inference** or understand an **implication** means to come to a logical conclusion based upon the facts that are given. Information that is implied is not stated. Therefore, you must look at the facts and details to arrive at a logical conclusion.

One technique to help determine which statement is a logical conclusion in a multiple choice test is to treat each answer choice as if it were a true/false question. Go back and reread to determine whether the answer choices could be true or false based upon the information that is presented in the passage. Be careful not to assume more than what is stated, but rely upon what is stated and your own background knowledge to help you make the right choice. Also, **be especially careful to read the question!** Sometimes, you will be asked to locate an inference that <u>cannot</u> be reached. In that case, you must look for the <u>false</u> answer rather than the true answer.

When drawing conclusions and making inferences, be sure that you understand the literal meaning of the passage. Begin by stating the topic and main idea. Pay close attention to the details. Think like a detective and use the details (clues) to arrive at the correct conclusion.

Also, be careful not to call a statement an inference or a conclusion simply because you strongly agree with that statement. In other words, do not let your own biases cause you to see things in the text that are not there or to jump too far with your logic.

> **Example**
> Truman's critics argue that the war might have ended even without the atomic bombings. They maintain that the Japanese economy would have been strangled by a continued naval blockade and forced to surrender by conventional firebombing. The revisionists also contend that the President had options apart from using the bombs. They believe that it might have been possible to induce a Japanese surrender by a demonstration of the atomic bomb's power or by providing a more specific warning of the damage it could produce or by guaranteeing the emperor's position in postwar Japan. (Adapted from J. Martin et al., *America and Its Peoples*, 5th ed., New York: Longman: 2004.)
>
> A conclusion that can be drawn from this passage is
>
> A. Truman was not a popular president.
> B. The navy did not blockade Japan.
> C. The Japanese witnessed a demonstration of the atomic bomb.
> D. After the atomic bombing, the war with Japan ended.

Look at each choice carefully, rereading the passage to determine if each statement is true or false.

A. *Truman was not a popular president.* Is there any information in the passage to support the idea that Truman was either popular or unpopular? The passage mentions Truman's critics, but every president, even popular ones, has critics. This statement is not supported by the passage. (False)

B. *The navy did not blockade Japan.* The passage does not say whether the navy blockaded Japan or not. It simply says, "the Japanese economy would have been strangled by a continued naval blockade." This statement is not supported by information in the passage. (False)

C. *The Japanese witnessed a demonstration of the atomic bomb.* This statement is the opposite of what the passage stated. In the passage, the argument states that the atomic bombing of Japan may not have been necessary because "it might have been possible to induce a Japanese surrender by a demonstration of the atomic bomb's power." Obviously, this did not happen. (False)

D. *After the atomic bombing, the war with Japan ended.* The passage states, "Truman's critics argue that the war might have ended even without the atomic bombings." The phrase "even without the atomic bombings" implies that the bombings took place and ended the war. This statement is true, and the correct answer.

▶▶▎ *Secrets to Success*

- *Look at the facts and details to arrive at a logical conclusion.*
- *Treat each answer choice as if it were a true/false question.*
- *Read the question very carefully to make sure you are being asked to locate true rather than false answers.*
- *Go back and reread to determine whether the answer choices could be true or false based upon the information that is presented in the passage.*
- *Do not assume more than what is stated in the passage, and do not select an inference simply because you agree with that statement.*
- *Rely upon your own background knowledge to help you make the right choice.*

SECTION 2 ◆ DIAGNOSTIC: INFERENCES AND CONCLUSIONS

Read the passages and apply the strategies described above for inferences and conclusions. When you are done, check your work with the answers immediately following the diagnostic. Even if you get a perfect score here, go ahead and complete the exercises in this section; they are designed to help build confidence and to give you practice for future test success.

Read the passages and answer the questions that follow.

PASSAGE #1

Time is especially linked to status considerations, and the importance of being on time varies with the status of the individual you are visiting. If the person is extremely important, you had better be there on time or even early just in case he or she is able to see you before schedule. Junior executives, for example, must be on time for conferences with senior executives, but it is even more important to be on time for the company president or the CEO. Senior executives, however, may be late for conferences with their juniors but not for conferences with the president. (DeVito, *Interpersonal Communication*, 6th ed.)

5

1. Which of the following conclusions can be drawn from the passage?
   A. The higher a person's status, the more important it is for a visitor to be on time for a meeting with that person.
   B. The higher a person's status, the less likely it is that they will wait for you.
   C. People with lower status must wait longer than people with higher status.
   D. Making people wait a long time will give a low status person higher status.

2. According to the passage, which of the following conclusions cannot be true?
   A. Junior executives must be on time for all persons of higher status.
   B. Even senior executives must be on time for some meetings.
   C. Senior executives have equal status with the company president or CEO.
   D. A CEO has as much status as a company president.

PASSAGE #2

In one experiment, Daniel Lehrman of Rutgers University found that when a male blond ring dove was isolated from females, it soon began to bow and coo to a stuffed model of a female—a model that had previously been ignored. When the model was replaced by a rolled-up cloth, he began to court the cloth; and when this was removed the sex-crazed dove distracted his attention to a corner of the cage, where it could at least focus its gaze. (R. Wallace, *Biology: The World of Life*, 4th ed., Glenview, NJ: Scott Foresman, 1987.)

5

3. Which of the following conclusions can be drawn from the passage?
   A. The experiment shows how all blond ring doves mate.
   B. Male ring doves have a very strong instinct to court.
   C. All male ring doves will court by bowing and cooing.
   D. Male blond ring doves do not have a high level of intelligence.

4. According to the passage, which of the following conclusions cannot be true?
   A. A male blond ring dove will try to court another female even if it is a model.
   B. The male blond ring dove has a strong drive to mate.
   C. The male blond ring dove cannot tell the difference between a live mate and a stuffed model.
   D. The male blond ring dove will exhibit mating behaviors even without a live female present.

PASSAGE #3

Bush infuriated environmentalists, who had been pleased with Clinton's efforts to protect America's national heritage. And, catering to the interests of oil companies, the new administration fought to promote drilling in the protected Arctic National Wildlife

Refuge, even in the face of estimates that there was very little oil there to be found. When his own Environmental Protection Agency (EPA) issued a report in mid-2002 linking the use of fossil fuel to global warming, Bush dismissed the study by declaring that he had "read the report put out by the bureaucracy," making it clear that he had no confidence in the judgments of the scientists working for the EPA. (G. Nash et al., *The American People: Creating a Nation and a Society*, 6th ed., New York: Longman, 2004.)

    5

5. Which of the following conclusions can be drawn from the passage?
    A. Environmentalists wanted to help oil companies drill in protected areas.
    B. The EPA's report was inaccurate.
    C. Research has been conducted regarding the presence of oil in the Arctic National Wildlife Refuge.
    D. Bush didn't want the EPA to study global warming.

6. What does the following sentence suggest about the environmentalists? "Bush infuriated environmentalists, who had been pleased with Clinton's efforts to protect America's national heritage."
    A. Environmentalists approved of the EPA's report.
    B. In comparison to Bush, Clinton was considered a better environmental president by environmentalists.
    C. America's national heritage is infuriating environmentalists.
    D. Because of Bush's actions, environmentalists were angry at Clinton's efforts to protect the environment.

PASSAGE #4

Managed care plans have agreements with certain physicians, hospitals, and health care providers to give a range of services to plan members at a reduced cost. There are three basic types of managed care plans: health maintenance organizations (HMOs), point-of-service plans (POSs), and preferred provider organizations (PPOs). The PPO, in my opinion, is the best type of managed care plan because it merges the best features of traditional health insurance and HMOs. As in traditional plans, participants in a PPO may pay premiums, deductibles, and co-payments, but the co-pay under a PPO is lower. The best part of a PPO, though, is its flexibility: participants may choose their physicians and services from a list of preferred providers, or they may go outside the plan for care if they wish. (Adapted from Pruitt and Stein, *Healthstyles*, Boston: Allyn and Bacon, 2001.)

    5

    10

7. Which of the following conclusions can be drawn from the passage?
    A. A PPO costs less overall than an HMO.
    B. People with HMO and POS plans may not be able to choose their own physician.
    C. Traditional plans pay no deductibles.
    D. People in PPOs must choose their physicians only from a list of preferred providers.

Answers to Diagnostic
    1. A   2. C   3. B   4. C   5. C   6. B   7. B

SECTION 2 ◆ EXERCISES: INFERENCES AND CONCLUSIONS

Use the following exercises to practice reading for inferences and conclusions.

PASSAGE #1

Read the passage and answer the questions that follow.

During the seventeenth and eighteenth centuries, the process of childbirth in colonial America was conducted by women. The typical woman gave birth to her children at home, while female relatives and neighbors clustered at her bedside to offer support and encouragement.

Most women were assisted in childbirth not by a doctor but by a midwife. Most 5 midwives were older women who relied on practical experience in delivering children. One midwife, Martha Ballard, who practiced in Augusta, Maine, delivered 996 babies with only 4 recorded fatalities. Skilled midwives were highly valued. Communities tried to attract experienced midwives by offering a salary or a rent-free house. In addition to assisting in childbirth, midwives helped deliver the offspring 10 of animals, attended the baptisms and burials of infants, and testified in court cases of illegitimate babies.

During labor, midwives administered no painkillers except for alcohol. Pain in childbirth was considered God's punishment for Eve's sin of eating the forbidden fruit in the Garden of Eden. Women were merely advised to have patience, to pray, and during 15 labor, to restrain their groans and cries which upset the people near them.

After delivery, new mothers were often treated to a banquet. At one such event, visitors feasted on boiled pork, beef, poultry, roast beef, turkey pie, and tarts. Women from well-to-do families were then expected to spend three to four weeks in bed convalescing. Their attendants kept the fireplace burning and wrapped them in a heavy blanket in 20 order to help them sweat out "poisons." Women from poorer families were generally back at work in one or two days. (Adapted from James Kirby Martin et al., *America and Its Peoples*, New York: Longman, 2004.)

1. A conclusion that can be drawn from this passage is that during the seventeenth and eighteenth centuries,
   A. midwives had children themselves.
   B. midwives received high salaries.
   C. doctors did not want to deliver babies.
   D. women from different social classes had different post-childbirth experiences.

2. What does the following sentence from the second paragraph suggest about midwives?

   "Skilled midwives were highly valued." (line 8)

   A. Skilled midwives were superior to doctors.
   B. Skilled midwives delivered babies without medicating the mothers.
   C. Skilled midwives were scarce.
   D. Midwives gave religious guidance to mothers.

PASSAGE #2

Read the passage and answer the question that follows.

In the 1980s, a long-running TV public service advertisement showed a father confronting his son with what is obviously the boy's drug paraphernalia. The father asks his son incredulously, "Where did you learn to do this?" The son, half in tears, replies, "From you, okay? I learned it from watching you!" Observational learning, which results simply from watching others, clearly appears to be a factor in an adolescent's willingness to experiment with drugs and alcohol.   5

Andrews and her colleagues found that adolescents' relationships with their parents influence whether they will model the substance use patterns of the parents. Specifically, they found that adolescents who had a positive relationship with their mothers modeled her use (or nonuse) of cigarettes, and those who had a close relationship   10 with their fathers modeled the father's marijuana use (or nonuse). Similarly, those who had a negative relationship with their parents were less likely to model their parents' use of drugs or alcohol. Although some of the more complex results of this study depended on the age and sex of the adolescent, the general findings can be understood by thinking about them from the three levels of analysis and their   15 interactions.

At the level of the brain, observing someone engage in a behavior causes you to store new memories, which involves the hippocampus and related brain systems. These memories later can guide behavior, as they do in all types of imitation. At the level of the person, if you are motivated to observe someone, you are likely to   20 be paying more attention to him or her and, therefore, increasing the likelihood of your learning from that person and remembering what you learn. At the level of the group, you are more likely to be captivated by models who have certain attractive characteristics.

In this case, adolescents who had a positive relationship with their parents were more   25 likely to do what their parents did; if their parents didn't smoke, the adolescents were less likely to do so. The events at these levels interact. Children who enjoy a positive relationship with their parents may agree with their parents' higher status than do children who have a negative relationship with their parents. Thus, the former group of children probably increases the amount of attention they give to their parents' behavior.   30 (Adapted from Stephen M. Kosslyn and Robin S. Rosenberg, *Psychology*, 2nd ed., Boston: Allyn and Bacon, 2004.)

3. A conclusion that can be drawn from this passage is that
   A. adolescents model their parents' behavior.
   B. the more a child pays attention to his or her parents, the more likely it is that the child will pick up the parents' bad habits.
   C. parents who drink set a poor example for their children.
   D. adolescents are willing to experiment with drugs and alcohol.

PASSAGE #3

Read the passage and answer the questions that follow.

Deborah Tannen, sociologist and author, explains the differences in the listening behavior of men and women. Women seek to build rapport and establish a closer relationship and so use listening to achieve these ends. For example, women use more listening cues that let the other person know they are paying attention and are interested. On the other hand, men not only use fewer listening cues but interrupt more and will often change the topic to one they know more about or one that is less relational or people-oriented to one that is more factual, for example, sports, statistics, economic developments, or political problems. Men, research shows, play up their expertise, emphasize it, and use it to dominate the conversation. Women play down their expertise. Research shows that men communicate with women in the same way they do with other men. Men are not showing disrespect for their female conversational partners, but are simply communicating as they normally do. Women, too, communicate as they do not only with men but also with other women.

Tannen argues that the goal of a man in conversation is to be accorded respect, and so he seeks to display his knowledge and expertise even if he has to change the topic from one he knows little about to one he knows a great deal about. A woman, on the other hand, seeks to be liked, and so she expresses agreement and less frequently interrupts to take her turn as speaker.

Men and women also show that they are listening in different ways. A woman is more apt to give lots of listening cues, such as interjecting, "yeah, uh-uh," nodding in agreement, and smiling. A man is more likely to listen quietly, without giving lots of listening cues as feedback. Tannen also argues, however, that men do listen less to women than women listen to men. The reason is that listening places the person in an inferior position whereas speaking places the person in a superior position. There is no evidence to show that these differences represent any negative motives on the part of men to prove themselves superior or of women to ingratiate themselves. Rather, these differences in listening are largely the result of the way in which men and women have been socialized. (Adapted from Joseph A. DeVito, *Essentials of Human Communication*, 3rd ed., New York: Longman, 1999.)

5

10

15

20

25

4. A conclusion that can be drawn from this passage is that
   A. men are naturally more aggressive than women, a fact that influences their listening styles.
   B. women and men do not communicate well.
   C. men are less likely than women to tolerate being uncomfortable in a conversation.
   D. in conversation, women are more likely to discuss people and relationships than men are.

5. What does the following suggest about the way people listen?

   "Rather, these differences in listening are largely the result of the way in which men and women have been socialized." (lines 26–27)

   A. Men and women have inherently different listening styles.
   B. People could change their bad listening habits if they seek professional help.
   C. Men disrespect women because society tells them to.
   D. Men's and women's listening styles are learned rather than natural.

PASSAGE #4

Read the passage and answer the questions that follow.

On April 20, 1999, a school shooting of such immense proportions occurred which radically, if not permanently, altered public thinking and debate about student safety and security. After months of planning and preparation, 18-year-old Eric Harris and 17-year-old Dylan Klebold armed themselves with guns and explosives and headed off to Columbine High School in Littleton, Colorado, to celebrate Adolph Hitler's birthday in a manner fitting their hero. By the time the assault ended with self-inflicted fatal gunshots, a dozen students and one teacher lay dead.   5

In understanding the horrific actions of schoolyard snipers, it is as important to examine friendships as it is to delve into family background. At Columbine, Harris and Klebold were generally seen as geeks or nerds, from the point of view of any of the large student cliques—the jocks, the punks, etc. Though excluded from mainstream student culture, they banded together and bonded together with several of their fellow outcasts in what they came to call the "Trench Coat Mafia." The image they attempted to create was clearly one of power and dominance—the barbaric incivility, the forces of darkness, the preoccupation with Hitler, the celebration of evil and villainy. Harris and Klebold desperately wanted to feel important; and in the preparations they made to murder their classmates, the two shooters got their wish. For more than a year, they plotted and planned, colluded and conspired to put one over on their schoolmates, teachers, and parents. They amassed an arsenal of weapons, strategized about logistics, and made final preparations—yet, until it was too late, not a single adult got wind of what Harris and Klebold intended to do.   10   15   20

Birds of a feather may kill together. Harris, the leader, would likely have enjoyed the respect and admiration from Klebold, who in turn would have felt uplifted by the praise he received from his revered buddy. In their relationship, the two boys got from one another what was otherwise missing from their lives—they felt special, they gained a sense of belonging, they were united against the world. As Harris remarked, as he and his friend made last-minute preparations to commit mass murder: "This is just a two-man war against everything else." (Adapted from James Alan Fox and Jack Levin, *The Will to Kill*, Boston: Allyn and Bacon, 2001.)   25

6. A conclusion that can be drawn from this passage is that
   A. it is important to understand family background and friendships of students who commit school shootings.
   B. students who are outcasts are likely to commit acts of violence.
   C. schools are not safe.
   D. young people who are preoccupied with Hitler are mentally unstable.

7. What does the following sentence from the third paragraph suggest about Harris and Klebold's motivation to commit mass murder?

   "This is just a two-man war against everything else." (lines 26–27)

   A. They might not have gone on their murderous rampage if they had been able to join the military or to go to military school.
   B. They wanted to show that they were important.

C. Their rage was reasonable.

D. They thought they could win.

PASSAGE #5

Read the passage and answer the question that follows.

Few people work constantly at their jobs. Most of us take breaks and, at least once in a while, goof off. We meet fellow workers at the water cooler, and we talk in the hallway. Much of this interaction is good for the company, for it bonds us to fellow workers and ties us to our jobs. Our personal lives may even cross over into our workday. Some of us make personal calls from the office. Bosses know that we need to check in with our child's preschool or make arrangements for a babysitter. They expect such calls. Some even wink as we make a date or nod as we arrange to have our car worked on. And most bosses make personal calls of their own from time to time. It's the abuse that bothers bosses, and it's not surprising that they fire anyone who talks on the phone all day for personal reasons. 5

10

The latest wrinkle at work is *cyberslacking*, using computers at work for personal purposes. Most workers fritter away some of their workday online. They trade stocks, download music, gamble, and play games. They read books, shop, exchange jokes, send personal e-mail, and visit online red-light districts. Some cyberslackers even operate their own businesses online. Others spend most of their "working" hours battling virtual enemies. One computer programmer became a national champion playing *Starcraft* at work. Companies have struck back. Xerox fired 40 employees for downloading pornography at work. Dow Chemical fired 200 "workers" for cyberloafing. Then there is the cybersleuth. With specialized software, cybersleuths can examine everything employees read online, everything they write, and every web site they visit. They can even bring up every word they've erased. What some workers don't know (and what some of us forget) is that "delete" does not mean *delete*. Our computer keeps a hidden diary, even of what we've erased. With a few clicks, the cybersleuth, like magic ink, makes our "deleted" information visible, exposing our hidden diary for anyone to read. (Adapted from James M. Henslin, *Sociology*, 6th ed., Boston: Allyn and Bacon, 2003.) 15

20

8. A conclusion that can be drawn from this passage is that

   A. most employees are expected to work the entire time they are on the premises.

   B. employers are probably unaware of how much time employees use to make personal phone calls at work.

   C. with the right software, an employer can view all of an employee's e-mails, even the personal ones.

   D. viewing pornography online is tolerated if it does not interfere with work.

PASSAGE #6

Read the passage and answer the questions that follow.

The analysis of DNA from fossils provides an opportunity to better understand extinct life and to trace the ancestry of genes found in modern organisms, including humans. Scientists have reported finding fragments of ancient DNA from many fossils, including a 40-million-year-old insect preserved in amber (fossilized plant resin), a 65-million-year-old dinosaur fossil, and a 30,000-year-old fossil arm bone of an extinct member of the human family tree (one of a group found in northern Europe called the Neanderthals).   5

In early autumn of 1991, two hikers working their way along the edge of a melting glacier in the high Alps of northern Italy found what seemed to be the weathered remains of an unlucky mountain climber. It was a man clothed in hand-sewn leather, frozen in glacial ice. Next to him were a bow and several arrows, a wooden backpack,   10
and a metal ax. A closer look turned up a leather pouch and other tools. The "Ice Man" turned out to be a leftover from the Stone Age, a young hunter who may have died from exhaustion and exposure some 5000 years ago.

Although scientists knew that the Ice Man was ancient, they did not know where he was from. In 1994, researchers reported that mitochondrial DNA from the Ice Man   15
closely matched that of modern central and northern Europeans, not Native Americans. Currently, the Ice Man remains frozen in the anatomy department of the University of Innsbruck. Continuing analysis of his DNA may provide more clues about his place in human evolution.

Science advances by the ebb and flow of ideas. Hypotheses are proposed, predictions   20
made, and test results evaluated. Too often, however, the advance is highlighted by the popular press as though it involves only a forward march, and the importance of disproving a hypotheses is lost. Some of the research on fossilized DNA illustrates this key aspect of science. Because it is difficult to obtain uncontaminated samples from fossils, ancient DNA is very challenging. Every report of success in isolating ancient   25
DNA has been met with skepticism and further analyses to make sure the DNA traces were not contaminated with DNA from bacteria, fungi, or other organisms. DNA is unlikely to remain intact, except when organisms fossilize in extremely cold or dry places where organic material tends to be preserved. Contamination is a potential pitfall even in ideal conditions. (Adapted from Neil A. Campbell, Lawrence G. Mitchell, and   30
Jane B. Reece, *Biology*, 3rd ed., San Francisco: Benjamin Cummings, 2000.)

9. It can be inferred that
    A. the Ice Man was probably out hunting when he was overcome by a snowstorm.
    B. the mitochondrial DNA of central and northern Europeans has changed very little over the last 5000 years.
    C. Neanderthals were not as well adapted to the earth as homo sapiens, and so they died off.
    D. the discovery of the Ice Man disproved many scientists' theories about ancient man.

10. A conclusion that can be drawn from this passage is that
    A. scientists would be more skeptical of DNA obtained from a fossil found in a rainforest than of DNA from a fossil found in the desert.
    B. the Ice Man is one of the oldest humans ever discovered.
    C. global warming must have caused the melting of the glacier where the Ice Man was found.
    D. the DNA of ancient insects preserved in amber is unlikely to be contaminated by other organisms.

PASSAGE #7

Read the passage and answer the questions that follow.

Today television is the most prevalent means used by candidates to reach voters. Thomas Patterson stresses that "today's presidential campaign is essentially a mass media campaign. . . . It is not exaggeration to say that, for the majority of voters, the campaign has little reality apart from its media version."

The most important goal of any media campaign is simply to get attention. Media coverage is determined by two factors: (1) how candidates use their advertising budget, and (2) the "free" attention they get as newsmakers. The first, obviously, is relatively easy to control; the second is more difficult but not impossible. Almost every logistical decision in a campaign—where to eat breakfast, whom to include on the rostrum, when to announce a major policy proposal—is calculated according to its intended media impact. About half the total budget for a presidential or senatorial campaign will be used for television advertising. 5

10

Candidates attempt to manipulate their images through advertising and image building, but they have less control over the other aspect of the media, news coverage. To be sure, most campaigns have press aides who feed "canned" news releases to reporters. Still, the media largely determine for themselves what is happening in a campaign. Campaign coverage seems to be a constant interplay between hard news about what candidates say and do and the human interest angle, which most journalists think sells newspapers or interests television viewers. (Adapted from George C. Edwards, Martin P. Wattenberg, and Robert L. Lineberry, *Government in America*, 9th ed., New York: Longman, 2000.) 15

11. A conclusion that can be drawn from this passage is that
     A. presidential candidates who do not receive much "free" media attention are unlikely to reach enough voters to win the election.
     B. most people are more interested in hard news about candidates than in personal stories about them.
     C. the press looks for opportunities to discredit presidential candidates.
     D. presidential candidates often criticize each other in their television advertisements.

12. What does the following sentence suggest about political campaigns?

     "It is not exaggeration to say that, for the majority of voters, the campaign has little reality apart from its media version." (lines 3–4)

     A. Campaigns are like television shows.
     B. Voters believe everything they see on television and read in the newspapers.
     C. The media's coverage of a campaign is very influential.
     D. Most people are too lazy to check sources other than the media for information about presidential candidates.

PASSAGE #8

Read the passage and answer the question that follows.

The most common stimulant is caffeine, which is contained in coffee, tea, cola drinks, and even chocolate. Caffeine is a mild stimulant that is often abused. Nonetheless, it is a drug and should be recognized as one that can lead to health problems.

Caffeine is absorbed rather quickly into the bloodstream and reaches a peak blood level in about thirty to sixty minutes. It increases mental alertness and provides a feeling of energy. However, high doses of caffeine can overstimulate and cause nervousness and increased heart rate. Caffeine can also cause sleeplessness, excitement, and irritability. In some cases, high doses of caffeine can induce convulsions.

5

Coffee or cola drinking, let alone chocolate eating, cannot be considered drug abuse by most commonly accepted standards. But some individuals seek out caffeine for its own sake in over-the-counter products and in illegal substances to produce a caffeine "high." Because it is not considered a dangerous drug, the opportunities for caffeine abuse are often overlooked. (David J. Anspaugh and Gene Ezell, *Teaching Today's Health*, 7th ed., San Francisco: Benjamin Cummings, 2004.)

10

13. A conclusion that can be drawn from this passage is that
   A. caffeine should be regulated by the Food and Drug Administration like other drugs are.
   B. people can get addicted to the caffeine in chocolate.
   C. some people abuse caffeine.
   D. caffeine is not dangerous.

PASSAGE #9

Read the passage and answer the question that follows.

Hate sites began on the Internet in the mid-1990s, and their numbers expanded rapidly. Now hate groups in general across the nation are on the rise because of the Internet. Hate sites advocate violence toward immigrants, Jews, Arabs, gays, abortion providers, and others. Through the Internet, disturbed minds effectively fuel hatred, violence, sexism, racism, and terrorism. Never before has there been such an intensive way for deprived people to gather to reinforce their prejudices and hatred. In one analysis of hate speech sites, the researchers found sophisticated use of persuasive strategies. The hate sites generally started with an objective approach that was straightforward and neutral in which they reinforced and strengthened the hate ideas that people already have. The Internet provides a forum for people with prejudicial attitudes to speak out and act out. Hate-mongers can create an online world where they reign supreme, a world of similar minds, where they can gather with others to feel that their way is right and where they can design severe disruption for the on-ground world. (Adapted from Leonard J. Shedletsky and Joan E. Aitken, *Human Communication on the Internet*, Boston: Allyn and Bacon, 2004.)

5

10

14. A conclusion that can be drawn from this passage is that
   A. the Internet has made it easier for hate groups to gather like-minded people.
   B. Internet hate sites are developed by unsophisticated or uneducated people.
   C. hate sites encourage people to kill Jews, Arabs, gays, and abortion providers.
   D. terrorists use the Internet to encourage suicide bombings.

PASSAGE #10

Read the passage and answer the questions that follow.

Evaluation research on drug education prevention programs done over the last thirty years indicates that these programs have not been effective. In fact, the findings state that these programs essentially had no effect on the drug problem. Although studies of the more recently developed programs are more optimistic, the findings still do not provide strong evidence of highly effective programs.   5

The goals of these programs have been to affect three basic areas: knowledge, attitudes, and behavior. The programs have had some success in increasing knowledge and, to a lesser extent, attitudes towards drugs; however, increases in knowledge and changed attitudes do not mean much if the actual drug behavior is not affected. In fact, those programs that only increase knowledge tend to reduce anxiety and fear of drugs and   10 may actually increase the likelihood of drug use. For example, one approach in the past was to provide students with complete information about all the possibilities of drug abuse, from the names of every street drug, to how the drugs are usually ingested, to detailed descriptions of possible effects of drugs and possible consequences of an overdose. Given the inquiring nature of children, such an approach could well amount   15 to a primer on how to take drugs, not how to avoid them.

The only effective approach to drug education is one in which children come to see that drug abuse constitutes unnecessary and self-abusive consequences. Too often, the real appeal of such drugs as marijuana or alcohol is dismissed by asking children to take up a sport or go bike riding or learn to play a musical instrument. Such suggestions   20 are fine as far as they go, but they often fail to take into account the personal problems that may tempt children into drug abuse.

Education programs that address social influence show the most promise in reducing or delaying the onset of drug use. Psychological approaches in which social influences and skills are stressed are more effective than other approaches. The most effective   25 programs in influencing both attitudes and behavior are peer programs that include either refusal skills—with more direct emphasis on behavior—or social and life skills, or both.

The use of scare tactics in any health education program, including drug abuse education programs, is counterproductive. Children soon learn to recognize the difference   30 between fact and possible fiction. Attempts to equate the dangers of marijuana with those of heroin, suggestions that any drug can kill or permanently impair an individual, and other dire warnings, no matter how true, are often disregarded as propaganda. (David J. Anspaugh and Gene Ezell, *Teaching Today's Health*, 7th ed., San Francisco: Benjamin Cummings, 2004.)

15. A conclusion that can be drawn from this passage is that
    A. telling children to take up a sport instead of drugs is an effective tactic.
    B. sometimes, drug prevention programs provide misleading information about drugs.
    C. the best approach for drug education is to avoid approaching it at all.
    D. programs that increase knowledge about drugs are very successful.

16. What conclusion can be reached regarding the following statement about scare tactics?

"The use of scare tactics in any health education program, including drug abuse education programs, is counterproductive." (lines 28–29)

A. Frightening children can cause psychological problems.
B. Scare tactics may make drugs appealing.
C. Children know more about drugs than their teachers do.
D. The most successful drug abuse education programs do not use scare tactics.

PASSAGE #11

Read the passage and answer the questions that follow.

Matt Drudge was 30 years old when he broke his first story about Monica Lewinsky's relationship with President Clinton, which would become the biggest political scandal of the 1990s. Drudge had never been trained in journalism nor hired by any media outlet. He had neither verified the story nor done any extensive research on it. All he had to go on was the rumor that *Newsweek* had been working on this story and had decided not to print it in that week's issue. But for Drudge, a rumor was good enough to report on. No editor was going to tell him that he needed confirmation, as Drudge worked on his own. He didn't have to worry about the damage to his publication because he didn't have one; he relied instead on getting the "Drudge Report" out through an e-mail list and by posting it on his web site. When Drudge hit the enter button on his computer to post the Lewinsky story, he knew his life would be changed forever, and for quite some time so would the nation's. 5
10

Matt Drudge and his brand of cyber reporting have changed the whole news cycle in America. Journalists who are working on a scoop know they can quickly lose an exclusive story if someone like Drudge gets wind of it and posts the headline on the Internet. As a result, a number of newspapers immediately post their most important stories on their web site rather than waiting until the next morning. The *Dallas Morning News* made big headlines when they rushed a story onto the web about a White House steward testifying that he had seen President Clinton and Monica Lewinsky in a compromising position. The next day the paper had egg on its face, however, when the steward's lawyer strongly denied the story and the paper was forced to retract it. Similarly, Drudge found himself in trouble when he accused White House aide Sidney Blumenthal of spouse abuse. He quickly pulled the story and apologized when he realized it was planted by politically motivated Republican operatives, but not before Blumenthal hit him with a $30 million libel suit. 15
20
25

Opinions on Matt Drudge and his reporting techniques vary widely. Because of his penchant for reporting rumors and gossip, the *New York Times* called him "the nation's chief mischief maker." Others have dubbed him the first Internet superstar and praised how he has paved the way for communication power to be transferred from media giants to anyone with a modem. However one views him, it is clear that Matt Drudge has made a difference. (Adapted from George C. Edwards, Martin P. Wattenberg, and Robert L. Lineberry, *Government in America*, 9th ed., New York: Longman, 2000.) 30

17. A conclusion that can be drawn from this passage is that
    A. Matt Drudge made the Internet a player in news reporting.
    B. Matt Drudge is an entertainer.
    C. Matt Drudge gets away with libel.
    D. Power players appreciate seeing stories about themselves on Drudge's site.

18. A conclusion that can be drawn from the first paragraph of this passage is that
    A. Matt Drudge is a troublemaker.
    B. Drudge does not always confirm stories before publishing them.
    C. Drudge enjoyed gathering and spreading rumors.
    D. Drudge broke the story about Monica Lewinsky's relationship with President Clinton.

PASSAGE #12

Read the passage and answer the questions that follow.

Forest decline is not a new phenomenon. During the past two centuries, our forests have experienced several declines, with different species affected. What sets the current decline apart from all others is differences among the symptoms in the past and the similarity of symptoms among species today. Past declines could be attributed to natural stresses, such as drought and disease. What causes forest decline and dieback today is   5
not established, but the widespread similarity of symptoms suggests a common cause—air pollution. All of the affected forests are in the path of pollutants from industrial and urban sources.

Forests close to the point of origin of pollutants experience the most direct effects of air pollution, and their decline and death can be directly attributed to it. Little evidence   10
exists that acid precipitation alone is the cause of forest decline and death at distant points. The effects of acid deposition, however, can so weaken trees that they succumb to other stresses such as drought and insect attack. The stressed forests of Fraser fir in the Great Smoky Mountains succumbed to the attacks of the introduced balsam woolly adelgid. The once deep, fragrant stands of Fraser fir, especially on the windward side   15
and peaks of the Great Smoky Mountains, are now stands of skeleton trees.

Air pollution and acid rain also are altering succession by changing the species composition of forests. Just as the chestnut blight shifted dominance in the central hardwood forest from chestnut to oaks, so is air pollution shifting dominance from pines and other conifers to leaf-shedding trees more tolerant of air pollution. (Adapted from   20
Robert Leo Smith and Thomas M. Smith, *Elements of Ecology*, 5th ed., San Francisco: Benjamin Cummings, 2003.)

19. An inference that <u>cannot</u> be made from this passage is that
    A. the balsam woolly adelgid is an insect.
    B. pine trees are susceptible to the effects of air pollution.
    C. forest decline cannot be directly attributed to air pollution.
    D. healthy trees can sometimes fight off attacks of disease and drought.

20. What does the following sentence suggest?

"All of the affected forests are in the path of pollutants from industrial and urban sources." (lines 7–8)

A. Air pollution is probably responsible for the damage to these forests.
B. All of the other forests beyond the reach of these pollutants are healthy.
C. Eventually, all trees in the path of these pollutants will die.
D. The polluters should be held responsible for the damage to the forests.

SECTION 3 ◆ ASSESSING SUPPORT FOR REASONING AND ARGUMENT

When an author makes a claim about something, it is expected that the claim will be supported with details that are relevant and logical, and it will provide sufficient factual information. Critical thinkers evaluate the author's support, looking for data and facts that prove the author's point.

This section tests your ability to recognize the difference between *adequate* and *inadequate* support, *relevant* and *irrelevant* support, and *objective* and *emotional* support for an argument. You will be given a passage to read; you will then be expected to choose a statement that offers the best support for an author's claim or an option that describes a support as *adequate*, *inadequate*, *relevant*, or *irrelevant*.

Check details against the main pattern of organization. The same event will provide different relevant details based on how the ideas are organized. For example, narrative passages may include different time order details than a process that relies on ordered steps in a series.

Check to match that generalized or broad statements are followed by specific examples or illustrations.

Check the logic of inferences and implications by matching conclusions to evidence.

What kind of support is offered in the following examples?

Example #1
Year-round schools have been huckstered as a way to raise students' achievement and a cure-all for what ails education. The year-round school proposal, however, does not get to the heart of our educational difficulties. It just relieves some school officials from attacking the real problems that plague their school systems. I am fed up with fads and with all self-aggrandizing individuals who, like vultures, have targeted the rich educational terrain looking to pick its bones at the expense of our students, parents and all taxpayers. The school system should not be used as a political smokescreen to buy time for those school officials who need to show taxpayers that they are doing "something." (Dorothy Rubin, "Should Students Attend School Year Round? No," from K. McWhorter, *Reading Across the Disciplines*, New York: Longman, 2005.)

Topic: Year-Round Schooling

Main Idea: Students should not attend school year round.

What kind of support is offered for the author's claim that students should not attend school year round?

A. Objective (factual)
B. Emotional (opinions)

The support given to the author's claim is B, Emotional. Rather than presenting logical and relevant reasons why year-round school is a bad idea, the author has simply given her own opinions. Some of the details have little to do with the topic and are therefore irrelevant. The supporting details must be related to the topic.

> **Example #2**
> Year-round school offers two important benefits. The most important is continuity of instruction that currently is split by a two-month summer break. Everyone who has attended school, and certainly everyone who has taught school, recognizes that much is forgotten over the summer and that tedious review in the fall wastes time. Not surprisingly, a great deal of research substantiates this observation. Research also shows that the vast majority of the more than 2,700 year-round schools show improved academic success. (Daniel Domenech, "Should Students Attend School Year Round? Yes," from K. McWhorter, *Reading Across the Disciplines*, New York: Longman, 2005.)

Topic: Year-Round Schooling

Main Idea: Students should attend school year round.

The author's claim that students should attend school year round is

   A. inadequately supported because it lacks evidence and explanation.
   B. adequately supported by factual details.

The author presents facts and data to support his claim, pointing out two important benefits of year-round school, and cites that research done on this issue shows that 2,700 year-round schools show improved academic success. The correct answer is B, adequately supported by factual details.

Which sentence offers the best support for the author's claim, "Year-round school offers two important benefits"?

   A. Not surprisingly, a great deal of research substantiates this observation.
   B. Everyone who has attended school, and certainly everyone who has taught school, recognizes that much is forgotten over the summer and that tedious review in the fall wastes time.
   C. Research also shows that the vast majority of the more than 2,700 year-round schools show improved academic success.

The correct answer is C, Research also shows that the vast majority of the more than 2,700 year-round schools show improved academic success. This statement offers proof that year-round schooling has benefits. Choices A and B are not as strong in their evidence that year-round school has important benefits.

▶▶❘ *Secrets to Success*

- *Make sure that the literal meaning of the passage is clearly understood by stating the topic, the main idea, and the author's claim.*
- *Go back into the passage and look for supporting details that prove or support the author's claim.*
- *Look for specific examples or illustrations of the author's claim.*
- *Look for opinions.*
- *Check to make sure that the supporting details are related to the issue.*
- *Check to make sure the author's claim is logical and based on facts and not opinions.*

SECTION 3 ◆ DIAGNOSTIC: ASSESSING SUPPORT FOR REASONING AND ARGUMENT

Read the passages and apply the strategies described above for reasoning and argument. When you are done, check your work with the answers immediately following the diagnostic. Even if you get a perfect score here, go ahead and complete the exercises in this section; they are designed to help build confidence and to give you practice for future test success.

Read the passages and answer the questions that follow.

PASSAGE #1

Forest decline is not a new phenomenon. During the past two centuries, our forests have experienced several declines, with different species affected. What sets the current decline apart from all others is differences among the symptoms in the past and the similarity of symptoms among species today. Past declines could be attributed to natural stresses, such as drought and disease. What causes forest decline and dieback today is not established,   5
but the widespread similarity of symptoms suggests a common cause—air pollution. All of the affected forests are in the path of pollutants from industrial and urban sources.

Forests close to the point of origin of pollutants experience the most direct effects of air pollution, and their decline and death can be directly attributed to it. Little evidence exists that acid precipitation alone is the cause of forest decline and death at distant   10
points. The effects of acid deposition, however, can so weaken trees that they succumb to other stresses such as drought and insect attack. The stressed forests of Fraser fir in the Great Smoky Mountains succumb to the attacks of the introduced balsam woolly adelgid. The once deep, fragrant stands of Fraser fir, especially on the windward side and peaks of the Great Smoky Mountains, are now stands of skeleton trees.   15

Air pollution and acid rain also are altering succession by changing the species composition of forests. Just as the chestnut blight shifted dominance in the central hardwood forest from chestnut to oaks, so is air pollution shifting dominance from pines and other conifers to leaf-shedding trees more tolerant of air pollution. (Adapted from Robert Leo Smith and Thomas M. Smith, *Elements of Ecology*, 5th ed., San Francisco: Benjamin Cummings, 2003.)

1. The author's claim that, "What causes forest decline and dieback today is not established, but the widespread similarity of symptoms suggests a common cause—air pollution," is
   A. inadequately supported based upon opinion.
   B. adequately supported based upon facts.

2. Throughout the passage, which type of support is offered for the author's claim that, "What causes forest decline and dieback today is not established, but the widespread similarity of symptoms suggests a common cause—air pollution"?
   A. Objective
   B. Emotional

3. Which statement offers the best support for the author's claim that, "What causes forest decline and dieback today is not established, but the widespread similarity of symptoms suggests a common cause—air pollution"?
   A. All of the affected forests are in the path of pollutants from industrial and urban sources.
   B. The effects of acid deposition, however, can so weaken trees that they succumb to other stresses such as drought and insect attack.
   C. Air pollution and acid rain also are altering succession by changing the species composition of forests.
   D. During the past two centuries, our forests have experienced several declines, with different species affected.

PASSAGE #2

September 11, 2001

Today, our fellow citizens, our way of life, our very freedom came under attack in a series of deliberate and deadly terrorist acts. The victims were in airplanes or in their offices: secretaries, business men and women, military and federal workers, moms and dads, friends and neighbors. Thousands of lives were suddenly ended by evil, despicable acts of terror.   5

The pictures of airplanes flying into buildings, fires burning, and huge structures collapsing have filled us with disbelief, terrible sadness and a quiet, unyielding anger. These acts of mass murder were intended to frighten our nation into chaos and retreat. But they have failed.   10

Terrorist attacks can shake the foundations of our biggest buildings, but they cannot touch the foundation of America. These acts shatter steel but they cannot dent the steel of American resolve.

Today, our nation saw evil, the very worst of human nature, and we responded with the best of America, with the daring of our rescue workers, with the caring for strangers   15
and neighbors who came to give blood and helped in any way they could. (From President George W. Bush's speech on September 11, 2001, in James Kirby Martin et al., *America and Its Peoples*, 5th ed., New York: Longman, 2004.)

4. The authors' claim that, "These acts of mass murder were intended to frighten our nation into chaos and retreat. But they have failed" is
   A. inadequately supported based upon opinion.
   B. adequately supported based upon facts.

5. Throughout the passage, which type of support is offered for the authors' claim that, "Terrorist attacks can shake the foundations of our biggest buildings, but they cannot touch the foundation of America"?
   A. Objective
   B. Emotional

6. Which statement offers the best support for the authors' claim that, "These acts shatter steel but they cannot dent the steel of American resolve"?
   A. These acts of mass murder were intended to frighten our nation into chaos and retreat.
   B. The victims were in airplanes or in their offices: secretaries, business men and women, military and federal workers, moms and dads, friends and neighbors.
   C. The pictures of airplanes flying into buildings, fires burning, and huge structures collapsing have filled us with disbelief, terrible sadness and a quiet, unyielding anger.
   D. Today, our nation saw evil, the very worst of human nature, and we responded with the best of America, with the daring of our rescue workers, with the caring for strangers and neighbors who came to give blood and helped in any way they could.

7. The authors' claim that, "Terrorist attacks can shake the foundations of our biggest buildings, but they cannot touch the foundation of America" is
   A. inadequately supported based upon opinion.
   B. adequately supported based upon facts.

Answers to Diagnostic
   1. B   2. A   3. A   4. A   5. B   6. D   7. A

SECTION 3 ◆ EXERCISES: ASSESSING SUPPORT FOR REASONING AND ARGUMENT

Use the following exercises to practice reading for assessing support for reasoning and argument.

PASSAGE #1

Read the passage and answer the questions that follow.

Everywhere it occurred, industrialization drove society from an agricultural to an urban way of life. The old system, in which peasant families worked the fields during the summer and did their cottage industry work in the winter to their own standards and at their own pace, slowly disappeared. In its place came urban life tied to the factory system. The factory was a place where for long hours people did repetitive tasks using 5 machines to process large amounts of raw materials. This was an efficient way to make a lot of high-quality goods cheaply. But the factories were often dangerous places, and the lifestyle connected to them had a terrible effect on the human condition.

In the factory system, the workers worked, and the owners made profits. The owners wanted to make the most they could from their investment and to get the most work 10 they could from their employees. The workers, in turn, felt that they deserved more of the profits because their labor made production possible. This was a situation guaranteed to produce conflict, especially given the wretched conditions the workers faced in the first stages of industrialization.

The early factories were miserable places, featuring bad lighting, lack of ventilation, 15 dangerous machines, and frequent breakdowns. Safety standards were practically nonexistent, and workers in various industries could expect to contract serious diseases; for example, laborers working with lead paint developed lung problems, pewter workers fell ill to palsy, miners suffered black lung disease, and operators of primitive machines lost fingers, hands, and even lives. Not until late in the nineteenth century did health and disability insurance come into effect. In some factories workers who suffered accidents were deemed to be at fault; and since there was little job security, a worker could be fired for almost any reason.   20

The demand for plentiful and cheap labor led to the widespread employment of women and children who worked long hours. Girls as young as 6 years old were used to haul   25
carts of coal in Lancashire mines, and boys and girls of 5 years of age worked in textile mills, where their nimble little fingers could easily untangle jams in the machines. When they were not laboring, the working families lived in horrid conditions in Manchester, England. There were no sanitary, water, or medical services for the workers, and working families were crammed 12 and 15 individuals to a room in damp, dark cellars. Bad   30
diet, alcoholism, cholera, and typhus reduced lifespans in the industrial cities. (Brummet, Palmira, et al., *Civilization: Past and Present*, New York: Longman, 2000.)

1. Throughout the passage, which type of support is offered for the authors' conclusion that "But the factories were often dangerous places, and the lifestyle connected to them had a terrible effect on the human condition"? (lines 7–8)
    A. Objective
    B. Emotional

2. The authors' claim that "This was a situation guaranteed to produce conflict, especially given the wretched conditions the workers faced in the first stages of industrialization" (lines 12–14) is
    A. inadequately supported because it lacks evidence and explanation.
    B. adequately supported by factual details.

3. Which statement offers the best support for the authors' claim that "The demand for plentiful and cheap labor led to the widespread employment of women and children who worked long hours" (lines 24–25)?
    A. Women made up the majority of the workplace in textile mills.
    B. Children were fast workers.
    C. Women worked in textile mills from 5 a.m. to 7:30 p.m., 14½ hours, 6 days a week.
    D. Women earned higher wages in factories than they could in other jobs.

PASSAGE #2

Read the passage and answer the questions that follow.

If you have ever stayed up late, say, studying or partying, and then awakened early the next morning, you have probably experienced sleep deprivation. In fact, you may be sleep deprived right now. If so, you have company. Many adults do not get enough sleep (defined as 8 hours). Sleep deprivation affects us in at least three important psychological areas: attention, mood, and performance.   5

Sleep deprivation affects the ability to perform tasks requiring sustained attention. Young adults who volunteered for a sleep deprivation study were allowed to sleep for only 5 hours each night, for a total of 7 nights. After 3 nights of restricted sleep, volunteers complained of cognitive, emotional, and physical difficulties. Moreover, their performance on a visual motor task declined after only 2 nights of restricted sleep. Visual motor tasks usually require participants to concentrate on detecting a change in a particular stimulus, and then to respond as quickly as they can after they perceive the change by pressing a button. Although you may be able to perform short mental tasks normally when sleep deprived, if a task requires sustained attention and a motor response, your performance will suffer. Driving a car is an example of such a task. In fact, in a survey by the National Sleep Foundation, 25% of the respondents reported that they had at some time fallen asleep at the wheel; sleepy drivers account for at least 100,000 car crashes each year.

Moods are also affected by sleep deprivation. Those who sleep less than 6 hours each weekday night are more likely to report being impatient or aggravated when faced with common minor frustrations such as being stuck in traffic or having to wait in line, and they were more dissatisfied with life in general, according to the National Sleep Foundation. The loss of even one night's sleep can lead to increases in the next day's level of cortisol. Cortisol helps the body meet the demands of stress. However, sleep deprivation can lead to a change in cortisol levels that, in turn, alters other biological functions. Regularly increased cortisol levels affect memory and cause a decrease in the immune system.

And what about a series of all-nighters, when you get no sleep at all, as might occur during finals period? Results from volunteers who have gone without sleep for long stretches (finally sleeping after staying awake anywhere from 4 to 11 days) show profound psychological changes, such as hallucinations, feelings of losing control or going crazy, anxiety, and paranoia. Morevoer, going without sleep alters the normal circadian rhythms of changes in temperature, metabolism, and hormone secretion. Results of a study on sleep-deprived humans found a different pattern of brain activation when learning verbal material, compared to the pattern of activation when not sleep deprived, suggesting an attempt to compensate for the brain changes induced by sleep deprivation. (Adapted from Stephen M. Kosslyn and Robin S. Rosenberg, *Psychology*, Boston: Allyn and Bacon, 2004.)

4. The authors' claim that "Sleep deprivation affects the ability to perform tasks requiring sustained attention" (line 6) is
   A. inadequately supported based on personal opinion.
   B. adequately supported based on factual details.

5. Throughout the passage, which type of support is offered for the authors' conclusion that "Sleep deprivation affects us in at least three important psychological areas: attention, mood, and performance"? (lines 4–5)
   A. Objective
   B. Emotional

6. Which statement offers the best support for the authors' claim that "Many adults do not get enough sleep (defined as 8 hours)"? (lines 3–4)
   A. In today's world of overscheduled lives and 10-hour workdays, no one can claim to be getting a natural amount of sleep.
   B. Older adults sleep less than younger adults and children.

C. Many adults claim to be so sleepy during the day that their daily activities are affected.

D. A 2002 survey by the National Sleep Foundation found that two out of three people are sleeping fewer than 6 hours each night.

PASSAGE #3

Read the passage and answer the questions that follow.

Almost everyone agrees that the use of drugs to enhance sports performance is unfair. Safeguards have been put in place, and the detection of drugs in a winner's body disqualifies that person from competition.

Now comes genetic engineering. With the human genome mapped and technology following rapidly, it is likely that inserting genetic materials in athletes can increase their 5 bulked-up muscle mass or their oxygen-carrying capacity. They will be able to run faster, to jump higher, and to throw further. Where the record for the 26.2 mile marathon is about 2 hours, someone may be able to run it in an hour and a half. The record for the 100-meter sprint, currently at 9.79 seconds, could drop to 6 seconds. The risks to health would be high. As the president of a biomedical ethics research in- 10 stitute said, inserting genetic materials "is like firing at the bull's-eye of a target with shotgun pellets." When you inject the material, you don't know its exact effects. You might want to strengthen the shoulder muscles of a javelin thrower, for example, but you might enlarge that person's heart, too. Suppose that you add the gene for human growth hormone, but it turns out that you can't regulate it. The individual could end 15 up with a gigantic head, jaw, hands, and feet.

With health risks high, would athletes take the risk? There is no doubt about the answer. Nearly 200 U.S. athletes who were aspiring for the Olympics were asked if they would take a banned substance that would guarantee them victory in every competition for the next five years—but at the end of the five years it would cause their death. More 20 than half said they would take it.

As genetic manipulation becomes more like a rifle shot than a shotgun blast—and we are closing in on that day—some athletes will seize the opportunity to increase their advantage. Others, seeing this, will do the same. The rush for genetic manipulation will be on. (James M. Henslin, *Sociology*, 6th ed., Boston: Allyn and Bacon, 2003.) 25

7. Throughout the passage, which type of support is offered for the author's conclusion that "As genetic manipulation becomes more like a rifle shot than a shotgun blast—and we are closing in on that day—some athletes will seize the opportunity to increase their advantage"? (lines 22–24)
   A. Objective
   B. Emotional

8. The author's claim that "When you inject the material, you don't know its exact effects" (line 12) is
   A. inadequately supported because it lacks evidence.
   B. adequately supported with relevant details.

9. The author's claim that "With the human genome mapped and technology following rapidly, it is likely that inserting genetic materials in athletes can increase their bulked-up muscle mass or their oxygen-carrying capacity" (lines 4–6) is
   A. adequately supported by factual detail.
   B. inadequately supported because it is based on generalizations.

10. Which statement offers the best support for the author's claim that "The risks to health would be high"? (line 10)
   A. When you inject the material, you don't know its exact effects.
   B. Genetic modifications to make muscles strong may put a strain on bones.
   C. Injecting red blood cells improves endurance, but the risks are blood clots, bacterial infection, and congestive heart failure.
   D. Injecting artificial genes to help a sprinter's muscles bulge with energy could result in pulled muscles and broken bones.

KEEP IN MIND ◆ SUMMARY OF CHAPTER 4

Fact and Opinion

In reading texts and on tests of reading comprehension, there are several rules to keep in mind when determining whether a statement is a fact or an opinion. Learning the rules can help you choose the correct answer.

- Look for adjectives that describe people, places, things, or events.
- Ask: Is this provable?
- Look for attitudes, prejudices, and beliefs.
- Don't confuse opinions in quotes with the fact that someone said it.
- If a sentence is both fact and opinion, consider it opinion unless you have an option to choose "fact and opinion."

Inferences and Conclusions

To make an inference means to come to a logical conclusion based upon the facts that are given. Information that is implied is not stated. To arrive at a logical conclusion:

- Look at the facts and details to arrive at a logical conclusion.
- Treat each answer choice as if it were a true/false question.
- Go back and reread to determine whether the answer choices could be true or false based upon the information that is presented in the passage.
- Do not assume more than what is stated in the passage.
- Rely upon your own background knowledge to help you make the right choice.

Part Three: Writing Workbook

Chapter 1: Concept Skills
Questions on the Essays / Paragraphs (Questions 1–10)

The Skill

This item tests your ability to identify the main idea of a passage and find the best thesis statement or topic sentence which expresses this idea.

In order to find the main idea, you should first ask yourself what the passage is about. Are some words or ideas frequently repeated throughout the text? This is the subject or **Topic** of the sentence. Next you should try to find out what the author is trying to say about this topic. The author's point about the topic is referred to as a **Controlling Idea**. When you put these two ideas together (the topic + the controlling idea) you have discovered the most important point of the passage, the **Main Idea**.

The topic sentence and the thesis statement are both single sentences which express the main idea of a passage, but they serve different purposes. The topic sentence is the main idea expressed in a sentence for a single paragraph. On the other hand, the thesis statement is the main idea for a piece of writing that consists of more than one paragraph.

Topic Sentence
The topic sentence states the main idea of a paragraph. The topic sentence is often the first sentence of a paragraph, but this is not always the case. The following is an example of a paragraph in which the topic sentence has been omitted.

_____. _Women seek to build rapport and establish a closer relationship_ and so use **listening** to achieve these ends. For example, **women** use more **listening** cues that let the other person know they are paying attention and are interested. _On the other hand, men not only use fewer **listening** cues but interrupt more_ and will often change the topic to one they know more about or one that is less relational or people-oriented to one that is more factual, for example, sports, statistics, economic developments, or political problems. Research shows that **men** play up their expertise, emphasize it, and use it to dominate the conversation. **Women** play down their expertise. (Adapted from Joseph A. DeVito, *Essentials of Human Communication*, 3rd ed., New York: Longman, 1999.)

In order to find the best topic sentence for this paragraph, we must first identify the main idea. Here we see the idea of how men and women listen repeated throughout the passage. This is the passage's topic.

Next, we have to decide what point the author is trying to make about men's and women's listening styles. We can do this by looking for the details the author uses. In this passage, the two major details deal with how women use listening to build relationships, while men use more fact-based, less interpersonal listening techniques. These details show that there are differences in the way men and women use listening. This is the controlling idea. When we put the topic (how men and women listen) together with the controlling idea (there are differences), we get the main idea which is that there are differences in the ways men and women listen. A good topic sentence to go in the blank would be a sentence that expresses this idea in a single sentence.

When selecting the topic sentence from a list of possibilities, keep in mind that all the details must support the topic. This means that you should look for the idea that is large enough to encompass all the major details, but not one that is so general that it goes beyond what the author is trying to say about the topic. A topic sentence which only mentioned how women listen, for example, would be too limited or narrow because it doesn't mention the differences in men's style. One that talked about how all creatures listen would be too large or broad because we are only contrasting men and women. Also, topic sentences cannot be a specific detail or a fact. These facts and details are used to support the more general statement, the main idea.

Thesis Statement
The thesis statement states the main idea of an essay. The thesis statement is a sentence that usually appears in the introductory paragraph of a piece of writing, often at the end of the introductory paragraph, though this is not always the case. After the introduction, the body paragraphs of the essay support the thesis statement. Each body paragraph has a topic sentence supported by details arranged in a specific pattern. We can visualize main ideas and where they are located by following the chart on the next page:

The thesis statement does two things:

1. Tells the readers what the limited subject will be (topic)
2. Gives the writer's point, opinion, idea, or attitude about the limited subject (controlling idea)

In addition to revealing the limited subject and the writer's point about the subject, the thesis can also list the supporting points in the same sentence. Here's an example:

> Attending community college was the best decision I have ever made because of the excellent teachers, the convenient location, and the affordable cost.

The topic: Attending community college
The controlling idea: was the best decision I have ever made
Supporting points: because of the excellent teachers, the convenient location, and the affordable cost.

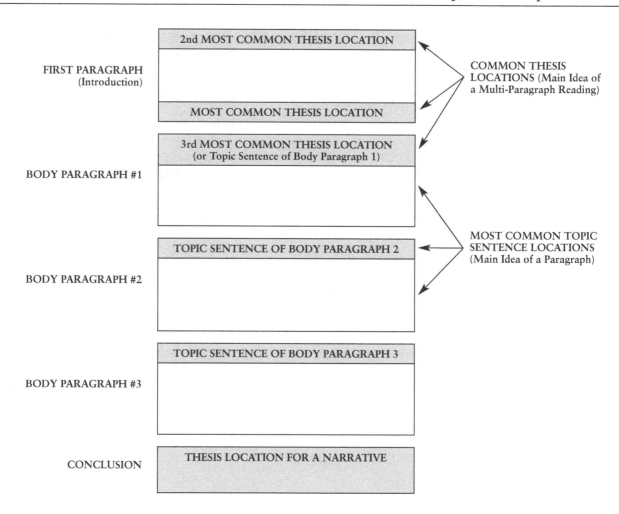

As you read the following passage, notice how the thesis statement (in bold) expresses the main idea and lists the points (underlined) that will be covered in the body. Also, look at how each body paragraph has a topic sentence (in bold), which is supported by proof details.

If you have ever stayed up late, say, studying or partying, and then awakened early the next morning, you have probably experienced sleep deprivation. In fact, you may be sleep deprived right now. If so, you have company. Many adults do not get enough sleep (defined as 8 hours). **Sleep deprivation affects us in at least three important psychological areas: <u>attention</u>, <u>mood</u>, and <u>performance</u>.**

One psychological area affected by sleep deprivation is the ability to perform tasks requiring sustained <u>attention</u>. Young adults who volunteered for a sleep deprivation study were allowed to sleep for only 5 hours each night, for a total of 7 nights. After 3 nights of restricted sleep, volunteers complained of cognitive, emotional, and physical difficulties. Moreover, their performance on a visual motor task declined after only 2 nights of restricted sleep. Visual motor tasks usually require participants to concentrate on detecting a change in a particular stimulus, and then to respond as quickly as they can after they perceive the change by pressing a button. Although you may be able to perform short mental tasks normally when sleep deprived, if a task requires sustained attention and a motor response, your performance will suffer. Driving a car is an example of such a task. In fact, in a survey by the National Sleep Foundation, 25% of the respondents reported that they had at some time fallen asleep at the wheel; sleepy drivers account for at least 100,000 car crashes each year.

<u>Moods</u> **are also affected by sleep deprivation.** Those who sleep less than 6 hours each weekday night are more likely to report being impatient or aggravated when faced with common minor frustrations such as being stuck in traffic or having to wait in line, and they were more dissatisfied with life in general, according to the National Sleep Foundation. The loss of even one night's sleep can lead to increases in the next day's level of cortisol. Cortisol helps the body meet the demands of stress. However, sleep deprivation can lead to a change in cortisol levels that, in turn, alters other biological functions. Regularly increased cortisol levels affect memory and cause a decrease in the immune system.

In addition to attention and mood, sleep deprivation affects <u>performance</u>. Many students take a series of all-nighters, when you get no sleep at all, as might occur during finals period. Results from volunteers who have gone without sleep for long stretches (finally sleeping after staying awake anywhere from 4 to 11 days) show profound psychological changes, such as hallucinations, feelings of losing control or going crazy, anxiety, and paranoia. Moreover, going without sleep alters the normal circadian rhythms of changes in temperature, metabolism, and hormone secretion. Results of a study on sleep-deprived humans found a different pattern of brain activation when learning verbal material, compared to the pattern of activation when not sleep deprived, suggesting an attempt to compensate for the brain changes induced by sleep deprivation. (Adapted from Stephen M. Kosslyn and Robin S. Rosenberg, *Psychology*, Boston: Allyn and Bacon, 2004.)

The Test Question

You will be tested on your ability to identify the best thesis statement or topic sentence in a passage of approximately 200 words. Incorrect answers may be too narrow and not include all the major supporting details, or they may be too broad and not limited to the scope of the passage.

▶▶ *Secrets to Success*

- *When looking for the main idea, ask: What is the topic (subject) of the passage?*
- *What do the most important sentences in the rest of the reading have in common?*
- *Look for repeated words and ideas.*
- *What is the author's most important point about that topic?*
- *Look for a broad statement that sounds like an important point the author is making.*
- *Ask yourself: Do all of the other sentences tell more about this sentence?*

SECTION 1 ◆ DIAGNOSTIC: THE TOPIC SENTENCE

Read the passages and apply the strategies described above for finding the topic sentence. When you are done, check your work with the answers immediately following the diagnostic. Even if you get a perfect score here, go ahead and complete the exercises in this section; they are designed to help build confidence and to give you practice for future test success.

PASSAGE #1

Read the passage and answer the question that follows.

[1]_____.

[2]Some instructors, for example, have a teaching style that promotes social interaction among students. [3]An instructor may organize small group activities, encourage class participation, or require students to work in pairs or teams to complete a specific task. [4]A lecture class is an example. [5]Other instructors offer little or no opportunity for social interaction. [6]Some instructors are very applied; they teach by example. [7]Others are more conceptual; they focus on presenting ideas, rules, theories, and so forth. [8]To an extent, of course, the subject matter also dictates how the instructor teaches. [9]_____ a biology instructor has a large body of factual information to present and may feel he or she has little time to schedule group interaction. [10]Some instructors' teaching styles are boring. [11]Once you are aware of your learning style and then consider the instructor's teaching style, you can begin to understand why you can learn better from one instructor than another and why you feel more comfortable in certain instructors' classes than others. (Adapted from Kathleen McWhorter, *Study and Critical Thinking Skills in College*, 5th ed., New York: Longman, 2003.)

1. Which sentence, if inserted in the blank labeled number 1, is the **best** main idea or topic sentence?
   A. Learning from both textbooks and lectures is the biggest challenge you face as a college student.
   B. The reasons instructors don't tell their students how to learn is simple.
   C. Just as each student has his or her own learning style, so does each instructor have his or her own teaching style.
   D. Variations in how people learn are known as learning styles.

PASSAGE #2

Read the passage and answer the question that follows.

[1]_____.

[2]As early as the 1920s, psychologists attempted to teach language to chimpanzees to find out whether they could communicate. [3]Chimps don't have the appropriate vocal apparatus to produce spoken language, so researchers had to devise other methods of communication. [4]For instance, a chimp named Washoe was taught a highly simplified version of American Sign Language. [5]In addition, a chimp named Sarah was taught to manipulate symbols on a magnetic board. [6]Skeptics wondered if the chimps' combination of gestures and symbols constituted any kind of meaningful language. [7]Recent research has provided more solid insights into the language capabilities of chimps. [8]Bonobos and chimps can be raised together. [9]Sue Savage-Rumbaugh and her team work primarily with *bonobos*, a species of great ape that is evolutionarily nearer to humans than even the common chimpanzees. [10]Remarkably, two of the bonobos in her studies, Kanzi and Mulika, learned the meanings of plastic symbols at the same time. [11]They did not receive direct training; rather, they acquired the symbols by watching humans and other bonobos. [12]_____ Kanzi and Mulika can understand some spoken English. [13]For example, when Kanzi hears a spoken word, he is able to locate either the symbol for the word or a picture of the object. (Adapted from Richard J. Gerrig and Philip G. Zimbardo, *Psychology and Life*, 16th ed., Boston: Allyn and Bacon, 2002.)

2. Which sentence, if inserted in the blank labeled number 1, is the **best** main idea or topic sentence?
    A. Bonobos are more intelligent than chimpanzees because bonobos are closer to humans in their evolution.
    B. Research over the years has demonstrated that bonobos and chimpanzees can understand some spoken English words.
    C. Researchers derive much satisfaction from teaching language to apes.
    D. Some chimps can communicate with sign language and plastic symbols.

PASSAGE #3

Read the passage and answer the question that follows.

1 _____.

[2]The relationship between temperature and assault is actually strongest in the late evening and early morning hours, from 9 p.m. to 3 a.m. [3]One explanation is that people are more likely to commit assault when they are out and about. [4]That is, in warmer weather, people are usually outdoors more and, therefore, are also more "available" as assault victims. [5]In the 9 p.m. to 3 a.m. hours, people are typically not working or bound by other responsibilities. [6]The time of day is another factor. [7]Furthermore, by the late evening hours, people may have been drinking alcohol or using other substances that lower their inhibition to aggression. [8]Substance abuse is a big problem in our society. [9]Another part of the explanation is the way in which people cope with and interpret the discomfort associated with high temperatures. [10]As the day goes on, it may be harder to remember, "I'm feeling this way because it's hot" and just conclude, "I'm feeling this way because this person is making me crazy." [11]_____, assaults decline when temperatures become very hot. [12]Researchers have speculated that at very high temperatures, people might experience sufficient discomfort to withdraw from abrasive situations rather than stay and fight. (Adapted from Richard J. Gerrig and Philip G. Zimbardo, *Psychology and Life*, 16th ed., Boston: Allyn and Bacon, 2002.)

3. Which sentence, if inserted in the blank labeled number 1, is the **best** main idea or topic sentence?
    A. Inappropriate levels of serotonin may impair the brain's ability to regulate aggressive behavior.
    B. Aggression is behavior that causes psychological or physical harm to another individual.
    C. Many individuals use aggression to solve their problems.
    D. Psychologists have learned that there is a strong relationship between how cold or hot it is and how likely it is that people will commit assaults.

PASSAGE #4

Read the passage and answer the question that follows.

1 _____.

[2]The Hare Indians of Colville Lake are a small group of Canadian Inuit. [3]Savishinsky lived with the Hare Indians to study them. [4]They survive by hunting, trapping, and fishing in one of the harshest environments in the world. [5]_____, dogs are economically useful. [6]Dog teams give the Inuit a means for travel during the harshest seasons of the year. [7]The tempera-

tures are extremely cold, and the winters are long and severe. [8]Finding food can be difficult. [9]The Inuit estimate that six dogs are required for travel, and some households have as many as four dog teams, with an average of 6.2 dogs per team. [10]The dogs are a frequent topic of conversation. [11]More than being only economically useful, dogs play a significant role in people's emotional lives. [12]Members of the community constantly compare and comment on the care, condition, and growth of one another's animals. [13]They note special qualities of size, strength, color, speed, and alertness. [14]Emotional displays, uncommon among the Hare, are significant between people and their dogs. [15]All people participate in the affectionate and concerned treatment of young dogs. (Adapted from Barbara D. Miller, *Cultural Anthropology*, 2nd ed., Boston: Allyn and Bacon, 2002.)

4. Which sentence, if inserted in the blank labeled number 1, is the **best** main idea or topic sentence?
   A. Inuit refers to the people formerly called Eskimos.
   B. Dogs play a significant role in the lives of the Hare Indians.
   C. The roots of the Inuit dog, or Qimmiq, date back 4,000 years, possibly more.
   D. The Inuit sled dog is bred for its overwhelming desire to work.

PASSAGE #5

Read the passage and answer the question that follows.

[1] _____ .

[2]The robin searches for food by selecting only those items that provide the greatest energy return for the energy expended. [3]This can be illustrated by the robin's behavior, which has four parts. [4]First, the robin has to decide where to hunt for food. [5]Once on the lawn, it has to search for food items. [6]Because the robin forages on lawns, it is vulnerable to pesticide poisoning. [7]Having located some potential food, the robin has to decide whether to pursue it. [8]If it begins pursuit by pecking, the robin has to attempt a capture, in which it might or might not be successful. [9]If a food item is too large, it requires too much time to handle; if it is too small, it does not deliver enough energy to cover the costs of capture. [10]The robin should reject or ignore less valuable items, such as small beetles and caterpillars, and give preference to small and medium-sized earthworms. [11]_____ by capturing an earthworm, the robin earns some units of energy. [12]These more valuable food items would be classified as preferred food. [13]If the robin fails to find suitable and sufficient food in the area of the lawn it is searching, it leaves to search elsewhere. [14]If successful, the bird probably will return until the spot is no longer an economical place to feed. (Adapted from Robert Leo Smith and Thomas M. Smith, *Elements of Ecology*, 5th ed., San Francisco: Benjamin Cummings, 2003.)

5. Which sentence, if inserted in the blank labeled number 1, is the **best** main idea or topic sentence?
   A. To the robin, time is energy.
   B. The robin is noted for feeding in lawns where it finds earthworms.
   C. Robins eat different types of food depending on the time of day; in the morning they eat earthworms, and in the afternoon they eat fruits and berries.
   D. The American robin is a common occupant of residential areas during the breeding season.

PASSAGE #6

Read the passage and answer the question that follows.

¹_____.

²Beach-nesting birds such as the piping plover and the least tern are so disturbed by bathers and dune buggies that both species are in danger of extinction. ³Other terns and shore birds are subjected to competition for nest sites and to egg predators by rapidly growing populations of large gulls. ⁴These gulls are highly tolerant of humans and thrive on human garbage. ⁵Sea turtles and the horseshoe crab, dependent on sandy beaches for nesting sites, find themselves evicted. ⁶_____, they are declining rapidly. ⁷Furthermore, each incoming tide brings onto the beaches feces-contaminated water that makes them unhealthy for humans and wildlife alike. ⁸This contaminated water comes from a number of different sources, such as sewer over-flows, failing private and commercial septic systems, animal and wildlife waste, and swimmers' illnesses. ⁹The oceans have become dumping grounds. ¹⁰Major chronic pollutants are oil that is released from tanker accidents, seepage from offshore drilling and other sources, toxic ma-terials such as pesticides and heavy metals from industrial, urban, and agricultural sources. ¹¹The most devastating human activity in reefs is overfishing, especially in the Philippines and the Caribbean. ¹²Tides also carry in old fishing lines, plastic debris, and other wastes hazardous to wildlife. (Adapted from Robert Leo Smith, and Thomas M. Smith, *Elements of Ecology*, 5th ed., San Francisco: Benjamin Cummings, 2003.)

6. Which sentence, if inserted in the blank labeled number 1, is the **best** main idea or topic sentence?
   A. Oil has become a major pollutant of the seas.
   B. Where the land meets the sea, we find the complex world of the seashore.
   C. Human intrusion onto the seashore has had serious effects on wildlife of the sandy shores.
   D. Ocean bathers face the risk of respiratory infections and gastroenteritis due to water pollution.

PASSAGE #7

Read the passage and answer the question that follows.

¹_____.

²About 21 million people trace their origin to Mexico, 3 million to Puerto Rico, 1 million to Cuba, and almost 5 million to Central or South America, primarily Venezuela or Colombia. ³Officially tallied at 35 million in the year 2000 census, the actual number of Latinos is higher because, not surprisingly, many who are in the country illegally avoid contact with both public officials and census forms. ⁴Each year, more than 1 million people are apprehended at the bor-der or at points inland and are deported to Mexico. ⁵Perhaps another million or so manage to enter the United States. ⁶_____ many migrate for temporary work and then return to their homes and families. ⁷To gain an understanding of how vast these numbers are, we can note that there are millions more Latinos in the United States than there are Canadians in Canada (31 million). ⁸To Midwesterners, such a comparison often comes as a surprise, for Latinos are absent from vast stretches of mid-America. ⁹Sixty-nine percent are concentrated in just four states: California, Texas, New York, and Florida. ¹⁰In the next twenty-five years, changes in the U.S. racial-ethnic mix will be dramatic. (Adapted from James M. Henslin, *So-ciology*, 6th ed., Boston: Allyn and Bacon, 2003.)

7. Which sentence, if inserted in the blank labeled number 1, is the **best** main idea or topic sentence?
    A. In the United States, 20 million people speak Spanish at home.
    B. Today Latinos are a growing minority group in the United States.
    C. People from different Latin nations feel little in common with one another.
    D. *Latino* refers to ethnic groups, not race.

Answers and Explanations to Diagnostic: The Topic Sentence

1. Answer   C
This passage gives examples of different teaching styles.

False choices
    Choice A leads the reader to think that the paragraph will be about learning from both textbooks and lectures.
    Choice B indicates that the paragraph will discuss reasons instructors don't tell students how to learn.
    Choice D defines learning style. A fact cannot be a topic sentence.

2. Answer   B
The passage describes research done over the years that has taught researchers that bonobos and chimpanzees can understand some English.

False choices
    Choice A leads the reader to believe that the entire paragraph will contrast the intelligence of bonobos and chimpanzees. While the author mentions that bonobos are evolutionarily closer to humans and indicates that bonobos are better at recognizing English, this is not the focus of the paragraph.
    Choice C refers to the satisfaction researchers derive from this work; however, the topic is not covered in the paragraph.
    Choice D is a fact from the paragraph, not the main idea.

3. Answer   D
This passage explains the relationship between temperature and assaults.

False choices
    Choice A refers to serotonin levels in the brain as a factor that contributes to aggressive behavior, but this is not covered in the passage.
    Choice B defines the term "aggression." Definitions are not main idea sentences.
    Choice C is too general in its statement that many people use aggression to solve problems. This paragraph clearly explains that there is a correlation between temperature and assaults.

4. Answer   B
The passage tells the reader how dogs are economically and emotionally helpful to the Hare Indians.

False choices
    Choice A provides a definition of Inuit. Since it is a fact, the definition cannot be a topic sentence.
    Choice C speaks of the root of the Inuit dog. While the paragraph is about these dogs, it does not discuss the history and evolution of the species.
    Choice D gives the reason that the sled dog is bred; however, the paragraph does not describe sled dog breeding.

5. Answer   A

The passage explains that the robin should find food without expending too much energy.

False choices

Choice B gives a fact about robins—that they look for earthworms on lawns. A topic sentence may not be a fact.

Choice C also gives a fact about what robins eat at different times of the day.

Choice D leads the reader to believe that the paragraph will talk about the kinds of residential areas the robin occupies, not the way it feeds.

6. Answer   C

The passage explains the effects of human intrusion on the seashore.

False choices

Choice A leads the reader to believe that the passage will focus on the effects of oil pollution on the oceans.

Choice B indicates that the discussion will be about the "complex world of the seashore." This might include the various plants and animals that live at the water's edge or in the sand.

Choice D tells the reader that the passage will talk about the risks ocean bathers face as a result of ocean pollution. Risks to bathers is mentioned in the passage, but it is not the main idea.

7. Answer   B

This passage gives specific information on how the Latino population is increasing in the United States.

False choices

Choice A presents a fact, which cannot be a topic sentence.

Choice C leads the reader to think that the paragraph will discuss the fact that people from different Latin countries do not have much in common; however, the passage focuses on population, not commonalities.

Choice D tells the reader the meaning of *Latino*. This is a definition, not a topic sentence.

SECTION 1 ◆ EXERCISES: THE TOPIC SENTENCE

PASSAGE #1

Read the passage and answer the question that follows.

¹ _____.

²First of all, because e-mail messages are informal and quick, writers may be sloppy in transferring their thoughts to the screen. ³Misspellings and ungrammatical sentences can project a negative image if users do not take time to edit what they write on e-mail. ⁴Second, the messages are sent and read online, often leaving no paper trail at all. ⁵As a result, some important messages are forgotten or lost. ⁶It is easy to read your electronic mail and delete it instead of printing out a copy of the message to keep in a file or filing the message electronically in your e-mail file folder. ⁷Although generally thought of as a quick method of communication, e-mail's efficiency is only as good as the recipient's care in routinely checking e-mail messages. ⁸Electronic communication can be slow if people don't check their messages. ⁹Moreover, you

have no privacy. [10]Another disadvantage is the increasing use of e-mail as a replacement for the personal contact of a phone call or face-to-face meeting. [11]The 1986 Electronic Communications Privacy Act considers e-mail to be the property of the company paying for the mail system. [12]_____, writing on a computer screen often encourages people to drop inhibitions and write things in e-mail that they would never write in a paper letter or say over the telephone. (Adapted from Kristin R. Woolever, *Writing for the Technical Professions*, 2nd ed., New York: Longman, 2002.)

1. Which sentence, if inserted in the blank labeled number 1, is the **best** main idea or topic sentence?
   A. Electronic mail is a beneficial form of communication.
   B. When using e-mail to communicate in the workplace, always maintain a level of professionalism and courtesy.
   C. Although electronic mail has become a medium of choice for business communication, e-mail has disadvantages for users.
   D. At work, people are using e-mail as a primary form of communication.

PASSAGE #2

Read the passage and answer the question that follows.

[1]_____.

[2]Although women have served in every branch of the armed services since World War II, two differences between the treatment of men and women in the military persist. [3]First, only men must register for the draft when they turn eighteen. [4]In 1981, the Supreme Court ruled that male-only registration for the military did not violate the Fifth Amendment. [5]Second, statutes and regulations also prohibit women from serving in combat. [6]A breach exists between policy and practice, however, as the Persian Gulf war showed. [7]Women piloted helicopters at the front and helped to operate antimissile systems; some were taken as prisoners of war. [8]_____, women are not permitted to serve as combat pilots in the navy and air force and to serve on navy warships. [9]They are still not permitted to serve in ground combat units in the army or marines. [10]These actions have reopened the debate over whether women should serve in combat. [11]Others argue that men will not be able to fight effectively beside wounded or dying women. [12]Critics of these views point out that some women surpass men in body strength and that we do not know how well men and women will fight together. [13]Some experts insist that because women, on the average, have less body strength than men, they are less suited for combat. [14]This debate is not only a controversy about ability, but it also touches on the question of whether engaging in combat is a burden or a privilege. (Adapted from George C. Edwards, Martin P. Wattenberg, and Robert L. Lineberry, *Government in America*, 9th ed., New York: Longman, 2000.)

2. Which sentence, if inserted in the blank labeled number 1, is the **best** main idea or topic sentence?
   A. Women have overcome many obstacles to serving in the military.
   B. The U.S. has had a volunteer military force since 1973.
   C. Women are less suited for combat than men.
   D. Military service is still a controversial issue of gender equality.

PASSAGE #3

Read the passage and answer the question that follows.

1 _____.

²Jaime Escalante taught calculus in an East Los Angeles inner-city school that was plagued with poverty, crime, drugs, and gangs. ³As a result of his methods, his students earned the highest Advanced Placement scores in the city. ⁴_____, Escalante had to open his students' minds to the possibility of success in learning. ⁵Most Latino students were tracked into craft classes where they made jewelry and birdhouses. ⁶Escalante felt that his students were talented and needed an opportunity to show it. ⁷Also, the students needed to see learning as a way out of the barrio, as a path to good jobs. ⁸By arranging for foundations to provide money for students to attend colleges of their choice, Escalante showed students that if they did well, their poverty would not stop them. ⁹When Escalante first came to the United States, he worked as a busboy and attended Pasadena Community College. ¹⁰Escalante also changed the system of instruction. ¹¹Before class, his students did "warm-ups," hand clapping and foot stomping to a rock song. ¹²To foster team identity, students wore team jackets, caps, and T-shirts with logos that identified them as part of the math team. ¹³He had his students think of themselves as a team, of him as the coach, and the national math exams as a sort of Olympics for which they were preparing. ¹⁴Escalante thought it was important to teach his classes in English, not Spanish. ¹⁵Escalante demonstrated that a teacher can motivate students to believe in their ability to achieve at high levels, no matter how great their problems. (Adapted from James M. Henslin, *Sociology*, 6th ed., Boston: Allyn and Bacon, 2003.)

3. Which sentence, if inserted in the blank labeled number 1, is the **best** main idea or topic sentence?
   A. Jaime Escalante, the Bolivian who did not know how to speak English when he came to the U.S., graduated from California State University in 1974 with a bachelor's degree in mathematics and electronics.
   B. Jaime Escalante's dramatic success in teaching calculus to students in an East Los Angeles inner-city school plagued with poverty, crime, drugs, and gangs, was a result of changes he made to classroom instruction.
   C. The story of Jaime Escalante's success in teaching calculus to low-income Latino high school students in Los Angeles was the subject of the movie *Stand and Deliver*.
   D. Jaime Escalante believed that all a person needs to succeed is desire that comes from within.

PASSAGE #4

Read the passage and answer the question that follows.

1 _____.

²Anorexia nervosa literally means loss of appetite, but this is a misnomer. ³The anorexic individual approaches weight loss with a fervor, convinced that her body is too large. ⁴A person with anorexia nervosa is hungry, but he or she denies the hunger because of an irrational fear of becoming fat. ⁵Therefore, the first characteristic is a significant weight loss due to a relentless drive for thinness. ⁶She is unable to recognize that her appearance is abnormal. ⁷She will insist that her emaciated figure is just right or is too fat. ⁸There is a strong argument that eating disorders are a form of addiction. ⁹This condition is more than a simple eating disorder. ¹⁰_____, anorexia is a distinct psychological disorder with a wide range of psychological

disturbances. [11]Anorexics are typically compulsive, perfectionistic, and very competitive. [12]Food preoccupation and rituals and compulsive exercising are other characteristics. [13]The anorexic sometimes suffers from low self-image due to a feeling of incompetence, so she becomes consumed with losing weight to demonstrate to herself and others that she is in total control. [14]Additional features of the disease develop from the effects of starvation over time. [15]Untreated anorexia can be fatal. [16]Causes of death include starvation, infections due to poor nutrition, irregular heartbeat due to potassium deficiency, and suicide due to depression. (Adapted from David J. Anspaugh and Gene Ezell, *Teaching Today's Health*, 7th ed., San Francisco: Pearson, 2004.)

4. Which sentence, if inserted in the blank labeled number 1, is the **best** main idea or topic sentence?
   A. Eating disorders are one of the most common psychological problems facing young women around the world.
   B. Some of the physical symptoms of anorexia nervosa are directly related to the effects of starvation.
   C. Anorexia nervosa has the poorest prognosis of all the eating disorders; however, the prognosis is moderately improved if the disorder is detected and treated in its early stages.
   D. The central features of anorexia nervosa are a complex mixture of symptoms.

PASSAGE #5

Read the passage and answer the question that follows.

[1]_____.
[2]Bare-knuckle boxing, the forerunner of modern boxing, was a brutal, bloody sport. [3]Two men fought bare-fisted until one could not continue. [4]A round lasted until one of the men knocked or threw down his opponent. [5]At that point, both men rested for thirty seconds and then started to fight again. [6]Fights often lasted over one hundred rounds and as long as seven or eight hours. [7]After such a fight, it took months for the fighters to recover. [8]During the 1800s, boxing underwent a series of reforms. [9]There have been periodic efforts to outlaw the sport. [10]The challenge system was replaced by modern promotional techniques. [11]Fighters deserted bare-fisted combat and started wearing gloves. [12]Most importantly, professional boxers adopted the Marquis of Queensberry Rules, which standardized a round at three minutes, allowing a one-minute rest period between rounds, and outlawed all wrestling throws and holds. [13]_____, the fight to the finish was replaced with a fight to a decision over a specified number of rounds. [14]A bell and a referee told fighters when to fight and when to rest. [15]Currently there are eight major professional divisions. [16]Although the new rules did not reduce the violence, they did provide for more orderly bouts. (Adapted from James Kirby Martin et al., *America and Its Peoples*, 5th ed., New York: Longman, 2003.)

5. Which sentence, if inserted in the blank labeled number 1, is the **best** main idea or topic sentence?
   A. Boxing originated when a person first lifted a fist against another in competition.
   B. Boxing began as a largely unstructured sport, but by 1900 new rules had standardized the sport.
   C. The sport of boxing did not catch on in the United States until the late 1800s.
   D. Boxing is one of the most popular sports in the history of modern sport.

PASSAGE #6

Read the passage and answer the question that follows.

1 _____.

²For example, with eye movements you can seek feedback. ³In talking with someone, you look at her or him intently, as if to say, "Well, what do you think?" ⁴Your pupils enlarge when you are interested or emotionally aroused. ⁵You can also inform the other person that the channel of communication is open and that he or she should now speak. ⁶You see this in the college class-room, when the instructor asks a question and then locks eyes with a student. ⁷Without saying anything, the instructor expects that student to answer the question and the student knows it.⁸Eye movements may also signal the nature of a relationship, whether positive (an attentive glance) or negative (eye avoidance). ⁹_____, you can signal your power through visual dominance behavior. ¹⁰The average speaker, for example, maintains a high level of eye contact while listening and a lower level while speaking. ¹¹When people want to signal dominance, they may reverse this pattern: maintaining a high level of eye contact while talking but a lower level while listening. ¹²Eye contact can also change the psychological distance between yourself and another person. ¹³When you catch someone's eye at a party, for example, you become psychologically close even though far apart. ¹⁴By avoiding eye contact—even when physically close as in a crowded eleva-tor—you increase the psychological distance between you. (Adapted from Joseph A. DeVito, *Essentials of Human Communication*, 3rd ed., New York: Longman, 1999.)

6. Which sentence, if inserted in the blank labeled number 1, is the **best** main idea or topic sentence?
   A. Eye movements have been widely researched.
   B. Eye movements communicate a variety of messages.
   C. Eye messages vary from one culture to another.
   D. The eyes are regarded as the most important nonverbal message system.

PASSAGE #7

Read the passage and answer the question that follows.

1 _____.

²It even drinks seawater, which is much saltier than its body fluids. ³Few animals can tolerate such salty liquid because the salt draws water out of their tissues, and they become severely dehydrated. ⁴An albatross can thrive on salt water because it has special salt-excreting glands in its nostrils. ⁵The glands dispose of excess salts, allowing the bird to eat salty fish and squid and drink all it needs without ever visiting land. ⁶Their scientific name, *Diomedea exulans*, means exiled warrior in Greek. ⁷_____ its remarkable salt tolerance, the wandering al-batross has extraordinary flight abilities specially suited to its seafaring life. ⁸Its wingspan is greater than that of any other bird—about 3.6 meters (nearly twelve feet). ⁹Most birds have to flap their wings to stay up in the air very long, but the albatross's long wings provide so much lift that the bird can stay aloft for hours by gliding up and down on wind currents. ¹⁰The wandering albatross spends most of its time in an area of high winds and rough seas, far from land, often alone on the open ocean. ¹¹The winds carry it from west to east, and in a year's time, an albatross may circle the globe, seeing little land except New Zealand and the tip of South America. (Adapted from Neil A. Campbell, Lawrence G. Mitchell, and Jane B. Reece, *Biology*, 3rd ed., San Francisco: Benjamin Cummings, 2000.)

7. Which sentence, if inserted in the blank labeled number 1, is the **best** main idea or topic sentence?
   A. Only a few birds can live at sea, but the albatross is a model of fitness for its environment.
   B. Albatrosses frequent areas where steady winds blow over the ocean.
   C. The albatross's body has special structural adaptations.
   D. An albatross takes full advantage of the energy of ocean winds to stay aloft.

PASSAGE #8

Read the passage and answer the question that follows.

1 _____.

[2]Testosterone is a male hormone that causes a general buildup in muscle and bone mass during puberty in males and maintains masculine traits throughout life. [3]Anabolic steroids are synthetic variants of the male hormone testosterone. [4]Pharmaceutical companies first produced and marketed anabolic steroids in the early 1950s as a treatment for certain diseases that destroy body muscle. [5]About a decade later, some athletes began using anabolic steroids to build up their muscles quickly and enhance their performance with less hard work. [6]It is not surprising that some of the heaviest users are weight lifters, football players, and body builders. [7]Today, anabolic steroids, along with other drugs, are banned by most athletic organizations. [8]Black market sales bring in up to $400 million a year. [9]Medical research indicates that these substances can cause serious physical and mental problems. [10]Overdosing in males can cause acne, baldness, and breast development. [11]Mental effects can range from mood swings to deep depression. [12]Internally, there may be liver damage leading to cancer. [13]_____, anabolic steroids can make blood cholesterol levels rise, perhaps increasing a user's chances of developing serious cardiovascular problems. [14]Heavy users may also experience a reduced sex drive and become infertile because anabolic steroids often make the body reduce its normal output of sex hormones. (Adapted from Neil A. Campbell, Lawrence G. Mitchell, and Jane B. Reece, *Biology*, 3rd ed., San Francisco: Benjamin Cummings, 2000.)

8. Which sentence, if inserted in the blank labeled number 1, is the **best** main idea or topic sentence?
   A. Athletes who use anabolic steroids to increase body mass should not be allowed to compete.
   B. The only way to promote fair athletic competition is to test the athletes for anabolic steroids.
   C. While using anabolic steroids is a fast way to increase general body size, their health hazards support the argument for banning their use in athletics.
   D. There are many ways to increase your strength or improve your appearance.

PASSAGE #9

Read the passage and answer the question that follows.

1 _____.

[2]In most cases, the child continually learns from the parent. [3]In the area of computer and Internet-mediated communication, however, the child may be able to teach the parent. [4]_____, one five-year-old learned a graphics program before she could read. [5]The child taught herself how to operate the rather intuitive program. [6]Not only did the computer provide the child with a valuable learning process, but the parents totally depended on the child

when they wanted to use the program she knew. [7]In another case, a young boy taught his parents how to use PowerPoint. [8]The examples are endless. [9]Children are more apt to interact with the computer as if it were alive. [10]A child may be able to understand a concept differently from the parent, and the role reversal of the child-as-teacher can be an important way the computer and the Internet can enhance a child's self-esteem. [11]The child and parent alike may feel positive toward themselves when they are able to learn new things, master a program, or win an Internet game. [12]Their self-confidence may increase when others seek their advice, for example, because they are the family computer experts. (Adapted from Leonard J. Shedletsky and Joan E. Aitken, *Human Communication on the Internet*, Boston: Allyn and Bacon, 2004.)

9. Which sentence, if inserted in the blank labeled number 1, is the **best** main idea or topic sentence?
   A. Young children often relate to the computer in creative and fun ways.
   B. Sharing information and teaching each other about their computer and the Internet can strengthen the parent-child relationship.
   C. The lure of computers can come between family members.
   D. The computer can have positive and negative effects on the family.

PASSAGE #10

Read the passage and answer the question that follows.

1 _____.

[2]Highlighting is a strategy for condensing textbook material and emphasizing what is important. [3]_____, the process of highlighting forces you to sift through what you have read to identify important information. [4]This sifting or sorting is an active thought process; you are forced to weigh and evaluate what you read. [5]One mistake to avoid is highlighting almost every idea on a page. [6]Another benefit of highlighting is that it keeps you physically active while you are reading. [7]In addition, highlighting can help you discover the organization of facts and ideas as well as their connections and relationships. [8]Highlighting demonstrates to you whether you have understood a passage you have just read. [9]When combined with annotation, highlighting is a quick and easy way to review so that you do not have to reread everything when studying for an exam. [10]If you highlight 20 percent of a chapter, you will be able to avoid rereading 80 percent of the material. [11]If it normally takes two hours to read a chapter, you should be able to review a highlighted chapter in less than a half hour. [12]Highlighting has many benefits, but it is not by itself a sufficient study method; you must process the information by organizing it, expressing it in your own words, and testing yourself periodically. (Adapted from Kathleen T. McWhorter, *Study and Critical Thinking Skills in College*, 5th ed., New York: Longman, 2003.)

10. Which sentence, if inserted in the blank labeled number 1, is the **best** main idea or topic sentence?
    A. If you have understood a paragraph or section, then your highlighting should be fast and efficient.
    B. To highlight textbook material most efficiently, apply these guidelines.
    C. College students should know how to highlight their textbooks properly.
    D. Highlighting is an extremely effective way of making a textbook review manageable.

SECTION 2 ◆ SUPPORTING DETAILS

The Skill

This item tests your ability to recognize whether or not an idea is supported adequately. A supporting detail is not an opinion, a restatement of the main idea, or a generality. Instead, supporting details relate to the main idea and support the ideas presented. Details answer the six questions used by writers: who, what, when, where, why, and how. The details give reasons; examples; explanations; descriptive characteristics; events or activities; people, places and objects; and particulars about an item or situation. Some of the details are considered major support while others that are not as important are minor details.

It is important to be able to recognize which are the major details and which are the minor details. Major details connect strongly with the topic sentence, provide substantial information, and are specific. The minor details are the sentences that support the major details. If your topic sentence stated, "Three teachers in my life shaped my future," then the three major support statements would probably name a teacher and specifically state how he or she helped shape your life. The minor details would give an example, a reason, an explanation, or a particular point of information that would make that teacher's special effect on your life more clear. An example is done for you below.

(1) Three teachers in my life shaped my future. (2) **Mrs. Rhine, my sixth grade teacher, taught me to believe in my abilities and to be happy using them.** (3) A new world opened up to me because of Mrs. Rhine's encouragement and her stimulating and creative student assignments. (4) Though I had only been an average student in the earlier grades, throughout the sixth grade my grades improved steadily, and I earned the right to be in the honors section in junior high school. (5) **The second teacher that affected my life was Mr. Ponte because he taught me to question what people stated and to observe the world with a questioning eye.** (6) **The third teacher that had an effect on me was Dr. Schillit because he taught me to set goals, to see the wonders of the world, and to challenge myself to go further.** (7) He continuously challenged me to try new ideas and to think of the possibilities for my life. (8) Without the influence of these three teachers, I would not be the person I am today.

Here is a concept map of the passage:

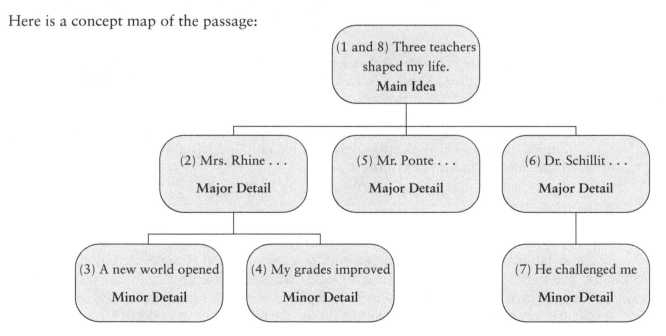

The topic sentence is sentence 1 and is repeated as a conclusion in sentence 8. The major details are the three sentences in bold naming the teachers and stating the effect they had (sentences 2, 5, and 6). The minor details (sentences 3, 4, and 7) give a little more information about the major details in order to help the reader understand more easily.

In this passage, the first major detail in sentence 2 is supported by minor details in sentences 3 and 4, and the last major detail in sentence 6 is supported by the minor details in sentence 7. This is a very typical pattern. If the question asks, "Which sentence gives details that support sentence X," generally, the answer will be the number of the next sentence or the sentence after that. For example, if the question asked about sentence 5, the answer would probably be 6. If 6 was not an option, the answer would likely be 7.

The other type of question you are likely to come across in this section will ask which sentence does not have sufficient details. In the example above, the second major detail in sentence 5 has no following minor detail sentences that show how the teacher challenged the student. Instead, sentence 6 begins a new major detail. In this case, sentence number 5 does not have adequate support.

Read the following two paragraphs. Which one is adequately supported?

Sample 1

> Caffeine, a common stimulant found in coffee, tea, cola drinks, and even chocolate, is a drug and should be recognized as one that can lead to health problems. Because it is not viewed as a dangerous drug, caffeine use for its own sake is overlooked.

Sample 2

> Caffeine, a common stimulant found in coffee, tea, cola drinks, and even chocolate, is a drug and should be recognized as one that can lead to health problems. Caffeine increases mental alertness and provides a feeling of energy. However, high doses of caffeine can over stimulate and cause nervousness and increased heart rate. Caffeine can also cause sleeplessness, excitement, and irritability. In some cases, high doses of caffeine can induce convulsions. Because it is not viewed as a dangerous drug, caffeine use for its own sake is overlooked. (Adapted from David J. Anspaugh and Gene Ezell, *Teaching Today's Health*, 7th ed., San Francisco: Benjamin Cummings, 2004.)

Sample 1 does not provide any supporting details explaining the possible health problems from caffeine use; however, Sample 2 does. Three statements give examples of the kinds of problems a person who uses caffeine might have:

> However, high doses of caffeine can over stimulate and cause nervousness and increased heart rate. Caffeine can also cause sleeplessness, excitement, and irritability. In some cases, high doses of caffeine can induce convulsions.

The Test Question
You will be tested on your ability to recognize adequate supporting details in one of two ways:

1. You may be asked to identify which sentence in a passage is NOT supported by sufficient details. You must decide if a statement is a general statement that needs additional support.
2. You may be given several sentences and asked to choose which sentence provides support for a specified sentence in the passage. You must choose the best statement of detail for a general idea.

> ### ▶▶⊨ *Secrets to Success*
>
> - ***Major details*** *tell us more information about the main idea.*
> - ***Minor details*** *tell us more about the major details.*
> - *To find supporting details, pay close attention to the <u>first sentence of each paragraph</u>. They often contain major details that support the main idea. They are also usually topic sentences that tell you what kind of information to expect in the paragraph.*
> - *Supporting sentences generally <u>immediately follow</u> the sentence they support. When choosing an answer, it is best to pick the sentence directly after or the one after that if that is not a possibility.*
> - *Supporting details answer questions such as who, what, when, where, why, and how. To find supporting details, look for:*
>
>   **R**easons   **E**xamples   **C**haracteristics
>   **A**nalysis and explanations   **P**eople and places   **S**enses

SECTION 2 ◆ DIAGNOSTIC: SUPPORTING DETAILS

Read the passages and apply the strategies described above for finding supporting details. When you are done, check your work with the answers immediately following the diagnostic. Even if you get a perfect score here, go ahead and complete the exercises in this section; they are designed to help build confidence and to give you practice for future test success.

PASSAGE #1

Read the passage and answer the question that follows.

¹_____.

²Some instructors, for example, have a teaching style that promotes social interaction among students. ³An instructor may organize small group activities, encourage class participation, or require students to work in pairs or teams to complete a specific task. ⁴A lecture class is an example. ⁵Other instructors offer little or no opportunity for social interaction. ⁶Some instructors are very applied; they teach by example. ⁷Others are more conceptual; they focus on presenting ideas, rules, theories, and so forth. ⁸To an extent, of course, the subject matter also dictates how the instructor teaches. ⁹_____ a biology instructor has a large body of factual information to present and may feel he or she has little time to schedule group interaction. ¹⁰Some instructors' teaching styles are boring. ¹¹Once you are aware of your learning style and then consider the instructor's teaching style, you can begin to understand why you can learn better from one instructor than another and why you feel more comfortable in certain instructors' classes than others. (Adapted from Kathleen McWhorter, *Study and Critical Thinking Skills in College,* 5th ed., New York: Longman, 2003.)

1. Which sentence provides specific support for sentence 8 in the passage?
   A. Some instructors' teaching styles are boring. (sentence 10)
   B. _____, a biology instructor has a large body of factual information to present and may feel he or she has little time to schedule group interaction. (sentence 9)

C. Once you are aware of your learning style and then consider the instructor's teaching style, you can begin to understand why you can learn better from one instructor than another and why you feel more comfortable in certain instructors' classes than others. (sentence 11)

D. A lecture class is an example. (sentence 4)

PASSAGE #2

Read the passage and answer the question that follows.

1 _____.

[2]As early as the 1920s, psychologists attempted to teach language to chimpanzees to find out whether they could communicate. [3]Chimps don't have the appropriate vocal apparatus to produce spoken language, so researchers had to devise other methods of communication. [4]For instance, a chimp named Washoe was taught a highly simplified version of American Sign Language. [5]In addition, a chimp named Sarah was taught to manipulate symbols on a magnetic board. [6]Skeptics wondered if the chimps' combination of gestures and symbols constituted any kind of meaningful language. [7]Recent research has provided more solid insights into the language capabilities of chimps. [8]Bonobos and chimps can be raised together. [9]Sue Savage-Rumbaugh and her team work primarily with *bonobos*, a species of great ape that is evolutionarily nearer to humans than even the common chimpanzees. [10]Remarkably, two of the bonobos in her studies, Kanzi and Mulika, learned the meanings of plastic symbols at the same time. [11]They did not receive direct training; rather, they acquired the symbols by watching humans and other bonobos. [12]_____ Kanzi and Mulika can understand some spoken English. [13]For example, when Kanzi hears a spoken word, he is able to locate either the symbol for the word or a picture of the object. (Adapted from Richard J. Gerrig and Philip G. Zimbardo, *Psychology and Life*, 16th ed., Boston: Allyn and Bacon, 2002.)

2. Which sentence provides specific support for sentence 3 in the passage?
   A. In addition, a chimp named Sarah was taught to manipulate symbols on a magnetic board. (sentence 5)
   B. Skeptics wondered if the chimps' combination of gestures and symbols constituted any kind of meaningful language. (sentence 6)
   C. Recent research has provided more solid insights into the language capabilities of chimps. (sentence 7)
   D. Bonobos and chimps can be raised together. (sentence 8)

PASSAGE #3

Read the passage and answer the question that follows.

1 _____.

[2]The relationship between temperature and assault is actually strongest in the late evening and early morning hours, from 9 p.m. to 3 a.m. [3]One explanation is that people are more likely to commit assault when they are out and about. [4]That is, in warmer weather, people are usually outdoors more and, therefore, are also more "available" as assault victims. [5]In the 9 p.m. to 3 a.m. hours, people are typically not working or bound by other responsibilities. [6]The time of day is another factor. [7]Furthermore, by the late evening hours, people may have been drinking alcohol or using other substances that lower their inhibition to aggression. [8]Substance

abuse is a big problem in our society. [9]Another part of the explanation is the way in which people cope with and interpret the discomfort associated with high temperatures. [10]As the day goes on, it may be harder to remember, "I'm feeling this way because it's hot" and just conclude, "I'm feeling this way because this person is making me crazy." [11]_____, assaults decline when temperatures become very hot. [12]Researchers have speculated that at very high temperatures, people might experience sufficient discomfort to withdraw from abrasive situations rather than stay and fight. (Adapted from Richard J. Gerrig and Philip G. Zimbardo, *Psychology and Life*, 16th ed., Boston: Allyn and Bacon, 2002.)

3. Which of the numbered sentences is not supported by sufficient specific details?
   A. 2
   B. 6
   C. 9
   D. 12

PASSAGE #4

Read the passage and answer the question that follows.

[1]_____.

[2]The Hare Indians of Colville Lake are a small group of Canadian Inuit. [3]Savishinsky lived with the Hare Indians to study them. [4]They survive by hunting, trapping, and fishing in one of the harshest environments in the world. [5]_____, dogs are economically useful. [6]Dog teams give the Inuit a means for travel during the harshest seasons of the year. [7]The temperatures are extremely cold, and the winters are long and severe. [8]Finding food can be difficult. [9]The Inuit estimate that six dogs are required for travel, and some households have as many as four dog teams, with an average of 6.2 dogs per team. [10]The dogs are a frequent topic of conversation. [11]More than being only economically useful, dogs play a significant role in people's emotional lives. [12]Members of the community constantly compare and comment on the care, condition, and growth of one another's animals. [13]They note special qualities of size, strength, color, speed, and alertness. [14]Emotional displays, uncommon among the Hare, are significant between people and their dogs. [15]All people participate in the affectionate and concerned treatment of young dogs. (Adapted from Barbara D. Miller, *Cultural Anthropology*, 2nd ed., Boston: Allyn and Bacon, 2002.)

4. Which of the numbered sentences is not supported by sufficient specific details?
   A. 3
   B. 5
   C. 10
   D. 12

PASSAGE #5

Read the passage and answer the question that follows.

[1]_____.

[2]The robin searches for food by selecting only those items that provide the greatest energy return for the energy expended. [3]This can be illustrated by the robin's behavior, which has four parts.

⁴First, the robin has to decide where to hunt for food. ⁵Once on the lawn, it has to search for food items. ⁶Because the robin forages on lawns, it is vulnerable to pesticide poisoning. ⁷Having located some potential food, the robin has to decide whether to pursue it. ⁸If it begins pursuit by pecking, the robin has to attempt a capture, in which it might or might not be successful. ⁹If a food item is too large, it requires too much time to handle; if it is too small, it does not deliver enough energy to cover the costs of capture. ¹⁰The robin should reject or ignore less valuable items, such as small beetles and caterpillars, and give preference to small and medium-sized earthworms. ¹¹_____ by capturing an earthworm, the robin earns some units of energy. ¹²These more valuable food items would be classified as preferred food. ¹³If the robin fails to find suitable and sufficient food in the area of the lawn it is searching, it leaves to search elsewhere. ¹⁴If successful, the bird probably will return until the spot is no longer an economical place to feed. (Adapted from Robert Leo Smith and Thomas M. Smith, *Elements of Ecology*, 5th ed., San Francisco: Benjamin Cummings, 2003.)

5. Which sentence provides specific support for sentence 3 in the passage?
    A. The robin searches for food by selecting only those items that provide the greatest energy return for the energy expended. (sentence 2)
    B. Once on the lawn, it has to search for food items. (sentence 5)
    C. Because the robin forages on lawns, it is vulnerable to pesticide poisoning. (sentence 6)
    D. These more valuable food items would be classified as preferred food. (sentence 12)

PASSAGE #6

Read the passage and answer the question that follows.

¹_____.
²Beach-nesting birds such as the piping plover and the least tern are so disturbed by bathers and dune buggies that both species are in danger of extinction. ³Other terns and shore birds are subjected to competition for nest sites and to egg predators by rapidly growing populations of large gulls. ⁴These gulls are highly tolerant of humans and thrive on human garbage. ⁵Sea turtles and the horseshoe crab, dependent on sandy beaches for nesting sites, find themselves evicted. ⁶_____, they are declining rapidly. ⁷Furthermore, each incoming tide brings onto the beaches feces-contaminated water that makes them unhealthy for humans and wildlife alike. ⁸This contaminated water comes from a number of different sources, such as sewer overflows, failing private and commercial septic systems, animal and wildlife waste, and swimmers' illnesses. ⁹The oceans have become dumping grounds. ¹⁰Major chronic pollutants are oil that is released from tanker accidents, seepage from offshore drilling and other sources, toxic materials such as pesticides and heavy metals from industrial, urban, and agricultural sources. ¹¹The most devastating human activity in reefs is overfishing, especially in the Philippines and the Caribbean. ¹²Tides also carry in old fishing lines, plastic debris, and other wastes hazardous to wildlife. (Adapted from Robert Leo Smith and Thomas M. Smith, *Elements of Ecology*, 5th ed., San Francisco: Benjamin Cummings, 2003.)

6. Which sentence provides specific support for sentence 7 in the passage?
    A. The oceans have become dumping grounds. (sentence 9)
    B. Major chronic pollutants are oil that is released from tanker accidents, seepage from offshore drilling and other sources, toxic materials such as pesticides and heavy metals from industrial, urban, and agricultural sources. (sentence 10)

C. This contaminated water comes from a number of different sources, such as sewer overflows, failing private and commercial septic systems, animal and wildlife waste, and swimmers' illnesses. (sentence 8)

D. Tides also carry in old fishing lines, plastic debris, and other wastes hazardous to wildlife. (sentence 12)

PASSAGE #7

Read the passage and answer the question that follows.

¹_____.

²About 21 million people trace their origin to Mexico, 3 million to Puerto Rico, 1 million to Cuba, and almost 5 million to Central or South America, primarily Venezuela or Colombia. ³Officially tallied at 35 million in the year 2000 census, the actual number of Latinos is higher because, not surprisingly, many who are in the country illegally avoid contact with both public officials and census forms. ⁴Each year, more than 1 million people are apprehended at the border or at points inland and are deported to Mexico. ⁵Perhaps another million or so manage to enter the United States. ⁶_____ many migrate for temporary work and then return to their homes and families. ⁷To gain an understanding of how vast these numbers are, we can note that there are millions more Latinos in the United States than there are Canadians in Canada (31 million). ⁸To Midwesterners, such a comparison often comes as a surprise, for Latinos are absent from vast stretches of mid-America. ⁹Sixty-nine percent are concentrated in just four states: California, Texas, New York, and Florida. ¹⁰In the next twenty-five years, changes in the U.S. racial-ethnic mix will be dramatic. (Adapted from James M. Henslin, *Sociology*, 6th ed., Boston: Allyn and Bacon, 2003.)

7. Which sentence provides specific support for sentence 3 in the passage?
   A. 5
   B. 7
   C. 8
   D. 9

Answers and Explanations to Diagnostic: Supporting Details

1. Answer   B

Sentence 9 gives an example for sentence 8. Sentence 9 explains that a biology teacher may teach a certain way because he or she has so much factual material to cover.

False choices

Choice A is a statement of opinion and does not support sentence 8.

Choice C is the concluding statement of the paragraph, not a supporting statement.

Choice D supports sentence 5, a class where there is no opportunity for social interaction.

2. Answer   A

Sentence 3 introduces the idea that researchers had to devise ways to communicate with chimps and bonobos because they can't talk. Sentence 5 gives a supporting example; a chimp was taught to manipulate symbols on a magnetic board.

False choices

Choice B introduces a new point about the researchers' skepticism about whether chimps were learning meaningful language.

Choice C supports the sentence before it. Recent research is showing that chimps do have language capabilities.

Choice D does not support any sentence in the paragraph.

3. Answer   D

Sentence 12 introduces an opinion of researchers for the reasons that keep people from assaulting others when the temperature is higher. This is not supported by specific details.

False choices

> Choice A is supported by sentence 3.
> Choice B is supported by sentence 5.
> Choice C is supported by sentence 10.

4. Answer   A

Sentence 3 mentions that the researcher Savishinsky lived with the Hare Indians to study them. No further explanation is given on this point.

False choices

> Choice B is supported by sentence 6.
> Choice C is supported by sentence 12.
> Choice D is supported by sentence 13.

5. Answer   B

Sentence 5 is one of the steps in the process introduced by sentence 3.

False choices

> Choice A provides specific support for the topic sentence.
> Choice C does not support any sentence in the paragraph.
> Choice D provides specific support for sentence 11.

6. Answer   C

Sentence 8 describes where the contaminated water comes from, supporting sentence 7, which explains that incoming tide brings feces-contaminated water to the beaches.

False choices

> Choice A makes a general statement, not a specific supporting statement for sentence 7.
> Choice B talks about oil pollution and does not support sentence 7.
> Choice D describes debris carried in by tides, such as plastic and fishing lines. It does not talk about human or animal waste products.

7. Answer   A

Sentence 3 explains that the number of Latinos is higher than the number tallied by the census taken in 2000 because of those who come to the U.S. illegally and avoid census forms. Sentence 5 supports sentence 3 by stating that about a million people enter illegally.

False choices

> Choice B does not support sentence 3. Sentence 7 provides an example of comparison to show how large the Latino population is.
> Choice C supports sentence 7.
> Choice D supports sentence 8.

SECTION 2 ◆ EXERCISES: SUPPORTING DETAILS

PASSAGE #1

Read the passage and answer the question that follows.

¹_____.

²First of all, because e-mail messages are informal and quick, writers may be sloppy in trans-ferring their thoughts to the screen. ³Misspellings and ungrammatical sentences can project a negative image if users do not take time to edit what they write on e-mail. ⁴Second, the mes-sages are sent and read online, often leaving no paper trail at all. ⁵As a result, some important messages are forgotten or lost. ⁶It is easy to read your electronic mail and delete it instead of printing out a copy of the message to keep in a file or filing the message electronically in your e-mail file folder. ⁷Although generally thought of as a quick method of communication, e-mail's efficiency is only as good as the recipient's care in routinely checking e-mail messages. ⁸Electronic communication can be slow if people don't check their messages. ⁹Moreover, you have no privacy. ¹⁰Another disadvantage is the increasing use of e-mail as a replacement for the personal contact of a phone call or face-to-face meeting. ¹¹The 1986 Electronic Commu-nications Privacy Act considers e-mail to be the property of the company paying for the mail system. ¹²_____, writing on a computer screen often encourages people to drop inhibi-tions and write things in e-mail that they would never write in a paper letter or say over the telephone. (Adapted from Kristin R. Woolever, *Writing for the Technical Professions*, 2nd ed., New York: Longman, 2002.)

1. Which of the numbered sentences is not supported by sufficient specific details?
   A. 9
   B. 4
   C. 2
   D. 7

PASSAGE #2

Read the passage and answer the question that follows.

¹_____.

²Although women have served in every branch of the armed services since World War II, two differences between the treatment of men and women in the military persist. ³First, only men must register for the draft when they turn eighteen. ⁴In 1981, the Supreme Court ruled that male-only registration for the military did not violate the Fifth Amendment. ⁵Second, statutes and regulations also prohibit women from serving in combat. ⁶A breach exists between policy and practice, however, as the Persian Gulf War showed. ⁷Women piloted helicopters at the front and helped to operate antimissile systems; some were taken as prisoners of war. ⁸_____, women are not permitted to serve as combat pilots in the navy and air force and to serve on navy warships. ⁹They are still not permitted to serve in ground combat units in the army or marines. ¹⁰These actions have reopened the debate over whether women should serve in combat. ¹¹Others argue that men will not be able to fight effectively beside wounded or dying women. ¹²Critics of these views point out that some women surpass men in body strength

and that we do not know how well men and women will fight together. [13]Some experts insist that because women, on the average, have less body strength than men, they are less suited for combat. [14]This debate is not only a controversy about ability, but it also touches on the question of whether engaging in combat is a burden or a privilege. (Adapted from George C. Edwards, Martin P. Wattenberg, and Robert L. Lineberry, *Government in America*, 9th ed., New York: Longman, 2000.)

2. Which of the numbered sentences is not supported by sufficient specific details?
   A. 10
   B. 14
   C. 6
   D. 2

PASSAGE #3

Read the passage and answer the question that follows.

[1]_____.
[2]Jaime Escalante taught calculus in an East Los Angeles inner-city school that was plagued with poverty, crime, drugs, and gangs. [3]As a result of his methods, his students earned the highest Advanced Placement scores in the city. [4]_____, Escalante had to open his students' minds to the possibility of success in learning. [5]Most Latino students were tracked into craft classes where they made jewelry and birdhouses. [6]Escalante felt that his students were talented and needed an opportunity to show it. [7]Also, the students needed to see learning as a way out of the barrio, as a path to good jobs. [8]By arranging for foundations to provide money for students to attend colleges of their choice, Escalante showed students that if they did well, their poverty would not stop them. [9]When Escalante first came to the United States, he worked as a busboy and attended Pasadena Community College. [10]Escalante also changed the system of instruction. [11]Before class, his students did "warm-ups," hand clapping and foot stomping to a rock song. [12]To foster team identity, students wore team jackets, caps, and T-shirts with logos that identified them as part of the math team. [13]He had his students think of themselves as a team, of him as the coach, and the national math exams as a sort of Olympics for which they were preparing. [14]Escalante thought it was important to teach his classes in English, not Spanish. [15]Escalante demonstrated that a teacher can motivate students to believe in their ability to achieve at high levels, no matter how great their problems. (Adapted from James M. Henslin, *Sociology*, 6th ed., Boston: Allyn and Bacon, 2003.)

3. Which sentence provides specific support for sentence 10 in the passage?
   A. As a result of his methods, his students earned the highest Advanced Placement scores in the city. (sentence 3)
   B. Escalante felt that his students were talented and needed an opportunity to show it. (sentence 6)
   C. Most Latino students were tracked into craft classes where they made jewelry and birdhouses. (sentence 5)
   D. Before class, his students did "warm-ups," hand clapping and foot stomping to a rock song. (sentence 11)

PASSAGE #4

Read the passage and answer the question that follows.

¹_____.
²Anorexia nervosa literally means loss of appetite, but this is a misnomer. ³The anorexic individual approaches weight loss with a fervor, convinced that her body is too large. ⁴A person with anorexia nervosa is hungry, but he or she denies the hunger because of an irrational fear of becoming fat. ⁵Therefore, the first characteristic is a significant weight loss due to a relentless drive for thinness. ⁶She is unable to recognize that her appearance is abnormal. ⁷She will insist that her emaciated figure is just right or is too fat. ⁸There is a strong argument that eating disorders are a form of addiction. ⁹This condition is more than a simple eating disorder. ¹⁰_____, anorexia is a distinct psychological disorder with a wide range of psychological disturbances. ¹¹Anorexics are typically compulsive, perfectionistic, and very competitive. ¹²Food preoccupation and rituals and compulsive exercising are other characteristics. ¹³The anorexic sometimes suffers from low self-image due to a feeling of incompetence, so she becomes consumed with losing weight to demonstrate to herself and others that she is in total control. ¹⁴Additional features of the disease develop from the effects of starvation over time. ¹⁵Untreated anorexia can be fatal. ¹⁶Causes of death include starvation, infections due to poor nutrition, irregular heartbeat due to potassium deficiency, and suicide due to depression. (Adapted from David J. Anspaugh and Gene Ezell, *Teaching Today's Health*, 7th ed., San Francisco: Pearson, 2004.)

4. Which sentence provides specific support for sentence 9 in the passage?
   A. A person with anorexia nervosa is hungry, but he or she denies the hunger because of an irrational fear of becoming fat. (sentence 4)
   B. Anorexia nervosa literally means loss of appetite, but this is a misnomer. (sentence 2)
   C. _____, anorexia is a distinct psychological disorder with a wide range of psychological disturbances. (sentence 10)
   D. Therefore, the first characteristic is a significant weight loss due to a relentless drive for thinness. (sentence 5)

PASSAGE #5

Read the passage and answer the question that follows.

¹_____.
²Bare-knuckle boxing, the forerunner of modern boxing, was a brutal, bloody sport. ³Two men fought bare-fisted until one could not continue. ⁴A round lasted until one of the men knocked or threw down his opponent. ⁵At that point, both men rested for thirty seconds and then started to fight again. ⁶Fights often lasted over one hundred rounds and as long as seven or eight hours. ⁷After such a fight, it took months for the fighters to recover. ⁸During the 1800s, boxing underwent a series of reforms. ⁹There have been periodic efforts to outlaw the sport. ¹⁰The challenge system was replaced by modern promotional techniques. ¹¹Fighters deserted bare-fisted combat and started wearing gloves. ¹²Most importantly, professional boxers adopted the Marquis of Queensberry Rules, which standardized a round at three minutes, allowing a one-minute rest period between rounds, and outlawed all wrestling throws and holds. ¹³_____, the fight to the finish was replaced with a fight to a decision over a specified number of rounds. ¹⁴A bell and a referee told fighters when to fight and when to rest. ¹⁵Cur-

rently there are eight major professional divisions. [16]Although the new rules did not reduce the violence, they did provide for more orderly bouts. (Adapted from James Kirby Martin et al., *America and Its Peoples*, 5th ed., New York: Longman, 2003.)

5. Which of the numbered sentences is not supported by sufficient specific details?
   A. 8
   B. 2
   C. 9
   D. 12

PASSAGE #6

Read the passage and answer the question that follows.

[1] _____.

[2]For example, with eye movements you can seek feedback. [3]In talking with someone, you look at her or him intently, as if to say, "Well, what do you think?" [4]Your pupils enlarge when you are interested or emotionally aroused. [5]You can also inform the other person that the channel of communication is open and that he or she should now speak. [6]You see this in the college classroom, when the instructor asks a question and then locks eyes with a student. [7]Without saying anything, the instructor expects that student to answer the question and the student knows it.[8]Eye movements may also signal the nature of a relationship, whether positive (an attentive glance) or negative (eye avoidance). [9]_____, you can signal your power through visual dominance behavior. [10]The average speaker, for example, maintains a high level of eye contact while listening and a lower level while speaking. [11]When people want to signal dominance, they may reverse this pattern: maintaining a high level of eye contact while talking but a lower level while listening. [12]Eye contact can also change the psychological distance between yourself and another person. [13]When you catch someone's eye at a party, for example, you become psychologically close even though far apart. [14]By avoiding eye contact—even when physically close as in a crowded elevator—you increase the psychological distance between you. (Adapted from Joseph A. DeVito, *Essentials of Human Communication*, 3rd ed., New York: Longman, 1999.)

6. Which of the numbered sentences is not supported by sufficient specific details?
   A. 12
   B. 6
   C. 8
   D. 2

PASSAGE #7

Read the passage and answer the question that follows.

[1] _____.

[2]It even drinks seawater, which is much saltier than its body fluids. [3]Few animals can tolerate such salty liquid because the salt draws water out of their tissues, and they become severely dehydrated. [4]An albatross can thrive on salt water because it has special salt-excreting glands in its nostrils. [5]The glands dispose of excess salts, allowing the bird to eat salty fish and squid and drink all it needs without ever visiting land. [6]Their scientific name, *Diomedea exulans*, means exiled warrior in Greek. [7]_____ its remarkable salt tolerance, the wandering albatross has extraordinary flight abilities specially suited to its seafaring life. [8]Its wingspan is

greater than that of any other bird—about 3.6 meters (nearly twelve feet). [9]Most birds have to flap their wings to stay up in the air very long, but the albatross's long wings provide so much lift that the bird can stay aloft for hours by gliding up and down on wind currents. [10]The wandering albatross spends most of its time in an area of high winds and rough seas, far from land, often alone on the open ocean. [11]The winds carry it from west to east, and in a year's time, an albatross may circle the globe, seeing little land except New Zealand and the tip of South America. (Adapted from Neil A. Campbell, Lawrence G. Mitchell, and Jane B. Reece, *Biology*, 3rd ed., San Francisco: Benjamin Cummings, 2000.)

7. Which sentence provides specific support for sentence 4 in the passage?
   A. It even drinks seawater, which is much saltier than its body fluids. (sentence 2)
   B. The glands dispose of excess salts, allowing the bird to eat salty fish and squid and drink all it needs without ever visiting land. (sentence 5)
   C. Few animals can tolerate such salty liquid because the salt draws water out of their tissues, and they become severely dehydrated. (sentence 3)
   D. The wandering albatross spends most of its time in an area of high winds and rough seas, far from land, often alone on the open ocean. (sentence 10)

PASSAGE #8

Read the passage and answer the question that follows.

[1]_____.

[2]Testosterone is a male hormone that causes a general buildup in muscle and bone mass during puberty in males and maintains masculine traits throughout life. [3]Anabolic steroids are synthetic variants of the male hormone testosterone. [4]Pharmaceutical companies first produced and marketed anabolic steroids in the early 1950s as a treatment for certain diseases that destroy body muscle. [5]About a decade later, some athletes began using anabolic steroids to build up their muscles quickly and enhance their performance with less hard work. [6]It is not surprising that some of the heaviest users are weight lifters, football players, and body builders. [7]Today, anabolic steroids, along with other drugs, are banned by most athletic organizations. [8]Black market sales bring in up to $400 million a year. [9]Medical research indicates that these substances can cause serious physical and mental problems. [10]Overdosing in males can cause acne, baldness, and breast development. [11]Mental effects can range from mood swings to deep depression. [12]Internally, there may be liver damage leading to cancer. [13]_____, anabolic steroids can make blood cholesterol levels rise, perhaps increasing a user's chances of developing serious cardiovascular problems. [14]Heavy users may also experience a reduced sex drive and become infertile because anabolic steroids often make the body reduce its normal output of sex hormones. (Adapted from Neil A. Campbell, Lawrence G. Mitchell, and Jane B. Reece, *Biology*, 3rd ed., San Francisco: Benjamin Cummings, 2000.)

8. Which sentence provides specific support for sentence 9 in the passage?
   A. _____, anabolic steroids can make blood cholesterol levels rise, perhaps increasing a user's chances of developing serious cardiovascular problems. (sentence 13)
   B. Today, anabolic steroids, along with other drugs, are banned by most athletic organizations. (sentence 7)
   C. It is not surprising that some of the heaviest users are weight lifters, football players, and body builders. (sentence 6)
   D. Anabolic steroids are synthetic variants of the male hormone testosterone. (sentence 3)

PASSAGE #9

Read the passage and answer the question that follows.

1 _____.

2In most cases, the child continually learns from the parent. 3In the area of computer and Internet-mediated communication, however, the child may be able to teach the parent. 4_____, one five-year-old learned a graphics program before she could read. 5The child taught herself how to operate the rather intuitive program. 6Not only did the computer provide the child with a valuable learning process, but the parents totally depended on the child when they wanted to use the program she knew. 7In another case, a young boy taught his parents how to use PowerPoint. 8The examples are endless. 9Children are more apt to interact with the computer as if it were alive. 10A child may be able to understand a concept differently from the parent, and the role reversal of the child-as-teacher can be an important way the computer and the Internet can enhance a child's self-esteem. 11The child and parent alike may feel positive toward themselves when they are able to learn new things, master a program, or win an Internet game. 12Their self-confidence may increase when others seek their advice, for example, because they are the family computer experts. (Adapted from Leonard J. Shedletsky and Joan E. Aitken, *Human Communication on the Internet*, Boston: Allyn and Bacon, 2004.)

9. Which of the numbered sentences is not supported by specific details?
    A. 3
    B. 4
    C. 5
    D. 9

PASSAGE #10

Read the passage and answer the question that follows.

1 _____.

2Highlighting is a strategy for condensing textbook material and emphasizing what is important. 3_____, the process of highlighting forces you to sift through what you have read to identify important information. 4This sifting or sorting is an active thought process; you are forced to weigh and evaluate what you read. 5One mistake to avoid is highlighting almost every idea on a page. 6Another benefit of highlighting is that it keeps you physically active while you are reading. 7In addition, highlighting can help you discover the organization of facts and ideas as well as their connections and relationships. 8Highlighting demonstrates to you whether you have understood a passage you have just read. 9When combined with annotation, highlighting is a quick and easy way to review so that you do not have to reread everything when studying for an exam. 10If you highlight 20 percent of a chapter, you will be able to avoid rereading 80 percent of the material. 11If it normally takes two hours to read a chapter, you should be able to review a highlighted chapter in less than a half hour. 12Highlighting has many benefits, but it is not by itself a sufficient study method; you must process the information by organizing it, expressing it in your own words, and testing yourself periodically. (Adapted from Kathleen T. McWhorter, *Study and Critical Thinking Skills in College*, 5th ed., New York: Longman, 2003.)

10. Which sentence provides specific support for sentence 3 in the passage?
   A. If you highlight 20 percent of a chapter, you will be able to avoid rereading 80 percent of the material. (sentence 10)
   B. This sifting or sorting is an active thought process; you are forced to weigh and evaluate what you read. (sentence 4)
   C. Highlighting is a strategy for condensing textbook material and emphasizing what is important. (sentence 2)
   D. One mistake to avoid is highlighting almost every idea on a page. (sentence 5)

SECTION 3 ◆ LOGICAL PATTERNS	
Skill Tested	Arranges ideas and supporting details in a logical pattern

The Skill

This item tests your ability to arrange ideas and supporting details in a logical pattern. A well-organized piece of writing is easy to read and understand because it follows a plan or pattern of organization. When writing does not follow a pattern of organization, the ideas do not seem to fit together, so the piece is difficult to read and understand. Your ability to recognize plans of organization will help you discover the correct answer to the test questions on this skill.

You may have learned patterns of organization for writing paragraphs or essays in your English class. Two characteristics of good organization are the order in which the details are presented and the use of patterns of development. Sometimes order and method overlap or are combined in a piece of writing.

Order

Order refers to the method used to organize the supporting material. Three commonly used methods are time order, spatial order, and order of importance.

Time Order	Details are listed as they happen in time
Spatial Order	Details are organized according to their physical positions
Order of Importance	Details are written from least important to most important, simplest to most difficult, or most familiar to least familiar

Patterns

Patterns are plans of development. Some essays follow one pattern throughout while others use several patterns to develop individual paragraphs within the essay.

Pattern	Supporting Details
Description	Creates a word picture of a person, place, thing, or emotion through the use of sensory words (sight, touch, taste, smell, sound)
Narration	Tells a story
Illustration	Uses specific examples to support or present a main idea
Process	Tells how to do something or how something is done by breaking the process into steps or stages

Cause and Effect	Explains reasons (cause) or results (effect) of a particular situation or event
Comparison/Contrast	Shows how people, places, things, events, or ideas are similar (comparison) or how they are different (contrast)
Classification	Analyzes a subject according to a single organizing principle, breaking the subject into categories or types
Definition	Gives the meaning of a word in a variety of ways, including its formal definition and extending the meaning by using other patterns of development
Argument/Persuasion	Makes a clear statement of the author's position and supports that position with details that convince or persuade the reader that the position is correct and possibly to take action

Once you are familiar with these organizational patterns you will be better able to identify the pattern and use the best arrangement of ideas. Always check the topic sentence or thesis statement. This sentence will often give you a clue about the overall pattern of the passage and the order in which the major details should be listed. For example, if you have selected "Attending community college was the best decision I have ever made because of the excellent teachers, the convenient location, and the affordable cost" as your thesis statement, you would expect that the logical arrangement of the major details would start with the excellent teachers, continue with the convenient location, and end with the affordable cost.

Transition words can also help you determine the pattern. A detailed list of these can be found in chapter 1, section 5. If you were asked to arrange three sentences into a logical order, it would make sense to check these three sentences and the sentence that preceded them for transitions. Take the following for example:

(1) Good readers prepare to read by using one of the two previewing methods before they settle down to their serious reading. (2) **The first** is to scan the whole chapter to get an understanding of the topic and the aspects covered in the reading. (3) **The second** is to survey specific parts of the chapter or article to find out information about topics covered in the reading. (4) **After** completing either of these previews, you should take a minute to think about your prior knowledge of the subject in order to pull the knowledge from your memory.

You can check to see if sentences 2, 3, and 4 are in the correct order by first noticing the preceding sentence, in this case, sentence 1. This sentence prepares us for two methods. Sentence 2 starts with the first of the two methods mentioned earlier, so this is correct. Next, note any transition words. Sentences 2, 3, and 4 use the transition words *first*, *second*, and *after* in the correct order. Therefore, this is the correct arrangement of the sentences.

The Test Question

You will be tested on your ability to recognize adequate supporting details in one of two ways:

1. You will be given a passage to read and asked to select the most logical arrangement or sequence of several sentences. Each choice will contain the same sentences, but they will be arranged in a different order. You need to decide which set expresses the idea most logically.
2. You will be given a short passage and asked to figure out the most logical placement of an additional sentence.

▶▶▌ *Secrets to Success*

- *Identify the topic and main idea of the passage.*
- *Learn the transitional phrases associated with each pattern.*
- *If you must arrange sentences in the proper order, be sure to look at the sentences that come before and after those sentences in the text for clues.*
- *Be aware that not all sentences have transitional phrases. For this reason, always ask,* What is the relationship between the sentences?

SECTION 3 ◆ DIAGNOSTIC: LOGICAL PATTERNS

Read the passages and apply the strategies described above for finding logical patterns. When you are done, check your work with the answers immediately following the diagnostic. Even if you get a perfect score here, go ahead and complete the exercises in this section; they are designed to help build confidence and to give you practice for future test success.

PASSAGE #1

Read the passage and answer the question that follows.

1 _____.

[2]Some instructors, for example, have a teaching style that promotes social interaction among students. [3]An instructor may organize small group activities, encourage class participation, or require students to work in pairs or teams to complete a specific task. [4]A lecture class is an example. [5]Other instructors offer little or no opportunity for social interaction. [6]Some instructors are very applied; they teach by example. [7]Others are more conceptual; they focus on presenting ideas, rules, theories, and so forth. [8]To an extent, of course, the subject matter also dictates how the instructor teaches. [9]_____ a biology instructor has a large body of factual information to present and may feel he or she has little time to schedule group interaction. [10]Some instructors' teaching styles are boring. [11]Once you are aware of your learning style and then consider the instructor's teaching style, you can begin to understand why you can learn better from one instructor than another and why you feel more comfortable in certain instructors' classes than others. (Adapted from Kathleen McWhorter, *Study and Critical Thinking Skills in College*, 5th ed., New York: Longman, 2003.)

1. Select the arrangement of sentences 3, 4, and 5 that provides the most logical sequence of ideas and supporting details in the paragraph. If no change is needed, select option A.
   A. An instructor may organize small group activities, encourage class participation, or require students to work in pairs or teams to complete a specific task. A lecture class is an example. Other instructors offer little or no opportunity for social interaction.
   B. An instructor may organize small group activities, encourage class participation, or require students to work in pairs or teams to complete a specific task. Other instructors offer little or no opportunity for social interaction. A lecture class is an example.
   C. Other instructors offer little or no opportunity for social interaction. An instructor may organize small group activities, encourage class participation, or require students to work in pairs or teams to complete a specific task. A lecture class is an example.

D. A lecture class is an example. An instructor may organize small groups, encourage class participation, or require students to work in pairs or teams to complete a specific task. Other instructors offer little or no opportunity for social interaction.

PASSAGE #2

Read the passage and answer the question that follows.

1 _____.

[2]As early as the 1920s, psychologists attempted to teach language to chimpanzees to find out whether they could communicate. [3]Chimps don't have the appropriate vocal apparatus to produce spoken language, so researchers had to devise other methods of communication. [4]For instance, a chimp named Washoe was taught a highly simplified version of American Sign Language. [5]In addition, a chimp named Sarah was taught to manipulate symbols on a magnetic board. [6]Skeptics wondered if the chimps' combination of gestures and symbols constituted any kind of meaningful language. [7]Recent research has provided more solid insights into the language capabilities of chimps. [8]Bonobos and chimps can be raised together. [9]Sue Savage-Rumbaugh and her team work primarily with *bonobos*, a species of great ape that is evolutionarily nearer to humans than even the common chimpanzees. [10]Remarkably, two of the bonobos in her studies, Kanzi and Mulika, learned the meanings of plastic symbols at the same time. [11]They did not receive direct training; rather, they acquired the symbols by watching humans and other bonobos. [12]_____ Kanzi and Mulika can understand some spoken English. [13]For example, when Kanzi hears a spoken word, he is able to locate either the symbol for the word or a picture of the object. (Adapted from Richard J. Gerrig and Philip G. Zimbardo, *Psychology and Life*, 16th ed., Boston: Allyn and Bacon, 2002.)

2. Select the arrangement of sentences 9, 10, and 11 that provides the most logical sequence of ideas and supporting details in the paragraph. If no change is needed, select option A.
   A. Sue Savage-Rumbaugh and her team work primarily with *bonobos*, a species of great ape that is evolutionarily nearer to humans than even the common chimpanzees. Remarkably, two of the bonobos in her studies, Kanzi and Mulika, learned the meanings of plastic symbols at the same time. They did not receive direct training; rather, they acquired the symbols by watching humans and other bonobos.
   B. Remarkably, two of the bonobos in her studies, Kanzi and Mulika, learned the meanings of plastic symbols at the same time. They did not receive direct training; rather they acquired the symbols by watching humans and other bonobos. Sue Savage-Rumbaugh and her team work primarily with *bonobos*, a species of great ape that is evolutionarily nearer to humans than even the common chimpanzees.
   C. They did not receive direct training; rather they acquired the symbols by watching humans and other bonobos. Remarkably, two of the bonobos in her studies, Kanzi and Mulika, learned the meanings of the plastic symbols at the same time. Sue Savage-Rumbaugh and her team work primarily with *bonobos*, a species of great ape that is evolutionarily nearer to humans than even common chimpanzees.
   D. Sue Savage-Rumbaugh and her team work primarily with *bonobos*, a species of great ape that is evolutionarily nearer to humans than even common chimpanzees. They did not receive direct training; rather they acquired the symbols by watching humans and other bonobos. Remarkably, two of the bonobos in her studies, Kanzi and Mulika, learned the meanings of the plastic symbols at the same time.

PASSAGE #3

Read the passage and answer the question that follows.

1
_____.

²The relationship between temperature and assault is actually strongest in the late evening and early morning hours, from 9 p.m. to 3 a.m. ³One explanation is that people are more likely to commit assault when they are out and about. ⁴That is, in warmer weather, people are usually outdoors more and, therefore, are also more "available" as assault victims. ⁵In the 9 p.m. to 3 a.m. hours, people are typically not working or bound by other responsibilities. ⁶The time of day is another factor. ⁷Furthermore, by the late evening hours, people may have been drinking alcohol or using other substances that lower their inhibition to aggression. ⁸Substance abuse is a big problem in our society. ⁹Another part of the explanation is the way in which people cope with and interpret the discomfort associated with high temperatures. ¹⁰As the day goes on, it may be harder to remember, "I'm feeling this way because it's hot" and just conclude, "I'm feeling this way because this person is making me crazy." ¹¹_____, assaults decline when temperatures become very hot. ¹²Researchers have speculated that at very high temperatures, people might experience sufficient discomfort to withdraw from abrasive situations rather than stay and fight. (Adapted from Richard J. Gerrig and Philip G. Zimbardo, *Psychology and Life*, 16th ed., Boston: Allyn and Bacon, 2002.)

3. Select the arrangement of sentences 5, 6, and 7 that provides the most logical sequence of ideas and supporting details in the paragraph. If no change is needed, select option A.
   A. In the 9 p.m. to 3 a.m. hours, people are typically not working or bound by other responsibilities. The time of day is another factor. Furthermore, by the late evening hours, people may have been drinking alcohol or using other substances that lower their inhibition to aggression.
   B. Furthermore, by the late evening hours, people may have been drinking alcohol or using other substances that lower their inhibition to aggression. The time of day is another factor. In the 9 p.m. to 3 a.m. hours, people are typically not working or bound by other responsibilities.
   C. In the 9 p.m. to 3 a.m. hours, people are typically not working or bound by other responsibilities. Furthermore, by the late evening hours, people may have been drinking alcohol or using other substances that lower their inhibition to aggression. The time of day is another factor.
   D. The time of day is another factor. In the 9 p.m. to 3 a.m. hours, people are typically not working or bound by other responsibilities. Furthermore, by the late evening hours, people may have been drinking alcohol or using other substances that lower their inhibition to aggression.

PASSAGE #4

Read the passage and answer the question that follows.

1
_____.

²The Hare Indians of Colville Lake are a small group of Canadian Inuit. ³Savishinsky lived with the Hare Indians to study them. ⁴They survive by hunting, trapping, and fishing in one of the harshest environments in the world. ⁵_____, dogs are economically useful. ⁶Dog teams give the Inuit a means for travel during the harshest seasons of the year. ⁷The tempera-

tures are extremely cold, and the winters are long and severe. [8]Finding food can be difficult. [9]The Inuit estimate that six dogs are required for travel, and some households have as many as four dog teams, with an average of 6.2 dogs per team. [10]The dogs are a frequent topic of conversation. [11]More than being only economically useful, dogs play a significant role in people's emotional lives. [12]Members of the community constantly compare and comment on the care, condition, and growth of one another's animals. [13]They note special qualities of size, strength, color, speed, and alertness. [14]Emotional displays, uncommon among the Hare, are significant between people and their dogs. [15]All people participate in the affectionate and concerned treatment of young dogs. (Adapted from Barbara D. Miller, *Cultural Anthropology*, 2nd ed., Boston: Allyn and Bacon, 2002.)

4. Select the arrangement of sentences 10, 11, and 12 that provides the most logical sequence of ideas and supporting details in the paragraph. If no change is needed, select option A.
    A. The dogs are a frequent topic of conversation. More than being only economically useful, dogs play a significant role in people's emotional lives. Members of the community constantly compare and comment on the care, condition, and growth of one another's animals.
    B. Members of the community constantly compare and comment on the care, condition, and growth of one another's animals. More than being only economically useful, dogs play a significant role in people's emotional lives. The dogs are a frequent topic of conversation.
    C. More than being only economically useful, dogs play a significant role in people's emotional lives. The dogs are a frequent topic of conversation. Members of the community constantly compare and comment on the care, condition, and growth of one another's animals.
    D. Members of the community constantly compare and comment on the care, condition, and growth of one another's animals. The dogs are a frequent topic of conversation. More than being only economically useful, dogs play a significant role in people's emotional lives.

PASSAGE #5

Read the passage and answer the question that follows.

[1] _____.

[2]The robin searches for food by selecting only those items that provide the greatest energy return for the energy expended. [3]This can be illustrated by the robin's behavior, which has four parts. [4]First, the robin has to decide where to hunt for food. [5]Once on the lawn, it has to search for food items. [6]Because the robin forages on lawns, it is vulnerable to pesticide poisoning. [7]Having located some potential food, the robin has to decide whether to pursue it. [8]If it begins pursuit by pecking, the robin has to attempt a capture, in which it might or might not be successful. [9]If a food item is too large, it requires too much time to handle; if it is too small, it does not deliver enough energy to cover the costs of capture. [10]The robin should reject or ignore less valuable items, such as small beetles and caterpillars, and give preference to small and medium-sized earthworms. [11]_____ by capturing an earthworm, the robin earns some units of energy. [12]These more valuable food items would be classified as preferred food. [13]If the robin fails to find suitable and sufficient food in the area of the lawn it is searching, it leaves to search elsewhere. [14]If successful, the bird probably will return until the spot is no longer an economical place to feed. (Adapted from Robert Leo Smith and Thomas M. Smith, *Elements of Ecology*, 5th ed., San Francisco: Benjamin Cummings, 2003.)

5. Which is the best placement for the sentence below to make the sequence of ideas in the paragraph clear?

   It stands stock-still with its head cocked to one side as though listening for its prey but actually discovering it by sight.

   A. Immediately after sentence 5
   B. Immediately after sentence 9
   C. Immediately before sentence 12
   D. Immediately after sentence 12

PASSAGE #6

Read the passage and answer the question that follows.

¹_____.

²Beach-nesting birds such as the piping plover and the least tern are so disturbed by bathers and dune buggies that both species are in danger of extinction. ³Other terns and shore birds are subjected to competition for nest sites and to egg predators by rapidly growing populations of large gulls. ⁴These gulls are highly tolerant of humans and thrive on human garbage. ⁵Sea turtles and the horseshoe crab, dependent on sandy beaches for nesting sites, find themselves evicted. ⁶_____, they are declining rapidly. ⁷Furthermore, each incoming tide brings onto the beaches feces-contaminated water that makes them unhealthy for humans and wildlife alike. ⁸This contaminated water comes from a number of different sources, such as sewer overflows, failing private and commercial septic systems, animal and wildlife waste, and swimmers' illnesses. ⁹The oceans have become dumping grounds. ¹⁰Major chronic pollutants are oil that is released from tanker accidents, seepage from offshore drilling and other sources, toxic materials such as pesticides and heavy metals from industrial, urban, and agricultural sources. ¹¹The most devastating human activity in reefs is overfishing, especially in the Philippines and the Caribbean. ¹²Tides also carry in old fishing lines, plastic debris, and other wastes hazardous to wildlife. (Adapted from Robert Leo Smith and Thomas M. Smith, *Elements of Ecology*, 5th ed., San Francisco: Benjamin Cummings, 2003.)

6. Which is the best placement for the sentence below to make the sequence of ideas in the paragraph clear?

   Increase in the development of coastal housing such as condominiums destroy the sea turtles' nesting habitat, and the lights from these homes disorient the turtle hatchlings so that many do not make it safely to the ocean.

   A. Immediately after sentence 3
   B. Immediately before sentence 6
   C. Immediately before sentence 9
   D. Immediately after sentence 12

PASSAGE #7

Read the passage and answer the question that follows.

¹_____.

²About 21 million people trace their origin to Mexico, 3 million to Puerto Rico, 1 million to Cuba, and almost 5 million to Central or South America, primarily Venezuela or Colombia.

[3]Officially tallied at 35 million in the year 2000 census, the actual number of Latinos is higher because, not surprisingly, many who are in the country illegally avoid contact with both public officials and census forms. [4]Each year, more than 1 million people are apprehended at the border or at points inland and are deported to Mexico. [5]Perhaps another million or so manage to enter the United States. [6]_____ many migrate for temporary work and then return to their homes and families. [7]To gain an understanding of how vast these numbers are, we can note that there are millions more Latinos in the United States than there are Canadians in Canada (31 million). [8]To Midwesterners, such a comparison often comes as a surprise, for Latinos are absent from vast stretches of mid-America. [9]Sixty-nine percent are concentrated in just four states: California, Texas, New York, and Florida. [10]In the next twenty-five years, changes in the U.S. racial-ethnic mix will be dramatic. (Adapted from James M. Henslin, *Sociology*, 6th ed., Boston: Allyn and Bacon, 2003.)

7. Which is the best placement for the sentence below to make the sequence of ideas in the paragraph clear?

Latinos are the largest minority group in several major cities, including Los Angeles, San Antonio, Miami, and Houston.

A. Immediately after sentence 2
B. Immediately before sentence 6
C. Immediately before sentence 8
D. Immediately after sentence 9

Answers and Explanations to Diagnostic: Logical Patterns
Some of the questions in this section ask you to select the arrangement of sentences that provides the most logical sequence of ideas and supporting details in the passage. For those questions, only the correct answer is explained. All other options do not provide a logical sequence of ideas.

1. Answer   B
The first sentence in the sequence supports sentence 2. This first sentence provides an example of ways in which an instructor may promote social interaction among students. The next sentence explains another teaching style, which offers little opportunity for social interaction. The last sentence gives the lecture class as an example of the teaching style that does not offer social interaction.

2. Answer   A
This series of sentences gives an example of how recent research has provided insights into language capabilities of chimps. The first sentence explains that Savage-Rumbaugh and her team worked with bonobos; this species is closer to humans than common chimpanzees. The next sentence gives the example of two bonobos who learned meanings of plastic symbols at the same time. The last sentence emphasizes that these two bonobos learned the meanings of the plastic symbols without direct instruction, further supporting the fact that these animals do have language capabilities as proved by the research.

3. Answer   D
These three sentences provide support and explanation for the time of day as a factor contributing to assault. The first sentence makes the point that the time of day is another factor. The next sentence explains that people are usually not bound by work or other responsibilities between 9 p.m. and 3

a.m. Finally, the last sentence supports the one before it by suggesting that some people are more likely to be drinking or using other substances during those hours.

4. Answer   C

This group of sentences begins by making the point that dogs play an important part in the emotional lives of the Hare Indians. The next sentence provides support by explaining that people talk about their dogs. This is elaborated on in the sentence that follows; people in the community compare their dogs and comment on the dogs' condition and growth.

5. Answer   A

This sentence, which describes the way the robin looks for prey, should follow sentence 5. Sentence 5 tells the reader that the second step in the robin's quest for food is that it must search for food once on the lawn.

False choices

Choice B would place the sentence at a later point in the process, after the robin has captured its prey.
Choice C would place the sentence after the robin had caught an earthworm. Since the sentence refers to the robin's actions before catching prey, choice C would not be in the appropriate sequence.
Choice D also places the sentence out of sequence. Sentence 12 talks about the earthworm as preferred food, not the hunting process.

6. Answer   B

Sentence 5 tells the reader that the sea turtles find themselves evicted from their nesting sites on the beach. The suggested sentence further develops this idea by explaining that coastal housing has destroyed the turtles' habitat and that the lights from these homes confuse the baby turtles who, as a result, may not make it to the ocean.

False choices

Choice A would place the sentence about sea turtles after the statement about sea birds, which compete for nest sites and are subjected to egg predators.
Choice C would place the sentence about sea turtles before the sentence that describes the ocean as a dumping ground, which does not correspond.
Choice D would place the sentence at the end of the passage after sentence 12, which gives examples of materials washed in by the tide. This does not make the sequence of ideas clear.

7. Answer   D

This sentence logically follows sentence 9, which offers the statistic that 69 percent of Latinos in the United States live in four states: California, Texas, New York, and Florida. The suggested sentence then lists the major cities in which Latinos are the largest minority groups.

False choices

Choice A places the sentence after sentence 2. Sentence 2 gives the numbers of Latinos who trace their origins to various countries. This has nothing to do with the suggested sentence.
Choice B places the suggested sentence before sentence 6. Sentence 6 suggests one way in which Latinos come to the U.S.—to work and then to return home. The two sentences do not support each other.
Choice C places the suggested sentence before sentence 8. Sentence 7 compares the number of Latinos in the U. S. to the number of Canadians in Canada. The suggested sentence does add information to make the sequence of ideas clearer.

SECTION 3 ◆ EXERCISES: LOGICAL PATTERNS

PASSAGE #1

Read the passage and answer the question that follows.

[1] _____.

[2]First of all, because e-mail messages are informal and quick, writers may be sloppy in transferring their thoughts to the screen. [3]Misspellings and ungrammatical sentences can project a negative image if users do not take time to edit what they write on e-mail. [4]Second, the messages are sent and read online, often leaving no paper trail at all. [5]As a result, some important messages are forgotten or lost. [6]It is easy to read your electronic mail and delete it instead of printing out a copy of the message to keep in a file or filing the message electronically in your e-mail file folder. [7]Although generally thought of as a quick method of communication, e-mail's efficiency is only as good as the recipient's care in routinely checking e-mail messages. [8]Electronic communication can be slow if people don't check their messages. [9]Moreover, you have no privacy. [10]Another disadvantage is the increasing use of e-mail as a replacement for the personal contact of a phone call or face-to-face meeting. [11]The 1986 Electronic Communications Privacy Act considers e-mail to be the property of the company paying for the mail system. [12]_____, writing on a computer screen often encourages people to drop inhibitions and write things in e-mail that they would never write in a paper letter or say over the telephone. (Adapted from Kristin R. Woolever, *Writing for the Technical Professions*, 2nd ed., New York: Longman, 2002.)

1. Select the arrangement of sentences 4, 5, and 6 that provides the most logical sequence of ideas and supporting details in the paragraph. If no change is needed, select option A.
   A. Second, the messages are sent and read online, often leaving no paper trail at all. As a result, some important messages are forgotten or lost. It is easy to read your electronic mail and delete it instead of printing out a copy of the message to keep in a file or filing the message electronically in your e-mail file folder.
   B. Second, the messages are sent and read online, often leaving no paper trail at all. It is easy to read your electronic mail and delete it instead of printing out a copy of the message to keep in a file or filing the message electronically in your e-mail file folder. As a result, some important messages are forgotten or lost.
   C. It is easy to read your electronic mail and delete it instead of printing out a copy of the message to keep in a file or filing the message electronically in your e-mail file folder. As a result, some important messages are forgotten or lost. Second, the messages are sent and read online, often leaving no paper trail at all.
   D. As a result, some important messages are forgotten or lost. Second, the messages are sent and read online, often leaving no paper trail at all. It is easy to read your electronic mail and delete it instead of printing out a copy of the message to keep in a file or filing the message electronically in your e-mail file folder.

PASSAGE #2

Read the passage and answer the question that follows.

[1] _____.

[2]Although women have served in every branch of the armed services since World War II, two differences between the treatment of men and women in the military persist. [3]First, only men

must register for the draft when they turn eighteen. [4]In 1981, the Supreme Court ruled that male-only registration for the military did not violate the Fifth Amendment. [5]Second, statutes and regulations also prohibit women from serving in combat. [6]A breach exists between policy and practice, however, as the Persian Gulf War showed. [7]Women piloted helicopters at the front and helped to operate antimissile systems; some were taken as prisoners of war. [8]_____, women are not permitted to serve as combat pilots in the navy and air force and to serve on navy warships. [9]They are still not permitted to serve in ground combat units in the army or marines. [10]These actions have reopened the debate over whether women should serve in combat. [11]Others argue that men will not be able to fight effectively beside wounded or dying women. [12]Critics of these views point out that some women surpass men in body strength and that we do not know how well men and women will fight together. [13]Some experts insist that because women, on the average, have less body strength than men, they are less suited for combat. [14]This debate is not only a controversy about ability, but it also touches on the question of whether engaging in combat is a burden or a privilege. (Adapted from George C. Edwards, Martin P. Wattenberg, and Robert L. Lineberry, *Government in America*, 9th ed., New York: Longman, 2000.)

2. Select the arrangement of sentences 11, 12, and 13 that provides the most logical sequence of ideas and supporting details in the paragraph. If no change is needed, select option A.
   A. Others argue that men will not be able to fight effectively beside wounded or dying women. Critics of these views point out that some women surpass men in body strength and that we do not know how well men and women will fight together. Some experts insist that because women, on the average, have less body strength than men, they are less suited for combat.
   B. Critics of these views point out that some women surpass men in body strength and that we do not know how well men and women will fight together. Some experts insist that because women, on the average, have less body strength than men, they are less suited for combat. Others argue that men will not be able to fight effectively beside wounded or dying women.
   C. Some experts insist that because women, on the average, have less body strength than men, they are less suited for combat. Others argue that men will not be able to fight effectively beside wounded or dying women. Critics of these views point out that some women surpass men in body strength and that we do not know how well men and women will fight together.
   D. Some experts insist that because women, on the average, have less body strength than men, they are less suited for combat. Critics of these views point out that some women surpass men in body strength and that we do not know how well men and women will fight together. Others argue that men will not be able to fight effectively beside wounded or dying women.

PASSAGE #3

Read the passage and answer the question that follows.

[1]_____.
[2]Jaime Escalante taught calculus in an East Los Angeles inner-city school that was plagued with poverty, crime, drugs, and gangs. [3]As a result of his methods, his students earned the highest Advanced Placement scores in the city. [4]_____, Escalante had to open his students' minds to the possibility of success in learning. [5]Most Latino students were tracked into craft classes where they made jewelry and birdhouses. [6]Escalante felt that his students were talented and needed an opportunity to show it. [7]Also, the students needed to see learning as a way out

of the barrio, as a path to good jobs. [8]By arranging for foundations to provide money for students to attend colleges of their choice, Escalante showed students that if they did well, their poverty would not stop them. [9]When Escalante first came to the United States, he worked as a busboy and attended Pasadena Community College. [10]Escalante also changed the system of instruction. [11]Before class, his students did "warm-ups," hand clapping and foot stomping to a rock song. [12]To foster team identity, students wore team jackets, caps, and T-shirts with logos that identified them as part of the math team. [13]He had his students think of themselves as a team, of him as the coach, and the national math exams as a sort of Olympics for which they were preparing. [14]Escalante thought it was important to teach his classes in English, not Spanish. [15]Escalante demonstrated that a teacher can motivate students to believe in their ability to achieve at high levels, no matter how great their problems. (Adapted from James M. Henslin, *Sociology*, 6th ed., Boston: Allyn and Bacon, 2003.)

3. Select the arrangement of sentences 11, 12, and 13 that provides the most logical sequence of ideas and supporting details in the paragraph. If no change is needed, select option A.
    A. Before class, his students did "warm-ups," hand clapping and foot stomping to a rock song. To foster team identity, students wore team jackets, caps, and T-shirts with logos that identified them as part of the math team. He had his students think of themselves as a team, of him as the coach, and the national math exams as a sort of Olympics for which they were preparing.
    B. He had his students think of themselves as a team, of him as the coach, and the national math exams as a sort of Olympics for which they were preparing. To foster team identity, students wore team jackets, caps, and T-shirts with logos that identified them as part of the math team. Before class, his students did "warm-ups," hand clapping and foot stomping to a rock song.
    C. To foster team identity, students wore team jackets, caps, and T-shirts with logos that identified them as part of the math team. Before class, his students did "warm-ups," hand clapping and foot stomping to a rock song. He had his students think of themselves as a team, of him as the coach, and the national math exams as a sort of Olympics for which they were preparing.
    D. He had his students think of themselves as a team, of him as the coach, and the national math exams as a sort of Olympics for which they were preparing. Before class, his students did "warm-ups," hand clapping and foot stomping to a rock song. To foster team identity, students wore team jackets, caps, and T-shirts with logos that identified them as part of the math team.

PASSAGE #4

Read the passage and answer the question that follows.

1 _____.

[2]Anorexia nervosa literally means loss of appetite, but this is a misnomer. [3]The anorexic individual approaches weight loss with a fervor, convinced that her body is too large. [4]A person with anorexia nervosa is hungry, but he or she denies the hunger because of an irrational fear of becoming fat. [5]Therefore, the first characteristic is a significant weight loss due to a relentless drive for thinness. [6]She is unable to recognize that her appearance is abnormal. [7]She will insist that her emaciated figure is just right or is too fat. [8]There is a strong argument that eating disorders are a form of addiction. [9]This condition is more than a simple eating disorder.

[10]_____, anorexia is a distinct psychological disorder with a wide range of psychological disturbances. [11]Anorexics are typically compulsive, perfectionistic, and very competitive. [12]Food preoccupation and rituals and compulsive exercising are other characteristics. [13]The anorexic sometimes suffers from low self-image due to a feeling of incompetence, so she becomes consumed with losing weight to demonstrate to herself and others that she is in total control. [14]Additional features of the disease develop from the effects of starvation over time. [15]Untreated anorexia can be fatal. [16]Causes of death include starvation, infections due to poor nutrition, irregular heartbeat due to potassium deficiency, and suicide due to depression. (Adapted from David J. Anspaugh and Gene Ezell, *Teaching Today's Health*, 7th ed., San Francisco: Pearson, 2004.)

4. Select the arrangement of sentences 3, 4, and 5 that provides the most logical sequence of ideas and supporting details in the paragraph. If no change is needed, select option A.
   A. The anorexic individual approaches weight loss with a fervor, convinced that her body is too large. A person with anorexia nervosa is hungry, but he or she denies the hunger because of an irrational fear of becoming fat. Therefore, the first characteristic is a significant weight loss due to a relentless drive for thinness.
   B. Therefore, the first characteristic is a significant weight loss due to a relentless drive for thinness. The anorexic individual approaches weight loss with a fervor, convinced that her body is too large. A person with anorexia nervosa is hungry, but he or she denies the hunger because of an irrational fear of becoming fat.
   C. A person with anorexia nervosa is hungry, but he or she denies the hunger because of an irrational fear of becoming fat. Therefore, the first characteristic is a significant weight loss due to a relentless drive for thinness. The anorexic individual approaches weight loss with a fervor, convinced that her body is too large.
   D. The anorexic individual approaches weight loss with a fervor, convinced that her body is too large. Therefore, the first characteristic is a significant weight loss due to a relentless drive for thinness. A person with anorexia nervosa is hungry, but he or she denies the hunger because of an irrational fear of becoming fat.

PASSAGE #5
Read the passage and answer the question that follows.

[1]_____.

[2]Bare-knuckle boxing, the forerunner of modern boxing, was a brutal, bloody sport. [3]Two men fought bare-fisted until one could not continue. [4]A round lasted until one of the men knocked or threw down his opponent. [5]At that point, both men rested for thirty seconds and then started to fight again. [6]Fights often lasted over one hundred rounds and as long as seven or eight hours. [7]After such a fight, it took months for the fighters to recover. [8]During the 1800s, boxing underwent a series of reforms. [9]There have been periodic efforts to outlaw the sport. [10]The challenge system was replaced by modern promotional techniques. [11]Fighters deserted bare-fisted combat and started wearing gloves. [12]Most importantly, professional boxers adopted the Marquis of Queensberry Rules, which standardized a round at three minutes, allowing a one-minute rest period between rounds, and outlawed all wrestling throws and holds. [13]_____, the fight to the finish was replaced with a fight to a decision over a specified number of rounds. [14]A bell and a referee told fighters when to fight and when to rest. [15]Currently there are eight major professional divisions. [16]Although the new rules did not reduce

the violence, they did provide for more orderly bouts. (Adapted from James Kirby Martin et al., *America and Its Peoples*, 5th ed., New York: Longman, 2003.)

5. Select the arrangement of sentences 3, 4, and 5 that provides the most logical sequence of ideas and supporting details in the paragraph. If no change is needed, select option A.
   A. Two men fought bare-fisted until one could not continue. A round lasted until one of the men knocked or threw down his opponent. At that point, both men rested for thirty seconds and then started to fight again.
   B. At that point, both men rested for thirty seconds and then started to fight again. Two men fought bare-fisted until one could not continue. A round lasted until one of the men knocked or threw down his opponent.
   C. A round lasted until one of the men knocked or threw down his opponent. At that point, both men rested for thirty seconds and then started to fight again. Two men fought bare-fisted until one could not continue.
   D. A round lasted until one of the men knocked or threw down his opponent. Two men fought bare-fisted until one could not continue. At that point, both men rested for thirty seconds and then started to fight again.

PASSAGE #6

Read the passage and answer the question that follows.

1 _____.

[2]For example, with eye movements you can seek feedback. [3]In talking with someone, you look at her or him intently, as if to say, "Well, what do you think?" [4]Your pupils enlarge when you are interested or emotionally aroused. [5]You can also inform the other person that the channel of communication is open and that he or she should now speak. [6]You see this in the college classroom, when the instructor asks a question and then locks eyes with a student. [7]Without saying anything, the instructor expects that student to answer the question and the student knows it. [8]Eye movements may also signal the nature of a relationship, whether positive (an attentive glance) or negative (eye avoidance). [9]_____, you can signal your power through visual dominance behavior. [10]The average speaker, for example, maintains a high level of eye contact while listening and a lower level while speaking. [11]When people want to signal dominance, they may reverse this pattern: maintaining a high level of eye contact while talking but a lower level while listening. [12]Eye contact can also change the psychological distance between yourself and another person. [13]When you catch someone's eye at a party, for example, you become psychologically close even though far apart. [14]By avoiding eye contact—even when physically close as in a crowded elevator—you increase the psychological distance between you. (Adapted from Joseph A. DeVito, *Essentials of Human Communication*, 3rd ed., New York: Longman, 1999.)

6. Which is the best placement for the sentence below to make the sequence of ideas in the paragraph clear?

   When you avoid eye contact, such as looking away from a couple fighting, you help others maintain their privacy.

   A. Immediately after sentence 11
   B. Immediately after sentence 12
   C. Immediately after sentence 13
   D. Immediately after sentence 14

PASSAGE # 7

Read the passage and answer the question that follows.

1 _____.

²It even drinks seawater, which is much saltier than its body fluids. ³Few animals can tolerate such salty liquid because the salt draws water out of their tissues, and they become severely dehydrated. ⁴An albatross can thrive on salt water because it has special salt-excreting glands in its nostrils. ⁵The glands dispose of excess salts, allowing the bird to eat salty fish and squid and drink all it needs without ever visiting land. ⁶Their scientific name, *Diomedea exulans*, means exiled warrior in Greek. ⁷_____ its remarkable salt tolerance, the wandering albatross has extraordinary flight abilities specially suited to its seafaring life. ⁸Its wingspan is greater than that of any other bird—about 3.6 meters (nearly twelve feet). ⁹Most birds have to flap their wings to stay up in the air very long, but the albatross's long wings provide so much lift that the bird can stay aloft for hours by gliding up and down on wind currents. ¹⁰The wandering albatross spends most of its time in an area of high winds and rough seas, far from land, often alone on the open ocean. ¹¹The winds carry it from west to east, and in a year's time, an albatross may circle the globe, seeing little land except New Zealand and the tip of South America. (Adapted from Neil A. Campbell, Lawrence G. Mitchell, and Jane B. Reece, *Biology*, 3rd ed., San Francisco: Benjamin Cummings, 2000.)

7. Which is the best placement for the sentence below to make the sequence of ideas in the paragraph clear?

   The albatross's feathers insulate it against the chill of the strong sea wind, and its wings remain dry because they are lightly coated with oil.

   A. Immediately after sentence 8
   B. Immediately after sentence 9
   C. Immediately after sentence 10
   D. Immediately after sentence 11

PASSAGE #8

Read the passage and answer the question that follows.

1 _____.

²Testosterone is a male hormone that causes a general buildup in muscle and bone mass during puberty in males and maintains masculine traits throughout life. ³Anabolic steroids are synthetic variants of the male hormone testosterone. ⁴Pharmaceutical companies first produced and marketed anabolic steroids in the early 1950s as a treatment for certain diseases that destroy body muscle. ⁵About a decade later, some athletes began using anabolic steroids to build up their muscles quickly and enhance their performance with less hard work. ⁶It is not surprising that some of the heaviest users are weight lifters, football players, and body builders. ⁷Today, anabolic steroids, along with other drugs, are banned by most athletic organizations. ⁸Black market sales bring in up to $400 million a year. ⁹Medical research indicates that these substances can cause serious physical and mental problems. ¹⁰Overdosing in males can cause acne, baldness, and breast development. ¹¹Mental effects can range from mood swings to deep depression. ¹²Internally, there may be liver damage leading to cancer. ¹³_____, anabolic steroids can make blood cholesterol levels rise, perhaps increasing a user's chances of developing serious cardiovascular problems. ¹⁴Heavy users may also experience a reduced sex drive

and become infertile because anabolic steroids often make the body reduce its normal output of sex hormones. (Adapted from Neil A. Campbell, Lawrence G. Mitchell, and Jane B. Reece, *Biology*, 3rd ed., San Francisco: Benjamin Cummings, 2000.)

8. Which is the best placement for the sentence below to make the sequence of ideas in the paragraph clear?

   Another effect of steroids on mind and behavior is known as "roid rage," which is severe, aggressive behavior that may result in violence, such as fighting or destroying property.

   A. Immediately after sentence 11
   B. Immediately after sentence 12
   C. Immediately after sentence 13
   D. Immediately after sentence 14

PASSAGE #9

Read the passage and answer the question that follows.

1 _____.

²In most cases, the child continually learns from the parent. ³In the area of computer and Internet-mediated communication, however, the child may be able to teach the parent. ⁴_____, one five-year-old learned a graphics program before she could read. ⁵The child taught herself how to operate the rather intuitive program. ⁶Not only did the computer provide the child with a valuable learning process, but the parents totally depended on the child when they wanted to use the program she knew. ⁷In another case, a young boy taught his parents how to use PowerPoint. ⁸The examples are endless. ⁹Children are more apt to interact with the computer as if it were alive. ¹⁰A child may be able to understand a concept differently from the parent, and the role reversal of the child-as-teacher can be an important way the computer and the Internet can enhance a child's self-esteem. ¹¹The child and parent alike may feel positive toward themselves when they are able to learn new things, master a program, or win an Internet game. ¹²Their self-confidence may increase when others seek their advice, for example, because they are the family computer experts. (Adapted from Leonard J. Shedletsky and Joan E. Aitken, *Human Communication on the Internet*, Boston: Allyn and Bacon, 2004.)

9. Which is the best placement for the sentence below to make the sequence of ideas in the paragraph clear?

   A preteen taught his parents how to download music to their computer, set up a music library, and upload songs to their iPod.

   A. Immediately after sentence 1
   B. Immediately after sentence 4
   C. Immediately after sentence 5
   D. Immediately after sentence 7

PASSAGE #10

Read the passage and answer the question that follows.

1 _____.

²Highlighting is a strategy for condensing textbook material and emphasizing what is important. ³_____, the process of highlighting forces you to sift through what you have read

to identify important information. [4]This sifting or sorting is an active thought process; you are forced to weigh and evaluate what you read. [5]One mistake to avoid is highlighting almost every idea on a page. [6]Another benefit of highlighting is that it keeps you physically active while you are reading. [7]In addition, highlighting can help you discover the organization of facts and ideas as well as their connections and relationships. [8]Highlighting demonstrates to you whether you have understood a passage you have just read. [9]When combined with annotation, highlighting is a quick and easy way to review so that you do not have to reread everything when studying for an exam. [10]If you highlight 20 percent of a chapter, you will be able to avoid rereading 80 percent of the material. [11]If it normally takes two hours to read a chapter, you should be able to review a highlighted chapter in less than a half hour. [12]Highlighting has many benefits, but it is not by itself a sufficient study method; you must process the information by organizing it, expressing it in your own words, and testing yourself periodically. (Adapted from Kathleen T. McWhorter, *Study and Critical Thinking Skills in College*, 5th ed., New York: Longman, 2003.)

10. Which is the best placement for the sentence below to make the sequence of ideas in the paragraph clear?

    If you have difficulty highlighting, or your highlighting is not helpful or meaningful after you have finished reading, you will know that you did not understand the passage.

    A. Immediately after sentence 9
    B. Immediately after sentence 6
    C. Immediately after sentence 8
    D. Immediately after sentence 7

SECTION 4 ◆ RELEVANCE OF DETAILS	
Competency 1.4	Conceptual and Organizational Skills
Skill Tested	**Identifies supporting material that is relevant or irrelevant to the thesis statement or topic sentence**

The Skill

This skill tests your ability to distinguish between elements that do and do not provide adequate and relevant support for the thesis statement or topic sentence. In addition, the skill tests your ability to understand how sentences work together to provide unity.

Details that are irrelevant do not relate to the main idea being expressed in the topic or thesis statement. For example, if the topic sentence is about the differences in spoken communication styles between men and women, then all the details must relate to

- men and women
- spoken communication styles
- differences

There should be no discussion about other species (like chimpanzees or pets); there should be no details about non-spoken communication (like hugging or frowning); and there should be no information about similarities.

The following questions can help you determine if a detail is relevant or not.

- What is the writing trying to say, explain, or prove?
- How does this sentence help explain or prove the writer's point?
- What is the logical pattern used by the writer?
- How does this sentence explain or complete that pattern?
- Does this sentence talk about a different topic or pattern?

The Test Question

You will be asked to read a passage of approximately 200 words and then choose the sentence that is the **least** relevant to the thesis statement or topic sentence.

 Secrets to Success

- *Always keep the main idea of the passage in mind. All the sentences in the passage should support the topic and the point the author is making about it.*
- *When making your choice, keep in mind that the sentence that is least relevant will not seem to support the sentence(s) before it. The point may be an interesting detail, but as you read the passage, you will wonder why the sentence is there.*

SECTION 4 ◆ DIAGNOSTIC: RELEVANCE OF DETAILS

Read the passages and apply the strategies described above for finding relevant details. When you are done, check your work with the answers immediately following the diagnostic. Even if you get a perfect score here, go ahead and complete the exercises in this section; they are designed to help build confidence and to give you practice for future test success.

PASSAGE #1

Read the passage and answer the question that follows.

1 _____.

[2]Some instructors, for example, have a teaching style that promotes social interaction among students. [3]An instructor may organize small group activities, encourage class participation, or require students to work in pairs or teams to complete a specific task. [4]A lecture class is an example. [5]Other instructors offer little or no opportunity for social interaction. [6]Some instructors are very applied; they teach by example. [7]Others are more conceptual; they focus on presenting ideas, rules, theories, and so forth. [8]To an extent, of course, the subject matter also dictates how the instructor teaches. [9]_____ a biology instructor has a large body of factual information to present and may feel he or she has little time to schedule group interaction. [10]Some instructors' teaching styles are boring. [11]Once you are aware of your learning style and then consider the instructor's teaching style, you can begin to understand why you can learn better from one instructor than another and why you feel more comfortable in certain instructors' classes than others. (Adapted from Kathleen McWhorter, *Study and Critical Thinking Skills in College*, 5th ed., New York: Longman, 2003.)

1. Which numbered sentence is **least** relevant to the passage?
   A. 2
   B. 4
   C. 8
   D. 10

PASSAGE #2

Read the passage and answer the question that follows.

1 _____ .

[2]As early as the 1920s, psychologists attempted to teach language to chimpanzees to find out whether they could communicate. [3]Chimps don't have the appropriate vocal apparatus to produce spoken language, so researchers had to devise other methods of communication. [4]For instance, a chimp named Washoe was taught a highly simplified version of American Sign Language. [5]In addition, a chimp named Sarah was taught to manipulate symbols on a magnetic board. [6]Skeptics wondered if the chimps' combination of gestures and symbols constituted any kind of meaningful language. [7]Recent research has provided more solid insights into the language capabilities of chimps. [8]Bonobos and chimps can be raised together. [9]Sue Savage-Rumbaugh and her team work primarily with *bonobos*, a species of great ape that is evolutionarily nearer to humans than even the common chimpanzees. [10]Remarkably, two of the bonobos in her studies, Kanzi and Mulika, learned the meanings of plastic symbols at the same time. [11]They did not receive direct training; rather, they acquired the symbols by watching humans and other bonobos. [12]_____ Kanzi and Mulika can understand some spoken English. [13]For example, when Kanzi hears a spoken word, he is able to locate either the symbol for the word or a picture of the object. (Adapted from Richard J. Gerrig and Philip G. Zimbardo, *Psychology and Life*, 16th ed., Boston: Allyn and Bacon, 2002.)

2. Which numbered sentence is **least** relevant to the passage?
   A. 2
   B. 3
   C. 8
   D. 12

PASSAGE #3

Read the passage and answer the question that follows.

1 _____ .

[2]The relationship between temperature and assault is actually strongest in the late evening and early morning hours, from 9 p.m. to 3 a.m. [3]One explanation is that people are more likely to commit assault when they are out and about. [4]That is, in warmer weather, people are usually outdoors more and, therefore, are also more "available" as assault victims. [5]In the 9 p.m. to 3 a.m. hours, people are typically not working or bound by other responsibilities. [6]The time of day is another factor. [7]Furthermore, by the late evening hours, people may have been drinking alcohol or using other substances that lower their inhibition to aggression. [8]Substance abuse is a big problem in our society. [9]Another part of the explanation is the way in which people cope with and interpret the discomfort associated with high temperatures. [10]As the day

goes on, it may be harder to remember, "I'm feeling this way because it's hot" and just conclude, "I'm feeling this way because this person is making me crazy." [11]_____, assaults decline when temperatures become very hot. [12]Researchers have speculated that at very high temperatures, people might experience sufficient discomfort to withdraw from abrasive situations rather than stay and fight. (Adapted from Richard J. Gerrig and Philip G. Zimbardo, *Psychology and Life*, 16th ed., Boston: Allyn and Bacon, 2002.)

3. Which numbered sentence is **least** relevant to the passage?
   A. 8
   B. 10
   C. 11
   D. 12

PASSAGE #4

Read the passage and answer the question that follows.

[1]_____.

[2]The Hare Indians of Colville Lake are a small group of Canadian Inuit. [3]Savishinsky lived with the Hare Indians to study them. [4]They survive by hunting, trapping, and fishing in one of the harshest environments in the world. [5]_____, dogs are economically useful. [6]Dog teams give the Inuit a means for travel during the harshest seasons of the year. [7]The temperatures are extremely cold, and the winters are long and severe. [8]Finding food can be difficult. [9]The Inuit estimate that six dogs are required for travel, and some households have as many as four dog teams, with an average of 6.2 dogs per team. [10]The dogs are a frequent topic of conversation. [11]More than being only economically useful, dogs play a significant role in people's emotional lives. [12]Members of the community constantly compare and comment on the care, condition, and growth of one another's animals. [13]They note special qualities of size, strength, color, speed, and alertness. [14]Emotional displays, uncommon among the Hare, are significant between people and their dogs. [15]All people participate in the affectionate and concerned treatment of young dogs. (Adapted from Barbara D. Miller, *Cultural Anthropology*, 2nd ed., Boston: Allyn and Bacon, 2002.)

4. Which numbered sentence is **least** relevant to the passage?
   A. 3
   B. 4
   C. 7
   D. 8

PASSAGE #5

Read the passage and answer the question that follows.

[1]_____.

[2]The robin searches for food by selecting only those items that provide the greatest energy return for the energy expended. [3]This can be illustrated by the robin's behavior, which has four parts. [4]First, the robin has to decide where to hunt for food. [5]Once on the lawn, it has to search

for food items. [6]Because the robin forages on lawns, it is vulnerable to pesticide poisoning. [7]Having located some potential food, the robin has to decide whether to pursue it. [8]If it begins pursuit by pecking, the robin has to attempt a capture, in which it might or might not be successful. [9]If a food item is too large, it requires too much time to handle; if it is too small, it does not deliver enough energy to cover the costs of capture. [10]The robin should reject or ignore less valuable items, such as small beetles and caterpillars, and give preference to small and medium-sized earthworms. [11]_____ by capturing an earthworm, the robin earns some units of energy. [12]These more valuable food items would be classified as preferred food. [13]If the robin fails to find suitable and sufficient food in the area of the lawn it is searching, it leaves to search elsewhere. [14]If successful, the bird probably will return until the spot is no longer an economical place to feed. (Adapted from Robert Leo Smith and Thomas M. Smith, *Elements of Ecology*, 5th ed., San Francisco: Benjamin Cummings, 2003.)

5. Which numbered sentence is **least** relevant to the passage?
    A. 2
    B. 6
    C. 11
    D. 13

PASSAGE #6

Read the passage and answer the question that follows.

[1]_____.

[2]Beach-nesting birds such as the piping plover and the least tern are so disturbed by bathers and dune buggies that both species are in danger of extinction. [3]Other terns and shore birds are subjected to competition for nest sites and to egg predators by rapidly growing populations of large gulls. [4]These gulls are highly tolerant of humans and thrive on human garbage. [5]Sea turtles and the horseshoe crab, dependent on sandy beaches for nesting sites, find themselves evicted. [6]_____, they are declining rapidly. [7]Furthermore, each incoming tide brings onto the beaches feces-contaminated water that makes them unhealthy for humans and wildlife alike. [8]This contaminated water comes from a number of different sources, such as sewer overflows, failing private and commercial septic systems, animal and wildlife waste, and swimmers' illnesses. [9]The oceans have become dumping grounds. [10]Major chronic pollutants are oil that is released from tanker accidents, seepage from offshore drilling and other sources, toxic materials such as pesticides and heavy metals from industrial, urban, and agricultural sources. [11]The most devastating human activity in reefs is overfishing, especially in the Philippines and the Caribbean. [12]Tides also carry in old fishing lines, plastic debris, and other wastes hazardous to wildlife. (Adapted from Robert Leo Smith and Thomas M. Smith, *Elements of Ecology*, 5th ed., San Francisco: Benjamin Cummings, 2003.)

6. Which numbered sentence is **least** relevant to the passage?
    A. 4
    B. 6
    C. 10
    D. 11

PASSAGE #7

Read the passage and answer the question that follows.

> ¹_____.
> ²About 21 million people trace their origin to Mexico, 3 million to Puerto Rico, 1 million to Cuba, and almost 5 million to Central or South America, primarily Venezuela or Colombia. ³Officially tallied at 35 million in the year 2000 census, the actual number of Latinos is higher because, not surprisingly, many who are in the country illegally avoid contact with both public officials and census forms. ⁴Each year, more than 1 million people are apprehended at the border or at points inland and are deported to Mexico. ⁵Perhaps another million or so manage to enter the United States. ⁶_____ many migrate for temporary work and then return to their homes and families. ⁷To gain an understanding of how vast these numbers are, we can note that there are millions more Latinos in the United States than there are Canadians in Canada (31 million). ⁸To Midwesterners, such a comparison often comes as a surprise, for Latinos are absent from vast stretches of mid-America. ⁹Sixty-nine percent are concentrated in just four states: California, Texas, New York, and Florida. ¹⁰In the next twenty-five years, changes in the U.S. racial-ethnic mix will be dramatic. (Adapted from James M. Henslin, *Sociology*, 6th ed., Boston: Allyn and Bacon, 2003.)

7. Which numbered sentence is **least** relevant to the passage?
    A. 10
    B. 9
    C. 3
    D. 2

Answers and Explanations to Diagnostic: Relevance of Details

1. Answer   D
This statement is an opinion that is not supported. Whether or not an instructor's style of teaching is boring does not support the purpose of the passage, which is to explain that each instructor has a particular teaching style that is sometimes dependent on the kind of material he or she has to cover.

False choices
    Choice A provides the first example in support of instructors' different teaching styles.
    Choice B offers an example of a teaching style that offers no opportunity for social interaction.
    Choice C is a relevant detail that makes the point that it is the subject matter that affects the way an instructor teaches.

2. Answer   C
The passage offers no information about bonobos and chimpanzees being raised together and whether or not that fact influences their understanding of English.

False choices
    Choice A is a fact that is relevant to the passage. The statement tells the reader that the first research done to teach chimpanzees language was attempted in the 1920s.
    Choice B is another relevant point to the passage. It explains that researchers had to develop methods to communicate with chimps because they cannot speak.
    Choice D states that two bonobos, Kanzi and Mulika, can both understand some spoken English. This is a relevant statement that is a finding of current research.

3. Answer   A

The opinion that substance abuse is a big problem in our society has nothing to do with the main idea of the passage. The passage discusses the relationship between temperature and assault.

False choices

Choice B is relevant because it supports sentence 9. The sentence gives an example of how people cope with the discomfort of high temperatures.

Choice C adds an important finding regarding temperature and assault. People are less likely to assault one another when the temperatures are very hot.

Choice D builds on the previous statement and is relevant to the passage. The sentence explains that researchers suggest that people are uncomfortable in very hot weather, and, therefore, they would rather withdraw than stay and fight.

4. Answer   A

Sentence 3 tells the reader that a person named Savishinsky lived with the Hare Indians to study them; however, no other information related to this fact is presented in the passage. Therefore, it is not relevant to the passage.

False choices

Choice B is relevant because it tells the reader how the Hare Indians survive in their harsh environment, thus giving background for the necessity of their dogs.

Choice C builds on the idea that winters are harsh and that dogs help the Hare travel during that time.

Choice D is also relevant by adding that finding food during the harsh winter is difficult. This adds to the description of the cold and isolation that the Hare experience.

5. Answer   B

The paragraph illustrates why it is important for the robin to conserve its energy while hunting for prey. The passage includes the steps the robin takes to hunt. However, the topic of pesticides is not relevant to the discussion.

False choices

Choice A sets up the premise of the passage.

Choice C is relevant because it explains that by catching an earthworm, the robin has expended the least amount of energy for the more valuable food.

Choice D is another step in the robin's process of searching for food, which is explained in the passage.

6. Answer   D

This sentence about overfishing in the Caribbean and the Philippines has nothing to do with the subject of the paragraph. The paragraph tells the reader about problems on the beaches for humans and animals.

False choices

Choice A is relevant because it further supports the sea gull encroachment on the territory needed by other sea birds.

Choice B gives the effect of the previous sentence. The sea turtles and horseshoe crabs are losing their nesting sites on the beaches; therefore, their populations are declining.

Choice C presents another support for problems on the beaches: oil as a major, chronic pollutant.

7. Answer   A

The passage explains that Latinos are the largest minority in the United States. It does not make projections for the next 25 years for Latinos or any other group. Therefore, the sentence is not relevant.

False choices

Choice B is relevant because it supplies data on the large number of Latinos who live in four states.
Choice C supports the main idea of the passage by providing data on the number of Latinos counted by the census; in addition, it explains that the number is larger due to illegal immigration.
Choice D presents data that is relevant to the main idea. It lists the numbers of Latinos who trace their origins to Mexico, Puerto Rico, Cuba, Central America, and South America.

SECTION 4 ◆ EXERCISES: RELEVANCE OF DETAILS

PASSAGE #1

Read the passage and answer the question that follows.

¹_____.

²First of all, because e-mail messages are informal and quick, writers may be sloppy in transferring their thoughts to the screen. ³Misspellings and ungrammatical sentences can project a negative image if users do not take time to edit what they write on e-mail. ⁴Second, the messages are sent and read online, often leaving no paper trail at all. ⁵As a result, some important messages are forgotten or lost. ⁶It is easy to read your electronic mail and delete it instead of printing out a copy of the message to keep in a file or filing the message electronically in your e-mail file folder. ⁷Although generally thought of as a quick method of communication, e-mail's efficiency is only as good as the recipient's care in routinely checking e-mail messages. ⁸Electronic communication can be slow if people don't check their messages. ⁹Moreover, you have no privacy. ¹⁰Another disadvantage is the increasing use of e-mail as a replacement for personal contact of a phone call or face-to-face meeting. ¹¹The 1986 Electronic Communications Privacy Act considers e-mail to be the property of the company paying for the mail system. ¹²_____, writing on a computer screen often encourages people to drop inhibitions and write things in e-mail that they would never write in a paper letter or say over the telephone. (Adapted from Kristin R. Woolever, *Writing for the Technical Professions*, 2nd ed., New York: Longman, 2002.)

1. Which numbered sentence is **least** relevant to the passage?
   A. 5
   B. 3
   C. 8
   D. 11

PASSAGE #2

Read the passage and answer the question that follows.

¹_____.

²Although women have served in every branch of the armed services since World War II, two differences between the treatment of men and women in the military persist. ³First, only men must register for the draft when they turn eighteen. ⁴In 1981, the Supreme Court ruled that male-only registration for the military did not violate the Fifth Amendment. ⁵Second, statutes and reg-

ulations also prohibit women from serving in combat. [6]A breach exists between policy and practice, however, as the Persian Gulf war showed. [7]Women piloted helicopters at the front and helped to operate antimissile systems; some were taken as prisoners of war. [8]_____, women are not permitted to serve as combat pilots in the navy and air force and to serve on navy warships. [9]They are still not permitted to serve in ground combat units in the army or marines. [10]These actions have reopened the debate over whether women should serve in combat. [11]Others argue that men will not be able to fight effectively beside wounded or dying women. [12]Critics of these views point out that some women surpass men in body strength and that we do not know how well men and women will fight together. [13]Some experts insist that because women, on the average, have less body strength than men, they are less suited for combat. [14]This debate is not only a controversy about ability, but it also touches on the question of whether engaging in combat is a burden or a privilege. (Adapted from George C. Edwards, Martin P. Wattenberg, and Robert L. Lineberry, *Government in America*, 9th ed., New York: Longman, 2000.)

2. Which numbered sentence is **least** relevant to the passage?
   A. 14
   B. 4
   C. 3
   D. 10

PASSAGE #3

Read the passage and answer the question that follows.

[1] _____.

[2]Jaime Escalante taught calculus in an East Los Angeles inner-city school that was plagued with poverty, crime, drugs, and gangs. [3]As a result of his methods, his students earned the highest Advanced Placement scores in the city. [4]_____, Escalante had to open his students' minds to the possibility of success in learning. [5]Most Latino students were tracked into craft classes where they made jewelry and birdhouses. [6]Escalante felt that his students were talented and needed an opportunity to show it. [7]Also, the students needed to see learning as a way out of the barrio, as a path to good jobs. [8]By arranging for foundations to provide money for students to attend colleges of their choice, Escalante showed students that if they did well, their poverty would not stop them. [9]When Escalante first came to the United States, he worked as a busboy and attended Pasadena Community College. [10]Escalante also changed the system of instruction. [11]Before class, his students did "warm-ups," hand clapping and foot stomping to a rock song. [12]To foster team identity, students wore team jackets, caps, and T-shirts with logos that identified them as part of the math team. [13]He had his students think of themselves as a team, of him as the coach, and the national math exams as a sort of Olympics for which they were preparing. [14]Escalante thought it was important to teach his classes in English, not Spanish. [15]Escalante demonstrated that a teacher can motivate students to believe in their ability to achieve at high levels, no matter how great their problems. (Adapted from James M. Henslin, *Sociology*, 6th ed., Boston: Allyn and Bacon, 2003.)

3. Which numbered sentence is **least** relevant to the passage?
   A. 9
   B. 3
   C. 7
   D. 5

PASSAGE #4

Read the passage and answer the question that follows.

1 _____.

[2]Anorexia nervosa literally means loss of appetite, but this is a misnomer. [3]The anorexic individual approaches weight loss with a fervor, convinced that her body is too large. [4]A person with anorexia nervosa is hungry, but he or she denies the hunger because of an irrational fear of becoming fat. [5]Therefore, the first characteristic is a significant weight loss due to a relentless drive for thinness. [6]She is unable to recognize that her appearance is abnormal. [7]She will insist that her emaciated figure is just right or is too fat. [8]There is a strong argument that eating disorders are a form of addiction. [9]This condition is more than a simple eating disorder. [10]_____, anorexia is a distinct psychological disorder with a wide range of psychological disturbances. [11]Anorexics are typically compulsive, perfectionistic, and very competitive. [12]Food preoccupation and rituals and compulsive exercising are other characteristics. [13]The anorexic sometimes suffers from low self-image due to a feeling of incompetence, so she becomes consumed with losing weight to demonstrate to herself and others that she is in total control. [14]Additional features of the disease develop from the effects of starvation over time. [15]Untreated anorexia can be fatal. [16]Causes of death include starvation, infections due to poor nutrition, irregular heartbeat due to potassium deficiency, and suicide due to depression. (Adapted from David J. Anspaugh and Gene Ezell, *Teaching Today's Health*, 7th ed., San Francisco: Pearson, 2004.)

4. Which numbered sentence is **least** relevant to the passage?
    A. 8
    B. 9
    C. 12
    D. 15

PASSAGE #5

Read the passage and answer the question that follows.

1 _____.

[2]Bare-knuckle boxing, the forerunner of modern boxing, was a brutal, bloody sport. [3]Two men fought bare-fisted until one could not continue. [4]A round lasted until one of the men knocked or threw down his opponent. [5]At that point, both men rested for thirty seconds and then started to fight again. [6]Fights often lasted over one hundred rounds and as long as seven or eight hours. [7]After such a fight, it took months for the fighters to recover. [8]During the 1800s, boxing underwent a series of reforms. [9]There have been periodic efforts to outlaw the sport. [10]The challenge system was replaced by modern promotional techniques. [11]Fighters deserted bare-fisted combat and started wearing gloves. [12]Most importantly, professional boxers adopted the Marquis of Queensberry Rules, which standardized a round at three minutes, allowing a one-minute rest period between rounds, and outlawed all wrestling throws and holds. [13]_____, the fight to the finish was replaced with a fight to a decision over a specified number of rounds. [14]A bell and a referee told fighters when to fight and when to rest. [15]Currently there are eight major professional divisions. [16]Although the new rules did not reduce the violence, they did provide for more orderly bouts. (Adapted from James Kirby Martin et al., *America and Its Peoples*, 5th ed., New York: Longman, 2003.)

5. Which numbered sentence is **least** relevant to the passage?
   A. 11
   B. 3
   C. 15
   D. 6

PASSAGE #6

Read the passage and answer the question that follows.

1 _____.

²For example, with eye movements you can seek feedback. ³In talking with someone, you look at her or him intently, as if to say, "Well, what do you think?" ⁴Your pupils enlarge when you are interested or emotionally aroused. ⁵You can also inform the other person that the channel of communication is open and that he or she should now speak. ⁶You see this in the college classroom, when the instructor asks a question and then locks eyes with a student. ⁷Without saying anything, the instructor expects that student to answer the question and the student knows it. ⁸Eye movements may also signal the nature of a relationship, whether positive (an attentive glance) or negative (eye avoidance). ⁹_____, you can signal your power through visual dominance behavior. ¹⁰The average speaker, for example, maintains a high level of eye contact while listening and a lower level while speaking. ¹¹When people want to signal dominance, they may reverse this pattern: maintaining a high level of eye contact while talking but a lower level while listening. ¹²Eye contact can also change the psychological distance between yourself and another person. ¹³When you catch someone's eye at a party, for example, you become psychologically close even though far apart. ¹⁴By avoiding eye contact—even when physically close as in a crowded elevator—you increase the psychological distance between you. (Adapted from Joseph A. DeVito, *Essentials of Human Communication*, 3rd ed., New York: Longman, 1999.)

6. Which numbered sentence is **least** relevant to the passage?
   A. 7
   B. 5
   C. 4
   D. 10

PASSAGE # 7

Read the passage and answer the question that follows.

1 _____.

²It even drinks seawater, which is much saltier than its body fluids. ³Few animals can tolerate such salty liquid, because the salt draws water out of their tissues, and they become severely dehydrated. ⁴An albatross can thrive on salt water because it has special salt-excreting glands in its nostrils. ⁵The glands dispose of excess salts, allowing the bird to eat salty fish and squid and drink all it needs without ever visiting land. ⁶Their scientific name, *Diomedea exulans*, means exiled warrior in Greek. ⁷_____ its remarkable salt tolerance, the wandering albatross has extraordinary flight abilities specially suited to its seafaring life. ⁸Its wingspan is greater than that of any other bird—about 3.6 meters (nearly twelve feet). ⁹Most birds have to flap their wings to stay up in the air very long, but the albatross's long wings provide so

much lift that the bird can stay aloft for hours by gliding up and down on wind currents. [10]The wandering albatross spends most of its time in an area of high winds and rough seas, far from land, often alone on the open ocean. [11]The winds carry it from west to east, and in a year's time, an albatross may circle the globe, seeing little land except New Zealand and the tip of South America. (Adapted from Neil A. Campbell, Lawrence G. Mitchell, and Jane B. Reece, *Biology*, 3rd ed., San Francisco: Benjamin Cummings, 2000.)

7. Which numbered sentence is **least** relevant to the passage?
   A. 3
   B. 8
   C. 10
   D. 6

PASSAGE #8

Read the passage and answer the question that follows.

[1]_____.
[2]Testosterone is a male hormone that causes a general buildup in muscle and bone mass during puberty in males and maintains masculine traits throughout life. [3]Anabolic steroids are synthetic variants of the male hormone testosterone. [4]Pharmaceutical companies first produced and marketed anabolic steroids in the early 1950s as a treatment for certain diseases that destroy body muscle. [5]About a decade later, some athletes began using anabolic steroids to build up their muscles quickly and enhance their performance with less hard work. [6]It is not surprising that some of the heaviest users are weight lifters, football players, and body builders. [7]Today, anabolic steroids, along with other drugs, are banned by most athletic organizations. [8]Black market sales bring in up to $400 million a year. [9]Medical research indicates that these substances can cause serious physical and mental problems. [10]Overdosing in males can cause acne, baldness, and breast development. [11]Mental effects can range from mood swings to deep depression. [12]Internally, there may be liver damage leading to cancer. [13]_____, anabolic steroids can make blood cholesterol levels rise, perhaps increasing a user's chances of developing serious cardiovascular problems. [14]Heavy users may also experience a reduced sex drive and become infertile because anabolic steroids often make the body reduce its normal output of sex hormones. (Adapted from Neil A. Campbell, Lawrence G. Mitchell, and Jane B. Reece, *Biology*, 3rd ed., San Francisco: Benjamin Cummings, 2000.)

8. Which numbered sentence is **least** relevant to the passage?
   A. 2
   B. 8
   C. 4
   D. 3

PASSAGE #9

Read the passage and answer the question that follows.

[1]_____.
[2]In most cases, the child continually learns from the parent. [3]In the area of computer and Internet-mediated communication, however, the child may be able to teach the parent.

⁴_____, one five-year-old learned a graphics program before she could read. ⁵The child taught herself how to operate the rather intuitive program. ⁶Not only did the computer provide the child with a valuable learning process, but the parents totally depended on the child when they wanted to use the program she knew. ⁷In another case, a young boy taught his parents how to use PowerPoint. ⁸The examples are endless. ⁹Children are more apt to interact with the computer as if it were alive. ¹⁰A child may be able to understand a concept differently from the parent, and the role reversal of the child-as-teacher can be an important way the computer and the Internet can enhance a child's self-esteem. ¹¹The child and parent alike may feel positive toward themselves when they are able to learn new things, master a program, or win an Internet game. ¹²Their self-confidence may increase when others seek their advice, for example, because they are the family computer experts. (Adapted from Leonard J. Shedletsky and Joan E. Aitken, *Human Communication on the Internet*, Boston: Allyn and Bacon, 2004.)

9. Which numbered sentence is **least** relevant to the passage?
   A. 9
   B. 3
   C. 12
   D. 4

PASSAGE #10

Read the passage and answer the question that follows.

¹_____.
²Highlighting is a strategy for condensing textbook material and emphasizing what is important. ³_____, the process of highlighting forces you to sift through what you have read to identify important information. ⁴This sifting or sorting is an active thought process; you are forced to weigh and evaluate what you read. ⁵One mistake to avoid is highlighting almost every idea on a page. ⁶Another benefit of highlighting is that it keeps you physically active while you are reading. ⁷In addition, highlighting can help you discover the organization of facts and ideas as well as their connections and relationships. ⁸Highlighting demonstrates to you whether you have understood a passage you have just read. ⁹When combined with annotation, highlighting is a quick and easy way to review so that you do not have to reread everything when studying for an exam. ¹⁰If you highlight 20 percent of a chapter, you will be able to avoid rereading 80 percent of the material. ¹¹If it normally takes two hours to read a chapter, you should be able to review a highlighted chapter in less than a half hour. ¹²Highlighting has many benefits, but it is not by itself a sufficient study method; you must process the information by organizing it, expressing it in your own words, and testing yourself periodically. (Adapted from Kathleen T. McWhorter, *Study and Critical Thinking Skills in College*, 5th ed., New York: Longman, 2003.)

10. Which numbered sentence is **least** relevant to the passage?
    A. 3
    B. 7
    C. 9
    D. 5

SECTION 5 ◆ TRANSITIONAL DEVICES

Competency 1.5   Conceptual and Organizational Skills
Skill Tested   **Recognizes effective transitional devices within the context of the passage**

The Skill

This item tests your ability to identify effective transitions that reflect the organization pattern used in a piece of writing. Transitions are words that connect one idea to another so that they flow smoothly and logically. They tell you the logical relationship of ideas **within** and **between** sentences. Transitional devices can appear at the beginning of a sentence or somewhere within a sentence.

Study the following chart of transition words and phrases so that you will recognize them in the test question.

Relationship Expressed	Transition Words and Phrases
Addition	also, in addition, too, moreover, and, besides, furthermore, equally important, then, finally, first, next, second
Example	for example, for instance, thus, as an illustration, namely, specifically, to illustrate
Contrast	yet, but, however, on the one hand/on the other hand, nevertheless, conversely, in contrast, still, although, despite that, on the contrary, otherwise, whereas
Comparison	similarly, likewise, in the same way
Concession	of course, certainly, granted, although it is true that, I admit that, it may appear that
Emphasis	indeed, in fact, of course
Place	here, there, above, below, beyond, closer to, far, near, nearby, to the left, to the right
Result	therefore, thus, consequently, as a result, so
Summary	in summary, in conclusion, finally, hence, on the whole, to summarize, as mentioned earlier, in other words, in short, therefore
Time	first, second, third, next, then, finally, after, afterwards, before, soon, later, meanwhile, subsequently, immediately, eventually, currently, after a while, earlier, presently, simultaneously, when, shortly

Here is an example of a passage that effectively uses transitions, most of which are underlined.

The carefully planned wedding quickly turned into a disaster. <u>After</u> months of phone calls to the florists, photographer, minister, and caterer, the day seemed perfectly planned. <u>In fact</u>, the weather forecaster predicted a beautiful, picture perfect day. _____, an unexpected summer rainstorm drove the wedding party off the beach after the bride, groom, minister, family, and guests had been thoroughly soaked. <u>Furthermore</u>, as if the rain and wind were not enough to ruin the day, the groom became violently ill with food poisoning and had to be hospitalized on his wedding night.

The test will ask that you choose the best transition to fill in a blank. A good way to try to pick the best transition word would be to carefully read the words around the blank before looking at the possible answers. Try to fill in a word that makes logical sense to you and then look at your choices. Pick the word that best matches the one you have already thought of.

In the example above, notice that the words on the left side of the blank refer to a perfect day, and on the other side, a rainstorm. These two ideas are in contrast with each other. Perhaps you thought of the word *but* or *although* as a possible word to place in the blank. You should then look over the possible answers and choose the word that means about the same thing as the word you chose.

The Test Question

You will be given a passage of approximately 200 words containing numbered sentences, one of which contains a blank or underlined transitional word or phrase. You will be asked to choose the best word or phrase that, if inserted into the blank, would make the relationship of the ideas clear.

> ▶▶▌ **Secrets to Success**
>
> - *Ask yourself:* What is the author trying to tell me about the relationship between these two sentences?
> - *Try to guess the relationship before you look over your options; then, choose the transition which best matches your guess.*
> - *Remember, if two or more words in your choices have the same relationship meaning, they cannot be correct. For example, if your choices were so, however, therefore, and as a result, you would know the correct answer would have to be however because the other three words mean the same thing.*

SECTION 5 ◆ DIAGNOSTIC: TRANSITIONAL DEVICES

Read the passages and apply the strategies described above for identifying transitional devices. When you are done, check your work with the answers immediately following the diagnostic. Even if you get a perfect score here, go ahead and complete the exercises in this section; they are designed to help build confidence and to give you practice for future test success.

PASSAGE #1

Read the passage and answer the question that follows.

¹ _____ .

²Some instructors, for example, have a teaching style that promotes social interaction among students. ³An instructor may organize small group activities, encourage class participation, or require students to work in pairs or teams to complete a specific task. ⁴A lecture class is an example. ⁵Other instructors offer little or no opportunity for social interaction. ⁶Some instructors are very applied; they teach by example. ⁷Others are more conceptual; they focus on presenting ideas, rules, theories, and so forth. ⁸To an extent, of course, the subject matter also dictates how the instructor teaches. ⁹_____ a biology instructor has a large body of factual information to present and may feel he or she has little time to schedule group interaction. ¹⁰Some

instructors' teaching styles are boring. [11]Once you are aware of your learning style and then consider the instructor's teaching style, you can begin to understand why you can learn better from one instructor than another and why you feel more comfortable in certain instructors' classes than others. (Adapted from Kathleen McWhorter, *Study and Critical Thinking Skills in College*, 5th ed., New York: Longman, 2003.)

1. Which word or phrase, if inserted in the blank in sentence 9, would make the relationship of the ideas clear?
   A. Therefore,
   B. However,
   C. In contrast,
   D. For example,

PASSAGE #2

Read the passage and answer the question that follows.

[1]_____.
[2]As early as the 1920s, psychologists attempted to teach language to chimpanzees to find out whether they could communicate. [3]Chimps don't have the appropriate vocal apparatus to produce spoken language, so researchers had to devise other methods of communication. [4]For instance, a chimp named Washoe was taught a highly simplified version of American Sign Language. [5]In addition, a chimp named Sarah was taught to manipulate symbols on a magnetic board. [6]Skeptics wondered if the chimps' combination of gestures and symbols constituted any kind of meaningful language. [7]Recent research has provided more solid insights into the language capabilities of chimps. [8]Bonobos and chimps can be raised together. [9]Sue Savage-Rumbaugh and her team work primarily with *bonobos*, a species of great ape that is evolutionarily nearer to humans than even the common chimpanzees. [10]Remarkably, two of the bonobos in her studies, Kanzi and Mulika, learned the meanings of plastic symbols at the same time. [11]They did not receive direct training; rather, they acquired the symbols by watching humans and other bonobos. [12]_____ Kanzi and Mulika can understand some spoken English. [13]For example, when Kanzi hears a spoken word, he is able to locate either the symbol for the word or a picture of the object. (Adapted from Richard J. Gerrig and Philip G. Zimbardo, *Psychology and Life*, 16th ed., Boston: Allyn and Bacon, 2002.)

2. Which word or phrase, if inserted in the blank in sentence 12, would make the relationship of the ideas clear?
   A. In contrast,
   B. Moreover,
   C. Next,
   D. In conclusion,

PASSAGE #3

Read the passage and answer the question that follows.

[1]_____.
[2]The relationship between temperature and assault is actually strongest in the late evening and early morning hours, from 9 p.m. to 3 a.m. [3]One explanation is that people are more likely to

commit assault when they are out and about. [4]That is, in warmer weather, people are usually outdoors more and, therefore, are also more "available" as assault victims. [5]In the 9 p.m. to 3 a.m. hours, people are typically not working or bound by other responsibilities. [6]The time of day is another factor. [7]Furthermore, by the late evening hours, people may have been drinking alcohol or using other substances that lower their inhibition to aggression. [8]Substance abuse is a big problem in our society. [9]Another part of the explanation is the way in which people cope with and interpret the discomfort associated with high temperatures. [10]As the day goes on, it may be harder to remember, "I'm feeling this way because it's hot" and just conclude, "I'm feeling this way because this person is making me crazy." [11]_____, assaults decline when temperatures become very hot. [12]Researchers have speculated that at very high temperatures, people might experience sufficient discomfort to withdraw from abrasive situations rather than stay and fight. (Adapted from Richard J. Gerrig and Philip G. Zimbardo, *Psychology and Life*, 16th ed., Boston: Allyn and Bacon, 2002.)

3. Which word or phrase, if inserted in the blank in sentence 11, would make the relationship of the ideas clear?
   A. On the other hand,
   B. In fact,
   C. Now,
   D. In conclusion,

PASSAGE #4

Read the passage and answer the question that follows.

[1]_____.
[2]The Hare Indians of Colville Lake are a small group of Canadian Inuit. [3]Savishinsky lived with the Hare Indians to study them. [4]They survive by hunting, trapping, and fishing in one of the harshest environments in the world. [5]_____, dogs are economically useful. [6]Dog teams give the Inuit a means for travel during the harshest seasons of the year. [7]The temperatures are extremely cold, and the winters are long and severe. [8]Finding food can be difficult. [9]The Inuit estimate that six dogs are required for travel, and some households have as many as four dog teams, with an average of 6.2 dogs per team. [10]The dogs are a frequent topic of conversation. [11]More than being only economically useful, dogs play a significant role in people's emotional lives. [12]Members of the community constantly compare and comment on the care, condition, and growth of one another's animals. [13]They note special qualities of size, strength, color, speed, and alertness. [14]Emotional displays, uncommon among the hare, are significant between people and their dogs. [15]All people participate in the affectionate and concerned treatment of young dogs. (Adapted from Barbara D. Miller, *Cultural Anthropology*, 2nd ed., Boston: Allyn and Bacon, 2002.)

4. Which word or phrase, if inserted in the blank in sentence 5, would make the relationship of the ideas clear?
   A. In contrast,
   B. Then,
   C. First of all,
   D. Nevertheless,

PASSAGE #5

Read the passage and answer the question that follows.

1 _____.

²The robin searches for food by selecting only those items that provide the greatest energy return for the energy expended. ³This can be illustrated by the robin's behavior, which has four parts. ⁴First, the robin has to decide where to hunt for food. ⁵Once on the lawn, it has to search for food items. ⁶Because the robin forages on lawns, it is vulnerable to pesticide poisoning. ⁷Having located some potential food, the robin has to decide whether to pursue it. ⁸If it begins pursuit by pecking, the robin has to attempt a capture, in which it might or might not be successful. ⁹If a food item is too large, it requires too much time to handle; if it is too small, it does not deliver enough energy to cover the costs of capture. ¹⁰The robin should reject or ignore less valuable items, such as small beetles and caterpillars, and give preference to small and medium-sized earthworms. ¹¹_____ by capturing an earthworm, the robin earns some units of energy. ¹²These more valuable food items would be classified as preferred food. ¹³If the robin fails to find suitable and sufficient food in the area of the lawn it is searching, it leaves to search elsewhere. ¹⁴If successful, the bird probably will return until the spot is no longer an economical place to feed. (Adapted from Robert Leo Smith and Thomas M. Smith, *Elements of Ecology*, 5th ed., San Francisco: Benjamin Cummings, 2003.)

5. Which word or phrase, if inserted in the blank in sentence 11, would make the relationship of the ideas clear?
   A. However,
   B. On the other hand,
   C. Therefore,
   D. In conclusion,

PASSAGE #6

Read the passage and answer the question that follows.

1 _____.

²Beach-nesting birds such as the piping plover and the least tern are so disturbed by bathers and dune buggies that both species are in danger of extinction. ³Other terns and shore birds are subjected to competition for nest sites and to egg predators by rapidly growing populations of large gulls. ⁴These gulls are highly tolerant of humans and thrive on human garbage. ⁵Sea turtles and the horseshoe crab, dependent on sandy beaches for nesting sites, find themselves evicted. ⁶_____, they are declining rapidly. ⁷Furthermore, each incoming tide brings onto the beaches feces-contaminated water that makes them unhealthy for humans and wildlife alike. ⁸This contaminated water comes from a number of different sources, such as sewer overflows, failing private and commercial septic systems, animal and wildlife waste, and swimmers' illnesses. ⁹The oceans have become dumping grounds. ¹⁰Major chronic pollutants are oil that is released from tanker accidents, seepage from offshore drilling and other sources, toxic materials such as pesticides and heavy metals from industrial, urban, and agricultural sources. ¹¹The most devastating human activity in reefs is overfishing, especially in the Philippines and the Caribbean. ¹²Tides also carry in old fishing lines, plastic debris, and other wastes hazardous to wildlife. (Adapted from Robert Leo Smith and Thomas M. Smith, *Elements of Ecology*, 5th ed., San Francisco: Benjamin Cummings, 2003.)

6. Which word or phrase, if inserted in the blank in sentence 6, would make the relationship of the ideas clear?
   A. For example,
   B. Finally,
   C. Similarly,
   D. Consequently,

PASSAGE #7

Read the passage and answer the question that follows.

¹_____.
²About 21 million people trace their origin to Mexico, 3 million to Puerto Rico, 1 million to Cuba, and almost 5 million to Central or South America, primarily Venezuela or Colombia. ³Officially tallied at 35 million in the year 2000 census, the actual number of Latinos is higher because, not surprisingly, many who are in the country illegally avoid contact with both public officials and census forms. ⁴Each year, more than 1 million people are apprehended at the border or at points inland and are deported to Mexico. ⁵Perhaps another million or so manage to enter the United States. ⁶_____ many migrate for temporary work and then return to their homes and families. ⁷To gain an understanding of how vast these numbers are, we can note that there are millions more Latinos in the United States than there are Canadians in Canada (31 million). ⁸To Midwesterners, such a comparison often comes as a surprise, for Latinos are absent from vast stretches of mid-America. ⁹Sixty-nine percent are concentrated in just four states: California, Texas, New York, and Florida. ¹⁰In the next twenty-five years, changes in the U.S. racial-ethnic mix will be dramatic. (Adapted from James M. Henslin, *Sociology*, 6th ed., Boston: Allyn and Bacon, 2003.)

7. Which word or phrase, if inserted in the blank in sentence 6, would make the relationship of the ideas clear?
   A. Nevertheless,
   B. In addition,
   C. In other words,
   D. Nearby,

Answers and Explanations to Diagnostic: Transitional Devices

1. Answer   D

"For example" is the transition that makes the relationship between ideas clear. The sentence is an example of how an instructor's subject matter dictates how he or she teaches.

False choices
   Choice A, "Therefore," suggests a result, not an example.
   Choice B, "However," suggests a contrast, not an example.
   Choice C, "In contrast," suggests a contrast, not an example.

2. Answer   B

"Moreover" is the appropriate transition word to make the relationship of ideas clear. The sentence adds information about what the two bonobos learned. In the previous sentence, the reader learns that they learned symbols by watching people and other bonobos. This sentence adds that they can understand some spoken English.

False choices
   Choice A, "In contrast," suggests that a contrast is being made.
   Choice C, "Next," leads the reader to think that the sentence is part of a sequence.
   Choice D, "In conclusion," indicates that the sentence is providing a summary or a conclusion for the paragraph.

3. Answer   A

"On the other hand" is the appropriate transition for making the relationship of ideas clear. The sentence points out a contrast. Although people are more likely to assault when the weather is warm, in contrast, they are less likely to assault when the weather is hot.

False choices
   Choice B, "In fact," indicates that an example is being given.
   Choice C, "Now," is a word used to express time, not contrast.
   Choice D, "In conclusion," indicates that the sentence is providing a summary or a conclusion for the paragraph.

4. Answer   C

"First of all" is the appropriate transition for making the relationship of ideas clear. It indicates that the first supporting idea is being introduced. In the passage, the reader learns that dogs are economically useful for the Hare Indians.

False choices
   Choice A, "In contrast," indicates that a contrast is being made.
   Choice B, "Then," is used to express time.
   Choice D, "Nevertheless," expresses contrast.

5. Answer   C

"Therefore" is the appropriate transition word to make the relationship of ideas clear. "Therefore" expresses the effect of the robin's ignoring less valuable prey and preferring earthworms.

False choices
   Choice A, "However," suggests a contrast, not an effect.
   Choice B, "On the other hand," also suggests a contrast, not an effect.
   Choice D, "In conclusion," indicates that the sentence is providing a summary or a conclusion for the paragraph.

6. Answer   D

"Consequently" is the appropriate transition word to make the relationship of ideas clear. "Consequently" expresses a result or effect. The sentence explains the effect of the loss of habitat of sea turtles and horseshoe crabs.

False choices
   Choice A, "For example," indicates that the sentence will provide an example.
   Choice B, "Finally," is used to express the last item in a sequence or the last idea.
   Choice C, "Similarly," suggests that a comparison is being made.

7. Answer   B

"In addition" is the appropriate transition for making the relationship of ideas clear. "In addition" tells the reader that another detail is being added. The sentence provides more supporting information for the fact that there are more Latinos in the U.S. than the 2000 census indicates.

False choices
Choice A, "Nevertheless," expresses a contrast.
Choice C, "In other words," is used to restate a point or give a conclusion.
Choice D, "Nearby," is used when describing a spatial relationship.

SECTION 5 ◆ EXERCISES: TRANSITIONAL DEVICES

PASSAGE #1

Read the passage and answer the question that follows.

1 _____.

²First of all, because e-mail messages are informal and quick, writers may be sloppy in transferring their thoughts to the screen. ³Misspellings and ungrammatical sentences can project a negative image if users do not take time to edit what they write on e-mail. ⁴Second, the messages are sent and read online, often leaving no paper trail at all. ⁵As a result, some important messages are forgotten or lost. ⁶It is easy to read your electronic mail and delete it instead of printing out a copy of the message to keep in a file or filing the message electronically in your e-mail file folder. ⁷Although generally thought of as a quick method of communication, e-mail's efficiency is only as good as the recipient's care in routinely checking e-mail messages. ⁸Electronic communication can be slow if people don't check their messages. ⁹Moreover, you have no privacy. ¹⁰Another disadvantage is the increasing use of e-mail as a replacement for personal contact of a phone call or face-to-face meeting. ¹¹The 1986 Electronic Communications Privacy Act considers e-mail to be the property of the company paying for the mail system. ¹²_____, writing on a computer screen often encourages people to drop inhibitions and write things in e-mail that they would never write in a paper letter or say over the telephone. (Adapted from Kristin R. Woolever, *Writing for the Technical Professions*, 2nd ed., New York: Longman, 2002.)

1. Which word or phrase, if inserted in the blank in sentence 12, would make the relationship of the ideas within the sentence clear?
   A. In contrast
   B. In conclusion
   C. Finally
   D. For example

PASSAGE #2

Read the passage and answer the question that follows.

1 _____.

²Although women have served in every branch of the armed services since World War II, two differences between the treatment of men and women in the military persist. ³First, only men must register for the draft when they turn eighteen. ⁴In 1981, the Supreme Court ruled that male-only registration for the military did not violate the Fifth Amendment. ⁵Second, statutes and regulations also prohibit women from serving in combat. ⁶A breach exists between policy and practice, however, as the Persian Gulf War showed. ⁷Women piloted helicopters at the front and helped to operate antimissile systems; some were taken as prisoners of war. ⁸_____, women

are not permitted to serve as combat pilots in the navy and air force and to serve on navy warships. ⁹They are still not permitted to serve in ground combat units in the army or marines. ¹⁰These actions have reopened the debate over whether women should serve in combat. ¹¹Others argue that men will not be able to fight effectively beside wounded or dying women. ¹²Critics of these views point out that some women surpass men in body strength and that we do not know how well men and women will fight together. ¹³Some experts insist that because women, on the average, have less body strength than men, they are less suited for combat. ¹⁴This debate is not only a controversy about ability, but it also touches on the question of whether engaging in combat is a burden or a privilege. (Adapted from George C. Edwards, Martin P. Wattenberg, and Robert L. Lineberry, *Government in America*, 9th ed., New York: Longman, 2000.)

2. Which word or phrase, if inserted in the blank in sentence 8, would make the relationship of the ideas within the sentence clear?
   A. Therefore
   B. In conclusion
   C. For example
   D. However

PASSAGE #3

Read the passage and answer the question that follows.

1 _____.

²Jaime Escalante taught calculus in an East Los Angeles inner-city school that was plagued with poverty, crime, drugs, and gangs. ³As a result of his methods, his students earned the highest Advanced Placement scores in the city. ⁴_____, Escalante had to open his students' minds to the possibility of success in learning. ⁵Most Latino students were tracked into craft classes where they made jewelry and birdhouses. ⁶Escalante felt that his students were talented and needed an opportunity to show it. ⁷Also, the students needed to see learning as a way out of the barrio, as a path to good jobs. ⁸By arranging for foundations to provide money for students to attend colleges of their choice, Escalante showed students that if they did well, their poverty would not stop them. ⁹When Escalante first came to the United States, he worked as a busboy and attended Pasadena Community College. ¹⁰Escalante also changed the system of instruction. ¹¹Before class, his students did "warm-ups," hand clapping and foot stomping to a rock song. ¹²To foster team identity, students wore team jackets, caps, and T-shirts with logos that identified them as part of the math team. ¹³He had his students think of themselves as a team, of him as the coach, and the national math exams as a sort of Olympics for which they were preparing. ¹⁴Escalante thought it was important to teach his classes in English, not Spanish. ¹⁵Escalante demonstrated that a teacher can motivate students to believe in their ability to achieve at high levels, no matter how great their problems. (Adapted from James M. Henslin, *Sociology*, 6th ed., Boston: Allyn and Bacon, 2003.)

3. Which word or phrase, if inserted in the blank in sentence 4, would make the relationship of the ideas within the sentence clear?
   A. First
   B. Then
   C. Next
   D. Consequently

PASSAGE #4

Read the passage and answer the question that follows.

1 _____.

²Anorexia nervosa literally means loss of appetite, but this is a misnomer. ³The anorexic individual approaches weight loss with a fervor, convinced that her body is too large. ⁴A person with anorexia nervosa is hungry, but he or she denies the hunger because of an irrational fear of becoming fat. ⁵Therefore, the first characteristic is a significant weight loss due to a relentless drive for thinness. ⁶She is unable to recognize that her appearance is abnormal. ⁷She will insist that her emaciated figure is just right or is too fat. ⁸There is a strong argument that eating disorders are a form of addiction. ⁹This condition is more than a simple eating disorder. ¹⁰_____, anorexia is a distinct psychological disorder with a wide range of psychological disturbances. ¹¹Anorexics are typically compulsive, perfectionistic, and very competitive. ¹²Food preoccupation and rituals and compulsive exercising are other characteristics. ¹³The anorexic sometimes suffers from low self-image due to a feeling of incompetence, so she becomes consumed with losing weight to demonstrate to herself and others that she is in total control. ¹⁴Additional features of the disease develop from the effects of starvation over time. ¹⁵Untreated anorexia can be fatal. ¹⁶Causes of death include starvation, infections due to poor nutrition, irregular heartbeat due to potassium deficiency, and suicide due to depression. (Adapted from David J. Anspaugh and Gene Ezell, *Teaching Today's Health*, 7th ed., San Francisco: Pearson, 2004.)

4. Which word or phrase, if inserted in the blank in sentence 10, would make the relationship of the ideas within the sentence clear?
   A. Consequently
   B. In fact
   C. Meanwhile
   D. However

PASSAGE #5

Read the passage and answer the question that follows.

1 _____.

²Bare-knuckle boxing, the forerunner of modern boxing, was a brutal, bloody sport. ³Two men fought bare-fisted until one could not continue. ⁴A round lasted until one of the men knocked or threw down his opponent. ⁵At that point, both men rested for thirty seconds and then started to fight again. ⁶Fights often lasted over one hundred rounds and as long as seven or eight hours. ⁷After such a fight, it took months for the fighters to recover. ⁸During the 1800s, boxing underwent a series of reforms. ⁹There have been periodic efforts to outlaw the sport. ¹⁰The challenge system was replaced by modern promotional techniques. ¹¹Fighters deserted bare-fisted combat and started wearing gloves. ¹²Most importantly, professional boxers adopted the Marquis of Queensberry Rules, which standardized a round at three minutes, allowing a one-minute rest period between rounds, and outlawed all wrestling throws and holds. ¹³_____, the fight to the finish was replaced with a fight to a decision over a specified number of rounds. ¹⁴A bell and a referee told fighters when to fight and when to rest. ¹⁵Currently there are eight major professional divisions. ¹⁶Although the new rules did not reduce the violence, they did provide for more orderly bouts. (Adapted from James Kirby Martin et al., *America and Its Peoples*, 5th ed., New York: Longman, 2003.)

5. Which word or phrase, if inserted in the blank in sentence 13, would make the relationship of the ideas within the sentence clear?
    A. In short
    B. Specifically
    C. However
    D. In addition

PASSAGE #6

Read the passage and answer the question that follows.

1 _____.
²For example, with eye movements you can seek feedback. ³In talking with someone, you look at her or him intently, as if to say, "Well, what do you think?" ⁴Your pupils enlarge when you are interested or emotionally aroused. ⁵You can also inform the other person that the channel of communication is open and that he or she should now speak. ⁶You see this in the college classroom, when the instructor asks a question and then locks eyes with a student. ⁷Without saying anything, the instructor expects that student to answer the question and the student knows it. ⁸Eye movements may also signal the nature of a relationship, whether positive (an attentive glance) or negative (eye avoidance). ⁹_____, you can signal your power through visual dominance behavior. ¹⁰The average speaker, for example, maintains a high level of eye contact while listening and a lower level while speaking. ¹¹When people want to signal dominance, they may reverse this pattern: maintaining a high level of eye contact while talking but a lower level while listening. ¹²Eye contact can also change the psychological distance between yourself and another person. ¹³When you catch someone's eye at a party, for example, you become psychologically close even though far apart. ¹⁴By avoiding eye contact—even when physically close as in a crowded elevator—you increase the psychological distance between you. (Adapted from Joseph A. DeVito, *Essentials of Human Communication*, 3rd ed., New York: Longman, 1999.)

6. Which word or phrase, if inserted in the blank in sentence 9, would make the relationship of the ideas within the sentence clear?
    A. However
    B. Afterwards
    C. Moreover
    D. As a result

PASSAGE #7

Read the passage and answer the question that follows.

1 _____.
²It even drinks seawater, which is much saltier than its body fluids. ³Few animals can tolerate such salty liquid because the salt draws water out of their tissues, and they become severely dehydrated. ⁴An albatross can thrive on salt water because it has special salt-excreting glands in its nostrils. ⁵The glands dispose of excess salts, allowing the bird to eat salty fish and squid and drink all it needs without ever visiting land. ⁶Their scientific name, *Diomedea exulans*,

means exiled warrior in Greek. [7]_____ its remarkable salt tolerance, the wandering albatross has extraordinary flight abilities specially suited to its seafaring life. [8]Its wingspan is greater than that of any other bird—about 3.6 meters (nearly twelve feet). [9]Most birds have to flap their wings to stay up in the air very long, but the albatross's long wings provide so much lift that the bird can stay aloft for hours by gliding up and down on wind currents. [10]The wandering albatross spends most of its time in an area of high winds and rough seas, far from land, often alone on the open ocean. [11]The winds carry it from west to east, and in a year's time, an albatross may circle the globe, seeing little land except New Zealand and the tip of South America. (Adapted from Neil A. Campbell, Lawrence G. Mitchell, and Jane B. Reece, *Biology*, 3rd ed., San Francisco: Benjamin Cummings, 2000.)

7. Which word or phrase, if inserted in the blank in sentence 7, would make the relationship of the ideas within the sentence clear?
   A. In contrast to
   B. Along with
   C. Finally
   D. Because of

PASSAGE #8

Read the passage and answer the question that follows.

[1]_____.
[2]Testosterone is a male hormone that causes a general buildup in muscle and bone mass during puberty in males and maintains masculine traits throughout life. [3]Anabolic steroids are synthetic variants of the male hormone testosterone. [4]Pharmaceutical companies first produced and marketed anabolic steroids in the early 1950s as a treatment for certain diseases that destroy body muscle. [5]About a decade later, some athletes began using anabolic steroids to build up their muscles quickly and enhance their performance with less hard work. [6]It is not surprising that some of the heaviest users are weight lifters, football players, and body builders. [7]Today, anabolic steroids, along with other drugs, are banned by most athletic organizations. [8]Black market sales bring in up to $400 million a year. [9]Medical research indicates that these substances can cause serious physical and mental problems. [10]Overdosing in males can cause acne, baldness, and breast development. [11]Mental effects can range from mood swings to deep depression. [12]Internally, there may be liver damage leading to cancer. [13]_____, anabolic steroids can make blood cholesterol levels rise, perhaps increasing a user's chances of developing serious cardiovascular problems. [14]Heavy users may also experience a reduced sex drive and become infertile because anabolic steroids often make the body reduce its normal output of sex hormones. (Adapted from Neil A. Campbell, Lawrence G. Mitchell, and Jane B. Reece, *Biology*, 3rd ed., San Francisco: Benjamin Cummings, 2000.)

8. Which word or phrase, if inserted in the blank in sentence 13, would make the relationship of the ideas within the sentence clear?
   A. Moreover
   B. Consequently
   C. However
   D. Nevertheless

PASSAGE #9

Read the passage and answer the question that follows.

1 _____.

²In most cases, the child continually learns from the parent. ³In the area of computer and Internet-mediated communication, however, the child may be able to teach the parent. ⁴_____, one five-year-old learned a graphics program before she could read. ⁵The child taught herself how to operate the rather intuitive program. ⁶Not only did the computer provide the child with a valuable learning process, but the parents totally depended on the child when they wanted to use the program she knew. ⁷In another case, a young boy taught his parents how to use PowerPoint. ⁸The examples are endless. ⁹Children are more apt to interact with the computer as if it were alive. ¹⁰A child may be able to understand a concept differently from the parent, and the role reversal of the child-as-teacher can be an important way the computer and the Internet can enhance a child's self-esteem. ¹¹The child and parent alike may feel positive toward themselves when they are able to learn new things, master a program, or win an Internet game. ¹²Their self-confidence may increase when others seek their advice, for example, because they are the family computer experts. (Adapted from Leonard J. Shedletsky and Joan E. Aitken, *Human Communication on the Internet*, Boston: Allyn and Bacon, 2004.)

9. Which word or phrase, if inserted in the blank in sentence 4, would make the relationship of the ideas within the sentence clear?
    A. Then
    B. Nevertheless
    C. Meanwhile
    D. For example

PASSAGE #10

Read the passage and answer the question that follows.

1 _____.

²Highlighting is a strategy for condensing textbook material and emphasizing what is important. ³_____, the process of highlighting forces you to sift through what you have read to identify important information. ⁴This sifting or sorting is an active thought process; you are forced to weigh and evaluate what you read. ⁵One mistake to avoid is highlighting almost every idea on a page. ⁶Another benefit of highlighting is that it keeps you physically active while you are reading. ⁷In addition, highlighting can help you discover the organization of facts and ideas as well as their connections and relationships. ⁸Highlighting demonstrates to you whether you have understood a passage you have just read. ⁹When combined with annotation, highlighting is a quick and easy way to review so that you do not have to reread everything when studying for an exam. ¹⁰If you highlight 20 percent of a chapter, you will be able to avoid rereading 80 percent of the material. ¹¹If it normally takes two hours to read a chapter, you should be able to review a highlighted chapter in less than a half hour. ¹²Highlighting has many benefits, but it is not by itself a sufficient study method; you must process the information by organizing it, expressing it in your own words, and testing yourself periodically. (Adapted

from Kathleen T. McWhorter, *Study and Critical Thinking Skills in College*, 5th ed., New York: Longman, 2003.)

10. Which word or phrase, if inserted in the blank in sentence 3, would make the relationship of the ideas within the sentence clear?
    A. Besides
    B. Thus
    C. First
    D. Also

Chapter 2: Important Skills to Focus On

1. *Uses Coordination and Subordination Effectively*
2. *Avoids Fragments, Comma Splices, and Fused Sentences*
3. *Maintains Agreement between Subjects and Verbs*
4. *Maintains Pronoun and Antecedent Agreement*
5. *Maintains Clear Pronoun Reference*
6. *Uses Proper Pronoun Case Forms*
7. *Avoids Inappropriate Pronoun Shifts*
8. *Avoids Shifts in Verb Tense*
9. *Uses Modifiers Correctly*
10. *Uses Standard Punctuation*

Introduction

The next section of the Writing Exit Exam—usually beginning with Question 11 and continuing on through Question 40 or the end of the test—focuses on grammar and usage skills. Many of these skills are related to the systems of Subjects and Verbs, Clauses, and Pronouns, and their concepts overlap. Thus, by focusing on these systems and their related skills, you can learn them more easily as similar information is repeated and recycled. Furthermore, understanding these related skills will be very beneficial to you because they can help you answer a good number of the questions on the Writing Exit Exam correctly. In fact, of the typical 30 questions on grammar and usage, more than half can be understood by understanding these basic grammar systems. Therefore, the better you know these systems, the better your chances of passing the test will be. Finally, these related skills also comprise a good number of the grammar and usage errors that students make in their essay. Thus, understanding these basic grammar systems will make your writing more grammatical, which will make it more likely that you pass the Exit Exam Writing Sample.

This chapter will be organized by first briefly introducing a specific question type addressed on the exit exam and then focusing on example test questions for you to try. For more detailed explanation of the grammar behind each question, please refer to the Parts of Speech Review Appendix.

SECTION 1 ◆ COORDINATION AND SUBORDINATION

The Skill

On the Writing Exit Exam, there are usually two questions on coordination and subordination. This item tests your ability to combine sentences and clauses effectively according to how they are related. Just so you know, coordination means linking independent clauses together, and subordination means linking dependent clauses to independent clauses. Please refer to The Parts of Speech Appendix for much more detailed information on how to join clauses.

The keys to answering these questions correctly are the following:

1. Knowing what the linking words *mean*. Fortunately, you probably know most of them.
2. To a lesser extent, knowing how to punctuate them.

Use the following linking words <u>after a comma</u> to join independent clauses:

, for	To give a reason (means "because") • Sandra is running every evening, **for** she is training for a marathon.
, and	To show additional information
, nor	To give a negative choice (means "or," but for a negative choice) • Sandra never run a marathon, **nor** has she trained for one before.
, but , yet	To show contrast or difference • John eats anything he wants, **yet** he never gains weight.
, or	To show a choice
, so	To give a result (means "therefore")

Use the following linking words (conjunctive adverbs) <u>after a semicolon</u> to join independent clauses. Put a <u>comma</u> after the word itself:

; in addition, ; also, ; furthermore, ; likewise, ; moreover,	To show additional information (means "and") • John eats bacon and eggs for breakfast; **moreover,** he often has fast food for lunch. • John eats bacon and eggs for breakfast; **likewise,** he often has fast food for lunch.
; however, ; in contrast, ; on the other hand, ; nevertheless,	To show contrast or difference (means "but") • John eats anything he wants; **however,** he never gains weight.
; meanwhile, ; then,	To show time (means "at the same time but in another place") • Sandra runs ten miles; **meanwhile,** her husband cooks a healthy dinner.
; therefore, ; consequently, ; thus, ; as a result,	To give a result or effect (means "so") • Sandra is training for a marathon; **thus,** she is running every evening.
; for example,	To provide an example of something • Exercise has many benefits; **for example,** it improves the cardio-vascular system, helps control weight, and reduces the chances of diabetes.

Use the following words to <u>create a dependent clause</u> by adding a subject and verb (complement). The resulting clause must be linked to an independent clause.

➤ If the dependent clause comes first, separate it from the independent clause with a comma.
➤ If the independent clause comes first, do not use a comma.

although since though while whereas	**To show contrast or difference (means "but")** • *Although* John eats anything he wants, he never gains weight. • John never gains weight *although* he eats anything he wants.
after as as soon as once while when whenever	**To show time** • *As* Sandra runs her ten miles, her husband cooks a healthy dinner. • Sandra's husband cooks a healthy dinner *as* she runs ten miles.
because since so that	**To give a reason or cause** • *Because* Sandra is training for a marathon, she is running every evening. • Sandra is running every evening *because* she is training for a marathon.
even if if if only provided that unless whether	**To show condition** • *Provided that* Sandra continues to train hard, she will successfully complete the marathon. • Sandra will successfully complete the marathon *provided that* she continues to train hard.

Select the right word to refer to the right noun.

➤ Clauses giving "extra information" should be set off with commas.
➤ Clauses giving information that is <u>necessary</u> should not be set off with commas.

who (subject) whom (object)	**Use for a person** • Sandra, *who* is training for a marathon, is running every evening. • John is the kind of person **who can eat anything and not gain weight.**
that , which,	**Use for things or people in general** • A marathon is a race *that* covers 26 miles. • Marathons, **which cover 26 miles,** are grueling physical tests.
where	**Use for places** • The beach is the place **where Sandra runs.**

The Test Question
You can be tested on your ability to use subordination and coordination in two different ways:

1. You may be given a sentence from which a linking word has been omitted. You must choose the most effective word or phrase suggested by the context of the sentence.
2. You may be given three versions of the same sentence and asked to pick the one that best expresses the relationship between ideas within the sentence.

SECTION 1 ◆ DIAGNOSTIC: COORDINATION AND SUBORDINATION

For each of the following questions, choose the most effective word or phrase within the context suggested by the sentence. When you are done, check your work with the answers immediately following the diagnostic. Even if you get a perfect score here, go ahead and complete the exercises in this section; they are designed to help build confidence and to give you practice for future test success.

1. Matt was going to major in electrical engineering, _____ when he found out the number of math courses he would have to take, he changed his mind.
   A. or
   B. for
   C. nor
   D. but

2. My mother, _____ was the oldest of five siblings, had to quit school and get a job to help the family financially.
   A. which
   B. who
   C. that
   D. what

3. The homes in our neighborhood were badly damaged from the hurricane last year; _____, this year we bought hurricane shutters for all of our windows.
   A. next
   B. likewise
   C. on the other hand
   D. consequently

4. _____ the lines to buy tickets for the movie at Muvico were so long, Dad used the automated ticket machine.
   A. Although
   B. Unless
   C. Because
   D. Until

DIRECTIONS: *For each of the following questions, choose the sentence that expresses the thought most clearly and effectively and that has no error in structure.*

5.
   A. Since I had not played football in high school and spent most of my time in practice, I would have ended up going out and getting in trouble.
   B. As long as I had not played football in high school and spent most of my time in practice, I would have ended up going out and getting in trouble.
   C. If I had not played football in high school and spent most of my time in practice, I would have ended up going out and getting in trouble.

6.

    A. Danielle has been able to rise above her drug addiction and financial instability although it is an ongoing battle for her.

    B. Danielle has been able to rise above her drug addiction and financial instability because it is an ongoing battle for her.

    C. Danielle has been able to rise above her drug addiction and financial instability so that it is an ongoing battle for her.

7.

    A. I do not have a car, but I have to depend on other people and public transportation to get me where I need to go.

    B. I do not have a car, so I have to depend on other people and public transportation to get me where I need to go.

    C. I do not have a car, or I have to depend on other people and public transportation to get me where I need to go.

Answers and Explanations to Diagnostic: Coordination and Subordination

For each of the following questions, the correct definition for each transitional phrase is provided, and the correct relationship between ideas is explained; however, only the definitions for the false choices are given.

1. Answer   D

But: contrast. The first independent clause tells what Matt had planned to study. The second independent clause sets up the contrast between his original plan and his decision to change that plan.

    A. Or   choice between two persons, places, things, or ideas

    B. For   reason/cause

    C. Nor   negative choice

2. Answer   B

Who: pronoun used at the beginning of the adjective clause "who was the oldest of five siblings." "Who" is the word used to refer to a person.

    A. Which   pronoun used at the beginning of an adjective clause to describe a place, thing, or animal

    C. That   pronoun used at the beginning of an adjective clause to describe a place, thing, or animal; can be used to refer to people in general

    D. What   pronoun meaning "that which"

3. Answer   D

Consequently: result. The second independent clause gives the result of the first.

    A. Next   transition word meaning "immediately following," as in time, order, or sequence

    B. Likewise   transition word meaning "similarly" or "also"

    C. On the other hand   transition phrase indicating contrast

4. Answer   C

Because: reason. The dependent clause that begins the sentence gives the reason for the independent clause that follows it.

A.	Although	subordinating conjunction indicating contrast
B.	Unless	subordinating conjunction meaning "except on the condition that"
D.	Until	subordinating conjunction meaning "before or up to the time that"

5. Answer   C

If: cause and effect. The dependent clause that begins the sentence sets up the condition necessary for a result.

A.	Since	subordinating conjunction indicating reason
B.	As long as	subordinating conjunction meaning "during the time that" or "on the condition that"

6. Answer   A

Although: contrast meaning "regardless of the fact that." The dependent clause that follows the independent clause sets up a contrast.

B.	Because	subordinating conjunction indicating a reason for something
C.	So that	subordinating conjunction meaning "in order that"

7. Answer   B

So: result or effect. The first independent clause establishes the cause; the second independent clause is the effect.

A.	But	coordinating conjunction meaning "however"
C.	Or	coordinating conjunction indicating a choice

SECTION 1 ◆ EXERCISES: COORDINATION AND SUBORDINATION

DIRECTIONS: *For each of the following questions, choose the most effective word or phrase within the context suggested by the sentence.*

1. _____ having a baby can be a joyous event for a couple, it can cause a strain on their relationship.
   A. Although
   B. Whenever
   C. Besides
   D. If

2. Our class plans to study Spanish at the University of Seville during the summer; _____, we intend to see the famous historical sites.
   A. therefore
   B. finally
   C. conversely
   D. moreover

3. Surfing the Internet has increased in popularity among teens and young adults, _____ they spend less time watching television.
   A. yet
   B. nor
   C. so
   D. or

4. The telemarketing company is looking for a person _____ can work on weekends.
   A. which
   B. who
   C. that
   D. what

5. Andrea's job as a nurse's aid at the hospital is very demanding; _____, she can take only two college classes each semester.
   A. however
   B. therefore
   C. finally
   D. certainly

DIRECTIONS: *For each of the following questions, choose the sentence that expresses the thought most clearly and effectively and that has no error in structure.*

6.
   A. Because the bus was late, I missed my first class.
   B. Although the bus was late, I missed my first class.
   C. While the bus was late, I missed my first class.

7.
   A. Whereas I receive my two-year degree from the community college, I plan to transfer to a four-year university.
   B. Since I receive my two-year degree from the community college, I plan to transfer to a four-year university.
   C. After I receive my two-year degree from the community college, I plan to transfer to a four-year university.

8.
   A. The pilot who is flying this airplane served in the Air Force before becoming a commercial pilot.
   B. The pilot which is flying this airplane served in the Air Force before becoming a commercial pilot.
   C. The pilot that is flying this airplane served in the Air Force before becoming a commercial pilot.

9.

    A. In my reading class, I have to learn fifty new words every week where I can improve my vocabulary.

    B. In my reading class, I have to learn fifty new words every week so that I can improve my vocabulary.

    C. In my reading class, I have to learn fifty new words every week since I can improve my vocabulary.

10.

    A. My friends and I like to eat fast food whereas most of the choices are high in calories.

    B. My friends and I like to eat fast food so that most of the choices are high in calories.

    C. My friends and I like to eat fast food even though most of the choices are high in calories.

SECTION 2 ◆ FRAGMENTS, COMMA SPLICES, AND FUSED SENTENCES (RUN-ONS)

The Skills

Sentence errors occur when the rules of punctuating and combining clauses are not followed. Please refer to The Parts of Speech Appendix for much more detailed information on dependent and independent clauses.

This item tests your ability to recognize three sentence errors: fragments, comma splices, and fused sentences (or run-ons).

Fragments

A fragment may look like a sentence because it begins with a capital letter and ends with a period, but if you read the word group more carefully, you'll notice that the thought is incomplete. Fragments are often pieces of information that were separated from an independent clause.

It is often easy to spot fragments if you read the question starting with the last sentence first. That way, fragments stick out and make less sense.

The most common types of fragments and how to fix them are as follows.

    1. <u>Dependent Clause Fragment</u>—A dependent clause cannot be punctuated as though it were a sentence. To fix these, you must connect them either to the previous or to the next independent clause. Here are some examples.

<table>
<tr><td align="center">Fragment</td><td align="center">Independent Clause</td></tr>
</table>

    • *Incorrect:* If the dependent <u>clause</u> <u>comes</u> first. <u>You</u> <u>should separate</u> it from the independent clause with a comma.

    • *Correct:* If the dependent <u>clause</u> <u>comes</u> first, <u>you</u> <u>should separate</u> it from the independent clause with a comma.

    • *Correct:* <u>You</u> <u>should separate</u> the dependent clause from the independent clause with a comma *if* the dependent <u>clause</u> <u>comes</u> first.

Independent Clause   Fragment

- *Incorrect:* James <u>could not drive</u> home after class. *Because* <u>he</u> <u>lost</u> his keys.
- *Correct:* James <u>could not drive</u> home after class *because* <u>he</u> <u>lost</u> his keys.
- *Correct:* *Because* <u>James</u> <u>lost</u> his keys, he <u>could not drive</u> home after class.

Independent Clause   Fragment

- *Incorrect:* James <u>made</u> it to the meeting. *Although* <u>he</u> <u>was</u> late.
- *Correct:* James <u>made</u> it to the meeting *although* <u>he</u> <u>was</u> late.
- *Correct:* *Although* <u>James</u> <u>was</u> late, <u>he</u> <u>made</u> it to the meeting on time.
  *Note: the word "although" always begins a dependent clause.

2. <u>Phrase Fragments</u>—Phrases do not have subjects or verbs, so they cannot be punctuated as though they were sentences. These fragments must be connected to either the previous sentence or to the next one, whichever one makes more sense.

Independent Clause   Fragment

- *Incorrect:* <u>Brian</u> <u>pulled</u> a muscle. *Trying* to lift the weight.
- *Correct:* <u>Brian</u> <u>pulled</u> a muscle *trying* to lift the weight.
- *Correct:* Trying to lift the weight, <u>Brian</u> <u>pulled</u> a muscle.

Fragment   Independent Clause

- *Incorrect:* At the beginning of the semester in my writing class. <u>We</u> <u>learned</u> about subjects and verbs.
- *Correct:* At the beginning of the semester in my writing class, <u>we</u> <u>learned</u> about subjects and verbs.
- *Correct:* <u>We</u> <u>learned</u> about subjects and verbs at the beginning of the semester in my writing class.

Be especially careful of fragments caused by a LIST following "such as."

Independent Clause   Fragment

- *Incorrect:* When <u>I</u> <u>went</u> on a diet, <u>I</u> <u>had</u> to give up my favorite foods. Such as pizza, chocolate candy, and ice cream.
- *Correct:* When <u>I</u> <u>went</u> on a diet, <u>I</u> <u>had</u> to give up my favorite foods, such as pizza, chocolate candy, and ice cream.

Comma Splices

Independent clauses can be joined with a COMMA + a coordinating conjunction. Coordinating conjunctions can be remembered as FANBOYS (for, and, nor, but, or, yet, so). A comma splice is an error in which a comma by itself with no FANBOYS is used to join two independent clauses. To fix comma splices, simply apply one of the 4 methods explained in The Parts of Speech Appendix for linking independent clauses:

➢ **Replace the comma with a period.**
➢ **Replace the comma with a semicolon (;).**
➢ **Add a FANBOYS after the comma.**
➢ **Make one of the 2 independent clauses dependent.**

To find comma splices, stop at EVERY comma. If you can add a FANBOYS after the comma, you have a comma splice. This trick does not find <u>all</u> comma splices, but it finds most of them.

The following sentences are examples of the comma splice and its correction.

                   Independent Clause   **Independent Clause**

- *Incorrect:* <u>Joining</u> independent clauses <u>is</u> not hard, <u>you</u> just <u>have</u> to watch out for comma splices and run-on sentences.
- *Correct:* <u>Joining</u> independent clauses <u>is</u> not hard. <u>You</u> just <u>have</u> to watch out for comma splices and run-on sentences.

                   Independent Clause   **Independent Clause**

- *Incorrect:* Comma <u>splices</u> are very common, however, <u>they</u> <u>are</u> easy to fix.
- *Correct:* Comma splices are very common; however, they are easy to fix.

                   Independent Clause   **Independent Clause**

- *Incorrect:* <u>Paul</u> did not have his own car, <u>he</u> <u>had</u> to share a car with his sister.
- *Correct:* <u>Paul</u> <u>did not have</u> his own car, **so** <u>he</u> <u>had</u> to share a car with his sister.

                   Dependent Clause   **Independent Clause**

- *Correct:* *Because* <u>Paul</u> did not have his own car, <u>he</u> <u>had</u> to share a car with his sister.

Fused Sentences (Run-Ons)

A fused sentence consists of two independent clauses with no punctuation or FANBOYS to indicate where the one ends and the second one begins. Read the following examples and corrections.

It is often easy to spot fused sentences if you read the question quietly aloud and listen for where your voice naturally drops. Punctuation is often needed there.

                   Independent Clause   **Independent Clause**

- *Incorrect:* In the summer, afternoon <u>thunderstorms</u> <u>are</u> common <u>driving</u> in heavy rain on the highway <u>can be</u> dangerous.
- *Correct:* In the summer, afternoon <u>thunderstorms</u> <u>are</u> common. <u>Driving</u> in heavy rain <u>can be</u> treacherous.
- *Correct:* In the summer, afternoon <u>thunderstorms</u> <u>are</u> common; <u>driving</u> in heavy rain <u>can be</u> treacherous.

                   Independent Clause   **Independent Clause**

- *Incorrect:* This <u>type</u> of error <u>is</u> very confusing <u>it's</u> hard to follow the writer's train of thought.
- *Correct:* This <u>type</u> of error <u>is</u> very confusing *because* <u>it's</u> hard to follow the writer's train of thought.
- *Correct:* This <u>type</u> of error <u>is</u> very confusing; <u>it's</u> hard to follow the writer's train of thought.
- *Correct:* This <u>type</u> of error <u>is</u> very confusing. <u>It's</u> hard to follow the writer's train of thought.

The Test Question

You can be tested on your ability to recognize fragments, comma splices, and fused sentences in two different ways.

1. You will be given a set of ideas with one underlined portion that indicates a possible error. The error may include a sentence fragment, a comma splice, or a fused sentence. You will be asked to choose the option that corrects the underlined portion.
2. You will be given a set of ideas with three underlined portions that could contain a possible fragment, comma splice, or fused sentence. Check each one of them for possible errors.

Keep in mind the possibility that the sentence is correct.

SECTION 2 ◆ DIAGNOSTIC: FRAGMENTS, COMMA SPLICES, AND FUSED SENTENCES (RUN-ONS)

For each of the following questions, choose the option that corrects an error in the underlined portion(s). If no error exists, choose "No change is necessary." When you are done, check your work with the answers immediately following the diagnostic. Even if you get a perfect score here, go ahead and complete the exercises in this section; they are designed to help build confidence and to give you practice for future test success.

1. When we go to the <u>mall, we</u> buy just about anything we <u>like, for example,</u> we buy clothes,
   A   B

   hats, shoes, and <u>jewelry, anything</u> that catches our eye.
                    C

   A. mall. We
   B. like; for example,
   C. jewelry. Anything
   D. No change is necessary.

2. My grandparents and parents lived in <u>Colombia when</u> it was a safe <u>country, but</u> this country
                                          A   B

   has changed <u>dramatically, now</u> it is not safe to be anywhere outside of one's own house.
               C

   A. Colombia. When
   B. country; but
   C. dramatically. Now
   D. No change is necessary.

3. At my cousin's fifteenth birthday party, while I was dancing to a bachata song with a
   handsome <u>guest. I</u> suddenly fell to the <u>floor. When</u> I stood <u>up, I</u> saw that the heel of my
            A   B   C

   favorite shoe had broken off completely.
   A. guest, I
   B. floor, when
   C. up; I
   D. No change is necessary.

4. I chose to attend a community <u>college, because</u> I do not <u>think that</u> I should pay more money
                                 A   B

   at a university for the same books and classes offered at the community <u>college. Also,</u> I can
                                                                            C

   save money on gas and living expenses by living at home to attend school.
   A. college because
   B. think. That
   C. college, also,
   D. No change is necessary.

5. During our vacation, the weather was not very <u>cooperative it</u> rained most of the time.
   A. cooperative, it
   B. cooperative; it
   C. cooperative and, it
   D. No change is necessary.

6. As a student, I need a flexible work <u>schedule however</u> my boss schedules me to work when I have classes.
   A. schedule, however,
   B. schedule, however;
   C. schedule; however,
   D. No change is necessary.

7. If a police officer suspects that you have been driving while <u>drunk, the</u> officer has the right to pull you over and give you a breath test.
   A. drunk. The
   B. drunk; the
   C. drunk, and the
   D. No change is necessary.

Answers and Explanations to Diagnostic: Fragments, Comma Splices, and Fused Sentences (Run-ons)

1. Answer   B
Choice B places a semicolon after "like." This corrects the comma splice in the sentence. Two independent clauses cannot be connected with a comma alone.

False choices
   A An introductory subordinate clause is followed by a comma. Placing a period after "mall" would make the introductory subordinate clause into a fragment.
   C Placing a period after "jewelry" would create a fragment of the modifier "anything that catches our eye."

2. Answer   C
Replacing the comma with a period and capitalizing "Now" corrects the comma splice error.

False choices
   A The subordinate clause "when it was a safe country" belongs with the independent clause that begins the sentence. The logic of the sentence is lost if that clause is placed at the beginning of the next sentence.
   B "But" is a coordinating conjunction used to join two independent clauses. The punctuation rule requires a comma before "but," not a semicolon.

3. Answer   A
Choice A corrects the fragment error in the sentence. The sentence begins with a prepositional phrase followed by a dependent clause.

False choices
   B Placing a comma after "floor" would create a comma splice error.
   C Placing a semicolon after the word "up" would create a fragment of the introductory dependent clause "When I stood up."

4. Answer   A

No comma is necessary when the dependent clause follows the independent clause.

False choices

    B   Placing a period after "think" creates a dependent clause fragment of the rest of the sentence "that I should pay more money at a university for the same books and classes offered at the community college."

    C   Placing a comma after "college" creates a comma splice.

5. Answer   B

The semicolon placed after "cooperative" corrects the fused sentence.

False choices

    A   Placing a comma after "cooperative" creates a comma splice.

    C   The comma should be placed before the coordinating conjunction, in this case "and," when used to join two independent clauses.

6. Answer   C

This choice corrects the fused sentence by adding a semicolon, a conjunctive adverb, and a comma.

False choices

    A   A comma placed after "schedule" creates a comma splice.

    B   The semicolon is misplaced; it belongs before "however," which should be followed by a comma.

7. Answer   D

This sentence is correctly punctuated.

False choices

    A   Placing a period after "drunk" makes the introductory dependent clause into a fragment.

    B   Placing a semicolon after "drunk" makes the introductory dependent clause into a fragment.

    C   Adding a comma and the word "and" to the sentence changes the sentence into a fragment.

SECTION 2 ◆ EXERCISES: FRAGMENTS, COMMA SPLICES, AND FUSED SENTENCES (RUN-ONS)

 Test Taking Hint

Pay particular attention to the way these questions are made. Notice that there are three words underlined in the stem of the question. Each of these underlined words is labeled in alphabetical order "A" through "C." Notice that each of the answer options is also labeled "A" through "C." The labels in the question are directly matched to the answer options. So the option labeled "A" is only going to replace the word in the question labeled "A." The same is true for "B" and "C." This labeling system means that word "A" does not have anything to do with option "B" or "C." Just be aware of this as you take the test.

DIRECTIONS: *For each of the following questions, choose the option that corrects an error in the underlined portion(s). If no error exists, choose "No change is necessary."*

1. Some people do not have the patience to revise their writing, so they just recopy their rough <u>draft; and</u> hand it in to the instructor.
   A. draft. And
   B. draft and
   C. draft, and,
   D. No change is necessary.

2. While walking on the <u>beach I</u> saw a lone sea gull with a fish hook through its jaw.
   A. beach; I
   B. beach. I
   C. beach, I
   D. No change is necessary.

3. My dial-up Internet connection was <u>slow, so</u> I switched my service to cable <u>modem now</u>
                                          A   B
   searching <u>online is</u> quick and easy.
                   C
   A. slow; so
   B. modem; now
   C. online, is
   D. No change is necessary.

4. Last Tuesday night, two servers did not show up at the <u>restaurant, therefore</u> I had to take on extra tables.
   A. restaurant; therefore,
   B. restaurant, therefore;
   C. restaurant, therefore,
   D. No change is necessary.

5. Because I could not catch the <u>cockroach that</u> ran under my <u>bed, I was</u> too nervous to go to
                                       A   B
   <u>sleep and</u> decided to wait up for it to come out of its hiding place.
        C
   A. cockroach, that
   B. bed. I
   C. sleep, and
   D. No change is necessary.

6. Although Azaleas is a full-time college <u>student; she</u> has a <u>husband and</u> two young children to
                                             A   B
   take <u>care of, which</u> takes up much of her time.
              C
   A. student, she
   B. husband, and
   C. care of; which
   D. No change is necessary.

7. I used to play basketball every night with my <u>friends studying</u> is my evening activity now that I am in college.
   A. friends, studying
   B. friends. Studying
   C. friends, studying;
   D. No change is necessary.

8. After sitting through three classes in a <u>row, I</u> get very hungry and <u>sleepy. As a result,</u> all I
                                       A   B

   think about is <u>food, not</u> the content of the lectures.
                       C
   A. row. I
   B. sleepy, as a result;
   C. food; not
   D. No change is necessary.

9. Jon used to be very <u>skinny, but</u> since he joined a <u>gym, he</u> has put on significant muscle <u>mass,</u>
                              A   B   C

   <u>and</u> likes to wear muscle shirts to show off.
   A. skinny, but,
   B. gym; he
   C. mass and
   D. No change is necessary.

10. Danielle spends all the money that she earns on her job on designer clothes, shoes, and <u>purses,</u>
    <u>for example</u> last week she spent $350 on a pair of faded, worn-out looking jeans with holes cut out of the knees.
    A. purses; for example,
    B. purses, for example,
    C. purses, for example;
    D. No change is necessary.

11. I do not have a printer at <u>home, so</u> I saved my paper on a <u>disk, when</u> I tried to open the disk
                                              A   B

    in the lab at <u>school, I</u> discovered that I had saved my work in a different program.
                          C
    A. home so,
    B. disk; when
    C. school. I
    D. No change is necessary.

12. Don bought a new hybrid <u>car, he</u> claims that he gets 45 miles per <u>gallon unlike</u> his old <u>car that</u>
                                            A   B   C

    got 19 miles per gallon.
    A. car; he
    B. gallon; unlike
    C. car, that
    D. No change is necessary.

13. Now that my best friend has become a <u>vegetarian, she</u> does not want <u>to go to</u> any of the
                                            A   B

    <u>restaurants where</u> we used to eat.
             C
    A. vegetarian; she
    B. to go, to
    C. restaurants, where
    D. No change is necessary.

14. Whenever the people who live in the apartment above mine have a <u>party. They</u> play their music
    so loudly that my walls vibrate to the beat.
    A. party, they,
    B. party, they
    C. party, and they
    D. No change is necessary.

15. Every Saturday, each of the children in Tamika's family has chores <u>to do such as</u> cleaning the
    bathrooms, changing the sheets, and doing the laundry.
    A. to do, such as
    B. to do; such as,
    C. to do. Such as
    D. No change is necessary

16. Marcellus left his English <u>book in</u> the <u>classroom, when</u> he came back to get <u>it, the</u> book was gone.
                                  A   B   C
    A. book. In
    B. classroom; when
    C. it. The
    D. No change is necessary.

17. After Annabelle <u>graduates, she</u> plans to look for a nursing position in a <u>hospital rather</u> than
                                A   B
    in a nursing <u>home, the</u> salary is better at a hospital.
                      C
    A. graduates; she
    B. hospital. Rather
    C. home. The
    D. No change is necessary.

18. At our college, students may not withdraw from more than three <u>courses during</u> their
                                                          A

    <u>enrollment, this</u> does not include courses dropped during the drop and add <u>period at</u> the
         B   C
    beginning of the semester when students can drop classes without penalty.
    A. courses. During
    B. enrollment; this
    C. period. At
    D. No change is necessary.

19. In order to pay for my car <u>expenses, which</u> <u>include:</u> insurance, gas, and <u>repairs, I</u> must have a
                                            A   B   C

part-time job.
   A. expenses; which
   B. include insurance
   C. repairs. I
   D. No change is necessary.

20. The United States culture, through images in the print and electronic media, promotes
slimness in <u>women as</u> the <u>ideal; to</u> try to attain that <u>appearance; some</u> young women become
                     A   B   C

anorexic.
   A. women, as
   B. ideal, to
   C. appearance, some
   D. No change is necessary.

SECTION 3 ◆ AGREEMENT BETWEEN SUBJECTS AND VERBS

On the grammar section of the Writing Exit Exam, you will get one or more questions in which you are expected to evaluate whether or not the <u>subject</u> is the right one given the <u>verb</u>, or vice-versa. In other words, you are expected to evaluate whether or not the subject and the verb agree. Please review The Parts of Speech Appendix for more detailed information about Verbs, Subjects, Prepositional Phrases, and Dependent Clauses. The following is a list of things to watch out for to successfully answer subject/verb agreement questions.

1. <u>**Watch out for DROPPED "S" ENDINGS and WAS/WERE errors**</u>—In simple present tense, verbs all have the same ending for every person EXCEPT for **he/she/it and nouns that can be referred to as he/she/it.** In those cases, there is an "s" at the end of the verb. Also, "be" linking verbs in the past tense can cause problems.

SINGULAR		PLURAL	
<u>SUBJECT</u>	<u>VERB</u>	<u>SUBJECT</u>	<u>VERB</u>
I	have / don't / am / was	WE	have / don't / are / were
YOU	have / don't / are / were	YOU (ALL)	have / don't / are / were
HE / SHE / IT (the student, peace, writing, etc.)	ha<u>s</u> / do<u>es</u>n't / is / was	THEY (the students, our neighbors, the assignments, etc.)	have / don't / are / were

- *Incorrect:* <u>Our teacher</u> <u>give</u> too much work.
                      Subject   Verb
- *Correct:* <u>Our teacher</u> <u>giveS</u> too much work.

- *Incorrect:* My <u>son</u> <u>have</u> to clean the cats' litter box, and my <u>daughter</u> <u>have</u> to fill their food and water dishes.
- *Correct:* My <u>son</u> <u>haS</u> to clean the cats' litter box, and my <u>daughter</u> <u>haS</u> to fill their food and water dishes.

- *Incorrect:* My <u>son</u> <u>don't know</u> what <u>he</u> <u>want</u> to be when <u>he</u> <u>grow</u> up.
- *Correct:* My <u>son</u> <u>doeSn't know</u> what <u>he</u> <u>wantS</u> to be when <u>he</u> <u>growS</u> up.

- *Incorrect:* When <u>we</u> <u>was</u> little, my sister and <u>I</u> <u>slept</u> in the same bed.
- *Correct:* When <u>we</u> <u>WERE</u> little, my sister and <u>I</u> <u>slept</u> in the same bed.

2. <u>Watch out for these SINGULAR SUBJECTS,</u> especially when prepositional phrases or other structures separate these subjects from the verb. In present tense, there is ALWAYS an "S" at the end of the verb with these subjects. With linking verbs in the past tense, the verb is always WAS.

"Body" words	"One" words	Others
Anybody Nobody Everybody Somebody	Every One (Of) One (Of) Everyone Anyone No One None (Of)	Either (Of) Neither (Of) Each (Of)

DO NOT GET CONFUSED AND MAKE THE OBJECT OF A PREPOSITION AGREE WITH THE VERB! IT'S BEST TO CROSS PREPOSITIONAL PHRASES OUT OF THE SENTENCE.

- *Incorrect:* Each of the students are going to pass the Exit Exam.
- *Correct:* <u>Each</u> (~~of the students~~) <u>is going</u> to pass the Exit Exam.

- *Incorrect:* The student with the most classes and the best grades have to try the hardest.
- *Correct:* The <u>student</u> (~~with the most classes and the best grades~~) <u>has</u> to try the hardest.

- *Incorrect:* After the sweetness of low prices diminish, the bitterness of poor labor and craftsmanship remain.
- *Correct:* After the <u>sweetness</u> (~~of low prices~~) <u>diminishes</u>, the <u>bitterness</u> (~~of poor labor and craftsmanship~~) <u>remains</u>.

3. <u>Watch out for overuse of "THERE IS"</u>—"There" is an <u>adverb</u>! It cannot be the subject of a sentence. The subject of "THERE IS" comes <u>after</u> the verb. If the subject is plural, make sure you use THERE ARE.

- *Incorrect:* There's too many dogs in my neighborhood.
- *Correct:* There <u>are</u> too many <u>dogs</u> in my neighborhood.
  - ➢ Try turning the sentence around to see the structure better:
    - ○ "Too many <u>dogs</u> <u>are</u> there in my neighborhood."

- *Incorrect:* There's some cherries in the refrigerator.
- *Correct:* There <u>are</u> some <u>cherries</u> in the refrigerator.
  - ➢ Try turning the sentence around to see the structure better:
    - ○ "Some <u>cherries</u> <u>are</u> there in the refrigerator."

4. <u>Watch out for ADJECTIVE CLAUSES</u>—The verb in an adjective clause must agree with the noun that's being described (its antecedent).

- <u>Students</u> [<u>who</u> <u>have</u> to leave class early] <u>should</u> always <u>inform</u> me ahead of time.
  - ➢ In this case, the adjective clause "who have to leave early" is referring to "students." Therefore, the verb in the adjective clause agrees with "students."

- A <u>student</u> [<u>who</u> <u>has</u> to leave class early] <u>should</u> always <u>inform</u> me ahead of time.
  - ➢ In this case, the adjective clause "who has to leave early" is referring to "student." Therefore, the verb in the adjective clause agrees with "student."

5. <u>Watch out for EITHER / OR and NEITHER / NOR combinations</u>—With those structures, the verb agrees with the subject closest to it.

- *Neither* my <u>sister</u> *nor* <u>I</u> <u>have</u> any children of our own.
  - ➢ The verb agrees with "I" (have) rather than "sister" (has) because "I" is the closest one to the verb.

- *Either* the <u>vegetables</u> *or* the <u>meat</u> <u>has</u> gone bad.
  - ➢ The verb agrees with "meat" (has) rather than "vegetables" (have) because "meat" is the closest one to the verb.

The Test Question

You will be given a sentence with three underlined parts, which may contain a subject-verb agreement error. If the original sentence contains an error, you must choose the answer that corrects the error in the underlined portion. If the sentence is correct, choose "No change is necessary."

SECTION 3 ◆ DIAGNOSTIC: AGREEMENT BETWEEN SUBJECTS AND VERBS

In each of the following questions, choose the option that corrects an error in the underlined portion(s). If no error exists, choose "No change is necessary." When you are done, check your work with the answers immediately following the diagnostic. Even if you get a perfect score here, go ahead and complete the exercises in this section; they are designed to help build confidence and to give you practice for future test success.

1. Under the stack of papers and books on my desk <u>is</u> my homework assignment, but my wallet
A

   as well as my driver's license <u>are</u> missing, and my friends <u>expect</u> me to drive to school today.
B   C

   A. are
   B. is
   C. expects
   D. No change is necessary.

2. There <u>is</u> some chips on the kitchen counter, and other snacks <u>are</u> in the cabinet; also, if anyone
A   B

   <u>wants</u> soda, we only have cola.
C

   A. are
   B. is
   C. want
   D. No change is necessary.

3. At graduation, the audience <u>disrespect</u> the speaker by talking during his speech; no one <u>seems</u>
A   B

   to dignify the event or <u>shows</u> respect for the people being honored.
C

   A. disrespects
   B. seem
   C. show
   D. No change is necessary.

4. Neither your ear mitts nor your knit cap <u>are</u> warm enough to keep your head warm while you
A

   are in Alaska, so you should buy a fake fur hat that <u>covers</u> your ears; a warm pair of boots <u>is</u>
B   C

   another item you should take with you.
   A. is
   B. cover
   C. are
   D. No change is necessary.

5. A carrying case and an A/C adaptor <u>are</u> included with your portable DVD player; not only do
A

   you get these items, but for no extra charge <u>are</u> the remote control and headphones, so the
B

   only thing left to buy <u>are</u> batteries.
C

   A. is
   B. is
   C. is
   D. No change is necessary.

6. One of my favorite television shows <u>is</u> *CSI Las Vegas* because Grissom's team <u>works</u> so well
   A   B

   together, and the crimes <u>are</u> difficult for me to figure out.
   C

   A. are
   B. work
   C. is
   D. No change is necessary.

7. Every meal at our favorite Thai restaurant <u>is</u> not only delicious to eat, but also beautiful to
   A

   look at; every entrée <u>have</u> a unique presentation with vegetables that <u>are</u> cut into shapes of
   B   C

   leaves and flowers.
   A. are
   B. has
   C. is
   D. No change is necessary.

Answers and Explanations to Diagnostic: Subject and Verb Agreement

1. Answer   B
The subject of the clause after "but" is "wallet," which is singular. Don't be fooled by thinking "as well as" is the same as "and."

False choices
  A The sentence begins with a series of prepositional phrases and, therefore, does not follow the usual subject-verb sentence pattern. The subject and verb are inverted; in other words, the subject comes after the verb. "My homework assignment" is the subject, so the verb must be singular, not plural.
  C The subject of the verb "expect" is plural ("friends"), so the verb must be in the third person plural form.

2. Answer   A
The word "there" does not function as a subject. Therefore, in this sentence, the subject and verb are inverted. The subject is "chips," so to agree, the verb must be the plural "are."

False choices
  B The subject "snacks" is plural and does not agree with the singular verb form "is."
  C The subject "anyone" is singular and does not agree with the plural verb form "want."

3. Answer   A
The subject "audience" is acting as a group, so the correct verb form is "disrespects," third person singular.

False choices
  B In the second main clause of the sentence, the subject is "no one." Because "no one" is singular, it does not agree with the plural verb form "seem."
  C The subject of the verb is "no one," which does not agree with the plural verb form "show."

4. Answer   A

With a "neither-nor" compound subject, the subject closest to the verb determines the form of the verb. In this sentence, "cap" follows "nor," so the verb must be singular, "is."

False choices

    B The dependent clause beginning with "that" modifies "hat." Therefore, the verb should agree with the singular "hat." "Cover" is the plural form.

    C The verb should agree with "pair," not "boots." "Boots" is in the prepositional phrase and in this case does not affect the subject-verb agreement. The verb form should not be "are," which is plural.

5. Answer   C

The verb "are" does not agree with the singular subject "thing."

False choices

    A The verb form "is" does not agree with the two subjects "carrying case" and "A/C adaptor."

    B The two subjects "remote control" and "headphones" follow the verb in this part of the sentence, so the verb must be plural, "are."

6. Answer   D

All of the subjects and verbs in the sentence agree.

False choices

    A The subject "one" is singular, so the verb must be singular, not plural.

    B The subject of the verb "works" is "team," which is singular.

    C The subject of the verb "are" is "crimes," which is plural.

7. Answer   B

The verb "has" agrees with the singular subject "entrée."

False choices

    A The singular subject "meal" requires a singular verb "is," not "are."

    C In this sentence, the verb follows the relative pronoun "that." The relative pronoun refers to a noun that comes before it in the sentence, "vegetables." Since the noun is plural, the verb form must also be plural, "are." (The dependent clause modifies "vegetables.")

SECTION 3 ◆ EXERCISES: AGREEMENT BETWEEN SUBJECTS AND VERBS

DIRECTIONS: *In each of the following questions, choose the option that corrects an error in the underlined portion(s). If no error exists, choose "No change is necessary."*

    1. Neither my keys nor my MP3 player <u>were</u> on the counter; maybe my roommates, who <u>have</u>
                                    A   B
       <u>been</u> home all afternoon, know where either of them <u>is</u>.
        C

    A. was

    B. has been

    C. were

    D. No change is necessary.

2. The committee <u>disagree</u> on the dates we <u>have</u> chosen for our yearly event; we must decide

                       A   B

    soon because each of the speakers <u>need</u> two months' notification.

                                   C

A. disagrees
B. has
C. needs
D. No change is necessary.

3. The Golden Cockatoo is one of the few stores in town that <u>specializes</u> in selling tropical birds;

                                               A

    my family <u>enjoys</u> going there because each of the birds on display <u>have</u> its own perch outside

               B   C

    their cages.

A. specialize
B. enjoy
C. has
D. No change is necessary.

4. The Department of Science and Engineering library <u>sponsors</u> a lecture series that <u>have become</u>

                                           A   B

    so popular that none of the people I know <u>have been</u> able to get tickets.

                                          C

A. sponsor
B. has become
C. has been
D. No change is necessary.

5. There <u>are</u> many different food options to choose from for lunch, but Joe, along with his

             A

    brother, <u>prefers</u> peanut butter and jelly, which <u>are</u> his favorite.

            B   C

A. is
B. prefer
C. is
D. No change is necessary.

6. *Stand and Deliver* <u>tell</u> a story of a dedicated math teacher; the movie <u>focuses</u> on his work with

                           A   B

    students who <u>come</u> from poor backgrounds.

                      C

A. tells
B. focus
C. comes
D. No change is necessary.

7. Diseases such as mumps and measles <u>have</u> been almost completely eradicated; however,
                                          A

    AIDS scientists from all over the world, who <u>performs</u> research every day, <u>have</u> not been able
                                                  B   C

    to find a cure.
    A. has
    B. perform
    C. has
    D. No change is necessary.

8. The number of students in my class <u>has</u> dropped from thirty to nine; anatomy and physiology
                                          A

    <u>is</u> a difficult subject, and few <u>passes</u> the course.
    B   C
    A. have
    B. are
    C. pass
    D. No change is necessary.

9. The slaughter of elephants for their tusks <u>has</u> caused a decline in the elephant population; the
                                                 A

    tusks <u>are</u> used to make jewelry and other precious items on which artisans <u>carve</u> intricate
          B   C

    designs.
    A. have
    B. is
    C. carves
    D. No change is necessary.

10. Shelters for abused women <u>offers</u> a place where single women or mothers and children <u>go</u> to
                               A   B

    escape the person who <u>wants</u> to harm them.
                           C
    A. offer
    B. goes
    C. want
    D. No change is necessary.

11. Refreshments on short flights <u>are</u> inadequate; a beverage and a small package of salted peanuts
                                   A

    <u>does</u> not satisfy the hunger that most travelers <u>experience</u>.
     B   C
    A. is
    B. do
    C. experiences
    D. No change is necessary.

12. Briana, along with her family, <u>have</u> recently moved to this area; she <u>wants</u> to buy a large piece
                    A   B

    of property in the country where she <u>plans</u> to build a large home and barn.
                                           C

    A. has
    B. want
    C. plan
    D. No change is necessary.

13. My new glasses <u>hurt</u> my nose; my blue jeans with the red stitching <u>are</u> too tight, but every one
                     A   B

    of my tattoos <u>look</u> just fine.
                    C

    A. hurts
    B. is
    C. looks
    D. No change is necessary.

14. Our accommodations at the hotel <u>has</u> been confirmed, so now one of us <u>needs</u> to book our
                                   A   B

    flight; then we can figure out how much money the trip <u>costs</u>.
                                                C

    A. have
    B. need
    C. cost
    D. No change is necessary.

15. Although statistics <u>are</u> difficult for me, mathematics <u>seems</u> easy; languages, like Spanish or
                          A   B

    French, <u>present</u> no problem at all since I lived in Venezuela and Paris.
                  C

    A. is
    B. seem
    C. presents
    D. No change is necessary.

16. Many students from the Bahamas <u>have come</u> to study in South Florida because the weather is
                                         A

    similar; in addition, there <u>are</u> a variety of schools that <u>offer</u> college degrees.
                                 B   C

    A. has come
    B. is
    C. offers
    D. No change is necessary.

17. Many foods and beverages that we enjoy today <u>come</u> from other countries; for example, the
                                                    A
    French, who <u>is</u> known for their cuisine, <u>have</u> given us café au lait, soufflés, baguettes (French
               B   C
    bread), petit fours, and fondue.
    A. comes
    B. are
    C. has
    D. No change is necessary.

18. The news of your accomplishments <u>make</u> us very proud; Automaticlabs <u>is</u> a new company
                                        A   B
    with enormous potential, and with you as president, the future of the business <u>looks</u> bright.
                                                                                      C
    A. makes
    B. are
    C. look
    D. No change is necessary.

19. A number of squirrels <u>live</u> in my neighborhood, and many of the neighbors <u>enjoy</u> watching
                             A   B
    them; unfortunately, a few of them <u>gets</u> run over by cars.
                                          C
    A. lives
    B. enjoys
    C. get
    D. No change is necessary.

20. On July 4th, most of the country <u>celebrates</u>; outdoor picnics and barbeques <u>are</u> popular
                                         A   B
    daytime activities while at night, fireworks displays <u>attract</u> people of all ages.
                                                              C
    A. celebrate
    B. is
    C. attracts
    D. No change is necessary.

SECTION 4 ◆ PRONOUN AND ANTECEDENT AGREEMENT

A pronoun is a general word that stands for some other word in the sentence. A pronoun is a word that is used to replace a noun or another pronoun. When the pronoun refers to a word that appears earlier in a sentence, then that word is called the pronoun's <u>antecedent</u>. Please refer to The Parts of Speech Appendix for more detailed information on pronouns.

The Skill
This item tests your ability to identify and correct errors in pronoun and antecedent agreement. There are certain situations that tend to lead to this error, so understanding those situations should help you recognize errors with pronoun agreement.

1. <u>Watch out for overuse of THEY, THEIR, and THEM</u>—Unlike most other languages, English does not have a good *neutral* third person singular pronoun. We have *he, she, it,* and *one.* If we do not know the sex of the person we are referring to, we often use *their/them/they,* which are **plural**. However, this is not appropriate if the original pronoun we use is *singular.*

   Make sure all instances of THEY/THEIR/THEM are referring to a <u>plural</u> word in the sentence.

   The following **personal pronouns** are **always singular** and so must be referred to with singular pronouns (**his or her, him or her, he or she**):

"Body" words	"One" words	Others
Anybody Nobody Everybody Somebody	Every One (Of) One (Of) Everyone Anyone No One None (Of)	Either (Of) Neither (Of) Each (Of)

   - *Incorrect:* **Someone** left **their** books in the classroom.
     ➤ "Someone" is SINGULAR, so it cannot be referred to with THEIR.
   Correct: **Someone** left **his or her** books in the classroom.
     ➤ Only use "his" if the antecedent is clearly male; only use "her" if the antecedent is clearly female. If the antecedent is neutral, use both: *his or her.*

   - *Incorrect:* **Nobody** should be alone on **their** birthday.
   - *Correct:* **Nobody** should be alone on **his or her** birthday.

   - *Incorrect:* **Anybody** would be proud to have **their** picture taken with the Queen.
   - *Correct:* **Anybody** would be proud to have **his or her** picture taken with the Queen.

   - *Incorrect:* **Everyone** who finishes the 5K race is a winner, regardless of how **they** place in the race.
   - *Correct:* **Everyone** who finishes the 5K race is a winner, regardless of how **he or she** places in the race.

   Watch out for "of" prepositional phrases! Be sure to cross out those prepositions so that you do not get distracted by their objects.

   - *Incorrect:* **One** of the employees left **their** sunglasses in the bathroom.
   - *Correct:* **One** (~~of the employees~~) left **his or her** sunglasses in the bathroom.

   Be careful! This does not mean that THEY/THEIR/THEM is always wrong in a sentence.

- *Correct:* **Kelly and Scott** ordered **their** wedding cake from a family-run bakery.
- *Correct:* The **children** should leave **their** shoes in the hallway.

2. <u>**Some pronouns can be EITHER SINGULAR OR PLURAL depending on how they are used**</u>— They include some, any, all, more, and most.

   - *Correct:* **Some people** prefer to own **their** own homes while others prefer to rent.
     ➤ The fact that "some" is describing "people" shows that it is plural.
   - *Correct:* **Most of the sweaters** in my closet have lost **their** shape.
     ➤ The fact that "most" is describing "sweaters" shows that it is plural.
   - *Correct:* **Some of the gas** spilled out of **its** container.
     ➤ The fact that "some" is being used with "gas" shows that it is singular.

3. <u>**Watch out for SINGULAR COLLECTIVE NOUNS—they are referred to as "IT"**</u>—Collective nouns are groups of things that are acting as a single unit. For example, a family may be composed of more than one member, but the word "family" itself is singular and so must be referred to as **it/its.** Some common examples include:

Class	Family	Gang	Jury
Committee	Firm	Government	School
Company	Flock	Group	Team

   - *Incorrect:* The basketball **team** won **their** first game of the season last week.
   - *Correct:* The basketball **team** won **its** first game of the season last week.

   - *Incorrect:* The **group** of schoolchildren made **their** way across the street.
   - *Correct:* The **group** of schoolchildren made **its** way across the street.

   If the collective noun is plural, refer to it as "they/their."
   - *Correct:* The **committees** got together for **their** annual meeting.

4. <u>**Watch out for EITHER / OR and NEITHER / NOR combinations**</u>—In the section on subject and verb agreement, you learned that with the word groups either/or and neither/nor, the verb always agrees in number with the closer of the two subjects. Pronoun agreement with these words works in the same way. **The pronoun should agree with the closest noun in the combination.**

   Correct: **Either** the *employees or the supervisor, Mrs. Jones,* left **her** day planner in the office.

   Correct: **Neither** the *ocean nor the sandy beaches* will ever lose **their** appeal to college students on spring break.

The Test Question

You will be presented with one or two sentences that have one or three underlined parts that may reflect a pronoun-antecedent agreement error. If the original sentence contains an error, you must choose the option that corrects the error in an underlined part. If the sentence is correct, choose "No change is necessary."

SECTION 4 ◆ DIAGNOSTIC: PRONOUN AND ANTECEDENT AGREEMENT

For each of the following questions, choose the option that corrects an error in the underlined portion(s). If no error exists, then choose "No change is necessary." When you are done, check your work with the answers immediately following the diagnostic. Even if you get a perfect score here, go ahead and complete the exercises in this section; they are designed to help build confidence and to give you practice for future test success.

1. Each group will have three minutes for <u>their</u> presentation.
   A. our
   B. your
   C. its
   D. No change is necessary.

2. A student should register early to get the courses at the times <u>you</u> would like.
   A. they
   B. he or she
   C. we
   D. No change is necessary.

3. The jury in the Michael Jackson case took <u>their</u> time to come to a unanimous verdict.
   A. its
   B. his
   C. our
   D. No change is necessary.

4. When lifting heavy weights, Joe must maintain his concentration so <u>you</u> won't get hurt.
   A. one
   B. we
   C. he
   D. No change is necessary.

5. Each year, the teens in the neighborhood stockpile fireworks to create <u>their</u> own display;
   A

   however, <u>they</u> do not realize that <u>we</u> could get hurt.
   B   C
   A. you
   B. you
   C. they
   D. No change is necessary.

6. Any woman who purchased a knock-off designer purse wasted <u>their</u> money; <u>its</u> stitching easily
   A   B

   comes loose, and <u>its</u> zippers get stuck or break.
   C
   A. her
   B. their
   C. your
   D. No change is necessary.

7. Our culture stresses the importance of physical perfection in women, so <u>they</u> try many
                                                                          A
different kinds of diets and get plastic surgery to alter <u>our</u> looks; few seem to appreciate <u>their</u>
                                                          B   C
inner beauty.
   A. she
   B. their
   C. her
   D. No change is necessary.

Answers and Explanations to Diagnostic: Pronoun and Antecedent Agreement

1. Answer   C
The correct pronoun is the singular "its," which agrees with the singular antecedent "each group."
The antecedent is third person singular, so the matching pronoun must also be a third person singular
form. Choice A is second person plural, and Choice B is second person singular.

2. Answer   B
In this sentence, the pronoun "he or she" agrees with its antecedent "student." Both are third person
singular. Choice A, "they" is a third person plural pronoun, and Choice C, "we" is a second person
plural pronoun.

3. Answer   A
The pronoun "its" agrees with the antecedent "jury." "Jury" is a collective noun that can be singular
or plural depending on its use. When referring to the individuals of the jury acting as a unit, the pronoun should be singular. Since the gender of the jury is unknown, "his" would be an inappropriate
choice. Choice C, "our," is second person plural.

4. Answer   C
The pronoun "he" refers to the antecedent "Joe." Since Joe is male, we can use "he" rather than
"one." "We" is a second person plural pronoun.

5. Answer   C
All of the pronoun choices in the sentence refer to the antecedent "teens." Therefore, they should all
be third person plural forms.

6. Answer   A
The pronoun for choice A should agree with the antecedent "woman," so "her" is the correct choice.
The second two pronouns in the sentence both refer to "purse," so they are the same, "its."

7. Answer   B
The pronoun "their" agrees with its antecedent, "women." All of the choices refer to "women" and,
therefore, should be third person plural forms.

SECTION 4 ◆ EXERCISES: PRONOUN AND ANTECEDENT AGREEMENT

DIRECTIONS: For each of the following questions, choose the option that corrects an error in the underlined portion(s). If no error exists, choose "No change is necessary."

1. Each passenger wanting to board the plane to Tampa must present <u>their</u> identification to the airline representative.
   A. her
   B. its
   C. our
   D. No change is necessary.

2. Either the band or the choir will give <u>its</u> performance first.
   A. their
   B. her
   C. his
   D. No change is necessary.

3. The company gives each of <u>their</u> employees a bonus at the end of the year.
   A. his
   B. its
   C. her
   D. No change is necessary.

4. Even though the weather conditions were not optimal, neither the surfers nor the boater changed <u>its</u> plans for a day on the ocean.
   A. their
   B. our
   C. his
   D. No change is necessary.

5. Pete has a successful landscaping business because the employees work hard, and <u>its</u> prices are fair.
   A. their
   B. his
   C. our
   D. No change is necessary.

6. Andrea and Sebastian do not seem to understand the concepts presented in <u>their</u> algebra class.
   A

   They have gone for tutoring in the math lab, but <u>it</u> has not helped <u>him.</u>
   B   C

   A. his
   B. he
   C. them
   D. No change is necessary.

7. The downtown improvement committee has presented <u>their</u> decision to tear down the existing
                                                        A

    strip mall and build a park. <u>It</u> wanted to give each child a place where <u>he</u> could play.
                                  B   C

    A. its
    B. They
    C. they
    D. No change is necessary.

8. The neighbor's pool was crowded with children who came to celebrate Brian's third birthday
    party with <u>him</u>. Each child was given an inflated toy to help <u>him</u> float in the water; as well,
                A   B
    each child's parent went in the pool with <u>their</u> child.
                                               C

    A. them
    B. them
    C. his or her
    D. No change is necessary.

9. The professor was angry with the class because no one brought <u>his or her</u> book to class;
                                                                   A

    therefore, neither the students nor the professor could do <u>their</u> lesson for the day. As a result,
                                                                B

    the professor gave <u>them</u> a lengthy homework assignment.
                        C

    A. their
    B. his
    C. him or her
    D. No change is necessary.

10. If anyone wants tickets to the game, <u>he or she</u> can buy <u>his or hers</u> online, at a ticket outlet, or
                                          A   B

    at the stadium. Because the tickets are selling fast, buy <u>them</u> as soon as possible.
                                                              C

    A. they
    B. them
    C. it
    D. No change is necessary.

SECTION 5 ◆ CLEAR PRONOUN REFERENCE

The Skill

When a pronoun is used, it must have a clear antecedent in the sentence. If not, then the reference is not clear. This item tests your ability to identify unclear pronoun reference and to recognize that a pronoun refers to a specific word or phrase, not a whole idea. A pronoun can refer to only one antecedent and must do so clearly without any confusion. Please review The Parts of Speech Appendix for more explanation about pronouns.

There are two instances in which errors are made in pronoun reference.

1. <u>Unclear Antecedents</u>—A pronoun can refer to only one antecedent and should do so without causing confusion. Sometimes, though, a sentence with several nouns and pronouns can cause problems with pronoun reference if it is not clear which of those nouns the pronoun is referring to.

   - *Incorrect:* The **computer** sat on the **desk** next to the **filing cabinet**. After Karen put her bag on **it**, she began to type her essay.
      ➤ Did Karen put her bag on the desk or on the filing cabinet? The pronoun "it" could refer to either one.
   - *Correct:* The computer sat on the **desk** next to the **filing cabinet**. After Karen put her bag on **the desk**, she began to type her essay.
   - *Correct:* The computer sat on the **desk** next to the **filing cabinet**. After Karen put her bag on **the filing cabinet**, she began to type her essay.

   - *Incorrect:* **Heather** told **Kimberly** that **she** should ask Ryan out for a date.
      ➤ "She" could refer to either Heather or Kimberly.
   - *Correct:* **Heather** told **Kimberly** that **she, Heather,** should ask Ryan out for a date.

2. <u>Missing Antecedents</u>—Remember: every pronoun must have an antecedent in the sentence that clearly matches the pronoun.
   - *Incorrect:* At Busch Gardens, **they** have wonderful roller coasters.
      ➤ Who is they?
   - *Correct:* Busch Gardens has wonderful roller coasters.

   - *Incorrect:* At the flea market, **they** have bargains on many different kinds of products.
      ➤ Who is they?
   - *Correct:* At the flea market, **the vendors** have bargains on many different kinds of products.

The Test Question
You will be presented with one or two sentences with one or three underlined parts that may contain a pronoun reference error. If the original sentence passage contains an error, you must choose the option that corrects an underlined part. If the sentence is correct, choose "No change is necessary."

SECTION 5 ◆ DIAGNOSTIC: CLEAR PRONOUN REFERENCE

For each of the following questions, choose the option that corrects an error in the underlined portion(s). If no error exists, then choose "No change is necessary." When you are done, check your work with the answers immediately following the diagnostic. Even if you get a perfect score here, go ahead and complete the exercises in this section; they are designed to help build confidence and to give you practice for future test success.

1. Greg beat Brandon at basketball when <u>he</u> had not even played for several months.
   A. the team
   B. he, Greg,
   C. the coach
   D. No change is necessary.

2. Melissa, whose book was stolen, told the instructor that <u>she</u> should report the theft.
   A. the class
   B. she, Melissa,
   C. the thief
   D. No change is necessary.

3. While I was carrying my essay to English class during the rainstorm, <u>it</u> made the ink run, and as a result, the essay was unreadable.
   A. the weather
   B. the essay
   C. the rain
   D. No change is necessary.

4. On the radio, <u>it</u> said that traffic on I-75 would be backed up for miles.
   A. the radio
   B. the traffic report
   C. the traffic reporter
   D. No change is necessary.

5. Sean had to take the CD player out of the car and fix <u>it</u>.
   A. the CD player
   B. Sean
   C. the CD
   D. No change is necessary.

6. Halfway through the movie, the bucket of popcorn was empty, but we were tired of eating <u>it</u> anyway.
   A. the bucket
   B. the popcorn
   C. the movie
   D. No change is necessary.

7. Caroline called Pat, <u>her</u> boss, to explain why <u>she</u> did not come to the meeting yesterday and
                     A   B
   was sorry to have missed <u>it</u>.
                   C
   A. their
   B. she, Caroline,
   C. them
   D. No change is necessary.

Answers and Explanations to Diagnostic: Clear Pronoun Reference

1. Answer   B

Two males are mentioned in the sentence, and although the reader may know that Greg is the one who had not played recently, there is no clue to that fact in the sentence as it is written. Repeating the name of the person intended clarifies any possible confusion.

2. Answer   B

Two people are mentioned in the sentence, Melissa and the instructor. The reader does not know to whom the pronoun "she" refers. Repeating the name of the person intended clarifies any possible confusion.

3. Answer   C

The use of the pronoun "it" is confusing because the pronoun does not appear to refer to anything in the sentence. The pronoun refers to the rain from the storm.

4. Answer   C

The use of the pronoun "it" does not specify who said the traffic would be backed up. "The traffic reporter" specifies what is meant by "it."

5. Answer   A

Although the reader may know that Sean was going to fix the CD player, not the car, there is no clue to that fact as the sentence is written. Therefore, replacing "it" with "the CD player" clarifies any confusion.

6. Answer   B

Although the reader may realize that "it" refers to the popcorn, not the bucket, there is no clue to that fact in the sentence as written; therefore, replacing "it" with "the popcorn" corrects any confusion.

7. Answer   B

The reader may realize that the pronoun "she" refers to Caroline, but there is no clue to that fact in the sentence as it is written. Repeating the name of the person next to the pronoun, "she, Caroline" helps to correct any confusion.

SECTION 5 ◆ EXERCISES: CLEAR PRONOUN REFERENCE

DIRECTIONS: *For each of the following questions, choose the option that corrects an error in the underlined portion(s). If no error exists, choose "No change is necessary."*

1. Yesterday, when I went for my job interview at the bank, <u>they</u> asked me difficult questions.
    A. he
    B. the manager
    C. the bank
    D. No change is necessary.

2. After carefully measuring the wall for a spot to hang the poster, Steve hammered the hook into the wall, and now <u>it</u> is crooked.
    A. the wall
    B. spot
    C. the poster
    D. No change is necessary.

3. Tavar's phone rang ten times, but <u>it</u> did not answer.
    A. Tavar
    B. the phone
    C. they
    D. No change is necessary.

4. On the radio, <u>they</u> says that one lane of the Interstate will be closed for repairs for a year.
   A. the newspaper
   B. the newscaster
   C. the article
   D. No change is necessary.

5. Bill, the foreman of the construction company, is concerned about safety in the large building. <u>They have had</u> three accidents in the past week.
   A. It has had
   B. She has had
   C. Members of his crew have had
   D. No change is necessary.

6. In the writing lab, <u>they</u> showed me how to edit my paper; <u>this</u> was helpful to me because now
                             A   B
   I know how to do <u>it</u>.
                  C
   A. the lab assistants
   B. the lab
   C. them
   D. No change is necessary.

7. Augusto had to take so many college preparatory courses that he thought he would never finish <u>it</u>; <u>they</u> frustrated him because <u>they</u> were not interesting.
                 A B   C
   A. them
   B. it
   C. it was
   D. No change is necessary.

8. The boss told <u>her</u> employee, Doreen, that <u>she</u> was the best worker <u>she</u> had.
                   A   B   C
   A. their
   B. she, Doreen,
   C. they
   D. No change is necessary.

9. Mr. Linger instructed Jim, his reference specialist, to develop a virtual library tour for <u>his</u> new students even if the tour took less than an hour.
   A. the tour's
   B. their
   C. Mr. Linger's
   D. No change is necessary.

10. Learning how to lift weights properly is important; <u>it requires</u> concentration because the lifter
                                                                A

can accidentally lose <u>his</u> grip and drop the weight on <u>himself</u>.
                        B   C

A. they require
B. its
C. itself
D. No change is necessary.

SECTION 6 ◆ PRONOUN CASE FORM

The Skill
Some pronouns are always subjects, meaning they do some action in the sentence or take a verb. Some pronouns are always objects, which means they are not doing any action in the sentence. Still others are possessives, showing ownership. You cannot mix these pronouns up. Please review The Parts of Speech Appendix information on subjects and prepositional phrases for more detailed explanation of subjects and objects. The pronouns that cause case errors are listed below:

SUBJECT PRONOUNS always have a verb	OBJECT PRONOUNS never have a verb	POSSESSIVES never have an apostrophe
I	ME	MINE
YOU	YOU	YOURS
HE	HIM	HIS
SHE	HER	HER
IT	IT	ITS
WE	US	OURS
THEY	THEM	THEIRS
WHO	WHOM	

Certain situations tend to cause errors in pronoun case.

1. <u>Watch out for COMPOUND SUBJECTS</u>—If you have 2 subjects working with the same verb, you have a compound subject. If one (or both) of those subjects is a pronoun, <u>it must be in subjective case.</u>

    Match each pronoun by itself to the verb and errors become obvious:

    • *Incorrect:* My <u>sister and me</u> <u>grew up</u> in Central Florida.
      ➢ "Me" grew up in Central Florida???
    • *Correct:* My <u>sister and I</u> <u>grew up</u> in Central Florida.
      ➢ "I" grew up in Central Florida.

    • *Incorrect:* <u>Him and his brother</u> <u>work</u> at Publix.
      ➢ "Him" works at Publix???
    • *Correct:* <u>He and his brother</u> <u>work</u> at Publix.
      ➢ "He" works at Publix

2. <u>**Watch out for COMPOUND OBJECTS**</u>—If you have 2 objects working together, you have a compound object. If one (or both) of those objects is a pronoun, <u>it must be in objective case</u>.

   Use just the pronoun in the sentence by itself and errors become obvious:

   - *Incorrect:* Our <u>kids</u> <u>made</u> my **husband and I** a nice card for our anniversary.
     ➣ Our kids made "I" a nice card???
   - *Correct:* Our <u>kids</u> <u>made</u> my **husband and me** a nice card for our anniversary.
     ➣ Our kids made "Me" a nice card.

   - *Incorrect:* My son asked us to give **he and his sister** a new TV.
     ➣ My son asked us to give "He" a new TV???
   - *Correct:* My son asked us to give **him and his sister** a new TV.
     ➣ My son asked us to give "Him" a new TV.

3. <u>**POSSESSIVE PRONOUNS do NOT take APOSTROPHES**</u>—They are already possessive, so they do not need the apostrophe added to nouns to show ownership.

   If a pronoun has an apostrophe, it is a CONTRACTION (it's = it is)

   - *Incorrect:* The black cat with the loud purr is **our's**.
     ➣ The black cat is **our is???**
   - *Correct:* The black cat with the loud purr is **ours**.

   - *Incorrect:* **Your's** is the next pizza to be delivered.
     ➣ **Your is** is the next pizza to be delivered???
   - *Correct:* **Yours** is the next pizza to be delivered.

4. <u>**Watch out for WHO VS. WHOM**</u>—Remember: "who" is a SUBJECT and "whom" is an OBJECT.

   - *Incorrect:* <u>I</u> <u>don't know</u> (**who** <u>you</u> <u>are talking</u> to).
     ➣ In this case, the "who" in the sentence is not doing any action. It is the "you" that's doing the talking.
   - *Correct:* <u>I</u> <u>don't know</u> (**whom** <u>you</u> <u>are talking</u> to).

   - *Incorrect:* <u>We</u> <u>were trying</u> to decide (**whom gave** us the bottle of wine).
     ➣ In this case, the subject that goes with the verb "gave" is "whom," but whom cannot be a subject.
   - *Correct:* <u>We</u> <u>were trying</u> to decide (**who** <u>gave</u> us the bottle of wine).

   - *Incorrect:* My <u>sister,</u> (**who** <u>everyone</u> <u>loves</u> to be around), <u>does not look</u> like me.
     ➣ In this case, the "who" in the sentence is not doing any action. "Everyone" loves, so the "who" has no verb associated with it.
   - *Correct:* My <u>sister,</u> (**whom** <u>everyone</u> <u>loves</u> to be around), <u>does not look</u> like me.

5. <u>**Watch out for Pronouns in COMPARISONS**</u>—When you compare 2 things using "as" or "than," and you use a pronoun at the end of the sentence, you have to know which case to use.

   To figure this out, **finish the sentence in your head,** and the correct pronoun will be obvious.

- *Incorrect:* My sister is shorter **than me.**
  ➤ "Finish" the sentence: My sister is shorter than me is?????
- *Correct:* My sister is shorter **than I.**
  ➤ "Finish" the sentence: My sister is shorter than I am.

- *Incorrect:* My sister likes shopping much more **than me.**
- *Correct:* My sister likes shopping much more **than I (do).**

- *Incorrect:* My sister is not very tall. My husband is as short **as her.**
- *Correct:* My sister is not very tall. My husband is as short **as she (is).**

The Test Question

You will be presented with three underlined pronouns in a sentence. You must determine if the sentence is correct as written or choose the answer that corrects the underlined part. If the sentence is correct, choose "No change is necessary."

SECTION 6 ◆ DIAGNOSTIC: PRONOUN CASE FORM

For each of the following questions, choose the option that corrects an error in the underlined portion. If no error exists, then choose "No change is necessary." When you are done, check your work with the answers immediately following the diagnostic. Even if you get a perfect score here, go ahead and complete the exercises in this section; they are designed to help build confidence and to give you practice for future test success.

1. My reading class started out with twenty-five students, but by midterm, only <u>me</u> and ten other
                                                                                              A

   students remained; even though the class is small, the instructor can give <u>me and them</u> more
                                                                                              B

   individual attention, which is better for <u>us</u>.
                                              C
   A. I
   B. I and they
   C. we
   D. No change is necessary.

2. Every Saturday, my dad makes <u>my brother and I</u> mow the lawn and trim any overgrown
                                   A

   plants; in the summer, <u>he and I</u> jump in the pool to cool off when <u>he and I</u> are finished doing
                           B   C

   yard work.
   A. my brother and me
   B. him and me
   C. him and me
   D. No change is necessary.

3. James and <u>I</u> both like wrestling; although James has been wrestling longer than I have, he was
            A

   surprised when the coach picked <u>me</u> instead of <u>he</u> to be captain of the team.
                                  B   C

   A. me
   B. I
   C. him
   D. No change is necessary.

4. The art appreciation lecture class is so long that <u>we</u> students <u>whom</u> sit in the back of the
                                                   A   B

   lecture hall tend to lose concentration; those of <u>us</u> who want to learn try to get to class early
                                                        C

   to sit in the front.
   A. us
   B. who
   C. we
   D. No change is necessary.

5. Three players, Tania, Abbey, and <u>me</u>, will be able to play on the team if we pass this course;
                                   A

   the semester has been tough for <u>them and me</u>, but <u>they and</u> I feel confident of our success.
                                       B   C

   A. I
   B. they and I
   C. them and me
   D. No change is necessary.

6. My two children, Matthew and Leanne, are very different. For example, <u>she</u> is much blonder
                                                                A

   than <u>him</u>, and he is much bigger than <u>she</u> is.
         B   C

   A. her
   B. he
   C. her
   D. No change is necessary.

7. <u>My</u> car may be older than <u>your's</u>, but <u>it</u> runs better.
      A   B   C

   A. me
   B. yours
   C. she
   D. No change is necessary.

Answers and Explanations to Diagnostic: Pronoun Case Form

1. Answer   A
"I" as well as "ten other students" is the subject of the verb "remained."

False choices
    A "Me and them" are the objects of the verb "can give."
    B "Us" is the object of the preposition "for."

2. Answer   A
"My brother and me" are objects of the verb "makes."

False choices
    B "He and I" is the subject of the verb "jump."
    C "He and I" is the subject of the verb "are finished."

3. Answer   C
"Him" is the object of the preposition "of."

False choices
    A "James and I" is the subject of the verb "like."
    C "Me" is the object of the verb "picked."

4. Answer   B
"Who" is the subject of the verb "sit."

False choices
    A "We" is a subject pronoun that is part of the subject "students."
    C "Us" is the object of the preposition "of."

5. Answer   A
"Tania, Abbey, and I" renames the subject "players." The pronoun "I" is a subject pronoun.

False choices
    B "Them and me" are objects of the preposition "for."
    C "They and I" are subjects of the verb "feel."

6. Answer   B
If you "mentally" finish the first part of the second sentence, you'll notice that "him" is an object pronoun trying to work with the verb "is." It should be "than he."
False choices
    A "She" is the subject of the verb "is."
    C "She" is the subject of the verb "is."

7. Answer   B
"Your's" is not the right form of the possessive pronoun. No apostrophe is needed since it's already possessive.

False choices
    A "My" is the right form for "car."
    C There is no reason to refer to the car as "she." The car was not given a personal name in the sentence.

SECTION 6 ◆ EXERCISES: PRONOUN CASE FORM

DIRECTIONS: *For each of the following questions, choose the option that corrects an error in the underlined portion(s). If no error exists, choose "No change is necessary."*

1. Between you and <u>I</u>, I would rather go to the football game with you and <u>her</u> because <u>we</u> get
      A   B   C
   along so well.
   A. me
   B. she
   C. us
   D. No change is necessary.

2. My dad, <u>who</u> helps me out with some of my expenses, gave fifty dollars to my brother Ben
            A
   and <u>I</u>; both <u>he</u> and I appreciate the help.
       B   C
   A. whom
   B. me
   C. him
   D. No change is necessary.

3. We took our midterms last week. Between the two of <u>us</u>, Jeff did better in chemistry; however,
                                                       A
   English and math were easy for <u>him</u> and <u>I</u>.
                                   B   C
   A. us
   B. he
   C. me
   D. No change is necessary.

4. Curly, our new puppy, enjoyed the new ball that Pete and <u>he</u> brought her; <u>she</u> and the boys
                                                            A   B
   played together until the dog and <u>them</u> were exhausted.
                                      C
   A. him
   B. her
   C. they
   D. No change is necessary.

5. The police stopped <u>me</u> and Alex and found some pills in the car. The pills belonged to Alex, <u>who</u>
                       A   B
   has epilepsy and must be on medication. Unfortunately, the officers did not believe him or <u>I</u>.
                                                                                               C
   A. I
   B. whom
   C. me
   D. No change is necessary.

6. My parents are planning a trip to Alaska, for the two of <u>them</u> have not had a vacation in
                                                               A
   several years. <u>They</u> both could use some time away from <u>us</u> children.
                   B   C
   A. they
   B. Them
   C. we
   D. No change is necessary.

7. Tom and <u>me</u> will be the first to test the new lightweight training shoes on the track; the coach
            A
   chose <u>him and me</u> because he knew our times would improve with <u>them</u>.
         B   C
   A. I
   B. he and I
   C. they
   D. No change is necessary.

8. Since <u>they</u> both have long blond hair, from a distance I could not tell whether Shannon or <u>her</u>
          A   B
   was walking across campus. <u>They</u> look like sisters.
                               C
   A. them
   B. she
   C. Them
   D. No change is necessary.

9. The teachers told <u>us</u> students that we must not bring beverages into the computer lab; anyone
                      A
   of <u>us</u> <u>who</u> does will be asked to leave.
      B   C
   A. we
   B. ourselves
   C. whom
   D. No change is necessary.

10. In our department at work, anyone <u>who</u> wants to can contribute a dollar a week to our lottery
                                      A
    pool. This way <u>us</u> employees have a better chance of winning when all of <u>us</u> chip in.
                    B   C
    A. whom
    B. we
    C. we
    D. No change is necessary.

SECTION 7 ◆ PRONOUN SHIFTS

A pronoun is a general word that stands for some other noun or pronoun in the sentence. If an author starts out using one pronoun, he cannot change that pronoun usage to another for no good reason.

That author must remain consistent with his pronoun use. In other words, the author cannot shift pronouns in the sentence for no good reason. Please refer to The Parts of Speech Appendix for more detailed information on pronouns.

The Skill

This item tests your ability to identify and correct pronoun shifts. A pronoun shift in a sentence occurs when the main pronoun in the sentence is replaced by another. This changes the point of view. Here are some tips to recognize pronoun shifts:

1. <u>**If one of the pronouns in the sentence is different, check it**</u>—Make sure it has been changed for a good reason.

   - *Incorrect:* When <u>I</u> exercise, <u>I</u> prefer long walks outside to workouts in the gym because <u>**you**</u> can save expensive monthly fees.
     ➤ In this example, the sentence starts out "I" and then unnecessarily shifts to "you" at the end. To correct the sentence, make all the pronouns the same.
   - *Correct:* When <u>I</u> exercise, <u>I</u> prefer long walks outside to workouts in the gym because <u>I</u> can save expensive monthly fees.

2. <u>**Make sure you understand how to use the pronoun ONE**</u>—We do not use this form that much in speech, so it might look odd to you if you see it on the exam. The pronoun "one" basically means "a person." It can be used correctly in several ways, as these examples show.

   - *Correct:* When <u>one</u> travels to San Antonio, <u>he or she</u> should take <u>his or her</u> comfortable walking shoes.
   - *Correct:* When <u>one</u> travels to San Antonio, <u>one</u> should take <u>one's</u> comfortable walking shoes.
   - *Incorrect:* When <u>one</u> travels to San Antonio, <u>one</u> should take <u>**your**</u> comfortable walking shoes.
     ➤ In this sentence, the "your" is an inappropriate shift because there is no reason to change to "your."

The Test Question

You will be given one or two sentences with one or three underlined parts that may contain an inappropriate pronoun shift. If the original sentence contains an error, you must choose the answer that corrects the error in an underlined part. If the sentence is correct, choose "No change is necessary."

> *Tip: *If you are given a sentence with 3 underlined pronouns, look for the one that is different. Often, that one is incorrect while the other 2 are correct.*

SECTION 7 ◆ DIAGNOSTIC: PRONOUN SHIFTS

For each of the following questions, choose the option that corrects an error in the underlined portion(s). If no error exists, choose "No change is necessary." When you are done, check your work with the answers immediately following the diagnostic. Even if you get a perfect score here, go ahead and complete the exercises in this section; they are designed to help build confidence and to give you practice for future test success.

1. Some people are not satisfied with what <u>they</u> have; <u>you</u> want more material things or <u>they</u>
                                         A   B   C

   wish to be like someone else.
   A. you
   B. they
   C. we
   D. No change is necessary.

2. I would like to be Oprah Winfrey for a brief time because <u>you</u> would have a chef making all
                                                              A

   <u>my</u> meals and <u>my</u> own personal hair, nail, and makeup artist.
    B   C
   A. I
   B. your
   C. her
   D. No change is necessary.

3. When I shop at the mall, <u>I</u> wear comfortable clothes because <u>I</u> need to be able to easily slip my
                                 A   B

   clothes off and on as <u>you</u> are constantly changing in the dressing rooms.
                         C
   A. you
   B. you
   C. I
   D. No change is necessary.

4. This summer, <u>she</u> started looking for work as soon as the semester ended, and in no time <u>she</u>
                     A   B

   found a job; taking this approach gave <u>one</u> an advantage over people who waited several
                                                     C

   weeks.
   A. they
   B. they
   C. her
   D. No change is necessary.

5. To avoid theft, <u>one</u> should never leave <u>your</u> valuable possessions in plain view in a car; also,
                 A   B

   <u>you</u> should never leave a wallet or a purse inside the vehicle.
    C
   A. you
   B. his or her
   C. one
   D. No change is necessary.

6. <u>You</u> can get rid of ants without <u>their</u> having to use pesticides by putting baking soda in the
     A   B

   places where they are entering <u>your</u> house.
                                  C

   A. One
   B. your
   C. one's
   D. No change is necessary.

7. Every Sunday afternoon, Tamika does her laundry at her mother's house, so <u>she</u> can save
                                                                     A

   money, <u>she</u> can spend time with her brother and sister, and she can help cook the family
           B

   dinner; Tamika feels that it is important to spend time with <u>your</u> family.
                                                       C

   A. they
   B. you
   C. her
   D. No change is necessary.

Answers and Explanations to Diagnostic: Pronoun Shifts

1. Answer   B
The third person plural is established with the pronoun "they." To correct the shifted pronoun "you," replace it with "they."

2. Answer   A
The first person "I" is established in the sentence. "I" corrects the shifted pronoun "you."

3. Answer   C
The first person singular pronoun form is established with the use of "I." The shifted pronoun "you" can be corrected by replacing it with "I."

4. Answer   C
The third person pronoun "she" is established in the sentence. Replacing "one" with "her" corrects the shift in person.

5. Answer   A
The second person is established with "you" and "your." The shifted pronoun "one" can be corrected by replacing it with "you."

6. Answer   B
The pronoun "you" determines second person. Replacing the shifted pronoun "their" with "your" corrects the error.

7. Answer   C
The noun "Tamika" establishes third person in the sentence. The shifted pronoun "your" can be corrected by replacing it with "her."

SECTION 7 ◆ EXERCISES: PRONOUN SHIFTS

DIRECTIONS: *For each of the following questions, choose the option that corrects an error in the underlined portion(s). If no error exists, choose "No change is necessary."*

1. If <u>you</u> want to succeed in college, <u>one</u> must set aside sufficient time to study; also, <u>you</u> should
       A   B   C

    not take too many credits each semester.
    A. one
    B. you
    C. they
    D. No change is necessary.

2. Professor Morrison told <u>us</u> that <u>we</u> have to turn in <u>your</u> research papers on Friday.
                                    A   B   C
    A. me
    B. you
    C. our
    D. No change is necessary.

3. Teenagers enjoy trying out a variety of changes to <u>their</u> appearance; <u>they</u> may get a tattoo, or
                                                        A   B

    sometimes <u>one</u> may try out a new hairstyle or hair color.
                    C
    A. one's
    B. he
    C. they
    D. No change is necessary.

4. When my brother was in high school, <u>you</u> were required to do thirty hours of service learning;
                                            A

    <u>he</u> did <u>his</u> hours by volunteering at the computer lab in the library.
      B   C
    A. he
    B. one
    C. our
    D. No change is necessary.

5. A full-time student who also works has to budget <u>his</u> time so that <u>you</u> can make <u>his</u> education
                                               A   B   C

    a priority.
    A. their
    B. he
    C. you
    D. No change is necessary.

6. The furniture deliverymen are coming this morning, so <u>we</u> have to make room in <u>our</u> den for
                                                       A   B

   the new sofa and chairs; now, when <u>he</u> invites friends over, we will not have to bring in chairs
                                         C

   from the kitchen to sit on.
   A. they
   B. your
   C. we
   D. No change is necessary.

7. Some people who participate in extreme sports put <u>their</u> lives in danger, but <u>they</u> like the rush
                                          A   B

   <u>you</u> get.
    C
   A. your
   B. you
   C. they
   D. No change is necessary.

8. Many people I know are a little nervous about flying even though <u>we</u> realize that airport
                                                    A

   security has improved; however, this has not stopped <u>them</u> from flying for business or for <u>their</u>
                                            B   C

   vacation.
   A. they
   B. him
   C. his
   D. No change is necessary.

9. Many college students know more about using computers than <u>their</u> parents do; it is not
                                                  A

   unusual for <u>them</u> to get a phone call from a parent asking for <u>their</u> help.
                B   C
   A. one's
   B. I
   C. your
   D. No change is necessary.

10. My truck is <u>my</u> most prized possession, but <u>you</u> have to work so that <u>I</u> can pay for the
                  A   B   C

   insurance and maintenance.
   A. one's
   B. I
   C. you
   D. No change is necessary.

SECTION 8 ◆ SHIFTS IN VERB TENSE

The Skill

If a person starts out using one verb tense, such as present tense, that person cannot change to past tense or some other tense for no good reason. The author must maintain consistent verb tense. In other words, the author cannot shift between verb tenses inappropriately. For more detailed information on how to find verbs, please refer to The Parts of Speech Appendix.

This item tests your ability to recognize when verb tenses have shifted for no good reason. Here are pointers to help you recognize verb tense shifts and problem areas to watch out for.

1. **If one of the verb tenses in the sentence is different, check it**—Make sure it has been changed for a good reason.
   - *Incorrect:* We all **wanted** to go golfing and **were looking** forward to it, but then it **starts** to rain.
     - ➤ In this example, the sentence starts out using the past tense and then unnecessarily shifts to the present at the end. The action is in the past throughout the sentence, so that shift is unnecessary. To correct the sentence, put all verbs in the past tense.
   - *Correct:* We all **wanted** to go golfing and **were looking** forward to it, but then it **started** to rain.

2. **Make sure you understand how to use HAD + VERB (Past Perfect)**—Here is an instance in which a change in verb tense is necessary. Sometimes you have a sentence in which two actions occur in the past. To show that one of the actions happened <u>before</u> the other, use <u>had + verb</u> for that action, which is called the past perfect tense. The later action should be in past tense.

   - *Incorrect:* She **had gone** to the bookstore after she **had registered** for her classes.
   - *Correct:* She **went** to the bookstore after she **had registered*** for her classes.
     - ➤ The correct version shows that registering for class happened first, before she went to the bookstore. Therefore, the first verb is <u>had registered</u>.
       *Note: It would also be correct to say "after she <u>registered</u> for classes." The word "after" establishes which action came first, so it is not required to use the past perfect.

3. **Make sure you understand how to use HAVE/HAS + VERB (Present Perfect)**—If an event started in the past and continues into the present and possibly even the future, then use <u>have/has + verb</u>.
   - *Incorrect:* I **live** in Tampa now. In fact, I **lived** in Florida my whole life, but I never **went** to Disney.
   - *Correct:* I **live** in Tampa now. In fact, I **have lived** in Florida my whole life, but I **have never been** to Disney.
     - ➤ The first verb "<u>live</u>" establishes just present tense. However, the next two verbs have to use <u>have + verb</u> or present perfect because those events started in the past and continue until today. The living in Florida is not over yet, so simple past cannot be used.

The Test Question

You will be given one or two sentences in which either one or three underlined parts may have an error in verb tense. If the original sentence contains an error, you must choose the answer that corrects an error in the underlined part. If the verbs are used correctly, choose the option "No change is necessary."

> Tip: *If you are given a sentence with 3 underlined verbs, look for the one that has a different tense. Often, that one is incorrect while the other 2 are correct.

SECTION 8 ◆ DIAGNOSTIC: SHIFTS IN VERB TENSE

Choose the option that corrects an error in the underlined portion(s). If no error exists, choose "No change is necessary." When you are done, check your work with the answers immediately following the diagnostic. Even if you get a perfect score here, go ahead and complete the exercises in this section; they are designed to help build confidence and to give you practice for future test success.

1. Shortboards are very fast, so they <u>gain</u> speed quickly, and when the surfer <u>made</u> a turn, called
                                          A   B
   a cutback, the board <u>slashes</u> through the wave, ripping it and creating spray.
                          C

   A. gained
   B. makes
   C. slashed
   D. No change is necessary.

2. Gabriel Garcia Marquez <u>wrote</u> about the rural areas of Colombia and <u>describes</u> the places
                             A   B
   and people in so much detail that the reader <u>thinks</u> he or she is there.
                                                 C

   A. writes
   B. described
   C. thought
   D. No change is necessary.

3. After Rasheed Wallace <u>play</u> basketball in college for two years, he <u>got drafted</u> into the NBA
                           A   B
   to play for Portland; six years later, he <u>was transferred</u> to the Detroit Pistons.
                                              C

   A. played
   B. gets drafted
   C. is transferring
   D. No change is necessary.

4. Several years ago, Jamie <u>was living</u> out of his truck, which frequently <u>broke</u> down, and eating
                              A   B
   the unwanted leftovers from customers at the restaurant where he <u>works</u>.
                                                                     C

   A. is living
   B. breaks
   C. worked
   D. No change is necessary.

5. Gonzalo likes to make people laugh, and he <u>enjoyed</u> the time they are with him.
   A. was enjoying
   B. would enjoy
   C. enjoys
   D. No change is necessary.

6. My cousin Derreck has planned his future step-by-step; so far, he <u>has completed</u> his goals of attending college and playing football.
   A. complete
   B. had completed
   C. was completing
   D. No change is necessary.

7. Dr. Mark, a physician who is on the admissions board of a prestigious medical university, <u>had activated</u> my aspiration to be a doctor because he is an African-American who has achieved success despite many setbacks in his life.
   A. had been activating
   B. was activating
   C. has activated
   D. No change is necessary.

Answers and Explanations to Diagnostic: Shifts in Verb Tense

1. Answer   B
All of the ideas in the sentence are expressed in the present tense; "made" should be changed to "makes" to correct the shift.

2. Answer   A
All of the ideas in the sentence are expressed in the present tense. "Wrote" should be changed to "writes" to correct the shift.

3. Answer   A
The verb "play" in the sentence is missing –ed to show that the verb expresses the past tense.

4. Answer   C
To correct the verb tense shift, "works" should be changed to "worked," the past tense form of the verb "work."

5. Answer   C
The correct verb form is "enjoys" because the ideas in the sentence are expressed in the present tense.

6. Answer   D
There are no verb shifts in this sentence.

7. Answer   C
The present perfect form of the verb "has activated" is required in this sentence. "Had activated" is the past perfect form.

SECTION 8 ◆ EXERCISES: SHIFTS IN VERB TENSE

DIRECTIONS: *Choose the option that corrects an error in the underlined portion(s). If no error exists, choose "No change is necessary."*

1. Whenever I take a test, I <u>become</u> so nervous that I <u>forgot</u> everything that I <u>know.</u>
                                A   B   C
   A. became
   B. forget
   C. knew
   D. No change is necessary.

2. After being punched on the back of his head by his opponent, the ice hockey player <u>fell</u> onto
                                                                               A
   his face on the ice and <u>suffered</u> a broken neck; right after it happened, the coach <u>suspends</u> the
                            B   C
   opponent.
   A. falls
   B. is suffering
   C. suspended
   D. No change is necessary.

3. A woman <u>is trying</u> to pay for eight hundred dollars worth of household items at a discount
                       A
   store with a counterfeit million dollar bill, but the cashier <u>alerted</u> the manager, who <u>called</u> the
                                                        B   C
   police.
   A. tried
   B. alerts
   C. had called
   D. No change is necessary.

4. Every day before I leave for school, I feed the dog and then <u>am taking</u> him for a walk.
   A. would take
   B. took
   C. take
   D. No change is necessary.

5. When Michael gets his college degree, he <u>worked</u> as an accountant in his father's company.
   A. does work
   B. will work
   C. would work
   D. No change is necessary.

6. When Carlos <u>has flown</u> his first solo flight as a pilot, he <u>forgot</u> his flight plan, <u>entered</u> the
                        A   B   C

airspace of the wrong airport, and had to call his instructor to help him get back.
   A. flew
   B. was forgetting
   C. has entered
   D. No change is necessary.

7. Bruce <u>started</u> to wash his truck after the rain had stopped.
   A. had started
   B. will start
   C. is starting
   D. No change is necessary.

8. While Mark <u>sleeps</u>, his younger brother threw a glass of cold water on him.
   A. is sleeping
   B. was sleeping
   C. would be sleeping
   D. No change is necessary.

9. If I <u>have seen</u> William tomorrow, I will tell him about our plans for the weekend.
   A. did see
   B. would see
   C. see
   D. No change is necessary.

10. Suzanne <u>does not work</u> at the bakery anymore; she <u>finds</u> a new job at a clothing store that she
                  A   B

<u>likes</u> better.
  C
   A. did not work
   B. found
   C. would like
   D. No change is necessary.

SECTION 9 ◆ MODIFIERS

<u>Modifiers</u> describe other words in the sentence. In essence, they are adjectives and adverbs. Adverbs are very mobile in a sentence, but adjectives are not. An adjective modifier should be placed as close as possible to the word it modifies. Please review the information on Adjectives and Adverbs in the Parts of Speech Review Appendix for more detailed information on modifiers.

The Skill
This item tests your ability to correctly place modifiers so that they are clearly describing what they are supposed to describe. The two types of errors using modifiers are the dangling modifier and the misplaced modifier.

The Dangling Modifier

The dangling modifier is a word or group of words (usually an adjective phrase or clause) that is not really describing anything in the sentence, as in the following examples:

- *Incorrect: Typing all night*, the paper was finished in time.
  - ➤ Modifiers are supposed to be placed next to the words they describe. Therefore, in this sentence, it sounds like THE PAPER was the one typing all night. This modifier is not actually describing anything in the sentence, so it's dangling.
- *Correct:* Typing all night, I finished the paper in time.

- *Incorrect: While driving through a wooded area outside the city,* a dog began to bark.
  - ➤ In this sentence, it sounds like the DOG was driving! The phrase, "While driving through a wooded area" is not describing anything in the sentence, so it's dangling.
- *Correct:* While driving through a wooded area outside the city, the woman heard a dog begin to bark.

- *Incorrect: Standing at the top of the hill,* the lights of the city twinkle like little stars.
  - ➤ In this sentence, it sounds like the LIGHTS are standing at the top of the hill! The modifier is not describing anything in the sentence, so it's dangling.
- *Correct: Standing at the top of the hill,* one can see the lights of the city twinkle like little stars.

The Misplaced Modifier

The misplaced modifier is a word or group of words that is simply in the wrong place (*misplaced*) in the sentence. Other words separate it from the word it is describing, as in these examples:

- *Incorrect:* Bob takes a towel to the gym *that is ragged and stained.*
  - ➤ The phrase *that is ragged and stained* is the misplaced modifier. The way the sentence is written, it sounds like the GYM is ragged and stained. The phrase needs to be placed <u>next to</u> "towel," which is what is really ragged and stained.
- *Correct:* Bob takes a ragged and stained towel to the gym.

- *Incorrect: Freshly cut in the morning,* Carlos gave Sandy a dozen red roses.
  - ➤ The phrase *freshly cut in the morning* is the misplaced modifier. The way the sentence is written, it sounds like CARLOS was freshly cut in the morning. The phrase needs to be placed <u>next to</u> "roses," which is what is really being modified.
- *Correct:* Carlos gave Sandy a dozen red roses that were freshly cut in the morning.

The Test Question

You will be given three versions of one sentence; two will have misplaced or dangling modifiers. You must choose the sentence in which the modifier is correctly placed.

- A. Catching the can of soda before it fell over, a messy spill was avoided.
- B. Catching the can of soda before it fell over, Jose avoided a messy spill.
- C. Catching the can of soda avoided a messy spill.

The modifier **Catching the can of soda before it fell over** is correctly placed in sentence B. Jose is the person who caught the can of soda.

SECTION 9 ◆ DIAGNOSTIC: MODIFIERS

Choose the sentence in which the modifier is correctly placed. When you are done, check your work with the answers immediately following the diagnostic. Even if you get a perfect score here, go ahead and complete the exercises in this section; they are designed to help build confidence and to give you practice for future test success.

1.
   A. Arriving home after two years of service in the navy, Turrell's family gave a surprise party for him.
   B. Arriving home after two years of service in the navy, Turrell was given a surprise party.
   C. Arriving home after two years of service in the navy, a big surprise party was given for Turrell.

2.
   A. While I was walking on the beach, a fishing boat came too close to shore and got stuck in the sand.
   B. While walking on the beach, a fishing boat came too close to shore and got stuck in the sand.
   C. While walking on the beach, a fishing boat got stuck in the sand because it came too close to shore.

3.
   A. Being sleepy, my sociology project did not get finished.
   B. Because I was sleepy, I did not finish my sociology project.
   C. Because of sleepiness, my sociology project did not get finished.

4.
   A. We ate a bucket, which were too spicy for me, of barbequed wings during the game.
   B. We ate a bucket of barbequed wings during the game, which were too spicy for me.
   C. During the game, we ate a bucket of barbequed wings, which were too spicy for me.

5.
   A. The pen ran out of ink that I just bought to write my essay.
   B. To write my essay, the pen ran out of ink that I just bought.
   C. The pen that I just bought to write my essay ran out of ink.

6.
   A. The palmetto bug that startled the students flew onto the teacher's head.
   B. The palmetto bug flew onto the teacher's head that startled the students.
   C. Onto the teacher's head that startled the students flew the palmetto bug.

7.
   A. The bottle of milk that was grabbed by the baby was hungry.
   B. The baby that was hungry grabbed the bottle of milk.
   C. The baby grabbed the bottle of milk that was hungry.

Answers and Explanations to Diagnostic: Modifiers

For each of these questions, to avoid needless repetition of information, only the correct option is explained. The type of error is also identified: dangling modifier or misplaced modifier.

1. Answer   B   Dangling Modifier

The modifier "Arriving home after two years of service" should be followed by the word it modifies, which is Turrell. In Choice A, the modifier modifies Turrell's family. In Choice C, the modifier is placed before "a surprise party," which indicates that the surprise party arrived home.

2. Answer   A   Dangling Modifier

The modifier "While I was walking on the beach" correctly identifies who was walking. In the false choices, it seems that the fishing boat was walking on the beach.

3. Answer   B   Dangling Modifier

The correct choice, "Because I was sleepy," identifies the person who did not finish the sociology project. In false choices A and C, the sociology project follows the modifier, making it seem as if the sociology project was sleepy.

4. Answer   C   Misplaced Modifier

The modifier "which were too spicy for me" must follow the words it modifies, "barbequed wings." In false choice A the modifier modifies "bucket," and in false choice C it modifies "game."

5. Answer   C   Misplaced Modifier

The modifier "that I just bought" must modify "pen." In the false choices, the modifier modifies "ink."

6. Answer   A   Misplaced Modifier

"That startled the students" is the modifier, which modifies "palmetto bug." In the false choices, the modifier modifies "head."

7. Answer   B   Misplaced Modifier

The modifier "that was hungry" modifies "baby," not "the bottle of milk" as in the false choices.

SECTION 9 ◆ EXERCISES: MODIFIERS

DIRECTIONS: Choose the sentence in which the modifier is correctly placed.

1.
   A. Having entered the gym, the screams of the crowd were overwhelming.
   B. Having entered the gym, the crowd's screams overwhelmed me.
   C. Having entered the gym, I was overwhelmed by the screams of the crowd.

2.
   A. To revise my paper, I need to rewrite it.
   B. To revise my paper, it needs to be rewritten.
   C. To revise my paper, rewriting is necessary.

3.
    A. While watching a movie on television, my friend called and asked me to go out.
    B. While I was watching a movie on television, my friend called and asked me to go out.
    C. My friend called and asked me to go out while watching a movie on television.

4.
    A. My dad, at the age of five, taught me to ride my bicycle without training wheels.
    B. My dad taught me to ride my bicycle without training wheels when I was five.
    C. At the age of five, my dad taught me to ride my bicycle without training wheels.

5.
    A. Riding on the escalator, I caught the heel of my shoe on one of the steps.
    B. Riding on the escalator, the heel of my shoe got caught on one of the steps.
    C. The heel of my shoe riding on the escalator got caught on one of the steps.

6.
    A. As a foreign student studying in the U.S., my mother does not get the chance to see me very often.
    B. My mother does not get the chance to see me very often as a foreign student studying in the U.S.
    C. As a foreign student studying in the U.S., I do not get the chance to see my mother very often.

7.
    A. After writing a check and signing the documents, we now owned the house.
    B. After writing a check and signing the documents, the house was now ours.
    C. The house, after writing a check and signing the documents, was now ours.

8.
    A. While fishing on the ocean with my friend, a barracuda jumped onto the boat.
    B. A barracuda jumped onto the boat while I was fishing on the ocean with my friend.
    C. A barracuda jumped onto the boat while fishing on the ocean with my friend.

9.
    A. Removing the label at the neckline, the T-shirt felt more comfortable.
    B. The T-shirt felt more comfortable at the neckline after removing the label.
    C. After I removed the label at the neckline, the T-shirt felt more comfortable.

10.
    A. Having run the red light, I got a ticket from the police officer.
    B. Having run the red light, the police officer gave me a ticket.
    C. The police officer, having run the red light, gave me a ticket.

SECTION 10 ◆ STANDARD PUNCTUATION—COMMAS, SEMICOLONS, APOSTROPHES, END MARKS

The Skill

This item tests your ability to use standard punctuation. You'll notice that we have already covered some of these punctuation rules in the previous two sections. Please refer to the Parts of Speech Appendix for more detailed information on punctuating phrases and clauses.

Commas

To understand comma errors, you first have to understand the comma RULES, several of which we have already learned. The most important comma usage falls under 6 rules, which you can think of as **FIESAD** rules. Each letter in **FIESAD** stands for a particular comma use.

1. <u>"F" stands for FANBOYS</u>—As we have already learned, when you use a FANBOYS to separate two independent clauses, you should put a comma first.
   - <u>Learning</u> to use commas correctly <u>is</u> easy, **but** <u>you</u> <u>must learn</u> the rules first.
     - ➢ Each clause is independent with its own subject and verb. Therefore, you need a comma.

   DO NOT put a comma if what comes after the FANBOYS is not an independent clause.
   - *Incorrect:* <u>I</u> always <u>get up</u> early on winter mornings, **and** *<u>have</u> my coffee outside on the pool deck.*
     - ➢ There is no subject in the part after the "and," so that is NOT an independent clause. This sentence simply has a compound verb (2 verbs, 1 subject).
   - *Correct:* <u>I</u> always <u>get up</u> early on winter mornings **and** <u>have</u> my coffee outside on the pool deck.

2. <u>"I" stands for INTRODUCTORY ELEMENTS</u>—**Anything** that introduces an Independent Clause should be set off with a comma.

   Introductory Words
   - *First*, <u>you</u> <u>should learn</u> the rules.
   - *Smiling*, the <u>woman</u> <u>held</u> the door for the man behind her.
   - *Exhausted*, the marathon <u>runner</u> <u>lay</u> down on the track after he crossed the finish line.
   - *James*, <u>I</u> <u>think</u> that <u>you</u> <u>should move</u> this paragraph to the end.

   Introductory Phrases
   - *Before the exit exam next Tuesday*, <u>you</u> <u>should have</u> a hearty breakfast.
   - *Shaking his fist in the air*, the angry <u>driver</u> <u>sped</u> around the slower car.
   - *Thrilled with his Exit Exam score*, the <u>man</u> <u>shouted</u>, "Yes!"
   - *To succeed in business*, <u>one</u> <u>needs</u> to maintain a network of business contacts.

   Introductory Adverb Clauses—Watch out that the adverb clause comes <u>before</u> the independent clause, though.
   - *Before <u>you</u> <u>submit</u> your paper*, <u>you</u> <u>should</u> always <u>proofread</u> for comma errors.
   - <u>You</u> <u>should</u> always <u>proofread</u> for comma errors *before <u>you</u> <u>submit</u> your paper*.

3. **"E" stands for EXTRA INFORMATION**—Any time you have "by the way" information, an interrupter, or extra information that doesn't give essential meaning to the sentence, you should set it off with commas. Basically, if you can imagine putting something in parentheses, it should be set off with commas.

- Marc, *my husband,* is a football fanatic.
- A special award was given to the leader of the company, *Mr. John Smith.*
- The mother cooks her toddler's favorite dish, *spaghetti with meatballs,* at least once a week.
- Your first paragraph is excellent. Your body paragraphs, *however,* do not have enough content.
- The Exit Exam for writing is the hardest of the three state exams, *in my opinion.*
- You like that movie? I like it, *too!*

Watch out for Adjective Clauses.

"Which" = Extra Information = Commas:
- <u>Rattlesnake</u>, **which** apparently <u>tastes</u> like chicken, <u>is</u> not something I <u>care</u> to eat.
- <u>St Catherine's Episcopal Day Care</u>, **which** <u>is located</u> in Jacksonville, Florida, <u>provides</u> preschoolers with many valuable learning experiences.

"That" = Necessary Information = NO Commas:
- The third <u>"F"</u> <u>was</u> the straw **that** <u>broke</u> the camel's back.
  - ➤ That information is essential to understanding "straw."
- <u>You</u> <u>should see</u> a doctor if <u>you</u> <u>have</u> a cough **that** <u>lasts</u> **more than 2 weeks.**
  - ➤ This clause is necessary: "cough." Not all coughs require a doctor's visit.

Other Adjective Clauses = Use Commas for Extra Information Only:
Extra Information:
- My <u>son</u>, *who* <u>eats</u> *as much as my husband and I do put together,* <u>is</u> quite thin.
- <u>Mr. Jones</u>, **whom** my <u>husband</u> <u>employed</u> last week, <u>is</u> an excellent worker.

Necessary Information:
- The <u>man</u> **who** <u>stole</u> my purse last week <u>is sitting</u> at the bar!
- *Necessary Information:* The <u>church</u> **where** <u>I</u> <u>got married</u> <u>burned</u> down recently.

4. **"S" stands for SERIES (lists)**
Lists of 3 or more—Any time you have a LIST (or series) of 3 or more items, you should separate the items with commas. As a rule, for 3 items, use 2 commas. For 4 items, use 3 commas. For 5 items, use 4 commas, etc.

- A person can learn to write well by **reading, studying, and practicing.** (3 items, 2 commas)
- The TOEFL exam tests **reading, writing, listening, speaking, and grammar.** (5 items, 4 commas)

Watch out for Adjectives in a Series NOT connected by a FANBOYS—Some adjectives can be placed in a series or list without needing commas while others DO need commas.

Use commas between adjectives under the following circumstances:
1. You can imagine putting "<u>and</u>" between the adjectives.
2. You can <u>rearrange</u> them.

- *Correct = Commas:* The **clean, fresh** scent of Mrs. Hendrick's laundry fragranced the morning air.
  - ➤ Test #1: <u>and</u>: "The **clean and fresh** scent" sounds okay.
  - ➤ Test #2: <u>rearrange</u>: "The fresh, clean scent" sounds okay.
- *Correct = No Commas:* She wore her **long black** hair in a French braid.
  - ➤ Test #1: <u>and</u>: "She wore her **long and black** hair" sounds odd.
  - ➤ Test #2: <u>rearrange</u>: "She wore her **black long** hair" sounds odd.

5. <u>**"A" stands for ADDRESS**</u>—Use commas to separate the elements of an address (except for between the state and the zip code). If the sentence continues after the name of the state, put a comma after the state.

   - As a child, I lived at 15 Maple Lane, Wilmington, North Carolina 21007.
   - As a child, I lived in Wilmington, North Carolina, but my parents moved us to Florida when I was in junior high school.

6. <u>**"D" stands for DATES**</u>—Use commas to separate the elements of a date.

   - For my back injury, I have a physical therapy appointment for Wednesday, November 18, 2009.

<u>Semicolons</u>

The semicolon is a relatively sophisticated mark of punctuation. By learning how to use semicolons, you can enhance the quality of your writing. They can be used in three basic ways:

1. <u>**Join Two Related Independent Clauses**</u>—Two independent clauses that are closely related in structure or in meaning can be nicely joined with a semicolon. Remember: a semicolon (;) is like a period in that both are used between independent clauses.

   - Cell phone <u>technology</u> <u>is</u> constantly <u>advancing</u>; the <u>phones</u> <u>are getting</u> smaller, but <u>they</u> <u>are</u> capable of more and more functions.

   Watch out for commas that separate independent clauses; if 2 independent clauses are separated with a comma, it must be followed by a FANBOYS. If you CAN put a FANBOYS after a comma and the sentence still makes sense, then you need a period, semicolon, or comma plus FANBOYS there.

   - *Incorrect:* The <u>movie</u> <u>was not</u> a thriller, <u>it</u> <u>was</u> an action film.
     - ➤ You could add the word "but" after the comma; therefore, that comma is not correct.
   - *Correct:* The <u>movie</u> <u>was not</u> a thriller; <u>it</u> <u>was</u> an action film.

2. <u>**Join Two Independent Clauses with a Conjunctive Adverb**</u>—Review Section 1 of this chapter for a list of common conjunctive adverbs and what they mean. **It is very common to use a semicolon before a conjunctive adverb.** Be sure to put a comma after the adverb!

   - <u>We</u> <u>love</u> eating outside at the café; **however,** sometimes <u>we</u> <u>cannot eat</u> outdoors because of the bothersome flies.

3. <u>Separate Items in a Series that Already Has Commas</u>—Semicolons do have one way in which they function more like commas than periods. If there is a list of items, and there are <u>commas</u> within the items of the list, then you should use semicolons to separate each item to prevent confusion.
   - *Incorrect:* Tracey bought paint brushes and canvas paper for art, a computer disk, a loose leaf notebook, and pens for English, and goggles, gloves, and a lab coat for biology.
   - *Correct:* Tracey bought paint brushes and canvas paper for **art;** a computer disk, a loose leaf notebook, and pens for **English;** and goggles, gloves, and a lab coat for biology.

<u>Apostrophes</u>
You probably already know how to use apostrophes for contractions, such as "can't" or "I'm," but you may be confused about how to use them for possession. There are several rules.

1. <u>Use an apostrophe + "S"</u> to show possession when the owner is **SINGULAR or DOES NOT END IN "S."**
   - The cats that belong to my daughter = **my daughter's cats (one daughter).**
   - The mother of my husband = **my husband's mother (one husband).**
   - The house that belongs to my neighbor = **my neighbor's house (one neighbor).**

2. <u>Put an apostrophe AFTER THE "S"</u> to show possession when the owner is **PLURAL or ENDS IN "S."**
   - The essays of my students = **my student<u>s'</u> essays (more than one student).**
   - The house that belongs to my parents = **my parents' house (two parents).**
   - The car that belongs to the Jones = **the Jones' car (Jones ends in "s").**

3. <u>Apostrophes for OTHER USES</u>
   Use an apostrophe for certain expressions of time.
   - He put in a hard day's work.
   - He lost a week's pay at the casino.
   - I got a terrible night's sleep!

   Use an apostrophe to pluralize letters and other expressions that are not normally pluralized.
   - When I was playing Scrabble with my husband, I drew four **e's** at one time.
   - You do not need to use a comma after all your **and's.**

4. <u>DO NOT USE AN APOSTROPHE FOR EVERY PLURAL!!!!</u> You only need apostrophes for possession and certain other uses.
   - *Incorrect:* We do expert tattoo<u>'s</u> and piercing<u>'s</u>.
   - *Correct:* We do expert tattoos and piercings.

5. <u>IT'S = IT IS; ITS = POSSESSION</u>
   - **It's** challenging to begin a new job in an unfamiliar city.
     ➢ It is challenging.
   - The dog gnawed on **its** bone.
     ➢ The bone belongs to the dog.

Colons

Colons (:) are used to call attention to some part of the sentence because they bring about a sudden stop in a sentence. They have the same effect as periods, but you do <u>not</u> have to use an independent clause after them. Capitalization of the first letter after a colon is optional.

- Once <u>I</u> <u>get</u> to the store, <u>I</u> <u>need</u> to buy the following items: *hairspray, deodorant, and mouthwash.*
- <u>I</u> <u>told</u> you: *<u>I</u> <u>am not going</u> to give you your allowance until <u>you</u> <u>clean</u> your room.*

Watch out for colons after phrases that are not part of a complete sentence!
- *Incorrect:* My <u>mother</u> <u>has</u> several health problems. ***Such as:*** *high blood pressure, high cholesterol, and diabetes.*
- *Correct:* My <u>mother</u> <u>has</u> several health problems: *high blood pressure, high cholesterol, and diabetes.*

Question Marks

You probably already know that question marks go at the ends of questions, but the question has to stand alone, not be embedded into a statement.

- *Incorrect:* <u>I</u> <u>wonder</u> *how many <u>students</u> <u>earn</u> bachelor's degrees each year in the US?*
- *Correct:* <u>I</u> <u>wonder</u> *how many <u>students</u> <u>earn</u> bachelor's degrees each year in the US.*

Quotations

A quotation represents a speaker's exact words. There are several things to remember about how to punctuate them.

1. ### Use a Comma Before the Quotation
   If the sentence continues on after the quotation, you should put a comma at the <u>end</u> of the quotation, too.

   - My father told **me, "You** should do what you love for your profession so that you go to work happy every day."
   - My father told **me, "You** should do what you love for your profession so that you go to work happy every day," and I followed that advice.

2. ### Put All End Punctuation INSIDE the Last Quotation Mark

   - *Incorrect:* The mayor said, "We need to take better care of our homeless<u>".</u>
   - *Correct:* The mayor said, "We need to take better care of our homeless."

The Test Question

You will be given two types of questions.

1. You will be given a sentence with one or three underlined parts. You must choose the option that corrects the error.
2. You will be given three versions of one sentence. You must choose the sentence that is correctly punctuated.

SECTION 10 ◆ DIAGNOSTIC: STANDARD PUNCTUATION—COMMAS, SEMICOLONS, APOSTROPHES, END MARKS

For each of the following questions, choose the option that corrects an error in the underlined portion(s). If no error exists, choose "No change is necessary." When you are done, check your work with the answers immediately following the diagnostic. Even if you get a perfect score here, go ahead and complete the exercises in this section; they are designed to help build confidence and to give you practice for future test success.

1. Bimini is the most relaxing place to fish; because, Bimini is practically deserted most of the
                                            A

   time, and I can go out on my boat and fish for hours without being bothered.
        B   C
   A. fish because
   B. time and
   C. boat, and
   D. No change is necessary.

2. In the past five years, drug dealer's and gangs have taken over my old neighborhood.
                                  A   B   C
   A. dealers
   B. gangs, have
   C. old, neighborhood
   D. No change is necessary.

3. When someone first walks into my room, he or she always says, "Wow! That's a nice guitar".
                                                           A   B   C
   A. says; "Wow!
   B. Thats'
   C. guitar."
   D. No change is necessary.

4. I enjoy playing soccer for a variety of reasons, soccer relieves my stress, helps me relax, and
                     A   B   C
   keeps me fit.
   A. soccer, for
   B. reasons; soccer
   C. stress. Helps
   D. No change is necessary.

5. A recent trip back to my old high school revealed a loss of innocence as I retraced my
                                     A   B

   wonderful teen years, the building was there, but the stone retaining wall and the grand old
                        C

   oak tree were not.
   A. school. Revealed
   B. innocence, as
   C. years. The
   D. No change is necessary.

For each of the following options, choose the sentence that is correctly punctuated.

6.
    A. In his senior year of high school, Michael went to Los Angeles to play baseball on a minor league field; in college, he played on fields in Pensacola and St. Petersburg.
    B. In his senior year of high school; Michael went to Los Angeles to play baseball on a minor league field; in college, he played on fields in Pensacola and St. Petersburg.
    C. In his senior year of high school; Michael went to Los Angeles to play baseball on a minor league field, in college, he played on fields in Pensacola and St. Petersburg.
    D. In his senior year of high school, Michael went to Los Angeles to play baseball on a minor league field, in college, he played on fields in Pensacola and St. Petersburg.

7.
    A. At our football teams' annual awards dinner, the coach gave a speech about the player who had improved the most William Hawling.
    B. At our football team's annual awards dinner, the coach gave a speech about the player who had improved the most, William Hawling.
    C. At our football teams' annual awards dinner; the coach gave a speech about the player who had improved the most, William Hawling.
    D. At our football team's annual awards dinner, the coach gave a speech about the player, who had improved the most William Hawling.

Answers and Explanations to Diagnostic: Standard Punctuation

1. Answer   A

No punctuation is required before this dependent clause that follows an independent clause.

False choices
    B   A comma and a coordinating conjunction are required to connect independent clauses.
    C   A comma is not needed to separate the compound verbs "can go" and "fish." The "and" connects the two verbs.

2. Answer   A

"Dealers" is the correct plural form of the noun "dealer." "Dealer's" is the possessive form.

False choices
    B   A comma is not used to separate a subject "gangs" from its verb, "have."
    C   A comma is not used to separate an adjective placed right before a noun.

3. Answer   C

The period is placed inside the quotation mark at the end of a sentence.

False choices
    A   A comma follows the signal verb introducing a direct quotation.
    B   "That's" is the contracted form of "that is."

4. Answer   B

The semicolon after "reasons" corrects the fused sentence.

False choices
    A   A comma is not required to separate a prepositional phrase from a direct object.
    C   Placing a period after "stress" creates a fragment at the end of the sentence. The sentence contains a series of phrases: "relieves my stress, helps me relax, and keeps me fit."

5. Answer   C

Placing a period after "years" corrects a comma splice error.

False choices

A   Placing a period after "school" creates a fragment of the first part of the sentence; the sentence created following "school" would be awkward.

B   No comma is necessary before a dependent clause that follows an independent clause.

6. Answer   A

The first issue is the punctuation after the word "school." A comma is required after a long introductory phrase. The next point to consider is the punctuation mark after "field." The semicolon is required to separate two independent clauses.

7. Answer   B

The first issue is the apostrophe used with the word "team." In this sentence, the word "team" is singular, so to make it possessive, an apostrophe and an "s" are placed at the end of the word: "team's." The next issue is the punctuation mark after "dinner." A comma is used after a long introductory phrase. Finally, a comma is required after the word "most" to set off the appositive that follows.

SECTION 10 ◆ EXERCISES: STANDARD PUNCTUATION—COMMAS, SEMICOLONS, APOSTROPHES, END MARKS

DIRECTIONS: *For each of the following questions, choose the option that corrects an error in the underlined portion(s). If no error exists, choose "No change is necessary."*

1. Patrice, who sits next to me in class, called to find out if our professor assigned an essay or a
                        A   B
    reading for homework?
                     C
    A. who sits next to me in class
    B. essay, or
    C. homework.
    D. No change is necessary.

2. Magdalene couldn't attend her English class, because her son had to be rushed to the
                    A   B
    hospital's emergency room.
        C
    A. could'nt
    B. class because
    C. hospitals'
    D. No change is necessary.

3. Since January 24, 1937 Bike Week has been held in Daytona Beach; this ten-day festival
                  A   B   C
    includes motorcycle races at Daytona International Speedway.
    A. January 24, 1937,
    B. Beach, this
    C. festival, includes
    D. No change is necessary.

4. <u>Although Doris</u> likes to eat her favorite flavors of low-carb <u>bars, such as,</u> s'mores, cookie
      A   B

crunch, and chocolate peanut <u>butter,</u> she has trouble digesting them.
                                C

A. Although, Doris
B. bars, such as
C. butter she
D. No change is necessary.

5. When Darryl received all <u>A's</u> last <u>semester, he</u> made the <u>Dean's List</u> for the first time in his life.
                             A   B   C

A. As'
B. semester; he
C. Deans' List
D. No change is necessary.

DIRECTIONS: *For each of the following questions, choose the sentence that is correctly punctuated.*

6.
A. As a student, Jessica was used to having summers and holidays off, so she was shocked to learn that she would get only two week's vacation on her first job after graduation.
B. As a student, Jessica was used to having summers and holidays off so she was shocked to learn that she would get only two week's vacation on her first job after graduation.
C. As a student, Jessica was used to having summers and holidays off so she was shocked to learn that she would get only two weeks' vacation on her first job after graduation.
D. As a student, Jessica was used to having summers and holidays off, so she was shocked to learn that she would get only two weeks' vacation on her first job after graduation.

7.
A. I can go to the movie but not dinner because somebody's coming to my house later.
B. I can go to the movie, but not dinner because somebody's coming to my house later.
C. I can go to the movie but not dinner because somebodys' coming to my house later.
D. I can go to the movie, but not dinner because somebodys' coming to my house later.

8.
A. Heather asked her boss if she could take a months' leave of absence to take care of her sick mother?
B. Heather asked her boss, if she could take a month's leave of absence to take care of her sick mother.
C. Heather asked her boss if she could take a month's leave of absence to take care of her sick mother.
D. Heather asked her boss if she could take a month's leave of absence to take care of her sick mother?

9.
A. Rabbits make wonderful pets and do not require much equipment; for example, a litter box, a hay manger, a food bowl, and a water bottle.
B. Rabbits make wonderful pets and do not require much equipment, for example, a litter box, a hay manger, a food bowl, and a water bottle.

C. Rabbits make wonderful pets, and do not require much equipment, for example, a litter box, a hay manger, a food bowl, and a water bottle.

D. Rabbits, make wonderful pets, and do not require much equipment; for example, a litter box, a hay manger, a food bowl, and a water bottle.

10.

A. The zircon gemstone was believed to have many powers, such as keeping evil spirits away and banishing grief and sadness from the mind.

B. The zircon gemstone was believed to have many powers, such as keeping evil spirits away, and banishing grief and sadness from the mind.

C. The zircon gemstone was believed to have many powers; such as, keeping evil spirits away and banishing grief and sadness from the mind.

D. The zircon gemstone was believed to have many powers, such as keeping evil spirits away, and, banishing grief and sadness from the mind.

Chapter 3: Other Important Skills

1. *Recognizes Parallel Structure*
2. *Recognizes Easily Confused and Misused Words*
3. *Uses Adjectives and Adverbs Correctly*
4. *Uses Appropriate Degree Forms of Adjectives and Adverbs*

Introduction

In addition to the important related skills covered in Chapter 2, there are other skills addressed by the Writing Exit Exam that you should become familiar with. You can prepare for the questions covering these skills by learning some tips or by what the test is most likely to focus on.

SECTION 1 ◆ PARALLEL STRUCTURE

The Skill

This item tests your ability to recognize parallel structure. When you place two or more words, phrases, or clauses together and connect them, each of those words, phrases, or clauses should be in the same grammatical form so that they balance. This balance occurs through repetition of the grammatical pattern. Read the following examples:

Parallel Words:

- *Not Parallel:* I love **thinking, writing,** and **to speak.**
  - ➤ There is a list of 3 things in this sentence. Two of them end in "ing" and the last does not. All 3 have to be in the same grammatical form.
- *Parallel:* I love **thinking, writing,** and **speaking.**
- *Parallel:* George spent the first day of his new job **moving shelves, packing boxes,** and **loading trucks.**

Parallel Phrases:

- Writing enables students **to record information, to learn concepts,** and **to share knowledge.**
- **Watching a concert in person** is more fun than **watching a concert on television.**
- This summer, I will either **visit my relatives in North Carolina** or **take classes at my college.**

Parallel Clauses:

- *Not parallel:* The new employee learned **that she would receive** excellent health benefits, **that she would get** two weeks' vacation, and **to expect** a raise every 6 months.
- *Parallel:* The new employee learned **that she would receive** excellent health benefits, **that she would get** two weeks' vacation, and **that she would get** a raise every 6 months.

The Test Question

You can be tested on your ability to recognize parallel structure in two different ways:

1. You may be given a sentence containing a blank. You must choose the correct word or phrase within the context suggested by the sentence that makes it grammatically parallel.

2. You may be given three versions of one sentence. You must choose the sentence that has no error in parallelism.

For each question, try to find a LIST of something. Select the answer in which the items in the list are in the same form.

SECTION 1 ◆ DIAGNOSTIC: PARALLEL STRUCTURE

For each of the following questions, choose the sentence that has no error in structure. When you are done, check your work with the answers immediately following the diagnostic. Even if you get a perfect score here, go ahead and complete the exercises in this section; they are designed to help build confidence and to give you practice for future test success.

1.
   A. To surprise me, my husband placed all the dirty clothes in the hamper, organizing the shoes in the closet, and changed the sheets on the bed.
   B. To surprise me, my husband placed all the dirty clothes in the hamper, organized the shoes in the closet, and the sheets on the bed.
   C. To surprise me, my husband placed all the dirty clothes in the hamper, organized the shoes in the closet, and changed the sheets on the bed.

2.
   A. As she walked closer to the village, to her amazement, she could see candlelight, she could hear adults conversing, and she could sense their happiness.
   B. As she walked closer to the village, to her amazement, she could see candlelight, was hearing adults conversing, and she could sense their happiness.
   C. As she walked closer to the village, to her amazement, she could see candlelight, she could hear adults conversing, and sensing their happiness.

3.
   A. Phillipe enjoys his new job at the stadium because he can see all the games for free, meeting some of the players, and get discount tickets for family and friends.
   B. Phillipe enjoys his new job at the stadium because he can see all the games for free, meet some of the players, and discount tickets are available for family and friends.
   C. Phillipe enjoys his new job at the stadium because he can see all the games for free, meet some of the players, and get discount tickets for family and friends.

4.
   A. I broke up with my boyfriend because he did not respect me, verbally abusive, and unfaithful.
   B. I broke up with my boyfriend because he was disrespectful, verbally abusive, and unfaithful.
   C. I broke up with my boyfriend because he was disrespectful, verbally abusive, and his unfaithful behavior.

DIRECTIONS: *For each of the following questions, choose the correct word or phrase within the context suggested by the sentence.*

5. Now that Javier is a college student, he worries about doing well on tests, _____ to class on time, and keeping up with assignments.
   A. get
   B. he gets
   C. got
   D. getting

6. The neighborhood in Detroit where I grew up has changed; the park has been converted to a zoo, my favorite gathering place has become a tattoo shop, and my neighbors _____ moved away.
   A. having
   B. they have
   C. have
   D. will have

7. I lost my volleyball scholarship because I _____ too many classes, I had a bad attitude, and I failed all my tests.
   A. missed
   B. am missing
   C. would miss
   D. miss

Answers and Explanations to Diagnostic: Parallel Structure
For each of these questions, to avoid needless repetition of information, only the correct option is explained.

1. Answer   C
At the end of each sentence is a series of verb phrases. The verbs that begin each of the phrases must be in the same verb tense, as they are in Choice C: placed, organized, and changed.

2. Answer   A
This sentence contains a series of independent clauses. Each of them should begin with "she could" and the base verb, as in Choice A: she could see the candlelight, she could hear adults conversing, and she could sense their happiness.

3. Answer   C
The series of details is contained in a dependent clause beginning with "because." The subject of that clause is "he," which is followed by the helping verb "can." These two words are not repeated in the series but are understood to apply to each word group. Each verb must be in its base form because it follows the helping verb "can." The detail that comes after each of the verbs has been formed with a direct object and a prepositional phrase.

4. Answer   B

The dependent clause that ends the sentence contains a list of words all of which must be adjectives to maintain parallel structure, as in Choice B: disrespectful, verbally abusive, and unfaithful.

5. Answer   D

To make the phrases that follow "he worries about" parallel, the verbs must be in the –ing form. Therefore, "getting" matches the verbs "doing" and "keeping."

6. Answer   C

This second part of this compound sentence contains a series of three independent clauses. In each of these clauses, the verbs must be in the present perfect tense. Each verb will contain both the present tense of have (has for singular and have for plural) and the past participle form of the verb. The correct answer, Choice C, supplies "have" to form the present perfect tense "have moved."

7. Answer   A

In this sentence, a series of clauses follows "because." Each of the clauses should be in the simple past tense to be parallel. Therefore, "missed," Choice A is correct.

SECTION 1 ◆ EXERCISES: PARALLEL STRUCTURE

DIRECTIONS: *For each of the following questions, choose the sentence that has no error in structure.*

1.
   A. Scott inserted his credit card in the slot, selected the grade of gas he wanted, and filled the gas tank.
   B. Scott inserting his credit card in the slot, selected the grade of gas he wanted, and filled the gas tank.
   C. Scott inserted his credit card in the slot, selecting the grade of gas he wanted, and filled the gas tank.

2.
   A. To plan their Saturday night at the movies, Gina and Andres look at the movie listings on-line, read the reviews, and they buy their tickets with a credit card.
   B. To plan their Saturday night at the movies, Gina and Andres look at the movie listings on-line, reading the reviews, and buying their tickets with a credit card.
   C. To plan their Saturday night at the movies, Gina and Andres look at the movie listings on-line, read the reviews, and buy their tickets with a credit card.

3.
   A. While studying for her psychology test, Francena had trouble concentrating because her friends were calling her, her brother's blasting stereo, and her dad mowing the lawn.
   B. While studying for her psychology test, Francena had trouble concentrating because her friends were calling her, her brother was blasting his stereo, and her dad was mowing the lawn.
   C. While studying for her psychology test, Francena had trouble concentrating because of phone calls from her friends, noise from her brother's stereo, and her dad was mowing the lawn.

4.
   A. Shiva's family follows three traditions when they enter their house: they take their shoes off, say hello to every person in the house, and hugging and kissing their elders.

   B. Shiva's family follows three traditions when they enter their house: they take their shoes off, they say hello to every person in the house, and they hug and kiss their elders.

   C. Shiva's family follows three traditions when they enter their house: taking their shoes off, say hello to every person in the house, and hugging and kissing their elders.

5.
   A. Every morning when Paulette wakes up, she brushes her teeth, takes a shower, and then she will walk the dog.

   B. Every morning when Paulette wakes up, she is brushing her teeth, takes a shower, and then will be walking the dog.

   C. Every morning when Paulette wakes up, she brushes her teeth, takes a shower, and then walks the dog.

DIRECTIONS: *For each of the following questions, choose the correct word or phrase within the context suggested by the sentence.*

6. Some methods students use to cheat are storing information on their cell phones, _____ answers on the inside of bottled water, and writing answers on the bottoms of their sneakers.
   A. tape
   B. taping
   C. they tape
   D. will tape

7. While taking a pleasurable swim in the ocean, Casey got stung by a Portuguese Man of War, _____ out in agony, and raced to the shore.
   A. is crying
   B. cries
   C. cried
   D. wanted to cry

8. After accumulating credit card debt I could not pay, I now pay for everything with cash and _____ a credit card for emergencies only.
   A. using
   B. used
   C. by using
   D. use

9. I am able to attend college full-time because of _____, a loan from the bank, and a monthly allowance from my parents.
   A. a tuition scholarship
   B. my ability to win a scholarship for tuition
   C. a scholarship for tuition
   D. receiving a scholarship for tuition

10. The dangers of the waves at Teahapoo, a surf spot off the coast of Tahiti, are the volume of the wave and _____.
    A. that the water is shallow
    B. the shallowness of the water
    C. shallow water
    D. water that is shallow

SECTION 2 ◆ CONFUSED OR MISUSED WORDS/PHRASES

The Skill

This item tests your ability to distinguish among words or phrases that are commonly misused or confused. Words that are often misused or confused may sound alike or look alike, but their spellings or meanings are different.

Some of these confused or misused words are more common than others, and they tend to show up more reliably in the Writing Exit Exam questions on confused or misused words. Therefore, you should become very familiar with those common misused words, and they are presented in a table for you below. In addition, you will find another table of other commonly confused words for your review.

MOST COMMONLY CONFUSED WORDS/PHRASES

1. **their**—possessive (*Their* names are John and Mary.)
   there—location (Put it over *there*.)
   they're—they are (*They're* familiar to me.)
2. **its**—possessive (The dog gnawed on *its* bone.)
   it's—it is (*It's* a mad world.)
3. **to**—part of prepositional phrase or to + verb (I went *to* London *to* see the queen.)
   too—excess, extra, or addition (I think it's *too* hot in here, *too.)*
   two—the number (We get two weeks' vacation.)
4. **then**—time (First we paid bills; *then,* we went for a swim.)
   than—comparison (This winter has been colder *than* usual.)
5. **your**—possessive (*Your* paper was great.)
   you're—you are (*You're* the best!)
6. **where**—location (*Where* have you been?)
   were—past tense linking verb (We *were* good friends.)
   wear—put on clothing (I *wear* skirts more often than pants.)
7. **whose**—possessive (*Whose* coat is this?)
   who's—who is (*Who's* having pizza?)
8. **would/should/could, etc. HAVE**—I *would have* tidied up if I had known you were coming over.
   would/should/could, etc. OF = Doesn't exist in English
9. **affect**—VERB: to influence (Studying *affects* test scores.)
   effect—NOUN: result (Studying has an *effect* on test scores.)
10. **lose**—misplace; not win (I hate it when I *lose* my keys.)
    loose—not secure or tight (The child had a *loose* tooth.)
11. **used to**—past habit (I *used to* watch cartoons on Saturday morning.)
    use to—utilize (You should *use* this *to* soothe dry skin.)

OTHER COMMONLY CONFUSED WORDS/PHRASES		
a, an	coarse, course	principle, principal
accept, except	complement, compliment	quit, quite, quiet
advice, advise	counsel, council, consul	rain, reign, rein
all right, alright	explicit, implicit	receipt, recipe
alot, a lot	good, well	right, rite, write
already, all ready	hear, here	roll, role
among, between	hole, whole	sense, since
are, our	idea, ideal	set, sit
bare, bear	knew, new	thorough, though
break, brake	know, no	through, threw, thorough
breath, breathe	much, many	waist, waste
capital, capitol	number, amount	weather, whether
choose, chose	passed, past	
cite, site, sight	personnel, personal	

The Test Question

The test question consists of a sentence containing three underlined words or phrases. You must choose the answer that corrects an error in one of the underlined portions.

SECTION 2 ◆ DIAGNOSTIC: CONFUSED OR MISUSED WORDS/PHRASES

Choose the most effective word word or phrase within the context suggested by the sentence(s). If no error exists, choose "No change is necessary." When you are done, check your work with the answers immediately following the diagnostic. Even if you get a perfect score here, go ahead and complete the exercises in this section; they are designed to help build confidence and to give you practice for future test success.

1. At the Halloween party, the host, who wore a ghost <u>costume</u>, told a scary <u>tale</u> about a <u>statute</u>
                                                             A   B   C
        that came alive and wreaked havoc on a small town in Idaho.
   A. custom
   B. tail
   C. statue
   D. No change is necessary.

2. Mark was able to <u>bear</u> the discomfort of getting a tattoo of an American eagle on his back,
                          A
   but after it was done, he was not <u>quite</u> sure <u>whether</u> he liked it.
                                  B   C
   A. bare
   B. quiet
   C. weather
   D. No change is necessary.

3. The children were <u>all together</u> surprised when they received <u>their</u> <u>presents</u>.
                              A   B   C
    A.   altogether
    B.   they're
    C.   presence
    D.   No change is necessary.

4. I hate <u>to</u> play games that I always <u>loose</u>. It's <u>no</u> fun.
              A   B   C
    A.   too
    B.   lose
    C.   know
    D.   No change is necessary.

5. After his <u>fourth</u> movie, the actor knew that he had a <u>flair</u> for his craft because he was
                  A   B
    receiving offers for better <u>rolls</u>.
                                   C
    A.   forth
    B.   flare
    C.   roles
    D.   No change is necessary.

6. As Joy began her <u>decent</u> from the <u>peak</u> of the mountain, she could see the <u>whole</u> canyon
                          A   B   C
    below her.
    A.   descent
    B.   peek
    C.   hole
    D.   No change is necessary.

7. The writer was so stubborn that he would not follow the editor's suggestion to <u>alter</u> the end
                                                                                        A
    of the book so that the hero would make it <u>through</u> enemy territory and successfully cross
                                                  B
    the <u>border</u>.
         C
    A.   altar
    B.   threw
    C.   boarder
    D.   No change is necessary.

Answers and Explanations to Diagnostic: Confused or Misused Words/Phrases

1. Answer   C
A "statue" is a three-dimensional form that is sculpted, modeled, or carved in a material such as clay, bronze, stone, or wood. A "statute" is an established rule or law.

False choices

 A "Custom" is a practice followed by a particular group or region; a "costume" is an outfit or disguise.

 B A "tale" is a story, and a "tail" is a posterior part of an animal.

2. Answer A

In the context of the sentence, "bear" means to endure while "bare" means naked.

False choices

 B "Quite" means to the greatest extent. "Quiet" is free of noise.

 C "Whether" means if; "weather" refers to conditions such as temperature, wind, clouds, and rain.

3. Answer A

"Altogether" means entirely. "All together" means at the same time.

False choices

 B "Their" is the possessive form of "they" used as a modifier before a noun. "They're" is the contracted form of "they are."

 C "Presents" are gifts. "Presence" means the immediate proximity of someone or something or the state of being present.

4. Answer B

"Loose" means not secure or tight. "Lose" means to not win.

False choices

 A "to" is part of the to + verb.

 C "No" is correct here in the negative.

5. Answer C

A "role" is the part of a character in a play. A "roll" has many definitions, such as a list of names or a small rounded form of bread.

False choices

 A "Fourth" is something that follows third in order, place, rank, or quality. "Forth" means to move forward.

 B "Flair" means a natural talent; a "flare" is a device for producing a bright light.

6. Answer A

"Descent" means the act of moving downward. "Decent" means appropriate, in good taste.

False choices

 B A "peak" is the highest point of a mountain; "peek" means a brief look.

 C "Whole" means all, the full extent, and "hole" is a hollowed place in something solid.

7. Answer D

No change is necessary.

False choices

 A "Alter" means to change; "altar" is a platform where religious ceremonies are enacted.

 B "Through" is a preposition meaning in one side and out the other. "Threw" is the past tense of the verb "throw," which means to hurl through the air.

 C A "border" is a part that forms the edge of something. A "boarder" is one who pays a fee for room and board.

SECTION 2 ◆ EXERCISES: CONFUSED OR MISUSED WORDS/PHRASES

DIRECTIONS: *Choose the most effective word or phrase within the context suggested by the sentence(s).*

> ✎ **Test Taking Hint**
>
> *Pay particular attention to the way these questions are made. Notice that there are three words underlined in the stem of the question. Each of these underlined words is labeled in alphabetical order "A" through "C." Notice that each of the answer options is also labeled "A" through "C." The labels in the question are directly matched to the answer options. So the option labeled "A" is only going to replace the word in the question labeled "A." The same is true for "B" and "C." This labeling system means that word "A" does not have anything to do with option "B" or "C." Just be aware of this as you take the test.*

1. All students are <u>supposed to</u> get <u>advice</u> from a counselor before pre-registration <u>has past</u>.
                A   B   C
   - A.   suppose to
   - B.   advise
   - C.   has passed

2. The <u>desserts</u> looked so <u>good</u> that I could not choose <u>among</u> the chocolate fudge brownie and
        A   B   C
   the strawberry cheesecake.
   - A.   deserts
   - B.   well
   - C.   between

3. I like to <u>sit</u> the TV remote control <u>right</u> next to my chair so I always know <u>where</u> it is.
          A   B   C
   - A.   set
   - B.   rite
   - C.   were

4. At the masquerade party, Derek received a large <u>amount</u> of <u>compliments</u> on his imaginative
                                          A   B
   <u>costume</u>.
  C
   - A.   number
   - B.   complements
   - C.   custom

5. I would like to take the Introduction to Psychology <u>course</u>, but <u>it's</u> <u>all ready</u> full.
                                             A   B   C
   - A.   coarse
   - B.   its
   - C.   already

6. <u>Stationary</u> sales have decreased <u>since</u> many people use e-mail to <u>write</u> to each other.
        A   B   C
    - A.   Stationery
    - B.   sense
    - C.   right

7. You <u>should have</u> tried to <u>except</u> <u>their</u> point of view.
                A   B   C
    - A.   should of
    - B.   accept
    - C.   they're

8. When I graduated from high school, my <u>principal</u> told me to always keep my <u>ideal</u> in <u>site</u>.
                                                  A   B   C
    - A.   principle
    - B.   idea
    - C.   sight

9. Watching <u>too</u> many violent movies can <u>effect</u> <u>your</u> attitude toward violence.
                  A   B   C
    - A.   to
    - B.   affect
    - C.   you're

10. <u>A lot</u> of people <u>loose</u> money <u>through</u> bad investments.
       A   B   C
    - A.   alot
    - B.   lose
    - C.   though

SECTION 3 ◆ ADJECTIVES AND ADVERBS

The Skill

This item tests your ability to understand the difference between the adjective and the adverb and to recognize which to use in the context of a sentence. Adjectives and adverbs are both modifiers, which means they are descriptive words. However, they modify different types of words. **Adjectives** modify nouns and pronouns. **Adverbs** modify verbs, adjectives, and other adverbs. Please see the Parts of Speech Appendix for more information on adjectives and adverbs.

Certain adjectives and adverbs predictably cause problems.

<u>Good / Well:</u>

"Good" is an adjective; it describes nouns.

"Well" is usually an adverb; it describes verbs, adjectives, and other adverbs; it answers the question "HOW."

- The <u>car</u> runs *well*.
  - ➤ *How* does it <u>run</u>?

- It <u>is</u> a *good* car.
  ➢ *What kind of* car?

- <u>He</u> <u>teaches</u> very *well*.
  ➢ *How* does he <u>teach</u>?

- <u>He</u> <u>is</u> a *good* teacher.
  ➢ *What kind of* teacher?

Bad / Badly
"Bad" is an adjective; it describes nouns.

"Badly" is usually an adverb; it describes verbs, adjectives, and other adverbs; it answers the question "HOW."

- That <u>fish</u> <u>smells</u> *bad*.
  ➢ *How* does the <u>fish</u> smell? "Bad" describes the *fish*, which is a noun.
  ➢ Notice the "sensory" verb. If you say the fish smells *badly*, it is like saying there is something wrong with the fish's nose, so he is unable to smell properly!

- The <u>fish</u> <u>was cooked</u> *badly*.
  ➢ *How* was the fish <u>cooked</u>?

- <u>I</u> <u>speak</u> Spanish *badly*.
  ➢ *How* do I <u>speak</u> Spanish?

- My <u>Spanish</u> <u>is</u> *bad*.
  ➢ *How* is my <u>Spanish</u>?

Well as an *Adjective* Describing *Health*
An important exception to the "well = adverb" rule concerns describing one's general health.

- How <u>are</u> <u>you</u>? Quite *well*, thanks.
  ➢ I'm in general good health.

- <u>I</u> <u>don't feel</u> *well*.
  ➢ My health is not good.

- <u>I</u> <u>feel</u> *good* around you.
  ➢ This means, "I feel <u>happy</u>," not "I feel in good health."

The Test Question
You will be presented with a sentence that contains one or three underlined adjectives and/or adverbs. You must decide if the sentence is correct as written or choose the answer that corrects an underlined part. If the sentence is correct, choose "No change is necessary."

SECTION 3 ◆ DIAGNOSTIC: ADJECTIVES AND ADVERBS

For each of the following questions, choose the option that corrects an error in the underlined portion(s). If no error exists, then choose "No change is necessary." When you are done, check your work with the answers immediately following the diagnostic. Even if you get a perfect score here, go ahead and complete the exercises in this section; they are designed to help build confidence and to give you practice for future test success.

1. My friend drove his <u>enormous</u> monster truck with 40-inch tires to the movie theatre; when
   A
   the movie was over, a man in a Porsche would not let him out because the man was waiting
   for a <u>real</u> good parking space nearby, so my friend put the truck in reverse and backed <u>directly</u>
   B   C
   onto the Porsche, then drove away.
   A. enormously
   B. really
   C. direct
   D. No change is necessary.

2. If a sky diver is not experienced and is not aware of how to breathe <u>correct</u>, he or she can pass
   A
   out in mid air; if this happens, the <u>unconscious</u> sky diver will fall through the air and,
   B
   therefore, will not be able to open the parachute <u>quickly</u>.
   C
   A. correctly
   B. unconsciously
   C. quick
   D. No change is necessary.

3. After three months of attending GED classes <u>regularly</u> and studying <u>diligently</u>, Elizabeth
   A   B
   passed the GED test <u>easy</u>.
   C
   A. regular
   B. diligent
   C. easily
   D. No change is necessary.

4. The streets in my neighborhood in Venezuela were not maintained <u>good</u>; driving was <u>perilous</u>
   A   B
   because of the jagged holes, which led to <u>recurring</u> automobile accidents.
   C
   A. well
   B. perilously
   C. recurrently
   D. No change is necessary.

5. The Christmas celebrations in Puerto Rico include foods that are prepared <u>special</u> for this
   A
   holiday, traditional music played <u>continuously</u> by radio stations, and "parrandas," songs sung
   B
   after midnight by <u>joyous</u> friends and neighbors.
   C

A. specially
B. continuous
C. joyously
D. No change is necessary.

6. While growing up in <u>imperfect</u> conditions, I made trips <u>frequent</u> to the pediatrician's office
                        A   B

with my brother since he was <u>constantly</u> ill.
                                  C

A. imperfectly
B. frequently
C. constant
D. No change is necessary.

7. My cousin Cameron grew up without water, heat, or electricity, the <u>mere</u> necessities that we
                                                                           A

take for granted; his apartment smelled <u>badly</u> from sewage because a pipe had exploded
                                                      B

<u>unexpectedly</u>, and the landlord never fixed it.
         C

A. merely
B. bad
C. unexpected
D. No change is necessary.

Answers and Explanations to Diagnostic: Adjectives and Adverbs

1. Answer   B
"Really" is an adverb that modifies the adjective "good." "Real" is an adjective.

False choices
   A "Enormous" is an adjective modifying "truck." "Enormously" is an adverb.
   C "Directly" is an adverb modifying the verb "backed." "Direct" is an adjective, which does not modify a verb.

2. Answer   A
"Correctly" is an adverb modifying the infinitive "to breathe." "Correct" is an adjective.

False choices
   B "Unconscious" is an adjective describing "sky diver."
   C "Quickly" is an adverb modifying "open." "Quick" is an adjective.

3. Answer   C
"Easily" is an adverb modifying the verb "passed." "Easy" is an adjective.

False choices
   A "Regularly" is an adverb modifying the verb "attending." "Regular" is an adjective.
   B "Diligently" is an adverb modifying the verb "studying." "Diligent" is an adjective.

4. Answer   A

"Well" is an adverb modifying the verb "maintained." "Good" is an adjective.

False choices

    B   "Perilous" is an adjective, required after the linking verb "was." "Perilously" is an adverb.

    C   "Recurring" is an adjective modifying "automobile accidents." "Recurrently" is an adverb.

5. Answer   A

"Specially" is an adverb modifying the verb "prepared." "Special" is an adjective.

False choices

    B   "Continuously" is an adverb modifying the verb "played." "Continuous" is an adjective.

    C   "Joyous" is an adjective modifying the nouns "friends and neighbors." "Joyously" is an adverb.

6. Answer   B

"Frequently" is an adverb modifying the verb "made." "Frequent" is an adjective.

False choices

    A   "Imperfect" is an adjective modifying the noun "conditions." "Imperfectly" is an adverb.

    C   "Constantly" is an adverb modifying the adjective "ill." "Constant" is an adjective.

7. Answer   B

"Bad" is an adjective following the linking verb "smelled." "Badly" is an adverb.

False choices

    A   "Mere" is an adjective modifying the noun "necessities."

    C   "Unexpectedly" is an adverb modifying the verb "had exploded." "Unexpected" is an adjective.

SECTION 3 ◆ EXERCISES: ADJECTIVES AND ADVERBS

DIRECTIONS: *For each of the following questions, choose the option that corrects an error in the underlined portion(s). If no error exists, choose "No change is necessary."*

1. The residents were asked to evacuate <u>peaceful</u> and <u>quietly</u> as possible to avoid <u>unnecessary</u>
                                   A   B   C

   panic.

   A. peacefully

   B. quiet

   C. unnecessarily

   D. No change is necessary.

2. Noel carried out the karate demonstration <u>flawlessly</u>; each move was executed <u>skillfully</u> and
                                                        A   B

   <u>artistic</u>.

     C

   A. flawless

   B. skillful

   C. artistically

   D. No change is necessary.

3. The contestants at the talent show performed <u>enthusiastically</u>, but Carrie sang her song so
   A

   <u>good</u> she should have won. Unfortunately, the judges were <u>extremely</u> harsh.
   B   C
   A. enthusiastic
   B. well
   C. extreme
   D. No change is necessary.

4. The food odor coming from the refrigerator was so <u>awfully</u> bad that no one wanted to
   A

   investigate, but we held our noses <u>tight</u> and opened the door to find a <u>disagreeably</u> sour carton
   B   C

   of milk.
   A. awful
   B. tightly
   C. disagreeable
   D. No change is necessary.

5. After Tiffany got her very <u>challenging</u> job at the insurance company, she enjoyed <u>frequent</u>
   A   B

   shopping trips to the mall, but she spent her money <u>frivolously</u>.
   C
   A. challenged
   B. frequently
   C. frivolous
   D. No change is necessary.

6. After the <u>disastrous</u> tropical storm, people came out of their homes to find fallen trees, broken
   A

   glass, and <u>severely</u> damaged roofs; the result was <u>real</u> bad.
   B   C
   A. disaster
   B. severe
   C. really
   D. No change is necessary.

7. The actress looked <u>really</u> <u>well</u> in her <u>unusual</u> designer gown, diamond studded shoes, and
   A   B   C

   exotic Tahitian pearl necklace.
   A. real
   B. good
   C. unusually
   D. No change is necessary.

8. Renzo felt <u>terribly</u> about having to miss several classes, but his mother was injured in a
                    A

    <u>horrible</u> car accident, and he <u>quickly</u> took the first plane to Peru.
        B   C
    A. terrible
    B. horribly
    C. quick
    D. No change is necessary.

9. Although he gets sick <u>infrequently</u>, this year Matt got the flu; he recovered <u>slowly</u>, but after
                                A   B

    two weeks, he felt <u>good</u> enough to return to his normal routine.
                         C
    A. seldomly
    B. slow
    C. well
    D. No change is necessary.

10. The crowd <u>sure</u> enjoyed the singer who sang <u>forcefully</u> and reached the high notes <u>perfectly</u>.
                 A   B   C
    A. surely
    B. forceful
    C. perfect
    D. No change is necessary.

SECTION 4 ◆ DEGREE FORMS OF ADJECTIVES AND ADVERBS

The Skill
This item tests your ability to recognize the difference between comparative and superlative forms of adjectives and adverbs and to use them correctly.

<u>Comparative</u>—This is the form used when comparing ***two things***.

   Adjective: My mother is **shorter** than my sister.
              Your baked lasagna is **more delicious** than my aunt's lasagna.

   Adverb: Our flight arrived **later** than we expected.
              Erin's picture was **more carefully** drawn than Linda's.

<u>Superlative</u>—This is the form used when comparing ***three or more things***.

   Adjective: My mother is the **shortest** person in the family.
              Your baked lasagna is the **most delicious** of all.

   Adverb: Our flight arrived the **latest** of all the flights scheduled that day.
              Erin's picture was the **most carefully** drawn of all.

How To Form Adjective Comparatives and Superlatives

To form comparatives and superlatives, you will need to know the number of syllables in the word you want to change.

1. <u>One Syllable</u>—If an adjective or adverb is only one syllable, add the "er" ending to form the comparative and the "est" ending to form the superlative. This rule also applies to adjectives that end in *y*; however, you need to change the *y* to *i* before adding the "er" or "est" ending.
   - John is **tall,** but Mary is **taller.**
   - Mary is **the tallest** girl in her class.

2. <u>Two Syllables</u>—If an adjective or adverb has more than one syllable, use the word <u>more</u> to make the comparative and the word <u>most</u> to make the superlative.
   - John is **more athletic** than Mary.
   - John is **the most athletic** boy in his class.

Irregular Forms of Adjectives

Some adjectives have irregular comparative and superlative forms. It's a good idea to memorize them.

Adjective	Comparative form	Superlative form
good/well	better	best
bad/badly	worse	worst
far	farther	farthest
ill	worse	worst
little (amount)	less	least
many	more	most
much	more	most

SECTION 4 ◆ DIAGNOSTIC: DEGREE FORMS OF ADJECTIVES AND ADVERBS

Choose the option that best completes the sentence. When you are done, check your work with the answers immediately following the diagnostic. Even if you get a perfect score here, go ahead and complete the exercises in this section; they are designed to help build confidence and to give you practice for future test success.

1. Nick needs to learn to be _____ with his money.
   A. carefuller
   B. more carefuller
   C. carefullest
   D. more careful

2. Cats seem to be _____ than dogs.
   A. more curiouser
   B. more curious
   C. curiouser
   D. most curious

3. That was the _____ movie I have ever seen.
   A. worse
   B. worst
   C. worstest
   D. most worst

4. The weather was _____ this spring than it was in the spring of last year.
   A. cooler
   B. coolest
   C. more cool
   D. more cooler

5. Hernan bought his girl friend the _____ BMW on the lot.
   A. more expensive
   B. expensivest
   C. most expensive
   D. most expensivist

6. I could not tell if Mother was _____ at me for coming home late or at my brother for not coming home at all last night.
   A. more angrier
   B. most angry
   C. angriest
   D. angrier

7. Although Helen likes her job at Chili's, she liked working at Applebee's _____.
   A. better
   B. best
   C. more better
   D. bestest

Answers and Explanations to Diagnostic: Degree Forms of Adjectives and Adverbs

1. Answer   D
The comparative "more careful" is the required form. Two-syllable adjectives not ending in –y often require the addition of "more" before the word for the comparative form.

2. Answer   B
The comparative "more curious" is required to compare cats to dogs. Adjectives of three or more syllables form the comparative by adding "more" before the word.

3. Answer   B
"Worst" is the superlative adjective form required because more than two movies are being compared, "the worst movie I have ever seen."

4. Answer   A
The spring weather in two different years is being compared in the sentence. One-syllable adjectives form the comparative by adding –er to the end of the word.

5. Answer   C
The superlative form "most expensive" is required. Adjectives of three or more syllables form the superlative by adding "most" before the word.

6. Answer   D
The comparative "angrier" is required. Two-syllable adjectives ending in –y form the comparative by adding –ier.

7. Answer   A
The comparative "better" is required to compare the two jobs. "Better" is the comparative form of the adjective "good."

SECTION 4 ◆ EXERCISES: DEGREE FORMS OF ADJECTIVES AND ADVERBS

DIRECTIONS: *For each of the following questions, choose the option that corrects an error in the underlined portion(s). If no error exists, choose "No change is necessary."*

1. Ronnie is the _____ of the two guitar players in the band.
   A. best
   B. more better
   C. better
   D. bestest

2. The Blue Ridge Mountains are among the _____ mountain ranges in the United States.
   A. more beautiful
   B. most beautiful
   C. beautifullest

3. Last year was the <u>worse</u> year since 1992 for the number of hurricanes in our state.
   A. worst
   B. most worst
   C. more worst
   D. No change is necessary.

4. My sister thinks that Brad Pitt is the <u>handsomest</u> actor in movies today.
   A. more handsome
   B. most handsome
   C. most handsomest
   D. No change is necessary.

5. Josh works out _____ than I do.
   A. most effectively
   B. more effective
   C. more effectively
   D. most effective

6. My house is _____ from the college than your house is.
   A. farthest
   B. more far
   C. most farthest
   D. farther

7. Debbie plans to study <u>more diligent</u> for the final than she did for the midterm.
   A. more diligently
   B. most diligently
   C. most diligent
   D. No change is necessary.

8. Hai performed his routine <u>more enthusiastically</u> than Kim.
   A. most enthusiastically
   B. more enthusiastic
   C. most enthusiastic
   D. No change is necessary.

9. These exercises are _____ than I thought they would be.
   A. more hard
   B. hardest
   C. harder
   D. more harder

10. Math is <u>more easier</u> for her than English is.
    A. more easy
    B. easier
    C. easiest
    D. No change is necessary.

Chapter 4: Additional Practice

1. *Standard Capitalization*
2. *Standard Verb Forms*
3. *Choosing Proper Expressions*
4. *Spelling*

SECTION 1 ◆ STANDARD CAPITALIZATION

The Skill

This item tests your ability to apply basic capitalization rules. Always capitalize the first word of a sentence.

The following chart summarizes some of these rules.

People

Names	Martin Luther King, Jr., Amy Tan, Gabriel Garcia Marquez
Job titles or positions: Capitalize when they immediately precede the individual's name or when they are honorary titles.	Professor Benjamin, Mayor Bloomberg, President Bush, Chairperson Grasso, Endowed Teaching Chair Hilton
Capitalize titles of **high-ranking government officials** used with or without their names. Use lower case if the reference is general.	The President will visit the Middle East. The second president was John Adams.
Family relationships NOTE: When using a word such as <u>mother</u> or <u>father</u>, do not capitalize it unless you are using the word in place of the person's name.	Uncle Tai, Aunt Bessie I called Father today to ask him for money for textbooks. I called my father today to ask him for money for textbooks.
Groups and languages	African-Americans, Asians, Native Americans, Aleuts, French, Hebrew, Latin, Arabic, English, Spanish

Places

Geographical locations NOTE: when using the words <u>north</u>, <u>south</u>, <u>east</u>, or <u>west</u> for directions, do not capitalize them.	Arizona, Palm Beach County, the Rocky Mountains, Honduras, Gulf of Mexico, Pacific Ocean, Australia, Haiti, College Avenue Jose plans to move west after he graduates. Jose's family lives in the West.

Places (continued)

Buildings, monuments (structures made by humans)	The Pentagon, Taj Mahal, Ritz Carlton Hotel, Philadelphia Museum of Art, Hoover Dam, Empire State Building, Golden Gate Bridge
Academic institutions, courses NOTE: Capitalize the title of a course but not the subject of the course	Michigan State University, University of Colorado, Valencia Community College History 101, Biology 2, English 2210 My favorite subject is <u>psychology</u>. I plan to take <u>Psychology 203</u> next semester.
Organizations, government agencies, institutions	Angel Flight, Internal Revenue Service, National Endowment for the Humanities, MADD, NFL

Things

Religious terms: religions and followers, holidays, holy books, words for deities	Islam, Christianity, Judaism, Buddhism, Easter, Ramadan, Yom Kippur, Kwanza, Allah, Bible, Torah, Koran, Book of Mormon, God, Vishnu
Historical periods, events, documents Time periods (days of week, months, holidays)	Civil War, Dark Ages, Great Depression Bill of Rights, the Constitution Sunday, July, Labor Day, Columbus Day, Thanksgiving
Company and product trademark™ names	Band-Aid, Microsoft, Apple, Verizon, Coke, Toyota, Nike, Big Mac, Levis
Awards	Oscars, Davis Cup, Grammy Awards, Nobel Prize, Pulitzer Prize
Planets, stars NOTE: Capitalize the word <u>earth</u> only when referring to it as a planet. Do not capitalize <u>earth</u> when used with <u>the</u> as in the earth's climate. Capitalize the words <u>earth</u>, <u>moon</u>, or <u>stars</u> in a sentence where they are used to refer to other astronomical bodies.	Little Dipper, Uranus, Earth, the Milky Way; Mars, Saturn, and Earth are planets in our solar system. The earth's atmosphere can support human life.
Major words in the titles of books, songs, plays, movies, articles. Always capitalize the the first word and the last word, but do not capitalize articles (a, an, the), short prepositions, or conjunctions in a title.	Lord of the Rings, Terminator, "I Can't Get No Satisfaction," The Godfather, Revenge of the Sith

The Test Question

You will be presented with a sentence with three underlined parts. If a sentence contains an error, you must choose the answer that corrects an underlined part. If the sentence is correct, choose "No change is necessary."

SECTION 1 ◆ DIAGNOSTIC: STANDARD CAPITALIZATION

For each of the following questions, choose the option that corrects an error in the underlined portion(s). If no error exists, choose "No change is necessary." When you are done, check your work with the answers immediately following the diagnostic. Even if you get a perfect score here, go ahead and complete the exercises in this section; they are designed to help build confidence and to give you practice for future test success.

1. My <u>uncle</u> came to the United States to teach <u>mathematics</u> at the <u>University</u>.
          A   B   C
    A. Uncle
    B. Mathematics
    C. university
    D. No change is necessary.

2. Kien Nguyen, the son of an anonymous soldier and a wealthy <u>south</u> Vietnamese <u>mother,</u>
                                                                 A   B

    gives an account of his difficult childhood in his book <u>The Unwanted</u>.
                                                              C
    A. South
    B. Mother
    C. unwanted
    D. No change is necessary.

3. In Sweden, the <u>Summer</u> solstice is a <u>national</u> holiday; the Swedish traditionally eat
                      A   B

    <u>strawberries</u> for dessert on that day.
          C
    A. summer
    B. National
    C. Strawberries
    D. No change is necessary.

4. The <u>red bush</u> is an exotic plant with needle-like leaves that was used to make tea
         A

    by the indigenous people of South Africa; in the late 1800s, <u>settlers</u> in <u>Cape Town</u>
                                                                    B   C

    discovered how this tea was made.
    A. Red Bush
    B. Settlers
    C. cape town
    D. No change is necessary.

5. A popular artificial sweetener on the market suitable for people with <u>Diabetes</u>

                             A

 is <u>Splenda</u>; it tastes just like sugar and contains maltodextrin and <u>sucralose</u>.

   B   C

  A. diabetes
  B. splenda
  C. Sucralose
  D. No change is necessary.

6. To get to the <u>airport</u>, go <u>North</u> on the <u>expressway</u> about twenty miles.

       A   B   C

  A. Airport
  B. north
  C. Expressway
  D. No change is necessary.

7. In 1978, Florida was designated a <u>sanctuary</u> for <u>manatees</u> by the Florida

               A   B

 Manatee Sanctuary Act; these animals are considered an <u>endangered species</u>.

                         C

  A. Sanctuary
  B. Manatees
  C. Endangered Species
  D. No change is necessary.

Answers and Explanations to Diagnostic: Standard Capitalization

1. Answer C

The word "university" is not capitalized unless it is part of its name.

False choices

 A The word "uncle" is not capitalized unless it comes before a person's name, such as Uncle Phil.

 B The word "mathematics" is not capitalized unless it is a name of a course, such as Intermediate Mathematics.

2. Answer A

"South" should be capitalized because it is part of the name of a region.

False choices

 B The word "mother" is not capitalized unless it is used in place of her name.

 C This word "Unwanted" is part of the title of a book. The last word of a title is always capitalized. It's a good idea to memorize the specific capitalization rules for titles.

3. Answer A

Names of seasons are not capitalized.

False choices

 B The common noun "national" does not have to be capitalized.

 C The common noun "strawberries" does not have to be capitalized.

4. Answer   D

All words are capitalized correctly in this sentence. "Red bush" and "settlers" are both common nouns and do not need to be capitalized.

5. Answer   A

Names of diseases are not usually capitalized.

False choices

    B "Splenda" is a brand name and should be capitalized.

    C The name of the artificial sweetener "sucralose" is a common noun and does not have to be capitalized.

6. Answer   B

Words indicating directions do not need to be capitalized.

False choices

    A "Airport" is a common noun in this sentence and does not need to be capitalized.

    C The common noun "expressway" does not require capitalization.

7. Answer   D

All capitalized words are correct. All of the word choices are common nouns.

SECTION 1 ◆ EXERCISES: STANDARD CAPITALIZATION

DIRECTIONS: For each of the following questions, choose the option that corrects an error in the underlined portion(s). If no error exists, choose "No change is necessary."

  1. Dan spent the first eight years of his life in the <u>northern</u> part of the United States, then

                                                          A

     he and his mother moved to the <u>South</u> during the <u>Summer</u>.

                                     B   C

    A. Northern

    B. south

    C. summer

    D. No change is necessary.

  2. This semester, Javier is taking <u>History</u>, <u>Psychology 101</u>, and <u>English</u>.

                                     A   B   C

    A. history

    B. psychology 101

    C. english

    D. No change is necessary.

  3. When I went to <u>high school</u>, anyone who did not follow the <u>Dress Code</u> was sent to

                             A   B

     the <u>principal's</u> office.

             C

    A. High school

    B. dress code

C. Principal's
D. No change is necessary.

4. To get to the <u>Chinese</u> restaurant, go <u>west</u> on Glades Road to <u>northwest</u> 20th Street.
                A   B   C

  A. chinese
  B. West
  C. Northwest
  D. No change is necessary.

5. All three of the <u>Lord Of The Rings</u> books, written by <u>J. R. R. Tolkien</u>, have been
                   A   B

adapted into successful movies that have won many <u>Oscars</u>.
                                       C

  A. Lord of the Rings
  B. J.r.r. Tolkien
  C. oscars
  D. No change is necessary.

6. I look forward to Sunday dinner after <u>church</u>; we all get together at my <u>Aunt's</u>
                               A   B

house, and she always serves my favorite, <u>Kraft brand macaroni and cheese</u>.
                                       C

  A. Church
  B. aunt's
  C. Kraft Brand Macaroni and Cheese
  D. No change is necessary.

7. The Declaration of Independence, written to justify America's <u>independence</u> from
                                              A

England, was approved by <u>Representatives</u> of the <u>American Colonies</u> in 1776 and
                              B   C

became one of the most respected documents in America.
  A. Independence
  B. representatives
  C. american colonies
  D. No change is necessary.

8. Each year, <u>companies</u> such as Budweiser, Charmin, and Staples pay over two
                A

million dollars to air a thirty-second <u>television</u> commercial to the 100 million viewers
                                         B

watching the <u>Super Bowl</u>.
                  C

  A. Companies
  B. Television
  C. Super bowl
  D. No change is necessary.

9. In a speech delivered to his supporters in January 2004, Howard Dean, <u>Governor</u> of
                                                                                    A
    Vermont, was publicly criticized for uncontrolled screaming. Some people felt that
    this speech, which was called <u>"I Have a Scream"</u> by Dean's critics, contributed to his
                                           B
    losing the <u>Presidential</u> nomination.
                     C
    A. governor
    B. "I have a scream"
    C. presidential
    D. No change is necessary.

10. Sheila and Dave spent a romantic <u>New Year's Eve</u> together on <u>Sanibel Island</u>, where
                                             A   B
    they watched a colorful fireworks display over the <u>Gulf of Mexico</u>.
                                                               C
    A. New year's eve
    B. Sanibel island
    C. gulf of Mexico
    D. No change is necessary.

SECTION 2 ◆ STANDARD VERB FORMS

The Skill
This item tests your ability to use standard forms of regular and irregular verbs. A standard form is
one that is considered correct in standard written English.

The difference between regular and irregular verb forms is that regular verbs follow specific rules to
show tense whereas irregular verbs do not. Therefore, irregular verb forms must be memorized.

To prepare for this skill, you need to know the regular and irregular forms for the present tense, past
tense, and past participle. The following chart shows the differences in their formations:

	Present	Past	Past Participle
Regular	-s or -es is added to the end of the verb when the subject is he, she, it, or a noun	-ed is added to the end of the verb	-ed is added to the end of the verb
Irregular	-s or -es is added to the end of the verb when the subject is he, she, it, or a noun	form must be memorized	form must be memorized

Regular and Irregular Verbs in the Present Tense
With the exception of the verb **be**, regular and irregular verbs form their present tenses in the same
way. The first chart shows the forms of the regular verb **attend** in the present tense. The second chart
shows the irregular verb **do** in the present tense.

	Singular Forms	Plural Forms
First person	I attend college at night.	We attend college at night.
Second person	You attend college at night.	You attend college at night.
Third person	He **attends** college at night. She **attends** college at night. The secretary **attends** college at night.	They attend college at night.

	Singular Forms	Plural Forms
First person	I do every assignment on time.	We do every assignment on time.
Second person	You do every assignment on time.	You do every assignment on time.
Third person	He **does** every assignment on time. She **does** every assignment on time. Brandon **does** every assignment on time.	They do every assignment on time.

Regular and Irregular Verbs in the Past Tense

In the past tense, regular verbs are formed by adding –ed to the end of the verb. However, irregular verb forms do not follow a specific rule and must be memorized. In the previous example, you saw how the present tense of the regular verb **attend** and the irregular verb **do** were formed. Look at how the past tense is formed for the same verbs.

Past tense of regular verb **attend**	Add –ed	attended
Past tense of irregular verb **do**	No rule	does

Regular and Irregular Verbs in the Past Participle

The past participle is used to form the present perfect and past perfect verb tenses. These verb tenses help to show the time relationship between two events. The past participles of regular verbs are formed the same way that their past tenses are formed; however, past participle forms of irregular verbs do not follow any specific rule. Therefore, you must memorize the irregular verb past participles.

The following charts show how the present perfect and past perfect tenses are formed with regular and irregular verbs.

	Formation with regular verb	Use in sentence
Present Perfect	has/have + past participle has attended, have attended	He **has attended** college since he moved to Florida.
Past Perfect	had + past participle had attended	She **had attended** a college in New Jersey before she moved to Florida.

	Formation with irregular verb	Use in sentence
Present Perfect	has/have + past participle has done, have done	He **has done** every assignment on the syllabus.
Past Perfect	had + past participle had done	She **had done** every assignment on the syllabus before it was due.

Here is a list of commonly used irregular verbs for you to study. Three forms are listed: the base form, the past tense form, and the past participle form

Base Form	Past Tense	Past Participle (following has/have/had)
be	was/were	been
become	became	become
break	broke	broken
bring	brought	brought
choose	chose	chosen
come	came	come
do	did	done
draw	drew	drawn
eat	ate	eaten
fall	fell	fallen
forget	forgot	forgotten
give	gave	given
go	went	gone
grow	grew	grown
have	had	had
hide	hid	hidden
know	knew	known
ride	rode	ridden
rise	rose	risen
run	ran	run
see	saw	seen
steal	stole	stolen
take	took	taken
tell	told	told
throw	threw	thrown
wear	wore	worn
write	wrote	written

The Test Question

You will be given a sentence with one or three underlined sections that may have an error in the use of standard verb forms. If the original sentence contains an error, you must choose the answer that corrects an error in the underlined section. If the verbs are used correctly, choose the option "No change is necessary."

SECTION 2 ◆ DIAGNOSTIC: STANDARD VERB FORMS

For each of the following questions, choose the option that corrects an error in the underlined portion(s). If no error exists, choose "No change is necessary." When you are done, check your work with the answers immediately following the diagnostic. Even if you get a perfect score here, go ahead and complete the exercises in this section; they are designed to help build confidence and to give you practice for future test success.

1. After Ashley <u>finished</u> her shopping at the mall, she could not <u>find</u> her car, and she realized
                     A   B

   that it was <u>stole</u>.
              C
   A. finish
   B. finds
   C. stolen
   D. No change is necessary.

2. Last year, I <u>come</u> to Florida to <u>study</u> and <u>gain</u> independence.
             A   B   C
   A. came
   B. studied
   C. gaining
   D. No change is necessary.

3. Our dog <u>ran</u> into the yard during the rainstorm; when he <u>came</u> back in, he <u>drug</u> in mud all
           A   B   C

   over the house.
   A. had ran
   B. had came
   C. dragged
   D. No change is necessary.

4. Loretta <u>had gone</u> without breakfast, so her stomach <u>be</u> rumbling all morning until she <u>ate</u>.
               A   B   C
   A. had went
   B. was
   C. eat
   D. No change is necessary.

5. Allen Iverson, the well-known basketball player, <u>has</u> great power; he <u>could go</u> anywhere he
                                                       A   B

   wants and <u>does</u> not have to wait to get in to restaurants, movies, and parties.
                   C
   A. have
   B. can go
   C. do
   D. No change is necessary.

6. Joe jumped into the lake where he <u>had swam</u> many times before, but he did not know that an
   alligator had made that same lake his new home.
   A. had swum
   B. had swimmed
   C. swum
   D. No change is necessary.

7. In London, some people <u>weeped</u> when they heard of the terrorist bombings on a bus and in the underground railway.
   A. weep
   B. wept
   C. wepted
   D. No change is necessary.

Answers and Explanations to Diagnostic: Standard Verb Forms

1. Answer   C
The past participle form of the verb "steal" is "stolen."

2. Answer   A
"Last year" calls for the simple past tense. "Come" must be changed to "came."

3. Answer   C
The simple past tense of the verb "drag" is "dragged," not "drug."

4. Answer   B
The verb "be" in the sentence is the base form of the verb; the sentence requires the past tense form of "be," which is "was."

5. Answer   B
The helping verb should be in the present tense, "can."

6. Answer   A
The past participle form of the verb "swim" is "swum" and it should be accompanied by "had" in this sentence.

7. Answer   B
The past form of the verb "weep" is "wept."

SECTION 2 ◆ EXERCISES: STANDARD VERB FORMS

DIRECTIONS: For each of the following questions, choose the option that corrects an error in the underlined portion(s). If no error exists, choose "No change is necessary."

1. I <u>slammed</u> on my brakes and <u>come</u> inches from being <u>hit</u> by the car that sped out of control.
   A. have slammed
   B. came
   C. hitted
   D. No change is necessary.

2. While the guerillas interrogated my grandfather, my grandmother <u>took</u> all the children, <u>hid</u> them under the bed in one of the rooms, and <u>locked</u> the door.
   A. taked
   B. hided
   C. lock
   D. No change is necessary.

3. As she <u>started</u> to climb the steps to reach the stage, Melissa <u>slipped</u> and <u>falled</u>, splashing the cranberry juice all over our vice president's new suit.
   A. start
   B. slips
   C. fell
   D. No change is necessary.

4. As soon as I <u>had approach</u> the dark street corner, I <u>heard</u> a strange noise and then <u>felt</u> a heavy blow to the back of my head, knocking me off my bicycle.
   A. had approached
   B. herd
   C. feel
   D. No change is necessary.

5. One night in the discount clothing store where I <u>worked</u>, a group of five people <u>came</u> in; three of them asked sales associates for help, and the other two <u>stealed</u> clothing by hiding it under their coats.
   A. working
   B. had came
   C. stole
   D. No change is necessary.

6. The babysitter for my two toddlers <u>was</u> late, the dog <u>dug</u> a huge hole under the fence, and the pipe under the sink <u>bursted</u>.
   A. been
   B. digged
   C. burst
   D. No change is necessary.

7. My friend has a ghost in her apartment: one night while we were watching television, a stack of CDs that had been piled up on a bookshelf <u>flown</u> across the room, hit the wall, and landed on the floor.
   A. flew
   B. flied
   C. flies
   D. No change is necessary.

8. Jessica <u>had forgotten</u> her sunscreen, so she <u>had become</u> very badly sunburned the day she <u>paddled</u> her kayak down the river.
   A. had forgot
   B. became
   C. paddles
   D. No change is necessary.

9. Last Sunday, Jodi <u>lays</u> on the beach soaking in the sun and listening to the waves break along the shore.
   A. laid
   B. layed

C. lay

D. No change is necessary.

10. We thought we <u>had brought</u> enough food to the barbeque, but some of the relatives <u>took</u> such huge portions that most of the ribs and chicken <u>had been ate</u> before all the guests arrived.

A. had brung

B. had took

C. had been eaten

D. No change is necessary.

SECTION 3 ◆ CHOOSING PROPER EXPRESSIONS

The Skill

This item tests your knowledge of the meanings of a variety of vocabulary words and their use within a sentence. You are being asked to choose the word that is used accurately and correctly.

For example, in the following sentence, which word is the best choice?

• Memorial Day is a day of **commendation** for those who have died in our nation's service.

• Memorial Day is a day of **remembrance** for those who have died in our nation's service.

Remembrance is the most accurate word choice. "Remembrance" is the act of honoring the memory of a person or event. "Commendation" means praise of someone's abilities or an award given to someone in recognition of an outstanding achievement.

The Test Question

The test question consists of a sentence that contains a missing word. You will be given three words to choose from; only one of the words is correct. Two of the three words may be similar in meaning. In that case, pick the one that expresses the meaning most accurately. One of the word choices may be clearly incorrect, and you can eliminate it immediately. If you are not sure which word is correct, look at the words surrounding the word in question. Use those words for clues to help you figure out the meaning.

Which word would you choose in the following sample question?

Although Jemi was a _____ tennis player, she quickly developed a strong backhand during her very first match.

A. mediocre   B. novice   C. courageous

The sentence sets up a contrast. You know that Jemi developed a strong backhand during her first tennis match. Therefore, she must be a new player. "Novice," which means beginner, is the correct answer. "Mediocre," meaning not exceptional in ability, is not appropriate because the sentence tells you that she had not played tennis before, so she has not previously shown her ability. "Courageous" suggests that she showed bravery, but the rest of the sentence does not support this.

A careful reading of the sentence and the use of context clues will help you choose the correct answer.

SECTION 3 ◆ DIAGNOSTIC: CHOOSING PROPER EXPRESSIONS

For each of the following questions, choose the most effective word or phrase based on the context suggested by the sentence(s). When you are done, check your work with the answers immediately following the diagnostic. Even if you get a perfect score here, go ahead and complete the exercises in this section; they are designed to help build confidence and to give you practice for future test success.

1. Gabriella was uncomfortable about giving her presentation in front of the class because she was _____ about her accent.
   - A.   apprehensive
   - B.   self-conscious
   - C.   arrogant

2. My favorite teachers are the ones who _____ me to do my best, not the ones who discourage me.
   - A.   instigate
   - B.   administer
   - C.   inspire

3. The boss was _____ because three of the five servers scheduled to work last Saturday night called in sick, and he could not find anyone to cover for them.
   - A.   elated
   - B.   irate
   - C.   indifferent

4. Although the instructor warned Kenny about the effects of _____, he waited until the night before the project was due to begin working on it.
   - A.   procrastination
   - B.   tenacity
   - C.   cowardice

5. The _____ effects of smoking cigarettes is well known, but some people smoke anyway.
   - A.   derogatory
   - B.   innocuous
   - C.   adverse

6. Despite the extremely hot summer temperatures, the tomato plants _____, supplying us with ripe, tasty tomatoes throughout the season.
   - A.   thrived
   - B.   languished
   - C.   gesticulated

7. Some people at the gym are so _____ that they spend most of their time posing in front of the mirror and staring at themselves.
   - A.   modest
   - B.   crude
   - C.   vain

Answers and Explanations to Diagnostic: Choosing Proper Expressions

1. Answer   B
"Self-conscious" means ill at ease.

False choices
    A   "Apprehensive" means fearful or uneasy.
    C   "Arrogant" means displaying a sense of superiority.

2. Answer   C
"Inspire" means to motivate.

False choices
    A   "Instigate" means to provoke or stir up.
    B   "Administer" is to manage, to take charge of.

3. Answer   B
"Irate" means extremely angry, enraged.

False choices
    A   "Elated" is proud, joyful.
    C   "Indifferent" means having no interest or concern.

4. Answer   A
"Procrastination" means to put off doing something.

False choices
    B   "Tenacity" is persistent determination.
    C   "Cowardice" means lack of courage.

5. Answer   C
"Adverse" means harmful or unfavorable.

False choices
    A   "Derogatory" means expressing a low opinion.
    B   "Innocuous" means harmless, having no adverse effects.

6. Answer   A
"Thrived" means to grow vigorously.

False choices
    B   "Languished" is to lose strength or vigor.
    C   "Gesticulated" means to say or express by making gestures.

7. Answer   C
"Vain" means excessively proud of one's appearance.

False choices
    A   "Modest" means having or showing a moderate estimation of one's own talents or abilities.
    B   "Crude" means blunt or offensive.

SECTION 3 ◆ EXERCISES: CHOOSING PROPER EXPRESSIONS

DIRECTIONS: *For each of the following questions, choose the most effective word or phrase based on the context suggested by the sentence(s).*

1. Good vision helps animals _____ their prey or predators from a distance.
   A. realize
   B. detect
   C. ignore

2. Although the computer has become _____ into our daily lives, most of us never think about it.
   A. integrated
   B. forced
   C. combined

3. Sleep enables the body to _____ itself by repairing the body.
   A. revise
   B. relieve
   C. restore

4. Research _____ that students who become involved with college activities tend to be more successful than those who do not.
   A. warns
   B. reveals
   C. conceals

5. An essential part of critical thinking is _____ fact from opinion.
   A. observing
   B. describing
   C. distinguishing

6. The movement for African-American pride found its cultural _____ in the Harlem Renaissance, which was a literary and artistic movement.
   A. expression
   B. explanation
   C. publication

7. While the September 11, 2001, attacks produced a surge of patriotism, national unity, and pride, they also _____ a new era of vulnerability.
   A. motivated
   B. created
   C. discouraged

8. Social scientists have seen a(n) _____ amount of change in marriage practices in the past fifty years.
   A. huge
   B. erudite
   C. significant

9. Body odor is only a problem if the culture defines it as such; if a person believes body odor is a problem, he or she will do something to _____ it.
   A.   invalidate
   B.   eradicate
   C.   restore

10. Test stress may _____ itself in distinct physical symptoms, such as a speeded-up heart rate, sweaty palms, and clouded thinking.
    A.   present
    B.   flaunt
    C.   mask

SECTION 4 ◆ STANDARD SPELLING

The Skill
This item tests your knowledge of the rules for Standard American English spelling and your ability to apply them. The words used on the test will include words commonly misspelled and those requiring knowledge of spelling rules.

The best way to improve your spelling is to track your own misspellings and to learn to use your dictionary frequently. Many misspellings are the simple confusion of vowel sounds, such as substituting "a" and "e" for each other. Sometimes a word may be spelled correctly, but it may be the wrong word, like **their** for **there**. There are standard spelling rules that you should learn.

Five Basic Spelling Rules

1. The **ie** rule. You may have heard the rhyme "Put an *i* before *e* except after *c* or when sounded like *ay* as in *neighbor* and *weigh*."

achieve	believe	chief	relieve	mischievous
ceiling	deceive	perceive	receive	receipt
freight	neighbor	vein	weigh	heir

2. The final **e** rule. Drop a final silent *e* before an ending beginning with a vowel (*a, e, i, o, u,* and here, *y*).

   write + ing = writing   fame + ous = famous   scare + y = scary

   Exception: mileage

   Keep the **e** in these situations:

   - After **c** and **g** before an ending beginning with *a* or *o*:
     noticeable   courageous   outrageous   vengeance

   - To avoid confusion with other words:
     dye + ing = dyeing   singe + ing = singeing

3. The final **y** rule. Change a final *y* to *i* before any ending except *–ing*.

   happy + ness = happiness   lady + es = ladies   cry + ing = crying

   Ignore the rule if a vowel precedes the *y*.
   chimn*eys*   ann*oy*ed   monk*eys*

   Exceptions: lay/laid   pay/paid   say/said

4. Double a final consonant before an ending that begins with a vowel (including *y*) if the original word does both of the following:

   * Ends in consonant-vowel-consonant
     drop/dropping   bat/batter

   * If more than one syllable is accented
     occur   occurred   occurrence
     begin   beginning   beginner

5. The let-it-alone rule. When adding beginnings or endings to words, do not add or drop letters unless you know that one of the spelling rules applies or that the word is irregular.
   disappear   misspell   statement   achievement

   (Adapted from Blanche Ellsworth and John A. Higgins, *English Simplified*, 9th ed., New York: Addison Wesley, 2001.)

Spelling Rules for Plurals

Making Nouns Plural. To form the plurals of most nouns, add an –s to the end of the word.
   machine + s = machines
   wave + s = waves
   notebook + s = notebooks
   Clark + s = Clarks

This general rule has several exceptions.

Exception 1: If the singular noun ends in –s, –ss, –sh, –ch, or –x, add –es to the end of the word.

bus	buses	kiss	kisses	wish	wishes
fox	foxes	church	churches	witch	witches

Exception 2: If the singular common noun ends in –o

* Add –s when the word ends in a vowel + –o
   radio   radios
   stereo   stereos
   Soprano   Sopranos

* Add –es when the word ends in a consonant + –o
   tomato   tomatoes
   veto   vetoes

NOTE: A few words that end in a consonant + o do not change in this way.
   solo   solos
   piano   pianos
   pro   pros
   memo   memos

Exception 3: If the singular noun ends in a consonant and –y, change the –y to –i and add –es.
   salary   salaries
   company   companies

Exception 4: If the singular noun ends in a vowel and –y, add –s.
   guy   guys
   day   days
   Gray   Grays

Exception 5: If the singular noun ends in –f or –fe, change the –f to a v and add –s or –es.

knife	knives
self	selves

NOTE: Some words ending in –f do not change:

belief	beliefs
chief	chiefs
staff	staffs

Exception 6: Some singular nouns have different plural forms and are considered irregular:

woman	women
man	men
child	children
foot	feet

Exception 7: With hyphenated nouns, add –s to the first word.

father-in-law	fathers-in-law
sister-in-law	sisters-in-law

100 Problem Words

absence	definite	management	pursue
acknowledge	description	maneuver	questionnaire
acquaintance	desperate	mathematics	reminisce
acquire	develop	meant	repetition
across	discipline	mischievous	restaurant
adolescence	doesn't	necessary	rhythm
amateur	eighth	ninety	ridiculous
analysis	erroneous	ninth	sacrifice
apologize	exaggerate	nucleus	schedule
apparent	excellent	omission	secretary
approximately	existence	opinion	sensible
argument	fascinating	opportunity	sincerely
article	forty	parallel	sophomore
auxiliary	fulfill	particularly	souvenir
business	guarantee	perform	supposed to
calendar	guidance	permanent	suppression
category	height	permissible	surprise
committee	hindrance	perseverance	synonym
competent	hypocrisy	persistent	tendency
condemn	independent	personally	tragedy
conscientious	indispensable	playwright	truly
courteous	irrelevant	prejudice	twelfth
criticism	irresistible	prevalent	unusually
criticize	knowledge	procedure	used to
curiosity	maintenance	psychology	vacuum

(From Blanche Ellsworth and John A. Higgins, *English Simplified*, 9th ed., New York: Addison Wesley, 2001.)

The Test Question

You will be presented with one or three underlined words in a sentence. In the sentence in which only one word is underlined, you must choose the correct spelling. If three words are underlined in the sentence, you must choose the option that is the correction for an error in one of the underlined portions. If the sentence is correct, choose "No change is necessary."

SECTION 4 ◆ DIAGNOSTIC: STANDARD SPELLING

For each of the following questions, choose the option that corrects an error in the underlined portion(s). If no error exists, choose "No change is necessary." When you are done, check your work with the answers immediately following the diagnostic. Even if you get a perfect score here, go ahead and complete the exercises in this section; they are designed to help build confidence and to give you practice for future test success.

1. Gene was <u>transfered</u> to the company's corporate office in Tampa; this was a <u>beneficial</u> move,
           A   B

   for he gained a <u>substantial</u> raise.
                    C
   A. transferred
   B. benificial
   C. substancial
   D. No change is necessary.

2. Jena refused to date men who <u>criticized</u> her <u>intelligence</u> and expected her to pay for <u>diner</u>.
                                   A   B   C
   A. critisized
   B. inteligence
   C. dinner
   D. No change is necessary.

3. At the end of the semester, Kim was <u>exhausted</u> but <u>exhillarated</u> because she was now <u>eligible</u>
                                        A   B   C

   for a scholarship.
   A. exausted
   B. exhilarated
   C. elligible
   D. No change is necessary.

4. The discovery of antibiotics has helped cure many <u>diseases</u>; however, some germ strains have
                                                       A

   become <u>resistent</u> to many antibiotics, and newer, stronger ones must be <u>developed</u>.
             B   C
   A. deseases
   B. resistant
   C. develloped
   D. No change is necessary.

5. When he was working out, Eric <u>accidentally</u> dropped a <u>dumbbell</u>, which greatly <u>embarassed</u>
                                                A   B   C
him.
   A. accidentaly
   B. dumbell
   C. embarrassed
   D. No change is necessary.

6. Adnan worked on his English <u>pronunciation</u> on a daily basis.
   A. pronounciation
   B. pronountiation
   C. pronounsiation
   D. No change is necessary.

7. Tennessee Williams was a famous North American <u>playright</u>.
   A. playwright
   B. playwrite
   C. playrite
   D. No change is necessary.

Answers and Explanations to Diagnostic: Standard Spelling

1. Answer   A
"Transfer" contains two syllables and a single vowel precedes the final consonant, so the *r* is doubled before adding an ending, as in "transferred."

2. Answer   C
The correct spelling contains the double consonant "n" in "dinner."

3. Answer   B
The correct spelling contains a silent "h" and a single "l," "exhilarated."

4. Answer   B
The correct spelling contains an –ant ending, "resistant."

5. Answer   C
"Embarrassed" has two sets of double consonants, two r's and two s's.

6. Answer   D
The correct spelling has only two o's: "pronunciation."

7. Answer   A
The trouble spot in this word is its ending, "wright." This word must be memorized.

SECTION 4 ◆ EXERCISES: STANDARD SPELLING

DIRECTIONS: *For each of the following questions, choose the option that corrects an error in the underlined portion(s). If no error exists, choose "No change is necessary."*

1. Some day, I hope to become a <u>knowledgable</u> physician.
   A. knowledgible
   B. knowledgeable
   C. knowlegeable
   D. No change is necessary.

2. The most difficult <u>descision</u> Carla had to make was to come to the United States on her own to attend college.
   A. decision
   B. dicision
   C. decishion
   D. No change is necessary.

3. It was <u>truley</u> a <u>privilege</u> to hear the President's <u>speech</u> in person.
           A   B   C
   A. truly
   B. priviledge
   C. speach
   D. No change is necessary.

4. Andy is <u>pursuing</u> a <u>career</u> as a <u>licenced</u> massage therapist.
             A   B   C
   A. persuing
   B. carreer
   C. licensed
   D. No change is necessary.

5. When my sister went to see her favorite band in concert, she was in <u>extasy</u>.
   A. exstasy
   B. ecstacy
   C. ecstasy
   D. No change is necessary.

6. Although Jolie has become a vegetarian, she has to have a burger <u>occasionally</u>.
   A. occassionally
   B. occasionaly
   C. occasinally
   D. No change is necessary.

7. A brief afternoon shower is a common <u>occurence</u> in the summer.
   A. occurrance
   B. occurrence
   C. ocurrence
   D. No change is necessary.

8. The <u>committee</u> was able to <u>accomodate</u> visitors at the meeting without <u>noticeable</u>
         A   B   C
   interruption.
   A. comittee
   B. accommodate
   C. noticable
   D. No change is necessary.

9. The team had an <u>arguement</u> about whether Edgar used good <u>judgment</u> when he <u>interfered</u>
                  A   B   C
   with the coach's directions.
   A. argument
   B. judgement
   C. interferred
   D. No change is necessary.

10. Luis had a guilty <u>conscience</u> after he saw how <u>embarassed</u> Natalie became when all the servers
                       A   B
    at the restaurant sang "Happy Birthday" as a <u>surprise</u>.
                                                C
    A. consience
    B. embarrassed
    C. suprise
    D. No change is necessary.

Thinking Through the Writing Sample

The second part of the Florida College Basic Skills Exit Test is a timed writing sample. You will be required to compose either an essay or a paragraph in 50 minutes. Writing under pressure can be stressful. However, if you apply the strategies in this section, you will be able to meet the challenge with confidence.

Understanding the Topics

You will be given a choice of at least two topics to write about. The topics can be either subjective or objective. If it is subjective, you can approach this subject by using personal experience. If it is objective, you can develop the topic by using information you know about it from something you have read or heard or something you have learned in a class. Although you may not know what the specific topics are before the test, you can understand how the topic is written and know the categories from which the topics are developed.

How the Topic Is Written

The topic consists of two parts: the subject and the qualifier, a word or phrase that limits the subject. You can narrow the subject down further, but you cannot change it. If you do not address the topic, your paper will be considered "off topic," and you run the risk of failing the exam. Here are some examples of subjective and objective topics.

Subjective Topics

1. A family tradition that you plan to continue

Subject	A family tradition
Qualifier	that you plan to continue

   Have any ideas popped into your mind when you heard the topic? What about a family reunion or a holiday celebration? A tradition from your ethnic or cultural background?

2. An experience that made you change something

Subject	An experience
Qualifier	that made you change something

3. A first impression that was either right or wrong

Subject	A first impression
Qualifier	that was either right or wrong

Objective Topics

1. A place that people should visit

Subject	A place
Qualifier	that people should visit

2. A job that is beneficial for a teenager

      Subject   A job

      Qualifier   that is beneficial for a teenager

3. A topic in the news that upsets people

      Subject   A topic in the news

      Qualifier   that upsets people

Subjects from Which Topics Are Developed

You can see that the subjective topics often focus on a place, person, object, or personal incident. Objective topics may address an event in the news, an issue people feel strongly about, a person who has contributed to society, or an activity people participate in.

Understanding How Your Essay Will Be Scored

The Graders

Your writing sample will be graded by one or more readers whom you may or may not know. The reader may be your instructor or another instructor at your college. You can be certain that all readers are qualified in the field of English instruction and have experience both in teaching and in grading college writing.

Keep in mind that the graders do not expect a perfect piece of writing. They think of the writing sample as a rough draft, not as one that you worked on over a period of time. The grader wants to see that you can write a passing paper. Therefore, don't worry if your paper is sloppy because you may have crossed words or sentences out. You're not being graded on neatness!

The Grading Method

The graders use a method called holistic scoring to assess your papers. With this method, the grader reads each paper all the way through without writing comments or marking errors. He or she scores the writing sample according to the criteria established by the state. This way, **each grader uses the same standards,** not the particular standards he or she may require in an English course. As a result, holistic scoring prevents a grader from focusing on finding errors. Instead a paper is graded as a "whole" piece of writing in a more objective way.

The Grading Criteria

A number system is used to grade the writing samples. The scores range from 1, the lowest, to 6, the highest. You will need to achieve a 3 or higher to pass the exam. The grader will decide how well you have demonstrated that you can

- state a main idea
- develop the main idea with specific and sufficient details and examples
- show connections between ideas by using transitional words and phrases
- use a clear pattern of organization
- express ideas logically
- show effective use of vocabulary
- vary sentence patterns
- use correct grammar, spelling, capitalization, and punctuation

These are the same skills that you have been learning and practicing in your college preparatory English class.

The graders use the official "Scoring Criteria for the Florida College Basic Skills Exit Writing Sample." The criteria gives readers an overview of the scores, so although a paper may not have all of the characteristics of a particular score, it will clearly fall into the high, middle, or low range of that score. The complete scoring criteria follows the sample essays you are about to read.

Sample Essays

To help you see how other students have handled the writing sample and how the paper has been scored, read the examples that follow. Although some students will be asked to write a paragraph, most are required to write an essay. Therefore, the examples you will read here are essays. The writer of each sample essay responded to the topic "An activity or hobby that you enjoy." Four student essays have been selected to illustrate a failing score, a minimum passing score ("3"), a mid-range passing score, and a high passing score.

Failing Score

Shopping is one of my activity I enjoy. I enjoy spending an afternoon at different malls. Shopping with my friend Shantell. Shantell is the only person I bring to the mall with me, because Shantell is a outspoken person. We also knows how to shop for good sales.

The first thing I do before I go to the mall is find out what can of sale the store is having. For example, I enjoy shopping at Old Navy and when I find out that Old Navy is having a sale. I call Shantell on the phone and we go right to the store. While we are in the store. I spend hours in the store. Looking around and trying on different items. There is sometimes when I go to the store and I do not have any money on me to buy the items, we will go right to the bank to talke money out.

Another reason I bring Shantell shopping with me, she is a outspoken person. For example, if I try on a out fix that do not look good on me. She will tell me right a way. She do not wait until some one tells me that the outfix do not look good. There are times we go to the mall and we just look around, for fun. Not only she is good friend to shop with. She is also a good friend you can talk with all the times.

Low Passing Score

Two outs, bottom of the 9th, bases loaded with the winning run up at the plate. I have been in many situations like that and I love the feeling of it. It is the game of baseball and it is my most favorite sport to play. I have been playing this sport for many years and it never gets boring to me.

I love to play baseball because it is a very exciting game that takes lots of skill and practice. Whenever I get a chance to go to the park and throw a ball with someone it makes my day because I feel like I'm getting ready for another big game I have to win.

Another reason why I love playing baseball is because it is a team sport. I love to cheer on my teammates when they make a good play or get a great hit. I always cheer them on because I feel like I make them feel real good about themselves and they will make another play or get another hit the next time.

A third reason why I love playing baseball is that it keeps me active. If it wasn't for baseball I would not be the person I am today. Baseball has made me an outgoing person with a great personality and it has given me a great sense of humor as well.

The last reason why I love baseball is that it can make me some money in the future. In a couple of years, if I'm good enough, a major league team could draft me and I could be very rich just for playing the sport I love best.

Baseball has been something I have wanted to play my whole life and it is something that I will play for the rest of my life. I love to play the game of baseball and I will never give it up for anything.

Mid-Range Passing Score

My favorite activity to do with my best friend is shopping. Shopping is something we do everyday. Clothes, accessories, jewelry, purses, shoes are all a part of our day when we are in the mall. When it comes to our items, most of them are designer brands. Coach, Louis Vuitton, Chanel, and Gucci sit in our closets, throughout our wardrobes. When we are not looking for designer items, we are buying cute, tacky t-shirts to wear on a not-so-dress up day. Shopping makes Jessica and I very happy and content. Shoes, clothes, jewelry and purses are all the items we buy to make our day better.

Clothes are an extremely big deal to Lisa and I. Between Juicy Couture, Rile, Rampage and XOXO, Lisa and I must own their whole line of clothes. To make the outfits a lot more fun, we buy accessories to go along with the outfits. Belts, chains, and headbands jazz our clothes up to make us look better. Jessica and I receive complements all the time for our cheesy accessories worn around our heads and waists. Clothes and accessories are only a few things that Lisa and I shop for.

Purses and jewelry are a very important asset to Lisa and I. Between the two of us, we must have at least 15 designer bags and a 100 different jewelry pieces. Chanel earrings, Gucci glasses, Louis Vuitton watches all shimmer on our wrists and ears. We also own a Tiffany and Company necklace, bracelet, and earring set. It is very special to us, so we only wear it on special occasions. Jessica has about four different Louis Vuitton styles and I have six different Coach purses. Having these expensive things makes Lisa and I feel good about ourselves because we work hard for all of these nice things. We buy everything with our own money that we worked for at our jobs.

Jessica and I really love to shop. We love the same things and share everything. All of these items seem important to us and we enjoy presenting them. It might seem conceited and vain to other people but we think it is better to spend our money on clothes than something else that could bet us into trouble. Shopping plays a big part in our lives and it is fun to do. We like to look nice for ourselves and other people, that is why shopping is our favorite activity to do.

Upper-Range Passing Score

When I was growing up I enjoyed many activities. For example, I used to play basketball and soccer with my friends, or just collecting baseball cards, but now that I am older I enjoy two activities that I do by myself: playing guitar and writing poems.

I started to play guitar when I was sixteen years old. It started as a hobby that I enjoyed during the summer when I was not in school and I would not be playing basketball. When I turned seventeen, I quit basketball and dedicated my spare time to improving my skills with the guitar. As time passed by I was more interested in playing guitar, I wanted to learn all of my favorite songs from Pink Floyd or Black Sabbath, but soon I learned that playing guitar was not easy; you have to dedicate time and be patient. Once I learned to play guitar decently, I found out that girls liked a guy who could play the songs they liked, so to meet more girls, I learned to play popular songs that they liked.

Playing guitar goes hand in hand with writing poems. I started to write poems when I was around twelve or thirteen years old. I wrote poems because I felt that I needed to express myself in some way.

I was a very shy kid and did not have many friends. I started writing about school and its problems, about meeting girls and falling in love. As years passed by and I lived more, my topics started to change. I wrote about lies, betrayal and very depressing experiences. My mom thought that I was having problems, but I was not. I just enjoyed writing about those subjects. When I was around seventeen, I started to write about experiencing with drugs. I could see that I was influenced by many artists but especially Pink Floyd. Also, by that time I started to date a lot more, so I started to write poems to girls. I kept a notebook with all the poems I wrote. Nowadays my writing has improved a lot. My topics vary from hate to love, from loneliness to friendship.

I enjoy playing guitar and writing poems because it is a way that I can relax. It is very peaceful to sit on my bed and just play guitar for hours or to write a poem about an experience I had. I have been playing guitar for almost ten years and it has made me more extroverted and organized. I have been writing poems maybe half of my life. It makes me happy because when I read a poem from when I was fifteen, it brings back memories. Above all, I enjoy playing guitar and writing poems because later I can see truly the person I am.

Scoring Criteria for the Florida College Basic Skills Exit Test Writing Sample

SCORE OF 6	• The paper has a clearly established main idea that the writer fully develops with specific details and examples. • Organization is notably logical and coherent. • Vocabulary and sentence structure are varied and effective. • Errors in sentence structure, usage, and mechanics are few and insignificant.
SCORE OF 5	• The paper has a clearly established main idea that is adequately developed and recognizable through specific details and/or examples. • Organization follows a logical and coherent pattern. • Vocabulary and sentence structure are mostly varied and effective. • Occasional errors in sentence structure, usage, and mechanics do not interfere with the writer's ability to communicate.
SCORE OF 4	• The paper has an adequately stated main idea that is developed with some specific details and examples. • Supporting ideas are presented in a mostly logical and coherent manner. • Vocabulary and sentence structure are somewhat varied and effective. • Occasional errors in sentence structure, usage, and mechanics may interfere with the writer's ability to communicate.
SCORE OF 3	• The paper states a main idea that is developed with generalizations or lists. • The paper may contain occasional lapses in logic and coherence and is mechanical. • Vocabulary and sentence structure are repetitious and often ineffective. • A variety of errors in sentence structure, usage, and mechanics sometimes interferes with the writer's ability to communicate.
SCORE OF 2	• The paper presents an incomplete or ambiguous main idea. • Support is developed with generalizations and lists. • Organization is mechanical. • The paper contains occasional lapses in logic and coherence. • Word choice is simplistic, and sentence structure is disjointed.

	• Errors in sentence structure, usage, and mechanics frequently interfere with the writer's ability to communicate.
SCORE OF 1	• The paper has no evident main idea.
	• Development is inadequate and/or irrelevant.
	• Organization is illogical and/or incoherent.
	• Vocabulary and sentence structure are garbled and confusing.
	• Significant and numerous errors in sentence structure, usage, and mechanics interfere with the writer's ability to communicate.

How to Prepare for the Writing Sample

1. Review the elements of a successful essay.

    You can find information on the parts of an essay in an appropriate English textbook, in the writing lab, or online. Many websites provide helpful information on essay writing.

2. Go over papers you've written.

    Look at all of the writing assignments you have completed in your writing class(es). What were your strengths and weaknesses? Did you have any problems with organizing your writing? Were there any grammar problems that seem to occur in more than one paper you've written? Do you make repeated punctuation errors? If you haven't paid much attention to comments your instructor made, read those comments and learn from them.

    If you aren't sure how to correct any problems you may have, get some help. Set up an appointment for a conference with your instructor. If you have a writing lab on your campus, set aside time to work on materials available there.

3. Practice, practice, practice

    You wouldn't sign up to run a marathon without training for it. You know that to become better at any skill you need to practice. The best way to prepare for a timed essay exam is to write as many timed essays as you can.

    • Simulate the conditions of the exam: find a quiet place where you will not be disturbed and use your watch or a clock to keep track of the time. Make note of the time you begin and the time you will finish. You might want to ask someone to signal you at specific intervals, such as at the 30 and 40 minute marks. Some people find it helpful to divide the minutes into stages; for example, if you had 50 minutes to write your essay you could use 10 minutes to brainstorm, 30 minutes to write the essay, and 10 minutes to proofread and correct. On the other hand, you may find that limiting your time this way gives you more stress. As you practice, you'll figure out how you can make the best use of the time you have.

    • Choose one of the topics mentioned in this section or make up one of your own and write an essay. Follow the steps in the writing process that work for you. Do you like to brainstorm, make a web, or do a scratch outline first? Work through the introduction, body paragraphs, and conclusion.

    • When you have finished, think about your performance. Did you have trouble figuring out what to say about the topic? Did you spend too much time on any one part of the essay? Were you able to finish in the allotted time? Were you stressed? Think about how you behaved while writing the essay. This will help you become aware of the things you need to work on, whether they are aspects of the writing process or feelings of stress.

4. Read the next section, which walks you through the exam step by step.

How to Survive the Writing Sample on Test Day

If you follow these 9 steps, you should be able to write a passing essay.

1. **Keep your eye on the time throughout the test.**
    In order to finish in the allotted time, you need to keep track of those minutes. Write down the time the test begins and ends. If you have practiced timed essays on your own, then you will know how to divide your time to complete the different parts of the essay-writing process. If you haven't practiced, you can try the 10-30-10 method: 10 minutes brainstorming, 30 minutes writing, 10 minutes proofreading/editing.

2. **Choose one topic and don't change it.**
    Read each of the topics carefully. Make sure you know what the topics mean. Once you've selected your topic, don't be tempted to switch topics after you have started to write even if you do not like the topic. You won't have enough time to start over.

    Remember, you don't have to feel strongly about the topic. If you have no connection to any of the topics, try choosing a subjective topic. Most people find these easier to write about. You can always draw from your experience or even invent one; the reader won't know whether it was true or not.

3. **Figure out what the topic is asking you to do.**
    Here is a hypothetical topic: Lessons that you have learned in college

    This topic tells you that "lessons" is to be the subject of your essay. The qualifier, "that you have learned in college," tells you that you are expected to write about lessons you learned in college, not general lessons that all students learn in college. The "you" in the topic is an indicator that you can write about yourself.

4. **Use a prewriting strategy to generate ideas for your paper.**
    Prewriting strategies help you avoid writer's block and help you organize your thoughts. You can create a list of ideas, do a map (also called mind map or cluster), or make a scratch outline. Using one of these strategies keeps you actively involved in the process, so you won't have time to stress out. When you feel that you have found something to say, narrow your ideas down to three main points that you can easily support.

    Applying one of the strategies to the sample topic, you may have arrived at three specific lessons you have learned, such as scheduling time to study, going to bed at a reasonable hour, and managing your money.

5. **Write your thesis and decide on a plan of development.**
    When you write your thesis, you will also be deciding your plan of development. Following a plan of development will make your essay logical and coherent.

    Which organizational plan could be used for our topic "Lessons that you have learned as a college student"? You might give <u>examples</u> of various lessons you've learned as a college student, such as study skills, time management, cooking, housekeeping, or financial responsibility. Another way of discussing the lessons you learned might be to <u>contrast</u> the way you used to be before you started college with the way you are now that you are in college. For example, you could talk about how you used to spend your money on entertainment and clothing, but now you spend your money on books and tuition.

One type of thesis statement that helps organize your essay is the thesis map. The thesis map is like a mini-outline of your essay. Here's an example:

> Since I have enrolled in college, I have learned to **be responsible** for my schoolwork, to **manage my time** better, and to **improve my study habits**.

This thesis lists three supporting points to be discussed in the essay. From this thesis, you can easily see that the first body paragraph will discuss how the writer learned to be responsible, the second body paragraph will discuss how the writer learned to manage his time, and the third body paragraph will discuss how the writer improved his study habits.

6. **Write your introductory paragraph.**
   The introductory paragraph will contain your lead-in and thesis statement. The lead-in gets your reader interested in the paper. Don't spend too much time thinking about writing an extensive, detailed introduction as you might if you were writing an essay at home with lots of time. Instead, use a few sentences to work up to the thesis. This paragraph and the following paragraph are the most important two paragraphs in your essay because they will influence the way a grader will score your paper. It is critical that you carefully proofread the introduction and the first body paragraph for errors. Be sure to get off to a good start by checking for mistakes!

   - To begin, think of a brief story (anecdote), give some background, use a quote that comes to mind, or ask a question or two.

   - Follow your lead-in with your thesis statement. Placing the <u>thesis at the end of the intro-duction</u> tells the reader exactly what to expect.

7. **Write your body paragraphs.**
   The body paragraphs will follow the organizational plan you have selected, which will be evident in your thesis. Plan on writing two to four body paragraphs for a short essay. Just as the thesis statement is the controlling idea for the entire essay, so also is a topic sentence the main idea for a particular body paragraph.

   - Each body paragraph should <u>start with a topic sentence</u> followed by details that support the topic sentence.

   - Use numerous specific details. For example, in our sample topic, one of the points of the thesis is that you have learned time management. To support this, tell specifically what things you did to manage your time, such as waking up to an alarm, setting aside three hours in the evening to study, and cutting down on television viewing.

   - Use transition words like *additionally, furthermore, then,* and *therefore* throughout the body paragraphs to help readers follow the train of your thoughts.

8. **Write your concluding paragraph.**
   The concluding paragraph draws your paper to a close and is typically the shortest paragraph in your essay.

   - For a short essay, you need only two or three sentences to conclude.

   - Restating the main idea of your essay (thesis statement) is useful as it reminds the reader of what he or she has read.

- To complete the concluding paragraph, you can point out the effects, the importance, or the benefits of your topic.

9. **Proofread and edit your essay.**

You want to be sure to set aside at least 10-15 minutes for reading what you have written. When the graders read your paper, they will be looking for your ability to use correct grammar and punctuation and write effective sentences as well as main idea, logic, organization, and supporting details. One proofreading technique people find helpful is to read the essay backwards. Begin with the last sentence and continue until you have read the first sentence. This method helps you see each sentence separately so that you can analyze it. When you read your paper through from beginning to end, you tend to focus on the content and miss possible errors.

- In the first two paragraphs, it is especially important to make sure you have as few errors as possible.

- Double check your thesis statement and topic sentences to make sure they are complete, error-free statements.

- If you double-space your essay, you'll find it easier to add, remove, or change information.

- If you know that you have trouble with punctuation or grammar, check your paper for those problems.

- Common grammar errors include

  - Comma Splices—Check each comma in your paper and decide if a coordinating conjunction (FANBOYS) could be placed there.

  - Fragments—Read from the bottom of your paper to the top (last sentence first) and check that each sentence has a subject and a verb and expresses a complete thought.

  - Pronoun Agreement—Check your paper for the words *they*, *their*, and *them*. These words are plurals, so the things they refer to must also be plural.

  - Commonly Confused Words—Know the difference between words that sound similar but are spelled differently: their/there/they're, its/it's, then/than

The following is a sample essay on the topic "Lessons you have learned in college."

Lessons I Learned My First Semester in College

Before starting college, I thought it would be easy, and I would not have much work; however, I was wrong. **My first semester of college changed the way I think of school by teaching me to be responsible for my schoolwork, to manage my time better, and to improve my study habits. (Thesis statement)**

The first thing I learned was to be responsible for my schoolwork. (Topic Sentence) In high school, I skipped class a lot, and I was able to make up the work I missed. On the other hand, when I skipped one day of math class in college, I fell far behind the rest of the class. Unlike high school, in college I can't make up a test that I missed. I didn't come to class for my first test in my reading class. I went to class the next day hoping to make the test up, but my teacher would not let me. Also, I learned to pay attention in class because if I didn't, I would miss something; the teachers in college don't repeat themselves. For example, one day in my English class, I was sitting in the back of the classroom drawing and not paying attention to what the teacher was saying. Then, when it came time to do the homework, I had no clue what to do, and I also got a bad grade on the test. Another responsibility I learned was to bring my book to class. In high school, the teacher let me borrow a book if I needed it, but in college, if I don't have my book, the teachers tell me to leave the class. I forgot to bring my book to my reading class, and the teacher told me she would see me at the next class. Responsibility for my schoolwork was one major lesson I learned this semester.

Another lesson I learned my first semester was to manage my time better. (Topic Sentence) I am a person who always puts off something until the last minute. For example, I put off finishing my English, reading, and math lab hours, and now I am running around trying to get them done, so I can pass my classes. I found that I am not the only one who did this because the labs are full. If I had known how to manage my time, I would have used the entire sixteen weeks to do my lab hours, not the last two weeks. Not only did I put my lab hours off, but I also put off my homework assignments until the last minute hoping that they would be easy, and I could get them done quickly. For example, in my English class, we had to write paragraphs and essays, and I would wait until the morning that they were due to start writing them. I learned my lesson when I did not do well on them. Another thing I learned about managing my time was to work my job around my classes. I go to school in the morning until 10 a.m. and then go to work just to come back to school at 1 p.m. to finish my classes. Since I work as a lifeguard, and the pools are not crowded during the winter, I found that I could work my hours around my classes. This first semester really taught me to manage my time wisely.

The last lesson I learned in my first semester of college was to improve my study habits. (Topic Sentence) Since the tests and work in college are more difficult than the work I was used to in high school, my study habits have to be totally different. In high school, I talked to my girl friend while I studied. I also watched television and chatted on the computer all while trying to study. When I started my first semester, I did all of those distracting things while studying, but I soon realized that in college I can't do that. For college work, I really need to concentrate and understand what I am reading. Another study habit I learned was to study for at least a few hours each night. In high school, I only studied for about a half hour and thought that was enough. In college, I need to study at least two hours a day. With better study habits, I should do much better next semester.

When I first came to college, my advisor told me, "Look around you and see who is sitting beside you because 50% of the students you see will not survive the first semester." I believe this is true. I **am thankful that in my first semester of college I learned to be responsible for my schoolwork, to manage my time better, and to improve my study habits.** (Concluding Statement) If I use these throughout my college experience, I should get through with no problem.

Topics for Practice Writing

1. A first impression that turned out to be *either* right *or* wrong

2. An important event that changed your life

3. A place where you can go to relax

4. An invention that people cannot live without

5. A problem that needs to be solved in your community

6. Necessary skills for being a successful student

7. A memorable vacation experience that you had

8. A possession that has special meaning to you

9. A valuable lesson you learned from participating in a sport *or* hobby

10. The importance of writing clearly and effectively

11. A family pet that you love

12. A celebrity who sets a positive *or* negative example for youth

Part Four:
Test-Taking Strategies

"It's not that I'm so smart; it's just that I stay with problems longer."

—Albert Einstein

The word "test" conjures up all kinds of different ideas, many of which are negative. Keep in mind, however, that a test is not intended to be a judgment of you as a person; it is simply a measurement of what information you know.

The best way to overcome the fear and anxiety you may have about passing this test is to become test-wise, that is, to learn the format of the questions that are on the test, to work through practice questions that are similar to those on the test, and to review the competencies that you will be tested on. *Thinking Through the Test* has everything you need to get ready for the exam.

The Reading Exit Exam consists of <u>36 multiple-choice questions</u> over four multi-paragraph readings. Each reading usually has approximately nine questions associated with it. The readings are usually fairly academic in nature but quite accessible. In other words, the subject matter of the readings is something one might encounter in a textbook, but it is often quite interesting, and the language and sentence structure of the readings is usually not overly academic. Sometimes, a narrative or even a humorous essay is used as one of the readings, but overall, the readings are similar to what one might see in a high-interest textbook on some subject. The questions concern the reading skills you have been learning as you go through the exercises in this book: Main Idea, Supporting Detail, Author's Purpose, Author's Tone, Patterns of Organization, Inferences and Conclusions, Vocabulary, and Fact and Opinion. Knowing as much as you can about the test before you take it can really reduce your test anxiety and make it much more likely that you will pass the test.

How to Prepare for the Exit Exam

1. Take the sample Pretest at the beginning of the book to find out what your strengths and weaknesses are before you begin working on the individual skills. This way, you will know which skills you need to spend more time acquiring.

2. Work through the sections of *Thinking Through the Test,* and make sure you understand the correct answers to the exercises. Be sure to follow the tips given in each section.

3. <u>Learn</u> the Patterns of Organization and the transitional words (key words) that accompany them from Chapter 2. There are more questions addressing this skill on the Exit Exam than any other, so make sure you comprehend this skill thoroughly.

4. <u>Learn</u> the most common words used to describe the author's tone in Chapter 3, section 3 of this text. Tone questions are not difficult as long as you know what the answer choices mean.

5. Take the practice Exit Exams in Part Four. After you score each test, analyze which skills you still need to work on. At the end of Part Five in this book, you'll find charts that show the skill tested in each of the questions as well as a Tracking Sheet to record your progress, strengths, and weaknesses. Use these tools to determine which skills need the most work.

6. Find extra help if you need it. Some people are uncomfortable about asking for help and want to tough it out alone. You don't have to! Go to your campus writing center; talk to an academic tutor. And most importantly, talk to your instructor!

7. Form a study group. You'll find that each person in the group has a particular strength to share. Studying with others not only helps academically, but also emotionally. You become a team in which the members support each other.

What to Do on the Day of the Test

1. **Get a Good Night's Sleep:** The night before the test, get a good night's sleep. Don't try to stay up all night studying. Pulling an "all-nighter" will disrupt your ability to think clearly. Overdosing on caffeinated products will make you shaky and hyper, and you won't be able to concentrate.

2. **Food:** Don't take your test on an empty stomach. You may not be hungry before the exam, but sooner or later your hunger is going to kick in and cloud your thinking. Eat something light but avoid foods that can increase stress, like caffeine and sugar-laden products. Another thing you can do is bring a snack with you, like a health bar.

3. **Time:** Arrive early. You don't want to get stuck in a traffic jam and risk being late. Bring something interesting with you to read so the wait won't be so nerve-wracking.

4. **Relaxation:** Try the square breathing technique while you wait. Practice relaxation techniques so that when the day of the test comes, you will be able to overcome your anxiety. Square breathing is one easy relaxation technique to master. Here's how you do it:

   • Close your eyes.
   • Take a slow, deep breath through your nose while you count to three.
   • Hold your breath while you count to three slowly.
   • Breathe out through your mouth, again counting to three slowly.
   • Hold your breath for three slow counts.

   Repeat this several times. You will be surprised to see how well this works to get rid of stress. Use it any time you feel anxious—and remember to use this method on the day of the test.

5. **Seating:** If you can, choose a seat away from distractions like doors or windows. Turn off your cell phone and put it out of sight so you won't be tempted to check for calls or messages. Also, avoid others in the room who show negative behavior, are not prepared, or are anxious.

6. **Materials:** Be sure to bring the materials required, such as a number 2 pencil and a scantron sheet.

7. **Anxiety:** Most people feel some anxiety at test time. Use that energy to motivate you to do your best. Don't turn that anxiety into negative self-talk. Turn negative thoughts, such as "I never do well on tests" or "Everyone else will do better than I will," into positive thoughts. When you find yourself thinking a negative thought, stop and replace it with a positive one. "I can pass this test with ease."

Specific Strategies for the Reading Skills Exit Exam

There are some specific tips you can follow to reduce your anxiety and improve your score on the Reading Skills Exit Exam.

1. **Note the TIME the test ends** so that you will finish the test on time.

2. **Look over the test to see how many questions and reading passages there are**—Usually there are 4 readings and 36 questions.

3. **Read the directions**—It's a good habit to make sure you understand what the test is measuring and how you should approach the test.

4. **PREVIEW each paragraph before you actually read it**—When you preview, you read the entire introductory paragraph, the first and last sentences of the body paragraphs, and the entire concluding paragraph. This technique usually helps you capture the main ideas (thesis statement for the reading as well as the topic sentences of the body paragraphs), which helps you focus on the most important information in the text. It also helps activate any background knowledge you may possess about the topic so that you are more ready to read new information about it.

5. **If you do not understand a reading passage, READ IT AGAIN**—One of the most common causes of anxiety on the Reading Skills Exit Exam is lack of comprehension of a particular reading passage. It can cause students to become insecure and miss even relatively easy questions from that passage. If you do not comprehend some passage, do not move on to the questions. Instead, read it again. If the reading is still incomprehensible, mark your spot on the answer key and move on to the next reading. Perhaps after successfully completing a different reading, you will be able to relax enough to come back to the one that was giving your problems and read it with ease.

6. **Focus on the QUESTIONS, not on the readings**—For each reading passage on the Reading Skills Exit Exam, more than half of the questions can usually be answered with minimal reading. Questions such as Relationship Within or Between Sentences, Fact and Opinion, and Word Choice can be answered by just reading the questions themselves.

7. **Know where to find the Main Ideas**—Main idea is <u>vital</u>. Misunderstanding the main idea can cause you to also miss the author's purpose, the overall pattern of organization, and supporting detail questions. Review Chapter 1, Part 1. If you are not sure about where the main idea is located, assume it is either the last sentence of the first paragraph, the first sentence of the first paragraph, or the first sentence of the second paragraph. If the reading is a narrative, you can expect to find the main idea somewhere in the conclusion.

8. **Purpose is VERY closely related to Main Idea**—Very often, the author's purpose is simply a restatement of the main idea. If a reading selection contains both an overall main idea question and a purpose question, compare the answers in the two questions to look for similarities.

9. **Locate the answers to Supporting Detail questions directly in the text**—Do NOT guess, and do not rely on memory. Before you select an answer to a supporting detail question, make sure you locate it directly in the text.

10. **Do NOT select a Tone Word answer if you do not know what it means**—Insecure students tend to select what looks like the hardest answer choice. Only do this if you can eliminate the other answer choices with 100% certainty.

11. **Fact and Opinion have NOTHING to do with True and False**—A fact is not necessarily true. It is just checkable. Similarly, an opinion is not necessarily wrong. It's just not verifiable the way it is written. Also, don't forget that reported speech (saying that someone else said something) is FACT.

12. **Watch out for Subtle Bias**—Does the author consider anything to be inherently positive or negative? If so, that's a subtle bias.

13. **Watch out for Personal Bias when doing Inference and Conclusion questions**—Do not call something an inference simply because you strongly believe it to be true. The text itself must support that inference. Also, do not leap too far in your logic when making an inference or reaching a conclusion. Again, the text itself must support any inference or conclusion that you draw.

Marking Your Answer Sheet

Most tests in college are taken with automatic scoring answer sheets. An answer sheet is usually made up of a line of bubbles or bars that you fill in with a pencil—NEVER USE A PEN. Also, many students do not realize that when the answer sheets are scanned for scores, any stray mark will be counted as a wrong answer; therefore, NEVER MARK OUTSIDE OF YOUR ANSWER CHOICES. Little marks, such as question marks or dashes, in the margins or anywhere on the test answer sheet, will all be read by the scanner as multiple answers and will be marked as wrong. If you must mark a question on your answer sheet, follow this suggestion: Once you have narrowed down your answer to two possible choices, make a diagonal slash in *one* of the bubbles, *but do not fill it in*. This way, when you have finished your test, you can go back and review the answers that have a slash. Also, if you run out of time, you will have one answer marked which may possibly be right. There are no penalties for guessing, but a blank will be marked as an incorrect answer.

Example

	A	B	C	D
1.	0	0	0	0

When you have completed the test, go back to the answers with a slash in them and reread the sections necessary to make a decision, looking for support for the answer.

Remember to fill in each bubble or bar neatly and completely. Do not bear down on the pencil to make a heavy mark. Answer sheet scanners can read ordinary pencil marks. If your mark is too dark, it makes it difficult to erase, and smudges can be read as wrong answers. For this reason, use a number 2 or higher pencil. A softer lead is more difficult to erase and leaves smudges.

Always bring to the test two sharpened pencils with good erasers that don't leave smudges when you erase an answer. A good pencil may cost a few pennies more, but the results make it worth the added minimal expense.

Choosing Answers

The best strategy for test taking is to answer all the questions, going once through the entire test without spending too much time on any one question. Narrow down your answer choices to the best two answers, and then go back into the reading selection to find support for one of the two. If the question is on one paragraph of the test, just reread that particular paragraph, do not read the entire passage again unless it is necessary.

After rereading, if you are still having difficulty answering a question, make an educated guess from the two best answers. The odds of getting it right are 50-50. Do not use "eeny-meeny-miney-moe" to decide. Remember, all the answers to the questions are in the passages. You just have to find them.

Keep Cool

If you find yourself getting frustrated over a question—or if you "blank," don't get upset—just make a slash through one of the possible correct answers and *move on*. Do all the easiest questions, then go back and revisit the hardest ones later.

Do not allow yourself to become angry, frustrated, or anxious over test questions. Keep a positive mental attitude by telling yourself, "The answer is there and I *will* find it." Sometimes leaving a passage and coming back to it later can actually help you to understand it better.

If you are feeling overwhelmed, take a few seconds for some deep breaths, and visualize yourself in a pleasant place, just long enough to relax your body. A relaxed body and mind can think much more clearly than one that is tense or worried. If you have problems dealing with stressful situations, like tests, then do some research on relaxation techniques and learn some strategies to help reduce your anxiety.

When you have finished the test, go back once more to make sure you have answered every question with one (and only one) answer. Make sure you have ended up on the correct number on your last answer. If you find that you are short by one or over by one number, work backwards, beginning at the end of the test, and go back over each answer until you find the one that you skipped or answered twice. Make slashes for your corrected answers, then go back and erase the answers you marked and fill in the slashes.

Always check your test over before you hand it in. However, this *does not* mean that you should retake the test or change your answers. Also, *never change an answer* unless you *are sure that the answer you have chosen is wrong*; your first choice on an answer is usually correct.

Avoid choosing answers that use words like *always, never, all,* or *none*. Unless the passage states that this is indeed the case, one cannot assume it to be true. For example, if a question were to ask:

A good testing strategy is:

A. skip questions that you don't know the answer to.
B. mark in the margins of your answer sheet.
C. never change an answer.
D. use a slash for an answer that you want to review later.

The correct answer is D, "use a slash for an answer that you want to review later." The paragraph stated, "Never change an answer unless you are sure that the answer you have chosen is wrong." So, there can be times when you will need to change an answer.

Also, when you see answer choices like "All of the above," "None of the above," or "No change is necessary," consider it as a possible correct answer, especially on tests where these options are not used often. They tend to be the correct answer. But always go back to check each of the other choices by rereading before choosing "all" or "none of the above."

Keep an Eye on the Clock

Monitor the time you have left to make sure you finish the test on time. Before reading each passage, look at the clock and estimate how much time you have left. If you have 30 minutes left and two passages to read and answer questions for, this allows you 10 to 15 minutes per passage.

If others finish before you, don't try to hurry to finish too. When you think you are done, and you still have time left, use that time to make sure that you have answered every question and to go over your answers. Try to allow yourself at least 5 to 10 minutes at the end of the test to check your answers.

It is not surprising that many good readers do poorly on tests. They tend to over-analyze the questions, thinking that the test is out to trick them, and the question is actually harder than it seems. This is rarely the case. Most test questions are very straightforward. If the answer you have chosen seems like the obvious choice, it is most likely the correct answer. Reading tests are not mind games; they are simply a measurement of your comprehension skills.

After you have checked over your answers, hand in your test. If you have followed the suggestions and applied the strategies in this book, you can hand in your paper with confidence, knowing that you were well prepared for success.

Finally, remember to congratulate yourself!

"Difficulties mastered are opportunities won."

—Winston Churchill

Part Four: Test-Taking Strategies

"It's not that I'm so smart; it's just that I stay with problems longer."

—Albert Einstein

Many students are plagued with test anxiety, meaning they feel as though they forget everything they learned as soon as a test form is put in front of them, and as a result, they often fail tests. The best way to overcome the fear and anxiety you may have about passing this test is to become test-wise, that is, to learn the format of the questions that are on the test, to work through practice questions that are similar to those on the test, and to review the competencies that you will be tested on. *Thinking Through the Test* has everything you need to get ready for the exam.

The Writing Exit Exam consists of <u>40 multiple-choice questions</u> broken down into two sections. The first section, usually consisting of 10 questions, offers two paragraphs or two brief essays, and asks questions about the readings' conceptual and organizational structure. Each reading usually has five questions associated with it. The second part of the test, usually consisting of 30 questions, tests your knowledge of a number of specific grammar and usage skills. Knowing as much as you can about the test before you take it can really reduce your test anxiety and make it much more likely that you will pass the test.

How to Prepare for the Exit Exam

1. Take the sample Pretest at the beginning of the book to find out what your strengths and weaknesses are before you begin working on the individual skills. This way, you will know which skills you need to spend more time acquiring. Make note of the skills you miss on the Tracking Sheet, located at the end of Part 6 of *Thinking Through the Test*.

2. If you have little or no background in English grammar, be sure to complete the Parts of Speech Review Appendix. This section will help you learn about the basic grammar so that learning about the concepts covered in *Thinking Through the Test* Workbook will be familiar to you.

3. Work through the sections of *Thinking Through the Test,* and make sure you understand the correct answers to the exercises. Be sure to follow the tips given in each section.

4. Take the practice Exit Exams in Part Four. After you score each test, analyze which skills you still need to work on. Note which questions you miss by logging them onto the Tracking Sheet at the end of section 6 to record your progress, strengths, and weaknesses. Use these tools to determine which skills need the most work.

5. Find extra help if you need it. Some people are uncomfortable about asking for help and want to tough it out alone. You don't have to! Go to your campus writing center; talk to an academic tutor. And most importantly, talk to your instructor!

6. Form a study group. You'll find that each person in the group has a particular strength to share. Studying with others not only helps academically, but also emotionally. You become a team in which the members support each other.

What to Do on the Day of the Test

1. **Get a Good Night's Sleep:** The night before the test, get a good night's sleep. Don't try to stay up all night studying. Pulling an "all-nighter" will disrupt your ability to think clearly. Overdosing on caffeinated products will make you shaky and hyper, and you won't be able to concentrate.

2. **Food:** Don't take your test on an empty stomach. You may not be hungry before the exam, but sooner or later your hunger is going to kick in and cloud your thinking. Eat something light but avoid foods that can increase stress, like caffeine and sugar-laden products. Another thing you can do is bring a snack with you, like a health bar.

3. **Time:** Arrive early. You don't want to get stuck in a traffic jam and risk being late. Bring something interesting with you to read so the wait won't be so nerve-wracking.

4. **Relaxation:** Try the square breathing technique while you wait. Practice relaxation techniques so that when the day of the test comes, you will be able to overcome your anxiety. Square breathing is one easy relaxation technique to master. Here's how you do it:
   - Close your eyes.
   - Take a slow, deep breath through your nose while you count to three.
   - Hold your breath while you count to three slowly.
   - Breathe out through your mouth, again counting to three slowly.
   - Hold your breath for three slow counts.

   Repeat this several times. You will be surprised to see how well this works to get rid of stress. Use it any time you feel anxious—and remember to use this method on the day of the test.

5. **Seating:** If you can, choose a seat away from distractions like doors or windows. Turn off your cell phone and put it out of sight so you won't be tempted to check for calls or messages. Also, avoid others in the room who show negative behavior, are not prepared, or are anxious.

6. **Materials:** Be sure to bring the materials required, such as a number 2 pencil and a scantron sheet.

7. **Anxiety:** Most people feel some anxiety at test time. Use that energy to motivate you to do your best. Don't turn that anxiety into negative self-talk. Turn negative thoughts, such as "I never do well on tests" or "Everyone else will do better than I will," into positive thoughts.

When you find yourself thinking a negative thought, stop and replace it with a positive one. "I can pass this test with ease."

Specific Strategies for the Writing Skills Exit Exam

There are some specific tips you can follow to reduce your anxiety and improve your score on the Reading Skills Exit Exam.

1. **Note the TIME the test ends** so that you will finish the test on time.

2. **Look over the test to see how many questions and reading passages there are**—Usually there are 2 readings with 4 or 5 questions each, and 30 to 32 grammar questions.

3. **Make sure that you know your school's policy about the writing sample**—Each school makes its own decision regarding whether students write an essay or a paragraph and regarding how much time is allotted to the writing sample. Make sure you know these policies ahead of time.

4. **Read the directions**—It's a good habit to make sure you understand what the test is measuring and how you should approach the test.

5. **PREVIEW each paragraph in the concept skills section (~ questions 1–10) before you actually read it**—When you preview, you read the entire introductory paragraph, the first and last sentences of the body paragraphs, and the entire concluding paragraph. This technique usually helps you capture the main ideas (thesis statement for the reading as well as the topic sentences of the body paragraphs), which helps you focus on the most important information in the text. It also helps activate any background knowledge you may possess about the topic so that you are more ready to read new information about it.

6. **Learn the ORDER in which the grammar questions are most likely to occur as well as the tips for each question:**

   • **Word Choice**—With this question, either you know it or you don't. Be sure to apply the word that most exactly fits the context. If you are not sure, pick a choice and move on.

   • **Commonly Confused Words**—Some of these words tend to show up on the test more than others. Be sure to learn the list of <u>most commonly confused words</u> and in Part 2, Chapter 3, Section 2.

   • **Uses Modifiers Correctly**—This test question tends to be quite easy. Remember: modifiers need to be placed as close as possible to the words they describe.

   • **Coordination and Subordination**—This question tends to be easy as long as you understand what each of the transition words means. Review Part 2, Chapter 2, Section 1 to make sure you know what the transition words mean.

   • **Parallel Structure**—Remember to look for the <u>list</u> and notice if any of the items in the list is in a form that is different from the others. The "different" item in the list tends to be unparallel.

   • **Avoids Fragments, Comma Splices, and Fused Sentences**—This test item is very important because <u>there are usually 4 questions</u> covering this skill. Make sure you understand very well how to combine clauses; go through the section on Clauses in the Parts of Speech Review Appendix. Also, make sure you study the tips for answering this question correctly in Part 2, Chapter 2, Section 2.

- **Uses Standard Verb Form**—Use the paragraphs and essays you have submitted to your instructor as a guide: did your instructor correct many of your verb forms? If so, make note of which ones and be sure to learn the standard form.

- **Avoids Inappropriate Shifts in Verb Tense**—Look for the verb in the sentence that is different in tense from the others. Is there a good <u>reason</u> for the author to have switched tenses? If not, the different one is the error.

- **Maintains Agreement between Subjects and Verbs**—This is a very important skill because there are usually at least two questions about subject and verb agreement, and because this skill is also related to another question, which is Pronoun and Antecedent Agreement. Make sure to learn the words that are always singular in Part 2, Chapter 2, Section 3 as well as the other tips from that section. Also, make sure you understand prepositional phrases. If you do not, please cover that section in the Parts of Speech Review Appendix.

- **Maintains Agreement between Pronoun and Antecedent**—This question is also very important. Be sure to watch out for THEY/THEIR/THEM to ensure that the word being referred to really is plural. Again, review the list of words that are always plural in Part 2, Chapter 2, Section 4.

- **Avoids Inappropriate Pronoun Shifts in Person**—This question tends to be easy. Look for the answer choice that is different from the others. Is there a good reason for the author to have switched persons? If not, then the different one is incorrect. Also, make sure you understand how to use the pronoun, "one."

- **Maintains Clear Pronoun References**—Remember that every pronoun must refer to some specific noun in the sentence. If you cannot match some pronoun to a specific noun in the sentence, the pronoun is an error.

- **Uses Proper Case Forms**—This is an important question. Make sure you know which pronouns are Subjects and which are Objects. Also, remember that the trouble seems to occur most often with <u>compound</u> structures. Remember the trick for compound subjects and objects with at least one pronoun: read the sentence with only one of the pronouns at a time. Errors will become obvious.

- **Uses Adjectives and Adverbs Correctly**—Learn the words that cause the most confusion in Chapter 2, Part 3, Section 3.

- **Uses Appropriate Degree Forms of Adjectives and Adverbs**—Make sure you are comfortable with comparing 2 things vs. comparing 3 or more things.

- **Uses Standard Spelling**—With this question, you either know it or you don't, and since there is almost always only ONE question on spelling, it is better to spend your time learning about other, more important skills.

- **Uses Standard Punctuation**—Be sure to review Part 2, Chapter 2, Section 10 for the most commonly asked punctuation questions. Learn the 6 Comma Rules, and be sure to understand how to use a semicolon (;).

- **Uses Standard Capitalization**—There is usually only one question on capitalization, but it is worth reviewing the general rules for capitalization in Part 2, Chapter 4, Section 1.

7. **Make sure you complete Part 3, Thinking Through the Writing Sample, for tips on how to write a passing paper.** In particular, focus on the <u>first 2 paragraphs</u> if you are writing an essay. Those paragraphs will help set you up to pass or fail. Make sure your topic sentences develop your thesis, and make sure to use descriptive content. For your conclusion, brief is best.

Marking Your Answer Sheet

Most tests in college are taken with automatic scoring answer sheets. An answer sheet is usually made up of a line of bubbles or bars that you fill in with a pencil—NEVER USE A PEN. Also, many students do not realize that when the answer sheets are scanned for scores, any stray mark will be counted as a wrong answer; therefore, NEVER MARK OUTSIDE OF YOUR ANSWER CHOICES. Little marks, such as question marks or dashes, in the margins or anywhere on the test answer sheet, will all be read by the scanner as multiple answers and will be marked as wrong. If you must mark a question on your answer sheet, follow this suggestion: Once you have narrowed down your answer to two possible choices, make a diagonal slash in *one* of the bubbles, *but do not fill it in*. This way, when you have finished your test, you can go back and review the answers that have a slash. Also, if you run out of time, you will have one answer marked which may possibly be right. There are no penalties for guessing, but a blank will be marked as an incorrect answer.

Example

	A	B	C	D
1.	0	0	0	0

When you have completed the test, go back to the answers with a slash in them and reread the sections necessary to make a decision, looking for support for the answer.

Remember to fill in each bubble or bar neatly and completely. Do not bear down on the pencil to make a heavy mark. Answer sheet scanners can read ordinary pencil marks. If your mark is too dark, it makes it difficult to erase, and smudges can be read as wrong answers. For this reason, use a number 2 or higher pencil. A softer lead is more difficult to erase and leaves smudges.

Always bring to the test two sharpened pencils with good erasers that don't leave smudges when you erase an answer. A good pencil may cost a few pennies more, but the results make it worth the added minimal expense.

Choosing Answers

The best strategy for test taking is to answer all the questions, going once through the entire test without spending too much time on any one question. Narrow down your answer choices to the best two answers, and then go back into the reading selection to find support for one of the two. If the question is on one paragraph of the test, just reread that particular paragraph; do not read the entire passage again unless it is necessary.

After rereading, if you are still having difficulty answering a question, make an educated guess from the two best answers. The odds of getting it right are 50-50. Do not use "eeny-meeny-miney-moe" to decide. Remember, all the answers to the questions are in the passages. You just have to find them.

Keep Cool

If you find yourself getting frustrated over a question—or if you "blank," don't get upset—just make a slash through one of the possible correct answers and *move on*. Do all the easiest questions, then go back and revisit the hardest ones later.

Do not allow yourself to become angry, frustrated, or anxious over test questions. Keep a positive mental attitude by telling yourself, "The answer is there and I *will* find it." Sometimes leaving a passage and coming back to it later can actually help you to understand it better.

If you are feeling overwhelmed, take a few seconds for some deep breaths, and visualize yourself in a pleasant place, just long enough to relax your body. A relaxed body and mind can think much more clearly than one that is tense or worried. If you have problems dealing with stressful situations, like tests, then do some research on relaxation techniques and learn some strategies to help reduce your anxiety.

When you have finished the test, go back once more to make sure you have answered every question with one (and only one) answer. Make sure you have ended up on the correct number on your last answer. If you find that you are short by one or over by one number, work backwards, beginning at the end of the test, and go back over each answer until you find the one that you skipped or answered twice. Make slashes for your corrected answers, then go back and erase the answers you marked and fill in the slashes.

Always check your test over before you hand it in. However, this *does not* mean that you should retake the test or change your answers. Also, *never change an answer* unless you *are sure that the answer you have chosen is wrong*; your first choice on an answer is usually correct.

Avoid choosing answers that use words like *always, never, all,* or *none*. Unless the passage states that this is indeed the case, one cannot assume it to be true. For example, if a question were to ask:

A good testing strategy is:

A. skip questions that you don't know the answer to.
B. mark in the margins of your answer sheet.
C. never change an answer.
D. use a slash for an answer that you want to review later.

The correct answer is D, "use a slash for an answer that you want to review later." The paragraph stated, "Never change an answer unless you are sure that the answer you have chosen is wrong." So, there can be times when you will need to change an answer.

Also, when you see answer choices like "All of the above," "None of the above," or "No change is necessary," consider it as a possible correct answer, especially on tests where these options are not used often. They tend to be the correct answer. But always go back to check each of the other choices by rereading before choosing "all" or "none of the above."

Keep an Eye on the Clock

Monitor the time you have left to make sure you finish the test on time. Before reading each passage, look at the clock and estimate how much time you have left. If you have 30 minutes left and two passages to read and answer questions for, this allows you 10 to 15 minutes per passage.

If others finish before you, don't try to hurry to finish too. When you think you are done, and you still have time left, use that time to make sure that you have answered every question and to go over your answers. Try to allow yourself at least 5 to 10 minutes at the end of the test to check your answers.

It is not surprising that many good readers do poorly on tests. They tend to over-analyze the questions, thinking that the test is out to trick them, and the question is actually harder than it seems. This is rarely the case. Most test questions are very straightforward. If the answer you have chosen seems like the obvious choice, it is most likely the correct answer. Reading tests are not mind games; they are simply a measurement of your comprehension skills.

After you have checked over your answers, hand in your test. If you have followed the suggestions and applied the strategies in this book, you can hand in your paper with confidence, knowing that you were well prepared for success.

Finally, remember to congratulate yourself!

"Difficulties mastered are opportunities won."

—Winston Churchill

Part Five:
Exit Exams—Reading

Instructions: This Exit Exam has 36 questions. Read each passage below and answer the questions that follow.

Snakes, like all reptiles, are cold-blooded. They need to maintain a certain body temperature to survive. Although snakes depend on the outside environment to give them the energy they need to maintain their body temperature within the range necessary for life processes, they are not passive prisoners of the constant variations in temperature. Snakes can control heat exchange between their bodies and their environments   5
by a combination of behavioral and physiological processes. For instance, a snake can control its absorption of the heat from the sun—and thereby its body temperature—by altering the color of its skin or changing the exposure of its body to the sun.

Many snakes can change their color. Because dark skin substantially increases the amount of solar energy that is absorbed, many snakes living in cooler parts of an area   10
are darker than those that live in warmer climates. Additionally, many snakes that live in warmer regions can change their color according to the amount of sun they get during changes in seasons. Some snakes use their color changing ability to increase sun exposure by having dark skin on their heads which they expose to the sun before other parts of their body. Warming the brain and the sensory organs such as the eyes and the   15
tongue first enhances a snake's ability to detect both danger and food. Finally, pregnant females of some species are darker than males and non-pregnant females to maintain warmer-than-normal body temperatures that speed up the development of embryos.

A second way that snakes control their absorption of the sun is by increasing or decreasing the amount of body area exposed to the sun. The snake can make its temper-   20
ature warmer than the outside air by lying at right angles to the direction of the sun and spreading and flattening to increase its body's surface area. When a snake's body has reached a suitable temperature, it avoids further heating by lightening its skin color, changing its position, and eventually moving underground. In addition, the temperature of the surface that the snake is in contact with is also important because a cool snake   25

can crawl on a warm rock or other surface and absorb its heat. (Adapted from Robert Leo Smith and Thomas M. Smith, *Elements of Ecology*, 5th ed., San Francisco: Benjamin Cummings, 2003.)

1. Which sentence best states the main idea of the passage?
   A. Snakes can control heat exchange between their bodies and their environments by a combination of behavioral and physiological processes.
   B. Snakes can change color to control absorption of the sun.
   C. Snakes, like all reptiles, are cold-blooded.
   D. Although snakes depend on the outside environment to give them the energy they need to maintain their body temperature, they are not passive prisoners of the constant variations in temperature.

2. In this passage, the author's purpose is
   A. to describe the ways that snakes can change color to control their absorption of the sun.
   B. to persuade readers that snakes are not passive prisoners of variations in temperature.
   C. to explain how snakes can change their color to control their absorption of the sun.
   D. to describe the ways that snakes can control heat exchange between their bodies and their environments.

3. The overall pattern of organization is
   A. listing.
   B. compare and contrast.
   C. cause and effect.
   D. illustration.

4. What is the relationship within this sentence from paragraph two? "Finally, pregnant females of some species are darker than males and non-pregnant females to maintain warmer-than-normal body temperatures that speed up the development of embryos."
   A. Illustration
   B. Listing
   C. Cause and effect
   D. Compare and contrast

5. According to the passage, which statement is true?
   A. Pregnant female snakes are lighter than non-pregnant females.
   B. A snake can alter the exposure of its body to the sun.
   C. Cool rocks will absorb the heat from the snakes' body.
   D. A snake can store body heat for long periods.

6. Is the following sentence a fact or an opinion? "Warming the brain and the sensory organs such as the eyes and the tongue first enhances a snake's ability to detect both danger and food."
   A. Fact
   B. Opinion

7. The author's claim that "Snakes can control heat exchange between their bodies and their environments by a combination of behavioral and physiological processes" is
   A. adequately supported by factual details.
   B. inadequately supported based upon opinions.

8. The tone of this passage can best be described as
   A. admiring.
   B. nostalgic.
   C. objective.
   D. ironic.

9. A conclusion that can be drawn from the passage is
   A. Snakes do not like to live in cold regions.
   B. Snakes can change color at will simply by deciding to do it.
   C. Snakes have a temperature that remains relatively constant.
   D. Snakes must constantly seek to find warmer or cooler environments to maintain their body temperature.

Read the passage below and answer the questions that follow.

Spielberg's journey is one version of the universal story of human development: A skinny kid beset by fears and with few friends becomes one of the most powerful figures in the global entertainment industry; from a family with a fragmented family life develops a man's resolve to make the best possible life for his own family.

Steven Spielberg was a perpetual new kid on the block. His father, Arnold, a pioneer   5
in the use of computers in engineering, was hardly ever around and, to make matters
worse, frequently uprooted his family, moving from Ohio to New Jersey, to Arizona,
and finally to Northern California. He was also, by all accounts, an unusual child, both
in his appearance (he had a large head and protruding ears) and in his fearful and awkward behavior. Spielberg himself has said that he "felt like an alien" throughout his   10
childhood. He desperately wanted to be accepted but didn't fit in. So, at age 12 he
began making films. Spielberg continued to make movies as a teenager, which helped
him gain acceptance by his peers.

When he was 16, Spielberg's parents divorced, and Spielberg blamed his father's constant traveling for the breakup. His father remarried, which deepened Spielberg's un-   15
happiness; he couldn't stand his father's second wife. Although he withdrew from his
father, he remained close with his mother, Leah, a concert pianist and artist. His split
with his father lasted some 15 years.

In many ways, Spielberg's films, like the rest of his life, are shaped by his childhood.
Spielberg himself has said about *E.T., The Extra-Terrestrial*, "The whole movie is really   20
about divorce. . . . Henry's (the main character's) ambition to find a father by bringing
E.T. into his life to fill some black hole—that was my struggle to find somebody to replace the dad who I felt had abandoned me." Many of Spielberg's other films include
children who are separated from their parents (such as the girl in *Poltergeist* and the
boy in *Close Encounters of the Third Kind*). *Back to the Future* might represent his   25
longings to change the past, if only he could. As he matured, Spielberg's identification
with oppressed people in general, not just oppressed children, led him to make movies
such as *The Color Purple*, *Schindler's List*, and *Amistad*.

Steven Spielberg married and had a child, but eventually divorced his first wife, actress
Amy Irving. His own experiences made him extremely sensitive to the effect of the di-   30

vorce on his son, Max, and he made every attempt to ensure that Max did not feel abandoned. When he married again, he became deeply involved with his family, which includes seven children, some of them adopted. His father Arnold became a well-loved grandfather as well. (Adapted from Stephen M. Kosslyn and Robin S. Rosenberg, *Psychology*, 2nd ed., Boston: Allyn and Bacon, 2004.)

10. The sentence which best states the main idea of the passage is
    A. The separation of Spielberg's parents caused him to make movies with characters who were divorced or abandoned.
    B. Spielberg's childhood influenced his career as a filmmaker and his personal life as a husband and a father.
    C. Spielberg's journey is one version of the universal story of human development.
    D. Spielberg's identification with oppressed people in general, not just oppressed children, led him to make movies.

11. What is the relationship within the following sentence? "He desperately wanted to be accepted but didn't fit in."
    A. Listing
    B. Time order
    C. Contrast
    D. Comparison

12. What is the relationship between these sentences? "He desperately wanted to be accepted but didn't fit in. So, at age 12 he began making films."
    A. Summary
    B. Time order
    C. Listing
    D. Cause and effect

13. The overall pattern of organization for this passage is
    A. cause and effect.
    B. time order.
    C. listing.
    D. illustration.

14. The author's purpose in writing this passage is
    A. to summarize Spielberg's career.
    B. to show how Spielberg's childhood affected his filmmaking career.
    C. to analyze the effect of divorce on children.
    D. to illustrate examples of the many films that Spielberg has made.

15. A conclusion that can be drawn from this passage is that
    A. Spielberg was not a good student in school.
    B. Spielberg's family moved frequently during his childhood because his parents had divorced.
    C. Spielberg expresses many of his feelings about his own life through his film characters.
    D. Spielberg's mother did not approve of his career in movies.

16. Which statement provides the best support for the author's claim that "In many ways, Spielberg's films, like the rest of his life, are shaped by his childhood"?
    A. Many of Spielberg's other films include children who are separated from their parents (such as the girl in *Poltergeist* and the boy in *Close Encounters of the Third Kind*).
    B. When he was 16, Spielberg's parents divorced, and Spielberg blamed his father's constant traveling for the breakup.
    C. He desperately wanted to be accepted but didn't fit in.
    D. Spielberg himself has said that he "felt like an alien" throughout his childhood.

17. According to the passage, Spielberg
    A. always knew he would be famous some day.
    B. got his ideas for the movie *The Color Purple* from observing his parents.
    C. became interested in filmmaking after his parents' divorce.
    D. modeled the character Henry in *E.T., The Extra-Terrestrial*, after himself as a child.

18. Is the following sentence a fact or an opinion? "Spielberg himself has said about *E.T., The Extra-Terrestrial*, 'The whole movie is really about divorce. . . . Henry's (the main character's) ambition to find a father by bringing E.T. into his life to fill some black hole—that was my struggle to find somebody to replace the dad who I felt had abandoned me.'"
    A. Fact
    B. Opinion

Read the passage below and answer the questions that follow.

There had been great athletes before; indeed probably the greatest all-around athlete of the twentieth century was Jim Thorpe, a Sac and Fox Indian who won both the pentathalon and the decathalon at the 1912 Olympic Games, made Walter Camp's All-American football team in 1912 and 1913, then played major league baseball for several years before becoming a pioneer founder and player in the National Football League. 5
But what truly made the 1920s a golden age was a coincidence—the emergence in a few short years of a remarkable collection of what today would be called superstars.

In football there was the University of Illinois's Harold "Red" Grange, who averaged over 10 yards a carry during his college career and who in one incredible quarter during the 1924 game between Illinois and Michigan carried the ball four times and scored a 10 touchdown each time, gaining in the process 263 yards. In prizefighting, heavyweight champion Jack Dempsey, the "Manassas Mauler," knocked out a succession of challengers in bloody battles only to be **deposed** in 1927 by "Gentleman Gene" Tunney, who gave him a 15-round boxing lesson and then, according to Tunney's own account, celebrated by consuming "several pots of tea." 15

During the same years, William "Big Bill" Tilden dominated tennis, winning the national singles title every year from 1920 to 1925 along with nearly every other tournament he entered. Beginning in 1923, Robert T. "Bobby" Jones ruled over the world of golf with equal authority, his climactic achievement being his capture of the amateur and open championships of both the United States and Great Britain in 1930. 20

A few women athletes dominated their sports during the Golden Age in similar fashion. In tennis Helen Wills was three times United States singles champion and the winner of the women's singles at Wimbledon eight times in the late 1920s and early 1930s. The swimmer Gertrude Ederle, holder of 18 world records by the time she was 17, swam the English Channel on her second attempt, in 1926. She was not only the first woman to do so, but she did it faster than any of the four men who had previously made it across.   25

However, the sports star among stars was "the Sultan of Swat," baseball's Babe Ruth. Ruth not only dominated baseball, he changed it from a game ruled by pitchers and low scores to one in which hitting was more greatly admired. Originally himself a brilliant pitcher, his incredible hitting ability made him more valuable in the outfield, where he could play every day. Before Ruth, John "Home Run" Baker was the most famous slugger; his greatest home run total was 12, achieved shortly before the Great War. Ruth hit 29 in 1919 and 54 in 1920, his first year with the New York Yankees. By 1923, he was so feared that he was given a base on balls more than half the times he appeared at the plate. (John A. Garraty and Mark C. Carnes, *The American Nation*, New York: Longman, 2000.)   30   35

19. The main idea of this passage is that
    A. many superstars dominated the field of football and baseball in the 1920s.
    B. women athletes were relatively new during the Golden Age of superstars.
    C. the 1920s were the Golden Age of athletic superstars.
    D. Jim Thorpe was one of the greatest athletes of all time.

20. The author's purpose in writing this passage is
    A. to give examples of the numerous superstar athletes in the 1920s.
    B. to analyze why so many athletes were superstars in the 1920s
    C. to compare women athletes to men athletes in the 1920s.
    D. to inform the reader about the history of athletic superstars.

21. A conclusion that can be drawn from the passage is that
    A. there were fewer female superstar athletes than male superstar athletes.
    B. Gertrude Ederle was the first person to swim the English Channel.
    C. William "Big Bill" Tilden won every tournament he entered.
    D. Jack Dempsey defeated "Gentleman Gene" Tunney for the world boxing championship.

22. The overall pattern of organization of this passage is
    A. statement and clarification.
    B. compare and contrast.
    C. spatial order.
    D. illustration.

23. The overall tone of this passage can best be described as
    A. ironic.
    B. sarcastic.
    C. nostalgic.
    D. irreverent.

24. What is the meaning of the word **deposed** in the following sentence? "In prizefighting, heavy-weight champion Jack Dempsey, the "Manassas Mauler," knocked out a succession of challengers in bloody battles only to be **deposed** in 1927 by "Gentleman Gene" Tunney, who gave him a 15-round boxing lesson and then, according to Tunney's own account, celebrated by consuming "several pots of tea"?
    A. Fought
    B. Defeated
    C. Challenged
    D. Taught

25. In this passage, the author is
    A. biased against the boxer "Gentleman Gene" Tunney.
    B. biased in favor of the New York Yankees.
    C. biased in favor of the superstar athletes of the 1920s.
    D. unbiased.

26. What is the relationship between the following sentences? "Before Ruth, John 'Home Run' Baker was the most famous slugger; his greatest home run total was 12, achieved shortly before the Great War. Ruth hit 29 in 1919 and 54 in 1920, his first year with the New York Yankees."
    A. Comparison
    B. Listing
    C. Example
    D. Contrast

27. What is the relationship within the following sentence? "She was not only the first woman to do so, but she did it faster than any of the four men who had previously made it across."
    A. Listing
    B. Contrast
    C. Comparison
    D. Time order

Read the passage below and answer the questions that follow.

Public opinion polling sounds scientific with its talk of random samples and sampling error; it is easy to take results for solid fact. But being an informed consumer of polls requires more than just a nuts-and-bolts knowledge of how they are conducted; you should think about whether the questions are fair and unbiased before making too much of the results. The good—or the harm—that polls do depends on how well the data are collected and how thoughtfully the data are interpreted.   5

Political scientist Benjamin Ginsberg has even argued that polls weaken democracy. He says that polls permit the government to think that it has taken public opinion into account when only passive, often ill-informed opinions have been counted. Polls substitute passive attitudes for active expressions of opinion, such as voting and letter writing, which take   10
work. Responding to a poll taker is a lazy way to claim that "my voice has been heard."

Polls can also weaken democracy by distorting the election process. They are often accused of creating a *bandwagon effect*. This term refers to voters who support a candi-   15 date merely because they see that others are doing so. Although only 2 percent of people in a recent CBS/*New York Times* poll said that poll results had influenced them, 26 percent said they thought others had been influenced (showing that Americans feel "It's always the other person who's susceptible.") Beyond this, polls play to the media's interest in who's hot and who's not. The issues of recent presidential campaigns have sometimes been drowned out by a steady flood of poll results.   20

Perhaps the most extensive criticism of polling is that by altering the wording of a question, pollsters can get pretty much the results they want. Sometimes subtle changes in question wording can produce dramatic differences. For example, a month before the start of the Gulf War, the percentage of the public who thought we should go to war was 18 percentage points higher in the ABC/*Washington Post* poll than the CBS/*New York Times* poll. The former poll asked whether the United States should go to war "at some point after January 15 or not," a relatively vague question; in contrast, the latter poll offered an alternative to war, asking whether the "U.S. should start military actions against Iraq, or should the U.S. wait longer to see if the trade embargo and other economic **sanctions** work." It is, therefore, important to evaluate carefully how questions are posed when reading public opinion data. (Adapted from George C. Edwards, Martin P. Wattenberg, and Robert L. Lineberry, *Government in America*, 9th ed., New York: Longman, 2000.)   25   30   35

28. The implied main idea of the passage is
   A. Critics of polls believe that polls can be harmful, depending on how the data is collected, interpreted, and used.
   B. Polls can get the results they want depending on how the questions are worded.
   C. Public opinion polling sounds scientific with its talk of random samples and sampling error; it is easy to take results for solid fact.
   D. Polls can weaken democracy because they create a bandwagon effect.

29. The overall pattern of organization for this passage is
   A. statement and clarification.
   B. compare and contrast.
   C. time order.
   D. listing.

30. What is the relationship between the following sentences? "Responding to a poll taker is a lazy way to claim that 'my voice has been heard.' Polls can also weaken democracy by distorting the election process."
   A. Classification
   B. Compare and contrast
   C. Addition
   D. Statement and clarification

31. In this passage, the author is
   A. biased in favor of using poll results as solid fact.
   B. biased in favor of understanding how poll data is collected and interpreted.
   C. biased against the media using poll results on television.
   D. unbiased.

32. What is the relationship between these sentences? "They are often accused of creating a *band-wagon effect*. This term refers to voters who support a candidate merely because they see that others are doing so."
   A. Addition
   B. Illustration
   C. Definition
   D. Statement and clarification

33. What does the word **sanctions** mean in the sentence, "The former poll asked whether the United States should go to war 'at some point after January 15 or not,' a relatively vague question; in contrast, the latter poll offered an alternative to war, asking whether the 'U.S. should start military actions against Iraq, or should the U.S. wait longer to see if the trade embargo and other economic **sanctions** work.'"
   A. Penalties
   B. Exports
   C. Businesses
   D. Situations

34. What is the relationship within the following sentence? "Although only 2 percent of people in a recent CBS/*New York Times* poll said that poll results had influenced them, 26 percent said they thought others had been influenced."
   A. Cause and effect
   B. Illustration
   C. Spatial order
   D. Compare and contrast

35. Throughout the passage, which type of support is offered for the author's claim that "The good—or the harm—that polls do depends on how well the data are collected and how thoughtfully the data are interpreted"?
   A. Objective
   B. Emotional

36. A conclusion that can be drawn from this passage is
   A. People can be influenced to vote for a candidate based upon the results of polls.
   B. Polls help the government find out what the people are thinking on many issues.
   C. The media uses polls to persuade the viewing public on certain issues.
   D. People who conduct polls are not honest about reporting the results correctly.

READING SKILLS EXIT EXAM #2

Instructions: This Exit Exam has 36 questions. Read each passage below and answer the questions that follow.

On average, American adults consume about 22 gallons of beer, 2 gallons of wine, and 1.5 gallons of spirits a year. Despite these high rates of consumption, many people are unaware of the harm excessive use of alcohol can cause. To combat these dangers, the United

States spends approximately $130 billion annually on problems related to alcoholism. However, alcoholism still creates serious problems for those who drink and their families.   5

Alcoholics can expect to live 10 to 12 years fewer than non-alcoholics. There are several reasons for this shortened life span. First, alcohol contains a high number of calories and no vital nutrients. Thus, alcoholics generally have a reduced appetite for nutritious food and inevitably suffer from vitamin deficiencies; as a result, their resistance to infectious diseases is lowered. Second, over a long period, large amounts of alcohol destroy liver   10
cells, which are replaced by scar tissue. This condition, called cirrhosis of the liver, is the cause of more than 27,000 deaths each year in the United States. Heavy drinking also contributes to heart ailments, and there is some evidence that alcohol contributes to the incidence of cancer. Finally, alcohol is implicated in thousands of suicides each year.

In 2004 more than 1,160,000 arrests, or about 12 percent of all non-serious crimes,   15
involved drunkenness or an offence related to violation of liquor laws. These criminal acts were minor, such as breaches of the peace, disorderly conduct, and vagrancy. In arrests for major crimes, drunkenness does not generally appear in the charges, although alcohol often contributes to criminal acts. Each year thousands of homicides are linked to alcohol use. In many homicide cases, alcohol is found in the victim, the   20
offender, or both. A significant percentage of male sex offenders are chronic alcoholics or were drinking at the time of the offense. The reasons for the strong link between drinking and arrests for serious crimes are not fully understood. It has been pointed out that alcohol, by removing inhibitions, may cause people to behave in unusual ways.

If only the victims of alcoholism were the alcoholics themselves, but other people, espe-   25
cially the families of alcoholics, also suffer. The emotional effect, which is part of any family crisis, is heightened when the crisis itself is socially defined as shameful. The effects of "acts of God," such as fires, illnesses, and accidents, on a family **elicit** sympathy, but those of alcoholism produce negative reactions. The children of an alcoholic parent frequently develop severe physical and emotional illnesses, and marriage to an alcoholic frequently   30
ends in divorce or desertion. Finally, because alcoholics are often unable to hold jobs, the outcome may be poverty for their families. (Adapted from William Kornblum and Joseph Julian, *Social Problems*, 13th ed., Upper Saddle River, NJ: Pearson Prentice Hall, 2009.)

1. Which sentence best states the main idea of the passage?
   A. American adults consume about 22 gallons of beer, 2 gallons of wine, and 1.5 gallons of spirits a year.
   B. The United States spends approximately $130 billion annually on problems related to alcoholism.
   C. Many people are unaware of the harm excessive use of alcohol can cause.
   D. Alcoholism creates serious problems for those who drink and their families.

2. The overall pattern of organization is
   A. compare and contrast.
   B. chronological
   C. listing.
   D. classification.

3. The implied main idea of paragraph 2 is that
   A. There are several reasons alcoholics do not live as long as non-drinkers.
   B. Vitamin deficiencies cause alcoholics to have little resistance to infectious diseases.
   C. Alcoholism can cause many serious problems.
   D. Cirrhosis of the liver leads to more than 27,000 deaths each year in the United States.

4. What is the relationship between the following sentences? "Each year thousands of homicides are linked to alcohol use. In many homicide cases, alcohol is found in the victim, the offender, or both."
   A. Cause and Effect
   B. Addition
   C. Statement and Clarification
   D. Generalization and Example

5. The author's purpose in writing this passage is
   A. to warn the reader about the damage alcohol can do to a person's health.
   B. to contrast the lives of alcoholics and non-alcoholics.
   C. to persuade the reader not to drink alcohol in excess.
   D. to give examples of some of the problems alcoholism can cause.

6. What is the meaning of the word **elicit** in the following sentence? "The effects of 'acts of God,' such as fires, illnesses, and accidents, on a family **elicit** sympathy, but those of alcoholism produce negative reactions."
   A. Require
   B. Create
   C. Exclude
   D. Justify

7. According to the passage, alcoholism
   A. can be passed down from parent to child.
   B. is the cause of more than 27,000 deaths each year in the United States.
   C. is more common in the United States than in other countries.
   D. can make a person more likely to develop an infectious disease.

8. A conclusion that can be drawn from the passage is
   A. The United States spends too little money on solving the problems associated with alcoholism.
   B. Vitamins help to build resistance to infectious diseases.
   C. Children of alcoholics grow up to be alcoholics themselves.
   D. Americans drink more alcohol than they should.

9. The author's claim that "alcoholism still creates serious problems for those who drink and their families" is
   A. adequately supported with relevant details.
   B. inadequately supported because it lacks evidence.

Read the passage below and answer the questions that follow.

Anyone from San Francisco who knew him believed that Charles E. Bolton was a gentleman. Mild-mannered and considerate, he always tucked a decorative handkerchief into his waistcoat pocket. Bolton made frequent trips to check on his mining property—the sign, people believed, of a savvy, well-to-do businessman. His friends, therefore, were stunned to learn of Bolton's arrest and true identity. He was, in reality, the notorious Black Bart, a   5
highwayman who stalked northern California between 1875 and 1883. In all, Bart robbed twenty-seven stagecoaches for the gold they carried. In classic English highwayman fashion, he sat astride a horse and greeted drivers with the demand, "Throw down the box!"

Black Bart was never vicious during his robberies. He extended great civility to lady passengers and always respected the sanctity of their purses. In fact, he left travelers alone   10
and stole only from large, impersonal institutions such as Wells Fargo and Company and the U.S. Postal Service. He carried a large shotgun to threaten drivers, but evidence later revealed that he kept it unloaded, fearing that it might accidentally go off and injure somebody. Bart also had a sense of humor and a somewhat skewed taste for the literary. Following each robbery, he left behind a poem usually deposited in the empty strongbox.   15

Wells Fargo detective James B. Hume tracked down Bart after he left behind one of his handkerchiefs. Hume discovered that Bart's real name was Bolles and not Bolton. Bart was arrested in 1883 and served jail time. After his release in 1888, he disappeared but may have managed one final heist of Wells Fargo money. His deeds reveal a frequent trend in the nineteenth-century West. Because railroads, mining companies, large cattle   20
outfits, bonanza farms, and banks often acquired vast wealth, some outlaws attacked the very institutions that offered others jobs.

Even so, the motives for western banditry, crime, and violence remain complex. Possibly for all his poetry and exaggerated manners, dandy Black Bart simply needed money to live on and robbed a stage when he found his wallet empty. Maybe he reveled in the   25
adventure and the notoriety. Perhaps like Robin Hood he targeted the rich and powerful that so often unjustly gained favor. Regardless, Bart hardly represents the typical western bandit. (Adapted from Gary Clayton Anderson and Kathleen P. Chamberlain, *Power and Promise: The Changing American West*, Prentice Hall, 2008.)

10. What is the implied main idea of this passage?
    A. Black Bart was able to trick his neighbors into thinking he was a respectable businessman.
    B. Many bandits in the nineteenth-century West only robbed because they truly needed the money.
    C. The motives for western banditry, crime, and violence remain complex.
    D. Black Bart was a very unusual western outlaw.

11. What is the relationship within the following sentence? "Because railroads, mining companies, large cattle outfits, bonanza farms, and banks often acquired vast wealth, some outlaws attacked the very institutions that offered others jobs."
    A. Listing
    B. Cause and effect
    C. Contrast
    D. Statement and clarification

12. What is the relationship between the following sentences? "Bolton made frequent trips to check on his mining property—the sign, people believed, of a savvy, well-to-do businessman. His friends, therefore, were stunned to learn of Bolton's arrest and true identity."
    A. Contrast
    B. Cause and effect
    C. Enumeration
    D. Generalization and example

13. According to the passage, which statement is NOT true about Black Bart?
    A. His neighbors thought he was a respectable businessperson before he was caught.
    B. He always left a poem after he committed a robbery.
    C. His real name was Charles E. Bolton.
    D. He never searched a lady's purse.

14. Which statement does NOT support the idea that "Black Bart was considerate to the people on the stagecoaches that he robbed?
    A. In fact, he left travelers alone and stole only from large, impersonal institutions such as Wells Fargo and Company and the U.S. Postal Service.
    B. Following each robbery, he left behind a poem usually deposited in the empty strongbox.
    C. He extended great civility to lady passengers and always respected the sanctity of their purses.
    D. He carried a large shotgun to threaten drivers, but evidence later revealed that he kept it unloaded, fearing that it might accidentally go off and injure somebody.

15. A conclusion that can be drawn from the passage is that Black Bart was
    A. not a violent man despite being an outlaw.
    B. not just looking for money and fame, but also the chance to avenge the poor.
    C. loved by his neighbors before they found out he was really a notorious bandit.
    D. well educated and an exceptionally good poet.

16. The tone of this passage can best be described as
    A. informative.
    B. reverent.
    C. satiric.
    D. nostalgic.

17. In this passage, the author is
    A. biased in favor of the bandits of the nineteenth-century West.
    B. biased in favor of the railroads, mining companies, large cattle outfits, bonanza farms, and banks.
    C. biased against Black Bart.
    D. unbiased.

18. Is the following sentence a fact or an opinion? "Perhaps like Robin Hood he targeted the rich and powerful that so often unjustly gained favor."

    A. Fact
    B. Opinion

Read the passage below and answer the questions that follow.

No biotechnology issue has raised more debate than that of genetically modified (GM) crops. What is this controversy about? In a nutshell, proponents of GM crops see in them the exciting potential to feed a hungry world and to lessen the environmental damage caused by such human practices as pesticide application. Overly cautious opponents of them only see the unlikely potential to harm human health and the possible disruption to the Earth's ecosystems.

One example of this debate can be seen in cotton plants. The genetically modified cotton plants contain genes from a bacterium called *Bacillus thuringienis* that is found naturally in the soil and produces proteins that are toxic to a number of insects. Collectively these proteins form a natural insecticide known as *Bt*, which has been sprayed on crops for years. In the 1990's, biotech firms were able to **splice** *Bt* genes into cotton crops with the result that these plants now produce their *own* insecticide. The results are clearly an environmentalist's dream. In one survey conducted in the American Southeast, farmers who planted *Bt* cotton reduced the amount of chemical pesticides they applied to their fields by 72 percent. They did this, moreover, while increasing cotton yields by more than 11 percent.

Despite such obvious benefits, some environmentalists are uneasy about the use of *Bt* seeds. They claim that those few insects that survive in *Bt*-enhanced fields are likely to produce offspring resistant to the natural toxin. This raises the prospect of the insecticide losing its effectiveness against insects over the long run. In order to calm those critics, the U.S. Environmental Agency requires that at least 20 percent of any farmer's crops must be non-*Bt* plants. This creates non-*Bt* "refugees" near the *Bt* fields that will provide habitat for bugs that will then mate with the *Bt*-resistant bugs, thus helping to ensure that the *Bt*-resistance does not spread. (Adapted from David Krogh, *Biology*, 3rd ed., Upper Saddle River, NJ: Pearson Prentice Hall, 2005.)

19. The implied main idea of this passage is that
    A. creating genetically modified crops can have unforeseen consequences.
    B. natural bacteria, such as *Bacillus thuringieni*s, can be combined with crops like cotton to produce a plant with its own insecticide.
    C. there are two sides to the debate about genetically modified crops that can be seen in the example of modified cotton.
    D. genetically modified crops will solve both human needs and environmental concerns.

20. The overall pattern of organization for this passage is
    A. cause and effect.
    B. compare and contrast.
    C. classification.
    D. simple listing.

21. What is the relationship within the sentence, "In the 1990's, biotech firms were able to splice *Bt* genes into cotton crops with the result that these plants now produce their *own* insecticide"?
    A. Addition
    B. Time order

C. Cause and effect

D. Compare and contrast

22. What is the relationship between these sentences? "In one survey conducted in the American Southeast, farmers who planted *Bt* cotton reduced the amount of chemical pesticides they applied to their fields by 72 percent. They did this, moreover, while increasing cotton yields by more than 11 percent."

A. Process

B. Addition

C. Cause and effect

D. Compare and contrast

23. The author's purpose is to

A. present two views on a controversial topic.

B. criticize the genetic modification of crops.

C. explain how biotech firms can create genetically modified crops.

D. persuade the reader to buy genetically modified foods.

24. In describing the opponents of genetically modified crops, the author's tone is

A. apathetic.

B. straightforward.

C. skeptical.

D. sympathetic.

25. In this passage, the author

A. is biased in favor of genetically modifying crops.

B. is biased against genetically modifying cotton plants.

C. is biased against biotech firms.

D. is unbiased.

26. Which of the following statements is an opinion?

A. Some environmentalists are uneasy about the use of *Bt* seeds.

B. The results are clearly an environmentalist's dream.

C. The genetically modified cotton plants contain genes from a bacterium called *Bacillus thuringienis*.

D. They claim that those few insects that survive in *Bt*-enhanced fields are likely to produce offspring resistant to the natural toxin.

27. As used in this sentence from paragraph two, "In the 1990's, biotech firms were able to **splice** *Bt* genes into cotton crops with the result that these plants now produce their *own* insecticide," the word **splice** most nearly means

A. grow.

B. join.

C. transform.

D. separate.

Read the passage below and answer the questions that follow.

One of the most important components of social structure is *status*. **Status** is a recognized position that a person occupies in society. A person's status determines where he or she fits in society in relationship to everyone else. Status may be based on or accompanied by wealth, power, prestige, or a combination of all of these.

Sociologists recognize two types of status. An **ascribed status** is one that is attached to   5
a person from birth or that a person assumes involuntarily later in life. The most prevalent ascribed statuses are based on family and kinship relations (for example, daughter or son), sex (male or female), and age. In addition, in some societies ascribed statuses are based on one's race or ethnicity. For example, skin color was used to designate ascribed status differences in South Africa under the system of apartheid.   10

In contrast, an **achieved status** is one based at least in part on a person's voluntary actions. Examples of achieved statuses in the United States are one's profession and level of education. Of course, one's family and kinship connections may influence one's profession and level of education. George W. Bush's and John Kerry's educational level and status are interrelated to their family of birth. However, these individuals had to   15
act voluntarily to achieve their status. (Adapted from Raymond Scupin and Christopher R. DeCorse, *Anthropology: A Global Perspective*, 6th ed., Upper Saddle River, NJ: Pearson Prentice Hall, 2007.)

28. Which sentence best states the main idea of the passage?
    A. Status may be based on or accompanied by wealth, power, prestige, or a combination of all of these.
    B. One of the most important components of social structure is *status*.
    C. An **ascribed status** is one that is attached to a person from birth or that a person assumes involuntarily later in life.
    D. Sociologists recognize two types of status.

29. Which sentence best states the main idea of the second paragraph?
    A. All societies recognize both *ascribed* and *achieved* statuses.
    B. An **ascribed status** is one that is attached to a person from birth or that a person assumes involuntarily later in life.
    C. The most prevalent ascribed statuses are based on family and kinship relations (for example, daughter or son), sex (male or female), and age.
    D. In addition, in some societies ascribed statuses are based on one's race or ethnicity.

30. The overall pattern of organization for this passage is
    A. spatial order.
    B. definition and example.
    C. classification.
    D. cause and effect.

31. What is the relationship within the following sentence? "Many anthropologists use the term *socioeconomic status* to refer to how a specific position is related to the division of labor, the political system, and other cultural variables."
    A. Comparison
    B. Definition

C. Contrast
D. Process

32. What is the relationship between the following sentences? "In contrast, an **achieved status** is one based at least in part on a person's voluntary actions. Examples of achieved statuses in the United States are one's profession and level of education."
A. Statement and clarification
B. Addition
C. Cause and effect
D. Generalization and example

33. The author's purpose in writing this passage is
A. to describe two types of statuses.
B. to define the meaning of status.
C. to contrast different cultures' definition of status.
D. to show how achieved status is superior to ascribed status.

34. A conclusion that can be drawn from the passage is that
A. all cultures measure status in the same way.
B. a person's achieved status is often influenced by their ascribed status.
C. achieved status is superior to ascribed status.
D. Americans value achieved status over ascribed.

35. The overall tone of this passage can best be described as
A. persuasive.
B. objective.
C. superior.
D. farcical.

36. Is the following sentence a fact or an opinion? "Examples of achieved statuses in the United States are one's profession and level of education."
A. Fact
B. Opinion

READING SKILLS EXIT EXAM #3

Instructions: This Exit Exam has 36 questions. Read each passage below and answer the questions that follow.

Although humans are omnivorous creatures with the ability to digest many types of plants and animals for nutrition, there are many differences in eating behaviors and food preferences throughout the world. Most Americans would be repulsed by the thought of eating insects and insect larvae, but many societies consider them to be delicacies. American culture also distinguishes between pets, which are not eaten, and farm animals, such as chickens, cows, and pigs, which can be eaten. However, other cultures of the world do not necessarily share these food preferences. Pigs, for example, are forbidden food in Jewish and most Arab cultures. This particular food taboo has several possible explanations.

5

One is that the Jews classify reality by placing things into distinguishable "mental boxes" based on their reading of the Bible. However, some things do not fit neatly into these distinguishable mental boxes. Some items are anomalous or ambiguous, so they fall between the basic categories that are used to define cultural reality. These anomalous items are usually treated as unclean, impure, unholy, polluted, or defiling. Edible animals are those that fit the description of the animals God created in the first chapter of the Bible, Genesis. Such animals include those that have cloven hoofs and chew cud. Pigs do have cloven hooves. However, since they do not chew cud, they fail to fit into the cultural classification of reality accepted by the ancient Israelites and are considered dirty or unfit to eat. Similarly, the "fish" that God created in Genesis swim in the water and have scales and fins, so they are fit to eat. However, since shellfish and eels lack fins and scales, they are considered unclean and unfit to eat.

Another possible explanation for the pig taboo is more practical and economic. In the hot, dry regions of the world, such as the Middle East, pigs are poorly adapted and extremely costly to raise. This is because unlike goats, sheep, or cattle, pigs are hard to herd and are not grazing animals. In places like Israel and some Arabic countries, the meat of pigs became forbidden. In contrast, in the cooler, wetter areas of the world that are more appropriate for pig raising, such as China and New Guinea, pig taboos are unknown, and pigs are the prized foods in those regions. (Adapted from Raymond Scupin and Christopher R. DeCorse, *Anthropology A Global Perspective*, 6th ed., Upper Saddle River, New Jersey: Pearson Education, Inc., 2008.)

1. Which sentence best states the implied main idea of the passage?
   A. Cultures have different food preferences and taboos.
   B. The Jewish and Arabic prohibition of pork can be explained by religion and economics.
   C. God's description of the animals He created in the book of Genesis led Jews to their food laws.
   D. Food preferences result from the circumstances under which the culture developed.

2. In this passage, the author's purpose is
   A. to explain why certain cultures have certain food preferences.
   B. to describe Middle Eastern food taboos.
   C. to explain why Jews and other Middle Easterners prohibit pork from their diets.
   D. To convince readers that food preferences and taboos are cultural and not universally accepted.

3. What is the overall pattern of organization of the passage?
   A. Compare and contrast
   B. Statement and clarification
   C. Process
   D. Simple listing

4. The author's claim that, "One is that the Jews classify reality by placing things into distinguishable 'mental boxes' based on their reading of the Bible," is
   A. adequately supported by a mix of fact and opinion.
   B. inadequately supported by opinion.

5. What is the relationship within this sentence in paragraph one? "Most Americans would be repulsed by the thought of eating insects and insect larvae, but many societies consider them to be delicacies."
    A. Cause and effect
    B. Compare and contrast
    C. Definition
    D. Addition

6. The tone of the passage can best be described as
    A. flippant.
    B. persuasive.
    C. reverent.
    D. objective.

7. What is the meaning of the word **anomalous** in the following sentence? "Some items are **anomalous** or ambiguous, so they fall between the basic categories that are used to define cultural reality."
    A. Unusual
    B. Dirty
    C. Unacceptable
    D. Detailed

8. Is the following statement from paragraph 3 a fact or an opinion? "In the hot, dry regions of the world, such as the Middle East, pigs are poorly adapted and extremely costly to raise"?
    A. Fact
    B. Opinion

9. A conclusion that can be drawn from the passage is
    A. Jews believe that God wrote the Bible.
    B. China and New Guinea would be inappropriate places to raise cattle, sheep, or goats.
    C. In some parts of the world, people eat animals that Americans would consider to be pets.
    D. If a person eats pork, he or she cannot be Jewish.

Read the passage below and answer the questions that follow.

In December 1347, rats infested with fleas carrying bubonic plague arrived on the island of Sicily, Italy. Soon these fleas began biting the people who lived on the island, infecting them with the plague. The disease began in the lymph glands of the groin or armpits, which slowly filled with pus and turned black. The inflammations were called buboes—hence the name bubonic plague—and their black color lent the plague its other name, the Black Death. Since it was carried by rodents, which were commonplace even in wealthy homes, hardly anyone was spared. It was an egalitarian disease—archbishops, dukes, lords of the manor, merchants, laborers, and peasants fell equally before it. For those who survived the pandemic, life seemed little more than an ongoing burial service. In many towns, traditional funeral services were abandoned, and the dead were buried in mass graves. By 1350, all of Europe, with the exception of a few territories far from traditional trade routes, was devastated by the disease. In Tuscany, the death rate in the cities was near 60 percent. In Florence, on June 24, 1348, the feast day of the city's patron saint, John the Baptist, 1,800 people reportedly died, and another 1,800 the next day—about 4 percent of the city's population in two days' time. Severe outbreaks of the plague erupted again in 1363, 1388-1390, and 1400.   15

Accounts of the time describe the surreal atmosphere of death and fear. Before the plague, it was common for friends and neighbors to gather in the house of someone who had died to mourn there and comfort the family. However, as the plague gained violence, these customs were either modified or laid aside altogether. More wretched still were the circumstances of the common people and of much of the middle class. Because they were confined to their homes either by hope of safety, by poverty, or by customary restriction to their own sections, they fell sick daily by the thousands. A great many died in the public streets, day and night; a large number perished in their homes, and it was only by the stench of their decaying bodies that they proclaimed their death to their neighbors. More out of fear of contagion rather than any charity they felt toward the dead, the neighbors would drag the corpses out of their homes and pile them in front of the doors to be collected. Huge trenches were dug in the crowded churchyards, and the new dead were piled in them, layer upon layer. Those writing during the plague years describe a world in virtual collapse as the Black Death stalked the streets. (Adapted from Henry M. Sayre, *Discovering the Humanities*, Upper Saddle River, New Jersey: Pearson Education, Inc., 2008.)   20   25   30

10. Which sentence best states the implied main idea of the passage?
    A. The plague was an equal-opportunity illness.
    B. Outbreaks of bubonic plague in 14th-century Europe devastated the population and culture.
    C. The bubonic plague led to many changes in European burial rites.
    D. Outbreaks of plague caused people to lose sympathy for their affected neighbors.

11. What is the relationship within the following sentence? "Huge trenches were dug in the crowded churchyards, and the new dead were piled in them, layer upon layer."
    A. Spatial order
    B. Addition
    C. Cause and effect
    D. Time order

12. What is the relationship between the following sentences? "More wretched still were the circumstances of the common people and of much of the middle class," and "A great many died in the public streets, day and night; a large number perished in their homes, and it was only by the stench of their decaying bodies that they proclaimed their death to their neighbors."
    A. Compare and contrast
    B. Definition and example
    C. Listing
    D. Statement and clarification

13. According to the passage,
    A. mourning a death was a private, family affair in pre-plague Europe.
    B. plague victims were buried in mass graves.

C. the Black Death turned people's armpits black.

D. wealthier classes had fewer rodents in their homes than poorer classes.

14. It can be inferred from the passage that
    A. the city of Florence was Christian during the time of the plague.
    B. nobody who contracted the plague survived.
    C. the Europeans knew the plague was spread by rodents and their fleas.
    D. big cities were better able to handle plague than smaller communities.

15. The tone of the passage can best be described as
    A. farcical.
    B. contemptuous.
    C. grim.
    D. optimistic.

16. Is the following sentence fact or opinion? "In Tuscany, the death rate in the cities was near 60 percent."
    A. Fact
    B. Opinion

17. In this passage, the author is
    A. biased against writers who describe the Black Death.
    B. biased in favor of pre-plague culture.
    C. biased against the effects of sudden and widespread death.
    D. unbiased.

18. What is the meaning of the word **pandemic** in the following sentence? "For those who survived the **pandemic,** life seemed little more than an ongoing burial service."
    A. Grief and despair caused by death
    B. A widespread disease outbreak
    C. Starvation
    D. A curse brought by God

Read the passage below and answer the questions that follow.

Grandparents usually take great pleasure in their grandchildren. The new role of grandparent gives their lives a sense of purpose and provides them with new experiences. There are a number of different grandparenting styles, however. Some of the most common are remote or detached, companionate and supportive, and involved and influential.

In the *remote or detached* relationship, the grandparents and grandchildren live far apart   5
and see each other infrequently, maintaining a largely ritualistic, symbolic relationship. For example, grandparents who are "distant figures" may see their grandchildren only on holidays or special occasions. Such relationships may be cordial but are also uninvolved and fleeting. While the biggest barrier to face-to-face contacts is living too far away, in other cases, grandparents are remote or detached because they're experiencing   10
health problems or their grandchildren's busy schedule makes it difficult to get together.

In the *companionate and supportive* style of grandparenting, grandparents see their grandchildren often, frequently do things with them, and offer them emotional and instrumental support (such as providing money), but they don't seek authority in the grandchild's life. These grandparents are typically on the maternal side of the family, are younger, and have more income than other grandparents—characteristics that might encourage meddling—but they avoid getting involved in parental child-rearing decisions. This style of grandparenting is the most common pattern. According to a national survey, most grandparents (68%) see a grandchild every one or two weeks. Eight in ten grandparents contact a grandchild by telephone at least once every couple of weeks, and 19% chat with a grandchild by e-mail every few weeks.

In the *involved and influential* grandparenting style, grandparents play an active role in their grandchildren's lives. They may be spontaneous and playful, but they also exert substantial authority over their grandchildren, imposing definite—and sometimes tough—rules. Black grandmothers, especially, say that they are concerned with teaching their grandchildren the value of education, providing emotional support, and involving them in the extended family and community activities. In general, grandparents are more likely to be involved if their grandchildren are struggling in school. They are also twice as likely to be influential in their grandchildren's lives if they had close relationships with their own grandparents. (Adapted from Nijole V. Benokraitis, *Marriages and Families, Changes, Choices, and Constraints*, 6th ed., Upper Saddle River, NJ: Pearson Education, Inc., 2008.)

19. Which sentence best states the main idea of paragraph 3?
    A. This style of grandparenting is the most common pattern.
    B. According to a national survey, most grandparents (68%) see a grandchild every one or two weeks.
    C. In the *companionate and supportive* style of grandparenting, grandparents see their grandchildren often, frequently do things with them, and offer them emotional and instrumental support (such as providing money), but they don't seek authority in the grandchild's life.
    D. These grandparents are typically on the maternal side of the family, are younger, and have more income than other grandparents—characteristics that might encourage meddling—but they avoid getting involved in parental child-rearing decisions.

20. In this passage, the author's purpose is
    A. to describe the best types of grandparenting.
    B. to persuade grandparents to be more involved with their grandchildren.
    C. to describe grandparents.
    D. to define and describe the most common grandparenting styles.

21. What is the relationship within the following sentence? "While the biggest barrier to face-to-face contacts is living too far away, in other cases, grandparents are remote or detached because they're experiencing health problems or their grandchildren's busy schedule makes it difficult to get together."
    A. Time order
    B. Compare and contrast
    C. Listing
    D. Spatial order

22. What is the overall pattern of organization of the passage?
    A. Process
    B. Generalization and example
    C. Classification
    D. Comparison and contrast

23. Is the following sentence fact or opinion? "The *companionate and supportive* style of grandparenting is the most common pattern."
    A. Fact
    B. Opinion

24. According to the passage,
    A. less than 10% of grandparents communicate with their grandkids by e-mail.
    B. grandparents are more likely to be involved if their grandchildren are doing well in school.
    C. *involved and influential* grandparents are playful and supportive but not authoritative.
    D. health problems cause some grandparents to be *remote or detached*.

25. It can be inferred from the passage that
    A. there are other grandparenting styles that are not described in this passage.
    B. the *involved and influential* style is superior to the other styles.
    C. a person's own experiences with grandparents rarely influences his or her own grandparenting style.
    D. *companionate and supportive* grandparents tend to come from the father's side of the family.

26. In this passage, the author is
    A. biased against *remote or detached* grandparents.
    B. biased in favor of *involved and influential* grandparents.
    C. biased in favor of black grandmothers.
    D. unbiased.

27. The statement, "The *companionate and supportive* style of grandparenting is the most common pattern," is
    A. adequately supported by mostly facts.
    B. inadequately supported by mostly opinions.

Read the passage below and answer the questions that follow.

We often hear a great deal about the trend toward globalization, but the term and its meanings are often not defined. Economic globalization means the growing tendency for goods and services to be produced in one nation or region and consumed in another. The largest of the companies that produce these goods and services are multinational corporations, often with many subsidiary corporations, that have their headquarters in one country but pursue business activities and profits in one or more foreign nations.   5

The growth of multinational corporations is associated with the tendency to export capital and jobs overseas where labor is cheaper and more plentiful. During the 1970s and 1980s, U.S. plants, factories, mills, and other industrial facilities suffered as capital was diverted abroad. Unable to maintain their competitive edge, many manufacturing   10 facilities closed. Especially hard hit were plants in the nation's older, single-industry cities and towns, most of which were located in the manufacturing belt of the Midwest.

The biggest losers in the decline in manufacturing have been industrial towns and cities in the Northeast and Midwest. When rubber mills in Akron, Ohio, and steel mills in Youngstown, Ohio, and the Pittsburgh areas shut their doors, the local economies were devastated. With few secondary industries to fall back on, these cities experienced severe economic and social upheavals during the recessions of the mid-1970s and early 1980s and 1990s. In the1970s, the steel mills in Gary, Indiana, employed almost 28,000 workers in relatively well-paid jobs with good benefits. Today, fewer than 8,000 workers are employed in the Gary mills. Nevertheless, modernization of the steel industry, leading to greater efficiency and quality control, may produce a turnaround. Steel exports are rising, and steel companies' profits are improving. (Adapted from William Kornblum and Joseph Julian, *Social Problems*, 13th ed., Upper Saddle River, NJ: Pearson Prentice Hall, 2009.)

15

20

28. Which of the following sentences best states the <u>implied</u> main idea of the passage?
    A. Although globalization initially devastated the U.S. steel industry, the industry is now experiencing a turnaround.
    B. As multinational corporations moved their production overseas, cities and industries of the American Mid- and Northwest declined.
    C. Globalization has many benefits for multinational corporations.
    D. Globalization has all but devastated the American Midwest.

29. What is the relationship between the following sentences? "In the1970s, the steel mills in Gary, Indiana, employed almost 28,000 workers in relatively well-paid jobs with good benefits. Today, fewer than 8,000 workers are employed in the Gary mills."
    A. Statement and clarification
    B. Compare and contrast
    C. Time order
    D. Cause and effect

30. What is the overall pattern of organization of the SECOND paragraph?
    A. Listing
    B. Cause and effect
    C. Spatial order
    D. Compare and contrast

31. The author's purpose in writing this passage is
    A. to show how the rise in multinational corporations impacted American industrial cities.
    B. to persuade the reader that globalization is negative for U.S. industry.
    C. to describe the post-globalization Midwest.
    D. to argue for sanctions against multinational corporations.

32. The author's tone in this passage can best be described as
    A. optimistic.
    B. morose.
    C. condescending.
    D. neutral.

33. The statement, "The biggest losers in the decline in manufacturing have been industrial towns and cities in the Northeast and Midwest," from the third paragraph is
   A. adequately supported by mostly facts.
   B. inadequately supported by mostly opinions.

34. Which of the following is a conclusion that can be reached regarding this passage?
   A. Multinational corporations tend to concentrate on just one industry.
   B. Before the 1970s, the American manufacturing belt had no economic or social problems.
   C. Multinational corporations pay their workers less than they would pay an American worker.
   D. If it weren't for multinational corporations, the manufacturing industries of the Midwest would be thriving.

35. Is the statement, "Nevertheless, modernization of the steel industry, leading to greater efficiency and quality control, may produce a turnaround" fact or opinion?
   A. Fact
   B. Opinion

36. What does the word **capital** mean in the sentence, "The growth of multinational corporations is associated with the tendency to export **capital** and jobs overseas where labor is cheaper and more plentiful"?
   A. Headquarters
   B. Culture
   C. Money and equipment
   D. Employees

Part Five:
Exit Exams—Writing

Read the entire passage carefully, then answer the questions. (Note: Intentional errors may have been included in the passage.)

(1) _____.

(2) At Columbine, 18-year-old Eric Harris and 17-year-old Dylan Klebold were generally seen as geeks or nerds from the point of view of any of the large student cliques—the jocks, the punks, etc. (3) Though excluded from mainstream student culture, they banded together and bonded together with several of their fellow outcasts in what they came to call the "Trench Coat Mafia." (4) As a result, trench coats became very popular attire among many students across the U. S. (5) The image they attempted to create was clearly one of power and dominance with their preoccupation with Hitler, the celebration of evil and villainy. (6) Harris and Klebold desperately wanted to feel important. (7) They amassed an arsenal of weapons, strategized about logistics, and made final preparations. (8) For more than a year, they plotted, planned, and conspired to put one over on their schoolmates, teachers, and parents. (9) In the preparations they made to murder their classmates, the two shooters got their wish. (10) Not a single adult got wind of what Harris and Klebold intended to do. (11) In their relationship, the two boys got from one another what was otherwise missing from their lives. (12) _____ they felt special, they gained a sense of belonging, and they were united against the world. (13) Family background can also be a factor in the actions of schoolyard snipers. (Adapted from James Alan Fox and Jack Levin, *The Will to Kill*, Boston: Allyn and Bacon, 2001.)

1. Which of the following sentences, if inserted into the blank labeled number 1, would provide the best thesis statement for the entire passage?
   A. On April 20, 1999, a school shooting occurred in Littleton, Colorado.
   B. In understanding the horrific actions of schoolyard snipers, it is important to examine friendships.
   C. The school shooting that occurred in Littleton, Colorado, altered the way people felt about school safety in many ways.
   D. Eric Harris and Dylan Klebold killed twelve students and one teacher on April 20, 1999.

2. Which of the numbered sentences is NOT supported by sufficient details?
   A. 6
   B. 8
   C. 11
   D. 13

3. Select the order of sentences 7, 8, and 9 that presents the details in the most logical sequence of ideas. If no change is necessary, select option A.
   A. They amassed an arsenal of weapons, strategized about logistics, and made final preparations. For more than a year, they plotted, planned, and conspired to put one over on their schoolmates, teachers, and parents. In the preparations they made to murder their classmates, the two shooters got their wish.
   B. For more than a year, they plotted, planned, and conspired to put one over on their schoolmates, teachers, and parents. In the preparations they made to murder their classmates, the two shooters got their wish. They amassed an arsenal of weapons, strategized about logistics, and made final preparations.
   C. In the preparations they made to murder their classmates, the two shooters got their wish. For more than a year, they plotted, planned, and conspired to put one over on their schoolmates, teachers, and parents. They amassed an arsenal of weapons, strategized about logistics, and made final preparations.
   D. They amassed an arsenal of weapons, strategized about logistics, and made final preparations. In the preparations they made to murder their classmates, the two shooters got their wish. For more than a year, they plotted, planned, and conspired to put one over on their schoolmates, teachers, and parents.

4. Which numbered sentence is the LEAST relevant to the passage?
   A. 2
   B. 4
   C. 5
   D. 12

5. Which word or phrase, if inserted into the blank in the sentence labeled number 12, would make the relationship between sentences 11 and 12 clear?
   A. As a result,
   B. However,
   C. Next,
   D. In summary,

Read the entire passage carefully, then answer the questions. (Note: Intentional errors may have been included in the passage.)

(1) _____.

(2) First of all, it may be difficult to meet the emotional needs of the child. (3) The demands of working and maintaining a home may be so overwhelming that a child's emotional needs may not be met adequately. (4) Telling a child that he or she is loved and demonstrating that love with quality time are ways to express love. (5) It also may be hard for the single parent to provide proper supervision for the child. (6) Making arrangements for the child's care and supervision is difficult and costly and may take a large share of the budget. (7) _____ because women tend to make less money than men, households headed by women can experience financial difficulties. (8) Finally, the single parent may experience unfulfilled emotional and sexual needs. (9) Unmet emotional needs can develop because of the lack of time to seek a relationship. (10) Because most single parents wish to hide their sexual involvement from their child, finding a time and place can present problems. (11) Divorce is not shameful as it used to be years ago. (12) It is important that single parents have sufficient financial, material, and emotional support to meet their own and their child's demands. (Adapted from David J. Anspaugh and Gene Ezell, *Teaching Today's Health*, 7th ed., San Francisco: Pearson, 2004.)

6. Which sentence, if inserted into the blank labeled number 1, would serve as the best thesis statement for the entire passage?
   A. There are over 11 million single parents in the United States.
   B. Divorce has many effects on a family.
   C. A single parent may experience a variety of problems.
   D. More than 15 million children are unsupervised from 3 to 8 p.m., which causes juvenile crime.

7. Which of the following sentences provides detailed support for sentence 6?
   A. Seventy-eight percent of mothers with 6–13-year-olds work full time.
   B. Full-time daycare often costs as much as college tuition at a public university, yet 1 out of 3 families with young children earn less than $25,000 per year.
   C. Parents who receive child support have higher incomes.
   D. Many custodial parents have no provisions for health insurance and health care costs.

8. Which is the best placement for the sentence below to make the sequence of ideas clearer?

    A child needs some quality time with the parent every day; interacting with the child, actively listening and talking with him or her, and keeping it pleasant is quality time.

    A. Before sentence 4
    B. After sentence 10
    C. After sentence 4
    D. Before sentence 8

9. Which numbered sentence is the LEAST relevant to the passage?
    A. 3
    B. 6
    C. 8
    D. 11

10. Which word or phrase, if inserted into the blank in sentence 7, would make clear the relationship of ideas between sentences 6 and 8?
    A. In addition,
    B. Nevertheless,
    C. Then,
    D. Incidentally,

11. DIRECTIONS: Choose the most effective word or phrase within the context suggested by the sentence.

    At the age of three, Mariah's _____ for singing was apparent; she first performed in public when she was six and began writing songs when she was in elementary school.

    A. affection
    B. stubbornness
    C. aptitude

12. DIRECTIONS: Choose the most effective word or phrase within the context suggested by the sentence.

    The attorney tried to _____ the truth about the crime by examining all the evidence and thoroughly questioning the witnesses.

    A. ascertain
    B. presume
    C. disregard

13. DIRECTIONS: Choose the option that corrects an error in the underlined portion(s). If no error exists, choose "No change is necessary."

    Some people cannot <u>accept</u> a <u>complement</u> because <u>they're</u> not used to being praised.
                  A   B   C

    A. except
    B. compliment
    C. their
    D. No change is necessary.

14. DIRECTIONS: Choose the option that corrects an error in the underlined portion(s). If no error exists, choose "No change is necessary."

Bryan <u>would of</u> shared an apartment with his girl friend, but his mom did not feel
                   A

<u>good</u> about the idea and <u>advised</u> against it.
  B   C

A. would have
B. well
C. adviced
D. No change is necessary.

15. DIRECTIONS: Choose the sentence in which the modifiers are correctly placed.
A. Uncle Fred finally found the restaurant driving around in his car.
B. The restaurant was found driving around in his car.
C. Driving around in his car, Uncle Fred finally found the restaurant.

16. DIRECTIONS: Choose the sentence in which the modifiers are correctly placed.
A. While watching a movie on television, the power went out.
B. While I was watching a movie on television, the power went out.
C. The power went out while watching a movie on television.

17. DIRECTIONS: Choose the sentence that expresses the thought most clearly and effectively and has no error in structure.
A. After the movie was over, we went to get pizza.
B. Although the movie was over, we went to get pizza.
C. While the movie was over, we went to get pizza.

18. DIRECTIONS: Choose the most effective word or phrase within the context suggested by the sentence.

When they play tennis doubles, Sean prefers to play the net position; _____, Rob likes the baseline position better.

A. finally
B. in addition
C. similarly
D. on the other hand

19. DIRECTIONS: Choose the most effective word or phrase within the context suggested by the sentence.

When I moved out, all of my bills became my responsibility, I could not control my freedom, and _____.

A. losing my volleyball scholarship.
B. I lost my volleyball scholarship.
C. lost my volleyball scholarship.

20. DIRECTIONS: Choose the sentence that has no error in structure.
   A. Living in my home in Venezuela was very different from living in my home in the United States with respect to size, maintaining the yard, and security.
   B. Living in my home in Venezuela was very different from living in my home in the United States with respect to the size of the rooms, the maintenance of the property, and security.
   C. Living in my home in Venezuela was very different from living in my home in the United States with respect to size, maintenance, and security.

21. DIRECTIONS: Choose the option that corrects an error in the underlined portion(s). If no error exists, choose "No change is necessary."

   Fashion design comes easy to <u>me I</u> can take something from the thrift store and make it look like it came from Saks Fifth Avenue.

   A. me for I
   B. me for, I
   C. me, for I
   D. No change is necessary.

22. DIRECTIONS: Choose the option that corrects an error in the underlined portion(s). If no error exists, choose "No change is necessary."

   Even though I am too old to play on a softball <u>team I</u> enjoy sitting in the <u>stands and</u>
                                            A   B

   watching my daughter play, cheering her <u>on, and</u> I remember how it used to be.
                                                 C

   A. team, I
   B. stands, and
   C. on and
   D. No change is necessary.

23. DIRECTIONS: Choose the option that corrects an error in the underlined portion(s). If no error exists, choose "No change is necessary."

   After three years of employment at <u>Kabooms. I</u> have found that the game of whirlyball can be fun or stressful to run, depending on how the people behave.

   A. Kabooms; I
   B. Kabooms I
   C. Kabooms, I
   D. No change is necessary.

24. DIRECTIONS: Choose the option that corrects an error in the underlined portion(s). If no error exists, choose "No change is necessary."

   When I am ordering at <u>Checkers, I</u> feel like I am competing with the sounds of the
                                     A

   traffic whizzing by about fifty feet from <u>me even</u> when I am <u>eating, I</u> still have to listen
                                            B   C

   to people honk their horns or yell at each other in their cars.

A. Checkers. I
B. me. Even
C. eating; I
D. No change is necessary.

25. DIRECTIONS: Choose the option that corrects an error in the underlined portion(s). If no error exists, choose "No change is necessary."

After two months of taking orders at the drive thru, Linda <u>had became</u> frustrated with the rudeness of the customers.

A. become
B. has became
C. had become
D. No change is necessary.

26. DIRECTIONS: Choose the option that corrects an error in the underlined portion(s). If no error exists, choose "No change is necessary."

First, Bobby <u>cooks</u> Melinda a gourmet meal, then he <u>asked</u> her to marry him;
            A   B

she <u>accepted</u> his proposal.
     C

A. cooked
B. had asked
C. accepting
D. No change is necessary.

27. DIRECTIONS: Choose the option that corrects an error in the underlined portion(s). If no error exists, choose "No change is necessary."

My favorite ride at Disney World, Big Thunder Canyon, takes me on a wild trip through an abandoned canyon mine at sixty miles per hour; my body <u>shook</u> in every direction.

A. shakes
B. had shaken
C. had shook
D. No change is necessary.

28. DIRECTIONS: Choose the option that corrects an error in the underlined portion(s). If no error exists, choose "No change is necessary."

After completing two years at the community college, each of the students in my class <u>plans</u>
                                                                          A

to get a four-year degree; a few of them <u>intends</u> to go out of state while most of them
                                               B

<u>choose</u> to transfer to a school in Florida.
  C

A. plan
B. intend
C. chooses
D. No change is necessary.

29. DIRECTIONS: Choose the option that corrects an error in the underlined portion(s). If no error exists, choose "No change is necessary."

Linda's new jeans, which she says <u>is</u> the latest fashion trend, <u>look</u> like someone <u>has</u> cut
                                  A   B   C

holes in the knees.

A. are
B. looks
C. have
D. No change is necessary.

30. DIRECTIONS: Choose the option that corrects an error in the underlined portion(s). If no error exists, choose "No change is necessary."

Every student should pay <u>his or her</u> fees before the semester begins; otherwise, <u>he or she</u>
                                 A   B

may be dropped from <u>their</u> classes.
                       C

A. their
B. they
C. his or her
D. No change is necessary.

31. DIRECTIONS: Choose the option that corrects an error in the underlined portion(s). If no error exists, choose "No change is necessary."

<u>I</u> have always liked meeting my friends at Don Carter's every Friday night, but now the
A

bowling alley is so crowded that <u>you</u> cannot get a lane as easily as <u>I</u> used to.
                                       B   C

A. We
B. I
C. you
D. No change is necessary.

32. Choose the option that corrects an error in the underlined portion(s). If no error exists, choose "No change is necessary."

At our restaurant, most of the customers <u>we</u> serve are senior citizens who are often rude
                                                         A

and short tempered toward <u>us</u>; although their behavior makes us angry, <u>I</u> have to provide
                                  B   C

good customer service by being patient with them.

A. I
B. me
C. we
D. No change is necessary.

33. Choose the option that corrects an error in the underlined portion(s). If no error exists, choose "No change is necessary."

The delivery room keeps Wildcard Systems running efficiently because <u>they distribute</u> the pre-paid credit cards to our customers.

A. the employees distribute
B. it distributes
C. the department distributes
D. No change is necessary.

34. DIRECTIONS: Choose the option that corrects an error in the underlined portion(s). If no error exists, choose "No change is necessary."

In honor of Tony and Mandi's college graduation, Pat, Kim, and <u>I</u> are planning a surprise
                                                                  A

party; the decision about the location is up to <u>me</u>, but <u>us</u> three will work together on
                                                     B   C

everything else.

A. me
B. I
C. we
D. No change is necessary.

35. DIRECTIONS: Choose the option that corrects an error in the underlined portion(s). If no error exists, choose "No change is necessary."

The toad jumped <u>quickly</u> into the pool of standing water and waited <u>patient</u> for a <u>tasty</u>
                        A   B   C

insect to gobble.

A. quick
B. patiently
C. tastily
D. No change is necessary.

36. DIRECTIONS: Choose the word or phrase that best completes the sentence.

Elijah's voice is the _____ in the choir.

A. loudliest
B. louder
C. loudlier
D. loudest

37. DIRECTIONS: Choose the option that corrects an error in the underlined portion(s). If no error exists, choose "No change is necessary."

Waiting at the dealership for my car to be repaired is an <u>inconvienence</u> to me.

A. inconveniance
B. inconvenyence
C. inconvenience
D. No change is necessary.

38. DIRECTIONS: Choose the option that corrects an error in the underlined portion(s). If no error exists, choose "No change is necessary."

She was the only <u>female, that</u> I have ever <u>known to</u> choose a male-dominated
              A   B

<u>career, automotive</u> engineering.
        C

A. female that
B. known, to
C. career; automotive engineering
D. No change is necessary.

39. DIRECTIONS: Choose the sentence that is correctly punctuated.
A. Lila asked when the research papers were due.
B. Lila asked when are the research papers due.
C. Lila asked when the research papers were due?

40. DIRECTIONS: Choose the option that corrects an error in the underlined portion(s). If no error exists, choose "No change is necessary."

My <u>doctor's</u> magazine subscriptions must have run out because the most recent
    A

<u>Reader's Digest</u>, *Time*, and *Sports Illustrated* are from the <u>Fall</u> of 2004.
  B   C

A. Doctor's
B. *Readers digest*
C. fall
D. No change is necessary.

WRITING SKILLS EXIT EXAM #2

Read the entire passage carefully, then answer the questions. (Note: Intentional errors may have been included in the passage.)

(1) _____.

(2) The earliest tales about mermaids date back to the eighth century B.C. (3) Throughout the

centuries, sailors have told stories of beautiful creatures with the upper body of a young woman and the lower body of a fish. (4) Curiously, "mermaid" contains two syllables that reveal the word's meaning: "mer" means "sea" and "maid" refers to a young woman. (5) Therefore, the term "mermaid" can be translated as "fish-like woman." (6) The two-part appearance of mermaids reflects their conflicting inner qualities. (7) On the one hand, they look friendly; on the other hand, they often behave unkindly and harm the humans whom they encounter. (8) In European folklore, mermaids are usually associated with danger, causing floods, drowning deaths among sailors, as well as shipwrecks. (9) One of the most famous mermaids in mythology is Lorelei, who reportedly dwells in the Rhine River near Germany and has lured many sailors to their deaths. (10) Indeed, for thousands of years, human beings have created myths like that of the mermaid to explain events that are difficult to understand, such as a natural disaster or a tragic accident. (11) Disney made a film titled *The Little Mermaid*. (12) Through mythology, people attempt to make sense of the world around them. (13) With its tales about Earth's mysterious waters, the myth of mermaids continues to intrigue human beings. (Adapted from *The History of "Mermaids,"* 11 May 2002 <http://rubens.anu.edu.au/student.projects/mermaids/homepage.html>. "Mermaids - Spirits or Goddesses?" 11 May 2002.)

1. Which of the following sentences, when inserted in the blank labeled number 1, is the best main idea or topic sentence for the passage?
   A. The myth of mermaids has fascinated human beings for ages, perhaps because it helps to explain the unexplainable.
   B. With their beautiful, mysterious appearance, mermaids attempt to lure sailors to their deaths.
   C. Lorelei is a famous mermaid who supposedly lives in the Rhine River near Germany.
   D. Mermaid mythology can be traced back to the eighth century B.C.

2. Which sentence provides the specific support for sentence 6 in the passage?
   A. The earliest tales about mermaids date back to the eighth century B.C. (sentence 2).
   B. On the one hand, they look friendly; on the other hand, they often behave unkindly and harm the humans whom they encounter (sentence 7).
   C. Indeed, for thousands of years, human beings have created myths like that of the mermaid to explain events that are difficult to understand, such as a natural disaster or a tragic accident (sentence 10).
   D. Disney made a film titled *The Little Mermaid* (sentence 11).

3. Select the arrangement of sentences 3, 4, and 5 that provides the most logical sequence of ideas and supporting details in the paragraph. If no change is needed, select option A.
   A. Throughout the centuries, sailors have told stories of beautiful creatures with the upper body of a young woman and the lower body of a fish. Curiously, "mermaid" contains two syllables that reveal the word's meaning: "mer" means "sea" and "maid" refers to a young woman. Therefore, the term "mermaid" can be translated as "fish-like woman."
   B. Curiously, "mermaid" contains two syllables that reveal the word's meaning: "mer" means "sea" and "maid" refers to a young woman. Throughout the centuries, sailors have told stories of beautiful creatures with the upper body of a young woman and the lower body of a fish. Therefore, the term "mermaid" can be translated as "fish-like woman."
   C. Therefore, the term "mermaid" can be translated as "fish-like woman." Curiously, "mermaid" contains two syllables that reveal the word's meaning: "mer" means "sea" and "maid" refers to a young woman. Throughout the centuries, sailors have told stories of beautiful creatures with the upper body of a young woman and the lower body of a fish.
   D. Therefore, the term "mermaid" can be translated as "fish-like woman." Throughout the centuries, sailors have told stories of beautiful creatures with the upper body of a young woman and the lower body of a fish. Curiously, "mermaid" contains two syllables that reveal the word's meaning: "mer" means "sea" and "maid" refers to a young woman.

4. Which numbered sentence is least relevant to the passage?
   A. Sentence 2
   B. Sentence 5
   C. Sentence 9
   D. Sentence 11

Read the entire passage carefully, then answer the questions. (Note: Intentional errors may have been included in the passage.)

(1) _____.

(2) Whereas the traditional artists of the eighteenth century portrayed idealized versions of people and places, the impressionists painted human subjects and landscapes in a natural, unstudied way.

(3) Some key elements of impressionism include the following: theme, nature, color, and brushstrokes, all of which differed sharply from those of traditional art. (4) To begin, impressionist themes concern everyday, slice-of-life subjects, not the grand historical, religious, and mythological subjects of traditional art. (5) _____, impressionist artists depicted nature more realistically and less dramatically than did the traditional artists. (6) The impressionists, moreover, used light, vibrant colors as opposed to the darker shades of traditional art. (7) When painting, impressionists applied quick brushstrokes that produced a spontaneous look as opposed to the precise, detailed

appearance of a traditional canvas. (8) Famous French impressionists include Claude Monet, Pierre Auguste Renoir, and Edgar Degas. (9) Although these impressionists differed in terms of their backgrounds, beliefs, and artistic styles, they shared the goal of creating a different way of viewing life and reflecting it on canvas. (10) Their paintings are now displayed in a few exclusive hotels. (11) Indeed, these artists, whose nontraditional style of painting developed in nineteenth-century France, have left a lasting impression on the art world. (Adapted from the following source: "Impressionism." 11 May 2002 <http://www.impressionism.org>.)

5. Which sentence, if inserted in the blank labeled 1, is the **best** main idea or topic sentence of the passage?
   A. Unlike traditional artists, impressionists portrayed everyday subjects.
   B. Impressionists painted with light colors instead of dark ones.
   C. Important features of impressionism include its theme, nature, color, and brushstrokes.
   D. Impressionism, a nontraditional style of painting that emerged in nineteenth-century France, strongly influenced the art world.

6. Select the arrangement of sentences 2, 3, and 4 that provides the most logical sequence of ideas and supporting details in the paragraph. If no change is needed, select option A.
   A. Whereas the traditional artists of the eighteenth century portrayed idealized versions of people and places, the impressionists painted human subjects and landscapes in a natural, unstudied way. Some key elements of impressionism include the following: theme, nature, color, and brushstrokes, all of which differed sharply from those of traditional art. To begin, impressionist themes concern everyday, slice-of-life subjects, not the grand historical, religious, and mythological subjects of traditional art.
   B. Whereas the traditional artists of the eighteenth century portrayed idealized versions of people and places, the impressionists painted human subjects and landscapes in a natural, unstudied way. To begin, impressionist themes concern everyday, slice-of-life subjects, not the grand historical, religious, and mythological subjects of traditional art. Some key elements of impressionism include the following: theme, nature, color, and brushstrokes, which differed sharply from those of traditional art.
   C. To begin, impressionist themes concern everyday, slice-of-life subjects, not the grand historical, religious, and mythological subjects of traditional art. Some key elements of impressionism include the following: theme, nature, color, and brushstrokes, which differed sharply from those of traditional art. Whereas the traditional artists of the eighteenth century portrayed idealized versions of people and places, the impressionists painted human subjects and landscapes in a natural, unstudied way.
   D. Some key elements of impressionism include the following: theme, nature, color, and brushstrokes, which differed sharply from those of traditional art. Whereas the traditional artists of the eighteenth century portrayed idealized versions of people and places, the impressionists painted human subjects and landscapes in a natural, unstudied way. To begin, impressionist themes concern everyday, slice-of-life subjects, not the grand historical, religious, and mythological subjects of traditional art.

7. Which numbered sentence is **least** relevant to the passage?
   A. Sentence 6
   B. Sentence 8
   C. Sentence 10
   D. Sentence 11

8. Which word or phrase, if inserted in the blank in sentence 5, would make the relationship of ideas in sentences 4 and 5 clearer?
   A. However
   B. Finally
   C. On the other hand
   D. In addition

9. DIRECTIONS: Choose the most effective word or phrase within the context suggested by the sentence.

   Although Jennifer mailed the gift several weeks ago, Tyler never _____ it.

   A. retrieved
   B. received
   C. redeemed

10. DIRECTIONS: Choose the most effective word or phrase within the context suggested by the sentence.

    Showing a great deal of _____, the award-winning author humbly thanked his fans for their support.

    A. vanity
    B. uncertainty
    C. modesty

11. DIRECTIONS: Choose the option that corrects an error in an underlined portion. If no error exists, choose "No change is necessary."

    The <u>weather</u> in the state <u>capital</u> is usually <u>ideal</u> at this time of year.
         A   B   C

    A. whether
    B. capitol
    C. idea
    D. No change is necessary.

12. DIRECTIONS: Choose the sentence in which the modifiers are correctly placed.
    A. Desmond devoured a juicy porterhouse steak grilled on Grandpa's stove.
    B. Grilled on Grandpa's stove, Desmond devoured a juicy porterhouse steak.
    C. Desmond, grilled on Grandpa's stove, devoured a juicy porterhouse steak.

13. DIRECTIONS: Choose the sentence in which the modifiers are correctly placed.
    A. Struggling to fly the dragon-shaped kite, a strong gust of wind carried it off into the branches of an old oak tree.
    B. A strong gust of wind carried off the dragon-shaped kite into the branches of an old oak tree struggling to fly it.
    C. As two young boys struggled to fly the dragon-shaped kite, a strong gust of wind carried it off into the branches of an old oak tree.

14. DIRECTIONS: Choose the most effective word or phrase within the context suggested by the sentence(s).

    The Olympic swimmer trained eight hours a day for several months; _____, she felt very confident about her upcoming performance.

    A. nevertheless
    B. besides
    C. similarly
    D. consequently

15. DIRECTIONS: Choose the sentence that most clearly expresses the thought without errors in sentence structure.
    A. In order that our family loves to read books, we visit the public library once a week.
    B. Because our family loves to read books, we visit the public library once a week.
    C. Even though our family loves to read books, we visit the public library once a week.

16. DIRECTIONS: Choose the sentence that has no errors in structure.
    A. In order to win the grand prize, a child must sell one hundred boxes of cookies and to volunteer twenty hours of community service.
    B. In order to win the grand prize, a child must sell one hundred boxes of cookies and volunteering twenty hours of community service.
    C. In order to win the grand prize, a child must sell one hundred boxes of cookies and volunteer twenty hours of community service.

17. DIRECTIONS: Choose the correct word or phrase within the context suggested by the sentence.

    On summer afternoons, the children enjoy running through the sprinkler, diving into the pool, and _____ in their fort.

    A. play
    B. playing
    C. to play
    D. and they play

18. DIRECTIONS: Choose the option that corrects an error in the underlined part(s) of the following sentences. If no error exists, choose "No change is necessary."

When the rain stopped <u>falling and</u> the sun once again <u>emerged. A</u> rainbow <u>appeared and</u>
                   A   B   C

produced magnificent colors in the sky.

A. falling. And
B. emerged, a
C. appeared. And
D. No change is necessary.

19. DIRECTIONS: Choose the option that corrects an error in the underlined part(s) of the following sentences. If no error exists, choose "No change is necessary."

Although Justin is only twelve years <u>old, he</u> helps his family a great <u>deal by</u> dusting and
                                 A   B

vacuuming the <u>house. Also</u> watches over his younger brothers.
                  C

A. old. He
B. deal by,
C. house. Also, he
D. No change is necessary.

20. DIRECTIONS: Choose the option that corrects an error in the underlined part(s) of the following sentences. If no error exists, choose "No change is necessary."

The elderly husband and wife walk five miles a <u>day, they</u> are in better shape than many people half their age.

A. day they
B. day so, they
C. day; they
D. No change is necessary.

21. DIRECTIONS: Choose the option that corrects an error in the underlined part(s) of the following sentences. If no error exists, choose "No change is necessary."

At his mother's <u>request, Ian</u> wears a helmet whenever he rides his motorized <u>scooter it</u> can
                      A   B

go as fast as fifteen miles per <u>hour, so</u> he travels carefully on it.
                                   C

A. request. Ian
B. scooter; it
C. hour so
D. No change is necessary.

22. DIRECTIONS: Choose the option that corrects an error in the underlined part(s) of the following sentences. If no error exists, choose "No change is necessary."

The little girl accidentally <u>ran</u> into the ottoman that she and her older brother <u>had broken</u>
                  A   B

yesterday during a game of tag; fortunately, she did not <u>get</u> hurt.
                                           C

A. run
B. had broke
C. got
D. No change is necessary.

23. DIRECTIONS: Choose the option that corrects an error in the underlined part(s) of the following sentences. If no error exists, choose "No change is necessary."

When Mom <u>come</u> home from work, I <u>ran</u> up to her and <u>gave</u> her a big hug.
             A   B   C

A. came
B. run
C. given
D. No change is necessary.

24. DIRECTIONS: Choose the option that corrects an error in the underlined part(s) of the following sentences. If no error exists, choose "No change is necessary."

Since its 1936 publication, *Gone with the Wind* <u>captivated</u> the interest of generations of readers.

A. captivates
B. was captivating
C. has captivated
D. No change is necessary.

25. DIRECTIONS: Choose the option that corrects an error in the underlined part(s) of the following sentences. If no error exists, choose "No change is necessary."

In the 1980s, rock groups like Bon Jovi and Whitesnake <u>play</u> at sold-out concerts; these
                                                         A

days, such groups, which some radio stations <u>call</u> "big hair bands," <u>are experiencing</u> a
                                               B   C

revival in their popularity.

A. played
B. called
C. were experiencing
D. No change is necessary.

26. DIRECTIONS: Choose the option that corrects an error in the underlined part(s) of the following sentences. If no error exists, choose "No change is necessary."

Either the tortoise or the hare <u>win</u> the long, challenging race.

   A. are winning
   B. were winning
   C. wins
   D. No change is necessary.

27. DIRECTIONS: Choose the option that corrects an error in the underlined part(s) of the following sentences. If no error exists, choose "No change is necessary."

One of the puppies <u>look</u> smaller than the others; interestingly, every litter <u>has</u> a runt that
                    A   B

often <u>captures</u> the hearts of both children and adults.
      C

   A. looks
   B. have
   C. capture
   D. No change is necessary.

28. DIRECTIONS: Choose the option that corrects an error in the underlined part(s) of the following sentences. If no error exists, choose "No change is necessary."

Each of the museum visitors <u>appears</u> surprised to discover that there <u>is</u> one dragonfly and
                             A   B

several butterflies in the painting that <u>portrays</u> city life.
                                         C

   A. appear
   B. are
   C. portray
   D. No change is necessary.

29. DIRECTIONS: Choose the option that corrects an error in the underlined part(s) of the following sentences. If no error exists, choose "No change is necessary."

The little boy enjoyed the circus thoroughly, but <u>he</u> especially loved the elephants because
                                                  A

<u>they</u> performed amazing stunts for <u>him</u> and all the other children.
  B   C

   A. they
   B. it
   C. her
   D. No change is necessary.

30. DIRECTIONS: Choose the option that corrects an error in the underlined part(s) of the following sentences. If no error exists, choose "No change is necessary."

Many of <u>us</u> have lived in this neighborhood since <u>we</u> graduated from college and started
      A   B

<u>their</u> families.
  C

A. them
B. you
C. our
D. No change is necessary.

31. DIRECTIONS: Choose the option that corrects an error in the underlined part(s) of the following sentences. If no error exists, choose "No change is necessary."

While preparing dinner, Darla listened to the CD <u>her</u> brothers had given her when <u>you</u>
                                           A   B

visited <u>them</u> in Maine.
      C

A. my
B. she
C. us
D. No change is necessary.

32. DIRECTIONS: Choose the option that corrects an error in the underlined part(s) of the following sentences. If no error exists, choose "No change is necessary."

Mr. Avery told Devin, <u>his</u> apprentice, that <u>he</u> needed to finish the repair of the switch and
                      A   B

check that <u>it</u> performed correctly.
          C

A. their
B. he, Devin,
C. they
D. No change is necessary.

33. DIRECTIONS: Choose the option that corrects an error in the underlined part(s) of the following sentences. If no error exists, choose "No change is necessary."

The boys and <u>her</u> love visiting the beach; <u>they</u> enjoy swimming, surfing, and tanning
             A   B

because such activities are fun and inexpensive for <u>them</u> to experience.
                                                C

A. she
B. them
C. they
D. No change is necessary.

34. DIRECTIONS: Choose the option that corrects an error in the underlined part(s) of the following sentences. If no error exists, choose "No change is necessary."

The <u>quietly</u> <u>elegant</u> essay <u>profound</u> touched the audience and won first prize in the
     A   B   C

student literary contest.

  A. quiet
  B. elegantly
  C. profoundly
  D. No change is necessary.

35. DIRECTIONS: Choose the option that corrects an error in the underlined part(s) of the following sentences. If no error exists, choose "No change is necessary."

Josh is the <u>powerfullest</u> of all the speakers on the debate team.

  A. more powerful
  B. most powerful
  C. most powerfullest
  D. No change is necessary.

36. DIRECTIONS: Choose the option that corrects an error in the underlined part(s) of the following sentences. If no error exists, choose "No change is necessary."

The <u>committee</u> <u>succeeded</u> in electing a <u>different</u> leader for next year.
     A   B   C

  A. comittee
  B. suceeded
  C. diferent
  D. No change is necessary.

37. DIRECTIONS: Choose the option that corrects an error in the underlined part(s) of the following sentences. If no error exists, choose "No change is necessary."

<u>Although Heather</u> wanted to attend her friend's baby <u>shower she</u> could not do <u>so because</u>
     A   B   C

she had to work.

  A. Although, Heather
  B. shower, she
  C. so, because
  D. No change is necessary.

38. DIRECTIONS: Choose the option that corrects an error in the underlined part(s) of the following sentences. If no error exists, choose "No change is necessary."

We enjoy listening to the news <u>programs and</u> classical music on the public radio
                       A

<u>station, so</u> we are going to make a contribution during the <u>next, fund-raising</u> campaign.
   B   C

- A. programs, and
- B. station so
- C. next fund-raising
- D. No change is necessary.

39. DIRECTIONS: Choose the option that corrects an error in the underlined part(s) of the following sentences. If no error exists, choose "No change is necessary."

I love snacking on <u>cold, sweet,</u> juicy <u>watermelon, surprisingly,</u> I even enjoy searching for
                 A   B

the black <u>seeds that</u> other people find annoying.
          C

- A. cold sweet
- B. watermelon; surprisingly,
- C. seeds, that
- D. No change is necessary.

40. DIRECTIONS: Choose the option that corrects an error in the underlined part(s) of the following sentences. If no error exists, choose "No change is necessary."

Having come from the <u>Philippines</u>, Amancia speaks a variety of languages, including
                     A

<u>English</u>, and she is looking forward to practicing her writing skills this <u>Fall</u>.
 B   C

- A. philippines
- B. english
- C. fall
- D. No change is necessary.

WRITING SKILLS EXIT EXAM #3

Read the entire passage carefully, then answer the questions. (Note: Intentional errors may have been included in the passage.)

(1) _____.

(2) Job candidates are tested in a variety of areas, including their appearance, qualifications, and

interpersonal skills. (3) The moment a candidate enters the waiting room, she is being evaluated. (4) To create a favorable first impression, she should arrive ten or more minutes early and wait patiently for the interview. (5) Ideally, the job seeker will have dressed in formal business attire, for doing so establishes a confident, professional image. (6) Unfortunately, casual clothes, such as blue jeans and tennis shoes, may suggest an indifferent attitude on the part of the interviewee. (7) Formal attire, like a tailored suit, shows that the candidate takes the position seriously. (8) Establishing a positive image through professional dress prepares the job seeker for the question and answer session of the interview. (9) During this stage, applicants should anticipate two types of questions: behavioral and ambition ones. (10) _____, behavioral questions assess one's teamwork skills and ability to deal with job conflicts. (11) Secondly, ambition questions focus on one's career plans. (12) By answering these questions honestly and sincerely, a candidate will favorably impress the interviewer. (13) Interviews can be nerve-wrecking experiences. (14) In brief, an interview is like a test for which job applicants must carefully prepare. (Adapted from the following source: Bacon, Su. "Expect Interviewers to Assess Everything." *Florida Times Union* 2 June 2002: H13)

1. Which of the following sentences, when inserted in the blank labeled number 1, is the best main idea or topic sentence for the passage?
   A. Business attire demonstrates that the candidate takes the interview seriously.
   B. Applicants should arrive at least ten minutes early to the interview.
   C. A job interview is like an exam for which applicants must carefully prepare.
   D. Candidates can expect to be asked behavioral and ambition questions.

2. Which sentence provides the specific support for sentence 3 in the passage?
   A. To create a favorable first impression, she should arrive ten or more minutes early and wait patiently for the interview (sentence 4).
   B. During this stage, applicants should anticipate two types of questions: behavioral and ambition ones (sentence 9).
   C. Secondly, ambition questions focus on one's career plans (sentence 11).
   D. By answering these questions honestly and sincerely, a candidate will favorably impress the interviewer (sentence 12).

3. Which numbered sentence is least relevant to the passage?
   A. Sentence 2
   B. Sentence 6
   C. Sentence 10
   D. Sentence 13

4. Which word or phrase, if inserted in the blank in sentence 10, would make
   the relationship of the ideas in sentences 9 and 10 clearer?
   A. Conversely
   B. First
   C. Therefore
   D. Also

Read the entire passage carefully, then answer the questions. (Note: Intentional errors may have been included in the passage.)

(1) _____.

(2) According to Bill Watterson, the creator of *Calvin and Hobbes*, engaging comic strips reflect their creators' curiosity and enthusiasm for learning. (3) In just a few panels, these cartoonists express readers' unspoken thoughts and feelings. (4) In addition, some comic strips, such as Charles Schulz's *Peanuts*, portray life from the point of view of children, inviting readers to look more innocently at the world. (5) Interestingly, comics are frequently referred to as the "funnies." (6) In fact, most comics contain humor, which involves the element of surprise. (7) Readers find humor in comics that not only surprise their expectations but also reveal a truth about life. (8) For instance, in a *Dilbert* comic strip by Scott Adams, Dilbert claims, "I have become one with my computer." (9) He then announces that he has achieved "a perfect blend of logic and emotion." (10) Just when Dilbert is about to say that he has reached a state of "Nirvana," his friend Dogbert exclaims, "Nerdvana." (11) Readers laugh at this surprisingly clever pun as they reflect on how difficult it is to achieve balance in their own lives. (12) _____, comic strips are a form of popular art that gives insight into life while entertaining audiences. (Adapted from the following sources: Watterson, Bill. *The Calvin and Hobbes Tenth Anniversary Book*. Kansas City, Missouri: Andrews and McMeel, a Universal Press Syndicate Company, 1995. Adams, Scott. *It's Obvious You Won't Survive by Your Wits Alone: A Dilbert Book*. Kansas City, Missouri: Andrews and McMeel, a Universal Press Syndicate Company, 1995.)

5. Which of the following sentences, if inserted in the blank labeled number 1, is the best
   main idea or topic sentence of the passage?
   A. The comics are found in the funnies section of the local newspaper.
   B. In some comic strips, characters become one with their computers.
   C. Comic strips are a form of popular art that both entertains audiences and offers insight
      into life.
   D. A few comics portray life from a child's point of view.

6. Which sentence provides the specific support for sentence 5 in the passage?
   A. According to Bill Watterson, the creator of *Calvin and Hobbes*, engaging comic strips reflect their creators' curiosity and enthusiasm for learning (sentence 2).
   B. In just a few panels, these cartoonists express readers' unspoken thoughts and feelings (sentence 3).
   C. In addition, some comic strips, such as Charles Schulz's *Peanuts*, portray life from the point of view of children, inviting readers to look more innocently at the world (sentence 4).
   D. In fact, most comics contain humor, which involves the element of surprise (sentence 6).

7. Select the arrangement of sentences 8, 9, and 10 that provides the most logical sequence of ideas and supporting details in the paragraph. If no change is necessary, select Option A.
   A. For instance, in a *Dilbert* comic strip by Scott Adams, Dilbert claims, "I have become one with my computer." He then announces that he has achieved "a perfect blend of logic and emotion." Just when Dilbert is about to say that he has reached a state of "Nirvana," his friend Dogbert exclaims, "Nerdvana."
   B. He then announces that he has achieved "a perfect blend of logic and emotion." Just when Dilbert is about to say that he has reached a state of "Nirvana," his friend Dogbert exclaims, "Nerdvana." For instance, in a *Dilbert* comic strip by Scott Adams, Dilbert claims, "I have become one with my computer."
   C. Just when Dilbert is about to say that he has reached a state of "Nirvana," his friend Dogbert exclaims, "Nerdvana." For instance, in a *Dilbert* comic strip by Scott Adams, Dilbert claims, "I have become one with my computer." He then announces that he has achieved "a perfect blend of logic and emotion."
   D. Just when Dilbert is about to say that he has reached a state of "Nirvana," his friend Dogbert exclaims, "Nerdvana." He then announces that he has achieved "a perfect blend of logic and emotion." For instance, in a *Dilbert* comic strip by Scott Adams, Dilbert claims, "I have become one with my computer."

8. Which word or phrase, if inserted in the blank in sentence 12, would make the relationship of the ideas in sentences 11 and 12 clearer?
   A. On the other hand
   B. Indeed
   C. For instance
   D. Next

9. DIRECTIONS: Choose the most effective word or phrase within the context suggested by the sentence.

   The mystery novel held its readers in _____.

   A. suspension
   B. suspicion
   C. suspense

10. DIRECTIONS: Choose the most effective word or phrase within the context suggested by the sentence.

    The lab assistant _____ through the microscope at the biological specimen.

A. scanned
B. peered
C. gawked

11. DIRECTIONS: Choose the option that corrects an error in an underlined portion. If no error exists, choose "no change is necessary."

It's a common occurrence for college students to <u>loose</u> <u>their</u> keys on campus.
 A   B   C

A. Its
B. lose
C. there
D. No change is necessary.

12. DIRECTIONS: Choose the sentence in which the modifiers are correctly placed.
A. Leaping from tree to tree in our backyard, the squirrel searched busily for food.
B. The squirrel searched busily for food leaping from tree to tree in our backyard.
C. The squirrel searched busily for food in our backyard leaping from tree to tree.

13. DIRECTIONS: Choose the sentence in which the modifiers are correctly placed.
A. Rowing the canoe across the lake, our oars made a gentle, swooshing sound in the water.
B. Our oars made a gentle, swooshing sound in the water rowing the canoe across the lake.
C. As Derrick and I rowed the canoe across the lake, our oars made a gentle, swooshing sound in the water.

14. DIRECTIONS: Choose the most effective word or phrase within the context suggested by the sentence(s).

Many drivers travel with a cell phone; _____, they no longer need to stop to use a pay phone at a telephone booth.

A. consequently
B. next
C. however
D. likewise

15. DIRECTIONS: Choose the sentence that most clearly expresses the thought without errors in structure.
A. If Veronica received three job offers this week, she did not accept any of them because she loves her current position.
B. Although Veronica received three job offers this week, she did not accept any of them because she loves her current position.
C. Provided that Veronica received three job offers this week, she did not accept any of them because she loves her current position.

16. DIRECTIONS: Choose the sentence that has no errors in structure.
A. The president wrote and to deliver an inspirational State of the Union address.
B. The president wrote and delivering an inspirational State of the Union address.
C. The president wrote and delivered an inspirational State of the Union address.

17. DIRECTIONS: Choose the correct word or phrase within the context suggested by the sentence.

At the popular club, strobe lights flicker in the smoky room, hip hop music lures people onto the dance floor, and dancers _____ in time to the music.

A. move
B. they move
C. to move
D. are moving

18. DIRECTIONS: Choose the option that corrects an error in the underlined portion(s). If no error exists, choose "no change is necessary."

If the light turns yellow at the busy <u>intersection. drivers</u> should stop as a safety precaution.

A. intersection drivers
B. intersection, drivers
C. intersection; drivers
D. No change is necessary.

19. DIRECTIONS: Choose the option that corrects an error in the underlined portion(s). If no error exists, choose "no change is necessary."

In the public <u>library, which</u> is located in downtown <u>Jacksonville, children</u> sit at Miss
        A   B

Roberta's <u>feet as</u> she reads a story about a mischievous monkey in an ice cream shop.
          C

A. library. Which
B. Jacksonville. Children
C. feet; as
D. No change is necessary.

20. DIRECTIONS: Choose the option that corrects an error in the underlined portion(s). If no error exists, choose "no change is necessary."

When Renata opened her mailbox, she discovered an envelope from her former college <u>roommate, the envelope</u> contained a wedding invitation.

A. roommate and the envelope
B. roommate and, the envelope
C. roommate; the envelope
D. No change is necessary.

21. DIRECTIONS: Choose the option that corrects an error in the underlined portion(s). If no error exists, choose "no change is necessary."

As the fire fighters drove the hook and ladder truck in the <u>parade, they</u> waved at a little
                                                            A

boy who watched them in <u>awe; suddenly,</u> they turned on the truck's <u>siren and</u> they rushed
                                    B   C

off in an emergency.

A. parade; they
B. awe, suddenly,
C. siren, and
D. No change is necessary.

22. DIRECTIONS: Choose the option that corrects an error in the underlined portion(s). If
    no error exists, choose "no change is necessary."

    Jordan <u>seen</u> an affordable motorcycle on the showroom floor and <u>bought</u> the bike so that
            A   B

    she <u>could ride</u> it to work.
        C

    A. saw
    B. had boughten
    C. could rode
    D. No change is necessary.

23. DIRECTIONS: Choose the option that corrects an error in the underlined portion(s). If
    no error exists, choose "no change is necessary."

    I <u>should have wore</u> a sweater to the theatre because I felt quite cold there.

    A. should wore
    B. should had worn
    C. should have worn
    D. No change is necessary.

24. DIRECTIONS: Choose the option that corrects an error in the underlined portion(s). If
    no error exists, choose "no change is necessary."

    In past decades, people <u>used</u> typewriters to prepare reports. Nowadays, most individuals
                                A

    <u>preferred</u> to type on a computer because they <u>can save</u> so much time.
     B   C

    A. use
    B. prefer
    C. could save
    D. No change is necessary.

25. DIRECTIONS: Choose the option that corrects an error in the underlined portion(s). If
    no error exists, choose "no change is necessary."

    Since the local museum opened its dinosaur exhibit last month, many parents <u>took</u> their
    children to see the fossils and skeletons on display.

A. take
B. were taking
C. have taken
D. No change is necessary.

26. DIRECTIONS: Choose the option that corrects an error in the underlined portion(s). If no error exists, choose "no change is necessary."

Neither the cookies nor the candy <u>interest</u> the determined dieter who prefers to snack on carrots and celery.

A. interests
B. are interesting
C. have interested
D. No change is necessary.

27. DIRECTIONS: Choose the option that corrects an error in the underlined portion(s). If no error exists, choose "no change is necessary."

Each of the blues musicians <u>perform</u> a thirty-minute set and <u>moves</u> the fans with soulful
                                   A   B

guitar playing that <u>fills</u> the entire amphitheatre.
                  C

A. performs
B. move
C. fill
D. No change is necessary.

28. DIRECTIONS: Choose the option that corrects an error in the underlined portion(s). If no error exists, choose "no change is necessary."

The superintendent of the schools <u>has exclaimed</u> that each school <u>is</u> responsible for
                                       A   B

making an "A" or a "B"; everybody <u>is working</u> hard to achieve this goal.
                                      C

A. have exclaimed
B. are
C. are working
D. No change is necessary.

29. DIRECTIONS: Choose the option that corrects an error in the underlined portion(s). If no error exists, choose "no change is necessary."

The sleeping dog awoke when <u>his</u> owners returned home; <u>she</u> patted <u>him</u> on the head.
                                    A   B   C

A. their
B. they
C. them
D. No change is necessary.

30. DIRECTIONS: Choose the option that corrects an error in the underlined portion(s). If no error exists, choose "no change is necessary."

When Mrs. McBride's students read a short story by Edgar Allen Poe, <u>they</u> asked
                                                                     A

<u>her</u> about <u>his</u> intriguing life.
 B   C

A. you
B. me
C. our
D. No change is necessary.

31. DIRECTIONS: Choose the option that corrects an error in the underlined portion(s). If no error exists, choose "no change is necessary."

The manager of the clothing department told <u>us</u> to display the sundress that had just
                                              A

arrived, so <u>we</u> placed <u>it</u> on a mannequin in the window.
             B   C

A. you
B. they
C. you
D. No change is necessary.

32. DIRECTIONS: Choose the option that corrects an error in the underlined portion(s). If no error exists, choose "no change is necessary."

The photographer told Steve, <u>his</u> assistant, that <u>he</u> needed to use a wide lens camera to
                               A   B

film the zebras in <u>their</u> natural habitat.
                     C

A. their
B. he, Steve,
C. its
D. No change is necessary.

33. DIRECTIONS: Choose the option that corrects an error in the underlined portion(s). If no error exists, choose "no change is necessary."

Between you and <u>me</u>, Paul and <u>her</u> have been dating for several years, but <u>they</u> do not plan
                  A   B   C

on marrying.

A. I
B. she
C. them
D. No change is necessary.

34. DIRECTIONS: Choose the option that corrects an error in the underlined portion(s). If no error exists, choose "no change is necessary."

Ashley's suit looked <u>tasteful</u> on her; it was <u>carefully</u> sewn by a <u>skillful</u> tailor.
                     A   B   C

A. tastefully
B. careful
C. skillfully
D. No change is necessary.

35. DIRECTIONS: Choose the option that corrects an error in the underlined portion(s). If no error exists, choose "no change is necessary."

Gabriel is the _____ of the two brothers.

A. younger
B. youngest
C. more young
D. most young

36. DIRECTIONS: Choose the option that corrects an error in the underlined portion(s). If no error exists, choose "no change is necessary."

I just <u>received</u> an e-mail from my sister who is a <u>sophomore</u> in <u>collage</u>.
          A   B   C

A. recieved
B. sophmore
C. college
D. No change is necessary.

37. DIRECTIONS: Choose the option that corrects an error in the underlined portion(s). If no error exists, choose "no change is necessary."

Bess works for a <u>cable company</u> in the <u>southwest</u> where she frequently speaks <u>Spanish</u>
                       A   B   C

with her customers.

A. Cable Company
B. Southwest
C. spanish
D. No change is necessary.

38. DIRECTIONS: Choose the option that corrects an error in the underlined portion(s). If no error exists, choose "no change is necessary."

Have you gotten <u>your</u> beauty sleep after a hard <u>weeks</u> <u>labor?</u>
$\qquad\qquad\qquad$ A $\qquad\qquad\qquad\qquad\qquad$ B $\qquad$ C

    A. you're
    B. week's
    C. labor.
    D. No change is necessary.

39. DIRECTIONS: Choose the option that corrects an error in the underlined portion(s). If no error exists, choose "no change is necessary."

<u>Because the</u> Smiths and Joneses have been close neighbors for over twenty <u>years they</u>
$\qquad$ A $\qquad\qquad\qquad\qquad\qquad\qquad\qquad\qquad\qquad\qquad\qquad\qquad\qquad\qquad\qquad\qquad$ B

occasionally baby sit each <u>other's</u> grandchildren.
$\qquad\qquad\qquad\qquad\qquad$ C

    A. Because, the
    B. years, they
    C. others
    D. No change is necessary.

40. DIRECTIONS: Choose the sentence that is correctly punctuated.
    A. Russell enjoys golf baseball, and tennis but he does not participate in contact sports like football.
    B. Russell enjoys golf baseball, and tennis, but he does not participate in contact sports like football.
    C. Russell enjoys golf, baseball, and tennis but he does not participate in contact sports like football.
    D. Russell enjoys golf, baseball, and tennis, but he does not participate in contact sports like football.

Part Six: Correspondence Charts for Test Questions and Tracking Sheets—Reading Skills

PRETEST CORRESPONDENCE CHART ◆ BY QUESTION NUMBER

Ques. No.	Skills	Ques. No.	Skills
1	Main Idea	19	Main Idea
2	Patterns of Organization	20	Fact and Opinion
3	Author's Purpose	21	Relationships Within a Sentence
4	Relationships Between Sentences	22	Patterns of Organization
5	Support for Reasoning and Argument	23	Author's Bias
6	Relationships Within a Sentence	24	Author's Tone
7	Author's Tone	25	Support for Reasoning and Argument
8	Main Idea	26	Relationships Between Sentences
9	Inferences and Conclusions	27	Inferences and Conclusions
10	Main Idea	28	Main Idea
11	Inferences and Conclusions	29	Relationships Within a Sentence
12	Supporting Details	30	Patterns of Organization
13	Word Meaning	31	Author's Bias
14	Fact and Opinion	32	Word Meaning
15	Support for Reasoning and Argument	33	Inferences and Conclusions
16	Patterns of Organization	34	Author's Tone
17	Relationships Within a Sentence	35	Fact and Opinion
18	Author's Purpose	36	Author's Purpose

READING PRETEST CORRESPONDENCE CHART ◆ BY SKILLS

Skills	Question Numbers				
Main Idea	1	8	10	19	28
Supporting Details	12				
Author's Purpose	3	18	36		
Patterns of Organization	2	16	22	30	
Relationships Within a Sentence	6	17	21	29	
Relationships Between Sentences	4	26			
Context Clues	13	32			
Author's Bias	23	31			
Author's Tone	7	24	34		
Fact and Opinion	14	20	35		
Inferences and Conclusions	9	11	27		
Support for Reasoning and Argument	5	15	25		

EXIT EXAM #1 QUESTION CORRESPONDENCE CHART
◆ BY QUESTION NUMBER

Ques. No.	Skills	Ques. No.	Skills
1	Main Idea	19	Main Idea
2	Author's Purpose	20	Author's Purpose
3	Patterns of Organization	21	Inferences and Conclusions
4	Relationships Within a Sentence	22	Patterns of Organization
5	Supporting Details	23	Author's Tone
6	Fact and Opinion	24	Word Meaning
7	Support for Reasoning and Argument	25	Author's Bias
8	Author's Tone	26	Relationships Between Sentences
9	Inferences and Conclusions	27	Relationships Within a Sentence
10	Main Idea	28	Main Idea
11	Relationships Within a Sentence	29	Patterns of Organization
12	Relationships Between Sentences	30	Relationships Between Sentences
13	Patterns of Organization	31	Author's Bias
14	Author's Purpose	32	Relationships Between Sentences
15	Inferences and Conclusions	33	Word Meaning
16	Support for Reasoning and Argument	34	Relationships Within a Sentence
17	Supporting Details	35	Support for Reasoning and Argument
18	Fact and Opinion	36	Inferences and Conclusions

EXIT EXAM #1 CORRESPONDENCE CHART ◆ BY SKILLS

Skills	Question Numbers			
Main Idea	1	10	19	28
Supporting Details	2	14	20	
Author's Purpose	5	17		
Patterns of Organization	3	13	22	29
Relationships Within a Sentence	4	11	27	34
Relationships Between Sentences	12	26	30	32
Word Meaning	24	33		
Author's Bias	25	31		
Author's Tone	8	23		
Fact and Opinion	6	18		
Inferences and Conclusions	9	15	21	36
Support for Reasoning and Argument	7	16	35	

EXIT EXAM #2 QUESTION CORRESPONDENCE CHART
◆ BY QUESTION NUMBER

Ques. No.	Skills	Ques. No.	Skills
1	Main Idea	19	Implied Main Idea
2	Patterns of Organization	20	Patterns of Organization
3	Implied Main Idea	21	Relationships Within a Sentence
4	Relationships Between Sentences	22	Relationships Between Sentences
5	Author's Purpose	23	Author's Purpose
6	Context Clues	24	Author's Tone
7	Supporting Details	25	Author's Bias
8	Inferences and Conclusions	26	Fact and Opinion
9	Support for Reasoning and Argument	27	Context Clues
10	Implied Main Idea	28	Main Idea
11	Relationships Within a Sentence	29	Main Idea
12	Relationships Between Sentences	30	Patterns of Organization
13	Supporting Details	31	Relationships Within a Sentence
14	Support for Reasoning and Argument	32	Relationships Between Sentences
15	Inferences and Conclusions	33	Author's Purpose
16	Author's Tone	34	Inferences and Conclusions
17	Author's Bias	35	Author's Tone
18	Fact and Opinion	36	Fact and Opinion

EXIT EXAM #2 CORRESPONDENCE CHART   ◆ BY SKILLS

Skills	Question Numbers					
Main Idea	1	3	10	19	28	29
Supporting Details	7	13				
Author's Purpose	5	23	33			
Patterns of Organization	2	20	30			
Relationships Within a Sentence	11	21	31			
Relationships Between Sentences	4	12	22	32		
Word Meaning	6	27				
Author's Bias	17	25				
Author's Tone	16	24	35			
Fact and Opinion	18	26	36			
Inferences and Conclusions	8	15	34			
Support for Reasoning and Argument	9	14				

EXIT EXAM #3 QUESTION CORRESPONDENCE CHART
◆ BY QUESTION NUMBER

Ques. No.	Skills	Ques. No.	Skills
1	Main Idea	19	Main Idea
2	Author's Purpose	20	Author's Purpose
3	Patterns of Organization	21	Relationships Within a Sentence
4	Support for Reasoning and Argument	22	Patterns of Organization
5	Relationships Within a Sentence	23	Fact and Opinion
6	Author's Tone	24	Supporting Details
7	Word Meaning	25	Inferences and Conclusions
8	Fact and Opinion	26	Author's Bias
9	Inferences and Conclusions	27	Support for Reasoning and Argument
10	Main Idea	28	Main Idea
11	Relationships Within a Sentence	29	Relationships Between Sentences
12	Relationships Between Sentences	30	Patterns of Organization
13	Supporting Details	31	Author's Purpose
14	Inferences and Conclusions	32	Author's Tone
15	Author's Tone	33	Support for Reasoning and Argument
16	Fact and Opinion	34	Inferences and Conclusions
17	Author's Bias	35	Fact and Opinion
18	Word Meaning	36	Word Meaning

EXIT EXAM #3 CORRESPONDENCE CHART ◆ BY SKILLS

Skills	Question Numbers			
Main Idea	1	10	19	28
Supporting Details	13	24		
Author's Purpose	2	20	31	
Patterns of Organization	3	22	30	
Relationships Within a Sentence	5	11	21	
Relationships Between Sentences	12	29		
Word Meaning	7	18	36	
Author's Bias	17	26		
Author's Tone	6	15	32	
Fact and Opinion	8	16	23	35
Inferences and Conclusions	9	14	25	34
Support for Reasoning and Argument	4	27	33	

Part Six: Correspondence Charts for Test Questions and Tracking Sheets—Writing Skills

Ques. No.	Skill Tested
1.	Identifies a thesis statement or topic sentence
2.	Recognizes adequate support provided by generalized and specific evidence
3.	Arranges ideas and supporting details in logical patterns
4.	Identifies supporting material that is relevant or irrelevant to the thesis statement or topic sentence
5.	Recognizes effective transitional devices within the context of a passage
6.	Identifies a thesis statement or topic sentence
7.	Recognizes adequate support provided by generalized and specific evidence
8.	Arranges ideas and supporting details in logical patterns
9.	Identifies supporting material that is relevant or irrelevant to the thesis statement or topic sentence
10.	Recognizes effective transitional devices within the context of a passage
11.	Chooses the appropriate word or expression in context
12.	Chooses the appropriate word or expression in context
13.	Recognizes commonly confused or misused words or phrases
14.	Recognizes commonly confused or misused words or phrases
15.	Uses modifiers correctly
16.	Uses modifiers correctly
17.	Uses coordination and subordination effectively
18.	Uses coordination and subordination effectively
19.	Recognizes parallel structure
20.	Recognizes parallel structure
21.	Avoids fragments, comma splices, and fused sentences
22.	Avoids fragments, comma splices, and fused sentences
23.	Avoids fragments, comma splices, and fused sentences
24.	Avoids fragments, comma splices, and fused sentences
25.	Uses standard verb forms
26.	Avoids inappropriate shifts in verb tense
27.	Avoids inappropriate shifts in verb tense
28.	Maintains agreement between subject and verb
29.	Maintains agreement between subject and verb
30.	Maintains agreement between pronoun and antecedent
31.	Avoids inappropriate pronoun shifts in person
32.	Avoids inappropriate pronoun shifts in person
33.	Maintains clear pronoun references
34.	Uses proper case forms
35.	Uses adjectives and adverbs correctly
36.	Uses appropriate degree forms of adjectives and adverbs
37.	Uses standard spelling
38.	Uses standard punctuation
39.	Uses standard punctuation
40.	Uses standard capitalization

PRETEST ◆ BY SKILL

Skill Tested	Question Number
Identifies a thesis statement or topic sentence	1, 6
Recognizes adequate support provided by generalized and specific evidence	2, 7
Arranges ideas and supporting details in logical patterns	3, 8
Identifies supporting material that is relevant or irrelevant to the thesis statement or topic sentence	4, 9
Recognizes effective transitional devices within the context of a passage	5, 10
Chooses the appropriate word or expression in context	11, 12
Recognizes commonly confused or misused words or phrases	13, 14
Uses modifiers correctly	15, 16
Uses coordination and subordination effectively	17, 18
Recognizes parallel structure	19, 20
Avoids fragments, comma splices, and fused sentences	21, 22, 23, 24
Uses standard verb forms	25
Avoids inappropriate shifts in verb tense	26, 27
Maintains agreement between subject and verb	28, 29
Maintains agreement between pronoun and antecedent	30
Avoids inappropriate pronoun shifts in person	31, 32
Maintains clear pronoun references	33
Uses proper case forms	34
Uses adjectives and adverbs correctly	35
Uses appropriate degree forms of adjectives and adverbs	36
Uses standard spelling	37
Uses standard punctuation	38, 39
Uses standard capitalization	40

EXIT EXAM #1 ◆ BY QUESTION NUMBER

Ques.
No. Skill Tested

1. Identifies a thesis statement or topic sentence
2. Recognizes adequate support provided by generalized and specific evidence
3. Arranges ideas and supporting details in logical patterns
4. Identifies supporting material that is relevant or irrelevant to the thesis statement or topic sentence
5. Recognizes effective transitional devices within the context of a passage
6. Identifies a thesis statement or topic sentence
7. Recognizes adequate support provided by generalized and specific evidence
8. Arranges ideas and supporting details in logical patterns
9. Identifies supporting material that is relevant or irrelevant to the thesis statement or topic sentence
10. Recognizes effective transitional devices within the context of a passage
11. Chooses the appropriate word or expression in context
12. Chooses the appropriate word or expression in context
13. Recognizes commonly confused or misused words or phrases
14. Recognizes commonly confused or misused words or phrases
15. Uses modifiers correctly
16. Uses modifiers correctly
17. Uses coordination and subordination effectively

Ques.
No. Skill Tested

18. Uses coordination and subordination effectively
19. Recognizes parallel structure
20. Recognizes parallel structure
21. Avoids fragments, comma splices, and fused sentences
22. Avoids fragments, comma splices, and fused sentences
23. Avoids fragments, comma splices, and fused sentences
24. Avoids fragments, comma splices, and fused sentences
25. Uses standard verb forms
26. Avoids inappropriate shifts in verb tense
27. Avoids inappropriate shifts in verb tense
28. Maintains agreement between subject and verb
29. Maintains agreement between subject and verb
30. Maintains agreement between pronoun and antecedent
31. Avoids inappropriate pronoun shifts in person
32. Avoids inappropriate pronoun shifts in person
33. Maintains clear pronoun references
34. Uses proper case forms
35. Uses adjectives and adverbs correctly
36. Uses appropriate degree forms of adjectives and adverbs
37. Uses standard spelling
38. Uses standard punctuation
39. Uses standard punctuation
40. Uses standard capitalization

EXIT EXAM #1 ◆ BY SKILL

Skill Tested	Question Number
Identifies a thesis statement or topic sentence	1, 6
Recognizes adequate support provided by generalized and specific evidence	2, 7
Arranges ideas and supporting details in logical patterns	3, 8
Identifies supporting material that is relevant or irrelevant to the thesis statement or topic sentence	4, 9
Recognizes effective transitional devices within the context of a passage	5, 10
Chooses the appropriate word or expression in context	11, 12
Recognizes commonly confused or misused words or phrases	13, 14
Uses modifiers correctly	15, 16
Uses coordination and subordination effectively	17, 18
Recognizes parallel structure	19, 20
Avoids fragments, comma splices, and fused sentences	21, 22, 23, 24
Uses standard verb forms	25
Avoids inappropriate shifts in verb tense	26, 27
Maintains agreement between subject and verb	28, 29
Maintains agreement between pronoun and antecedent	30
Avoids inappropriate pronoun shifts in person	31, 32
Maintains clear pronoun references	33
Uses proper case forms	34
Uses adjectives and adverbs correctly	35
Uses appropriate degree forms of adjectives and adverbs	36
Uses standard spelling	37
Uses standard punctuation	38, 39
Uses standard capitalization	40

EXIT EXAM #2 ◆ BY QUESTION NUMBER

Ques. No. Skill Tested

1. Identifies a thesis statement or topic sentence
2. Recognizes adequate support provided by generalized and specific evidence
3. Arranges ideas and supporting details in logical patterns
4. Identifies supporting material that is relevant or irrelevant to the thesis statement or topic sentence
5. Identifies a thesis statement or topic sentence
6. Arranges ideas and supporting details in logical patterns
7. Identifies supporting material that is relevant or irrelevant to the thesis statement or topic sentence
8. Recognizes effective transitional devices within the context of a passage
9. Chooses the appropriate word or expression in context
10. Chooses the appropriate word or expression in context
11. Recognizes commonly confused or misused words or phrases
12. Uses modifiers correctly
13. Uses modifiers correctly
14. Uses coordination and subordination effectively
15. Uses coordination and subordination effectively
16. Recognizes parallel structure
17. Recognizes parallel structure
18. Avoids fragments, comma splices, and fused sentences

Ques. No. Skill Tested

19. Avoids fragments, comma splices, and fused sentences
20. Avoids fragments, comma splices, and fused sentences
21. Avoids fragments, comma splices, and fused sentences
22. Uses standard verb forms
23. Avoids inappropriate shifts in verb tense
24. Avoids inappropriate shifts in verb tense
25. Avoids inappropriate shifts in verb tense
26. Maintains agreement between subject and verb
27. Maintains agreement between subject and verb
28. Maintains agreement between subject and verb
29. Maintains agreement between pronoun and antecedent
30. Avoids inappropriate pronoun shifts in person
31. Avoids inappropriate pronoun shifts in person
32. Maintains clear pronoun references
33. Uses proper case forms
34. Uses adjectives and adverbs correctly
35. Uses appropriate degree forms of adjectives and adverbs
36. Uses standard spelling
37. Uses standard punctuation
38. Uses standard punctuation
39. Uses standard punctuation
40. Uses standard capitalization

EXIT EXAM #2 ◆ BY SKILL

Skill Tested	Question Number
Identifies a thesis statement or topic sentence	1, 5
Recognizes adequate support provided by generalized and specific evidence	2
Arranges ideas and supporting details in logical patterns	3, 6
Identifies supporting material that is relevant or irrelevant to the thesis statement or topic sentence	4, 7
Recognizes effective transitional devices within the context of a passage	8
Chooses the appropriate word or expression in context	9, 10
Recognizes commonly confused or misused words or phrases	11
Uses modifiers correctly	12, 13
Uses coordination and subordination effectively	14, 15
Recognizes parallel structure	16, 17
Avoids fragments, comma splices, and fused sentences	18, 19, 20, 21
Uses standard verb forms	22
Avoids inappropriate shifts in verb tense	23, 24, 25
Maintains agreement between subject and verb	26, 27, 28
Maintains agreement between pronoun and antecedent	29
Avoids inappropriate pronoun shifts in person	30, 31
Maintains clear pronoun references	32
Uses proper case forms	33
Uses adjectives and adverbs correctly	34
Uses appropriate degree forms of adjectives and adverbs	35
Uses standard spelling	36
Uses standard punctuation	37, 38, 39
Uses standard capitalization	40

EXIT EXAM #3 ◆ BY QUESTION NUMBER

Ques. No.	Skill Tested	Ques. No.	Skill Tested
1.	Identifies a thesis statement or topic sentence	19.	Avoids fragments, comma splices, and fused sentences
2.	Recognizes adequate support provided by generalized and specific evidence	20.	Avoids fragments, comma splices, and fused sentences
3.	Identifies supporting material that is relevant or irrelevant to the thesis statement or topic sentence	21.	Avoids fragments, comma splices, and fused sentences
4.	Recognizes effective transitional devices within the context of a passage	22.	Uses standard verb forms
		23.	Uses standard verb forms
5.	Identifies a thesis statement or topic sentence	24.	Avoids inappropriate shifts in verb tense
6.	Recognizes adequate support provided by generalized and specific evidence	25.	Avoids inappropriate shifts in verb tense
7.	Arranges ideas and supporting details in logical patterns	26.	Maintains agreement between subject and verb
8.	Recognizes effective transitional devices within the context of a passage	27.	Maintains agreement between subject and verb
9.	Chooses the appropriate word or expression in context	28.	Maintains agreement between subject and verb
10.	Chooses the appropriate word or expression in context	29.	Maintains agreement between pronoun and antecedent
11.	Recognizes commonly confused or misused words or phrases	30.	Avoids inappropriate pronoun shifts in person
12.	Uses modifiers correctly	31.	Avoids inappropriate pronoun shifts in person
13.	Uses modifiers correctly	32.	Maintains clear pronoun references
14.	Uses coordination and subordination effectively	33.	Uses proper case forms
15.	Uses coordination and subordination effectively	34.	Uses adjectives and adverbs correctly
16.	Recognizes parallel structure	35.	Uses appropriate degree forms of adjectives and adverbs
17.	Recognizes parallel structure	36.	Uses standard spelling
18.	Avoids fragments, comma splices, and fused sentences	37.	Uses standard capitalization
		38.	Uses standard punctuation
		39.	Uses standard punctuation
		40.	Uses standard punctuation

EXIT EXAM #3 ◆ BY SKILL

Skill Tested	Question Number
Identifies a thesis statement or topic sentence	1, 5
Recognizes adequate support provided by generalized and specific evidence	2, 6
Arranges ideas and supporting details in logical patterns	7
Identifies supporting material that is relevant or irrelevant to the thesis statement or topic sentence	3
Recognizes effective transitional devices within the context of a passage	4, 8
Chooses the appropriate word or expression in context	9, 10
Recognizes commonly confused or misused words or phrases	11
Uses modifiers correctly	12, 13
Uses coordination and subordination effectively	14, 15
Recognizes parallel structure	16, 17
Avoids fragments, comma splices, and fused sentences	18, 19, 20, 21
Uses standard verb forms	22, 23
Avoids inappropriate shifts in verb tense	24, 25
Maintains agreement between subject and verb	26, 27, 28
Maintains agreement between pronoun and antecedent	29
Avoids inappropriate pronoun shifts in person	30, 31
Maintains clear pronoun references	32
Uses proper case forms	33
Uses adjectives and adverbs correctly	34
Uses appropriate degree forms of adjectives and adverbs	35
Uses standard spelling	36
Uses standard capitalization	37
Uses standard punctuation	38, 39, 40

TRACKING SHEET ◆ WRITING PRACTICE EXIT EXAMS

DIRECTIONS: Every time you take a Practice Exit Exam, you will fill in the number of errors you made for each type of skill. This way, you see which skills you need to practice before you take the real Exit Exam. Look on the back of this sheet for an example of how to complete the sheet.

	Pretest	Practice Exam #1	Practice Exam #2	Practice Exam #3
Capitalization				
Punctuation				
Spelling				
Adjectives and Adverbs				
Pronoun Agreement				
Pronoun Reference				
Pronoun Case				
Pronoun Consistency				
Subject/Verb Agreement				
Shifts in Verb Tense				
Standard Verb Form or Tense				
Fragments, Comma Splices, Run-Ons				
Parallel Structure				
Subordination and Coordination				
Modifiers				
Commonly Confused Words				
Word Choice				
Transitional Devices				
Relevant or Irrelevant Support				
Arranges Ideas into Logical Patterns				
Adequate Support				
Thesis Statement/Topic Sentence				

Part Seven: Answer Keys for Reading

ANSWER KEY TO PRETEST, WORKBOOK EXERCISES, AND EXIT EXAM

PRETEST – READING SKILLS

1.	C	2.	B	3.	C	4.	D	5.	B	6.	C
7.	A	8.	B	9.	A	10.	C	11.	B	12.	A
13.	C	14.	B	15.	A	16.	D	17.	C	18.	A
19.	A	20.	B	21.	D	22.	C	23.	D	24.	D
25.	B	26.	C	27.	C	28.	A	29.	B	30.	D
31.	A	32.	C	33.	C	34.	B	35.	A	36.	C

READING WORKBOOK

CHAPTER 1: CONCEPT SKILLS

1. The Main Idea

1.	A	2.	D	3.	C	4.	C	5.	A
6.	D	7.	B	8.	D	9.	A	10.	C

2. Supporting Details

1.	B	2.	D	3.	A	4.	B	5.	A
6.	C	7.	D	8.	C	9.	B	10.	B

3. Author's Purpose

1.	C	2.	B	3.	D	4.	A	5.	D
6.	D	7.	B	8.	A	9.	C	10.	C

CHAPTER 2: STRUCTURAL SKILLS

1. Patterns of Organization

1.	D	2.	B	3.	A	4.	C	5.	C
6.	D	7.	B	8.	A	9.	C	10.	D
11.	B	12.	A	13.	C	14.	B	15.	D
16.	C	17.	A	18.	B	19.	B	20.	D

2. Relationships *Within* a Sentence

1.	B	2.	D	3.	D	4.	A	5.	C
6.	A	7.	D	8.	B	9.	C	10.	C

3. Relationships *Between* Sentences

1.	D	2.	C	3.	C	4.	B	5.	A
6.	B	7.	D	8.	D	9.	D	10.	A

CHAPTER 3: LANGUAGE SKILLS

1. Word Choice: Context Clues

1.	B	2.	C	3.	D	4.	B	5.	A
6.	D	7.	A	8.	C	9.	B	10.	C

2. Biased Language

1.	D	2.	A	3.	D	4.	C	5.	B
6.	A	7.	C	8.	D	9.	B	10.	B

3. Tone of Passage

1.	C	2.	A	3.	B	4.	A	5.	A
6.	C	7.	B	8.	D	9.	C	10.	A

CHAPTER 4: REASONING SKILLS

1. Fact and Opinion

1.	C	2.	C	3.	B	4.	A	5.	B
6.	A	7.	B	8.	B	9.	A	10.	B

2. Inferences and Conclusions

1.	D	2.	C	3.	B	4.	D	5.	D
6.	A	7.	B	8.	C	9.	B	10.	A
11.	A	12.	C	13.	C	14.	A	15.	B
16.	D	17.	A	18.	B	19.	C	20.	B

3. Assessing Supports for Reasoning and Argument

1.	B	2.	A	3.	C	4.	B	5.	A
6.	D	7.	B	8.	A	9.	B	10.	C

Exit Exam #1 – Reading Skills

1.	A	2.	D	3.	A	4.	D	5.	B	6.	A
7.	A	8.	C	9.	D	10.	B	11.	C	12.	D
13.	A	14.	B	15.	C	16.	A	17.	D	18.	A
19.	C	20.	A	21.	A	22.	D	23.	C	24.	B
25.	C	26.	D	27.	B	28.	A	29.	D	30.	C
31.	B	32.	C	33.	A	34.	D	35.	B	36.	A

Exit Exam #2 – Reading Skills

1.	D	2.	C	3.	A	4.	C	5.	D	6.	B
7.	D	8.	B	9.	A	10.	D	11.	B	12.	B
13.	C	14.	B	15.	A	16.	A	17.	D	18.	B
19.	C	20.	B	21.	C	22.	B	23.	A	24.	C
25.	A	26.	B	27.	B	28.	D	29.	B	30.	C
31.	B	32.	D	33.	A	34.	B	35.	B	36.	A

Exit Exam #3 – Reading Skills

1.	B	2.	C	3.	D	4.	A	5.	B	6.	D
7.	A	8.	B	9.	C	10.	B	11.	B	12.	D
13.	B	14.	A	15.	C	16.	A	17.	C	18.	B
19.	C	20.	D	21.	B	22.	C	23.	A	24.	D
25.	A	26.	D	27.	A	28.	B	29.	C	30.	B
31.	A	32.	D	33.	A	34.	C	35.	B	36.	C

ANSWERS TO READING PRETEST *WITH* EXPLANATIONS

Pretest Answers with Explanations

1. Answer   C

Choices A, B, and D are details and do not cover everything discussed in the passage.

2. Answer   B

The information is organized by the type of carnivorous plant. Active trappers are discussed in paragraph two and passive trappers are discussed in paragraph three. Although some cause-and-effect examples are given, the overall pattern of how the information is presented is by classifying the types of carnivorous plants.

3. Answer   C

The author offers a detailed explanation of how the insects become trapped inside carnivorous plants. The author does more than give a definition; his focus is mostly upon the process that happens after the prey lands on the plant. Choice A is too narrow, dealing only with one type of carnivorous plant, and choice D is incorrect because the passage does not explain all of the effects (how the digestion of the insect helps the plant) of trapping prey.

4. Answer   D

The sentences describe two steps in the process of how a bladderwort traps its prey. It does not compare or contrast the two ideas, nor does it show a relationship of location (spatial order). The second statement doesn't clarify or explain the first.

5. Answer   B

The author supports his claim that carnivorous plants fall into two groups by giving examples of both active trappers and passive trappers and presenting facts about both types of plants.

6. Answer   C

The cause is the prey touching the tactile cells, and the effect is the trap door opening. It does not give an example of the first idea (when the prey touches the tactile cells) nor is it a summary of the process. The relationship is more than just listing facts in random order. In this sentence, the first action causes the second to happen.

7. Answer   A

Objective means an unbiased presentation of the facts. The author does not use emotional language to support the other tones, such as admiring, nostalgic, or reverent.

8. Answer   B

A is incorrect because it infers that the process is complicated, which is an opinion that may not be shared by others. Choice C only refers to one type of active trapper that is discussed in the paragraph. Choice D is incorrect

because the passage does not state that <u>all</u> active trappers have nectar glands.

9. Answer   A

In paragraph one, the author states that active trappers use rapid plant movements to open trap doors or to close traps. Since the Pitcher plant is a passive trapper, and a bladderwort is an active trapper, the pitcher plant would be slower at trapping its prey. Choice B is not discussed. Choice C is not accurate according to the passage. The passage does not state that <u>all</u> passive trappers have small trigger hairs to trap their prey, so D is incorrect.

10. Answer   C

Choice A presents a detail from the passage, not the implied main idea of the entire passage. Choice B does not have enough evidence from the text to support and does not capture the full main idea. Choice D is close, but it is a bit too narrow and does not include all of the information in the paragraph.

11. Answer   B

Choice A is false. The passage states that she studied medical technology in college and learned of numerous incidents of radioactive contamination at the plant. Choice C is false. Most women in the 1970s were traditional homemakers. The last sentence states that women who moved out of the role of homemaker endured a lack of respect. Choice D is not discussed. Choice B reflects Silkwood's efforts to expose worker safety problems at the plant.

12. Answer   A

Choice B was not discussed in the passage. Choice C is false because the passage states that Kerr-McGee knowingly manufactured defective nuclear products. Choice D is incorrect because she was not paid for her efforts to expose Kerr-McGee's unethical practices. A whistle-blower is a person who exposes unethical practices.

13. Answer   C

Paragraph 3 states, "Her **dismissive** treatment by some fellow workers, her employers, and the media also suggested the <u>lack of respect</u> that women had long endured." The other choices do not fit the meaning of the word.

14. Answer   B

This statement is not provable, as in the phrase "suggested the lack of respect," which is the author's interpretation of what her treatment suggested.

15. Answer   A

The author has provided numerous facts about what Karen Silkwood did to challenge one of the most powerful energy corporations in the country.

16. Answer   D
The details of the passage are in chronological (time) order, beginning with her childhood and ending with her death in 1974.

17. Answer   C
The action of her car's being forced off the road caused her death. Therefore, it is a cause-and-effect relationship. If the first event merely came before the second event but did not cause it, then time order would be correct. But in this case, the first event caused the second event to happen.

18. Answer   A
Choice B is too broad and does not focus on the topic of the passage, Karen Silkwood. Choice C is a conclusion that may be drawn from reading the passage, but was not the author's primary purpose in writing the passage. Choice D is a conclusion about one of the details of the passage.

19. Answer   A
Choices B, C, and D are all details that cover only one part of the passage. Choice A is broad enough to include all the information in the passage.

20. Answer   B
The phrase "may be viewed" is the author's own opinion and it is not a provable statement. Facts must be provable.

21. Answer   D
Since the father is nearly totally absent from the home scene, the result is that the children are raised mainly by the mother.

22. Answer   C
Most of the supporting details in this passage show the effects of salarymen's lives. Because they spend long hours at work and are expected to socialize after work, they go to nightclubs and do not spend time at home with their families. Another result is that the children are mainly raised by the mother.

23. Answer   D
The author reports on the research done on salarymen and does not express a judgment either for or against them. The author presents both the negative and the positive aspects of being a salaryman. Therefore, the passage is unbiased.

24. Answer   D
Straightforward is objective. The author has presented facts about salarymen without making judgments. There is no emotional language in the passage.

25. Answer   B
Choice A discusses Japanese boys and does not refer to salarymen. Choices C and D do not support the idea that salarymen work long hours.

26. Answer   C
The reason why salarymen eat dinner only a few times a year with their families is that they typically spend many hours after work at expensive nightclubs.

27. Answer   C
The question asks which conclusion can NOT be drawn, so it is asking for a false statement. Choices A, B, and D are all true based upon the information in the passage. C is correct because it assumes information that is not discussed in the passage. It cannot be inferred from the passage that Japanese mothers do not work outside of their homes.

28. Answer   A
Choice B is a detail because the passage discusses more than just factories. Choice C is a detail but does not cover all the information in the passage. Choice D can be concluded, but it is not the main point the author is making in the passage.

29. Answer   B
The second half of the sentence adds to the first half more information about the same topic. It states two separate facts about the factory system. It also uses a transition, "and."

30. Answer   D
The details of the passage are the effects of industrialization. The main idea is that industrialization caused many problems in society. The author's intent was to show this cause-and-effect relationship, not merely to list the problems during industrialization.

31. Answer   A
The author uses emotional language to describe the "horrid conditions" in early factories, describing them as "miserable places." Therefore, the author is biased against the early factories. Nothing in the passage suggests choice B or C. Choice D is incorrect because the author uses emotional language.

32. Answer   C
Choice C, *believed*, is the only word which makes sense in "workers who suffered accidents were believed to be at fault . . ."

33. Answer   C
The question asks which conclusion can NOT be drawn from the passage, so it is asking for a false statement. Choices A, B, and D are all true conclusions that can be drawn based upon the information in the passage. The passage does not state or imply that industrialization caused a decline in agriculture. Therefore, C is the correct answer.

34. Answer   B
The author is clearly critical of conditions in early factories and living conditions for working families during early industrialization. None of the other words accurately describe the author's tone.

35. Answer   A

The phrase "This situation was guaranteed to produce conflict" is not provable, and "wretched conditions" expresses a judgment or opinion. Choices A, C, and D are all provable statements; therefore, they are facts.

36. Answer   C

The main idea of the passage is that early industrialization had many negative effects on society. In this passage, it was the author's intent to show the negative effects of industrialization: poor working conditions, child labor, and poor health. Choice A is briefly mentioned in the first paragraph but is not explained. Choice B is incorrect because most of the details in the passage are not being used to compare industrialized society to agricultural society. Choice D is too narrow and focuses only on one aspect of the passage.

Note: All answers to diagnostics can be found within each chapter, immediately following the diagnostic.

ANSWERS TO EXERCISES IN THE READING WORKBOOK *WITH* EXPLANATIONS

CHAPTER 1: CONCEPT SKILLS

1. The Main Idea

1. Answer   A

The paragraph explains the reasons youths join gangs, which "contradict popular thinking on this subject."

False Choices

    B   This detail is provided in the introductory paragraph and explains the basis of the findings expressed in the passage.

    C   This is a supporting detail given in the first paragraph.

    D   This definition of street gangs is a paraphrase of the information in sentences 1–3.

2. Answer   D

The details in paragraph 3 support the idea that urban poverty causes individuals to develop a "defiant individualist" personality type. The topic sentence states: "Those who were gang members shared a personality type called a "defiant individualist." The rest of the paragraph provides details to describe this personality type.

False Choices

    A   In paragraph 3, street gang members are not portrayed as victims.

    B   While the passage states that poverty contributes to the development of a distinct personality type, it does not imply that these individuals would be successful if they weren't poor.

    C   As one of the five traits of the "defiant individualist" personality, competitiveness is a supporting detail and cannot be the main idea.

3. Answer   C

The second paragraph builds on the idea expressed in the first paragraph—that the commonly held perceptions about the reasons individuals join street gangs is not true.

False Choices

    A   This is a supporting detail and cannot be the main idea.

    B   This is a generalization that is argued in the paragraph, but it is not the main idea.

    D   This statement is another supporting detail of the paragraph and not the main idea.

4. Answer   C

Each paragraph of the passage gives examples of the First Ladies' activities while their husbands were presidents. The first paragraph introduces the idea that there is more to the job of First Lady than being the hostess at White House dinners. The second paragraph describes the roles of Abigail Adams, Dolly Madison, Edith Galt Wilson, Eleanor Roosevelt, Lady Bird Johnson, Rosalyn Carter, Nancy Reagan, and Barbara Bush. The last paragraph focuses on Hillary Clinton.

False Choices

    A   While this statement may be true, it is not the main idea of the paragraph.

    B   The information in the paragraph does not support the idea that the role of the First Lady has become more important in the past 50 years.

    D   The role of the media in the First Ladies' lives is not the focus of the passage. The only reference to the media is in the first paragraph, which mentions that the media "chronicles every word she speaks and every hairstyle she adopts."

5. Answer   A

Paragraph 2 describes what each of eight different First Ladies contributed. Lady Bird Johnson, Rosalyn Carter, Nancy Reagan, and Barbara Bush picked an issue while Abigail Adams and Dolly Madison counseled their husbands. Edith Galt Wilson and Eleanor Roosevelt had more involvement in helping their husbands run the government.

False Choices

    B   This is a supporting detail in the paragraph, not the main idea of paragraph 2.

    C   This is a supporting detail in the paragraph, not the main idea of paragraph 2.

    D   Not all of the details in the paragraph support this idea.

6. Answer   D

This statement summarizes the last part of the first sentence of the paragraph and is supported by the details.

False Choices
- A   The passage does not describe her as a "model" First Lady, but rather as a woman who held a leadership position.
- B   This is a supporting detail and cannot be the implied idea.
- C   No reference is made to Hillary Clinton's education or its impact on her activities.

7. Answer   B

The main idea of the passage is summarized in the last two sentences of the last paragraph.

False Choices
- A   This is a supporting detail explained in the first sentence of the third paragraph, so it cannot be the main idea of the passage.
- C   This is a generalization that is a misinterpretation of the information provided in the passage.
- D   The only mention of television in the passage is the reference to a 1980s public service advertisement. The scenario is used as an attention-getting device in the introductory paragraph.

8. Answer   D

The statement best explains the idea of paragraph 4.

False Choices
- A   This detail is not expressed in the paragraph. The paragraph states that adolescents who had a positive relationship with their parents would more likely do what their parents did. Therefore, in this positive relationship, if the parents didn't smoke, the adolescent was less likely to smoke.
- B   This statement is too general for the passage.
- C   This statement is the opposite of what is expressed in the passage.

9. Answer   A

This is expressed in the first sentence of the second paragraph and is supported by the details of the paragraph.

False Choices
- B   This sentence is a supporting detail in the paragraph and cannot be the main idea.
- C   The passage supports the idea that adolescents whose parents use drugs or alcohol will probably not copy their parents, unlike the statement that suggests that they "may or may not copy their parents."
- D   This is an opinion that is not supported by the information in the paragraph.

10. Answer   C

The third paragraph does explain the three levels that are affected by observational learning.

False Choices
- A   The passage says that at the level of the group, a person may be "captivated" by people who have characteristics that are attractive to them. This is a supporting detail, not a main idea.
- B   This statement is supplied as supporting evidence in the passage in the second sentence.
- D   This statement is a supporting detail and not the main idea.

2. Supporting Details

1. Answer   B

As stated in paragraph 4, whether ESP is a valid, reliable phenomenon will depend on the results of studies scientifically designed to prove it; if they show there is nothing to it, then ESP will be considered pseudopsychology. These studies are still underway, so ESP has not been completely proved or disproved.

False Choices
- A   To say that ESP is a pseudopsychology is to draw a conclusion not based on evidence from the passage. Pseudopsychology is "superstition or unsupported opinion pretending to be science." The passage states that experiments have not proved or disproved ESP, so ESP cannot yet be considered pseudopsychology.
- C   In the passage, no relationship is made among astrology, palm reading, and ESP.
- D   This statement is not mentioned anywhere in the passage.

2. Answer   D

The author defines pseudopsychology as "superstition" in sentence 5.

False Choices
- A   This is not true. The author states that pseudopsychology "is not a branch of psychology."
- B   No mention is made in the passage that pseudopsychology is a science.
- C   Pseudopsychology is not a study, it is a superstition.

3. Answer   A

In paragraph 4, the author explains that if a person involved in an ESP experiment has an unconscious bias towards a particular color of card, he or she might select that color more often; this would affect the results of the experiment.

False Choices
- B   ESP experiments must be set up properly to avoid bias and expectancy of effects, but whether or not these experiments are difficult to set up is not a supporting detail of the passage.
- C   The passage does not state that ESP experiments have shown that telepathy is largely guesswork.
- D   The passage does not state that telepathy experiments are a waste of time.

4. Answer   B

According to paragraph 4, a "better experiment" would eliminate these two problems. Visible clues could be avoided by putting the receiver and sender in different rooms. Unconscious bias could be avoided by including a control condition in which the receiver is told to guess cards when the receiver is not sending.

False Choices

A   Eliminating guesswork is only one aspect of designing a better experiment.

C   Playing cards are traditionally used in these kinds of experiments. Since the method already exists, it would not contribute to a "better" experiment.

D   Measuring the percentage of times the receiver chooses the correct card has been a method used in telepathy experiments and is not a new concept; therefore, it would not make a "better" experiment.

5. Answer   A

As quoted from the first paragraph in the passage, "the adult is only about the size of a house cat."

False Choices

B   According to the passage, they "look so much alike that even experts can have a difficult time of telling them apart."

C   The ranges of the two species overlap. (line 14)

D   According to lines 31–32, "they are separate species, despite the pronounced similarities in their body form and coloration.

6. Answer   C

The female warns an intruder by "raising her tail, stamping her forefeet, raking the ground with her claws, or even doing a handstand." (lines 7–8)

False Choices

None of the three are mentioned in the passage. Lines 7–8 do not include A, hissing; B, running in circles; or C, swishing her tail.

7. Answer   D

Biologists thought that all spotted skunks were the same species until 1960s studies of their sexual reproduction showed they were two species. (lines 19–21)

False Choices

A and B   Migration patterns and range overlap were not involved in the discovery that the species were different.

C   The passage does not mention any study done with the skunks' potent musk sprays.

8. Answer   C

In line 23, the passage describes the reproductive cycle of the western spotted skunk as including "delayed development."

False Choices

A   The western spotted skunk mates in the late summer and early fall. The blastocyst stays dormant in the female through the winter, and the young are born in May or June.

B   The reproductive cycles occur at different times. The eastern spotted skunk mates in late winter and gives birth between April and July. The western spotted skunk's reproductive cycle is explained in False Choice A.

D   The western spotted skunk's reproductive cycle is longer, not shorter.

9. Answer   B

The eastern and western spotted skunks are interesting because they illustrate "some important concepts about biological species." (lines 3–4)

False Choices

A   This is one aspect of the difference between the two skunks, not the only reason that they are interesting.

C   The passage does not mention anything about these skunks becoming extinct.

D   The markings of these skunks are similar, but it's not the sole reason they are interesting.

10. Answer   B

The most important discovery about the eastern and western spotted skunks is that they are different species. Until the 1960s, biologists thought that they were one species.

False Choices

A   The fact that their habitats overlapped was one of the pieces of information that made biologists think they were the same species.

C   The similarity in the appearance of the eastern and western spotted skunk contributed to the idea that the two were the same species.

D   Information about the western spotted skunk is given in the passage, not about how the eastern spotted skunk defends her young.

3. Author's Purpose

1. Answer   C

The topic sentence of this paragraph indicates that examples of the practical uses of fungi will be given in the paragraph. In fact, four examples are provided.

False Choices

A   The paragraph is not limited to describing foods that are fungi. It also explains that fungi produce antibiotics.

B   The paragraph does not discuss how fungi are used to ripen cheeses. The paragraph's purpose is not to describe a process.

D   No arguments are presented in the paragraph.

2. Answer   B

The first sentence of the passage gives the purpose of the passage: "John Castle's lifestyle gives us a glimpse into how the super-rich live."

False Choices

A   The reader may find his lifestyle appealing, but the passage does not attempt to persuade the reader that Castle's lifestyle is to be envied.

C   The author does not criticize Castle for wasting his money. Instead, he tells us the kinds of things Castle spends money on.

D   There is no attempt to inspire the reader to become wealthy. The reader may be impressed with Castle's wealth by reading about his estate, his ranch, or his yacht.

3. Answer   D

The passage does convince teachers that they must report suspected cases of child abuse and neglect. The first paragraph defines child abuse. The second paragraph informs teachers that they should become familiar with their state's laws. It encourages teachers to file a report. In fact, teachers can be fined or imprisoned if they do not make the report. The concluding paragraph reinforces the point about reporting child abuse, applying the "reasonable person" standard.

False Choices

A   Child abuse is defined in the first paragraph, but the entire passage is not definition.

B   This is a supporting detail covered in the second paragraph. It notes that each state has its own requirements, so teachers should become familiar with those in their state.

C   The passage does not discuss indicators of child abuse.

4. Answer   A

The passage contrasts cultural differences in criticizing in public. Competitive cultures like the United States readily criticize, while collectivist cultures such as Japan find public criticism uncomfortable.

False Choices

B   The passage does not give instruction about how to criticize effectively.

C   As a result of reading the passage, the reader may see that there are vast cultural differences regarding criticism and therefore may gain respect for those differences; however, persuasion is not the purpose of the paragraph.

D   As a byproduct of the discussion of the cultural differences in public criticism, the passage explains what people from different cultures may feel when they interpret criticism through their own cultural filter.

5. Answer   D

The passage illustrates the pubic roles of eight First Ladies. It begins with Abigail Adams and ends with Hillary Rodham Clinton.

False Choices

A   The readers may infer contrasts among the First Ladies as they read the passage. Some of the First Ladies were more directly involved in their husbands' career while others chose a particular issue to work on.

B   This is not a process paragraph explaining how the job of the First Lady is done.

C   The First Ladies in this passage were selected for their contributions; however, no attempt is made to convince the reader that they were feminists. The word "feminist" is not even mentioned in the passage. True, these were strong, capable women; however, assuming they were feminists would be the reader's opinion.

6. Answer   D

The purpose of the passage is clearly stated in the first sentence: "President Truman's decision to order the atomic bombings on the Japanese cities of Hiroshima and Nagasaki has been the subject of intense historical debate."

False Choices

A   The passage does not describe the effects of the atomic bombs on the people in the two Japanese cities.

B   Because the passage argues both sides of the debate, the reasons for dropping the atomic bombs is given; however, the paragraph is not solely about causes.

C   Both sides of the debate are presented without an attempt to persuade the reader one way or the other.

7. Answer   B

This passage explains the problems of single parenthood as stated in the first sentence of the passage: "A single parent may experience a variety of problems." Meeting the child's emotional needs, providing proper supervision, financial difficulties, and unmet emotional and sexual needs are examples.

False Choices

A   The passage does not argue that single parenthood has disadvantages.

C   Although the problems may make children's lives challenging, the passage does not persuade the reader that the children are suffering.

D   The passage presents the problems for parents, some of which affect the children, but the focus of the passage is not on the effects of divorce on children.

8. Answer   A

The passage clearly classifies the ineffective, harmful types of quick diets people try. The purpose is stated in the last sentence of the first paragraph: "This attitude results in choosing quick-weight-loss diets that are not effective and may be harmful."

False Choices

B   Certainly the information shared in the passage will persuade the reader that crash diets are harmful, but this is not the purpose.

C   In telling the reader about the different types of crash diets, the passage describes each one as a means of support.

D   At the end of the passage, the author suggests the proper way to lose weight in lines 18–19: lose weight slowly, eat properly and in moderation, and exercise.

9. Answer   C

The first sentence of this passage gives its purpose as contrast: "The dramatic difference between respective burial rites."

False Choices

A   The passage does not attempt to give the details behind the Egyptians' belief in the afterlife. Their beliefs are reflected in their burial rites.

B   The passage mentions that the pyramids were the core of the nobility's city of the dead as a supporting detail.

D   The tombs of the pharaohs are briefly described in supporting details in the passage.

10. Answer   C

The passage gives the reasons individuals join gangs. This information is a result of research done by an anthropologist who studied nearly forty street gangs in New York, Los Angeles, and Boston.

False Choices

A   The passage does not attempt to discourage youths from joining a gang.

B   The belief that all gang members come from homes with no authority figure is disproved by the information presented in the second paragraph of the passage. The study showed that equal numbers of gang members came from intact families. No attempt at argument is made.

D   The last paragraph defines the "defiant individualist" as the personality type gang members share. This description provides supporting detail for the main idea of the paragraph and is not the purpose of the passage.

CHAPTER 2: STRUCTURAL SKILLS

1. Patterns of Organization

1. Answer   D

The passage clearly states that it will provide suggestions for balancing work and school.

False Choices

A   The passage does not summarize the problems of a working student.

B   This passage is not organized around the reasons for attending school full-time rather than working and studying. The issue is not addressed at all.

C   Getting along with supervisors and coworkers is not a topic of this passage.

2. Answer   B

The passage explains that slavery was based on three factors: debt, crime, and war and conquest.

False Choices

A   One of the supporting examples is that the first people to be enslaved through warfare were women. This detail is a part of the war and conquest factor.

C   Most of the discussion is based on pre-modern forms of slavery. There is no contrast between the two in the passage.

3. Answer   A

The passage gives an extended definition of "cyberliteracy." Extended definition passages use a variety of methods to explain a term, such as example, contrast, cause and effect, process, and so on.

False Choices

B   Part of the passage contrasts online and written communication, but contrast is not the organizational pattern. Written communications, such as letters, give the writer a chance to think about what he or she wants to say. In contrast, electronic "discourse" is quick, more like oral communication.

C   Critical thinking is discussed to help define cyberliteracy. Electronic literacy requires that we understand that communication in the online word is different; it is neither purely print nor purely oral.

D   The passage does not tell how to become cyberliterate.

4. Answer   C

The passage offers examples of the forms of entertainment in the Roman Empire. The people enjoyed such things as chariot races and gladiator combats to the death. The spectacle of feeding humans to wild beasts was commonplace.

False Choices
  A   The passage is not organized around effects.
  B   One form of entertainment was the gladiatorial combats. This fact is used as one of the supporting examples.
  D   The passage does not attempt to analyze the Romans' preference for sadism and voyeurism in their entertainment.

5. Answer   C
The second paragraph explains that the Romans uninhibitedly enjoyed watching people being killed, either in gladiator combats or by beasts. These forms of entertainment were sadistic and voyeuristic.

False Choices
  A   In the second paragraph, the author makes the point that the Romans would have been "mystified" by the "anxieties people feel today about the make-believe violence in the movies and on television." However, that is a supporting point, not the pattern of organization of the paragraph.
  B   The paragraph gives examples of sadistic entertainment, but it does not define the term.
  D   The paragraph is not organized by describing Hollywood gladiator movies.

6. Answer   D
The topic sentence of the paragraph alerts the reader that the paragraph will describe a process: "Nonflowing bodies of water such as lakes become contaminated in stages."

False Choices
  A   The second sentence of the paragraph lists the types of chemical pollutants, but that is a supporting detail.
  B   The growth of algae is one of the stages of contamination. It is one part of the overall process explained in the paragraph.
  C   The paragraph does not give a definition of water pollution although it explains how nonflowing bodies of water become polluted.

7. Answer   B
The paragraph offers an explanation of panic disorder as an example of one type of anxiety disorder.

False Choices
  A   Agoraphobia is discussed toward the end of the paragraph, but it is not contrasted with panic attacks. The point made is that people who have panic attacks may become afraid to leave the house (agoraphobia).
  C   The paragraph does not discuss strategies recommended for dealing with panic attacks. The second paragraph explains how some people try to change their behavior to try to avoid future attacks.

  D   No causes of panic attacks are provided in the paragraph.

8. Answer   A
This passage gives examples of what people do to avoid or minimize their panic attacks by changing their behavior.

False Choices
  B   The second paragraph does not define panic disorder.
  C   No steps for treatment are covered in this paragraph.
  D   The paragraph describes ways people may go about changing their behavior to minimize the chance of having more attacks. However, the paragraph does not contrast them.

9. Answer   C
This passage provides an extended definition of plagiarism. The first paragraph gives the formal definition. Paragraph two provides an example. The third paragraph explains the possible effects of plagiarism and tells why it is a serious offense.

False Choices
  A   Analysis of a situation in which plagiarism occurs is not the organizational pattern of the passage. This is accomplished in paragraph two.
  B   The paragraph is not developed by listing.
  D   Paragraph two explains that you can reproduce parts of a paper you find on the Web without permission under copyright and fair use guidelines; however, this is a supporting detail in an example of plagiarism. The organizational pattern is not a description of the process of using information from the Web or any other process.

10. Answer   D
The third paragraph gives the reasons why plagiarism is a serious infraction. The topic sentence indicates this: "Plagiarism is a serious infraction in most settings." Plagiarism violates your obligation to yourself to be truthful, your obligation to society to produce accurate information, and your obligation to other students and researchers.

False Choices
  A   One effect of plagiarism on students is given in the paragraph as a supporting detail.
  B   The paragraph gives the reasonable criteria for ethical decision making. These are supporting details within the paragraph. Ethical decision making is not defined.
  C   The paragraph is not organized by contrast.

11. Answer   B
During the seventeenth and eighteenth centuries, women conducted the process of childbirth. This passage gives examples of their roles in that process.

False Choices

  A   The third paragraph offers a religious reason to explain pain in childbirth. This is a supporting detail in a discussion of the use of alcohol and no painkillers.

  C   The end of the fourth paragraph contrasts the convalescent period of women from well-to-do families and women from poorer families. This is a supporting detail.

  D   No dangers of childbirth are described in the passage.

12. Answer   A

Midwives assisted in childbirth, not doctors. The paragraph describes midwives with respect to their ages, their value, and their skills.

False choices

  B   No attempt is made to argue the advantages of midwives over doctors. The paragraph makes the point that doctors did not assist in childbirth.

  C   Martha Ballard's skills are offered as a supporting detail in the paragraph to illustrate that midwives had a lot of experience.

  D   The paragraph does not explain how the midwife assists a delivery.

13. Answer   C

The first sentence of the passage is the thesis, which indicates the contrast: "Deborah Tannen, sociologist and author, explains the differences in the listening behavior of men and women."

False Choices

  A   Illustration is used as support for the contrasts made.

  B   This point is only one of many supporting details in the discussion of contrasts between men and women.

  D   Tannen says that men communicate with men and women in the same way. A man's goal is to obtain respect and to show his knowledge, and he prefers to dominate a conversation. The author does not focus her discussion on how male listening behavior affects women.

14. Answer   B

In the first paragraph, the author contrasts the different listening cues men and women use. Women use more listening cues and let the other person know they are paying attention; on the other hand, men use fewer listening cues, interrupt more, and often change the topic to one they know more about.

False Choices

  A   The paragraph does not give examples of how men do not listen to women; it contrasts their listening behaviors.

  C   The paragraph does not explain the listening process women use to get close to a person.

  D   No mention of male disrespect for female conversational patterns is made in the paragraph.

15. Answer   D

The first paragraph provides background about the Columbine shootings; however, the rest of the passage analyzes Harris's and Klebold's friendship to understand their "horrific actions."

False Choices

  A   No attempt is made to provide the details of the shootings. The first paragraph merely mentions that a dozen students and one teacher died.

  B   The effects of these murders are not the primary organizational pattern. In the first paragraph, the author provides his opinion of the effect: "a school shooting of such immense proportions occurred which radically, if not permanently, altered public thinking and debate about student safety and security." (lines 1–3)

  C   In the second paragraph, the author explains that Harris and Klebold "plotted and planned, colluded and conspired." He adds that they amassed weapons, strategized, and made final preparations. These details of their preparations support the discussion of their efforts to feel important, but this process is not the organizational pattern of the passage.

16. Answer   C

The paragraph is a description of the process the fireflies use to signal mates. Each species has a specific pattern of flashes that are meant to lead the male to the female. Most females stop flashing after they mate.

False Choices

  A   An explanation of these patterns supplies necessary supporting details in the overall description of the process.

  B   At the end of the paragraph, the author explains that in a few species, mated females will continue to flash and attract males of other species. Then she "grabs and eats him." This information is provided as supporting detail for the description of the process.

  D   The paragraph does explain that the different species of fireflies flash in different patterns and colors. However, these details help to explain the process.

17. Answer   A

This passage explains the effects of some of the well-known quick-weight-loss diets, such as very-low-calorie diets, liquid-protein diets, and crash diets.

False Choices
- B   The passage does classify the types of diets, but the emphasis is on their effects.
- C   Paragraph 5 discusses the problems with prescription drugs. These are supporting details.
- D   No attempt is made to contrast any of the diets described. Each is discussed separately to establish its effects.

18. Answer   B

The third paragraph does, indeed, describe the effects of very-low-calorie diets. Such effects are metabolic imbalances, water and lean protein loss, and slowing of metabolism.

False Choices
- A   The paragraph explains the effects, not the process.
- C   A brief definition is provided in the first sentence of the paragraph, but the paragraph is not organized by definition.
- D   The reader could infer that very-low-calorie diets are harmful, but the passage does not argue against them.

19. Answer   B

The passage presents both sides of the argument regarding Truman's decision to use atomic bombs on Hiroshima and Nagasaki.

False Choices
- A   As part of the argument of Truman's defenders, reasons the bombings ended the war are given. (lines 9–10)
- C   Time order is not the organizational pattern of the passage.
- D   The passage is not organized around causes for dropping atomic bombs, but some of the reasons emerge within the arguments presented.

20. Answer   D

This paragraph is organized by supporting a generalization with examples. The topic sentence states that "fungi have a number of practical uses for humans."

False Choices
- A   The paragraph does not use process to organize its information.
- B   Fungi is not defined in the paragraph, and definition is not used as an organizational pattern.
- C   While the overall pattern is example, classification is used in the supporting details.

2. Relationships Within a Sentence

1. Answer   B

The dependent clause that begins the sentence sets up the cause, and the independent clause gives the effect. One group of people conquering another is the cause; the effect was the enslavement of some of the vanquished.

False Choices
- A   No contrast is established. Note the absence of words like "however," "on the other hand," and "in contrast."
- C   Process deals with steps or methods within a procedure and does not apply here.
- D   Words such as "in conclusion" or "finally" would be used in a summary, but they are not used in the sentence.

2. Answer   D

According to the passage, when one group conquered another, some of those conquered were enslaved. Women were the first group enslaved through warfare. The sentence lists the qualities for which women were valued as slaves.

False Choices
- A   The sentence does not summarize. Note that words such as "in conclusion," "in short," and "in summary" are not used.
- B   Addition is close to listing because every new item is an addition, but addition is not limited to listing. A list is a type of addition, so listing is more specific and a better choice.
- C   "Specifically" and "thus" are words used in sentences that clarify ideas.

3. Answer   D

The sentence expresses a cause-and-effect chain of events. The algae feed on inorganic pollutants (cause), which increases their growth (effect), and slime covers the water (effect).

False Choices
- A   Spatial order describes how something is arranged in space, which does not apply in this sentence.
- B   The sentence mentions the types of inorganic pollutants the algae eat; however, the pattern of the sentence is cause-and-effect.
- C   Addition is usually indicated by "also," "in addition," and "furthermore." None of these words are present in the sentence.

4. Answer   A

This sentence defines cyberliteracy. It contains the term "cyberliteracy" (class), "an electronic literacy" (differentia; that which differentiates it from other kinds of literacy).

False Choices
- B   With words like "combines" and "and," the sentence does have elements of addition, but the sentence uses the definition form.
- C   The effect of cyberliteracy is that it "changes how we read, speak, think, and interact with others." This effect is a part of the definition, which helps to clarify the term.

D   Words such as "in conclusion" and "finally" are clues that the sentence is a summary. This sentence does not summarize.

5. Answer   C

The sentence explains that men communicate with women the same way they do with other men. The sentence pattern is set up to be a comparison. Note the use of "the same way" as an indication that items are being compared.

False Choices
A   The phrases "for example" and "for instance" are used to indicate examples; in the sentence, information is compared rather than added.
B   The sentence does not show a cause-and-effect relationship. "If," "therefore," "as a result," and "so" are examples of words that are often used to express cause and effect.
D   Clarification involves an explanation of a point made, in this exercise, within a sentence. No clarification is expressed in the sentence.

6. Answer   A

The sentence begins with the transition "In addition," which alerts the reader that new information is being added. The sentence explains that midwives did other things "in addition" to assisting in childbirth, such as attending baptisms and burials of infants.

False Choices
B   Time is not an element of this sentence.
C   Listing is similar to addition; it is a type of addition. However, addition is the best choice because of the introductory phrase, which sets up the pattern for addition: "In addition to assisting childbirth."
D   The sentence does not summarize or draw a conclusion.

7. Answer   D

The prepositional phrase "After delivery," which begins the sentence, indicates time order. The rest of the sentence explains what happens after the mother delivers her child.

False Choices
A   There is no cause-and-effect relationship in the sentence. A banquet for the new mother was not an effect of her delivering her child.
B   The sentence does not provide a summary.
C   The relationship of ideas within this sentence is not addition.

8. Answer   B

The first part of the sentence makes the point that the boys' friendship gave them "what was otherwise missing from their lives." The rest of the sentence explains and clarifies what that means by providing more specific in-

formation—"they felt special, they gained a sense of belonging, they were united against the world."

False Choices
A   No comparisons are made in the sentence. Words that show comparison such as "in comparison," "similarly," or "in the same way" would not make sense if placed in the sentence.
C   The first part of the sentence does not contrast, or show a difference between, the second part of the sentence.
D   Time is not addressed in the sentence.

9. Answer   C

The sentence sets up a contrast between fireflies' flashing patterns. The first part of the sentence, which is an independent clause, explains that some fireflies flash more often than others or during different hours. The second part of the sentence is a dependent clause beginning with "while"; this word indicates a contrast. "Other species give fewer but longer flashes."

False Choices
A   A sentence of comparison shows similarities. This sentence shows differences.
B   No new information is added in this sentence.
D   Process deals with steps of methods within a procedure that does not apply.

10. Answer   C

Spatial order connects the ideas within this sentence. In the first part of the sentence, the reader is told that a causeway linked each pyramid to a temple. The second part of the sentence explains that a building was located "adjacent" to the pyramid.

False Choices
A   The sentence is not a simple list.
B   The locations of pyramids and accompanying buildings are described in the sentence, not time order.
D   The use of "and" within the sentence does suggest addition; however, descriptions such as "a processional causeway linked each pyramid to a temple" and "adjacent to the pyramid" clearly indicate spatial order.

3. Relationships Between Sentences

1. Answer   D

The first event ("inmates experience uncertainty and fear") causes the second event ("Therefore, they avoid contact with other prisoners and guards").

False Choices
A   The second sentence does not summarize the first.
B   There is no comparison of similarities between the two sentences.

C. Despite the fact that a process transition is used at the beginning of the first sentence ("First"), the author is showing a cause-and-effect relationship, not steps in a process.

2. Answer   C

The first sentence makes a point. The second sentence explains what the "partnership" means in more detail.

False Choices

A   There is no comparison of similarities between the first and second sentence.

B   The events in the first sentence do not cause the events in the second sentence to happen.

D   The second sentence does more than just restate the same idea—it explains the first idea more clearly with detail.

3. Answer   C

False Choices

A   Even though there is a difference in the amount of freight described in the first sentence and in the second sentence, the transition word "Later" indicates that the author is showing that as time went on, the amount of freight transported increased.

B   The second sentence does not provide an example of what is discussed in the first sentence.

D   Because of the dates and the transition word "Later," the author is trying to emphasize the progress of shipping over a period of time, rather than just giving additional information.

4. Answer   B

The first sentence describes what motivates people. The second sentence begins with the addition transition "moreover," indicating the author wishes to add more information to the point that was made in the first sentence.

False Choices

A   The second sentence does not provide an example of the first.

C   There is no cause-and-effect relationship between the ideas or events described in the two sentences.

D   The second sentence does not show a difference (contrast) between the ideas in the first.

5. Answer   A

The first sentence makes a general point about needs and how they will push you to reach a particular goal. The second sentence provides an example of one type of need: hunger.

False choices

B.   The second sentence does not summarize the information in the first one.

C.   There are no terms or words defined in either sentence.

D.   The second sentence does not compare any similarities to the first.

6. Answer   B

The second sentence describes what will happen if the female skunk's warnings are not heeded. The effect is described in the second sentence: she will spray odor with considerable accuracy.

False Choices

A   The second sentence does not show a contrast (difference) to the information in the first sentence.

C   The second sentence is not an example of what the first sentence is describing; it shows the effect of the skunk's warnings when they are not heeded.

D   The two sentences do not show similarities.

7. Answer   D

The second sentence shows the similarity between the two species by describing their similar appearance. Notice the transition word "both."

False Choices

A   The second sentence does more than just add information; it shows how the two species are alike in color and markings.

B   The second sentence does not give an example of the first.

C   The second sentence does not summarize what is in the first.

8. Answer   D

The time clues in these sentences show that the author is presenting a sequence of events: during the winter months, the blastocysts remain dormant, then in spring they resume growth.

False Choices

A.   The second sentence does more than add information; it presents the information in the order that it occurs.

B.   The second sentence does not restate the first.

C.   There are no terms defined in either sentence.

9. Answer   D

The first sentence states in the conclusion what Andrews and her colleagues found. The second sentence clarifies and specifies that conclusion by citing what adolescents who had a positive relationship with their mothers did in regard to cigarette use or nonuse.

False Choices

A.   The second sentence does more than just add information; it provides a specific example of the conclusion stated in the first sentence.

B.   The second sentence is neither a cause nor an effect of the ideas described in the first.

C. The first sentence is not a generalization. It is a specific finding of this study. The second sentence then goes on to clarify what the first one says.

10. Answer   A

The first sentence makes a general point. The second sentence explains what this means in more specific terms.

False Choices

B. Even though there is contrast in the second sentence, the question is asking for the relationship between the first and second sentences, not just within the second sentence. Remember that the relationship within one single sentence may not be the same as the relationship between two different sentences.

C. The second sentence does not show a cause or effect of the first one.

D. The second sentence does not summarize the information in the first one. The second sentence is much more detailed than the first.

CHAPTER 3: LANGUAGE SKILLS

1. Word Choice: Context Clues

NOTE: The explanatory answers will look a little different in this section. You will be provided with the definition of the underlined word from the question and, if needed, of the correct choice.

If you chose an incorrect option, you should look up the meaning of that word. Use this as an opportunity to develop your vocabulary and dictionary skills.

1. Answer   B

"Gravitate" means to be drawn to or attracted to something or someone. The sentence points out that future teachers who are not fond of any particular academic subject may be more attracted to teaching the lower grades. "Be attracted" was provided as a defnition.

2. Answer   C

"Dispel" means to cause to go away, to remove. The author of the passage attempts to remove several myths about teaching. "Remove" is a synonym.

3. Answer   D

"Incompetent" means without the skill or talent to do something; not qualified or suited for a purpose; not doing a good job; or having *inadequate* skills for the job.

4. Answer   B

"Prevalent" means widely or commonly accepted or practiced. Candidates use television as the most common method to reach voters. "Common" is a synonym.

5. Answer   A

"Manipulate" means to influence, manage, use, or *control* to one's advantage by artful or indirect means. Polit-

ical candidates attempt to control the images they want presented to the public through advertising and image building. "Control" is a synonym.

6. Answer   D

"Interplay" means a reciprocal (shared by both sides) action or reaction; interaction. Campaign coverage is an interaction between hard news and the human interest angle. "Interaction" is a synonym.

7. Answer   A

"Habitable" means fit to live in, *livable*. The passage discusses Africa's geography. The savannas (grassy plains) are the areas where people can live, as opposed to the jungle or desert. "Livable" is a synonym.

8. Answer   C

"Interspersed" means placed or mixed among other things; *scattered*. "Scattered" is a synonym.

9. Answer   B

"Humus" is a brown or black organic substance consisting of partially or wholly decayed vegetable or animal matter that provides nutrients for plants and increases the soil's ability to retain water. In the sentence, "or organic matter" follows the word "humus" and provides a context clue.

10. Answer   C

"Erosion" means the wearing away of material from the earth's surface by the action of water and wind. "Washing away" describes the effect of the torrential rains on soil.

2. Biased Language

1. Answer   D

The first item in the list of the passage's concluding sentence clearly states the author's bias for losing weight slowly.

False Choices

A   The author is biased against taking prescription drugs for weight loss because of evidence that they could cause heart damage.

B   The author is biased against the theory that a liquid-protein diet will control insulin levels and thus burn fat because no research supports this.

C   The author does not express an opinion on using prescription drugs, but he points out the fact that they can have harmful effects.

2. Answer   A

This paragraph describes the harmful effects of very-low-calorie diets, which can result in "serious" metabolic imbalances.

False Choices

B   The author believes in moderating food choices: "eat properly and in moderation."

C   The passage mentions that obese and overweight individuals resort to harmful diets; however, the author does not show a bias towards obesity.

D   The author expresses bias in the last sentence. Notice the judgment word "best."

3. Answer   D

The author believes that the plea-bargaining system "saves the state the time and money that would otherwise be spent on a trial." He is against spending money on trials.

False Choices

A   The author does not show a bias against live television trial coverage. He says that most cases do not go to trial. "Highly publicized trials are dramatic, but rare."

B   The author says that 90 percent of all cases are settled with plea bargaining. The defendant pleads guilty to a lesser crime. The author is not biased against this. He feels that it saves the state time and money and lets defendants plead guilty to a lesser charge.

C   The author makes no comment about the verdict of the O. J. Simpson murder trial.

4. Answer   C

The author is in favor of plea bargaining. He feels that it saves the state time and money and lets defendants plead guilty to a lesser charge.

False Choices

A   The author does not express a bias for or against television's portrayal of courts and trials. He comments that they are dramatic and not realistic.

B   No bias is expressed towards police and detective shows on television. The author says that television's portrayal of courts and trials is as unrealistic as police and detective shows.

D   The author is against trial by jury due to the expense.

5. Answer   B

The author expresses a bias for considering caffeine a drug, as stated in the last sentence of the introductory paragraph: "Nonetheless, it is a drug and should be recognized as one that can lead to health problems."

False Choices

A   According to the author, eating chocolate and drinking coffee and cola cannot be considered drug abuse; however, the author is not in favor of ingesting these substances if they are sought out to produce a caffeine high.

C   The author is biased against using caffeine to produce a "high."

D   The author is stating an opinion, that caffeine should be considered a drug.

6. Answer   A

The author is biased against employers' asking unlawful questions during an interview.

False Choices

B   The author does not express an opinion about answering direct questions. He says that if a person is confronted by unlawful questions, he or she should answer using the gentle method first. If that doesn't work, then the person should use a direct method of responding.

C   The passage does not mention closed questions.

D   It is legal for an employer to ask about whether the interviewee meets the legal age requirements of the job and whether he or she can provide proof of age. The author is not biased against legal questions.

7. Answer   C

The author is in favor of developing strategies to deal with unlawful questions.

False Choices

A   The author states that it is not a good idea to immediately tell the interviewer that he or she is asking an unlawful question because the interviewer may not be aware of the legality of various questions.

B   The author does not suggest that a person should answer an unlawful question to get a job. This is not addressed in the passage.

D   The author does not suggest that a person turn an employer in.

8. Answer   D

In this passage, the author is biased against hate sites. The reader can infer this from the comments made in the passage. For example, he says "Never before has there been such an intensive way for depraved people to gather and reinforce their prejudices and hatred."

False Choices

A   The author is not opposed to people's expressing opinions on the Internet. He is against people with prejudicial attitudes who speak and act out.

B   The author does not discuss penalties for creators of hate sites in this passage.

C   The author is using emotional language and clearly expresses opinion. This passage is very biased.

9. Answer   B

The author is in favor of unique experiences. He says that "predictability washes away spontaneity, changing the quality of our lives."

False Choices

A   The author feels that packaged travel tours are standardized and do not produce unique, spontaneous experiences.

C   The author is biased against *USA Today* news reporting because it gives "short, bland, unanalytic pieces" of information.

D   McDonald's is used as an example of the standardization of everyday life, which the author is biased against.

10. Answer   B

The author is biased against the standardization of everyday life. It causes predictability in life, which he feels changes the quality of our lives for the worse.

False Choices

A   The author says that shopping malls are another example of the standardization of our lives, which he is biased against; however, he does not express a bias against shopping in general.

C   The author is not against hamburgers; however, he does not like the "robotlike assembly of food" offered by McDonald's.

D   According to the author, "efficiency brings dependability." It also lowers prices. However, the author feels that it comes at a cost, which "washes away spontaneity."

3. Author's Tone

1. Answer   C

The tone of the passage is critical. The author criticizes the way our lives are being McDonaldized—made standard and predictable. For example, he states, "Predictability washes away spontaneity, changing the quality of our lives."

False Choices

A   Nothing in the passage is humorous.

B   In a way, the tone suggests pessimism. The author seems resigned to the fact that our social destiny is to be packaged. However, the overriding tone of the passage is critical.

D   The passage does not offer a sense of remembrance, of looking back to another time.

2. Answer   A

This passage provides information by explaining how to balance work and school.

False Choices

B   The author does not give the names of respected sources or significant statistics. Instead the tone is familiar and helpful.

C   Cautionary means to warn or beware and may even imply that the reader should change an action or behavior. Although the passage gives suggestions, they are not presented as a warning.

D   Sarcastic implies a cruel or mocking tone. The writer gives the information in a helpful way.

3. Answer   B

For the most part, the passage explains the mating habits of the different species of fireflies in an objective tone. The information is scientific and neutral with the exception of the subjective description of a species of firefly referred to as a "femme fatale."

False Choices

A   The passage may be interesting, but it is not funny.

C   The author is not negative or critical in his description of the material.

D   No techniques are used to establish an argumentative tone.

4. Answer   A

The passage presents the practical uses of fungi and is written in a neutral tone.

False Choices

B   Respectful is an emotional, subjective treatment and does not apply.

C   The author does not use excited, active language in the description.

D   The reader may be bored with the topic, but the tone is not boring. It is filled with relevant and interesting details, especially for someone who is interested in the topic.

5. Answer   A

Cautionary means to warn or beware and may even imply that the reader should change an action or behavior. The passage explains what can happen to a student or a researcher if he or she plagiarizes. It explains why plagiarism is such a serious offense.

False Choices

B   Defiance is an attitude that shows lack of fear or respect. No defiant language is used.

C   The term "annoyed" means to show mild anger, which does not apply to this passage.

D   The subject described in the passage does not evoke sadness.

6. Answer   C

In this passage, the author presents one side of an argument in a neutral way. He does not agree or disagree with the arguments made by Truman's critics.

False Choices

A   The author does not use a complaining tone.

B   The tone of the passage is not passionate but consistent with an objective presentation of information.

D   No attempt is made to be humorous.

7. Answer   B

"Tragic" accurately describes the tone of the passage, which graphically describes the events of the fatal shootings. Notice the emotional language in the first sentence.

False Choices

A   While the event caused sadness to those in Littleton, Colorado, it also touched hearts across the United States, but the passage does not use subjective words to create a sad tone.

C   The author does not use excited, active language.

D   There is nothing flattering about the description of Harris and Klebold or their crimes.

8. Answer   D

The writers of The Declaration of Independence knew they were composing an important document. This declaration established the original thirteen colonies as free and independent states no longer under the rule of Great Britain. They chose formal language to emphasize the importance and seriousness of the document.

False Choices

A   Reverent implies worshipful and does not apply to the passage.

B   Instead of looking back and remembering, the words in the passage look ahead to the "Acts and Things which Independent States may of right do."

C   The Declaration of Independence is a strong statement announcing the dissolution of all political connections between the colonies and England. Its words are stated with conviction.

9. Answer   C

This excerpt from President Bush's speech on September 11, 2001, was intended to inspire the people of the United States—to assure them that the terrorists have failed, that their acts "shatter steel but they cannot dent the steel of American resolve."

False Choices

A   The passage is not objective or impartial. Bush's language is strong and forceful.

B   Bush's language could also be described as passionate and emotional, yet the message was intended to unite the people of this country.

D   Parts of the passage were described graphically; however, overall, the tone goes beyond this.

10. Answer   A

The author describes the Tiwi custom of "covering up" the elderly women. The passage is filled with graphic, descriptive details and is written in a narrative style.

False Choices

B   The term "annoyed" means to show mild anger, which does not apply to this passage.

C   The passage does not use argumentative language.

D   The idea of "covering up" evokes an emotional response in the reader, but the tone of the passage is quieter.

CHAPTER 4: REASONING SKILLS

1. Fact and Opinion

1. Answer   C

The sentence is a generalization, as indicated by "even more spectacularly." This point is supported in the passage by the factual information in the sentences that follow it.

False Choices: Each of the other options is a statement that can be verified.

A and B can be verified by checking shipping records in 1816, 1817, 1840, and 1841.

D can be verified by checking prices of coffee in Cincinnati and in New Orleans in the years 1816 and 1818.

2. Answer   C

This statement is an opinion that speculates why Mendel chose to study garden peas. The word "probably" does not indicate that the point was verified.

False Choices: Each of the other options is a statement that can be verified.

A, B, and D can be researched and verified by reading about Gregor Mendel's life and discoveries.

3. Answer   B

The statement expresses the opinion of the author in his assumption that people are ignorant of African geography and environment. In addition, he assumes that people have misconceptions about African culture and history. The statement is the thesis of the passage, and the author supports his opinion with factual information.

4. Answer   A

This is a fact that can be verified by researching mosquitoes and tsetse flies as transmitters of diseases to humans.

5. Answer   B

This is an opinion that is not supported by fact. "Many Americans" is a generalization.

6. Answer   A

The sentence offers a statistic that can be checked by researching the number of votes that are submitted by mail in California.

7. Answer   B

This sentence sets up a cause-and-effect relationship that speculates what would happen if everyone voted electronically. The words "if," "may be," and "could" show that the sentence expresses an opinion.

8. Answer   B

A speculative cause-and-effect relationship is established in this sentence, indicating that an opinion is being given. No data is offered to support this claim.

9. Answer   A

This statement is a fact that can be verified by going to the Federal Election Commission website and locating the National Mail Voter Registration Form.

10. Answer   A

It is a fact that can be verified by checking to see whether these men made this argument when presenting their case to the Supreme Court.

2. Inferences and Conclusions

1. Answer   D

The conclusion that women from different social classes experienced different post-childbirth treatment is supported by details in the last paragraph. Regarding choice A, there is no mention in the passage as to whether or not midwives had children of their own. As for letter B, we know that skilled midwives received certain considerations, such as housing, but there is no indication as to their salaries. Letter C is false since we do not know why doctors did not typically deliver babies at that time. We only know that they did not.

2. Answer   C

The word "skilled," which means good at one's job, suggests that there weren't many midwives that were skilled or had years of experience delivering babies.

False Choices

- A   The abilities of doctors are not discussed. The passage explains that most women were assisted by midwives, not doctors.
- B   The use of medication was not considered a skill. The prevailing belief at that time was that the pain women experienced in childbirth was "God's punishment for Eve's sin of eating the forbidden fruit in the Garden of Eden." Therefore, women were offered alcohol to ease childbirth pain.
- D   Midwives did not provide religious guidance—with the exception of advising women to pray during labor. This was simply a reinforcement of the prevailing religious beliefs of the time.

3. Answer   B

This statement can be inferred from the information presented in paragraph 3 about how people learn from paying attention to others' behavior. The last sentence of that paragraph says, "you are more likely to be captivated by models who have certain attractive characteristics." Children who like their parents and enjoy a good relationship with them are more likely to pay attention to them, thus picking up their bad habits.

False Choices

- A   According to the passage, not all adolescents model their parents' behavior. The modeling behavior is attributed to whether or not adolescents have a positive or negative relationship with their parents.
- C   The passage does not make a judgment about whether or not parents who use alcohol set a poor example for their children. Andrews is more interested in the parent-child relationship and its effect on modeling parents' drug or alcohol use.
- D   The research shared in this passage does not conclude that all adolescents are willing to experiment with drugs and alcohol. Andrews wanted to know which adolescents would be most influenced by their parents' use of drugs or alcohol. Adolescents with positive relationships with their parents would most likely imitate parents' behavior.

4. Answer   D

The reading stresses that, "Men, research shows, play up their expertise, emphasize it, and use it to dominate the conversation. Women play down their expertise." Women also "seek to build rapport and establish a closer relationship," and so are more likely to discuss personal and relationship issues.

False Choices

- A   The passage states that men and women are socialized to listen differently; there is no mention that men are "naturally" more aggressive.
- B   Tannen discusses the differences in listening styles of men and women and supplies the reasons for this; however, she does not say that men and women do not communicate "well."
- C   There is no mention of this in the text. Men and women are equally likely to listen and discuss as they are socialized to do.

5. Answer   D

The quote is implying that society teaches men and women how to listen differently. Thus, people learn how to listen and converse based on what they learn from environmental social cues.

False Choices

- A   This says exactly the opposite of what the quote is implying.
- B   The passage does not suggest that people can or should seek professional help to change their listening styles.
- C   The passage does not say that men disrespect women. In fact, they listen to and converse with women in the same way they do men.

6. Answer   A

Many of the supports in this passage make this point. The entire second paragraph delves into Harris and Klebold's friendship and activities. The author explains that the two boys were viewed as outcasts, "geeks and nerds." Because they were excluded from the mainstream culture of the school, they bonded with other "outcasts" to form the "Trench Coat Mafia." Their image was one of power and dominance. The author goes on to explain how for more than a year, the two planned to kill teachers and students at their school and one day carried out their plan.

False Choices

- B   Not all students who are outcasts will commit acts of violence. This is a generalization that cannot be supported from the information in the passage.

C   Just because Harris and Kelbold succeeded at mass murder at their high school does not necessarily mean that this could happen at any high school. The event did bring the issue of safety to the forefront of concerns; however, the generalization that all schools are not safe is not supported in the passage.

D   This is an illogical conclusion.

7. Answer   B

This need to show that they were important is supported in lines 15–17: "Harris and Klebold desperately wanted to feel important; and in the preparations they made to murder their classmates, the two shooters got their wish."

False Choices

A   There is no mention of whether or not military school would have helped them.

C   While their anger may have been understandable, it was not reasonable, especially given the extreme way they expressed it. Rather, their rage was intimately connected to their relationship with each other.

D   Since they committed suicide, they did not seem to have a goal of "winning." Rather, they wanted to be seen as important.

8. Answer   C

The reading clarifies that "What some workers don't know (and what some of us forget) is that "delete" does not mean *delete*. Our computer keeps a hidden diary, even of what we've erased. With a few clicks, the cybersleuth, like magic ink, makes our "deleted" information visible, exposing our hidden diary for anyone to read." Furthermore, "With specialized software, cybersleuths can examine everything employees read online, everything they write, and every web site they visit." This would include e-mails.

False Choices

A   This statement contradicts paragraph one, which says that bosses know that workers conduct some personal business at work and that some interpersonal slacking even helps build work relationships. Bosses "wink as we make a date or nod as we arrange to have our car worked on."

B   Paragraph one clarifies that bosses only care about workers who abuse the phone privilege. "It's the abuse that bothers bosses, and it's not surprising that they fire anyone who talks on the phone all day for personal reasons." That implies that bosses only notice phone calls when they go too far, but they don't in general know how much time employees spend on the phone.

D   The passage implies the opposite since Xerox employees were fired for downloading pornography.

9. Answer   B

The reading states that "researchers reported that mitochondrial DNA from the Ice Man closely matched that of modern central and northern Europeans," implying that mitochondrial DNA has not changed much over the last 5,000 years.

False Choices

A   While his tools indicate he may have been hunting, we have no idea whether it was a snowstorm, an animal, or even an enemy that killed him.

C   The statement is not supported by the passage.

D   This statement is not supported by the passage.

10. Answer   A

According to the passage, "Every report of success in isolating ancient DNA has been met with skepticism and further analyses to make sure the DNA traces were not contaminated with DNA from bacteria, fungi, or other organisms." The passage further states that "DNA is unlikely to remain intact, except when organisms fossilize in extremely cold or dry places." Therefore, DNA from a fossil discovered in a wet, humid rainforest would be less trustworthy than DNA discovered in a hot, dry desert.

False Choices

B   The passage tells us that the "Ice Man" is ancient but does not state that he is the oldest human ever discovered. This statement is a false fact.

C   We don't know what caused the glacier to melt; it was August, so it may have been melting simply because it was summer.

D   While paragraph one reports that scientists have isolated such DNA, it does not say that such DNA is never contaminated.

◆

This section provides you with 20 items because of the difficulty of the type of question. Ten explanatory answers have been provided. Use the next ten questions to practice thinking through the test independently.

Think it through, use the explanatory answers as your models, and explain your own reasons for the choices you made. Compare your thinking to the definition of this skill at the beginning of the section in the workbook. *Thinking* about your thinking is an important tool. Therefore, only brief explanations of the remaining 10 questions have been provided.

11. Answer   A

The second and third paragraphs explain the importance of this "free" coverage, implying that without it, candidates do not receive enough media coverage to get their messages across to the public and therefore do not get elected.

12. Answer   C

The other answers reach too far in their logic or are not supported by the text.

13. Answer   C

The third paragraph states that "some individuals seek out caffeine for its own sake in over-the-counter products and in illegal substances to produce a caffeine 'high.'" The other answers are either contradicted by or not supported by the text.

14. Answer   A

The passage states that "Never before has there been such an intensive way for deprived people to gather to reinforce their prejudices and hatred." The other answers either reach too far in their logic or are not supported by the text.

15. Answer   B

This is implied in the last two sentences of the reading. The other answers are either contradicted by or not supported by the text.

16. Answer   D

Since scare tactics are counterproductive, the best programs probably do not use them. The other answers are not supported by the text.

17. Answer   A

The last paragraph discusses how Drudge "paved the way for communication power to be transferred from media giants to anyone with a modem."

18. Answer   B

The first paragraph shows that Drudge posted a story that was planted by someone's political enemy. Therefore, he did not confirm the story with the source.

19. Answer   C

This one requires that you read the question carefully. You are looking for the FALSE answer. The only one that is clearly false is C since the first sentence of the paragraph states the opposite indirectly.

20. Answer   A

The other answers either reach too far in their logic or are contradicted by the text.

3. Assessing Support for Reasoning and Argument

1. Answer   B

The passage is filled with emotional support to show that the factories were dangerous places. For example, factories are described as "miserable places" with "dangerous machines." Safety standards were "practically nonexistent." There was "little job security."

2. Answer   B

The author describes early factories in the following paragraph in detail.

3. Answer   C

This option provides specific information to support the author's claim. It gives the number of hours per day and per week and the number of days per week that the women worked in textile mills.

False Choices

    A   This is a broad statement that adds little to the sentence in the question.

    B   The statement is a generalization and is irrelevant.

    D   This detail is a broad statement and does not support the sentence.

4. Answer   B

The statement is adequately supported by details in the passage. For example, the second paragraph provides an illustration of that point by citing a sleep deprivation study done using young adult volunteers.

5. Answer   A

Many objective supporting details are given to explain the three areas affected by sleep deprivation: attention, mood, and performance. For example, paragraph four explains that going without sleep changes the normal circadian rhythms of the body. Throughout the passage, results of studies were provided.

6. Answer   D

This detail has concrete data that is verifiable, so it is the best statement of support.

False Choices

    A   This is a broad generalization that does not support the sentence.

    B   This may be a true statement, but no specific information is offered.

    C   The statement is not verified with specifics.

7. Answer   B

Most of the details provided in the passage are emotional. The author speculates on the effects of genetic manipulation. For example, the author suggests that inserting genetic materials in athletes could help them increase their ability, such as beating the two hour marathon record by a half hour. In paragraph three, the author speculates about adding the gene for growth hormone but not being able to regulate it.

8. Answer   A

The statement is not supported by evidence.

9. Answer   B

The author's claim is not adequately supported. No scientific data is offered to prove that athletes will be able to run faster. It is speculation.

10. Answer   C

This sentence gives an example of a type of material, red blood cells, that when injected, has specific risks: blood clots, bacterial infection, and congestive heart failure.

False Choices

A   This does not address health risks; it simply states that the effects of injecting a material are unknown.

B   In this sentence, "may" suggests a possibility but does not provide factual evidence for the author's claim.

D   This sentence offers a speculation of what could happen by injecting artificial genes to help increase a sprinter's muscles. It does not support the sentence with concrete evidence.

Part Eight: Answer Keys for Writing

ANSWER KEY TO PRETEST, WORKBOOK EXERCISES, AND EXIT EXAM

ANSWERS TO THE PRETEST

1.	C	2.	A	3.	B	4.	A	5.	D	6.	C
7.	C	8.	D	9.	D	10.	A	11.	B	12.	A
13.	B	14.	B	15.	C	16.	B	17.	A	18.	D
19.	C	20.	C	21.	A	22.	C	23.	B	24.	A
25.	A	26.	B	27.	B	28.	C	29.	B	30.	A
31.	C	32.	B	33.	C	34.	C	35.	A	36.	B
37.	D	38.	C	39.	B	40.	B				

ANSWERS TO THE WORKBOOK EXERCISES

CHAPTER 1: *CONCEPT SKILLS*

1. The Topic Sentence

1.	C	2.	D	3.	B	4.	D	5.	B
6.	B	7.	A	8.	C	9.	B	10.	D

2. Supporting Details

1.	A	2.	B	3.	D	4.	C	5.	C
6.	C	7.	B	8.	A	9.	D	10.	B

3. Logical Patterns

1.	B	2.	C	3.	B	4.	C	5.	A
6.	D	7.	B	8.	A	9.	D	10.	C

4. Relevance of Details

1.	D	2.	B	3.	A	4.	A	5.	C
6.	C	7.	D	8.	B	9.	A	10.	D

5. Transitional Devices

1.	C	2.	D	3.	A	4.	B	5.	D
6.	C	7.	B	8.	A	9.	D	10.	C

CHAPTER 2: *IMPORTANT SKILLS TO FOCUS ON*

1. Choosing Proper Expressions (Context Clues)

1.	A	2.	D	3.	C	4.	B	5.	B
6.	A	7.	C	8.	A	9.	B	10.	C

2. Fragments, Comma Splices, and Fused Sentences (Run-ons)

1.	B	2.	C	3.	B	4.	A	5.	D
6.	A	7.	B	8.	D	9.	C	10.	A
11.	B	12.	A	13.	D	14.	B	15.	A
16.	B	17.	C	18.	A	19.	B	20.	C

3. Subject and Verb Agreement

1.	A	2.	C	3.	C	4.	B	5.	C
6.	A	7.	B	8.	C	9.	D	10.	A
11.	B	12.	A	13.	C	14.	A	15.	A
16.	D	17.	B	18.	A	19.	C	20.	D

4. Pronoun and Antecedent Agreement

1.	A	2.	D	3.	B	4.	C	5.	B
6.	C	7.	A	8.	C	9.	B	10.	D

5. Clear Pronoun Reference

1.	B	2.	C	3.	A	4.	B	5.	C
6.	A	7.	A	8.	B	9.	C	10.	D

6. Pronoun Case Form

1.	A	2.	B	3.	C	4.	C	5.	C
6.	D	7.	A	8.	B	9.	D	10.	B

7. Pronoun Shifts

1.	B	2.	C	3.	C	4.	A	5.	B
6.	C	7.	C	8.	A	9.	D	10.	B

8. Shifts in Verb Tense

1.	B	2.	C	3.	A	4.	C	5.	B
6.	A	7.	D	8.	B	9.	C	10.	B

9. Modifiers

1.	C	2.	A	3.	B	4.	B	5.	A
6.	C	7.	A	8.	B	9.	C	10.	A

10. Standard Punctuation

1.	C	2.	B	3.	A	4.	B	5.	A
6.	D	7.	A	8.	C	9.	B	10.	A

CHAPTER 3: *OTHER IMPORTANT SKILLS*

1. Parallel Structure

1.	A	2.	C	3.	B	4.	B	5.	C
6.	B	7.	C	8.	D	9.	C	10.	B

2. Confused or Misused Words/Phrases

1.	C	2.	C	3.	A	4.	A	5.	C
6.	A	7.	B	8.	C	9.	B	10.	B

3. Adjectives and Adverbs

1.	A	2.	C	3.	B	4.	B	5.	D
6.	C	7.	B	8.	A	9.	C	10.	A

4. Degree Forms of Adjectives and Adverbs

1.	C	2.	B	3.	A	4.	B	5.	C
6.	D	7.	A	8.	D	9.	C	10.	B

CHAPTER 4: *ADDITIONAL PRACTICE*

1. Standard Capitalization

1.	C	2.	A	3.	B	4.	C	5.	A
6.	B	7.	B	8.	D	9.	C	10.	D

2. Standard Verb Forms

1.	B	2.	D	3.	C	4.	A	5.	C
6.	B	7.	A	8.	B	9.	C	10.	C

3. Choosing Proper Expressions (Context Clues)

1.	B	2.	A	3.	C	4.	B	5.	C
6.	A	7.	B	8.	C	9.	B	10.	A

4. Standard Spelling

1.	B	2.	A	3.	A	4.	C	5.	C
6.	D	7.	B	8.	B	9.	A	10.	B

ANSWERS TO EXIT EXAM #1

1.	B	2.	D	3.	C	4.	B	5.	A	6.	C
7.	B	8.	C	9.	D	10.	A	11.	C	12.	A
13.	B	14.	A	15.	C	16.	B	17.	A	18.	D
19.	B	20.	C	21.	C	22.	A	23.	C	24.	B
25.	C	26.	A	27.	A	28.	B	29.	A	30.	C
31.	B	32.	C	33.	A	34.	C	35.	B	36.	D
37.	C	38.	A	39.	A	40.	C				

ANSWERS TO EXIT EXAM #2

1.	A	2.	B	3.	A	4.	D	5.	D	6.	A
7.	C	8.	D	9.	B	10.	C	11.	D	12.	A
13.	C	14.	D	15.	B	16.	C	17.	B	18.	B
19.	C	20.	C	21.	B	22.	D	23.	A	24.	C
25.	A	26.	C	27.	A	28.	B	29.	D	30.	C
31.	B	32.	B	33.	A	34.	C	35.	B	36.	D
37.	B	38.	C	39.	B	40.	C				

ANSWERS TO EXIT EXAM #3

1.	C	2.	A	3.	D	4.	B	5.	C	6.	D
7.	A	8.	B	9.	C	10.	B	11.	B	12.	A
13.	C	14.	A	15.	B	16.	C	17.	A	18.	B
19.	D	20.	C	21.	C	22.	A	23.	C	24.	B
25.	C	26.	A	27.	A	28.	D	29.	B	30.	D
31.	D	32.	B	33.	B	34.	D	35.	A	36.	C
37.	B	38.	B	39.	B	40.	D				

ANSWERS TO WRITING PRETEST *WITH* EXPLANATIONS

1. **Skill tested:** Identifies a thesis statement or topic sentence. **Answer:** C. **Explanation:** Choice C is the best topic sentence for the passage. The authors use the Ice Man as an example to illustrate how DNA was used to find out information about him.

2. **Skill tested:** Recognizes adequate support provided by generalized and specific evidence. **Answer:** A. **Explanation:** No examples or other support is provided for the sentence.

3. **Skill tested:** Arranges ideas and supporting details in a logical pattern. **Answer:** B. **Explanation:** The pattern follows chronological order, describing the Ice Man and the items found along with him.

4. **Skill tested:** Identifies supporting material that is relevant or irrelevant to the thesis statement or topic sentence. **Answer:** A. **Explanation:** Sentence 12 adds information about a dinosaur fossil; however, it is neither supported by nor connected to the main idea of the passage.

5. **Skill tested:** Recognizes effective transitional devices within the context of the passage. **Answer:** D. **Explanation:** The word "currently" takes the reader from the story of the Ice Man discovery to his location at this time.

6. **Skill tested:** Identifies a thesis statement or topic sentence. **Answer:** C. **Explanation:** The paragraph explains the ways in which ethical standards are violated, which is best expressed in answer C.

7. **Skill tested:** Recognizes adequate support provided by generalized and specific evidence. **Answer:** C. **Explanation:** The passage does not discuss the systems for citing others' ideas.

8. **Skill tested:** Arranges ideas and supporting details in a logical pattern. **Answer:** D. **Explanation:** The sentences describe the ways in which plagiarism violates ethical standards. Transition words indicate the logical pattern. The second sentence of the group uses the transition word "also." "Finally" is used in the third sentence of the group to indicate that the idea is the last way.

9. **Skill tested:** Identifies supporting material that is relevant or irrelevant to the thesis statement or topic sentence. **Answer:** D. **Explanation:** Sentence 13 gives a specific effect on a student if he or she plagiarizes, but the passage does not discuss specific effects of plagiarism on an individual.

10. **Skill tested:** Recognizes effective transitional devices within the context of the passage. **Answer:** A. **Explanation:** The phrase "for example" is appropriate because the sentence introduces an example to illustrate the main idea.

11. **Skill tested:** Chooses the appropriate word or expression in context. **Answer:** B. **Explanation:** The word "deficient" means lacking or inadequate.

12. **Skill tested:** Chooses the appropriate word or expression in context. **Answer:** A. **Explanation:** The word "oblivious" means lacking a conscious awareness of. The sentence implies that the subject is no longer bothered by the noise of the planes flying overhead.

13. **Skill tested:** Recognizes commonly confused and misused words or phrases. **Answer:** B. **Explanation:** The possessive form "whose" is the correct word while the word in the sentence, "who's," is the contracted form of who + is.

14. **Skill tested:** Recognizes commonly confused and misused words or phrases. **Answer:** B. **Explanation:** The words "number" and "amount" are often confused. "Number" is used for things that can be counted while "amount" is used for things that are not countable. Therefore, "number" is correct because calories can be counted.

15. **Skill tested:** Uses modifiers correctly. **Answer:** C. **Explanation:** A modifier must have a word to modify. If not, it "dangles." Choice C places the modifier before the subject, "they," which clearly shows who was "sitting on the beach."

16. **Skill tested:** Uses modifiers correctly. **Answer:** B. **Explanation:** For clarity and meaning, a modifier must be placed next to the word or phrase that is being modified; otherwise, it is misplaced. Choice B places the modifier "that was moldy" next to "cheese spread," which is the word group it modifies.

17. **Skill tested:** Uses coordination and subordinating effectively. **Answer:** A. **Explanation:** This type of question requires that you carefully consider the relationship between ideas within the sentence. The sentence shows a cause and effect relationship best expressed by Choice A. The dependent clause that begins the sentence tells why.

18. **Skill tested:** Uses coordination and subordination effectively. **Answer:** D. **Explanation:** This sentence consists of two independent clauses connected with a

semicolon. The word that fills in the blank, a conjunctive adverb or transition word, must show a relationship between the two sentences. Choice D shows effect; as a result of the dog's aggression, it must be kept in a cage.

19. **Skill tested:** Recognizes parallel structure. **Answer:** C. **Explanation:** This sentence contains a list. When listing items in a sentence, you must be sure that each of the items is written in the same grammatical structure. The list could contain all words, all phrases, all clauses, or all sentences. In the sentence, the first two phrases in the list begin with –*ing* words, so the third item in the group should also. C is the only choice that has the same grammatical structure.

20. **Skill tested:** Recognizes parallel structure. **Answer:** C. **Explanation:** As in question 19, this sentence also contains a list, so once again you must choose the list that has structurally parallel items. Each of the items in the list in Choice C begins with the base form of a verb: ride, take, and borrow.

21. **Skill tested:** Avoids fragments, comma splices, and fused sentences. **Answer:** A. **Explanation:** You must determine whether the sentence has any of these problems: is incomplete (a fragment), has a comma separating two independent clauses (a comma splice), or lacks appropriate punctuation between two independent clauses (fused). The underlined portion of the sentence is the last word of the first sentence and the first word of a new sentence. Since it is not punctuated appropriately, it is considered a fused sentence. Choice A corrects the sentence by placing a period after the word "school" and capitalizing "Sometimes." This separates the two independent clauses correctly.

22. **Skill tested:** Avoids fragments, comma splices, and fused sentences. **Answer:** C. **Explanation:** You must determine whether the sentence has any of these problems: is incomplete (a fragment), has a comma separating two independent clauses (a comma splice), or lacks appropriate punctuation between two independent clauses (fused). This sentence offers three options. Choice C is correct. The comma between "pressure" and "if" creates a comma splice. The semi-colon corrects this error.

23. **Skill tested:** Avoids fragments, comma splices, and fused sentences. **Answer:** B. **Explanation:** You must determine whether the sentence has any of these problems: is incomplete (a fragment), has a comma separating two independent clauses (a comma splice), or lacks appropriate punctuation between two inde-

pendent clauses (fused). The underlined portion of the sentence is the last word of the first sentence and the first word of a new sentence. The second word group in the sentence is a fragment. Choice B corrects this fragment by replacing the period with a comma.

24. **Skill tested:** Avoids fragments, comma splices, and fused sentences. **Answer:** A. **Explanation:** You must determine whether the sentence has any of these problems: is incomplete (a fragment), has a comma separating two independent clauses (a comma splice), or lacks appropriate punctuation between two independent clauses (fused). This sentence offers three options. Choice A corrects the error, which is a fragment: "When my mother first came to the United States." This dependent clause begins the sentence, so it should be followed by a comma.

25. **Skill tested:** Uses standard verb forms. **Answer:** A. **Explanation:** The past participle of "spoke" is "spoken." This verb form, "had spoken," is necessary to show that the first action in the past was completed before the second action in the past.

26. **Skill tested:** Shift in verb tense. **Answer:** B. **Explanation:** This sentence contains a shift in verb tense. The three verbs in the sentence should all be in the simple past tense; however, B is not. Choice B, "looked," corrects "is looking."

27. **Skill tested:** Shift in verb tense. **Answer:** B. **Explanation:** The verb in the underlined portion of the sentence, "dive," is in the present tense, but the rest of the sentence is in the simple past tense. "Dove" is the past tense form of the verb "dive."

28. **Skill tested:** Subject and verb agreement. **Answer:** C. **Explanation:** This question tests your ability to determine whether the subject of an independent or dependent clause agrees with its verb. In this sentence, the problem is in the dependent clause "if there is any drug sales." The subject of that clause is "sales," which is plural, so the verb must be in the plural form, "are."

29. **Skill tested:** Subject and verb agreement. **Answer:** B. **Explanation:** This question tests your ability to determine whether the subject of an independent or dependent clause agrees with its verb. This error tests your knowledge of the rule for subject-verb agreement when *neither* and *nor* are used as subjects. In this situation, the word after "nor" determines the form of the verb. In this sentence, "flowers" follows nor. Because "flowers" is plural, the verb must be plural in form, "need."

30. **Skill tested:** Pronoun and antecedent agreement. **Answer:** A. **Explanation:** In the sentence the pronoun "their" is incorrect. "Their" is a plural pronoun, but the word it refers to, "each" (the subject of the sentence), is singular. The correction is "his or her." "His or her" is used because the reader does not know the gender of the children, so both the masculine and feminine forms of the pronoun are used separated by "or" to indicate it could be either gender.

31. **Skill tested:** Avoids inappropriate pronoun shifts in person. **Answer:** C. **Explanation:** Choice C corrects the shifted pronoun "you."

32. **Skill tested:** Avoids inappropriate pronoun shifts in person. **Answer:** B. **Explanation:** The pronoun "we" marks a shift from the other two pronouns, "they." To correct the shift in person, "they" should replace "we."

33. **Skill tested:** Maintains clear pronoun references. **Answer:** C. **Explanation:** In this sentence, the reader does not know what the pronoun "it" refers to. Choice C, "an antique car," replaces the pronoun with a specific noun.

34. **Skill tested:** Uses proper case forms. **Answer:** C. **Explanation:** Choice C corrects the incorrect pronoun "I." When a pronoun is an object of a preposition, it must be in the objective form. "Between" is a preposition, so the correct object pronoun must be "me."

35. **Skill tested:** Uses adjectives and adverbs correctly. **Answer:** A. **Explanation:** "Safely," the adverb, must be used to modify the verb "live." "Safe" is the adjective form.

36. **Skill tested:** Uses appropriate degree forms of adjectives and adverbs. **Answer:** B. **Explanation:** A comparison is implied in this sentence. The weather is not as good as it was; it is getting "worse." "Worse" is the correct comparative form.

37. **Skill tested:** Uses standard spelling. **Answer:** D. **Explanation:** "Broccoli" as it appears in the sentence is the correct spelling.

38. **Skill tested:** Uses standard punctuation. **Answer:** C. **Explanation:** The sentence begins with a dependent clause and ends with an independent clause. The independent clause contains compound verbs, "organizing" and "helping." No comma is needed to separate these compound verb phrases.

39. **Skill tested:** Uses standard punctuation. **Answer:** B. **Explanation:** This question tests your knowledge of the question mark and the apostrophe. The sentence is an indirect question, so no question mark is necessary. The apostrophe is needed to show possession; the jerseys belong to the team members. The apostrophe follows "members," indicating that "members" is a plural possessive.

40. **Skill tested:** Uses standard capitalization. **Answer:** B. **Explanation:** The South is a region of the country and is capitalized.

ANSWERS TO THE EXIT EXAM *WITH* EXPLANATIONS

1. **Skill tested:** Identifies a thesis statement or topic sentence. **Answer:** B. **Explanation:** The passage focuses on the friendship of Harris and Klebold as an example of "horrific actions of schoolyard snipers."

2. **Skill tested:** Recognizes adequate support provided by generalized and specific evidence. **Answer:** D. **Explanation:** No support is provided for the sentence about family background.

3. **Skill tested:** Arranges ideas and supporting details in a logical pattern. **Answer:** C. **Explanation:** The first sentence in the group makes a statement that the two boys wanted to feel important. This sentence supports the previous sentence (6). The next two sentences build on the first of the group.

4. **Skill tested:** Identifies supporting material that is relevant or irrelevant to the thesis statement or topic sentence. **Answer:** B. **Explanation:** The passage does not focus on how popular trench coats became because Harris and Klebold wore them.

5. **Skill tested:** Recognizes effective transitional devices within the context of the passage. **Answer:** A. **Explanation:** "As a result" indicates that the sentence is expressing the effect of the previous sentence.

6. **Skill tested:** Identifies a thesis statement or topic sentence. **Answer:** C. **Explanation:** The passage explains the various problems a single parent may experience.

7. **Skill tested:** Recognizes adequate support provided by generalized and specific evidence. **Answer:** B. **Explanation:** Sentence 6 points out that child care can be costly. Choice B provides information about the cost of full-time day care compared to family income.

8. **Skill tested:** Arranges ideas and supporting details in a logical pattern. **Answer:** C. **Explanation:** This detail

supports the sentence before it, sentence 4, which says that spending quality time with a child is a demonstration of love. This sentence gives an example of quality time as "interacting with the child, actively listening and talking with him or her."

9. **Skill tested:** Identifies supporting material that is relevant or irrelevant to the thesis statement or topic sentence. **Answer: D. Explanation:** The passage does not discuss how society views divorce, so the sentence is not relevant to the topic.

10. **Skill tested:** Recognizes effective transitional devices within the context of the passage. **Answer: A. Explanation:** Sentence 7 adds to the point made in sentence 6, so "in addition" is appropriate and effective.

11. **Skill tested:** Chooses the appropriate word or expression in context. **Answer: C. Explanation:** "Aptitude" means talent, a natural ability.

12. **Skill tested:** Chooses the appropriate word or expression in context. **Answer: A. Explanation:** "Ascertain" means to find out or learn with certainty, which is what the subject of the sentence tried to do.

13. **Skill tested:** Recognizes commonly confused or misused words or phrases. **Answer: B. Explanation:** "Compliment" and "complement" are often confused. A "compliment" is an expression of praise; a "complement" is something added that completes, such as adding some flowers to a beautifully set table.

14. **Skill tested:** Recognizes commonly confused or misused words or phrases. **Answer: A. Explanation:** "Would have" is the grammatically correct form.

15. **Skill tested:** Uses modifiers correctly. **Answer: C. Explanation:** For clarity of meaning, modifiers must be placed next to the word or phrase that is being modified; otherwise it is misplaced. Choice C places the modifier, "Driving around in his car," before the word(s) it modifies, "Uncle Fred."

16. **Skill tested:** Uses modifiers correctly. **Answer: B. Explanation:** A modifier must have a word or phrase to modify. If not, it "dangles." Choice B tells the reader who was watching the movie on television.

17. **Skill tested:** Uses coordination and subordination effectively. **Answer: A. Explanation:** This type of question requires that you carefully consider the relationship between ideas within the sentence. The sentence shows a time relationship best expressed by Choice A. "After" is used in the dependent clause to explain the sequence of actions in the sentence.

18. **Skill tested:** Uses coordination and subordination effectively. **Answer: D. Explanation:** The sentence contrasts the two positions that each person prefers in doubles tennis, so "on the other hand" is the appropriate choice to coordinate these two sentences.

19. **Skill tested:** Recognizes parallel structure. **Answer: B. Explanation:** The sentence contains a list. When listing items in a sentence, you must be sure that each of the items is written in the same grammatical structure. In other words, the list could contain all words, all phrases, all clauses, or all sentences. In this sentence, the list is a series of sentences, and Choice B is the only option that is a sentence.

20. **Skill tested:** Recognizes parallel structure. **Answer: C. Explanation:** This sentence contains a list. Each item in the list must be written in the same grammatical structure. In Choice C, all of the words in the list are nouns.

21. **Skill tested:** Avoids fragments, comma splices, and fused sentences. **Answer: C. Explanation:** This sentence fuses two independent clauses. One way to correct this problem is to add a comma and a coordinating conjunction between the two independent clauses. Choice C is the only answer that has the comma before the coordinating conjunction.

22. **Skill tested:** Avoids fragments, comma splices, and fused sentences. **Answer: A. Explanation:** The beginning of the sentence is a dependent clause. A comma must follow an introductory dependent clause. Therefore, Choice A is the option that corrects the error in the sentence.

23. **Skill tested:** Avoids fragments, comma splices, and fused sentences. **Answer: C. Explanation:** Choice C corrects the error in the sentence. "After three years of employment at Kabooms" is a dependent clause. Placing a period at the end of it creates a fragment. Always put a comma at the end of an introductory dependent clause.

24. **Skill tested:** Avoids fragments, comma splices, and fused sentences. **Answer: B. Explanation:** Two sentences are fused because there is no punctuation after the word "me," which ends the first sentence of the two. Choice B corrects the error with a period after "me" and a capital "E" to begin the next sentence.

25. **Skill tested:** Uses standard verb forms. **Answer: C. Explanation:** The past perfect verb tense is formed by combining "had" and the past participle verb form of "become": had + become.

26. **Skill tested:** Avoids inappropriate shifts in verb tense. **Answer:** A. **Explanation:** The sentence begins with the verb in the present tense but the verb shifts to the past in the second independent clause. The verb in the independent clause after the semicolon is also in the past tense. To keep the verb tense consistent in the sentence, the first verb must be changed to the past tense, "cooked."

27. **Skill tested:** Avoids inappropriate shifts in verb tense. **Answer:** A. **Explanation:** This sentence begins in the present tense with "takes" and finishes in the past with "took." Choice A corrects the verb shift, so both verbs are in the present tense.

28. **Skill tested:** Maintains agreement between subject and verb. **Answer:** B. **Explanation:** The subject of the independent clause beginning with "a few of them" is "few," which is plural. Therefore, the verb must be in the plural form, "intend." "Intends" is the third person singular form.

29. **Skill tested:** Maintains agreement between subject and verb. **Answer:** A. **Explanation:** The verb "are" agrees with the subject, "jeans." The dependent clause modifies "jeans," and the word "which" refers to "jeans," so the verb must be in the plural form.

30. **Skill tested:** Maintains agreement between pronoun and antecedent. **Answer:** C. **Explanation:** Pronouns must agree with their antecedents. In this sentence, the subject of the sentence is student, which is singular. All of the pronouns refer to that subject (the antecedent), so they must all be singular. "His or her" is the correction for "their."

31. **Skill tested:** Avoids inappropriate pronoun shifts in person. **Answer:** B. **Explanation:** The pronoun shifts from "I" to "you" and then back to "I." "You" should be replaced with "I" for consistency.

32. **Skill tested:** Avoids inappropriate pronoun shifts in person. **Answer:** C. **Explanation:** The pronoun shift in the sentence is "I." The other pronouns used are "we" and "us," both forms of the first person plural. To correct the error, "I" must be replaced with "we."

33. **Skill tested:** Maintains clear pronoun references. **Answer:** A. **Explanation:** In the sentence, the reader is not told what "they" refers to. The employees are the ones who distribute the credit cards.

34. **Skill tested:** Uses proper case forms. **Answer:** C. **Explanation:** An object pronoun cannot be used as a subject. The second independent clause in the sentence is compound; that is, it consists of two independent clauses joined by a comma and a coordinating conjunction. The subject follows the coordinating conjunction." The subject is "three," but a pronoun is used as part of the subject "three."

35. **Skill tested:** Uses adjectives and adverbs correctly. **Answer:** B. **Explanation:** "Patient" is an adjective, but in this sentence "patient" does not modify any noun in the sentence. The adverb "patiently" corrects the error.

36. **Skill tested:** Uses appropriate degree forms of adjectives and adverbs. **Answer:** D. **Explanation:** The sentence compares more than two things, so the superlative form must be used.

37. **Skill tested:** Uses standard spelling. **Answer:** C. **Explanation:** "Inconvenience" is spelled correctly.

38. **Skill tested:** Uses standard punctuation. **Answer:** A. **Explanation:** No comma should appear before a relative pronoun, in this case "that," which begins an essential dependent clause. The dependent clause "that I have ever known" is essential to the meaning of the sentence.

39. **Skill tested:** Uses standard punctuation. **Answer:** A. **Explanation:** The sentence contains an indirect question correctly punctuated with a period at the end of the sentence.

40. **Skill tested:** Uses standard capitalization. **Answer:** C. **Explanation:** Seasons are not capitalized.

ANSWERS TO EXERCISES IN THE WRITING WORKBOOK *WITH* EXPLANATIONS

CHAPTER 1: *CONCEPT SKILLS*

1. The Topic Sentence

1. Answer   C

This sentence is the best choice for the main idea because it summarizes all the supporting ideas in the passage. The passage gives six disadvantages of e-mail in a business environment.

2. Answer   D

This topic sentence is the best choice because it provides a summary of the supporting details in the passage that discuss gender equality in the military.

3. Answer   B

Jaime Escalante's success as a teacher was a result of the methods he used with his students to help them achieve. The passage gives examples of those methods.

4. Answer   D

The purpose of this paragraph is to describe the physical and psychological symptoms of anorexia nervosa. This topic sentence achieves that purpose.

5. Answer   B

The paragraph covers the history of the standardization of bare-knuckle boxing between the late 1800s and the early 1900s. Choice B clearly indicates this.

6. Answer   B

This topic sentence is an effective unifying summary of the supporting details in the paragraph. Examples of the different messages communicated by eye movements are provided.

7. Answer   A

The passage describes how the albatross is equipped to live at sea, and this topic sentence is the best summary of the topic. The paragraph explains the features of the albatross that help it survive: its salt tolerance and its wingspan.

8. Answer   C

This sentence works well as a topic sentence because it covers the reasons athletes use anabolic steroids and the effects they could experience.

9. Answer   B

The topic sentence reflects the content of the paragraph, which shows how parents and children can learn about computers from each other and increase their self-confidence, strengthening their relationship.

10. Answer   D

This topic sentence is effective for the content of the paragraph. The passage explains the benefits of highlighting.

2. Supporting Details

1. Answer   A

This sentence cites another disadvantage of e-mail, but the passage offers no discussion of the privacy issues and is, therefore, not supported.

2. Answer   B

This sentence brings up a new point, whether being able to serve in combat is a privilege or a burden, but the author does not discuss it.

3. Answer   D

Sentence 11 provides specific support for sentence 10 in the passage. It gives an example of a way Escalante changed his method of instruction.

4. Answer   C

Sentence 9 is a transitional sentence in the paragraph. It shifts the discussion of anorexia to more than an eating disorder. Sentence 10 adds the idea that it is a psychological disorder, too, with a wide range of disturbances. Thus, sentence 10 supports 9.

5. Answer   C

Periodic efforts to outlaw boxing are not discussed in the passage.

6. Answer   C

No support is provided for sentence 8, which says that eye movements can signal a positive or negative relationship.

7. Answer   B

The sentence that provides specific support for sentence 4 in the passage is sentence 5. It explains how the salt-excreting glands in the albatross dispose of excess salts.

8. Answer   A

Sentence 13 supports sentence 9 because it gives an example of a physical problem that can occur from using anabolic steroids. Sentence 9 introduces the idea that these substances can cause physical and mental problems.

9. Answer   D

Sentence 9 is not supported by specific details. No examples of how children interact with the computer as if it were alive are provided.

10. Answer   B

Sentence 4 provides specific support for sentence 3 in the passage. It explains what sifting and sorting is. Sentence 3 explains that highlighting is a process of sifting and sorting.

3. Logical Patterns

For this section, only the correct answer is explained. The question asks you to select the arrangement of sentences that provides the most logical sequence of ideas and supporting details in the paragraph. Therefore, it is unnecessary to explain why the other answers are false.

1. Answer   B

This is the best arrangement for the series of sentences. The passage gives the disadvantages of e-mail communication in the workplace. The first sentence of the group introduces the second disadvantage of the passage, which talks about the fact that e-mail provides no paper trail. The point made in sentence 6 should follow because it directly supports sentence 4; it explains the ease of reading and deleting e-mail instead of printing a copy for your files or moving it to an electronic folder. Sentence 5 begins with the transition "As a result." This phrase logically follows sentence 6 because it gives the effect of what happens when messages aren't printed or saved; they are forgotten or lost.

2. Answer   C

This group of sentences follows sentence 10, which introduces the idea that there is a debate over whether women should serve in combat. Sentence 13 presents the first point of debate, that women are less suited for combat because they have less body strength than men do. The sentence begins with the word "Some." It makes sense logically that sentence 11 should follow. The sentence begins with the word "Others," showing that another point of view is being expressed. Sentence 12 addresses the two previous opinions given in sentences 13 and 11 by stating that there are critics of both of those points.

3. Answer   B
Sentences 11, 12, and 13 are supporting details for sentence 10. Sentence 10 introduces the idea that Escalante changed the system of instruction that the students had experienced at their high school. Sentence 13 is logically the first point that supports this. His first step was to get the students to think of themselves as a team and of him as their coach because they were preparing for the national math exams. Next, he fostered team identity; sentence 12 gives examples of how this was accomplished. They wore hats and clothing items that identified them as a team. Moving from establishing their identity as a team and fostering that identity, Escalante had his students do warm-ups before each class, getting them ready to work together and learn.

4. Answer   C
The paragraph begins with a definition of anorexia nervosa as a loss of appetite in sentence 2 but explains that the meaning does not fit the disease. Sentence 4 supports this statement: a person with anorexia is hungry but denies it in fear of becoming fat. The use of the transition word "Therefore" beginning sentence 5 leads the reader to the effect of the fear as well as introduces the reader to the first characteristic of the illness: severe weight loss. Sentence 3 adds information about the anorexic's approach to weight loss.

5. Answer   A
The sequence of sentences in the passage is the most logical sequence. These sentences describe the stages of a bare-knuckle boxing fight. The other arrangements of sentences do not make sense as a sequential description.

6. Answer   D
The best placement for the sentence is immediately after sentence 14. Sentence 12 presents the detail that eye contact can change psychological distance between you and someone else. Sentence 13 gives the example of catching someone's eye at a party, which brings the two people psychologically close. Then sentence 14 explains how avoiding eye contact increases the psychological distance. The new sentence gives another example of increasing distance.

7. Answer   B
Sentence 7 in the passage begins the transition to a discussion of the albatross's flight abilities. Sentence 8 talks about the wingspan, and sentence 9 describes how the al-

batross's long wings give it sufficient lift to stay up in the air for hours. The new sentence explains how the feathers insulate it from the chill of the sea wind and how they keep the bird dry because they are coated with oil. This is an appropriate placement because it further explains how the albatross can handle the environmental conditions it is exposed to while gliding on wind currents over the ocean.

8. Answer   A
The sentence suggested for placement in the passage gives another effect of anabolic steroids on the mind. It supports the sentence immediately before it, sentence 11, which begins the discussion of the mental effects. Both sentences support sentence 9; this sentence refers to the serious physical and mental effects of anabolic steroids. Sentence 12 moves the discussion forward to the internal effects.

9. Answer   D
The best placement for the sentence is after sentence 7. It gives another example of how children can teach their parents how to use computer programs and Internet communication. Sentence 3 gives the main supporting detail, and sentences 4, 5, 6, and 7 provide the minor details. The suggested sentence would serve as the last example in the series. Sentence 8 summarizes the examples that were discussed.

10. Answer   C
The suggested sentence is best placed after sentence 8. Sentence 7 begins the discussion of another benefit of highlighting, a new supporting detail; it helps you discover how facts and ideas are organized and are connected. Sentence 8 adds another detail: highlighting shows you whether or not you have understood what you have read. The suggested sentence further supports this idea. The author says that if your highlighting was difficult or not helpful, then you did not understand the passage you read.

4. Relevance of Details

For each of the following explanatory answers, the topic sentence for each passage is provided as the first piece of information. A detail's relevance is best judged against the main idea, for good writing ties every detail either directly as a major point or indirectly as a minor point (that supports a major point) to the main idea.

1. Topic Sentence: Although electronic mail has become a medium of choice for business communication, e-mail has disadvantages for users.

Answer: D. The 1986 Electronic Communications Privacy Act considers e-mail to be the property of the company paying for the mail system.

The Electronic Communications Privacy Act is least relevant to the main idea as stated in the topic sentence. The paragraph does not discuss who "owns" the company's e-mail system.

2. Topic Sentence: Military service is still a controversial issue of gender equality.

Answer: B. In 1981, the Supreme Court ruled that male-only registration for the military did not violate the Fifth Amendment.

The beginning of the paragraph establishes that men and women are treated differently in the military. The first support is that only men must register for the draft when they turn 18. However, the history of the male-only registration for the military ruling moves the discussion off the main topic into another direction that is merely stated and not developed or related to the point of the paragraph.

3. Topic Sentence: Jaime Escalante's dramatic success in teaching calculus to students in an East Los Angeles inner-city school plagued with poverty, crime, drugs, and gangs was a result of changes he made to classroom instruction.

Answer: A. When Escalante first came to the United States, he worked as a busboy and attended Pasadena Community College.

This sentence does not support the topic sentence. It has nothing to do with the changes Escalante made to his instruction in the classroom. Instead it tells the reader about Escalante's past when he first came to this country.

4. Topic Sentence: The central features of anorexia nervosa are a complex mixture of symptoms.

Answer: A. There is a strong argument that eating disorders are a form of addiction.

This sentence is not relevant for two reasons. First, the passage does not discuss all eating disorders, just one, anorexia nervosa. Next, although the passage mentions the psychological aspects of the disorder, it neither lists addiction as one of the aspects nor attempts to provide any further discussion of that idea.

5. Topic Sentence: Boxing began as a largely unstructured sport, but by 1900, new rules standardized the sport.

Answer: C. Currently there are eight major professional divisions.

This sentence has no relationship to the discussion of the changes to boxing by 1900.

6. Topic Sentence: Eye movements communicate a variety of messages.

Answer: C. Your pupils enlarge when you are interested or emotionally involved.

The change in the size of a person's pupils is not supported in the passage. The passage focuses on eye movements, not the pupils.

7. Topic Sentence: Only a few birds can live at sea, but the albatross is a model of fitness for its environment.

Answer: D. Their scientific name, *Diomedea exulans*, means exiled warrior in Greek.

This is the least relevant sentence in the paragraph. While it is interesting to know the scientific name of the albatross, the information does not add to the details explaining how the albatross is well-suited for its environment.

8. Topic Sentence: While using anabolic steroids is a fast way to increase general body size, their health hazards support the argument for banning their use in athletics.

Answer: B. Black market sales bring in up to $400 million a year.

This sentence has no relevance to the passage. The illegal sale of anabolic steroids does not support the idea that steroids can be hazardous to a person's health.

9. Topic Sentence: Sharing information and teaching each other about their computer and the Internet can strengthen the parent-child relationship.

Answer: A. Children are more apt to interact with the computer as if it were alive.

This sentence is least relevant because the passage is about sharing information, not about how children interact with the computer. This does not help the reader understand how a child is able to master a program, whether through persistence or intuition.

10. Topic Sentence: Highlighting is an extremely effective way of making a textbook review manageable.

Answer: D. One mistake to avoid is highlighting almost every idea on the page.

The paragraph explains the many ways in which highlighting is effective. Its purpose is not to point out mistakes people make when highlighting.

5. Transitional Devices

1. Answer   C

"Finally" indicates that the last point is being made. In this passage, the final disadvantage of e-mail is that writing on a computer screen often encourages people to drop their inhibitions and write things in e-mail that they would not write in a letter or say on the phone.

2. Answer   D

"However" is the best choice, for it indicates contrast with the sentence that precedes it. Sentence 7 explains the services women performed during the Persian Gulf War and sentence 8 states that the policy does not allow them to serve as combat pilots in the navy and air force or on navy war ships.

3. Answer   A

"First" is the best choice because it indicates that the statement is the first in a series of details explaining the methods Escalante used with his students. His first task was to show his students that they could learn successfully.

4. Answer   B

"In fact" is the best choice because it clarifies the information presented in the sentence before it. Sentence 9 states that anorexia is more than a simple eating disorder. Sentence 10 begins with "In fact" to say that in actuality, anorexia is a distinct psychological disorder.

5. Answer   D

"In addition" indicates that new information of equal value is being added. In the passage, another change to bare-fisted boxing is added to the previous two already mentioned.

6. Answer   C

"Moreover" indicates an addition of information. In the passage, "Moreover" appropriately begins sentence 9, which adds a new detail expressing another way eye movements communicate.

7. Answer   B

"Along with" means in addition to. Sentence 7 in the passage uses "Along with" to show that the albatross not only has salt tolerance but also has extraordinary flight abilities.

8. Answer   A

"Moreover" indicates an addition of information. In the passage, sentence 13 adds another serious physical effect of overdosing on anabolic steroids.

9. Answer   D

"For example" alerts the reader that a specific support is going to follow a more general statement. In the passage, sentence 4 provides the first example to support the point that a child may be able to teach a parent a computer or Internet skill.

10. Answer   C

"First" indicates that a specific idea is going to be introduced. In this passage, "First" is used in the sentence to express the first benefit of highlighting.

CHAPTER 2: LANGUAGE SKILLS

1. Choosing Proper Expressions (Context Clues)

1. Answer   B

"Detect" means to discover the presence of. Good vision helps animals discover the presence of their prey or predators from a distance.

2. Answer   A

"Integrated" means incorporated into a larger unit. The computer has become incorporated into our daily lives. In other words, using a computer has become part of our lives without our thinking about it. We use the computer informally for e-mail, Internet searches, and chats. Many of us use computer technology in some way in the workplace.

3. Answer   C

"Restore" means to repair, to renew. The context of the sentence makes this an ideal choice. Sleep enables the body to renew itself by repairing the body.

4. Answer   B

"Reveals" means to make known, to show. The purpose of research is to prove a theory, so "reveals" makes sense within the context of the sentence.

5. Answer   C

"Distinguishing" means seeing the difference between. This is the best word based on the context of the sentence. Critical thinking involves being able to distinguish the difference between fact and opinion.

6. Answer   A

"Expression" means representation in words, art, or music. The context of the sentence makes this the best word. The Harlem Renaissance was a literary and artistic movement that expressed African-American pride.

7. Answer   B

"Created" means produced or caused. This word works well within the context of the sentence. A contrast is set up by the structure of the sentence in which the dependent clause that begins the sentence describes a more positive effect of the September 11 attacks. The second part of the sentence gives the negative effect: the attacks caused people to feel more vulnerable.

8. Answer   C

"Significant" means large, meaningful, important, or having a major effect. Within the context of the sentence, this is the best word choice. In the past fifty years, major changes in marriage practices have occurred and have been noted by social scientists.

9. Answer   B

"Eradicate" means destroy, do away with, get rid of. The context of the sentence makes this word an ideal choice. A person would get rid of body odor if he or she thought it was a problem.

10. Answer   A

"Present" has several meanings, but in this sentence it is used as a verb to mean show or make evident by showing. This is the best choice based on the context of the sentence. Test stress can present itself in distinct physical symptoms.

2. Confused or Misused Words/Phrases

For each of these questions, the definition for each underlined word in the sentence and the definition for its corresponding option is provided. Notice that the correct answer/definition is given first, followed by its counterpart definition. To clarify your understanding, you should insert the definitions into the sentence.

1. Answer   C
   has passed   has moved forward to catch up and then continued beyond (verb)
   has past   a nonstandard (incorrect) form of "has passed."

2. Answer   C
   between   measuring one thing with another, used with two items
   among   with each other, used with more than two items

3. Answer   A
   set   to put or place (verb)
   sit   to bend one's knees and rest on one's buttocks

4. Answer   A
   number   expression of a quantity, used with countable nouns
   amount   expression of a quantity, used with non-countable nouns

5. Answer   C
   already   by this time
   all ready   fully prepared

6. Answer   A
   stationery   envelopes and paper used for writing letters
   stationary   not moving

7. Answer   B
   accept   to approve of
   except   but, excluding

8. Answer   C
   sight   in view; at or within a reasonable time
   site   place of something

9. Answer   B
   affect   have an influence on or cause a change in (verb)
   effect   a result (noun)

10. Answer   B
    lose   to be unsuccessful in retaining possession of
    loose   not tight

CHAPTER 3: *SENTENCE SKILLS*

1. Modifiers

For each of these questions, to avoid needless repetition of information, only the correct option is explained. The type of error is also identified: dangling modifier or misplaced modifier.

1. Answer   C   Dangling Modifier
The modifier "Having entered the gym" must be followed by a noun or pronoun identifying the individual who entered the gym.

2. Answer   A   Dangling Modifier
The modifier "To revise my paper" must be followed by a noun or pronoun identifying the individual who needs to revise it. Otherwise, the modifier "dangles" because it doesn't have a reference.

3. Answer   B   Dangling Modifier
The modifier "While I was watching a movie on television" correctly identifies who was watching a movie on television.

4. Answer   B   Misplaced Modifier
The correct sentence identifies which of the two, the father or the son, was five when he learned to ride his bicycle without the training wheels. The clause "when I was five" corrects the sentence.

5. Answer   A   Dangling Modifier
The modifier "Riding on the escalator" must be followed by the person riding on the escalator. The correct sentence follows that modifier with "I."

6. Answer   C   Dangling Modifier
The foreign student is the person who does not get to see her mother; therefore, the modifier "As a foreign student studying in the U.S." should be followed by the pronoun "I."

7. Answer   A   Dangling Modifier
The pronoun "we" must follow the modifier "After writing a check and signing the documents" to indicate who wrote the check and signed the documents.

8. Answer   B   Dangling Modifier
The correct sentence supplies a subject "I" to identify who was fishing on the ocean with his friend.

9. Answer   C   Dangling Modifier
The reader needs to know who removed the label at the neckline of the T-shirt. Adding the word "I" to the modifier clarifies the sentence by identifying the actor in the sentence. Otherwise, the reader would think that the T-shirt removed its own label.

10. Answer   A   Dangling Modifier
The correct sentence supplies the pronoun "I" to indicate who ran the red light.

2. Coordination and Subordination

For each of the following questions, the correct definition for each transitional phrase is provided, and the correct relationship between ideas is explained.

1. Answer   A

Although: contrast. The dependent clause that begins the sentence suggests that having a baby can be joyous; the independent clause indicates the contrasting idea that it can strain a relationship.

2. Answer   D

Moreover: addition. The first independent clause explains the class' plan to study at the University of Seville in the summer. The second independent clause adds information: they also intend to see the famous historical sites.

3. Answer   C

So: cause and effect; indicates a result. The second independent clause gives the result of the first.

4. Answer   B

Who: relative pronoun used at the beginning of an adjective clause (dependent clause) to describe a person. The "who" clause modifies the word "person" at the end of the opening independent clause.

5. Answer   B

Therefore: cause and effect; indicates the effect. The independent clause that begins the sentence explains that Andrea's job is demanding. The effect, as stated in the second independent clause, is that she can only take two classes per semester.

6. Answer   A

Because: cause and effect. The dependent clause that begins the sentence gives the cause, "Because the bus was late." The independent clause that completes the sentence explains the effect: "I missed my first class."

7. Answer   C

After: time order; indicates that one thing occurs later than the other. In the sentence, the person plans to transfer to a four-year university "after" he or she receives a two-year degree from the community college.

8. Answer   A

Who: relative pronoun used at the beginning of an adjective clause (dependent clause) to describe a person. The clause "who is flying this airplane" modifies the word "pilot."

9. Answer   B

So that: cause and effect. The dependent clause "so that I can improve my vocabulary" is the effect of the independent clause that begins the sentence, explaining that the person has to learn fifty new words in reading class every week.

10. Answer   C

Even though: contrast. The sentence contrasts the knowledge that fast foods are high in calories with the decision to eat it despite this knowledge.

3. Parallel Structure

For each of these questions, to avoid needless repetition of information, only the correct option is explained.

1. Answer   A

The three verbs in the sentence are correctly expressed in the same past tense: inserted, selected, and filled.

2. Answer   C

The three verbs in the sentence are correctly expressed in the same present tense: look, read, and buy.

3. Answer   B

In this sentence, independent clauses are listed in the same grammatical structure: her friends were calling her, her brother was blasting his stereo, and her dad was mowing the lawn.

4. Answer   B

This sentence has a series of independent clauses in a list; each one begins with "they" and is followed by a verb in the present tense: take, say, and hug.

5. Answer   C

The sentence is grammatically parallel, with verb phrases used in a series: brushes her teeth, takes a shower, and walks the dog.

6. Answer   B

In this sentence, the verbs "storing" and "writing" must be balanced with "taping."

7. Answer   C

The answer, "cried," is consistent with the other verbs in the series, all in the past tense.

8. Answer   D

The verb "use" matches the verb "pay."

9. Answer   C

In this sentence, there are three noun phrases in a list that must be consistent in grammatical form; the phrases begin with a noun and end with a prepositional phrase. Therefore, "a scholarship for tuition" is the grammatically parallel answer.

10. Answer   B

Two noun phrases complete the sentence. To match grammatically, each of the items must begin with a noun and end in a prepositional phrase. "The shallowness of the water" is the correct match.

4. Fragments, Comma Splices, and Fused Sentences (Run-ons)

Due to the difficulty of this skill, twenty questions have been provided; however, only the first ten questions are explained. You will find two types of questions in this exercise. Some of the questions require that you decide whether the underlined portion needs to be corrected; if so, then you select from the options. The other type of question asks you to read each of the three underlined portions of a sentence for a possible error. The underlined portions are labeled in alphabetical order, "A" through "C." Each of the answer options is a possible replacement for the words in the question.

1. Answer   B

The semicolon in the original sentence is not correctly used; semicolons separate two independent clauses. The word group that comes after the semicolon is missing a subject, which makes it a fragment. This fragment "and hand it in to the instructor" is corrected by eliminating the punctuation at that point in the sentence.

2. Answer   C

A dependent clause begins this complex sentence. When a dependent clause comes at the beginning of a sentence, follow it with a comma.

3. Answer   B

This sentence contains three independent clauses. The last independent clause is not punctuated, creating a run-on error (fused). Choice B is the correction. The semicolon indicates that a new, related sentence is beginning: "now searching online is quick and easy."

4. Answer   A

"Therefore" is the conjunctive adverb used to join the two sentences. In this case, place a semicolon before "therefore" and follow it with a comma.

5. Answer   D

The sentence is correct as written.

6. Answer   A

A comma corrects the semicolon error in the sentence. Placing a semicolon after a dependent clause creates a fragment.

7. Answer   B

The sentence is fused. Placing a period between the first independent clause that ends with "friends" corrects the error. The first word of the next independent clause must be capitalized, "Studying."

8. Answer   D

The sentence is correct as written.

9. Answer   C

The compound verbs in the sentence, "put" and "likes," should not be separated by a comma.

10. Answer   A

The use of the semicolon is correct in this sentence because it separates two independent clauses. "For example" is the transitional expression that begins the second sentence. A comma is correctly placed after "For example."

11. Answer   B

The semicolon corrects the comma splice in the sentence.

12. Answer   A

A semicolon, not a comma, is required to separate two independent, related sentences.

13. Answer   D

The sentence is punctuated correctly as written.

14. Answer   B

The sentence beginning with "Whenever" and ending with "party" consists of two dependent clauses. It is a fragment. To correct the fragment, a comma should be added following "party."

15. Answer   A

A comma before the words "such as" indicates that the examples given are nonessential.

16. Answer   B

The semicolon after "classroom" separates the two independent clauses.

17. Answer   C

A period placed after "home" corrects the comma splice.

18. Answer   B

The semicolon corrects the comma splice error.

19. Answer   B

No punctuation is needed to separate a verb from its objects.

20. Answer   C

A comma should be used after an introductory phrase.

CHAPTER 4: *GRAMMAR SKILLS*
1. Standard Verb Forms

1. Answer   B

The verb "come" must be changed to the past tense "came" because the rest of the sentence is in the past tense.

2. Answer   D

The verbs in the sentence are correct. They are all in the past tense and use the correct past tense forms.

3. Answer   C

In this sentence, the incorrect past tense form of fall, "falled" is incorrect. "Fell" is the correct form.

4. Answer   A

The correct verb form to use with "had" is the past participle. "Approached" is the correct past participal form, so the answer is "had approached."

5. Answer   C

"Stealed" is not the correct past tense verb form of "steal." "Stole" is the correct form.

6. Answer   C

"Burst" is the correct past participle for the verb "burst."

7. Answer   A

The past tense of the verb "fly" is "flew."

8. Answer   B

The first part of the sentence uses the past perfect tense of the verb "had forgotten" to indicate that the action expressed occurred before the next action. "Had become" is incorrectly used in the next part of the sentence because her sunburn occurred later. The simple past "became" corrects the error.

9. Answer   C

"Lays" is an incorrect form of the verb "lie," meaning to recline. The phrase "Last Sunday," which begins the sentence, indicates that the action of the sentence is in the past. "Lay" is the past tense of "lie."

10. Answer   C

In this sentence, the past participle of the verb "eat" is incorrect. "Eaten" is the past participle, so the answer is "had been eaten."

2. Shifts in Verb Tense

1. Answer   B

The sentence is written in the present tense; therefore "forgot" must be changed to the present tense, "forget."

2. Answer   C

The actions in the sentence occurred in the past, so all of the verbs must be in the past tense. "Suspends" should be changed to "suspended."

3. Answer   A

In this sentence, the verbs should all be in the past tense. "Is trying" is in the present progressive tense and needs to be changed to "tried."

4. Answer   C

This sentence uses the simple present tense to express habitual action. In the sentence, the person performs the same activities, feeds the dog and takes him for a walk. The present progressive "am taking" should be replaced by the simple present "take."

5. Answer   B

The past tense of the verb "work" is incorrect in this sentence. The future is indicated; the second action of the sentence cannot happen until the first is completed. "Worked" should be changed to "will work."

6. Answer   A

All the verbs in this sentence should be in the past tense because the details of the sentence describe something that happened in the past. "Has flown" should be changed to "flew."

7. Answer   D

The sentence is correct. The use of the past and past perfect tenses show that one action in the past was completed before another action in the past.

8. Answer   B

This sentence explains that one action in the past occurred while another was still going on in the past.

"Sleeps" is in the present tense; the verb should be in the past progressive tense.

9. Answer   C

This sentence sets up an if . . . then condition. The present tense of the verb is the correct choice for the "if" clause that begins the sentence.

10. Answer   B

In this sentence, both the present and past tenses are used. In the first part of the sentence, the reader learns that Suzanne does not work at her previous job. She "found" a new job; this happened and was completed at some point in the past. Right now she likes it better than the job in the bakery.

3. Subject and Verb Agreement

1. Answer   A

"Was" is the correction for "were" in the sentence. When two subjects are joined by "neither . . . nor," the verb agrees with the closer subject (the word after "nor").

2. Answer   C

The subject of the dependent clause is "each," which is a singular indefinite pronoun. Therefore, the singular form of the verb, "needs," is required. When a singular indefinite pronoun is the subject of a sentence, the verb will always be singular. Don't be fooled by the prepositional phrase that may come between the subject and the verb. Even if the object of the prepositional phrase is a plural word, such as "speakers" in the question, you should disregard it.

3. Answer   C

"Each" is the subject of the dependent clause that begins with "because." "Each" is a singular subject, so the verb must be singular, "has." Don't be fooled by the prepositional phrase that may come between the subject and the verb. Even if the object of the prepositional phrase is a plural word, such as "birds" in the question, you should disregard it.

4. Answer   B

The dependent clause beginning with "that" modifies "lecture series," which is singular; although the word "series" may be plural, the compound noun "lecture series" is considered a unit. Therefore, the verb must be singular. The helping verb "have" should be changed to the singular "has."

5. Answer   C

The dependent clause in this sentence begins with "which"; "which" takes the place of the subject of the clause. Therefore, you need to find the word that "which" refers to: "peanut butter and jelly." Although "peanut butter and jelly" appears to be two items, it is viewed as one, so the verb should be in the singular form, "is."

6. Answer   A

The subject of the sentence, *Stand and Deliver*, is the name of a movie. Titles are considered singular, so the present tense verb form must be singular to agree with the subject. The third person singular present tense form of a regular verb ends with an –s, in this case "tells."

7. Answer   B
The verb is part of a dependent clause that begins with "who." You need to find the word that the clause modifies to determine whether the verb of the dependent clause is singular or plural. In this sentence, "who" refers to "scientists," so the plural form of the verb, "perform," is correct.

8. Answer   C
"Few" is the subject of the last independent clause in the sentence. "Few" is a plural indefinite pronoun, so the verb must also be in the plural form, "pass."

9. Answer   D
The sentence is correct.

10. Answer   A
The subject "shelters" requires a plural verb, "offer." Remember, plural verbs do not end in –s.

11. Answer   B
The second independent clause of the sentence has a compound subject: "a beverage and a small package of salted peanuts." The verb must be plural to agree: "do."

12. Answer   A
The subject of the sentence, "Briana," takes a singular verb, "has." The intervening prepositional phrase should be ignored.

13. Answer   C
The subject of the second independent clause in this compound sentence is "one," which is singular. The verb must be singular, "looks." The third person singular present tense form of a regular verb ends with –s.

14. Answer   A
"Accommodations" is the subject of the sentence and is plural, so the plural verb form must be used, "have."

15. Answer   A
The subject of the sentence, "statistics," is singular. The singular verb form "is" agrees.

16. Answer   B
"Is" is the correct verb which agrees with the subject "variety." This second independent clause in the sentence begins with the transition words "in addition." The word "there" is not a subject. In sentences that begin with "there is" or "there are," the subject usually follows the verb.

17. Answer   B
The dependent clause begins with "who." To determine whether this "who" subject is singular or plural, you must find the word the dependent clause modifies. It is "the French." "The French" is considered plural, so the verb form is plural, "are."

18. Answer   A
The subject of the sentence is "news," which is considered singular. The verb must also be singular, "makes." Remember, the third person singular present tense form of a regular verb ends with –s.

19. Answer   C
"Few" is the subject, which is a plural indefinite pronoun. Therefore, the subject should be plural, "get." The third person plural form in the present tense does not end in –s.

20. Answer   D
The sentence is correct.

4. Pronoun and Antecedent Agreement

1. Answer   A
"Each" is the singular subject of the sentence. The pronoun that refers to it must also be singular. Therefore, "their" is incorrect because it is a plural pronoun. Of the choices, "her" is the only possible correction. "Its" is not used to refer to people, and "our" is plural.

2. Answer   D
The sentence is correct. When two subjects are joined by "either . . . or," the pronoun must agree with the antecedent closest to the verb (after "or"). A band or choir is a thing, so "its" is the appropriate choice.

3. Answer   B
"Company" is the singular subject of the sentence to which the pronoun refers. For the pronoun to agree, it must be singular. In addition, "company" is a thing, so "its" is the correct choice, not "him" or "her."

4. Answer   C
The two subjects of the second part of the sentence are joined by "neither . . . nor." In this situation, the pronoun must agree with the word closest to the verb (after "nor"), which is "boater." Therefore, "his" is the correct choice, for it is the only one of the three choices that is singular.

5. Answer   B
The pronoun in this sentence refers to the subject, Pete. It must be the singular "his." This is the only possible answer because the other two choices are plural.

6. Answer   C
The pronoun "them" is the correction, replacing "him." The pronoun refers to the subject "They" (Andrea and Sebastian), so it must take the objective plural pronoun "them."

7. Answer   A
The pronoun "its" agrees with the subject "committee." "Committee" is considered singular in this sentence because the members are acting as a unit.

8. Answer   C
The pronoun must agree with the singular "parent." "His or her" is the correct choice. Without knowing the sex of the parent, the choice of "his or her" is appropriate.

9. Answer   B

The pronoun refers to the subject, "neither the students nor the professor." In this situation, the pronoun must agree with the word closest to the verb (after "nor"), which is the "professor." "Professor" is singular, so the pronoun that refers to it must also be singular. "His" is the correct choice.

10. Answer   D

The sentence is correct.

5. Pronoun Shifts

1. Answer   B

The second person viewpoint "you" is established in the sentence with "you," so the word "one" must be replaced with "you" to avoid a shift in perspective.

2. Answer   C

The sentence is written in the second person plural with the pronouns "us" and "we" and must be continued with the possessive form, "our."

3. Answer   C

The sentence is written in the third person plural viewpoint with the pronouns "their" and "they" and must be continued with by replacing "one" with "they."

4. Answer   A

The third person singular is established with the pronouns "he" and "his." Therefore, "you" must be replaced by "he" to avoid a shift in perspective.

5. Answer   B

The third person singular is established with the pronoun "his," which is used twice in the sentence. This perspective must be continued by replacing "you" with "he."

6. Answer   C

In this sentence, the second person plural is established with "we" and "our." To avoid a shift in perspective, "we" must replace the "he."

7. Answer   C

The third person plural is established with "their" and "they." To avoid a shift in person, "they" must replace "you."

8. Answer   A

Third person plural is established in this sentence with "them" and "their." Replacing "we" with "they" corrects a shift in person.

9. Answer   D

Third person plural is used consistently and properly throughout this sentence.

10. Answer   B

In this sentence, first person singular is established by "my" and "I." To avoid a shift in person, "you" must be replaced with "I."

6. Clear Pronoun Reference

1. Answer   B

The word "they" in the original sentence does not refer to any word in the sentence; its antecedent is missing. "The manager" provides the missing information. The manager is the one doing the interview.

2. Answer   C

In this sentence, there is no way to know what the pronoun "it" refers to. "The picture" is now crooked.

3. Answer   A

As the sentence is written, the pronoun "it" seems to refer to the phone, which cannot answer itself. "Tavar" should replace the pronoun to clarify that he did not answer the phone.

4. Answer   B

In this sentence, the pronoun "it" does not refer to any word in the sentence. The newspaper does not "say" anything; "the reporter" does.

5. Answer   C

As this sentence is written, it is difficult to know to what the pronoun "it" is referring. "It" should be replaced with "the table."

6. Answer   A

The pronoun "they" does not specify who helped edit the paper in the writing lab. Replacing "they" with "the lab assistants" clarifies this.

7. Answer   A

The use of the pronoun "it" is confusing because it does not appear to refer to anything in the sentence. The pronoun must refer to "college preparatory courses," so the pronoun "them" corrects any misunderstanding.

8. Answer   B

Two women are mentioned in this sentence, and although the reader may know that Doreen is the best worker, there is no clue to that fact in the sentence as it is written. Repeating the name of the person near the pronoun, "she, Doreen," clarifies any possible confusion.

9. Answer   C

Two men are mentioned in this sentence, and although the reader may know that the tour is for Mr. Linger's students, there is no clue to that fact in the sentence as it is written. Replacing the pronoun "his" with "Mr. Linger's" clarifies the meaning.

10. Answer   D

All of these pronouns clearly refer to their antecedents.

7. Pronoun Case Form

1. Answer   A

"Me" is the object of the preposition "between."

2. Answer   B

"Me" is the object of the preposition "to."

3. Answer   C

"Me" is the object of the preposition "for."

4. Answer   C

"They" is the subject of the verb "were exhausted."

5. Answer   C

"Me" is the direct object of the verb "believe."

6. Answer   D

All of the pronouns are used properly in the sentence. "Them" is the object of the preposition "to," "They" is the subject of the verb "use," and "us" is the object of the preposition "of."

7. Answer   A

"I" is the subject of the verb "will be."

8. Answer   B

"She" is the subject of the verb "was walking."

9. Answer   D

All of the pronouns are used properly in the sentence. "Us" is the object of the verb "told," "us" is the object of the preposition "of," and "who" is the subject of the verb "does."

10. Answer   B

"We" is the subject of the verb "have."

8. Adjectives and Adverbs

1. Answer   A

"Peacefully" is the adverb that modifies the infinitive verb "evacuate." "Peaceful" is an adjective.

2. Answer   C

"Artistically" is the adverb that modifies "was executed." "Artistic" is an adjective.

3. Answer   B

"Well" is an adverb modifying "sang." "Good" is an adjective.

4. Answer   B

"Tightly" is an adverb modifying "held." "Tight" is an adjective.

5. Answer   D

The adjectives and adverb are used correctly in this sentence. "Challenging" is an adjective modifying "job," "frequent" is an adjective modifying "shopping trips," and "frivolously" is an adverb modifying "spent."

6. Answer   C

"Really" is an adverb modifying the adjective "bad." "Real" is an adjective; it cannot modify another adjective.

7. Answer   B

"Good" is a predicate adjective describing the subject, "actress." Predicate adjectives describe the subject of the sentence through a linking verb such as "looked."

8. Answer   A

"Terrible" is a predicate adjective (also called a complement) describing the subject, "Renzo." Predicate adjectives describe the subject of the sentence through a linking verb such as "felt."

9. Answer   C

"Well" is an adverb modifying "felt." Although "felt" is a linking verb, the adverb "well" is used when referring to health.

10. Answer   A

"Surely" is an adverb modifying the verb "enjoyed." "Sure" is an adjective.

9. Degree Forms of Adjectives and Adverbs

1. Answer   C

The comparative "better" is required because "of the two guitar players" indicates a choice between two players.

2. Answer   B

The superlative "most beautiful" is required because the comparison is with more than two mountain ranges. The word "among" is used to describe more than two. Three syllable words form the superlative by adding "most" before the word.

3. Answer   A

The superlative "worst" is required because the comparison includes more than two years. "Since 1992" indicates more than two years.

4. Answer   B

The superlative "most handsome" is required because Brad Pitt is being compared to all actors, not just one other actor. Two-syllable words not ending in –y often require the addition of "most" before the word for the superlative form.

5. Answer   C

The comparative "more effectively" is required because Josh is being compared to one other person, "I." Words of three or more syllables form the comparative by adding "more" before the word.

6. Answer   D

The comparative "farther" is required because two distances are being compared.

7. Answer   A

The comparative adverb form "more diligently" is required. Studying for the final is compared to studying for the midterm. Words of three or more syllables form the comparative by adding "more" before the word.

8. Answer   D

The comparative form "more enthusiastically" is correctly used in the sentence. Hai's and Kim's routines are compared. Words of three or more syllables form the comparative by adding "more" before the word.

9. Answer   C

The comparative form "harder" is required to compare the difficulty of the exercises with the person's perception about how hard they might be. One-syllable words form the comparative by adding –er to the end of the word.

10. Answer   B

"Easier" is the required comparative form to compare math with English. One-syllable words ending in –y form the comparative by dropping –y and adding –ier.

10. Standard Spelling

1. Answer   B

There are three spelling issues that can be confusing with the word "knowledgeable": the silent "d," the addition of the suffix, and the choice of the suffix, -able or -ible. The suffix –ible is less commonly used than –able; therefore, it is a matter of memorizing the correct ending. When adding –able to a word that ends in –e that is not pronounced, usually you drop the –e; however, "knowledgeable" is one exception to this rule.

2. Answer   A

3. Answer   A

The word "truly" is an exception to the spelling rule. Usually, when you add –ly to a word ending in a vowel, you retain the vowel; however, you do drop the –e to spell "truly."

4. Answer   C

The word "license" is frequently misspelled. Most often the c and the s are reversed; however, in the incorrect choice c is used in place of s.

5. Answer   C

Although the word sounds as if it begins with ex, the correct spelling is "ecstasy." The word ending is –asy, not –acy.

6. Answer   D

The correct spelling involves double consonants.

7. Answer   B

The correct spelling involves double consonants.

8. Answer   B

The correct spelling involves double consonants.

9. Answer   A

The word "argue" does not retain the final –e before the suffix –ment.

10. Answer   B

The correct spelling involves two sets of double consonants.

11. Standard Punctuation

1. Answer   C

The sentence does not ask a direct question, so it does not require a question mark as end punctuation.

2. Answer   B

The comma before "because," between the first independent clause and the dependent clause that follows it, is not necessary.

3. Answer   A

Commas are used to separate elements of a date.

4. Answer   B

No comma is necessary after "such as."

5. Answer   D

The sentence is punctuated correctly.

For questions 6–10, only the correct option is explained to avoid unnecessary repetition of information.

6. Answer   D

The first punctuation issue is the comma after the word "off." This comma is required because along with the coordinating conjunction "so," it marks the separation between two separate complete sentences. The apostrophe used in "two weeks' vacation" is required. "Weeks'" is the plural of "week's." It is also a possessive. To form the possessive of a plural word ending in –s, you add an apostrophe after the –s.

7. Answer   A

In this sentence, no comma is required before "but" because the word does not begin another independent clause. The apostrophe is correctly placed after the y in "somebody's" to show possession.

8. Answer   C

The word "month's" requires an apostrophe because the word is possessive. Since it is only one month, the apostrophe is correctly placed after the h. The comma after "mother" indicates that the dependent clause is nonessential. The sentence is declarative, not a question, so a question mark is not required.

9. Answer   B

The semicolon after "equipment" is not necessary because it does not separate one independent clause from another. The semicolon is not used to introduce a list. The other error is the comma after "pets." This comma is not necessary because a separate independent clause does not come after the "and," which would indicate a compound sentence.

10. Answer   A

The sentence requires one comma placed after "powers" to set off the examples given. No comma is necessary after "away" to separate the two examples. The semicolon would not be used to introduce a series of examples. Finally, the two commas, one before and one after "and" in sentence D is incorrect; the first comma is not used to separate two examples, and the second comma is unnecessary.

12. Standard Capitalization

1. Answer   C
Seasons are not capitalized.

2. Answer   A
The word "history" should not be capitalized because it is not a specific course title.

3. Answer   A
Neither the "h" nor the "s" of the word "high school" needs to be capitalized. They are capitalized only when used with the name of the school.

4. Answer   C
The word "Northwest" is part of the name of a street address, so it should be capitalized.

5. Answer   A
The title of the book is not capitalized appropriately. Short prepositions and articles are not capitalized in titles of books and other works.

6. Answer   B
The word "aunt" is capitalized only when used in place of the person's name.

7. Answer   B
Official titles do not need to be capitalized when they are not accompanied by a person's name.

8. Answer   D
All words in this sentence are capitalized correctly.

9. Answer   C
The word "presidential" does not need to be capitalized. It is not used as a title.

10. Answer   D
All words in this sentence are capitalized correctly.

Appendix: Parts of Speech Review

1. *Verbs and Subjects*
2. *Nouns and Pronouns: Subjects versus Objects*
3. *Prepositional Phrases*
4. *Adjectives*
5. *Adverbs*
6. *Clauses*

Introduction

Before you begin learning about the grammar questions on the Writing Exit Exam, you first should know some basic grammar terminology and concepts that will very much help you understand what the test authors are looking for in each of the grammar questions. Many times, students get overwhelmed by all the "grammar terminology," or vocabulary used to describe grammar elements. In fact, there are just a few concepts that you really need to know in order to understand and describe what is going on with the grammar in a sentence. With that in mind, we will keep things as simple as possible. If you thoroughly understand the basic parts of speech—Verbs and Subjects, Nouns and Pronouns, Prepositional Phrases, Adjectives and Adverbs, and Clauses—you will be ready to learn about the specific grammar items typically covered on the Writing Exit Exam.

SECTION 1 ◆ VERBS AND SUBJECTS

Verbs and their subjects are the basic building blocks of sentences. Most students think they already know what a verb is—an action word, right? **However, you have to be careful: not all action words are verbs!**

1. <u>What is a VERB?</u> It is an action word **that <u>someone</u> or <u>something</u> in the sentence <u>is doing</u>.** If you see an action word in a sentence, but there is nobody or nothing that is actually <u>doing</u> that verb, then that action word is NOT a verb. It's actually something else.

2. <u>What is a SUBJECT?</u> It is the <u>someone</u> or <u>something</u> in the sentence that <u>is doing</u> some verb.

   • Olympic <u>athletes</u> <u>exercise</u> regularly.
      ➢ "Exercise" in this case is an action word, and it has a subject!
      ➢ WHO exercises? Athletes.

   • After dinner, the <u>kids</u> <u>loaded</u> the dishwasher.
      ➢ "Loaded" is an action word; does it have a subject?
      ➢ WHO loaded? The kids.

- The <u>Thompsons</u> <u>have</u> a new refrigerator, and <u>it</u> <u>is working</u> very well.
  - ➤ "Have" is an action word.
  - ➤ WHO has? The Thompsons.

  - ➤ "Is working" is an action word.
  - ➤ WHAT is working? It is working. "It," of course, is referring to the refrigerator.

- <u>Salt and pepper</u> <u>give</u> flavor to foods.
  - ➤ "Give" is an action word.
  - ➤ WHAT gives flavor to foods? Salt and pepper.

- Raising his hand, the <u>student</u> <u>asked</u> the teacher to repeat the question.
  - ➤ "Raising" is an action word.
  - ➤ WHO raising? Nobody, actually. It's not "the student." The sentence does not say, "The student WAS raising his hand." This is an example of an action word that is not a verb.

  - ➤ "Asked" is an action word.
  - ➤ WHO asked? The student.

  - ➤ "Repeat" is an action word, but notice the "to" in front of it.
  - ➤ WHO "to repeat?" Nobody. Nobody repeated anything. "To repeat" is an example of an action word that is not a verb.

  TIPS: *The verb usually comes AFTER the subject.
  *A sentence can have more than one verb and/or more than one subject.
  *To find subjects and verbs, find the action words first. Then, test whether or not someone or something is <u>doing</u> that action word.
  *"To + verb"(an infinitive) is NEVER a verb by itself.

3. <u>"Be" LINKING Verbs are ALWAYS verbs or parts of verbs:</u>

AM ARE WAS	WERE IS	*BE (not "to + be") *BEEN

*"Be" and "been" are always **parts** of verbs (i.e., <u>will be making</u>, <u>should have been done</u>)

- <u>I</u> <u>am</u> an English teacher.
  - ➤ "Am" is ALWAYS a verb.
  - ➤ "I" is the subject that "am."

- Right now, <u>you</u> <u>are learning</u> about subjects and verbs.
  - ➤ "Are" is ALWAYS a verb. "Learning" is part of the action, so the whole verb is "are learning."
  - ➤ "You" is the subject that is doing the learning.

- <u>It</u> <u>is</u> difficult for me to understand spoken Spanish.
  - ➤ "Is" is ALWAYS a verb.
  - ➤ WHAT is difficult? "It" is difficult.
  - ➤ "Spoken" is an action word, but there is no subject that goes with it. WHO or WHAT spoken? It is not a verb.

- **<u>Fruits and vegetables</u> <u><u>are</u></u> healthy and <u><u>should be eaten</u></u> every day.**
  - ➢ "Are" is ALWAYS a verb.
  - ➢ WHAT are healthy? Fruits and vegetables.
  - ➢ "Should be eaten" is a verb—"be" is a linking verb!
  - ➢ WHAT should be eaten? Fruits and vegetables.

- **<u>Learning</u> grammar <u><u>can be</u></u> easy.**
  - ➢ "Be" is ALWAYS a verb with can, must, will, should, etc.
  - ➢ WHAT can be easy? Learning grammar. Of those two words, the simple subject is "learning."
  - ➢ "Learning" is an action word, but WHO LEARNING? Nobody. There is no subject, so that is not a verb.

    *TIPS: *Verbs can be composed of more than one word.*
    An "ing" action word is NOT a verb UNLESS it is working with a linking verb (am, is, are, was, were, be, been).

SECTION 1 ◆ PRACTICE: FINDING VERBS AND SUBJECTS

For each of the following sentences, <u>underline</u> the simple subjects and <u>double-underline</u> the verbs that go with them.

1. Many students learn to type in high school.

2. Nowadays, typing is very important for many professions.

3. Computers have made it easier for everyone to type.

4. Some older students find computers to be very confusing and so avoid them.

5. Correcting mistakes on a computer is easier than on a typewriter.

6. Computers and printers are becoming less expensive.

7. Nowadays, many elementary schools teach typing rather than cursive handwriting.

8. Some schools issue students laptop computers and do not charge money for them.

9. Many employers these days expect their workers to be able to use computers.

10. After graduating from college, most students can use computers well.

Answers and Explanations to Practice: Finding Subjects and Verbs

1. <u>Students</u> <u><u>learn</u></u>
   "Learn" is an action. Who learns? Students learn. "Type" is not a verb because nobody in the sentence types, so it has no subject. "High school" is not doing any action, so it's not a subject.

2. <u>Typing</u> <u><u>is</u></u>
   "Is" is a linking verb, which is always a verb. What is (very important)? "Typing" is very important. "Professions" is not doing any action, so it's not a subject.

3. Computers <u>have made</u>
"Have made" is an action. What have made it easier? Computers have made it easier. "To type" is never a verb by itself. "Students" is not actually doing any action in the sentence, so it's not a subject.

4. Students <u>find, avoid</u>
"Find" is an action. Who find computers to be confusing? Some older students, but the simple subject is "students." "To be" is an action word, but "to + verb" by itself is never a verb. Nobody in the sentence "to be." Similarly, "confusing" looks like it may be an action word, but it's not. Nobody or nothing "confusing." "Avoid" is an action word. Who avoids? The students. This sentence has one subject but two verbs.

5. Correcting <u>is</u>
"Is" is a linking verb, which is always a verb. What is easier? Correcting mistakes on a computer is easier. Of all those words, the simple subject is "correcting." It's not "mistakes" because "mistakes" is not easier on a computer. "Correcting" mistakes is easier. "Typewriter" is not doing any action, so it's not a subject.

6. Computers and printers <u>are becoming</u>
"Are becoming" contains a linking verb, which is always a verb. What are become less expensive? "Computers and printers" are becoming less expensive.

7. Schools <u>teach</u>
"Teach" is an action word. Who or what teaches typing? Elementary schools teach typing. The simple subject is "schools." "Typing" and "handwriting" are not verbs because they do not have "be" linking verbs; an "ing" word is only a verb if it is accompanied by a linking verb. Also, nobody in the sentence "typing" or "handwriting," so if there are no subjects, they are not verbs.

8. Schools <u>issue, do not charge</u>
"Issue" is an action word. Who or what issues students laptop computers? Schools do. Neither "laptop computers" nor "students" are doing actions, so those words are not subjects. "Do not charge" is an action. Who does not charge? Again, schools. This sentence has one subject with two verbs.

9. Employers <u>expect</u>
"Expect" is an action word. Who expects? Employers expect. "To be able" and "to use" are never verbs by themselves. "Workers" and "computers" are not doing any action in the sentence, so it's not a subject.

10. Students <u>can use</u>
"Graduating" is an action word, but there is no <u>linking verb</u> working with it, so it is not a verb. "Can use" is an action. Who can use computers? Most students, and of those two words, students is the simple subject.

SECTION 2 ◆ NOUNS AND PRONOUNS: SUBJECTS VS. OBJECTS

Subjects are vitally important, but it is also important to distinguish them from other kinds of nouns so that you do not mix them up.

1. **What is a NOUN?** It is a **person** (WHO), **place**, or **thing** (WHAT).

2. <u>What are the **TWO WAYS** that **NOUNS WORK**?</u>
   • **Subjects**
   • **Objects**

3. <u>**What is a SUBJECT**</u>? It is the <u>**someone**</u> (WHO) or <u>**something**</u> (WHAT) that <u>is doing</u> some verb.

4. <u>**What is an OBJECT**</u>? Any person, place, or thing (any WHO or WHAT) **that is NOT doing some action** is an <u>object</u>.

5. <u>**What is a COMPOUND subject or object**</u>? It is when there are TWO OR MORE of them in the same structure (my *son* and his *friend*; for my *husband* and *me*; *salt* and *pepper*, etc.).

6. <u>**What is a PRONOUN**</u>? It is a <u>general</u> word that is used to replace a noun or another pronoun in the sentence (student = HE or SHE; students = THEY; belonging to US = OUR, etc).

7. <u>**What is the ANTECEDENT or REFERENT**</u>? When the pronoun refers to a word that appears earlier in a sentence, then that word is called the pronoun's antecedent.

8. <u>**What are the SUBJECT and OBJECT PRONOUNS?**</u>

SUBJECT PRONOUNS	OBJECT PRONOUNS
I write well.	This is for **ME**
YOU write well.	This is for **YOU**
HE writes well.	This is for **HIM**
SHE writes well.	This is for **HER***
IT writes well.	This is for **IT**
WE write well.	This is for **US**
THEY write well.	This is for **THEM**
WHO writes well?	**WHOM** is this for?

*"Her" is also a possessive pronoun (Her name is Mary), which is neither a subject nor an object.

> TIPS: *To test whether or not a pronoun is a subject or an object, put it before some verb (ex: I like it vs. Me like it).*
> *NOUNS usually answer the questions WHO or WHAT (make sure the WHO or WHAT is also a person, place, or thing!).*
> ***Compound pronouns** can cause big problems! "My mom and me went shopping" does not work because you can't say "Me went shopping" without sounding like a caveman. "Me" is always a subject, not an object.*

• **It** <u>is</u> easy to find the *subject* of a *sentence*.
   ➤ "Is" is a linking verb, which is ALWAYS a verb.
   ➤ The pronoun "It" is the subject that "is," and the antecedent or referent is "to find the subject of a sentence."
   ➤ *"Subject"* and *"sentence"* are objects because they are not doing some action.

• My **family** and I <u>will go</u> to the USF Bulls' opening *game* this *Saturday*.
   ➤ "Will go" is an action.
   ➤ "Family and I," which contains the pronoun "I," is the subject.
   ➤ *"Game"* and *"Saturday"* are objects because they are not doing some action.

- <u>We</u> always <u>tailgate</u> before the *game*.
  - ➤ "Tailgate" is an action.
  - ➤ WHO tailgates? "We" do, and the antecedent for the pronoun "we" is "my family and I."
  - ➤ "*Game*" is an object because it is not doing some action.

- Unfortunately for *us*, the **weather** <u>**is going to be**</u> terrible.
  - ➤ "Is going" is the action (notice the linking verb).
  - ➤ WHAT is going to be terrible? The weather.
  - ➤ "Us" is an object. It answers the question WHO, but it is not doing any action in the sentence. Notice that it's in the form of an object pronoun.
  - ➤ "Terrible" is NOT a noun. It is not a person, place, or thing. It is describing the weather.

SECTION 2 ◆ PRACTICE: FINDING SUBJECTS AND OBJECTS

For each of the following sentences, <u>underline</u> the simple subjects, <u>double-underline</u> the verbs that go with them, and circle the objects.

1. Last year, it rained from start to finish.

2. My husband bought rain ponchos for my daughter and me.

3. Rain makes it very uncomfortable for my family and me to watch the game.

4. In the past, my friends and I did not watch football.

5. My husband taught the rules of the game to my children and me.

6. He and his best friend sometimes go to games without us.

7. His best friend's wife and I sometimes play tennis without them.

8. My son and his friends sometimes get to the game before us.

9. Whom did you buy this soda for?

10. Who asked you to do that?

Answers and Explanations to Practice: Finding Subjects and Objects

1. <u>It</u> <u>rained</u>
   Objects: year, start, finish
   Each of these words answers the question WHAT, which is typically a question nouns answer.

2. <u>Husband</u> <u>bought</u>
   Objects: ponchos, daughter, me
   Each of these words answers the question WHAT, which is typically a question nouns answer. Notice that you cannot say, "for my daughter and I" because it would sound wrong to say, "for I." "Rain" is describing what kind of ponchos, and so is an adjective. "My" is a possessive, and it is also an adjective.

3. <u>Rain</u> <u>makes</u>
   Objects: it, family, me, game
   "Uncomfortable" is an adjective. "My" is a possessive, and it is an adjective. "To watch" is not a verb because "to + verb" is never a verb by itself.

4. <u>Friends, I</u> <u>did not watch</u>
   Objects: past, football
   Notice that you cannot say, "My friends and me did not watch" because it would sound wrong to say, "Me did not watch."

5. <u>Husband</u> <u>taught</u>
   Objects: rules, game, children, me
   "My" is a possessive, and it is an adjective.

6. <u>He, friend</u> <u>go</u>
   Objects: games, us
   "His" is a possessive, and it is an adjective. "Best" is an adjective describing "friend." "Sometimes" is an adverb telling when.

7. <u>Wife, I</u> <u>play</u>
   Objects: tennis, them
   "His" and "friend's" are possessives, which are adjectives. "Best" is an adjective describing "friend." "Sometimes" is an adverb telling when.

8. <u>Son, friends</u> <u>go</u>
   Objects: game, us
   "My" and "his" are possessives, and they are adjectives. "Sometimes" is an adverb telling when.

9. <u>You</u> <u>did buy</u>
   Objects: soda, whom. Question grammar is easier to understand if you turn the question into a statement. Thus, "You did buy this soda for whom." Clearly, "whom" is not doing any action, so that is why it is in object form.

10. <u>Who</u> <u>asked</u>
    Objects: you, that. "To do" is not a verb because "to + verb" is never a verb by itself.

SECTION 3 ◆ PREPOSITIONAL PHRASES

Sometimes, the presence of Prepositional Phrases in a sentence can confuse students about what the real Subject is. Learning to spot Prepositional Phrases can help you avoid being distracted by them so that you can find the true Subject and Verb.

<u>What is a PREPOSITIONAL PHRASE</u>? It is a group of words consisting of (at least) a **<u>preposition</u>** and an **<u>object</u>** (noun).

1. **<u>How do PREPOSITIONAL PHRASES function</u>?** They help describe things by telling WHERE, WHEN, WHY, HOW, and WHICH, etc.
   • The <u>cat</u> <u>is sleeping</u> (~~on the bed~~). (WHERE)

- (~~Before Wednesday's test~~), <u>you</u> <u>should take</u> the Practice Test. (WHEN)
- The <u>man</u> <u>divorced</u> his wife (~~for cheating~~) (~~on him~~). (WHY)
- The <u>students</u> (~~in my class~~) <u>pass</u> the Exit Exam (~~by studying hard~~). (HOW)
- The <u>people</u> (~~in the green jerseys~~) <u>are</u> Bulls fans. (WHICH)

2. **What are some common PREPOSITIONS?**

General Prepositions	
AT	IN
ABOUT	OF
BEFORE	ON
BY	TO
FOR	WITH
FROM	

LOCATION Prepositions	
ABOVE	NEAR
BELOW	THROUGH
BETWEEN	UNDER
INTO	

TIPS: *You can generally CROSS OUT prepositional phrases in sentences to see the true subject / verb structure.
*The OBJECT of a preposition can NEVER be a subject.
*If the object of a preposition is a pronoun, it MUST be an object pronoun.
*WHOM is an OBJECT PRONOUN!!! WHO is a SUBJECT.

3. **Why are "OF" prepositional phrases so important?** If they are located between the subject and the verb, they can cause students to misunderstand the true subject. Beware of the following:
✓ Either (of)
✓ Neither (of)
✓ Each (of)
✓ Every one (of)
✓ One (of)

- <u>Each</u> (~~of the girls~~) <u>has</u> her own style.
  ➤ Notice the "of" preposition. If you don't cross it out, you might get confused and think "girls" is the subject, which might cause you to use the wrong verb.

- The <u>lunchbox</u> (~~on the counter~~) <u>belongs</u> (~~to me~~).
  ➤ Notice how crossing out the prepositional phrases makes the simple subject/verb structure of the sentence clear.

- (~~For many years~~), <u>I</u> <u>taught</u> English (~~to speakers~~) (~~of other languages~~).

- <u>One</u> (~~of the children~~) (~~in my daughter's class~~) <u>has</u> a severe allergy (~~to peanuts~~).
  ➤ Notice the "of" preposition. If you don't cross it out, you might get confused and think "children" is the subject, which might cause you to use the wrong verb.

- (~~Before work~~), the <u>man</u> <u>bought</u> gas (~~at the 7-11~~) (~~near his house~~).

- (~~Whom~~) <u>are</u> <u>you</u> <u>talking</u> (~~to~~)?
  ➤ In this case, the preposition "to" and its object "whom" are separated.

- (~~To whom~~) <u>are</u> <u>you</u> <u>talking</u>?
  ➤ In this case, the preposition "to" and its object "whom" are together.

SECTION 3 ◆ PRACTICE: FINDING PREPOSITIONAL PHRASES

For each of the following sentences, <u>underline</u> the simple subjects and <u>double-underline</u> the verbs that go with them. Put the prepositional phrases in parentheses and cross them out.

1. On Valentine's Day, my husband always buys something special for my daughter and me.

2. All of the states in America have different laws about marriage.

3. By studying hard and by staying committed, you can succeed in college.

4. With whom was the man walking?

5. My sister was trying to point to an old boyfriend in the restaurant.

6. Every person in the United States is supposed to be treated equally in a court of law.

7. Several celebrities have written books about the abusive relationship between their parents and them.

8. I always have a cup of coffee in the morning.

9. Many of the teenagers in the neighborhood talk on the telephone to each other at night.

10. One of the kids in my neighborhood was arrested for breaking mailboxes.

Answers and Explanations to Practice: Finding Prepositional Phrases

1. <u>Husband</u> <u>buys</u>
   Prepositional Phrases: on Valentine's Day, for my daughter and me

2. <u>All</u> <u>have</u>
   Prepositional Phrases: of the states, in America, about marriage
   Be careful to cross out the prepositions! Otherwise, you'll think "states" is the subject, and it's not.

3. <u>You</u> <u>can succeed</u>
   Prepositional Phrases: by studying hard, by staying committed, in college

4. <u>Man</u> <u>was walking</u>
   Prepositional Phrases: with whom
   Turn the sentence into a statement to see the structure more easily: "The man was walking with whom." Notice that the object pronoun WHOM is used with this preposition since all prepositions take objects and not subjects.

5. <u>Sister</u> <u>was trying</u>
   Prepositional Phrases: to an old boyfriend, in the restaurant
   "To point" is actually a "to + verb" and not a prepositional phrase.

6. <u>Person</u> <u>is supposed (OR is supposed to be treated)</u>
   Prepositional Phrases: in the United States, in a court, of law
   Notice that if you don't cross out the prepositional phrase "in the United States," you might be tempted to call "states" the subject.

7. <u>Celebrities</u> <u>have written</u>
Prepositional Phrases: about the abusive relationship, between their parents and them

8. <u>I</u> <u>have</u>
Prepositional Phrases: of coffee, in the morning

9. <u>Teenagers</u> <u>talk</u>
Prepositional Phrases: of the teenagers, in the neighborhood, on the telephone, to each other, at night

10. <u>One</u> <u>was arrested</u>
Prepositional Phrases: of the kids, in my neighborhood, for breaking mailboxes

SECTION 4 ◆ ADJECTIVES

Like prepositional phrases, adjectives and adverbs are descriptive words. It is important to see how they are used so that you don't mix them up.

1. **What is an <u>ADJECTIVE</u>?** It is a word or group of words that **<u>describes</u>** a **<u>noun</u>**.

2. **What <u>QUESTIONS</u> do adjectives generally answer in a sentence?**
   ✓ **What kind of** (<u>He</u> <u>wore</u> a *baggy* shirt.)
   ✓ **How many** (The <u>woman</u> <u>owns</u> *several* pairs of shoes.)
   ✓ **Whose** (*My husband's* <u>mom</u> <u>loves</u> to quilt.)
   ✓ **Which** (<u>I'll</u> <u>take</u> *this* one.)
   ✓ **How after linking verbs** (<u>She</u> <u>looks</u> *sweet*, but <u>she</u> <u>is</u> actually very *mean.*)
      ○ Normally, "how" is a question that <u>adverbs</u> answer, but after <u>sensory verbs</u> (look, sound, feel, smell, seem, taste, etc.) and <u>linking verbs</u>, the adjectives that follow answer the question "how."

3. **Which <u>PRONOUNS</u> are <u>ADJECTIVES</u>?** **POSSESSIVE** pronouns: They answer the question **WHOSE.**

> This is MY class
> This is YOUR class
> This is HIS class
> This is HER* class
> The dog wagged ITS tail
> This is OUR class
> This is THEIR class

*"Her" is also an object pronoun.

TIPS: *Adjectives can often be crossed out of the sentence.*
Asking yourself "which question does this answer" helps you identify adjectives and adverbs.

• To me, <u>shopping</u> for *new* clothes <u>is</u> a *terrible* chore.
   ➤ *What kind of* clothes? *New* clothes.
   ➤ *What kind of* chore? A *terrible* chore.

- For *that* reason, I prefer *online* shopping.
  ➤ For *which* reason? For *that* reason.
  ➤ *What kind of* shopping? *Online* shopping.

- *Fifteen* years ago, *cell* phones were *uncommon*.
  ➤ *How many* years ago? *Fifteen* years ago.
  ➤ *What kind of* phones? *Cell* phones.
  ➤ *How* were cell phones? *Uncommon*.

- *Red* marks on *their* papers make *my* students feel *panicked*.
  ➤ *What kind of* marks? *Red* marks.
  ➤ On *whose* papers? On *their* papers.
  ➤ *Whose* students? *My* students.
  ➤ *How* does it make them feel? *Panicked*.

SECTION 4 ◆ PRACTICE: FINDING ADJECTIVES

For each of the following sentences, underline the simple subjects and double-underline the verbs that go with them. Circle the adjectives.

1. Sometimes, the internet at school is extremely slow.

2. I always grade my students' papers with colored pens.

3. My male cat is a coward.

4. My female cat is very brave; she growls at strange noises.

5. Being in an orderly house makes me happy.

6. In most cases, the most successful student studies hard.

7. I have terrible spatial perception, so my drawings look bad.

8. Fortunately, good teaching does not require good drawing skills.

9. One important teaching skill is computer literacy.

10. The best way to learn computer skills is to use the computer every day.

Answers and Explanations to Practice: Finding Adjectives

1. Internet is
   Adjectives: slow (*How* is the internet?)
   "Sometimes" and "extremely" are also descriptive words, but they are adverbs.

2. I grade
   Adjectives: my (*Whose* students?); students' (*Whose* papers?); colored (*What kind of* pens?)
   "Always" is also a descriptive word, but it is an adverb.

3. Cat is; he hides
   Adjectives: my (*Whose* cat?); male (*Which* cat or *what kind of* cat?)
   "Coward" is a noun (object—answers the question "What")

4. Cat <u>is</u>; <u>she</u> <u>growls</u>
   Adjectives: my (*Whose* cat?); female (*Which* cat or *what kind of* cat?); brave (*How* is she?); strange (*What kind of* noises?)
   "Very" is also a descriptive word, but it is an adverb.

5. <u>Being</u> <u>makes</u>
   Adjectives: orderly (*What kind of* house?); happy (*How* do I feel?)
   "In an orderly house" is a prepositional phrase, so the subject is NOT "house" because the object of a preposition can never be the subject of a sentence.

6. <u>Student</u> <u>studies</u>
   Adjectives: most (*Which* cases?); most successful (*Which* student or *What kind of* student?)
   "In most cases" is a prepositional phrase. "Hard" is also a descriptive word, but it is an adverb describing how the student studies.

7. <u>I</u> <u>have</u>; <u>drawings</u> <u>look</u>
   Adjectives: terrible (*What kind of* spatial perception?); spatial (*What kind of* perception?); my (*Whose* drawings?); bad (*How* do my drawings look?)
   "Fortunately" is also a descriptive word, but it is an adverb.

8. <u>Teaching</u> <u>does not require</u>
   Adjectives: good (*What kind of* teaching?); good (*What kind of* drawing skills?); drawing (*What kind of* skills?)

9. <u>Skill</u> <u>is</u>
   Adjectives: one (*How many* teaching skills?); important (*What kind of* teaching skill?); teaching (*What kind of* skill?); computer (*What kind of* literacy?)

10. <u>Way</u> <u>is</u>
    Adjectives: best (*Which* way?); computer (*What kind of* skills?); every (*Which* day(s)?)
    "To learn" and "to practice" are "to + verbs," so they are not verbs.

SECTION 5 ◆ ADVERBS

1. <u>What is an ADVERB?</u> It is a word or group of words that <u>describes verbs, adjectives,</u> and <u>other adverbs</u>.

2. <u>What QUESTIONS do adverbs generally answer in a sentence?</u>
   ✓ HOW (<u>You</u> <u>should work</u> *very carefully*)
   ✓ WHEN (<u>I</u> <u>will call</u> you *later*)
   ✓ WHERE (The <u>tissues</u> <u>are</u> *there*)
   ✓ WHY (<u>She</u> <u>cried</u> *because <u>she</u> <u>was</u> sad*)
   ✓ CONDITION (IF) (*If <u>you</u> <u>pass</u> the exit test,* <u>you</u> <u>can take</u> Comp I)

3. <u>Adverbs often end in "ly":</u> *Slowly, happily, sadly, quickly, badly,* etc.

4. <u>What are CONJUNCTIVE ADVERBS?</u> They are adverbs that <u>show relationships</u> between words, phrases, and sentences.

As a result,	However,	On the other hand,
Consequently,	Meanwhile,	Therefore,
Finally,	Moreover,	Then,
For example,	Nevertheless,	Thus,
Furthermore,		

- I <u>was</u> sick; *therefore*, I <u>stayed</u> home.
  ➤ "Therefore" shows **why** I stayed home.

- I <u>was</u> sick; *however*, I still <u>went</u> to work.
  ➤ "However" shows the <u>contrast</u> or unexpected result of being sick, which is that I stayed home.

- There <u>are</u> many <u>breeds</u> of dogs; *for example*, German <u>shepherds</u>, Labrador <u>retrievers</u>, and <u>poodles</u> <u>are</u> all common breeds.
  ➤ "For example" shows that the second part of the sentence is giving examples of the first part.

*Note: It is a good idea to put a period or a semicolon (;) before a conjunctive adverb so that you do not misuse it.

SECTION 5 ◆ PRACTICE: FINDING ADVERBS

For each of the following sentences, <u>underline</u> the simple subjects and <u>double-underline</u> the verbs that go with them. Circle the adverbs.

1. I jumped out of the way quickly to avoid the speeding car.

2. She did extremely well on her test.

3. Very soon, we will take our next test.

4. This essay is very poorly written.

5. I could very easily go to sleep right now; however, I have class soon.

6. She didn't get a trophy; therefore, she cried pitifully.

7. If you understand adverbs, you will understand clauses very well.

8. The freezing temperatures killed many of my plants; for example, my hibiscus and crotons are dead.

9. At the beginning of March, I will slowly begin to add plants to my yard again.

10. Many of my students study very well with loud music in the background.

Answers and Explanations to Practice: Finding Adverbs

1. <u>I</u> <u>jumped</u>
   Adverbs: quickly (*How* did I <u>jump</u>?)
   "To avoid" is a "to + verb," so it is not a verb. However, it is functioning as an adverb telling "why." "Speeding" is telling "*what kind of* car," so it's an adjective.

2. <u>She</u> <u>did</u>
   Adverbs: extremely (*How* well?); well (*How* did she do?)
   "On her test" is a prepositional phrase.

3. <u>We</u> <u>will take</u>
   Adverbs: very (*How* soon?); soon (*When* will we take our next test?)
   "Our" and "next" are both adjectives describing "test."

4. <u>Essay</u> <u>is written</u>
   Adverbs: very (*How* poorly written?); poorly (*How* is it written?)
   "This" is an adjective describing "essay."

5. <u>I</u> <u>could go</u>; <u>I</u> <u>have</u>
   Adverbs: very (*How* easily?); easily (*How* could I go?); right now (*When* could I go to sleep?)

6. <u>She</u> <u>didn't get</u>; <u>she</u> <u>cried</u>
   Adverbs: therefore (Conjunctive adverb showing the connection between her crying and not getting the trophy); pitifully (*How* did she cry?)
   "Trophy" is an object, not a subject, because the trophy is not doing any action in the sentence.

7. <u>You</u> <u>understand</u>; <u>you</u> <u>will understand</u>
   Adverbs: if you understand adverbs (*Under what condition* will you understand clauses?); very (*How* well?); well (*How* will you understand clauses?)

8. <u>Temperature</u> <u>killed</u>; <u>hibiscus, crotons</u> <u>are</u>
   Adverbs: for example (Conjunctive adverb showing the connection between the examples and the fact that many plants were killed)
   "Freezing" is an adjective describing "temperatures"; "of my plants" is a prepositional phrase; "dead" is an adjective describing "plants."

9. <u>I</u> <u>will begin</u>
   Adverbs: slowly (*How* will I begin?); again (*When* will I add them?)
   "At the beginning" and "of March" are prepositional phrases, but they are telling *when*, so they are also functioning as adverbs; "to add" is a "to + verb," so it is not a verb; "to my yard" is a prepositional phrase also functioning as an adverb telling *when*.

10. <u>Many</u> <u>study</u>
    Adverbs: very (*How* well?); well (*How* do they study?)
    "Of my students" is a prepositional phrase, so "students" cannot be the subject because it is the object of a preposition; "with loud music" and "in the background" are also prepositional phrases functioning as adverbs telling *how* and *where*.

SECTION 6 ◆ CLAUSES

Part 1—Independent Clauses

In order to teach you what a true sentence is, we have to explain **Independent and Dependent Clauses** to you. FOUR of the forty questions on the Exit Exam directly address incomplete sentences, more than any other question type on the test. Furthermore, by far the most common error that developing students commit in their writing is **Incomplete Sentences**, particularly **Comma Splices**. These errors are annoying to professors, and even worse, unflattering for you.

1. <u>What is a clause?</u> It is a group of related words with a subject and a verb. Not every clause is a sentence, but <u>every sentence has at least one clause.</u>

2. <u>What is an INDEPENDENT (or Main) CLAUSE?</u> An independent clause <u>makes sense by itself</u> and can be punctuated like a sentence. It can stand ALONE.

   • Every <u>sentence</u> <u>has</u> a clause. (a sentence = INDEPENDENT clause)

   • Some <u>sentences</u> <u>have</u> just one clause. (a sentence = INDEPENDENT clause)

   • Some <u>sentences</u> <u>have</u> just one clause, but <u>others</u> <u>have</u> more than one clause. (a sentence with 2 INDEPENDENT clauses)

3. <u>How can 2 (or more) Independent Clauses be joined together or put back to back?</u>
   ✓ Period.
      • Independent <u>clauses</u> <u>are</u> complete sentences. Dependent <u>clauses</u> <u>are not</u> complete sentences.
        ➤ Each sentence above is made up of one independent clause.

   ✓ Semicolon (;)
      • Independent <u>clauses</u> <u>are</u> complete sentences; **however,** dependent <u>clauses</u> <u>are not</u> complete sentences.
        ➤ Semicolons are like *periods*. They are used to join ideas that are closely related.
        ➤ It is very common to follow a semicolon with a *coordinating adverb* like "however," "therefore," or "for example."

   ✓ COMMA + Coordinating Conjunction
      • Independent <u>clauses</u> <u>are</u> complete sentences, **but** dependent <u>clauses</u> <u>are not</u> complete sentences.
        ➤ Learn **FANBOYS** to remember the list of coordinating conjunctions. ONLY THESE WORDS can be used after a comma to join independent clauses.

F	A	N	B	O	Y	S
O R	N D	O R	U T	R	E T	O

<u>NOTE:</u> **You do not need a comma before a FANBOYS unless you have TWO subjects and TWO verbs.**
   Ex: <u>The secretary</u> <u>filed</u> papers in the morning and <u>worked</u> on scheduling meetings in the afternoon.
   One subject (secretary) and two verbs (filed, worked) = ONE clause.

✓ Make one of the clauses DEPENDENT.
  • *Although* independent <u>clauses</u> <u>are</u> complete sentences, dependent <u>clauses</u> <u>are not</u> complete sentences.
    ➤ The first clause cannot be punctuated like a sentence because the word "although" makes it *dependent*. It has to be attached to an independent clause.

  TIPS: *If a sentence does not have at least one Independent Clause, it's not a sentence.*
     Semicolons (;) function like PERIODS, not like commas. Both sides of a semi-colon (;) must be Independent Clauses.
     You do not need a comma before a FANBOYS unless you have TWO subjects and TWO verbs (or two independent clauses, each with its own subject and verb).
     To see how many clauses you have, first find your subject and verb combinations. However many subject and verb combinations you have, that's how many clauses you have.

  • [<u>Some</u> (~~of the students~~)(~~in my class~~) <u>have</u> children], **but** [only a <u>few</u> <u>have</u> grandchildren.]
    ➤ There are 2 different subject/verb combinations, so there are 2 clauses.
    ➤ Each clause makes sense by itself, so they are both independent.
    ➤ The 2 independent clauses are joined <u>legally</u> with a <u>comma + FANBOYS.</u>

  • [<u>Some</u> (~~of my students~~) <u>have</u> full-time jobs and <u>are raising</u> children, too.]
    ➤ There are 2 verbs, but only <u>one</u> subject, so there is only one clause.
    ➤ Notice that there is <u>NO COMMA</u> after the "and" because it's not a joining 2 independent clauses.

SECTION 6.1 ◆ PRACTICE: FINDING INDEPENDENT CLAUSES

For each of the following sentences, <u>underline</u> the simple subjects and <u>double-underline</u> the verbs that go with them. That will tell you how many clauses there are. Then, put each clause in brackets and tell whether it is independent or dependent.

1. Mrs. Jones was married six times. However, her son and daughter both got married only once.

2. The two cats are sunning themselves next to the window. Each of them looks very content.

3. Mr. Jones was born in Milwaukee, but he was raised in Germany.

4. Americans are permitted to get a driver license when they are 16 years old.

5. The young boy could not speak any English, but he learned English very quickly by attending special classes at school.

6. During the Korean War, Mr. Jones served as a US Embassy guard in Ecuador, but he never shot anybody.

7. After the war, he returned to America and went to college on the GI Bill.

8. The GI Bill was a special college tuition program; it allowed veterans to go to college for very little money.

9. After they are discharged, many US soldiers go to school on the GI Bill.

10. One of the former soldiers in my class has awards for bravery, but he is very humble.

Answers and Explanations to Practice: Finding Independent Clauses

1. [Mrs. Jones <u>was married</u> six times.] [However, her <u>son</u> and <u>daughter</u> both <u>got married</u> only once.]
    There are two independent clauses joined with a period.

2. [The two <u>cats are sunning</u> themselves next to the window.] [<u>Each</u> of them <u>looks</u> very content.]
    There are two independent clauses joined with a period.

3. [<u>Mr. Jones was born</u> in Milwaukee], but [<u>he was raised</u> in Germany.]
    There are two independent clauses joined with a COMMA + FANBOYS.

4. [<u>Americans are permitted</u> to get a driver license] [when <u>they are</u> 16 years old.]
    The first clause is independent but the second is <u>dependent</u>. It cannot stand alone, but it is joined legally to an independent clause.

5. [The young <u>boy could not speak</u> any English], but [<u>he learned</u> English very quickly by attending special classes at school.]
    There are two independent clauses joined with a COMMA + FANBOYS.

6. [During the Korean War, <u>Mr. Jones served</u> as a US Embassy guard in Ecuador], but [<u>he</u> never <u>shot</u> anybody.]
    There are two independent clauses joined with a COMMA + FANBOYS.

7. [After the war, <u>he returned</u> to America and <u>went</u> to college on the GI Bill.]
    There is only one independent clause because there is only one subject. The two verbs go with that one subject.

8. [<u>The GI Bill was</u> a special college tuition program allowing veterans to go to college for very little money.]
    There is only one independent clause. "Allowing" is not a verb because it does not work with a linking verb. Instead, it is an adjective telling more about "program."

9. [After <u>they are discharged</u>], [many US <u>soldiers go</u> to school on the GI Bill.]
    There are two clauses. The first one is <u>dependent</u> because it cannot stand alone. The second clause is independent.

10. [<u>One</u> of the former soldiers in my class <u>has</u> awards for bravery], but [<u>he is</u> very humble.]
    There are two independent clauses joined with a COMMA + FANBOYS. Don't be distracted by the objects of the prepositions "of the former soldiers" and "in my class." The true subject is <u>one</u>.

Part 2—Dependent Clauses

1. <u>**What is a DEPENDENT CLAUSE?**</u> A DEPENDENT CLAUSE has a subject and verb, but it does not make sense all by itself. It must be **connected to an independent clause** in order to function.

    • **because <u>I</u> <u>said</u> so** (not a sentence = DEPENDENT clause)
    ➤ [<u>You need</u> to do it this way] [**because <u>I</u> <u>said</u> so.**]

- **which** <u>makes</u> me very happy (not a sentence = DEPENDENT clause)
  - ➤ [My <u>papers</u> <u>are</u> all graded], [**which** <u>makes</u> me very happy.]

- **while** <u>others</u> <u>have</u> more than one (not a sentence = DEPENDENT clause)
  - ➤ [Some <u>sentences</u> <u>have</u> only one clause] [**while** <u>others</u> <u>have</u> more than one.]

2. <u>**What types of Dependent Clauses are there?**</u> There are 3 kinds:

   ✓ <u>**Adverb clauses**</u>—Answer the Adverb Questions (WHERE, WHEN, WHY, HOW, and CONDITION) <u>or</u> clarify the relationship with the independent clause.
   - ○ Begin with an Adverb (not LY) followed by a subject/verb combination.
   - ○ Many look like prepositions, but they are followed by subject/verb combinations instead of an object.

   COMMON ADVERB CLAUSE INTRODUCERS (subordinating conjunctions)

After	Even though	Unless
Although	If	Until
As	Since	When
Because	So that	Whereas
Before	Though	While

   TIPS: *Adverb clauses are MOVEABLE. That's one way to identify them. If a dependent clause can be moved to the beginning or end of the sentence, it's an ADVERB.*
   *Adverb clauses CAN BE CROSSED OUT of the sentence to see the independent clause.
   [If the adverb <u>clause</u> <u>comes</u> BEFORE the independent clause**], [<u>you</u> <u>should put</u> a comma after the adverb clause.] In fact, ANYTHING that introduces the independent clause should be set off with a comma.*

- The <u>student</u> <u>asked</u> the teacher a question [*because* <u>he</u> <u>did not understand</u> clauses].
  - ➤ If the "because" were not there, then, "He did not understand clauses" would be independent. The "because" *creates* dependence.
  - ➤ The independent clause comes first, so no comma.
  - ➤ Notice that the adverb clause could be crossed out and the independent clause becomes obvious.

- [*Because* the <u>student</u> <u>did not understand</u> clauses], [<u>he</u> <u>asked</u> the teacher a question.]
  - ➤ The dependent clause comes <u>before</u> the independent clause, so a comma is necessary.

- [Many <u>students</u> <u>make</u> clause errors] [*although* <u>they</u> <u>are</u> easy to fix.]
  - ➤ If the "although" were not there, then, "They are easy to fix" would be independent. The "although" *creates* dependence.
  - ➤ The independent clause comes first, so no comma.
  - ➤ Notice that the adverb clause could be crossed out and the independent clause becomes obvious.

- [**Although** clause errors are easy to fix], [many students make them.]
  - ➤ The dependent clause comes <u>before</u> the independent clause, so a comma is necessary.

✓ **Adjective clauses**—Describe **nouns** and answer the Adjective Questions (WHAT KIND OF, HOW MANY, WHOSE, WHICH, and HOW).
   ○ **Often begin with THAT, WHICH, WHO, WHOM, or WHOSE**

   TIPS: *Adjective clauses CANNOT BE MOVED AROUND. That's one way to identify them. If they are moved, it becomes difficult to tell what noun they are describing.*
   They usually come AFTER THE NOUN or idea that is being described.
   Like adverb clauses, adjective clauses CAN GENERALLY BE CROSSED OUT of the sentence to see the independent clause.
   A "which" clause, [which gives extra information about some noun in the sentence], should be set off with COMMAS. Remember "comma which comma."

• [A dependent clause is a *clause*] (**that must be attached** to some independent clause).
   ➤ *The word "clause" is being described by the adjective clause. What kind of clause? One that must be attached.*
   ➤ *Notice that the adjective clause comes right after the noun it is describing.*
   ➤ *Notice that you can remove the adjective clause, but you can't move it around.*

• [A clause, (**which** always **has** a subject and a verb), can be either dependent or independent.]
   ➤ *The word "clause" is being described by the adjective clause.*
   ➤ *Notice that the adjective clause comes right after the noun it is describing.*
   ➤ *Notice that you can remove the adjective clause, but you can't move it around.*
   ➤ *Notice that the adjective clause appears in the middle of the independent clause. That is not uncommon.*
   ➤ *Notice that the clause begins with "which," so it is set off by commas.*

✓ **Noun clauses**—Tell WHO or WHAT (necessary to the sentence so can't be crossed out)
   ○ **Begin with THAT, HOW, WHY, WHEN, WHERE, WHO**

   TIPS: *Noun clauses OFTEN CANNOT BE CROSSED OUT OF THE SENTENCE.*
   Like all nouns, they function as either subjects or objects.

• [The student told the teacher (**that he was going** to be absent).]
   ➤ *The dependent clause answers the question WHAT and cannot be crossed out. It is part of the independent clause.*

• [(**What the child** said) was very important.]
   ➤ *WHAT was very important? What the child said. The noun clause is actually the subject of the sentence.*
   ➤ *Notice that it cannot be crossed out.*

• [The child was punished] ~~for (what he said)~~.
   ➤ *For WHAT was the child punished? For what he said. The noun clause is the object of the preposition "for."*
   ➤ *Since prepositional phrases can generally be crossed out, we can cross the noun clause out because it is part of the prepositional phrase.*

SECTION 6.2 ◆ PRACTICE: FINDING INDEPENDENT AND DEPENDENT CLAUSES

For each of the following sentences, <u>underline</u> the simple subjects and <u>double-underline</u> the verbs that go with them. That will tell you how many clauses there are. Then, put each clause in brackets and tell whether it is independent or dependent. For the dependent clauses, identify whether they are adverbs, adjectives, or nouns.

1. Although some Americans prefer hot tea, most prefer coffee.

2. The man always regretted that he did not learn Spanish, but his parents stopped speaking it when they came to America.

3. Our new neighbor lives by herself, but my old neighbor lived with his wife, whom he loved very much.

4. The office workers performed very well; therefore, they received a raise.

5. The man visited his father for the first time when he was 15 years old.

6. It was very awkward, but he was very happy because he learned that they had much in common.

7. After the party, the woman stayed up late talking to her best friend while her husband went to bed.

8. Before leaving the country, you should make sure to renew your passport.

9. My mother was very passionate and reactive whereas my father is much more analytical and careful in his response to something.

10. My sister, who lives up north, works at a bank.

Answers and Explanations to Practice: Finding Independent and Dependent Clauses

1. [*Although* some <u>Americans</u> <u>prefer</u> hot tea], [<u>most</u> <u>prefer</u> coffee].
   2 clauses: Adverb clause, independent clause.
   The comma is necessary because the dependent clause came first.
   Notice that the adverb clause is *moveable*. You could put it at the end of the sentence if you wanted.

2. [The <u>man</u> always <u>regretted</u> (*that* <u>he</u> <u>did not learn</u> Spanish)], but [his <u>parents</u> <u>stopped</u> speaking it] [*when* <u>they</u> <u>came</u> to America].
   4 clauses: Independent clause with noun clause embedded, independent clause, adverb clause.
   Notice the "comma + FANBOYS" between the two independent clauses.
   Notice that you cannot cut the noun clause out of its independent clause.
   Notice that the adverb clause is *moveable*.

3. [Our new <u>neighbor</u> <u>lives</u> by herself], but [my old <u>neighbor</u> <u>lived</u> with his wife], [*whom* <u>he</u> <u>loved</u> very much].
   3 clauses: Independent clause, independent clause, adjective clause describing "wife."
   Notice the "comma + FANBOYS" between the two independent clauses.
   Notice that *you cannot move* the adjective clause. You could cut it, though.

4. [The office <u>workers</u> <u>performed</u> very well]; [therefore, <u>they</u> <u>received</u> a raise].
   2 clauses: Independent clause, independent clause.

5. [The <u>man</u> <u>visited</u> his father for the first time] [*when* <u>he</u> <u>was</u> 15 years old].
   2 clauses: Independent clause, adverb clause.
   Notice that the adverb clause is *moveable.*

6. [<u>It</u> <u>was</u> very awkward], but [<u>he</u> <u>was</u> very happy] [*because* <u>he</u> <u>learned</u> (*that* <u>they</u> <u>had</u> much in common)].
   4 clauses: Independent clause, independent clause, adverb clause with embedded noun clause.
   Notice the "comma + FANBOYS" between the two independent clauses.
   Notice that the adverb clause is *moveable.* You could put it at the beginning of the sentence if you wanted to.
   Notice that there is no comma before "because" since the independent clause comes first.
   Notice that you cannot cut the noun clause out of the adverb clause.

7. [After the party, the <u>woman</u> <u>stayed</u> up late talking to her best friend] [*while* her <u>husband</u> <u>went</u> to bed].
   2 clauses: Independent clause, adverb clause.
   "After the party" is a prepositional phrase, not a clause. It has no subject/verb.
   Notice that the adverb clause is *moveable.* You could put it at the beginning of the sentence if you wanted to.
   Notice that there is no comma before "while" since the independent clause comes first.

8. [*Before* leaving the country, <u>you</u> <u>should renew</u> your passport.]
   2 clauses: Adverb clause, independent clause.
   Notice that the adverb clause is *moveable.*
   Notice that there is a *comma* after the adverb clause since it introduces the independent clause.

9. [My <u>mother</u> <u>was</u> very passionate and reactive] [*whereas* my <u>father</u> <u>is</u> much more analytical and careful].
   2 clauses: Independent clause, adverb clause
   Notice that the adverb clause is *moveable.*
   Notice that there is no comma before "whereas" since the independent clause comes first.

10. [My <u>sister</u>, (*who* <u>lives</u> up north), <u>works</u> at a bank].
    2 clauses: Independent clause with embedded adjective clause.
    Notice that you *cannot move* the adjective clause. However, you could cut it if you wanted to.